Lecture Notes in Computer Science

Lecture Notes in Artificial Intelligence 15685

Founding Editor

Jörg Siekmann

The series Lecture Notes in Artificial Intelligence (LNAI) was established in 1988 as a topical subseries of LNCS devoted to artificial intelligence.

The series publishes state-of-the-art research results at a high level. As with the LNCS mother series, the mission of the series is to serve the international R & D community by providing an invaluable service, mainly focused on the publication of conference and workshop proceedings and postproceedings.

Rem Collier · Alessandro Ricci · Vivek Nallur ·
Samuele Burattini · Andrea Omicini
Editors

Multi-Agent Systems

21st European Conference, EUMAS 2024
Dublin, Ireland, August 26–28, 2024
Proceedings

Springer

Editors
Rem Collier
University College Dublin
Dublin, Ireland

Alessandro Ricci
Università di Bologna
Cesena, Italy

Vivek Nallur
University College Dublin
Dublin, Ireland

Samuele Burattini
Università di Bologna
Cesena, Italy

Andrea Omicini
Università di Bologna
Cesena, Italy

ISSN 0302-9743 ISSN 1611-3349 (electronic)
Lecture Notes in Artificial Intelligence
ISBN 978-3-031-93929-7 ISBN 978-3-031-93930-3 (eBook)
https://doi.org/10.1007/978-3-031-93930-3

LNCS Sublibrary: SL7 – Artificial Intelligence

This Springer imprint is published by the registered company Springer Nature Switzerland AG
The registered company address is: Gewerbestrasse 11, 6330 Cham, Switzerland

Preface

This volume constitutes the proceedings of the 21st European Conference on Multi-Agent Systems (EUMAS 2024), held from the 26th to 28th August 2024 in Dublin, Ireland. The past two decades has seen a surge of interest in agent-based computing and Multi-Agent Systems (MAS). Agent-based computing is poised to be a key technology for building intelligent systems in the 21st century. The EUMAS conference series seeks to provide the primary forum for academics and practitioners in Europe to discuss current MAS research and applications.

EUMAS 2024 followed in the traditions of previous editions: Oxford 2003, Barcelona 2004, Brussels 2005, Lisbon 2006, Hammamet 2007, Bath 2008, Agia Napa 2009, Paris 2010, Maastrict 2011, Dublin 2012, Toulouse 2013, Prague 2014, Athens 2015, Valencia 2016, Evry 2017, Bergen 2018, Thessaloniki 2020 (virtual), Israel 2021 (virtual), Dusseldorf 2022, and Naples 2023. Like the previous editions, EUMAS 2024 aimed to bring together academic and industry researchers and practitioners who share an interest in Multi-Agent Systems. EUMAS is the flagship annual event of the European Association for Multi-Agent Systems (EURAMAS) and we thank the board for its kind support and encouragement.

The peer review process was carried out by 36 Programme Committee (PC) members who put an emphasis on both quality and relevance to the community. Each submission to EUMAS 2024 was peer reviewed by two PC members in a single-blind fashion. Out of 36 submissions, 27 papers were accepted as full papers for oral presentation. Additionally, 4 papers were accepted to a demo track as short papers. As special session on Agent Toolkits was also held at EUMAS 2024 with the submitted work to be published in a separate book.

In addition to the papers contained in this volume, the EUMAS 2024 programme was enriched by two wonderful keynote talks given by Franziska Klugl (Örebro University, Sweden) was entitled "Towards More Credible Agent-Based Simulations". The second keynote, given by Julian Padget (University of Bath, UK), was entitled "Governing complex commons: an accidental transdisciplinary tour".

Among the accepted papers, we chose the best ones based on their review scores during the conference and invited the authors to submit an extended version for fast-track publication in the Journal of Autonomous Agents and Multi-Agent Systems (JAAMAS). In addition, selected authors were invited to extend their contributions for a special issue of SN Computer Science.

We would like give our thanks to: the authors for submitting their work to EUMAS 2024; the PC members for reviewing the submissions; the participants and invited speakers for traveling to Dublin, listening to and giving great talks; the editors of JAAMAS and SN Computer Science; the local organizing committee; and our sponsors.

April 2025

Rem Collier
Alessandro Ricci
Vivek Nallur
Samuele Burattini
Andrea Omicini

Organization

Organizing Committee

Rem Collier	University College Dublin, Ireland
Alessandro Ricci	University of Bologna, Italy

Program Committee Chair

Andrea Omicini	University of Bologna, Italy

Special Track Chairs

Vivek Nallur	University College Dublin, Ireland
Samuele Burattini	University of Bologna, Italy

Programme Committee

Natasha Alechina	Utrecht University, Netherlands
Edmond Awad	University of Oxford, UK
Cristina Baroglio	University of Turin, Italy
Katharine Beaumont	University College Dublin, Ireland
Federico Bergenti	University of Parma, Italy
Lars Braubach	HSB Hochschule Bremen, Germany
Selmer Bringsjord	Rensselaer Polytechnic Institute, USA
Rafael C. Cardoso	University of Aberdeen, UK
Amit Chopra	Lancaster University, UK
Giovanni Ciatto	University of Bologna, Italy
Paul Davidsson	Malmö University, Sweden
Louise Dennis	University of Manchester, UK
Angelo Ferrando	University of Modena and Reggio Emilia, Italy
Paul Formosa	Macquarie University, Australia
Nicoletta Fornara	Università della Svizzera italiana, Switzerland
Davide Grossi	University of Groningen, Netherlands
Zahia Guessoum	University of Reims Champagne-Ardenne, France
Feyza Hafızoğlu	İstanbul Ticaret University, Turkey

Timotheus Kampik	Umeå University, Sweden
Viviana Mascardi	University of Genoa, Italy
Simon Mayer	University of St. Gallen, Switzerland
Conor Muldoon	Manchester Metropolitan University, UK
Aniello Murano	University of Naples Federico II, Italy
Vivek Nallur	University College Dublin, Ireland
Juan Carlos Nieves	Umeå University, Sweden
Maurice Pagnucco	UNSW Sydney, Australia
Georgios Papasotiropoulos	University of Warsaw, Poland
Pere Pardo	University of Luxembourg, Luxembourg
Ken Satoh	National Institute for Informatics, Japan
Sandip Sen	University of Tulsa, USA
Marija Slavkovik	University of Bergen, Norway
Sonja Smets	University of Amsterdam, Netherlands
Yang Song	California Institute of Technology, USA
Alexandru Sorici	National University of Science and Technology POLITEHNICA Bucharest, Romania
Leon van der Torre	University of Luxembourg, Luxembourg
Nicolas Verstaevel	Toulouse Capitole University, France

Contents

Engineering Multi-Agent Systems

Multi-Agent Based Simulation

MAiS: Exploiting JADE as a Multi-agent Simulator of the Immune System

Sanchayan Bhunia[1], Angelo Ferrando[1(✉)], Viviana Mascardi[1], and Chiara Vitale[2]

[1] Department of Computer Science, Bioengineering, Robotics and Systems Engineering (DIBRIS), University of Genova, Genoa, Italy
{angelo.ferrando,viviana.mascardi}@unige.it

[2] Department of Experimental Medicine (DIMES), University of Genova, Genoa, Italy
chiara.vitale@unige.it

Abstract. The immune system is the second most complex biological system after the brain. It consists in millions of cells, of various nature, interacting amongst them to keep the organism safe from external enemies (pathogens), such as viruses and bacteria. To better understand how the immune system works, and how it reacts to certain diseases and cures, simulations have been proposed over the years. Amongst them, we may find agent-based ones where the organism's actors, like cells, antibodies, viruses, and so on, are represented as agents. In this paper, we present the initial design and development of an agent-based simulation of the immune system using a well-known agent framework, JADE. We present the engineering choices we made and the instantiation of some steps of the secondary immune system response. We discuss the implementation in JADE, and we present some experimental results.

Keywords: Agent-based Simulation · Immune System · JADE

1 Introduction

The immune system of any multi-cellular organism is a very complex system with a lot of different T-cells playing important role to keep a body free from infections, such as those due to viruses. The goal of the virus is to hijack a cell and use its resources to make a copy of itself (replication) and to spread those replicas into other parts of the body. The immune system helps an organism to fight back the infection by searching for any virus signature moving from one cell to another. The immune system in general consists of multiple different cells with different behaviours: some of them immediately activate and contribute to eradicate the infection by different and complementary mechanisms, such as Phagocytes, T-cells, B-cells; some of them remember the signature of an infection, such as B-cells and Memory T-cells, and are essential to prevent similar infection in the future.

R. Collier et al. (Eds.): EUMAS 2024, LNAI 15685, pp. 3–20, 2025.
https://doi.org/10.1007/978-3-031-93930-3_1

The goal of this paper is to model some of the components of the immune system and as interacting agents using the Java Agent DEvelopment Framework (JADE [2]) and simulate a situation when the immune system is under attack from a virus. Agent-Based Model & Simulation (ABMS) is a well-known research area focused on simulating systems following a bottom-up approach, where agents are used to describe the actors of the simulation (for further readings on ABMS techniques a review can be found in [18]). Specifically, this work is about the engineering of an agent-based simulator in JADE. JADE is a well-known agent framework based in Java and used in many industrial applications for its being natively distributable, and having a shallow learning curve. We present an initial engineering and development of a small part of the immune system in JADE, namely the secondary immune response carried out by specialised Memory T-cells. We show the engineering process that brought us to the development of the digital twins cells as JADE agents, and how their behaviours have been coded as JADE behaviours. We recognise the part currently tackled in our integration in JADE is limited, and an over-simplification of how a realistic multi-cellular organism's immune system behaves; however, we decided to focus on the engineering aspects of finding suitable mappings amongst biological entities (cells) and digital ones (agents). Above all, we are interested in presenting the skeleton of an agent-based simulator, called MAiS (Multi-Agent immune System), which is going to serve us as a base for future developments and extensions that will be considered to properly model the actual immune system. Finally, we point out that no simulation of the immune system has ever been proposed in JADE.

The paper is structured as follows. Section 2 introduces background knowledge on JADE and immune system to make the paper as widely accessible as possible. Section 3 presents the engineering decisions made in the MAiS development, as well as the main reasons for implementing the latter on top of JADE. Section 4 presents the agents used in MAiS to represent the biological entities and how such agents work with each other. Section 5 reports the results obtained by carrying out experiments with MAiS. Section 6 positions the paper w.r.t. the state of the art. Finally, Sect. 8 concludes the paper and points out future directions.

2 Preliminaries

2.1 JADE

JADE[1] [2] is a widely used agent framework. By being based upon Java, it is easy to learn and to integrate to existing solutions. JADE is structured around the idea of agents, behaviours, and containers. Agents follow the standard meaning, as main actors of the system. Each agent runs on a different thread, and it communicates with the other agents through FIPA[2] compliant messages. Behaviours

[1] https://jade.tilab.com.
[2] http://www.fipa.org.

denote how the agents act, and how they achieve their goals. Containers represent the abstract environment where the agents live, and can be distributed over multiple machines. It is important to note, that agents can move amongst different containers. This is going to be exploited in the paper to simulate the passage of viruses and lymphocyte amongst different cells. Note that, since the containers can be deployed on different machines, the agents not only move, but their computations move as well. This aspect is of paramount importance in case the system to model becomes too big to be handled by a single machine; as it would happen for a realistic immune system comprised of millions of cells.

2.2 The Secondary Immune Response Scenario

The immune system is our second most complex system, after the brain. It involves many different actors (*i.e.*, cells of our body's tissues, pathogens like bacteria and viruses), each one with different features, capabilities and objectives. Depending on the scenario, and the current state of our organism, we may find ourselves with a complete different set of cells involved in defending us, and that carry out different tasks.

In this section we consider a simple – but correct – scenario, that will be used as the case study for the initial design and implementation of MAiS.

1. Some time ago, Alice got an infection from a virus V, which infected cells of tissue TIS (target cells). The infection fired a reaction from the immune system that, besides successfully fighting V, also activated the generation of Memory T-cells specific for V, that we name $MemT(V)$. Memory T-cells are a subset of T Lymphocytes and their primary function is augmented immune response once the pathogen that initially caused their generation (V in this scenario) attacks the body again. Memory T-cells may 'wander' in the blood and in tissues close to those that had been infected by the pathogen, even 30 years after the first infection.
2. Alice comes into contact with V again.
3. V enters her body via her mouth and tries to infect cells of tissue TIS again. It may succeed in this attempt with some infection success rate ISR. Let us suppose that one cell $C(TIS)_a$ becomes infected. Two events take place:
   (a) $C(TIS)_a$ becomes a virus-making factory: V can in fact use it to move to 'infectable neighbouring cells', and infect them. The amount and density of infectable neighbouring cells depends on TIS, on the point the virus entered the body, and on other factors.
   (b) $C(TIS)_a$ can be recognized as infected thanks to a peptide (an antigen) on its membrane surface, acting as a manifesto for its health state: when a cell is infected with a virus, it has pieces of antigens of that virus – the virus 'signature' – on its surface, not present when the cell is healthy.
4. One Memory T-cell trained to recognize V, $MemT(V)_b$, that was wandering close to $C(TIS)_a$, perceives pieces of V's antigen on the cell's membrane[3].

[3] Memory T-cells $MemT(V)$ recognize *only* antigens of V, since they are virus-specific.

5. $MemT(V)_b$ kills $C(TIS)_a$: this is the only way to stop the proliferation and spread of V.
6. Depending on TIS, cells may be re-generated (cellular replication) to cope with the fact that some amount of $C(TIS)$ infected cells were killed; replication may accelerate to re-establish some stable number of cells, or may not take place at all, depending on TIS. For example, cells of the nervous systems cannot be replicated (perennial cells), hepatic cells can, but only as a response of a serious damage and up to some extent (stable cells), blood cells are continuously replicated (labile cells). If the damage is too vast, even tissues with labile cells may not be able to restore at the healthy situation holding before the virus infection.

3 The Engineering of MAiS

MAiS has been engineered to be a highly scalable and distributed agent-based immune system simulator. Even though in this paper we only focus on a simple sub-process of the immune system's response, we tackle all the fundamental aspects of its full engineering. Specifically, we address how to represent the main immune system's components inside JADE. As we mentioned in the introduction, the main actors of the immune system are the cells. A cell does not only denote the building block of any organic system, but it also represents the point of attack for viruses as well (for replication). Because of its importance, we started the engineering of MAiS from the cells.

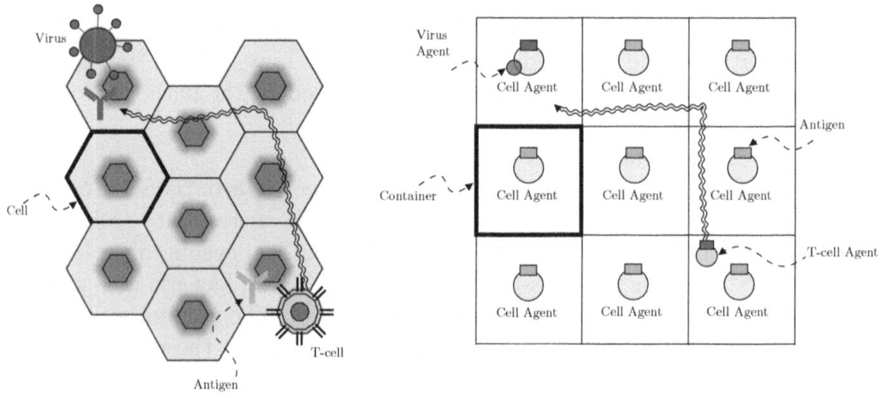

Fig. 1. Schematic of how the biological components (left) are mapped into MAiS (right).

Figure 1 graphically shows the engineering of the immune system's pillar components in MAiS. On the left, we may find a schematic representation of a region of cells in the organic system. While, on the right, we may find the counterpart in MAiS, where each cell is represented as an agent (Cell Agent). One important aspect to clarify is the locality of cells. Indeed, each cell is not an island, but is connected to other cells. This aspect has been mapped into MAiS by adding each Cell Agent inside a JADE container. Then, to maintain the positioning of the cells, the JADE containers are stored keeping the information about their neighbour containers (*i.e.*, neighbour cells). This can be schematically represented as a grid of containers (as shown in Fig. 1). We decided to specify a cell as the combination of a Cell Agent and a JADE container for two main reasons:

1. to exploit the agents' mobility feature of JADE;
2. to exploit the intrinsic distribution of containers in JADE.

Thanks to (i), if we denote a cell as a container, we can natively implement in JADE the movement of T-cells and viruses through the movement of T-Cell Agents and Virus Agents between containers. Such feature is available in JADE, and allows the agents to move between containers in a transparent way. This is very important both for T-cells, that need to move around the system searching for viruses, and for viruses as well, that need to replicate to neighbour cells. On the other hand, thanks to (ii), by denoting the cells as containers, we can distribute the latter on multiple machines. By doing that, we can exploit the computational power of cluster of machines as well as parallel computing. This aspect is of paramount importance when the immune system to model starts growing; since it would be increasingly hard for a single machine to handle millions of cells (*i.e.*, millions of agents). These two features make JADE a suitable candidate to specify distributed simulations of the immune system.

4 Agents

Now that we have clarified the topology of the immune system representation in JADE as a grid of containers, we can focus on the main actors of the immune system and their agent representation.

We have three different typology of agents: Cell Agents, T-Cell Agents, and Virus Agents.

4.1 Cell Agent

A Cell Agent, as the name suggests, represents a cell in the body of a multicellular organism. It lives inside a JADE container and has an identifying peptide (*i.e.*, the antigen) which is used by the immune system to verify the status of the cell (healthy or infected). In case a cell is detected as infected, the immune system reacts by killing such cell (by means of T-cells). The entire "identify and kill" process is necessary to avoid the propagation of the infection to other cells.

To represent this behaviour in MAiS, each Cell Agent stores its antigen information, and allows other agents in the system to interact with it. Such antigen is expressed by the cell antigen as string storing the peptide ammino sequence. T-Cell Agents can read such antigen to recognise if belonging to a known virus, or,

Virus Agents can replace cellular antigen with an own viral antigen to simulate the binding of the virus with the cell membrane (action performed by the virus for replicating itself through the cell). We discuss these two mechanics when we present the corresponding agents in the following sections. The identification carried out by a T-Cell Agent is obtained by checking the corresponding string antigen for a complete match (*i.e.*, the antigen peptide sequence has to be 100% equal to the one known by the T-cell).

In here, we present the behaviours of the Cell Agent, and how it communicates with the other agents in the MAS.

Let us focus on the behaviour first. A Cell Agent enacts three different behaviours, which correspond to three different states.

- **Healthy:** At the beginning of the simulation, the Cell Agent is healthy and has not been infected by any virus, yet. In this state, the Cell Agent listens for communications from any possible agent, including Virus Agents. This listening phase is obtained in JADE by the use of a Cyclic Behaviour[4], where the agent accepts communications from other agents in its container (*i.e.*, agents that are local to it). In this phase, a Virus Agent can move to the Cell Agent's container, and send a message to the latter triggering the infection. This causes the Cyclic Behaviour to be removed, and the Cell Agent's antigen to be modified according to the Virus Agent needs.
- **Infected:** After a Cell Agent has been infected by a Virus Agent, the only Cyclic Behaviour which remains listens to T-Cell Agents (since cannot be infected anymore by being already infected the behaviour listening for the Virus Agent is removed after the previous step). Such behaviour listens for messages from any T-Cell which is located inside the Cell Agent's container. When this happens, the T-Cell Agent asks the Cell Agent to communicate its own antigen, and if the antigen (which was previously modified by the virus) is recognised by the T-Cell Agent, the Cell Agent (along with its residing virus) is killed.
- **Regenerating:** After the Cell Agent has been killed by the T-Cell Agent, the Cell Agent can start a process of rebirth (induced by neighbour cells). Hence, a new Cell Agent is created to substitute the previously killed one. After that, the cell is considered healthy again and the process can restart.

We want to linger a bit longer on the regeneration phase. In particular, we have to point out that the act of regenerating a new cell is not a trivial process, and is not always possible in real life scenarios. Indeed, not all cells in the human body can be regenerated; an example are brain and heart cells, which once they are lost, for any reason, are not regenerated by the body (causing the affected organ to function in a more limited way, *i.e.*, never fully recovering). In MAiS, we are currently focusing on cells that can be regenerated, according to some regeneration factor (which of course would depend on the typology of the cell).

The other fundamental aspect of the Cell Agent is the communication with the other agents in the system. As we mentioned before, depending on which

[4] A behaviour which is cyclically executed by the JADE agent (until is not removed).

state the Cell Agent currently is, the communication may vary. When the Cell Agent is healthy, the infection from a Virus Agent can be triggered by message exchange. The same reasoning is followed with the T-Cell Agent as well, which can trigger the destruction of the cell and the virus by message exchange. Specifically, at the Cell Agent level, we may find three different kind of messages being exchanged:

- **Virus→Cell:** When the Virus Agent enters the Cell Agent's container, it sends a message to the Cell Agent informing the latter of the attack and requesting the Cell Agent to change. This is obtained in JADE by exchanging an `REQUEST` message[5] over a specific communication channel, named `Update_Antigen_Peptide`.
- **Cell↔T-Cell:** When a T-Cell Agent enters the Cell Agent's container, it sends a message to the Cell Agent asking to verify the cell's antigen. This is obtained in JADE by exchanging a `REQUEST` message over a specific communication channel, named `Antigen_Peptide_Verification`. Upon such request, the Cell Agent sends a message over the same channel informing the T-Cell of the current antigen peptide sequence.
- **T-Cell→Cell:** Finally, when a T-Cell Agent has killed a Cell Agent (along with its virus), it sends a message to the Cell Agent asking to start the regeneration process. This is obtained in JADE by exchanging an `INFORM` message over the `Start_Regeneration` communication channel (which triggers the cell regeneration).

4.2 T-Cell Agent

The T-Cell Agent is the agent which executes the task of identifying and killing infected cells. Upon initiation, the T-Cell Agent is created inside a random container. This is a mobile agent which can move from one container to another one. Such movement is allowed only between containers that are neighbours on the grid (as presented in Sect. 3). After moving to a new container, the T-Cell Agent asks the Cell Agent present in that container to verify its antigen peptide sequence. Upon retrieval of the antigen peptide, it performs an identification process to detect whether the cell has been infected by a virus known by the T-Cell Agent. If that is the case, it kills the Cell Agent present in that container and sends a request to the corresponding Cell Agent to start the regeneration process. After completing the killing step, the T-Cell Agent restarts moving to a new neighbour container and it repeats its Cyclic Behaviours.

As we did for the Cell Agent, let us focus on the behaviours of the T-Cell Agent. In more detail, a T-Cell agent enacts three different behaviours, which correspond to three different states.

- **Searching:** The T-Cell Agent's standard behaviour is to move between neighbour cells. This is obtained in JADE by instantiating a One-Shot Behaviour[6]

[5] A message with `INFORM` FIPA performative.

[6] A behaviour which is executed by the agent only once.

which makes the agent move from the current container to a neighbour one. This is obtained by calling the native JADE method `doMove()`, which moves the agent into a destination container (passed as argument). The movement is completely handled by the JADE framework, and makes the movement amongst different cell containers transparent to the T-Cell Agent.

- **Checking:** After completing the movement and having reached a new cell to inspect, the T-Cell Agent communicates with the Cell Agent inside the currently visited container asking for its antigen peptide sequence. This is implemented as a One-Shot behaviour and consists in not only the communication step with the Cell Agent, but in the verification of the antigen peptide sequence as well. After such identification is completed, if the T-Cell detected the antigen peptide as the one of the virus, then the T-Cell Agent carries on with the killing of the Cell Agent (along with its residing virus). Otherwise, the T-Cell Agent restarts moving as explained in the previous step, since the currently analysed cell is healthy (or is infected by a virus that is not recognisable by the T-Cell Agent[7]).
- **Killing:** In case the antigen peptide sequence of the analysed Cell Agent actually matches the one recognised by the T-Cell Agent, there is an infected cell to kill (to stop the replication). In JADE this is obtained by instantiating a One-Shot Behaviour calling the JADE native method `kill()`, which kills an agent in the MAS. After the Cell Agent, and its Virus Agent, have been killed, the T-Cell Agent communicates to the Cell Agent in the container asking to start the regeneration process. After that, it restarts moving.

The communication aspects which are relevant for the T-Cell Agent are the messages exchanged with the Cell Agent about the verification of the antigen peptide sequence. We have already explained how such message passing works in the previous section, where the T-Cell agent sends a `REQUEST` message over the `Antigen_Peptide_Verification` communication channel to the Cell Agent, and waits for the corresponding `INFORM` message containing the sequence to verify.

Figure 2 reports a Sequence Diagram on the interaction between a Cell Agent and a T-Cell Agent. Such diagram schematically presents the steps carried out by a T-Cell Agent w.r.t. a Cell Agent, as we explained previously. Note that, the diagram is very abstract. To be more precise, the `doMove()` method requires the name of the target container in advance (such information is stored inside each Cell Agent, which keeps track of both the current container, and the neighbour ones). The rest of the methods and messages used in the diagram have been presented before, and their meaning is straightforward.

[7] We have to keep in mind that a T-Cell Agent is specific for a single Virus Agent, it knows how to recognise and destroy only that kind of virus; all other viruses in the system are invisible to it.

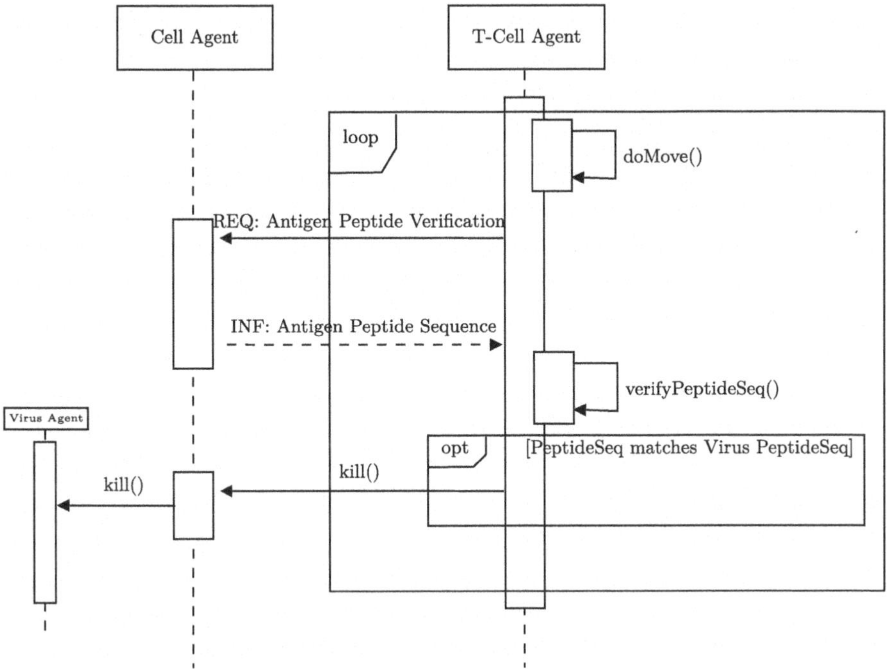

Fig. 2. Sequence diagram of the interaction amongst a Cells Agents and T-Cell Agents.

4.3 Virus Agent

The Virus Agent mimics a virus in real life whose goal is to replicate itself exploiting the resources of the host cells. Differently from the T-Cell Agent, the Virus Agent is not a mobile agent. In fact, it can only move by replicating itself to the adjacent cells. Like it happens in nature, the Virus Agent has a replication factor, which defines how many copies the Virus Agent can make of itself before destroying the host cell. Such replication factor is an input parameter of MAiS, and it can be customised to simulate different replication scenarios. The Virus Agent is spawn in a random container in the grid at the beginning of the simulation (naturally multiple viruses can be spawn at the same time). Subsequently, the Virus Agent asks the cell in such container to change its own antigen peptide sequence by marking that the virus is now present in that cell. Once the infection of the cell is completed, the Virus Agent starts replicating to the neighbour cells. This is obtained by spawning a random number (according to the replication factor) of instantiations of the Virus Agent in a random set of neighbour cells. Once a new Virus Agent is created inside a neighbour cell, then the same process described above is reiterated (*i.e.*, infection and replication, in this order). Since a cell could have been previously infected by another instance of the same virus, the Virus Agent also checks if the Cell Agent can, or not, be infected. In case this is not possible, then the Virus Agent stops replicating and dies. Otherwise, it infects the Cell Agent and continues its replication.

After a certain amount of time (which can be parameterised in MAiS), the Virus Agent kills the host Cell Agent and thereby commits suicide. Hence, once the resources of a cell have been completely consumed by the virus, the virus dies (*i.e.*, the corresponding Virus Agent is killed calling the `kill()` method).

Let us now focus on the behaviours of the Virus Agent. Specifically, such agent enacts three different behaviour, which correspond to three different states of the agent.

- **Infecting:** When an agent is born in a container, the first thing it does is to try to infect the hosting cell (*i.e.*, the Cell Agent inside the container). To achieve this in JADE, a One-Shot Behaviour is instantiated. Such behaviour has the task of communicating with the Cell Agent. In more detail, the Virus Agent informs the Cell Agent of being infected, and forcing the latter to change the antigen peptide sequence, consequently.
- **Cloning:** After the Cell Agent inside the container has been successfully infected, the Virus Agent starts spreading amongst the neighbour cells. This is obtained by means of another One-Shot Behaviour, which calls the JADE native `createNewAgent()` method to spawn new Virus Agents inside neighbour cells. Such method is used a random number of times, on a random number of neighbour cells (depending on the replication factor).
- **Killing:** After the cell has been infected, and the Virus Agent has successfully completed its cloning phase, the Virus Agent keeps feeding on the cell resources (simulated inside the Cell Agent). When such resources end, the Virus Agent kills the cell (by calling `kill()` method on the Cell Agent), and kills itself (by calling the `kill()` method on itself). This sequence of actions is performed inside a One-Shot Behaviour as well.

The only communication carried out by the Virus Agent is the one with the Cell Agent. The message passing involved in such communication are used to inform the Cell Agent that has been infected by a virus, and that the antigen peptide sequence needs to be updated. This is obtained by sending an `INFORM` message from the Virus Agent to the Cell Agent over the `Update_Antigen_Peptide` communication channel.

Figure 3 reports a Sequence Diagram of the interaction between a Cell Agent and a Virus Agent. Again, this diagram is very abstract, and serves us only to help the reader to better visualise the sequence of actions carried out by the Virus and Cell Agents. Note that, on the left, the diagram shows the actions concerning the infection of a cell. While on the right, it shows the resulting cloning phase of the virus on the neighbour containers (*i.e.*, neighbour cells, since each container contains one cell in the current definition).

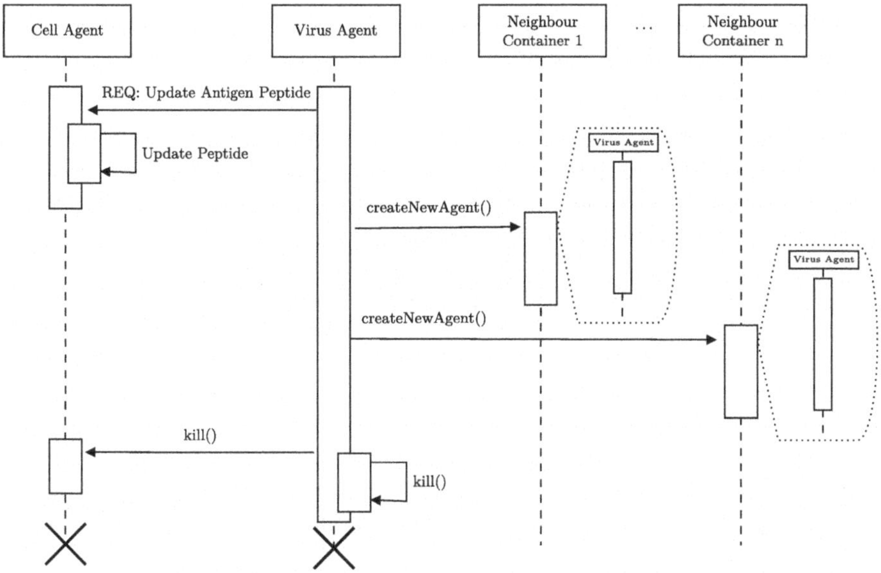

Fig. 3. Sequence diagram of the interaction amongst a Cells Agents and Virus Agents.

5 Experiments

An initial prototype of MAiS can be found as a publicly available GitHub repository[8]. In the current state, the tool can be customised through a list of parameters. Each parameter influences a different aspect of the simulation, and can be used to model different scenarios. The available parameters are the following:

- *GRID_SIZE*: the size of the grid of cells (as shown in Fig. 1, on the right).
- *T-CELL_SLEEP_TIME*: the number of milliseconds that T-Cell Agent stays in a cell before moving on with its exploration.
- *VIRUS_REPLICATION_TIME*: the number of milliseconds that a Virus Agent takes to perform replication (*i.e.*, between creation and replication).
- *VIRUS_REPLICATION_FACTOR*: the factor by which the virus multiplies.
- *CELL_IDENTIFYING_PEPTIDE*: the initial peptide of a healthy cell.
- *KILL_THE_CELL_AFTERWARD*: the number of milliseconds after which the Virus Agent kills the host cell.

Given the list of parameters presented above, we carried out experiments varying the two following parameters:

- **Grid Size:** Given an assumption of a square-shaped universe, the grid size represents the length of a side in unit grid.

[8] https://github.com/sanchayan721/Multi_agent_Immune_System.

– **Replication factor:** The replication factor of the virus (e.g., if the replication factor is n, then the virus makes n copies of itself to the adjacent containers in each cycle).

We perform some experiments with varying number of these *two* parameters while capturing the behaviour of the system as a whole. Moreover, we were interested in inspecting both the infection and death rate of the cells in the course of the simulation. Every consecutive simulation was created with an increasing number of containers (*i.e.*, cells), one Virus Agent and one T-Cell Agent. At the beginning of each simulation, the Virus Agent is dropped in a random container and starts replicating itself according to its replication factor parameter, while the T-Cell Agent, already present in the system since the beginning of the simulation, searches for the virus from one container to another. We also created a Monitor Agent to dynamically keep track of the number of infected and dead cells. Every 50 milliseconds, such agent collects the data and stores them into a *.csv* file. These log files are then used to plot the so obtained results; some of them are reported in Fig. 4. Note that, every simulation is stopped when there are no virus left in the system.

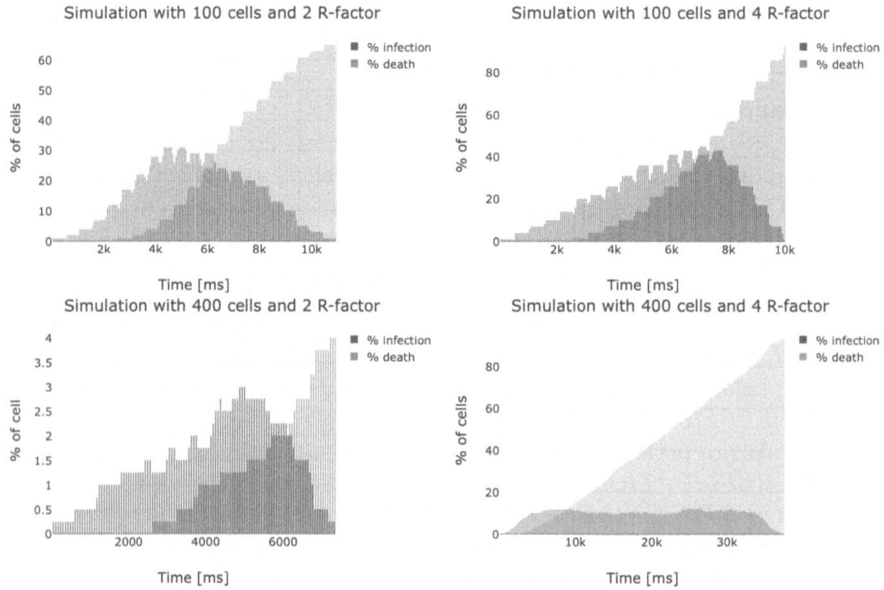

Fig. 4. Results obtained through our experiments.

Figure 4 reports four different scenarios that we have experimented. The first (top left) is a scenario with 100 cells (*i.e.*, 10×10 grid) and replication factor set to 2, the second (top right) with 100 cells and replication factor 4, the third (bottom left) with 400 cells (*i.e.*, 20×20 grid) and replication factor 2, and finally, the fourth (bottom right) with 400 cells and replication factor 4. In each scenario, we can observe how there is a delay between the percentage of infected cells, and the percentage of death cells. This derives by the intrinsic nature of infections, where a virus first infects a cell and then, after depriving the latter of all its resources, kills it. In most of the reported experiments (3 out of 4), the virus ends up killing most of the cells before being killed by the T-cell lymphocyte, or dying from starvation. Indeed, in all but the third scenario (bottom left), the percentage of death cells reaches 60% (top left), 80% (top right), and 90% (bottom right) of the total population of cells. In the third case, we have an example of simulation where the t-cell is capable of detecting the virus soon enough to stop its replication; in fact, in such simulation, the percentage of death cells reaches only 4% of the entire population. Another interesting aspect to note is the behaviour we obtain in the fourth scenario. In there, by having a large matrix (200×200 containers) and a high replication factor, the virus succeeds in replicating and is the scenario in fact where we obtain the highest percentage of death cells (since the fast replication is not successfully fought by the T-cell lymphocyte in such bigger area).

Before moving on with the related work section, we want to point out that MAiS is currently at the beginning of its development, and the experiments we carried out are only meant to show its initial results and to perform some empirical testing. We are already planning to build on top of MAiS, to enrich its features, and to experiment it on more challenging scenarios.

6 Related Work

Naturally, one cannot talk about agent-based simulation without citing Netlogo[9]. In fact, also in the context of simulating the immune system, we may find many applications based on Netlogo (a detailed review on the topic [4]). When considering such applications, the most relevant difference w.r.t. MAiS is scalability. Netlogo is mainly an academic centralised simulator, and it is hard to decentralise (only features to perform concurrent executions exist), which makes it not suitable when the number of agents to simulate grows too much.

One first category of works which are related to the one presented in this paper are the ones which belong to the area of Artificial Immune Systems (AIS). In [17], the authors present an intelligent multiagent model based on the artificial immune system, named AISIMAM. In [17], AISIMAM is not used to simulate how the immune system works, but as it happens in other disciplines, such as genetic programming, AISIMAM aims at exploiting mechanics which efficiently work in nature. Specifically, it applies them to a mine detection scenario. A similar work can be found in [1], where a MAS is designed to mimic the human immune system behaviour. Also here, the resulting model is applied to a certain domain of interest, which is power system reconfiguration and restoration. AIS have also been applied in the robotic scenario [6], where autonomous mobile robots emulate the natural behaviours of cells and molecules to realise

[9] http://www.netlogoweb.org.

their group behaviours (*i.e.*, cooperation). Similarly, in [9], AIS are also used to engineer the organisational layer in a MAS, when exploited with simulated robot soccer. Another scenario where AIS have found application in MAS is the flexible job shop scheduling problem (FJSP). In [21], the authors analyse similarities between FJSP and humoral immunity, which is one of the immune responses. Based on the similarities, a new immune multi-agent scheduling system (NIMASS) to solve the FJSP with the objective of minimizing the maximal completion time is presented. The Agent-Based Artificial Immune System (AbAIS) [12] is a framework that uses a hybrid architecture where heterogeneous agents evolve in a cellular automata environment and are modelled following a genetic approach. AbAIs is applied to intrusion detection systems (IDS). Finally, we can find AIS implemented in JADE as well. Also in such works, the aim is not to simulate the immune system, but to take inspiration from it to solve different tasks. We may find [16], where an AIS is developed in JADE and used in a process for gas purification from acidic components, or [8], where it is used to minimise the operational cost of microgrids and maximise the real-time response in grid-connected microgrids, or [10], where a mobile agent-based system architecture is proposed in JADE to monitor machine condition by imitating the human immune system, or finally [5], where the AIS in JADE is used to handle disturbance management in the monitoring and control of production systems.

Unlike MAiS, all these works are not interested in designing, engineering, and developing an agent-based simulation of the immune system; instead, they are examples of how to take inspiration from the immune system to solve general MAS problems.

The second category of works which are related to our contribution is those that present agent-based simulations of the immune system. Numerous existing works are on agent-based immune system models. CAFISS [20] models cell-to-cell interactions in a grid with each cell denoted by a bit string. In [20], the authors describe a Java-based implementation of a framework to model the immune system, particularly the attack by the human immunodeficiency virus (or HIV), using a complex adaptive systems model (CAS). The only downside of such a solution is that it is not very scalable; indeed, it has a large overhead caused by the use of separate threads for each cell. ImmSim [3,14] is a simulator based on cellular automata developed in APL2 [7]; the framework exploits task parallelism on distributed computers and because of this it is able to reduce execution time and supports large-scale simulations. ImmSim is also the base on which ImmunoGrid [13], and Sentinel [15], two other immune system simulators, have been built. Swarms [11] is a three-dimensional model of the human immune system and its response to exposure to the first and second viral antigens (implemented in BREVE [19], a physics-based ABMS engine).

For further reading on existing ABM techniques to simulate the immune system, a detailed review can be found in [18].

To the best of our knowledge, no agent-based immune system simulation has been proposed in JADE before.

7 Comparison with Existing Immune System Simulators

The study of immune system dynamics has been approached through various computational frameworks, each employing different methodologies to achieve scalability, granularity, and computational efficiency. While the previous section outlined key immune system simulators, this section provides a structured comparison to highlight the distinctions between MAiS and such established models.

MAiS leverages the distributed agent-based paradigm of JADE, offering a fine-grained, dynamic, and scalable alternative to existing models such as *ImmunoGrid* [13], *Sentinel* [15], *CAFISS* [20], and *ImmSim/Swarms* [3,11,14]. Table 1 summarises the key differences among these approaches, highlighting aspects such as modelling paradigms, computational frameworks, scalability, and real-time agent interactions.

Note that, ImmSim and Swarms are grouped together as they both employ a hybrid approach combining agent-based modeling and cellular automata, leveraging distributed task parallelism to simulate immune responses. While ImmSim focusses on stochastic immune interactions, Swarms introduces swarm intelligence principles, yet both share conceptual similarities in modelling emergent immune behaviours and distributed computation.

Table 1. Comparison of MAiS with existing immune system simulation frameworks

Framework	MAiS	ImmunoGrid [13]	Sentinel [15]	CAFISS [20]	ImmSim/Swarms [3,11,14]
Modelling Approach	Agent-Based (JADE)	System-Level Grid Computing	Cellular Automata	Complex Adaptive System (CAS)	Hybrid ABM + Cellular Automata
Computational Framework	JADE (Java)	Grid Computing (Distributed HPC)	Distributed Parallel Simulation	Java-based Grid Framework	Custom-built Simulators (APL2, BREVE)
Granularity	Individual cells (fine-grained)	System-level immune response	Mid-level (cell-tissue interactions)	Molecular-level modeling	Hybrid (cell-level & multi-scale)
Agent Mobility	Yes (native JADE migration)	No	No	No	Partial (Swarms has mobility)
Real-Time Interaction	Yes (dynamic agent adaptation)	No (batch-mode processing)	No (discrete simulation steps)	No (predefined agent rules)	Partial (Swarms has emergent behaviors)
Scalability	Distributed over multiple JADE containers	Requires HPC/Grid Infrastructure	Moderate scalability	High scalability but with overhead	Limited scalability
Use Cases	Cellular immune response, T-cell movement, localized infection control	Vaccine discovery, antigen processing, large-scale immune modeling	Immune response simulations (HIV, cancer, pathogen spread)	HIV immune response, system-level pathogen interactions	Multi-scale immune modeling (robotic swarms, viral antigen exposure)

Real-Time Agent Mobility. Most existing immune simulators rely on static models in which cells and pathogens interact within fixed spatial grids. MAiS introduces a real-time, autonomous migration of immune agents, which more accurately reflects biological processes such as T cell movement and infection spread (even though it is still a prototype at its initial stage).

Container-Based Distributed Execution. While frameworks like ImmunoGrid scale by distributing computations across high-performance clusters, MAiS utilises JADE's multi-container architecture, allowing immune agents to be dynamically distributed across multiple nodes. This enables a scalable execution model that does not depend on access to specialised computing infrastructure.

Asynchronous and Adaptive Interaction. ImmunoGrid and Sentinel use batch-mode updates where agent interactions occur at predefined steps. MAiS, in contrast, operates in an asynchronous event-driven manner, allowing agents to react dynamically to infections, immune activation, and pathogen evolution.

Scalability in a Distributed Agent-Based Framework. Existing models such as Sentinel and ImmSim achieve scalability through task parallelism and distributed computing but lack an integrated agent-based structure. MAiS scales by using distributed JADE containers, allowing agents to migrate dynamically across the computing nodes. This, theoretically speaking, supports larger-scale simulations while maintaining biological accuracy at the cellular level. Naturally, being MAiS at its infancy, this is a possible future direction, but is based on the agent-based nature of MAiS.

8 Conclusions and Future Work

In this paper, we present the building blocks of MAiS, an agent-based simulator built in JADE to reproduce the immune system of the human body in a distributed and scalable manner. We are well aware that the actual immune system is extremely complex and that MAiS only tackles a very specific aspect of it. However, the current work allowed us to focus on the initial engineering steps required to map the immune system in JADE. In fact, we showed how some of the main organic actors (cells, lymphocyte, and so on) can be mapped into their corresponding agent representation in JADE, and how a specific step of the immune system's response can be simulated through such agents. Moreover, we showed how the innate JADE agent's mobility and containers' distributability are key features of such a mapping.

As future directions, we plan to further expand MAiS by introducing additional immune agents and enriching their behavioural dynamics to better capture complex immune responses.

A key focus will be on systematically evaluating the scalability and distributed execution capabilities of JADE, assessing how these features influence simulation performance and biological accuracy. To achieve this, we will conduct benchmarking experiments with increasing agent populations and multi-container execution, providing empirical validation of MAiS's scalability advantages.

Furthermore, a structured performance comparison with existing agent-based simulators such as *ImmunoGrid*, *Sentinel*, and *ImmSim* will be performed to evaluate execution efficiency and computational overhead in large-scale immune simulations.

Beyond scalability, our aim is to enhance the biological fidelity of MAiS by incorporating more complex immune interactions, including cytokine signaling, antigen presentation mechanisms, and adaptive immune memory formation. These extensions will enable more biologically relevant simulations, positioning MAiS as a versatile framework for immune system modelling.

References

1. Belkacemi, R., Feliachi, A.: Multi-agent design for power distribution system reconfiguration based on the artificial immune system algorithm. In: International Symposium on Circuits and Systems (ISCAS 2010), 30 May–2 June 2010, Paris, France, pp. 3461–3464. IEEE (2010). https://doi.org/10.1109/ISCAS.2010.5537841
2. Bellifemine, F.L., Caire, G., Greenwood, D.: Developing Multi-agent Systems with JADE (Wiley Series in Agent Technology). Wiley (2007)
3. Bernaschi, M., Castiglione, F.: Design and implementation of an immune system simulator. Comput. Biol. Med. **31**(5), 303–331 (2001). https://doi.org/10.1016/S0010-4825(01)00011-7
4. Castiglione, F., Chiacchio, F., Pennisi, M., Russo, G., Motta, S., Pappalardo, F.: Agent-based modeling of the immune system: Netlogo, a promising framework. Biomed. Res. Int. **2014**, 907171 (2014). https://doi.org/10.1155/2014/907171
5. Darmoul, S., Pierreval, H., Gabouj, S.H.: An immune inspired multi agent system to handle disruptions in manufacturing production systems. In: International Conference on Industrial Engineering and Systems Management, IESM, vol. 2011 (2011)
6. Dioubate, M., Guanzheng, T., Toure Mohamed, L.: An artificial immune system based multi-agent model and its application to robot cooperation problem. In: 2008 7th World Congress on Intelligent Control and Automation, pp. 3033–3039 (2008). https://doi.org/10.1109/WCICA.2008.4593405
7. Falkoff, A.D.: The IBM family of APL systems. IBM Syst. J. **30**(4), 416–432 (1991). https://doi.org/10.1147/sj.304.0416
8. Harmouch, F.Z., Ebrahim, A.F., Esfahani, M.M., Krami, N., Hmina, N., Mohammed, O.A.: An optimal energy management system for real-time operation of multiagent-based microgrids using a t-cell algorithm. Energies **12**(15) (2019). https://doi.org/10.3390/en12153004, https://www.mdpi.com/1996-1073/12/15/3004
9. Hilaire, V., Koukam, A., Rodriguez, S.: An adaptative agent architecture for holonic multi-agent systems. ACM Trans. Auton. Adapt. Syst. **3**(1), 2:1–2:24 (2008). https://doi.org/10.1145/1342171.1342173
10. Hua, X.L., Gondal, I., Yaqub, F.: Mobile agent based artificial immune system for machine condition monitoring. In: 2013 IEEE 8th Conference on Industrial Electronics and Applications (ICIEA), pp. 108–113. IEEE (2013)

11. Jacob, C., Litorco, J., Lee, L.: Immunity through swarms: agent-based simulations of the human immune system. In: Nicosia, G., Cutello, V., Bentley, P.J., Timmis, J. (eds.) ICARIS 2004. LNCS, vol. 3239, pp. 400–412. Springer, Heidelberg (2004). https://doi.org/10.1007/978-3-540-30220-9_32
12. Ou, C.M., Ou, C., Wang, Y.T.: Agent-based artificial immune systems (ABAIS) for intrusion detections: inspiration from danger theory. In: Hakansson, A., Hartung, R. (eds.) Agent and Multi-Agent Systems in Distributed Systems - Digital Economy and E-Commerce. SCI, vol. 462, pp. 67–94. Springer, Cham (2013). https://doi.org/10.1007/978-3-642-35208-9_4
13. Pappalardo, F., et al.: ImmunoGrid, an integrative environment for large-scale simulation of the immune system for vaccine discovery, design and optimization. Briefings Bioinform. **10**(3), 330–340 (2009). https://doi.org/10.1093/bib/bbp014
14. Puzone, R., Kohler, B., Seiden, P., Celada, F.: IMMSIM, a flexible model for in machina experiments on immune system responses. Future Gener. Comput. Syst. **18**(7), 961–972 (2002). https://doi.org/10.1016/S0167-739X(02)00075-4
15. Robbins, M.J., Garrett, S.M.: Evaluating theories of immunological memory using large-scale simulations. In: Jacob, C., Pilat, M.L., Bentley, P.J., Timmis, J.I. (eds.) ICARIS 2005. LNCS, vol. 3627, pp. 193–206. Springer, Heidelberg (2005). https://doi.org/10.1007/11536444_15
16. Samigulina, G.A., Samigulina, Z.I.: Design of technology for prediction and control system based on artificial immune systems and the multi-agent platform JADE. In: Jezic, G., Chen-Burger, J., Kusek, M., Sperka, R., Howlett, R.J., Jain, L.C. (eds.) Agents and Multi-Agent Systems: Technologies and Applications 2020. SIST, vol. 186, pp. 143–153. Springer, Singapore (2020). https://doi.org/10.1007/978-981-15-5764-4_13
17. Sathyanath, S., Sahin, F.: Application of artificial immune system based intelligent multi agent model to a mine detection problem. In: IEEE International Conference on Systems, Man and Cybernetics. vol. 3, p. 6 (2002). https://doi.org/10.1109/ICSMC.2002.1176015
18. Shinde, S.B., Kurhekar, M.P.: Review of the systems biology of the immune system using agent-based models. IET Syst. Biol. **12**(3), 83–92 (2018)
19. Spector, L., Klein, J., Perry, C., Feinstein, M.: Emergence of collective behavior in evolving populations of flying agents. Genet. Program Evolvable Mach. **6**(1), 111–125 (2005). https://doi.org/10.1007/s10710-005-7620-3
20. Tay, J.C., Jhavar, A.: CAFISS: a complex adaptive framework for immune system simulation. In: Haddad, H., Liebrock, L.M., Omicini, A., Wainwright, R.L. (eds.) Proceedings of the 2005 ACM Symposium on Applied Computing (SAC), Santa Fe, New Mexico, USA, 13–17 March 2005, pp. 158–164. ACM (2005). https://doi.org/10.1145/1066677.1066716
21. Xiong, W., Fu, D.: A new immune multi-agent system for the flexible job shop scheduling problem. J. Intell. Manuf. **29**(4), 857–873 (2015). https://doi.org/10.1007/s10845-015-1137-2

Standardize Data Synchronization Policies for Distributed Agent-Based Simulations Using Proxies

Lucas Grosjean[1,2(✉)], Paul Breugnot[1,2], Alexis Drogoul[1], Bénédicte Herrmann[2], Nghi Quang Huynh[1,3], Christophe Lang[2], Nicolas Marilleau[1,2], and Laurent Philippe[2]

[1] UMI 209, UMMISCO, IRD, Sorbonne Université, Bondy, France
Lucas.grosjean@ird.fr
[2] Université Marie et Louis Pasteur, CNRS, institut FEMTO-ST, 25000 Besançon, France
[3] Can Tho University, Can Tho, Vietnam

Abstract. Agent-based modeling, or agent-based model (ABM), is a powerful tool that helps researchers understand complex and high-stakes problems, such as the impact of climate change, digital twins, or epidemiology issues. However, as the scale and/or the precision of these models increase, performance problems emerge when running large simulations on standard computers. Agent-based simulation platforms, can no longer run these large-scale models in a reasonable amount of time, or even cannot run them at all. To address these problems, ABM can be distributed using High-Performance Computing (HPC) techniques to divide the workload across multiple processors, speeding up the simulation execution. Distribution bring the need for defining data synchronization protocols between processors, and ways to access agents across processors to properly execute the distributed simulation. To tackle the issues introduced by the distribution of a model, we propose the concept of *proxy*: entities managing interactions between agents across distributed instances of a simulation and controlling access to agent data using *data synchronization policies*. The effectiveness is shown through a case study using the GAMA platform.

Keywords: Data synchronization · Distribution · Agent-based modeling

1 Introduction

Agent-based approaches are well suited to represent and understand complex systems. Agent Based Models (ABM) are indeed used in numerous contexts [1–5], to simulate the behavior of various systems and showcase the emergence of global trends from individuals, by modeling the behavior of individual agents and their interactions.

R. Collier et al. (Eds.): EUMAS 2024, LNAI 15685, pp. 21–38, 2025.
https://doi.org/10.1007/978-3-031-93930-3_2

However, as the scale and/or the precision of these models increase, performance problems emerge when running large simulations on standard computers. Since most agent-based simulation platforms run on these type of computer, the execution of large-scale models is sometimes no longer possible, or not possible within a reasonable time. In this case, the use of high-performance computing (HPC) techniques, by distributing the same simulation across multiple processors that does not shared memory, opens up interesting prospects for overcoming resource constraints and hardware limitations of large-scale simulation.

Thus, despite the intrinsically "distributed" nature of multi-agent systems, these systems describe a single world with synchronized interactions and shared data. Distributed agent-based simulations, for instance, require frequent synchronization operations, such as updating the state of the environment and the agents perceptions, that are not taken into account into the HPC Agent-based simulation platforms, making their distribution still challenging. The distribution of an ABM is therefore neither a trivial task, nor easily generalizable.

Some HPC Agent-based modeling and simulation platforms (HPC ABMS) emerged [6–14], proposing frameworks that help users designing distributed ABM and deal with some of the distribution issues. Several challenges however remains open.

A critical problematic in distributed ABM simulation is effectively managing data synchronization among the set of processors. As the agent set is split across the processors, it is often required for an agent to access other agents, located on different processors, to interact with them. While agents can be easily copied to make interactions possible, many issues arise from having multiple copies in the distributed simulation. Data synchronization is needed to ensure that interactions between agents follow rules or policies, keeping the distributed simulation coherent. The main focus of this article is thus on improving data synchronization in distributed simulations.

While data synchronization remains not supported in many HPC ABMS platforms, FPMAS [15] was the first platform to define data synchronization rules for distributed simulation. While their proposition represents a promising start, it lacks a formal frame to define these interactions and the interaction scheme is limited. This paper proposes solutions to address two critical challenges to take better account of data synchronization in distributed agent based simulations: (i) **Standardizing the way to describe ABM distribution**, to describe data synchronization in a standard, and (ii) **Taking user input in the process**, to adapt data synchronization policies to each model with input from the user. The contribution of this article is to introduce two new concepts:

- **Proxies:** entities acting as an agents unique contact point for other agents interacting with this agent
- **Data synchronization Policy:** a formal language/notation for specifying data synchronization across various levels (simulation, species, and individual) in distributed agent-based simulations

We introduce these two concepts as a way to provide a flexible, customized and standardized management of distributed interactions and to improve data synchronization following the targeted challenges. The GAMA Platform is our testing ground to validate the effectiveness and practicality of our data synchronization approaches and concepts.

To have a better understanding of the possible issues in distributing ABM, existing platforms are reviewed in Sect. 2: fully centralized ABM, distribution-oriented ABM, and ABM that were initially centralized but have been adapted for distribution purposes. Identifying implemented data synchronization solutions on these platforms is the objective of the review. In Sect. 3, we present *proxies* and how they can be used to improve the data synchronization policies in any ABM and how they can be used by users to adapt data synchronization policies to their needs. In Sect. 4, we show the use of proxies with a proof-of-concept ABM developed with the GAMA Platform. This section analyses synchronization policies implemented with proxies and their impact on coherence and performance in GAMA simulations. Lastly, we conclude in Sect. 5.

2 Data Synchronization in Distributed ABM

While the autonomous nature of agents might suggest that distributing ABM simulations is straightforward, this is however not the case. In the now relatively vast field of Agent-Based Modeling and Simulation (ABMS) [16–18], the development of distributed ABM simulations has not reached the same level of sophistication as centralized modeling. Some platforms are still specialized in distributing ABM like FPMAS [6], PDES-MAS [7], Pandora [8], MASS [9], FAME-core [10], Care HPS [11], FLAME and FLAME GPU [12]. While others, initially focused on centralized environments, have since been able to distribute simulation, e.g. Repast [19] with RepastHPC [13] and Mason [20] with D-MASON [14]. In the following, we analyze the issues arising when synchronizing data in a distributed ABM environment. This analysis builds upon existing work in the field through the previously cited platforms.

2.1 Coherence in Distributed Simulation

In distributed ABM simulations, keeping data consistent across processors during run time is a challenge for efficient large-scale simulations. Data synchronization ensures that agents access consistent data, from other processors and have access to coherent copy of data. Addressing this issue is crucial to maintain the coherence of large scale simulations.

To illustrate the state of data synchronization in the literature, we use the example of a Prey-Predator model [21] defined as:

"*Preys and Predators are moving around the space. If they have enough energy, Preys and Predators reproduce with other members of their population following a stochastic law (normal distribution). When a Predator is in range of an alive Prey with less than 25 energy, it kills and eats the Prey to consume its energy. A Predator cannot eat a prey with more than 25 energy, as it runs too*

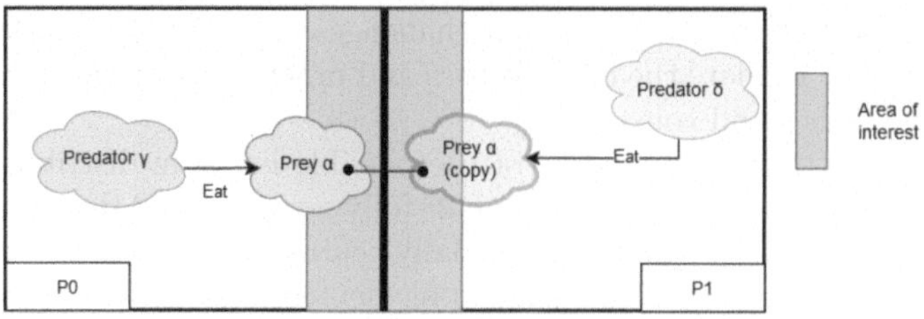

Fig. 1. Incoherence in a distributed Prey-Predator model: Prey α can be eated by two Predators at the same time on different processors.

fast. When a Prey or a Predator runs out of energy, it dies.". A sequential simulation of this model ensures that each predator always has an exclusive access to preys, so there is no need for explicit concurrency management in this case.

In distributed simulation, preys and predators are executed on different processors, as shown in Fig. 1. In order to allow Predator δ, running on P1, to interact with the Prey α, on P0, a copy of Prey α can be created on P1. Note that the concept of "copy" is known by different names in ABM literature, e.g., "proxy agent", "distant agent", or "copy agent". The introduction of a copy of Prey α can lead to this prey being consumed by two predators at the same time: Predator γ can consume Prey α and Predator δ can consume the copy agent. The incoherence in the distributed model generates biases that could violate rules of the ABM and potentially leads to wrong results compared to the centralized execution of the model. The distributed model architecture and data synchronization mechanisms can introduce inconsistencies in some models, if they do not fit correctly with the needs of the ABM.

2.2 Current Proposition in HPC ABMS

HPC ABMS platforms, like RepastHPC [13], Pandora [8], and D-Mason [20] use local and distant agents to access data across processors. They update the copy agent with the most recent data of the local agent between each step. This can however lead to inconsistencies as interactions with copy or local agent are treated identically. FLAME [22] uses a strong conservative messaging board to synchronize the data. It prevents incoherence at the cost of relying on the message board for all interactions. From an user point of view, it might be difficult to understand how data synchronization is performed on these HPC ABMS platforms.

In FPMAS [15], distant agents are created to ensure that every processor has access to agents needed to execute their simulation, updating the set of distant agents at each step. They define "synchronization modes" (see Table 1) to ensure data synchronization in interactions between agents and all agents follow the same mode in the simulation. Each mode has a purpose regarding data synchronization. Authors give these definitions [15]:

Table 1. Synchronization modes defined in FPMAS

Synchronization Mode	*self*	*local*		*distant*	
	write	read	write	read	write
GhostMode	T	T	T	T−1	×
GlobalGhostMode	T+1	T−1	×	T−1	×
HardSyncMode	T	T	T	T	T
PushGhostMode	T	T	T	T−1	T+1
PushGlobalGhostMode	T+1	T−1	T+1	T−1	T+1

- *GhostMode:* no restriction on local agent, distant agent cannot be written on, data are retrieved from the previous step only for read on distant agents.
- *GlobalGhostMode:* read always returns the state of the agent from the previous state; no write is allowed on any agent except on the agent itself.
- *HardSyncMode:* allows for all types of interactions between agents, but the consistency of read and write accesses is ensured using concurrent access algorithms. Any read or write operation on a remote agent requires communication with the processor that holds the local copy of that agent.
- *PushGhostMode:* same as *GhostMode*, but writes on distant agents are allowed. At the step end, all agents must retrieve the data from their copies and solve conflicts following an user provided conflict resolution mechanism.
- *GlobalPushGhostMode:* writes on agents are handled as distant writes in *PushGhostMode*, reads on agents return data from the previous step.

Depending on the ABM needs, the appropriate synchronization mode can be selected to cover different range of situations. In Fig. 1 a strong synchronization mode ("HardSyncMode") is appropriate. For ABM like the Flocking model a less restricting synchronization mode ("GhostMode") that requires less synchronization might be better. This work shows that the global behavior of a distributed ABM depends a lot on the choice of the synchronization mode.

2.3 Data Synchronization Policies

Synchronization modes are a first step to accurate and coherent distributed simulations. On the other hand, defining a global synchronization mode for all the agent is not flexible, as different agent behaviors may imply different types of interactions, and may lead to performance issues. For this reason, we introduce Data Synchronization Policy (or DSP) and we state that every agent need to have a different DSP, depending on its needs. Let us look at the previously defined Prey-Predator ABM example. The critical scenario requiring a strong DSP is when a predator attempts to access a remotely copied prey from another processor, i.e. when a *write* action is performed on a copy prey. The predator does not need strong synchronization since its behavior and interactions on its data happen without conflict. Thus, a solution with customised DSP for each agent or species of agents would be more suitable for distributed ABM. Since only the modelers possess the in-depth knowledge of their ABM critical interactions, their input is crucial to select the right DSP for each agent type. Moving forward, we need to break free from the limitation of a single global data synchronization mode to control synchronization at different levels.

Overcoming the DSP customization challenge requires the implementation of standardized and entirely manageable agent interaction mechanism. We hence have to manage the way agents are reached to introduce a data synchronization layer between interacting agents.

2.4 Standardized Synchronized Interactions Between Agents

Distributing an ABM is a complex and time-consuming process, which can deter people from using distributed ABM architectures. Most of the current architectures to distribute ABM force the modelers to modify the base code of their ABM to incorporate all the distribution related functions: communication between processors, partitioning of the workload, and data synchronization. Having a clear distinction between the ABM and its distribution follows the principle of separation of concerns, giving the modelers more ease in maintaining the project with two clearly identified sides: the ABM definition on one side and the distribution functions on the other. To this end, we identify key points to improve the data synchronization aspect of HPC ABMS:

- **Standardize interaction between agents:** agent interactions imply synchronizations, they must follow a well-defined standard that can describe most agent interactions in a simple way. It should allow any kind of interaction happening in the ABM to be translated and executed properly in a distributed context.
- **DSP customization:** HPC ABMS needs to be able to cover a large range of different DSP to match what modelers need in data synchronization. Data synchronization should be tailored to the specific needs of each ABM. As each species of agent has different needs, we must be able to define a DSP for each of them to improve the efficiency of the distributed simulation.

Those improvements are linked to the challenges previously stated in the introduction: (i) **Defining a standard way to describe the distribution of an ABM** and (ii) **Taking user's input in the distribution process**.

Overcoming the DSP customization challenge requires the implementation of a standardized and entirely manageable agent interaction mechanisms. We hence have to manage the way agents are reached to introduce a data synchronization layer between interacting agents.

3 Proxy: Standardize Interaction Between Agents

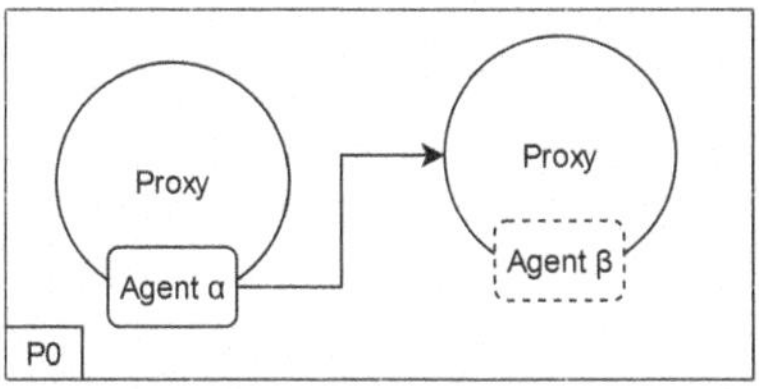

Fig. 2. When Agent α interacts with Agent β, it must go through Agent β's proxy first

To introduce a data synchronization layer for mediating agent interactions, we use **proxies**, a versatile concept enabling customization of DSP. This standardized and transparent approach leverages modelers' knowledge of simulated agent behavior to tailor synchronization within distributed simulations.

In ABM context, a proxy can be defined as an *"agent unique handle point for other agents interacting with this agent"*. In the interaction shown in Fig. 2, Agent α accesses unknowingly Agent β through its proxy. Every agent in the distributed simulation is assigned a proxy when created. Proxies ensure transparency in the interactions by hiding the process of reaching an agent and may be used to introduce control over the remote agent data. This approach was already introduced in [15] but is generalized here.

Algorithm 1. *Proxy* transparently indirecting to agent attributes

```
function GETATTRIBUTE(attributeName)
    return agent.getAttribute(attributeName)
function SETATTRIBUTE(attributeName, value)
    return agent.setAttribute(attributeName, value)
```

Algorithm 1 shows the basic implementation of a proxy. It simply implements the accessors of the agent attributes to act as a layer between interacting agents. It may be completed with any rules before and after the access to the agent attributes. For instance, rules to manage concurrency or data synchronization can be added in this layer.

3.1 Data Synchronization Policies with Proxies

DSP specifies how the attributes of an agent can be accessed by other agents depending on its location (local or distant) and the access type (read or write). The synchronization modes outlined by [15] define how agents access the data of other agents in a distributed simulation. We adapt the idea of synchronization mode and improve it by combining it with proxies. A DSP is introduced in the proxy of an agent. It controls who can read (access) and modify (write) the attributes of this agent. The agent itself does not perform action related to this control. Agent reaching another agent has to follow the DSP of the targeted agent. Figure 3 shows that DSP is set on the proxy of Agent β. In this example, the used DSP is "HardSyncMode", as introduced in Table 1. Access to Agent β

attributes is now determined by its DSP, when Agent α tries to access Agent β, the proxy of Agent β, the interaction follows its rule.

Algorithm 2 shows a possible implementation of a proxy, including a DSP. Whenever an agent tries to reach another agent data, startSync() and endSync() are called. These functions control how data access happens and are defined according to the current DSP of the proxy, startSync() and endSync() specific behavior depends on the DSP used. They can be customized to create a specific DSP according to the agent need.

Figure 4 shows how, depending on the state of an agent (local or distant), the data synchronization is different. In this figure, we use a DSP that allows only write and read operations on the local proxy agent and read operations on the distant proxy. No write operation is possible on a distant proxy with this DSP ("GhostMode" in FPMAS).

Our approach of defining DSP at the proxy level instead of simulation level allows the full customization of synchronization for any given agent in the distributed simulation. The approach allows to define a custom DSP for each agent according to its behavior and the opportunity to define three distinct customization levels:

- **Simulation level mode:** DSP can be applied to any agent of the simulation (approach originally defined in FPMAS platform).
- **Species level mode:** DSP can be applied for each type of agent depending on the behaviors and the needs of the species.
- **Individuals level mode:** DSP can be applied for individual agent depending on its behavior.

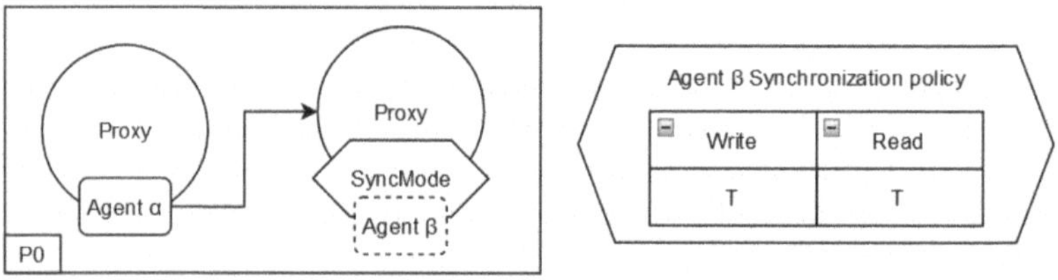

Fig. 3. When Agent α reaches Agent β, it must respect the DSP of Agent β to ensure the coherence of Agent β attributes.

Algorithm 2. *Proxy* implementation with DSP inclusion

```
function GETATTRIBUTE(attributeName)
    startSync()
    value = agent.getAttribute(attributeName)
    endSync()
    return value
function SETATTRIBUTE(attributeName, value)
    startSync()
    agent.setAttribute(attributeName, value)
    endSync()
```

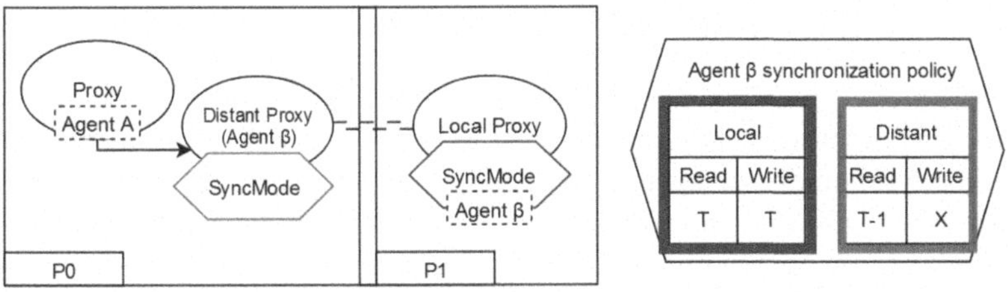

Fig. 4. Agent α interacts with a distant proxy of Agent β on P0. The interaction is following the DSP of the distant proxy of Agent β instead of the DSP of Agent β's local proxy on P1.

Note that the data synchronization requirement of the most restrictive agent determines the DSP at both the Simulation and Species levels. Specification of DSP allows to accurately define and describe the synchronization algorithms, chosen accordingly to the case study. Current data synchronization in HPC ABMS does not permit customization from the simulation level to the individual level. As far as our knowledge goes, there is no Domain-Specific Language (DSL) [23] to specify data synchronization in HPC ABMS platforms. Our approach promotes a DSL dedicated to the specification of a DSP according to the three previously defined levels using this notation:

DSP = LevelMode[AP,
Local(Read: ST;Write: ST),
Distant(Read: ST;Write: ST)]

where LevelMode ∈ [Simulation, Species, Individuals], AP (Activation Predicate) can be any predicate, ST (Synch Temporality) ∈ [..., T-1, T, T+1, ...] or X when the operation is not permitted.

We illustrate this notation on the Fig. 4, Agent β needs two distinct kinds of proxies: a local proxy for local Agent β on Processor 1, with a policy qualified by $Local(Read : T; Write : T)$, a distant proxy for the distant Agent β on Processor 0 with a policy qualified by $Distant(Read : T - 1; Write : X)$. The DSL for Agent β can now be fully defined as follows:

Individuals[Agent β, Local(Read: T; Write: T,
Distant(Read: T-1; Write: X)]

This notation is the root of a DSL to describe the distribution of an ABM, also opening a new perspective to distinguish *the thematic ABM* (representing the studied case) from *the distribution model* (specifying the distribution of the thematic model).

3.2 Illustration of DSP With the Prey-Predator Model

To illustrate the practical use of DSP in a real case scenario, we describe the possible DSP defintions that can be used for the defined Prey-Predator model.

The model defines two species with different behaviors. (i) Preys are shared and indivisible resources for predators; a strong DSP should be associated to preys to ensure competition constraints when the simulation is distributed. (ii) Predators have independent life cycle; they die only if they run out of energy, and they do not require specific synchronization. Figure 1 shows a distributed example of the model. The environment is divided into two subspaces with an overlapping zone (OLZ) [24], and any agent located in this OLZ is mirrored on the other processor, thus requiring the definition of a DSP.

Table 2. Data synchronization for Prey-Predator model.

Level mode	Concerned agent	Data Synchronization Policy			
		Local		Distant	
		Read	Write	Read	Write
Simulation level	Any agents	T	T	T	T
Species level	Prey	T	T	T	T
	Predator	T	T	T−1	X
Individual level	Prey with energy < 25	T	T	T	T
	Prey with energy > 25	T	T	T−1	X
	Predator	T	T	T−1	X
	Possible other DSP	?	?	?	?

Table 2 shows all the DSP that can be used for the Prey-Predator model. Any agent can choose to use the Simulation level DSP, any agent of a given species can choose the Species level DSP and any agent can choose a fitting Individual level DSP. An agent can only use one DSP at a time but can change DSP over time if needed. For a better understanding, let us examine the data presented in the table.

At *Simulation level*, the most constraining agent species in the model are preys. More specifically, preys that can be eaten by predators as specified by the rules of the model. This DSP can be assigned to any agent. It is defined as:

Simulation[Local(Read: T; Write: T),
Distant(Read: T; Write: T)]

At *Species level*, preys and predators have to follow respectively the DSP of their species, for Prey:

Species[Prey,Local(Read: T; Write: T),
Distant(Read: T; Write: T)]

and for Predator:

Species[Predator,Local(Read: T; Write: T),
Distant(Read: T-1; Write: X)]

At *Individual level*, preys could be divided into two sets depending on their state: (i) preys with less than 25 energy (ii) preys with more than 25 energy; predators have a unique state.

The preys with less than 25 energy require concurrent write operations to be managed, hence the following DSP:

Individuals[Prey, Energy $<$ 25,
Local(Read: T; Write: T),
Distant(Read: T; Write: T)]

Since their data are replicated across multiple processors and that they can be consumed by predators, it raises the risk of concurrent write conflicts (see Fig. 1). We adopt the name "DSP_HardSyncMode" for this DSP, aligning with the FPMAS definition in Table 1.

Preys with more than 25 energy do not require the same DSP as they cannot be eaten by predators, we can then set a less restricting DSP:

Individuals[Prey, Energy $>$ 25,
Local(Read: T; Write: T),
Distant(Read: T-1; Write: X)]

We adopt the name "DSP_GhostMode" for this DSP, aligning with the FPMAS definition in Table 1. Predators do not require any change from the DSP defined in Species level as there is no difference between predators at individual level. The three DSP (two preys and one predator) are assigned automatically to agents depending on their state.

We have presented the functioning of proxies and DSP. In the following, we depict how proxies and DSP make communication transparent to all agents.

4 Case Study With the GAMA Platform

We use the GAMA Platform [25] to demonstrate the use of proxies and DSP in a distributed context. This platform is an easy-to-use, open-source modeling and simulation environment for spatially explicit ABM. Despite being useful in many domains, GAMA does not provide any tool to distribute ABM across several processors. Being an active open-source platform makes GAMA a solid candidate to implement our approach using proxies and DSP. We use this platform to demonstrate the use of proxies and DSP using a distributed prey-predator model. Building upon the proven performance of the FPMAS platform [15], our research will mainly focus on the coherence of data in a distributed context. We developed solutions[1] to distribute instances of a model on multiple computers or cores. Note that these solutions are simple show-cases. We present concrete scenarios in which proxies help us solving synchronization issues in an ABM distribution.

4.1 Proof of Concept for DSP_HardSyncMode

We present here the result of our implementation of DSP_HardSyncMode in GAMA through a modified Prey-Predator model shown in Fig. 5a. It illustrates how the DSP_HardSyncMode is working in this situation. Now, when a predator attacks a prey, the energy level of the later decreases by 5. We use this attack mechanism only in this example. Prey0 is executed on P0 with 200 energy and is associated with DSP_HardSyncMode, and copied on P1 as Prey0_COPY. With DSP_HardSyncMode, every time Prey0_COPY is attacked, the change to the energy is reported to the original Prey0 agent on P0.

Fig. 5b is the graph of Prey0 energy over time. From it, we see that Prey0 is attacked by two predators, starting from Step 11 (the arbitrary step in which we make Prey0 available on P1). At Step 21, Prey0 has been killed by either Predator1 or Predator0. It implies that DSP_HardSyncMode is working as intended, as attacks from Predator1 are well reported on the value of Prey0 energy.

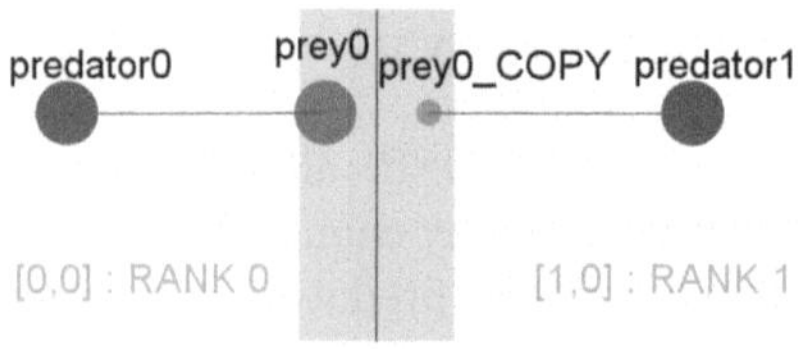

(a) Prey-Predator GAMA model. Prey0 is executed on P0 and copied on P1.

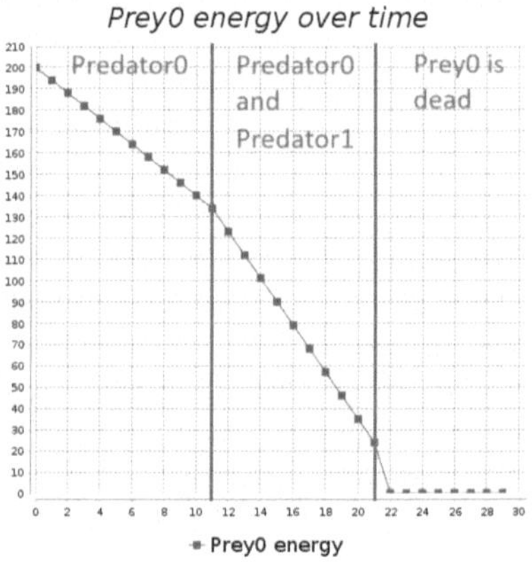

(b) Prey0 energy over time

Fig. 5. GAMA model proving the effectiveness of DSP_HardSyncMode in forwarding change made on prey0_COPY to the prey0

[1] https://github.com/LucasGrjs/Proxies_DSP.

4.2 Tailoring DSP: a Case-By-Case Approach

In this second case, we use the Prey-Predator model shown in Fig. 6a, using the same situation as in Fig. 1. In this model, Prey0 and Prey1 are shared between P0 and P1, bringing concurrent access. We show that with proxies and DSP, we can tailor the DSP of all agents depending on their needs while keeping the model coherent. Figure 6a shows 20 steps of the model execution.

Prey0 is assigned to DSP_HardSyncMode and Prey1 to DSP_GhostMode. Although Prey0 has an energy level above 25, we chose to set its DSP to DSP_HardSyncMode. This let the Prey0 energy decreases over time to reach the 25 energy threshold five steps later. With this setup, we ensure that Predator0 and Predator1 can compete to eat Prey0 fairly. Prey1 has 80 energy and then cannot be eaten by predators before the end of the model execution.

Figure 6b shows the number of preys eaten at each step on each processor over the execution duration of our model. It shows that Predator0 and Predator1 were competing for Prey0 in Step 6 and that Predator0 eats Prey0. Predator0 has however a significant advantage over Predator1: it is located on the same processor as Prey0, while Predator1 is on a different one. Communications between P1 and P0 introduce delays, which can affect the order in which requests for Prey0 are processed. This delay can give Predator0 a crucial advantage in eating Prey0 over Predator1. We experimented on the same model, this time by having the original Prey0 agent located on P1 and then sent on P0. Predator1 won Prey0 over Predator0 in that case.

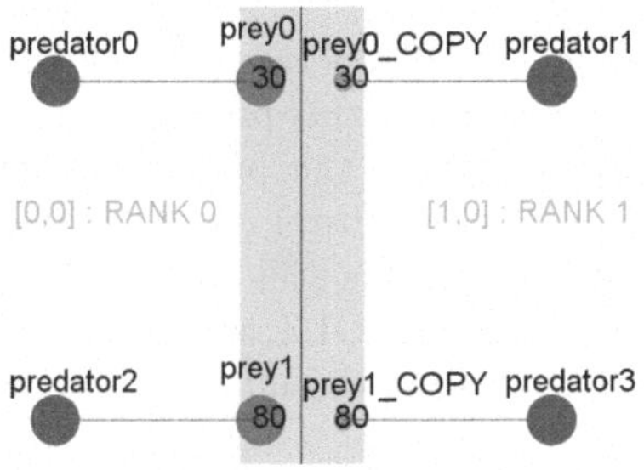

(a) GAMA model representing the issue raised in fig. 1. Prey0 and Prey1 are executed on P0 and copied on P1. Prey0 have 30 energy, Prey1 have 80 energy. We assigned DSP_GhostMode to Prey0 and DSP_HardSyncMode to Prey1.

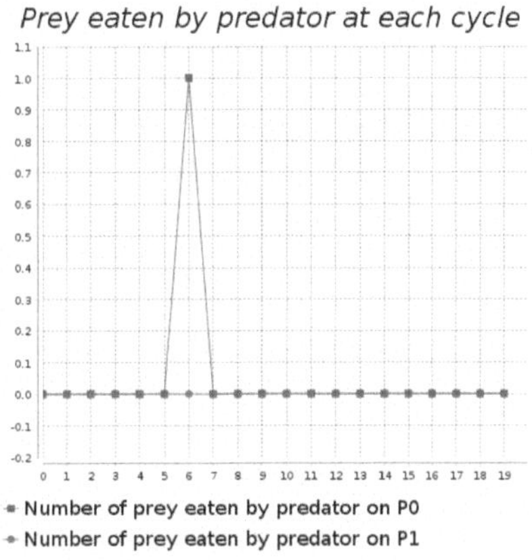

(b) Result of Figure 6a. Number of prey eaten on P0 and P1 at each step

Fig. 6. GAMA model showing how we are able to lower the restrictive level of Prey1 DSP by using different DSP depending on individual properties

This example does, in fact, demonstrate that once Predator0 consumes Prey0 on P0, it cannot be accessed or eaten again on any other processor. This implies that the issue of concurrent accesses between processors for this agent has likely been solved using proxies and DSP. While the whole situation has maintained coherence, we were able to lower the restrictive level of Prey1 DSP using a tailored DSP matching its needs. Using proxies and DSP correctly can improve the way data are synchronized in a distributed ABM.

4.3 DSP and Coherence: Concurrency Access and Change Forwarding

A second use of DSP in the distribution process of an ABM is to protect the coherence of the distributed ABM. For the sake of clarity in Fig. 7a, we have simplified the Prey-Predator model by removing the energy threshold. This induces a clear advantage to the predator which is able to kill the prey regardless of the prey energy reserves.

Figure 7a shows a simple situation where Prey0 and Prey1 are located on P0 and Predator0 and Predator1 are located on P1. We assigned DSP_GhostMode to Prey0 and DSP_HardSyncMode to Prey1. The difference between the two DSP is that DSP_HardSyncMode reports changes made on Prey1_COPY to Prey1 located on P0. This means that, when Predator1 eats Prey1_COPY on P1, Prey1 is effectively killed on P0. Changes to the copy would not be reported to the original agent if DSP_GhostMode was used. Here is a breakdown of what happened to Prey0 and Prey1 over time in this model:

- *Before Step 0:* Prey0 and Prey1 are located on the OLZ between P0 and P1, we copy the preys on P1 as they do not have a copy on this processor.
- *Step 0:* Prey0_COPY and Prey1_COPY are killed by the predators, only Prey1_COPY forwards the change to its original agent, Prey1 on P0 is killed. From this point Prey1 is dead in the simulation. Prey0 is still alive on P0.
- *Between Step 0 and Step 1:* Prey0 is still located in the OLZ, we copy Prey0 on P1 as Prey0 does not have a copy on P1, overriding the information that Prey0 has been killed at step 0.
- *Step 1:* Prey0_COPY is killed again.
- *Between Step 1 and Step 2:* Prey0 is copied again on P1.
- *Step 2:* Same as Step 1.

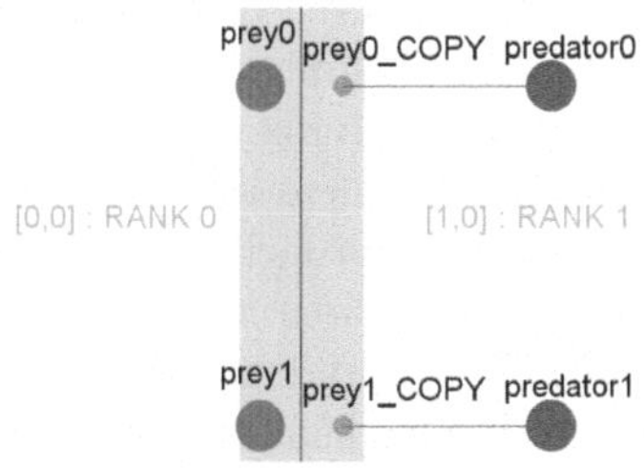

(a) GAMA model of Prey-Predator showcasing the use of DSP to protect the coherence of the distributed simulation. We assigned DSP_GhostMode to Prey0 and DSP_HardSyncMode to Prey1

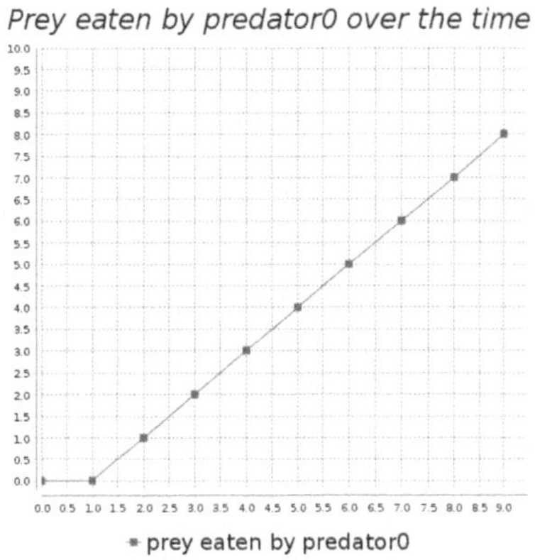

(b) Result of Figure 7a highlighting the coherence problem resulting from the non-forwarding changes made on a copy to the original agent on a critical aspect

Fig. 7. GAMA model showcasing the impact of not forwarding changes from copies to original agent on the coherence of the distributed simulation

Our experiment, in Fig. 7a, demonstrates that concurrent accesses to agent data isn't the only data synchronization issue. Managing how changes are reflected back to the original agent is required to ensure the coherence of the data. Figure 7b illustrates the incoherence introduced when changes are not forwarded from a copy to the original agent on a critical aspect of the agent (living state of the agent). Predator0 will be able to kill Prey0_COPY at every step of the simulation. DSP has then to integrate the notion of forwarding changes from copies to original agent to fully cover the data synchronization issue in distributed ABM. Some early concept have been theoretically introduced by FPMAS [15] with "PushGhostMode" to solve the forwarding of information from copies to the original agent: copies of an agent have to forward all changes to the original agent between step, original agent would have to merge all the states of its copies into one coherent state. This approach places a burden on the modeler, responsible for defining the merging state function.

DSP are not only meant to solve concurrent accesses over a resource in a distributed simulation, but also ensure the coherence of the simulation by synchronizing changes made to any copy agent with the original agent.

5 Conclusion

In this article, we present new concepts aimed at distributing ABM: *proxy* and *DSP*. Proxy is a flexible and transparent concept for managing interactions between agents across distributed instances of a simulation. Our use of proxies is to allow the usage of DSP more effectively, but we can think of other uses for proxies in centralized ABM. Proxies can be useful for data processing, ensuring the correctness of interactions, they can efficiently process relevant data and validate interactions before they are passed to the agent. This might reduce the risk of errors or inconsistencies in the overall simulation by giving more insight into the execution of a centralized or distributed model. We introduced DSP to define data synchronization for distributed simulation. Our approach of assigning agent-level DSP control through proxies offers control over three levels of data synchronization (simulation, species and individual). Modelers can tailor data flow for each species and individual within their simulation, using their expertise to achieve the desired level of coherence. Our implementation and testing within GAMA validates the effectiveness of this approach, paving the way for more controls over data synchronization in distributed ABM development. A recognized limitation of the proposed methodology is the computational cost of DSP and proxy in interaction between agents. To provide a detailed analysis of computational performance, future research will be dedicated to benchmarking the cost of our approach. If the computational cost is kept low, performance reductions may be a necessary trade-off for fine-grained data synchronization.

In the introduction of the article, we defined two critical challenges for improving ABM distribution:

- **Standardizing way to describe the distribution of ABM:** we have introduced a novel notation to define DSP in distributed simulations, species within those simulations, and individual entities. This DSP notation effectively addresses the challenge of data synchronization at various levels.
- **Taking user's input in the process:** with proxies and DSP, we have achieved customization of data synchronization for any individual in the simulation. User can then create and use new DSP adapted to the ABM needs enabling the definition of DSP based on individual agent states.

Future works will focus on defining new DSL to describe different parts of a distributed ABM. Ultimately, aiming to create a complete DSL that can describe the entire distribution of an ABM. This DSL will be the basis to address other critical challenges:

- **Distributing an ABM out-of-the-box:** making it easy to distribute an ABM without making changes to the base code of the model. We should be able to outsource distribution functions outside of the model definition.
- **Adapting the architecture to the user's skill level:** adjust the distribution architecture to modelers with diverse technical expertise. Our goal is to develop customizable, ready-to-use solutions for distributing ABM, allowing for improvement based on user needs.

References

1. Taillandier, F., et al.: An agent-based model to simulate inhabitants behavior during a flood event. Int. J. Disast. Risk Reduct. **64**, 102503 (2021). https://doi.org/10.1016/j.ijdrr.2021.102503. ISSN 22124209
2. Gaudou, B., et al.: COMOKIT: a modeling kit to understand, analyze, and compare the impacts of mitigation policies against the COVID19 epidemic at the scale of a city. Front. Public Health **8**, 563247 (2020). https://doi.org/10.3389/fpubh.2020.563247. ISSN 2296-2565
3. Daudé, E., et al.: ESCAPE: exploring by simulation cities awareness on population evacuation (2019)
4. Carley, K.M., et al.: BioWar: scalable agent-based model of bioattacks. IEEE Trans. Syst. Man Cybern.-Part A: Syst. Hum. **36**(2), 252–265 (2006)
5. Yun, T.-S., et al.: Agent-based model for urban administration: a case study of bridge construction and its traffic dispersion effect. J. Artif. Soc. Soc. Simul. **25**(4) (2022). https://doi.org/10.18564/jasss.4923. ISSN 1460-7425
6. Breugnot, P., et al.: A synchronized and dynamic distributed graph structure to allow the native distribution of Multi-Agent System simulations. In: 2021 29th Euromicro International Conference on Parallel, Distributed and Network-Based Processing (PDP), pp. 54–61. IEEE, Valladolid (2021). https://doi.org/10.1109/PDP52278.2021.00017. ISBN 978-1-66541-455-5
7. Suryanarayanan, V., Theodoropoulos, G., Lees, M.: PDESMAS: distributed simulation of multi-agent systems. Procedia Comput. Sci. **18**, 671–681 (2013). https://doi.org/10.1016/j.procs.2013.05.231. 2013 International Conference on Computational Science. ISSN 1877-0509
8. Rubio-Campillo, X.: Pandora: a versatile agent-based modelling platform for social simulation (2014)
9. Chuang, T., Fukuda, M.: A parallel multi-agent spatial simulation environment for cluster systems. In: 2013 IEEE 16th International Conference on Computational Science and Engineering, pp. 143–150. IEEE, Sydney (2013). https://doi.org/10.1109/CSE.2013.32. ISBN 978-0-7695-5096-1
10. Schimeczek, C., et al.: FAME-core: an open framework for distributed agent-based modelling of energy systems. J. Open Sour. Softw. **8**(84), 5087 (2023). https://doi.org/10.21105/joss.05087. ISSN 2475-9066
11. Borges, F., et al.: Care HPS: a high performance simulation tool for parallel and distributed agent-based modeling. Future Gener. Comput. Syst. **68**, 59–73 (2017). https://doi.org/10.1016/j.future.2016.08.015. ISSN 0167739X
12. Richmond, P., et al.: High performance cellular level agent-based simulation with FLAME for the GPU. Brief. Bioinform. **11**(3), 334–347 (2010). https://doi.org/10.1093/bib/bbp073. ISSN 1467-5463, 1477-4054
13. Collier, N., North, M.: Parallel agent-based simulation with repast for high performance computing. Simulation **89**(10), 1215–1235 (2013). https://doi.org/10.1177/0037549712462620. ISSN 0037-5497, 1741-3133
14. Cordasco, G., et al.: Designing computational steering facilities for distributed agent based simulations (2013). https://doi.org/10.1145/2486092.2486147
15. Breugnot, P., et al.: Data synchronization in distributed simulation of multi-agent systems (2022). https://doi.org/10.1007/978-3-031-18192-4_5. ISBN 978-3-031-18191-7
16. Abar, S., et al.: Agent based modelling and simulation tools: a review of the state-of-art software. Comput. Sci. Rev. **24**, 13–33 (2017). https://doi.org/10.1016/j.cosrev.2017.03.001. ISSN 15740137

17. Pal, C.-V., et al.: A review of platforms for the development of agent systems. ArXiv abs/2007.08961 (2020)
18. Wrona, Z., et al.: Overview of software agent platforms available in 2023. Information **14**(6), 348 (2023). https://doi.org/10.3390/info14060348. ISSN 2078-2489
19. North, M.J., et al.: Complex adaptive systems modeling with Repast Simphony. Complex Adapt. Syst. Model. **1**(1), 3 (2013). https://doi.org/10.1186/2194-3206-1-3. ISSN 2194-3206
20. Luke, S., et al.: MASON: a multiagent simulation environment. Simulation **81**(7), 517–527 (2005). https://doi.org/10.1177/0037549705058073. ISSN 0037-5497, 1741-3133
21. "Wilensky, U.: NetLogo predator prey game HubNet model. Center for Connected Learning and Computer-Based Modeling, Northwestern University, Evanston, IL (2002)
22. Chin, L.S., et al.: FLAME: an approach to the parallelisation of AgentBased applications (2012)
23. Mernik, M., Heering, J., Sloane, A.: When and how to develop domain-specific languages. ACM Comput. Surv. **37**, 316 (2005). https://doi.org/10.1145/1118890.1118892
24. Rousset, A., et al.: A survey on parallel and distributed multi-agent systems for high performance computing simulations. Comput. Sci. Rev. **22**, 27–46 (2016)
25. Taillandier, P., et al.: Building, composing and experimenting complex spatial models with the GAMA platform. GeoInformatica **23**(2), 299–322 (2018). https://doi.org/10.1007/s10707-018-00339-6. ISSN 1384-6175, 1573-7624

Data-Driven Agent-Based Modeling and Simulation of Price Competition in the Danish Pharmaceutical Market

Ruhollah Jamali[1(✉)] and Sanja Lazarova-Molnar[1,2]

[1] The Maersk Mc-Kinney Moller Institute, University of Southern Denmark, 5230 Odense, Denmark
{ruja,slmo}@mmmi.sdu.dk

[2] Institute of Applied Informatics and Formal Description Methods, Karlsruhe Institute of Technology, 76133 Karlsruhe, Germany
sanja.lazarova-molnar@kit.edu

Abstract. Agent-based modeling allows us to analyze the dynamics of economic systems by simulating the interactions and behaviors of entities in the system. However, developing agent-based models is challenging due to the complexity of economic systems. This complexity emerges from the variety of factors that influence the behaviors of entities within these systems. Data-driven techniques can facilitate the development process of agent-based models by integrating patterns derived from data into the model. In this paper, we use data-driven methods to identify key patterns and characteristics of market competitors and utilize these patterns to develop an agent-based model of price competition in the Danish pharmaceutical market as a case study.

Keywords: Agent-based modeling · Data-driven modeling · Competitive pricing · Price competition

1 Introduction

The pharmaceutical industry has experienced significant growth during the past two decades, with worldwide revenues totaling 1.48 trillion US dollars in 2022 [24]. Meanwhile, this industry is currently navigating complex trends such as global demand growth, new therapeutic modalities, and supply chain pressures [6]. These complexities underscore the importance of data-driven decision-making in this market. This solution can be achieved by developing a robust model of pharmaceutical price competition that helps to understand the dynamics of pricing strategies, competitive behavior, and market responses. The model could serve as a valuable tool for various stakeholders, including market competitors and regulatory authorities, enabling them to make informed decisions. It can also contribute to a more competitive and efficient market, benefiting consumers through lower medicine prices and improved medication access.

R. Collier et al. (Eds.): EUMAS 2024, LNAI 15685, pp. 39–54, 2025.
https://doi.org/10.1007/978-3-031-93930-3_3

Considering the European Union (EU), the pricing of medicines varies from country to country due to different regulatory procedures and market dynamics. However, the Danish pharmaceutical market is an intriguing case study for understanding the dynamics of medicine pricing in the EU. The pharmaceutical market in Denmark is characterized by a competitive interplay between generic and parallel imported medicines. Generic medicines contain the same active ingredients as their brand-name counterparts, offering consumers more choices, and often at lower prices [23]. On the other hand, parallel import involves the purchase of pharmaceuticals in one European Economic Area (EEA) country, where they are cheaper, and their resale in another EEA country, such as Denmark, where they are more expensive [15]. In this paper, we focus on modeling the pharmaceutical price competition of parallel imported medicines in Denmark as an intriguing case study.

To study the complex interplay and model the pharmaceutical price competition, we turn to Agent-Based Modeling (ABM), which recently gained attention in the field of economics [3]. Unlike traditional economic models that assume homogeneity and rationality, ABM embraces complexity theory [29]. It views the economy as a dynamic system composed of heterogeneous interacting agents/individuals, firms, or entities-each characterized by limited information and bounded rationality. These agents are not mere abstractions; they represent real-world actors with diverse behaviors and decision-making processes. In ABM, the dynamics of the entire system emerge from the interactions of these individual agents. For instance, agent-based models can simulate how consumers make purchasing decisions [8], how firms compete [19], or how financial markets evolve [10,25]. ABM provides a bottom-up approach to understanding economic systems by capturing the micro-level dynamics of the target system. Researchers can build, simulate, and analyze agent-based models that allow them to explore patterns, test hypotheses, and gain insights that conventional economic models might overlook [2,5].

While ABM offers a powerful framework for modeling complex systems, its effectiveness can be further enhanced by incorporating real-world data. Data-driven ABM combines the strengths of data-driven modeling and ABM, providing a unique approach to understanding complex systems such as the pharmaceutical market. Unlike traditional modeling techniques, data-driven ABM does not rely solely on theoretical assumptions or expert knowledge. In this approach, historical data that provide a rich source of information about the target system can be used to design, calibrate, and validate the models while ensuring their accuracy and reliability [22]. This approach allows capturing the intricacies and complexities of real-world phenomena, which are often overlooked in traditional economic models [25]. For instance, historical data can reveal pricing patterns or medicine trends in the pharmaceutical market. It can also shed light on the behaviors and decision-making processes of the agents, such as the pricing strategies of pharmaceutical companies or consumers' purchasing decisions.

This paper aims to enhance our understanding of the Danish pharmaceutical market by analyzing available historical data of the market. Our goal is to refine our existing model of price competition within this market. Previously, we employed a straightforward agent-based model based on an available game theory model of the market to study the pharmaceutical parallel trade market [11]. In this model, we developed an initial pricing function for agents representing competitors in the market. This allowed us to investigate scenarios where ABM can provide valuable insights [12]. Subsequently, we focused on developing a data-driven agent-based model of pharmaceutical price competition specifically for Denmark [13] as the framework of pharmaceutical products is different within countries in the EU. Our latest research focused on uncovering pricing patterns in the Danish pharmaceutical market to investigate how we can use this analysis to further develop the agent-based model of pharmaceutical price competition in Denmark [14]. Here, we focus on discovering competitors' characteristics in this market and developing an agent-based model that can replicate the price competition in the Danish pharmaceutical market.

The remainder of the paper is structured as follows: Sect. 2 provides related works and explains the Danish pharmaceutical market price competition framework. Section 3 outlines the available data sources and their properties, followed by a description of the data analysis procedure we employed. Section 4 discusses how the presented data analysis procedure can be used to develop the agent-based model of the market further, followed by a data-driven model of the market and simulation results. Finally, Sect. 5 summarizes the paper and outlines our future research directions.

2 Background and Literature Review

In Denmark, medicine prices are determined by the pharmaceutical companies that manufacture or import these medicines, and the prices are uniform across all pharmacies. The Danish Medicines Agency, which is the authority organization in Denmark, does not influence these prices. Prices are set for fortnights (14-day period), with changes reported to the Danish Medicines Agency every fortnight. This information is then disseminated to pharmacies and citizens via medicinpriser website. In the case of parallel imported medicines, pharmacies must offer the cheapest option, named A-price, due to the fact that the parallel imported medicines only differ in their brand. The pricing system of free competition and fortnight price changes fosters intense competition and leads to lower medicine prices in Denmark [1]. In this research, we focus on the competitive pricing dynamics within the market of parallel imported pharmaceuticals.

ABM has been widely used in the field of economic analysis [2,25]. The ability to model heterogeneous, boundedly rational agents and their complex interactions, along with insights from behavioral economics and empirical data, have significantly enhanced agent-based models' capacity to simulate emergent macroeconomic phenomena and complex economic system dynamics [25]. Following these advancements, data-driven modeling has emerged as a rapidly evolving field that leverages the power of modern computational capabilities and the availability of large datasets. This approach has been increasingly used in various fields, including economics, to refine the accuracy and predictive power of economic simulations further. In contrast to traditional modeling approaches that rely on predefined assumptions and theories, data-driven models are built directly from data, harnessing the power of data analysis methods and techniques to uncover patterns and relationships inherent in the data itself, which leads to more accurate and robust models.

A significant advancement in data-driven modeling is the use of machine learning techniques. Machine learning algorithms, such as neural networks, decision trees, and support vector machines, have been widely used to build predictive models from large datasets [4,9]. These models can capture complex, non-linear relationships that are often missed by traditional statistical methods. Moreover, the rise of big data has provided an unprecedented opportunity for data-driven modeling. With the availability of large, high-dimensional datasets, it is now possible to build models that can capture the complexity of real-world systems [21]. For example, in the field of economics, researchers have used big data to model and predict economic indicators, market trends, and consumer behavior [7,20,27].

In the development of agent-based models, data can be used to inform the design and behavior of agents, thereby leading to more accurate models. The availability of large-scale data can potentially change the way of developing agent-based models, from simple rules to being driven by data [16]. Data-driven ABM has demonstrated its applicability in different fields, such as rooftop solar adoption [30] and transit-oriented design [28]. This approach allows for a quantitative casual understanding of emergent phenomena through complex nonlinear dynamics at the macro level while also emphasizing the importance of validating models with empirical data to explain real-world phenomena [18].

3 Danish Pharmaceutical Market Data Overview and Analysis Procedure

In the following, we present a detailed overview of the dataset employed in our study. Subsequently, we explain our data analysis methodology, i.e., our approach to uncovering competitors' pricing behavior and patterns.

We utilized data from the Danish Health Data Authority, which is the authoritative source for health-related data in Denmark. The Danish Health Data Authority collects, processes, and publishes statistics and analyses on health and welfare, making it an ideal source for our research. Our dataset includes information pertaining to 427 parallel imported medicines within the Danish market, characterized by competitive dynamics involving two or more competitor companies vying for sales. Our dataset includes pricing data of 6 parallel trader companies and 79 original manufacturer companies are available. In the dataset, we observed varying degrees of competition: 132 medicines faced competition from two companies, meaning two competitors offered them. Similarly, 127 medicines were sold from three competitors, 73 medicines from four competitors, 73 medicines from five competitors, and 22 medicines from six competitors over the course of 27 fortnights (one year). In the time series representing each competitor's pricing behavior, there may be instances of 'Not a Number' (NaN) values. These NaN values indicate fortnights when the competitor opts not to participate in the market. Such non-participation could be due to various strategic reasons specific to the competitor company or the market conditions at that time.

3.1 Data Preprocessing

In the data preprocessing stage, we implemented two steps to ensure the quality and comparability of our dataset for further analysis. In the first step, we applied MinMax normalization to each medicine's pricing data to ensure a uniform pricing range across all medicines. This technique transformed the original pricing data into the range between 0 and 1, facilitating a more effective comparison of pricing patterns across different medicines' data. In the second step, we address the potential presence of NaN values in the pricing history of each company and our interest in discerning pricing patterns. We split the pricing time series into smaller segments from the point at which a competitor did not participate in the market. This process resulted in 2154 subsequent pricing time series in our dataset.

3.2 Data Analysis Procedure

We assumed that all original manufacturers share similar characteristics in our data analysis stage. Our primary focus was on identifying pricing characteristics specific to parallel traders. To achieve this, we conducted three data analysis steps. First, we examined general characteristics of competitors by analyzing the sizes of parallel traders, the quantity of medicines they sell, their participation in competitions, and the number of A-prices each competitor had. Next, we performed a pricing patterns analysis by applying time series clustering to segmented pricing time series of competitors in the market. Finally, we analyzed competitors' competitive behavior by investigating each company's reaction to market price. We detail each of these steps in the following.

General Characteristics of Competitors: For the first step, we investigate the sizes of parallel traders and their general pricing behaviors. For this, we first analyze the quantity of medicines each parallel trader sells. Here, Orifarm and 2care4, as large-scale parallel traders, were engaged in the majority of the competitions, each competing to sell almost 350 different parallel imported medicines. Medium-sized parallel traders, such as Abacus and Paranova, participated in approximately half of the competitions. Finally, Medartuum and Epione, which are smaller and newer companies, only participated in less than 50 of the competitions.

To further understand market dominance, we assess the number of A-prices secured by each competitor. Our findings indicate that Orifarm and 2care4 are particularly dominant in the market, as Orifarm secured 3541 A-prices and

2care4 secured 2990 A-prices. The original manufacturers follow closely, securing 2711 A-prices.

The analysis of the general pricing behaviors of competitors is illustrated in Fig. 1, where 1(a) illustrates the box plot of the price ranges that each competitor offers in their consecutive pricing behavior. Figure 1(b) provides insight into the pricing of each competitor involved in the market, considering all available pricing data.

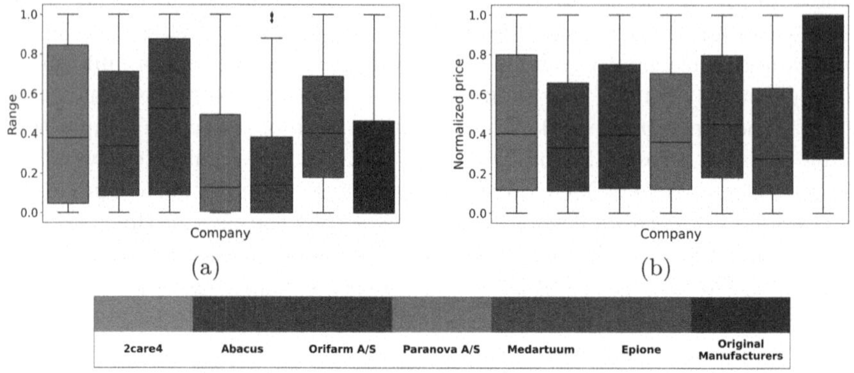

Fig. 1. Individual statistics of each competitor pricing behavior: (a) Box plot of price ranges across all available pricing time series for each competitor (b) Box plot of all available pricing data for each competitor in the market.

Pricing Patterns Analysis: The second step - pricing patterns analysis, is based on our prior research [14], which developed a methodology to analyze pricing patterns in the Danish pharmaceutical market using subsequence time series clustering. The whole process of this method involved collecting and preprocessing data, creating subsequences, applying the clustering method, and analyzing the resulting clusters, which was followed by conducting case studies on specific medicines to investigate the analysis results. In the current research, we refined our methodology by adjusting the subsequence creation step. Instead of manually creating subsequences with predefined lengths, we utilized time series segmentation using the Pelt method [17] available in the Ruptures library [26]. Time series segmentation is a method used to divide a time series into several smaller segments, each with certain characteristics. This technique is particularly useful when looking for patterns in the data, as it allows us to isolate and examine each segment individually. By applying the Pelt method to our dataset, we generated 7259 segmented time series. This approach not only addresses the issue of NaN values but also enhances our ability to detect and understand the pricing patterns of the companies in our dataset. Through this analysis, we determined that the optimal number of clusters for pricing patterns among competitors is five. Figure 2 demonstrates the clustering result of the pricing behavior of each parallel trader involved in the market.

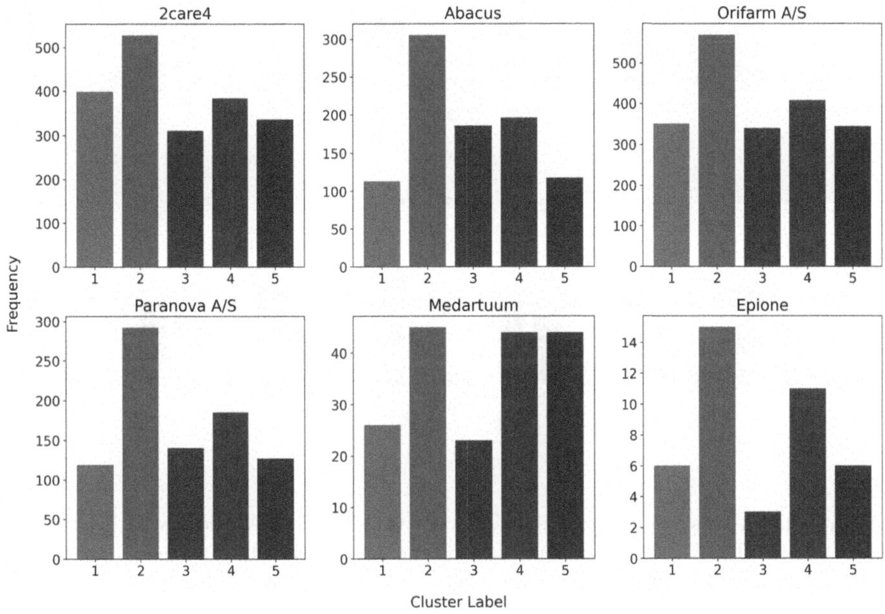

Fig. 2. Number of pricing segments in each cluster for trader companies

Competitive Behavior Analysis: In our last step, competitive behavior analysis, we examined each competitor's reactions based on their A-price status. Figure 3 illustrates the frequency of price adjustments over a fortnight, with panel (a) showing competitors holding the A-price and panel (b) depicting the behavior of each competitor when they do not have the A-price. Competitors had three pricing options: increase (I), decrease (D), or maintain (N) their current price.

This analysis informs the creation of agent-based models representing competitors with distinct decision-making rules, reflecting real-world strategies. The model may incorporate state-dependent behaviors, as data shows competitors adjust strategies based on A-price possession. Moreover, probabilistic decision-making can be implemented using observed frequencies of price changes (I, D, N) that enable realistic agent action representation. This approach captures the pricing dynamics of each competitor under different market conditions, allowing for a more accurate simulation of market behavior.

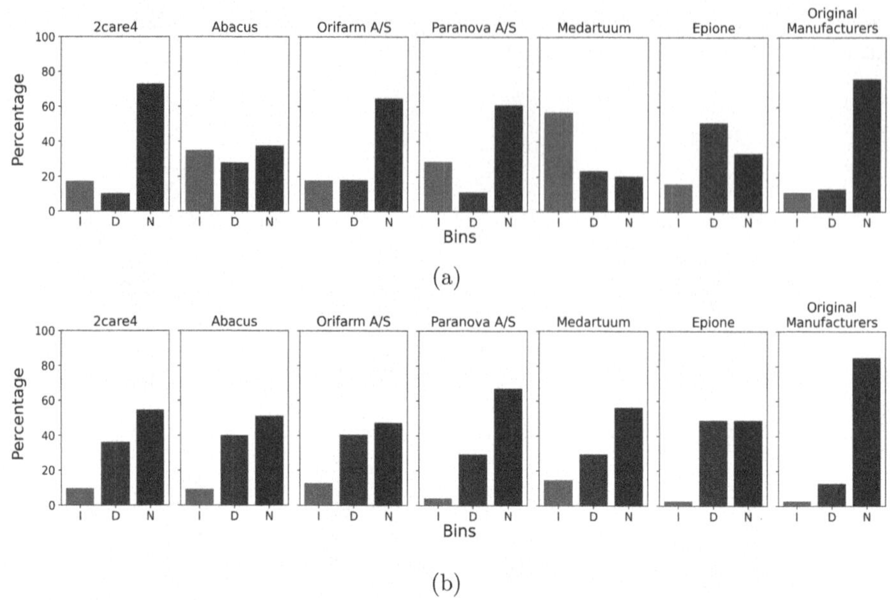

Fig. 3. Competitors pricing behavior when (a) they had the A-price vs (b) when they did not have the A-price of the market in the next fortnight. In these figures, "I" indicates an increase, "D" means a decrease, and "N" means no change.

4 A Case Study and Experimental Results

Previously, we developed an agent-based model of price competition in the Danish pharmaceutical market, considering expert knowledge and visual data insights [13]. Here, we aim to explain how developing the same model can be made more data-driven by employing some part of our data analysis approach outlined in Sect. 3.

The first data analysis step presented in Subsect. 3.2 investigates the general characteristics of the parallel traders. This information can be used to define the attributes of the agents representing parallel traders, indicating their general characteristics such as size and competitiveness. E.g., the number of medicines each parallel trader is involved in competing can be used to determine the participation probability attribute for the agents representing competitors, indicating the probability of their involvement in selling parallel traded medicines. This information can also be used to define an attribute representing agent size. Agents' sizes are categorical variables that can be either large-scale traders (e.g., Orifarm and 2care4), medium-sized traders (like Abacus and Paranova), or small-sized to present newer companies (such as Medartuum and Epione). The number of fortnights each company has the A-price can be incorporated into the model to define an attribute indicating the competitiveness of the agents representing competitors. Figure 1(a) and (b) show the average range of prices each competitor offers and the pricing range of each competitor involved in the market, respectively. The average range of prices and the pricing range of each competitor involved in the market provide insight into the variability and competitiveness of each competitor in the market.

The second data analysis step, as described in the previous Sect. 3.2, introduces an approach to uncovering pricing patterns in the Danish pharmaceutical market by applying time series clustering on segmented pricing times series from each company. In this step, each cluster represents a competitor's pricing pattern. Figure 2 illustrates the distribution of pricing segments across various clusters for six parallel trader competitors. A notable observation from this figure is the dominance of cluster 2 among all parallel traders. Subsequently, we conducted a time series analysis for each cluster, taking into account the cluster centers and the time series data within each cluster. Our analysis revealed that cluster 2 exhibits a pattern of competitive pricing at low market prices. This pattern suggests that parallel traders strive to maintain their prices at the most competitive levels, reflecting the constant competition in the market. Another notable finding is that the distribution of pricing clusters is largely similar across parallel traders of the same size. For instance, Orifarm and 2care4, the largest competitors in this market, exhibit a similar frequency of segments in each cluster, as depicted in Fig. 2. Similarly, Abacus and Paranova, two medium-to-large competitors, also display comparable cluster patterns. For the small competitor, Epione, Clusters 2 and 4 are the dominant ones, both of which indicate low prices and align with the fact that this company is seeking a bigger market share. This observation could provide insights into competitors' strategic pricing decisions and competitive positioning in the market.

In the final data analysis step, we focus on how each competitor reacts to their price position, specifically whether they have the A-price (the lowest price) or not. This analysis reveals significant differences in the behaviors of small, medium, and large companies. For instance, when Epione (a small company) has the A-price in the market, it frequently lowers its prices further over the next fortnight. In contrast, Medartuum, another small company, tended to increase their prices in the next fortnight. Large companies such as Orifarm and 2care4 did not change their price for the next fortnight when they had the A-price, suggesting a more standardized approach to pricing. However, Abacus displayed unique behavior with a uniform frequency, indicating that they do not have a dominant strategy in the market. In the case of not having the A-price of the market, the data analysis reveals that most companies typically do not alter their prices in the next fortnight. However, Epione acted as an exception by decreasing their prices most of the time. This suggests that smaller companies may employ different strategies compared to their larger competitors, which could be due to various factors such as market positioning, cost structures, or strategic objectives. Orifarm and Abacus, two other competitors, exhibit a balanced behavior characterized by either maintaining or decreasing their prices. This could indicate a more cautious approach to pricing when not having the A-price, possibly to avoid triggering price wars or to maintain a stable market position. Meanwhile, increasing prices while not having the A-price is a relatively uncommon behavior among competitors in the Danish pharmaceutical market. Based on these observations, we can create a pricing function to simulate competitors' pricing behavior and explore emergent market phenomena. However, for accurate emulation and predictive modeling, additional investigation considering each specific medicine is necessary.

In order to construct a general agent-based model that mirrors the competitive pricing dynamics in the Danish pharmaceutical market, it is vital to extract agents' behavioral characteristics from historical pricing data. These characteristics will form the foundation for modeling the behavior of the agents representing competitors within the model. For example, agents representing parallel traders might display behaviors such as regular price modifications to sustain competitiveness. In contrast, agents representing original manufacturers might exhibit behaviors like setting initial prices higher and adjusting them based on market demand. The agent-based model can also facilitate adaptability and learning over time. Agents can be programmed with learning algorithms that enable them to modify their strategies based on past experiences and market feedback. This adaptive capability allows agents to dynamically respond to changes in market conditions, regulatory policies, or competitor actions, thereby enhancing the model's predictive power and realism. Lastly, by basing agents' characteristics on observed pricing patterns and incorporating realistic decision-making processes and interactions, the agent-based model can serve as a valuable tool for understanding and predicting price competition dynamics in the Danish pharmaceutical market. In the following, we present an agent-based model of pricing competition in the Danish pharmaceutical market based on our data analysis to demonstrate how this analysis can be useful.

4.1 A Data-Driven Agent-Based Model of Pharmaceutical Price Competition

We focus on the share of A-prices among competitors. As noted earlier, multiple factors can affect the pricing behavior of a competitor in this market; however, the analysis in Sect. 3.2 could be a cumulative presentation of each competitor's pricing behavior. This means that companies adjusted their prices by considering all the factors, and the resulting behavior implicitly comprises those factors. To examine this hypothesis, we developed a pricing function for agents using the data analysis presented in Sect. 3.2 to investigate the performance of the simulation in replicating the real historical data. The resulting agent-based model is defined as follows:

Agents Types and Attributes

The model consists of two types of agents: Original Manufacturer and Parallel Trader agents. Original manufacturer agents have the following six attributes:

- **Starting Price Point** is the price an agent starts pricing a medicine. This attribute is derived from data, and it is the median price from all normalized historical pricing data available for each company.

- **Last Step A-price** gets a True/False value and indicates if the agent had the A-price in the last fortnight or not.
- **A-price Probabilities** is a list of three values indicating probabilities of different actions (increase, decrease, or keep) for price adjustment of agents when they had the A-price in the last step of the simulation. The values are derived from the analysis in Sect. 3.2.
- **NA-price Probabilities** is the same as A-price probabilities when the agent did not have the A-price in the last step of the simulation.
- **Price Increase Probability Distribution** is the probability distribution of the price increases derived from the available data of all original manufacturers. We employed kernel density estimation to estimate the probability density function.
- **Price Decrease Probability Distribution** is the same as the previous attribute but in the case of decreasing price.

Parallel trader agents have the same attributes as the original manufacturer, plus one additional attribute:

- **Participation Probability** indicates whether an agent participates in the market or not. The value of this attribute is derived from historical data, and it is basically the number of medicines a parallel trader participated in a competition divided by the total number of medicines.

Agents Behavior Rules

The second part of our agent-based model defines the behavior rules of agents. In this market, a company will sell the medicine if it has the A-price and otherwise, it will not. Therefore, we assume that the pricing method for both types of agents is the same. Agents check whether they had the A-price in the past fortnight. Depending on their status, they use either A-price probabilities or NA-price probabilities to determine their actions. Based on the selected action, agents might use the increase or decrease probability distribution to specify the amount of the price adjustment. Algorithm 1 shows the pseudocode of the pricing function in our model. For each medicine, all agents follow this price adjustment process to come up with their prices at each step. However, parallel traders, prior to this, decide if they will participate in the pricing competition or not based on the participation probability attribute. Original manufacturer agent participates in all price competitions.

Model Environment

The environment of our model is the Danish pharmaceutical market. To simplify the model, we did not consider any attribute related to the environment, as it does not significantly affect the agents' pricing behavior. This decision is based on the observation that external factors related to the environment, such as regulations, economic conditions, and market trends, are already implicitly captured in the historical pricing data to inform agents' behavior. Therefore, adding environmental attributes would not substantially change the simulation's outcome.

Algorithm 1. Pricing Adjustment Pseudocode for Agents

```
Price Adjustment Options ← ['increase', 'decrease', 'keep']
if Last step A-price is True then
    action ← random choice from options with A-price probabilities
else
    action ← random choice from options with NA-price probabilities
end if
if action is 'increase' then
    price adjustment ← random value from increase probability density function
else if action is 'decrease' then
    price adjustment ← random value from decrease probability density function
else
    price adjustment ← 0
end if
price ← current price + price adjustment
return price
```

Simulation of Price Competition in Danish Pharmaceutical Market After developing our data-driven agent-based model of the Danish pharmaceutical market, we used the model to simulate the Danish pharmaceutical market. As mentioned in Sect. 3, there are 79 original manufacturer companies and 6 parallel trader companies competing to sell their medicines in the market. Since, in most cases, original manufacturer companies demonstrate the same pricing behaviors, we considered the same characteristics for all of them and analyzed their available data in an aggregated way. Besides, we analyzed the available data of each parallel trader separately, as presented in Sect. 3. In the simulation, we considered that we have 427 medicines, the same as in the Danish pharmaceutical market. Therefore, we ran the model 427 times, each time for 32 steps (each step representing a fortnight), which is roughly the duration of one year and a half. In the simulation, we derived all agents' attributes from the data presented in Sect. 3. Since the starting price point is an input to the model derived from data, we did not consider the first three months (6 steps) of pricing information of agents in the simulation to decrease the impact of the starting price point on the final A-price analysis. Considering the remaining pricing data of agents (26 steps), which is equal to one year (the same as the data we had in data analysis), we counted the number of times each agent had the A-price of the market. We ran the simulation 42700 times (One hundred simulations per medicine) and divided the number of times each agent achieved the A-price by 100. Finally, we compared the results of the simulation with historical data. Figure 4 shows the bar chart, illustrating the number of times an agent got A-price, where (a) represents the historical data and (b) represents the simulated data.

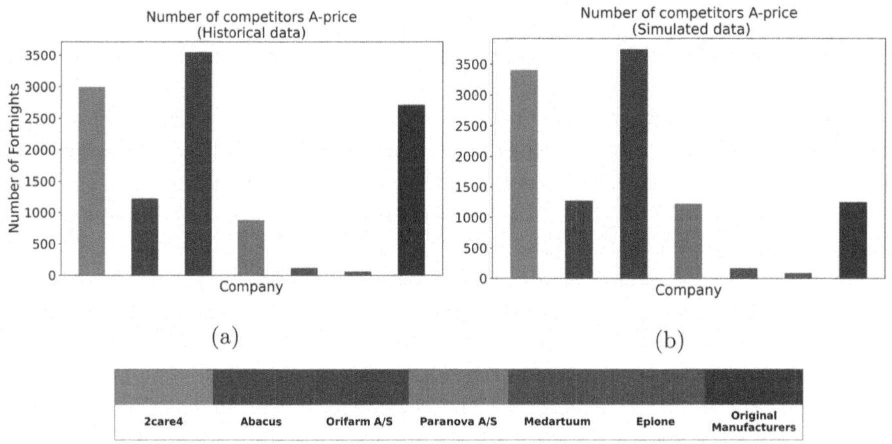

Fig. 4. Comparision of historical data and simulated data on number of competitors A-price: Bar chart of each number of fortnights a competitor has the A-price from (a) historical data and (b) simulated data.

Validation of Simulation Results

By analyzing these charts, it is evident that the distribution of A-prices among agents in the simulated data closely mirrors that of the historical data. This observation suggests that our model accurately captures the competitive dynamics of the Danish pharmaceutical market. However, we observed a lower number of A-prices for the original manufacturer agent in the simulations, which might be due to two main reasons. First, in our model, all 79 original manufacturers were considered as the same entity. This simplification might have caused some divergence from the real-world data, as it does not account for the potential differences in pricing behaviors among these manufacturers. Second, there might be periods in the real-world market where parallel traders cannot meet the market demand. In such cases, the original manufacturer becomes the only seller, which could lead to a higher frequency of achieving the A-price than what is observed in the simulated data. Generally, depending on the simulation goal, further refinement and validation through empirical data and real-world experimentation can enhance the model's accuracy and utility for stakeholders in the Danish pharmaceutical industry.

In conclusion, our goal with this case study was to demonstrate the potential of data-driven methods for developing agent-based models that can replicate the emergent macro results of complex systems, such as the Danish pharmaceutical market.

5 Summary and Outlook

In this research, we aim to highlight the application of data-driven methodologies in the development of agent-based models, as illustrated through a specific case study on price competition for parallel-traded medicines in the Danish pharmaceutical market. We utilized public market data to analyze competitor behavior and identify characteristics that could define agents in our model. We implemented three data analysis procedures, all of which rely solely on historical pricing data. The first procedure identified general competitor characteristics such as size, competitiveness, pricing range, and desired price range. The second procedure helped us discern pricing patterns in competitor behavior. The final procedure aided in the development of agents that statistically represent competitor behavior, enabling the study of emergent phenomena in the market. We discussed in detail how each analysis contributes to the development of an agent-based model. Finally, we developed an agent-based model of the market based on our data analysis procedures.

The design of the data analysis procedure can be tailored to the purpose of the agent-based model, facilitating the development of a data-driven model. For instance, in the context of price competition in the Danish pharmaceutical market, the model could be used to study emergent events such as A-price achievement, price equilibrium, or upcoming market competition. Alternatively, it could be used to optimize pricing decisions based on short or long-term goals, predicting competitor behavior under various scenarios. We demonstrated how the same data could serve different model development purposes.

In our future work, we aim to develop a framework for creating data-driven agent-based models to streamline the modeling process. We plan to present this framework with a focus on price competition in the Danish pharmaceutical market, further developing the model representing this market. Moreover, we believe that our proposed framework will not only enhance the understanding of the dynamics in the Danish pharmaceutical market but also provide valuable insights for other markets with similar structures. The methodologies and techniques we have developed could be applied to other sectors and markets, broadening the scope and impact of our research.

Acknowledgments. This work is partly funded by the Innovation Fund Denmark (IFD) under File No. 9065-00207B.

References

1. Agency, D.M.: Reimbursement and prices (2024). https://laegemiddelstyrelsen.dk/en/reimbursement/prices. Accessed 07 Mar 2024
2. Axtell, R.L., Farmer, J.D.: Agent-based modeling in economics and finance: past, present, and future. J. Econ. Lit. (2022)
3. Boero, R., Morini, M., Sonnessa, M., Terna, P.: Agent-Based Models of the Economy: From Theories to Applications. Springer (2015)
4. Breiman, L.: Statistical modeling: the two cultures (with comments and a rejoinder by the author). Stat. Sci. **16**(3), 199–231 (2001)
5. Delli Gatti, D., Fagiolo, G., Gallegati, M., Russo, A., Richiardi, M.G., et al.: Agent-Based Models in Economics: A Toolkit. Cambridge University Press (2018)

6. Dukart, H., Lanoue, L., Rezende, M., Rutten, P.: Emerging from disruption: the future of pharma operations strategy. Operations Practice, by McKinsey & Company (2022). https://www.mckinsey.com/capabilities/operations/our-insights/emerging-from-disruption-the-future-ofpharma-operations-strategy. Accessed 10 Dec 2022
7. Einav, L., Levin, J.: Economics in the age of big data. Science **346**(6210), 1243089 (2014)
8. Furaiji, F., Łatuszyńska, M.: Experimental study of consumer behavior using agent-based simulation. In: Problems, Methods and Tools in Experimental and Behavioral Economics: Computational Methods in Experimental Economics (CMEE) 2017 Conference, pp. 167–183. Springer (2018)
9. Hastie, T., Tibshirani, R., Friedman, J.H., Friedman, J.H.: The Elements of Statistical Learning: Data Mining, Inference, and Prediction, vol. 2. Springer (2009)
10. Iori, G., Porter, J.: Agent-based modeling for financial markets (2018)
11. Jamali, R., Lazarova-Molnar, S.: Towards agent-based simulation of the parallel trading market of pharmaceuticals. In: 2022 IEEE International Conference on Parallel & Distributed Processing with Applications, Big Data & Cloud Computing, Sustainable Computing & Communications, Social Computing & Networking (ISPA/BDCloud/SocialCom/SustainCom), pp. 173–181. IEEE (2022)
12. Jamali, R., Lazarova-Molnar, S.: Agent-based simulation of the pharmaceutical parallel trade market: A case study. Procedia Comput. Sci. **220**, 495–502 (2023)
13. Jamali, R., Lazarova-Molnar, S.: Towards developing an agent-based model of price competition in the European pharmaceutical parallel trade market. In: European Conference on Multi-agent Systems, pp. 200–213. Springer (2023)
14. Jamali, R., Lazarova-Molnar, S.: Uncovering competitor pricing patterns in the Danish pharmaceutical market via subsequence time series clustering: a case study. In: 2023 Winter Simulation Conference (WSC), pp. 793–804. IEEE (2023)
15. Kanavos, P., Costa-Font, J.: Pharmaceutical parallel trade in Europe: stakeholder and competition effects. Econ. policy **20**(44), 758–798 (2005)
16. Kavak, H.: A data-driven approach for modeling agents (2019)
17. Killick, R., Fearnhead, P., Eckley, I.A.: Optimal detection of changepoints with a linear computational cost. J. Am. Stat. Assoc. **107**(500), 1590–1598 (2012)
18. Lorenz, J.: Data-driven agent-based modeling in computational social science. In: Handbook of Computational Social Science, vol. 1, pp. 150–167. Routledge (2021)
19. Onozaki, T., Onozaki, T.: Agent-based model of market structure dynamics II. In: Nonlinearity, Bounded Rationality, and Heterogeneity: Some Aspects of Market Economies as Complex Systems, pp. 175–199 (2018)
20. Poledna, S., Miess, M.G., Hommes, C., Rabitsch, K.: Economic forecasting with an agent-based model. Eur. Econ. Rev. **151**, 104306 (2023)
21. Provost, F., Fawcett, T.: Data Science for Business: What You Need to Know About Data Mining and Data-Analytic Thinking. O'Reilly Media, Inc. (2013)
22. Sattenspiel, L., Dimka, J., Orbann, C.: Using cultural, historical, and epidemiological data to inform, calibrate, and verify model structures in agent-based simulations. Math. Biosci. Eng. **16**(4), 3071–3093 (2019)
23. Simoens, S.: A review of generic medicine pricing in Europe. GaBI J. **1**(1), 8–12 (2012)
24. Statista: Global pharmaceutical industry - statistics & facts (2023). https://www.statista.com/topics/1764/global-pharmaceutical-industry/#topicOverview. Accessed 01 Jan 2024

25. Steinbacher, M., et al.: Advances in the agent-based modeling of economic and social behavior. SN Bus. Econ. **1**(7), 1–24 (2021). https://doi.org/10.1007/s43546-021-00103-3
26. Truong, C., Oudre, L., Vayatis, N.: Selective review of offline change point detection methods. Signal Process. **167**, 107299 (2020)
27. Varian, H.R.: Big data: new tricks for econometrics. J. Econ. Perspect. **28**(2), 3–28 (2014)
28. Yang, L., van Dam, K.H.: Data-driven agent-based model development to support human-centric transit-oriented design. In: International Conference on Autonomous Agents and Multiagent Systems, pp. 60–66. Springer (2022)
29. Zellner, M.L.: Embracing complexity and uncertainty: the potential of agent-based modeling for environmental planning and policy. Plann. Theory Pract. **9**(4), 437–457 (2008)
30. Zhang, H., Vorobeychik, Y., Letchford, J., Lakkaraju, K.: Data-driven agent-based modeling, with application to rooftop solar adoption. Auton. Agent. Multi-Agent Syst. **30**(6), 1023–1049 (2016). https://doi.org/10.1007/s10458-016-9326-8

Multi-Agent Learning

Adversarial Search and Deep Learning for Strategic Settlement Placement in the "Settlers of Catan"

Diamantis Rafail Papadam(✉) and Georgios Chalkiadakis

School of Electrical and Computer Engineering, Technical University of Crete, Chania, Greece
{dpapadam,gchalkiadakis}@tuc.gr

Abstract. Despite recent deep neural network superhuman performance in many strategic board games, such as Chess and Go, there does not yet exist an algorithm that beats "Settlers of Catan" expert human players. Towards this direction, we present a combination of modern machine learning with a traditional tree-based adversarial search algorithm for initial settlement placement, and achieve performance that essentially matches the state-of-the-art. In particular, we use the n-player generalization of the classic Minimax search algorithm, known as Max^n, with the novelty that the evaluation function at the leaf nodes is the result of a forward pass in a trained convolutional neural network. Our work consists of two distinct parts that can work independently. The first is the use of the simple Max^n algorithm for the first time in this game setting. The second is the use of the neural network as an evaluation function for evaluating the initial settlement placement, and which could potentially be plugged into any adversarial search algorithm. After 10000 simulated games, which is a sufficient number to draw conclusions in this demanding strategic board game, we achieve performance close to the state-of-the-art; with the advantages that *(a)* our approach does not make use of any human-generated data corpus; and *(b)* that our approach's runtime is acceptable by human players, and much lower than the state-of-the-art's for initial placement in this domain.

Keywords: Deep Learning · Supervised Leaning · Adversarial Search · Multiagent Systems · Strategic Board Games · Settlers of Catan

1 Introduction

Nowadays, Artificial Intelligence (AI) research is heavily focusing on the use of Machine Learning (ML) methods, and in particular Deep Neural Networks (DNNs). Such research is actively growing within several domains including the strategic board games one.

Indeed, popular benchmarks for AI in strategic board games include Go [25] and Chess [26]; while recently, the "Settlers of Catan" (SoC) strategic board

R. Collier et al. (Eds.): EUMAS 2024, LNAI 15685, pp. 57–76, 2025.
https://doi.org/10.1007/978-3-031-93930-3_4

game has become an increasingly popular benchmark for AI and Multi-Agent Systems (MAS) research [3,10,30]. This is since it combines the following intriguing characteristics: stochasticity, large state space, non-zero-sum game, imperfect information (in the main phase), and multi-agent strategic environment.

SoC consists of two phases: The initial phase, where each player places two settlements and two roads for free; and the main phase where the action space is more complex. Detailed game rules can be found in [5].

Our main contributions in this paper are the following. Our first key contribution is employing the simple generalization of minimax, namely the Max^n algorithm [19], to perform initial settlement placement in SoC for the first time in the literature—via combining it with a trained deep neural network (DNN) which performs the evaluation at the leaf nodes before the tree backpropagation takes place. As such, our method aims to optimize the initial settlement placement via combining Max^n with a trained DNN—in particular, a Convolutional Neural Network (CNN) [2] chosen among several candidate DNN models via a meticulous process. Our agent overrides the initial settlement placement strategy of the JSettlers version 2.6.10 agent [20] (a well-known plan-based heuristic agent purpose-built for this domain), and retains its strategy during the main phase of the game. We show experimentally that optimizing the initial settlement placement via combining the simple Max^n algorithm (while employing generous pruning), with a trained CNN, while retaining the strategy of JSettlers version 2.6.10 for the main phase of the game, is enough to achieve performance close to the state-of-the-art for initial placement [11]. We consider the simplicity of our approach to be a key advantage. Moreover, the runtime of our algorithm is in the order of $\frac{1}{3}$ of a minute for the second initial settlement placement, and as such clearly acceptable to human competitors. This is in contrast to the runtime of the state-of-the-art which was reported to be in the order of 5 min for the same settlement placement.

A second key contribution to the SoC-related AI line of research, is indeed the use of DNNs to evaluate the initial settlement placement for each player. This new addition to the literature can be used not only to pave new paths for future work, but also to improve existing research, such as adversarial search algorithms that might benefit from our evaluator [11,16] or methods that do not take the initial phase into account at all [7,30].

As a final contribution, our three datasets illustrated in Sect. 3.4, are made public (along with our complete results) at the Open Science Framework (OSF).[1]

2 Background and Related Work

In this section, we initially provide some essential background on Max^n, and then review related work on strategic board games and especially SoC.

[1] For dataset $\mathcal{D}_2$, we also make public the *".soclog"* files of 2,000,000 simulated SoC games before processing.

2.1 Minimax for n Players (Max^n)

The Max^n algorithm [19] constitutes a generalization of Minimax that can be used in perfect information, sequential, non-zero-sum games with more than 2 players. Unlike Minimax, the codomain of the Max^n function is not a single value but rather a tuple of n values given that we have n players. In other words, the codomain is $\mathbb{R}^n$, while the domain can vary depending on how many dimensions and what type of data is required to describe the state space. Essentially, Max^n replaces the single value used by Minimax for each node with a vector of values; and uses as the backed-up value of a node k the utility vector of the successor with the highest value for the player choosing at k [23].

In some detail, Max^n is a function $V : \mathcal{S} \rightarrow \mathbb{R}^n$, where $\mathcal{S}$ is the set of all possible game states. In the scope of this paper, we have $n = 4$, but we illustrate the general case of the recursive Max^n algorithm:

$$V(s, p_i) = \begin{cases} u(s), & \text{if } s \text{ is a terminal state} \\ \max_{s' \leftarrow a_{p_i}(s)} \{V(s',\ p_{(i+1) \bmod n})_i\}, & \text{otherwise} \end{cases}$$

where: $p_i \in \{p_0, p_1, ..., p_{n-1}\}$ is the current player; s is the current state of the game; s' is the new state reached by some action a_{p_i} at s; $u(s)$ is the tuple of expected utilities in terminal state s; $V(s, p_i)$ is the Max^n score in state s and player p_i's turn. $\max_{s' \leftarrow a_{p_i}(s)} \{V(s', p_j)_i\}$ means that we are trying to maximize the i-th element (which corresponds to the score for the i-th player) of the tuple given by $V(s', p_j)$. We do that over the set of possible actions for player p_i, where each action leads to a new state s' as given by the function $a_{p_i}(s)$.

2.2 Strategic Board Games

Over the last decade, DNNs have pushed the state-of-the-art in many strategic board games by a lot (e.g., Chess, Go). They have not only been incorporated in traditional approaches [25], but have also been used independently [26]. A fairly recent survey on AI in the field of strategic board games was conducted by Duarte *et al.* [12].

Settlers of Catan. The first AI SoC agent to be able to compete against humans at a decent level was developed by Thomas R.S. as part of his Ph.D. thesis in 2003 [29]. The agent was named JSettlers as a combination of the names "Java" and "Settlers of Catan". The core of JSettler's decision-making process is an algorithm that estimates the building speed of available types of property (i.e., settlement, city, road, and development card), based on the hexes and ports that a player has access to. This building speed estimation is used for both the initial and the main phases of SoC. For the initial placement, JSettlers considers pairs of settlements, and for each of them calculates the sum of building speeds of each property type. Subsequently, the agent decides to build the pair that maximizes the building speed sum, starting with the settlement that is adjacent to the number tiles that are most likely to be activated. For the main phase, there are a lot of special cases. In general, during the early stages of the game, building speed estimates are considered for actions that maximize resource production; whereas, during the late stages of the game, building speed estimates are considered for actions that yield the most points. JSettlers gave rise to the 2007 JSettlers2 framework [20], heavily used for SoC research ever since.

An approach that managed to beat the JSettlers agents, even though trades were disallowed and the rules were simplified to make it a 2-player game, is that of Gendre and Kaneko [13]. Another noteworthy approach that did not simplify the rules of SoC, is that of Panousis [21]. In his thesis, a Monte Carlo Tree Search (MCTS) [4] approach that considers the main phase of the game was developed. Additionally, three approaches to solve the exploration-exploitation dilemma [22] were considered: UCT [17], Bayesian UCT [28], and myopic-VPI [8]. However, [21] was unable to beat the JSettlers agents. Similarly, Karamalegos [16], used the three aforementioned approaches as a foundation and improved the MCTS algorithm as part of his own thesis. In addition, to handle the full set of legal actions of the game, he merged MCTS that handles the main phase of SoC with an approach that still constitutes the state-of-the-art for the initial phase of the game [11] (see below). His results show an improvement compared to the work of [21], but his approach could not beat the JSettlers agents either.

In [3], the author uses supervised learning to predict player moves. To train her models, she incorporates linguistic data into the game state information. Furthermore, [3] develops a Multi-Layer Perceptron (MLP) architecture, a Long Short-term Memory Neural Network (LSTM) architecture, and combinations of the two. Even though the best neural network reaches an 88% prediction accuracy, the trained models were not tested against JSettlers. In [14], the trading policy of JSettlers agents is improved after thorough consideration of empirical data. Cuayáhuitl *et al.* [7] developed a strategic dialogue system using (deep) reinforcement learning (RL), empirically showcasing the effectiveness of their approach in negotiating trades. In the same research direction, Xenou *et al.* [30], developed a novel approach based on deep RL to negotiate trades. They used the concept of Q-decomposition [24] to calculate the Bellman Q-value function, and created an architecture that consists of $|\mathcal{A}|$ parallel LSTM neural networks, where $\mathcal{A}$ is the set of legal actions. Once the game state is fed into these networks and the outputs are produced, the final Q-value is computed as the maximum over all Q^i, where $i \in \{1, 2, ..., |\mathcal{A}|\}$. Moreover, at each iteration, the LSTM weights Q^i, are updated $\forall\, i \in \{1, 2, ..., |\mathcal{A}|\}$. Notably, the complete algorithm is able to train itself online (during gameplay), and the authors report a superior performance to that of the JSettlers agents.

Moving to approaches that handle the full set of actions, in [10], Dobre and Lascarides improved the traditional MCTS algorithm in two ways. Firstly, they broke the sampling policy into two steps: sampling over action types, and sampling over actions within the chosen action type. They empirically show that this two-step process speeds up the algorithm. Secondly, they implement tree parallelization [6] and make their approach much more time-efficient. In [9], the same authors extend the definition of the Partially Observable Monte Carlo Planning algorithm (POMCP) [27] to multi-agent environments.

We now focus on approaches that deal with the exact same problem we tackle: the initial settlement placement. In [15], Guhe and Lascarides improve the initial placement strategy as well as the strategy for choosing the next action during the main phase of the game. They show the dominance of their agent against JSettlers agents. Their created agent was named STAC [1] in subsequent publications of Lascarides *et al.* However, in the scope of this paper we call it "STAC-v1". Then, in Dodre and Lascarides [11], the authors further improve the initial placement strategy with an MCTS-based algorithm seeded with a human data corpus. Their new agent achieves a 30.43% win ratio after playing against three "STAC-v1" agents over 10,000 games. To the best of our knowledge, the agent of [11] is the state-of-the-art for initial settlement placement, and in the scope of this paper, we call it "STAC-v2". Note that the approaches that handle the full set of game rules, such as [10], do not report results where only the initial phase strategy is improved, thus they cannot be fairly compared against [11].

In version 2.5.0 of the JSettlers2 framework [20], released in 2022, certain components from the STAC project [1] were incorporated into the JSettlers agent; while the current JSettlers version is 2.6.10. However, the specific STAC parts integrated in JSettlers have not been specified, thus we cannot be certain about the initial placement strategy used by JSettlers 2.5.0 or 2.6.10. In our research, we used version 2.6.10 for playing in the main phase of the game after the initial placement phase. However, we do not use the JSettlers (and, as such, definitely neither STAC's [11,15]) initial placement strategy, but replace it with our own, which is the focus of this paper. Finally, we compare our results to the state-of-the-art [11]; and, as we report in Sect. 4, we manage to get close to it, while achieving a runtime that is faster by one order of magnitude.

3 Our Approach

As mentioned in the introduction, the focus of our work is on optimizing the initial settlement placement via combining Max^n with a trained deep neural network (in particular, a CNN), while retaining the strategy of JSettlers version 2.6.10 for the main phase of the game. In this section, we explain our approach in detail.

To begin, we note that we designed and trained six candidate DNN models—three MLPs and three CNNs. After a thorough training and empirical experimentation process (which we detail later in this section and in the online Appendices), we chose the *Small CNN* to be combined with the Max^n algorithm for initial settlement placement on the SoC board. Our resulting *Max^n-CNN* agent overrides the initial phase strategy of the JSettlers version 2.6.10 agent [20], while it retains its strategy during the main phase of the game.

In the rest of this section, we first present our *Max^n-CNN* algorithm that optimizes the initial settlement placement via the aforementioned Small CNN-Max^n integration (Sect. 3.1). Then, in Sect. 3.2 we provide the details on how we produced the data from simulated games to train the DNNs; in Sect. 3.3 we detail how we preprocessed the data to maximize the effectiveness of the DNNs; in Sect. 3.4 we describe the three datasets we created for use in this paper and beyond; in Sect. 3.5 we present the six candidate model architectures we designed and tested; and in Sect. 3.6, we describe our models' training process in detail.

3.1 The Max^n-CNN Algorithm in Detail

We present the initial settlement placement decision-making process of our *Max^n-CNN* agent in Algorithm 1. Whenever a leaf node is reached, Algorithm 1 calls Algorithm 2 for initial placement evaluation by the CNN. On the other hand, when Algorithm 1 is in a non-leaf node, it calls Algorithm 3 to prune the Max^n tree according to the current depth and recursively moves to the next settlement placement nodes. Algorithm 2 performs the CNN evaluation by sending the completed initial placement game state to a python server via localhost. Moreover, Algorithm 3 performs the pruning according to the scores calculated by Algorithm 4 (a JSettlers2 framework [20] algorithm, presented in the Appendix).

To describe the algorithms in greater detail, Algorithm 1, begins by checking the number of settlements that are left to be placed. If this number is zero, then it calls Algorithm 2 which performs the leaf node evaluation with the use of our trained CNN. On the other hand, if this number is above zero, it figures out which player's turn it is. Furthermore, it retrieves a list of all available settlement placements for that player and calls Algorithm 3 to prune those settlement placements according to the current depth. In its main part, it recursively calls itself for each available move in the pruned options and chooses the settlement placement that maximizes the score for the current player. Finally, it returns the four scores, one for each player, that resulted from the chosen settlement placement along with that placement.

Algorithm 2 creates an array with the neural network input before preprocessing, as shown in the first 4 rows of Table 1, and sends it to a python server through localhost, as described in the end of this section. The server preprocesses the input, performs the forward pass, and responds with the result which is an array of the 4 predicted float scores. Finally, before returning the 4 computed scores, Algorithm 2 multiplies each score with 100000 and keeps the integer part, thus accounting for 5 decimal digits.

Algorithm 3 begins by computing the *size* of the pruned settlement placement options using the formula $\lceil \frac{30}{d^{1.46}} \rceil$. This calculation, results in a pruned *size* of 30, 11, 7, 4, 3, 3, 2, 2, for depth $d = 1, 2, 3, 4, 5, 6, 7, 8$ respectively. In reality, we take the $min\left(\lceil \frac{30}{d^{1.46}} \rceil, potential.size()\right)$, in case the enumerator is chosen to be too large. Moreover, a hashtable where each potential settlement is mapped to an initial score of 0 is created, and Algorithm 4 is called to perform the scoring. Furthermore, a trivial function is used to sort the potential settlement placements according to the calculated scores. Finally, an array with the previously calculated *size* (number of most promising options) is returned.

Algorithm 1: Max^n with CNN as Evaluation Function (*Max^n-CNN*)

```
Input: int settlements_rem, int depth, SOCGame game
Output: int[] scores, settlement move
Function Maxⁿ− CNN(settlements_rem, depth, game):
    int player ← −1;
    if settlements_rem = 0 then
        return {evaluateBoard(game), null}; // Evaluation performed by CNN (Alg. 2)
    else if settlements_rem = 8 or settlements_rem = 1 then
        player ← 0;
    else if settlements_rem = 7 or settlements_rem = 2 then
        player ← 1;
    else if settlements_rem = 6 or settlements_rem = 3 then
        player ← 2;
    else
        player ← 3;
    end
    settlement[] potential ← game.getLegalSettlements(player); // Legal settlements
    // Sort & prune legal settlement moves with a heuristic function (Alg. 3)
    settlement[] moves ← prunePotential(potential, depth, player, game);
    int best ← −1; int[] scores ← {0, 0, 0, 0}; settlement move ← null;
    // Recursion for each possible move in the pruned moves
    for settl in moves do
        game.putPiece(settl);
        road = planRoad(player); // JSettlers heuristic for road building decision
        game.putPiece(road);
        local_score = Maxⁿ− CNN(settlements_rem − 1, depth + 1, game)[0];
        game.removePiece(road);
        game.removePiece(settl);
        if local_score[player] > best then
            best ← local_score[player];
            scores ← local_score;
            move ← settl;
        end
    end
    return {scores, move};
end
```

Algorithm 2: Evaluate Completed Initial Phase with CNN

```
Input: SOCGame game
Output: int[] scores
Function evaluateBoard(game):
    int[] scores ← new int[4];
    int[] NN_input ← new int[200];
    NN_input[0 : 37] ← game.getHexLayout();
    NN_input[38 : 74] ← game.getNumLayout();
    NN_input[75 : 146] ← game.getRoads();
    NN_input[147 : 200] ← game.getSettlements();
    // Send data through socket and receive CNN evaluation result
    float[] NN_output ← send_data_to_NN(NN_input);
    for i ← 0 to 3 do
        scores[i] ← (int)(100000 · NN_output[i]); // We consider 5 decimal digits
    end
    return scores;
end
```

After careful consideration of preliminary results, as well as inspiration from [11] that proceeds in the same way, we decided to use our *Max^n-CNN* approach only for the second settlement placement. The reason is that in the first settlement placement, the state space is huge; hence our pruning heuristic, which is

Algorithm 3: Prune Potential Settlements

```
Input: settlement[] potential, int depth, int player, SOCGame game
Output: settlement[] pruned
Function prunePotential(potential, depth, player, game):
    int size ← min(⌈30 / depth^1.46⌉, potential.size());
    Hashtable<settlement, int> nodes;
    for settl in potential do
        nodes.add(settl, 0);
    end
    // JSettlers heuristic for settlement evaluation (Alg. 4)
    scoreNodesForSettl(nodes, player, game, 10, 5, 10); // Updates nodes
    // Keep the size best settlement spots in sorted order
    settlement[] pruned ← sort_and_prune(nodes, size);
    return pruned;
end
```

very simplistic in our approach, plays a very important role. Conversely, when the state space is smaller, less pruning is required, and hence one does not heavily rely on the effectiveness of the pruning heuristic.

Regarding the speed of our algorithm, it is able to evaluate approximately 450 $\frac{\text{leaf nodes}}{\text{second}}$. This may seem slow but it is important to note that the bottleneck of our method is the forward pass through the CNN which is done by an *NVIDIA GeForce RTX 2080 Ti*, as well as the socket communication explained in the next paragraph. Note also that, in most Catan tournaments, players have 1–3 min per initial settlement placement, while our algorithm reaches a decision within ≈20.5 s in the worst case, as shown in the Appendix. " This allows our method to be readily employed in a tournament—either to be used for supporting the decisions of a human player if this is not prohibited by competition rules, or to allow human spectators to observe in real time Catan softbots that employ our method while playing the game. By contrast, as we mention in Sect. 4 below, the state-of-the-art algorithm [11] requires 300 s to reach a decision regarding the initial settlement placement, and as such is impractical for use in a real-world Catan tournament.

Integration of CNN with Max^n To allow the Max^n algorithm [19] to communicate with our CNN, we use a socket. When a tree leaf is reached by Max^n in Java, the completed initial phase game state, composed of 200 features, shown in the first 4 rows of Table 1, is sent to a Python server that holds the trained CNN. The Python server, preprocesses these features to create the required input of 1141 features, shown in Table 2. Moreover, it runs a forward pass to compute 4 float numbers, representing the expected *Final Scores*, and sends these back to the Java Max^n algorithm for tree backpropagation.

3.2 Data Creation

One of the necessary elements for any supervised learning algorithm is data. In the scope of our research, we used the JSettlers2 framework [20] and simulated 3,500,000 games of SoC with 2 types of agents: JSettlers Agent (places initial settlements heuristically); Random Agent (places initial settlements uniformly at random). Nevertheless, during the main phase of SoC, both of these agents use the JSettlers version 2.6.10 strategy [20].

To create sparse data, we simulated: 2,500,000 Games Consisting of 4 Random Agents; 500,000 Games Consisting of 3 Random Agents & 1 JSettlers Agent; 500,000 Games Consisting of 4 JSettlers Agents.

Using available functionality, we stored these games in *".soclog"* files. Afterwards, through parsing, we extracted the data that is relevant to our work. In Table 1, we present the extracted features (i.e., those before preprocessing).

Table 1. Extracted *".soclog"* files data. Descriptions are as in JSettlers2 [20].

Feature	Number	Domain	Description
Hex Layout	37	$\{0, 1, ..., 213\}$	Desert Hexes $\rightarrow$ 0
			Water Hexes $\rightarrow$ 6
			Resource Hexes $\rightarrow$ $\{1, ..., 5\}$
			3:1 Port Hexes $\rightarrow$ $\{7, ..., 15\}$
			2:1 Port Hexes $\rightarrow$ $\{16, ..., 213\}$
Number Layout	37	$\{-1, 0, ..., 9\}$	$-1 \rightarrow$ No Number Tile
			0 $\rightarrow$ Number Tile 2
			1 $\rightarrow$ Number Tile 3
			2 $\rightarrow$ Number Tile 4
			3 $\rightarrow$ Number Tile 5
			4 $\rightarrow$ Number Tile 6
			5 $\rightarrow$ Number Tile 8
			6 $\rightarrow$ Number Tile 9
			7 $\rightarrow$ Number Tile 10
			8 $\rightarrow$ Number Tile 11
			9 $\rightarrow$ Number Tile 12
Roads	72	$\{0, 1, ..., 4\}$	0 $\rightarrow$ No Road Built
			1 $\rightarrow$ Road Belongs to Player 1
			2 $\rightarrow$ Road Belongs to Player 2
			3 $\rightarrow$ Road Belongs to Player 3
			4 $\rightarrow$ Road Belongs to Player 4
Settlements	54	$\{0, 1, ..., 4\}$	0 $\rightarrow$ No Settlement Built
			1 $\rightarrow$ Settlement Belongs to Player 1
			2 $\rightarrow$ Settlement Belongs to Player 2
			3 $\rightarrow$ Settlement Belongs to Player 3
			4 $\rightarrow$ Settlement Belongs to Player 4
Final Scores	4	$\{2, 3, ..., 12\}$	The final player scores.
			Even though 10 points are needed to win,
			the highest possible score is 12 points.

There are $37+37+72+54 = 200$ input features (*Hex Layout*, *Number Layout*, *Roads*, *Settlements*) and 4 output features (the *Final Scores*). The *Hex Layout* constitutes the arrangement of hexagonal terrain tiles that make up the game board. The *Number Layout* constitutes the arrangement of number tiles that are placed on top of hexagonal terrain tiles; and which get activated according to the rolled dice sum. The *Roads* correspond to edges and contain the information about road ownership, and the *Settlements* correspond to intersections and contain the information about settlement ownership.

3.3 Data Preprocessing

Having extracted all the meaningful data, as explained in Sect. 3.2 and summarized in Table 1, we then preprocess it so that the DNNs can utilize it better. Notice that: *Hex Layout* → Categorical Data (13 domain values); *Number Layout* → Numerical Data; *Roads* → Categorical Data (5 domain values); *Settlements* → Categorical Data (5 domain values); *Final Scores* → Numerical Data.

To begin with, we allowed the *Hex Layout* feature to take 13 values only. Specifically: 5 values for the resource hexes; 1 value for the water hexes; 1 value for the desert hexes; 1 value for the 3:1 ports irrespective of their $\{7, ..., 15\}$ JSettlers2 codification; and 5 values for the 2:1 ports, irrespective of their $\{16, ..., 213\}$ JSettlers2 codification, depending on the port resource type.

Moreover, we wanted the network to be able to utilize spatial information. For this reason, we represented *Hex Layout* and *Number Layout* as 7×7 matrices, where any cell that is not part of the initial 37 tiles is set to zero. Additionally, we used one-hot encoding for the categorical data, which heavily increased the total number of features, but also the accuracy of our neural network. We do not show any results without one-hot encoding, because they were significantly worse, as it is well-established to be the case. Finally, we empirically found that transforming *Number Layout* tiles by mapping them to their corresponding probabilities of being activated after a dice roll, works better for the neural network. The exact transformation is as follows—where, the first number in a row corresponds to a *Number Layout* code in the JSettlers2 framework (see Table 1); the second number corresponds to the actual number found on a *Number Layout* tile; and the third number is the code we use, corresponding to the P probability of the tile marked with the second number getting activated:

- $-1 \rightarrow$ No number tile $\rightarrow 0$
- $0 \rightarrow 2 \rightarrow 3;\ P(\{\text{dice sum equals } 2\}) = 1/36 \approx 0.03$
- $1 \rightarrow 3 \rightarrow 6;\ P(\{\text{dice sum equals } 3\}) = 2/36 \approx 0.06$
- $2 \rightarrow 4 \rightarrow 8;\ P(\{\text{dice sum equals } 4\}) = 3/36 \approx 0.08$
- $3 \rightarrow 5 \rightarrow 11;\ P(\{\text{dice sum equals } 5\}) = 4/36 \approx 0.11$
- $4 \rightarrow 6 \rightarrow 14;\ P(\{\text{dice sum equals } 6\}) = 5/36 \approx 0.14$
- $5 \rightarrow 8 \rightarrow 14;\ P(\{\text{dice sum equals } 8\}) = 5/36 \approx 0.14$
- $6 \rightarrow 9 \rightarrow 11;\ P(\{\text{dice sum equals } 9\}) = 4/36 \approx 0.11$
- $7 \rightarrow 10 \rightarrow 8;\ P(\{\text{dice sum equals } 10\}) = 3/36 \approx 0.08$
- $8 \rightarrow 11 \rightarrow 6;\ P(\{\text{dice sum equals } 11\}) = 2/36 \approx 0.06$
- $9 \rightarrow 12 \rightarrow 3;\ P(\{\text{dice sum equals } 12\}) = 1/36 \approx 0.03$

The only feature that was not preprocessed is that of the *Final Scores*, which represents the DNN output. After preprocessing, there are $588+49+288+216 = 1141$ final input features and 4 final output features. Intuitively, we want our DNN to take the completed initial placement phase as input, and output the expected *Final Scores*: $E[s_1, s_2, s_3, s_4 \,|\, \text{initial placement}]$, where s_1, s_2, s_3, s_4 are the final player scores. The input format of the DNN is as in Table 2.

Table 2. Preprocessed DNN Input

Feature	Number	Domain
Hex Layout	$7 \times 7 \times 12 = 588$	$\{0, 1\}$
Number Layout	$7 \times 7 = 49$	$\{0, 3, 6, 8, 11, 14\}$
Roads	$72 \times 4 = 288$	$\{0, 1\}$
Settlements	$54 \times 4 = 216$	$\{0, 1\}$

3.4 Dataset Creation

As presented in Sect. 3.2, we simulated a total of 3,500,000 SoC games. From these games, we created 3 datasets shown in Table 3, which we made available at this Open Science Framework (OSF) project. Dataset $\mathcal{D}_1$ was created to test the different architectures in games where the initial placement is always uniformly random, and dataset $\mathcal{D}_2$ was created as a representative subset of dataset $\mathcal{D}_3$, to allow for faster hyperparameter optimization.

Table 3. Datasets used for Training

Dataset	Total Size	Description
$\mathcal{D}_1$	1,000,000	Games with 4 Random Agents
$\mathcal{D}_2$	2,000,000	1,000,000 games with 4 Random Agents 500,000 Games with 3 Random Agents & 1 JSettlers Agent 500,000 Games with 4 JSettlers Agents
$\mathcal{D}_3$	3,500,000	All created games presented in Sect. 3.2

3.5 Model Architectures

As mentioned, we created and tested 6 DNNs: a *Small MLP* with $1,432,836$ parameters; a *Medium MLP* with $6,762,452$ parameters; a *Large MLP* with $17,067,316$ parameters; a *Small CNN* with $1,401,460$ parameters; a *Medium CNN* with $4,646,524$ parameters; and a *Large CNN* with $16,528,512$ parameters.

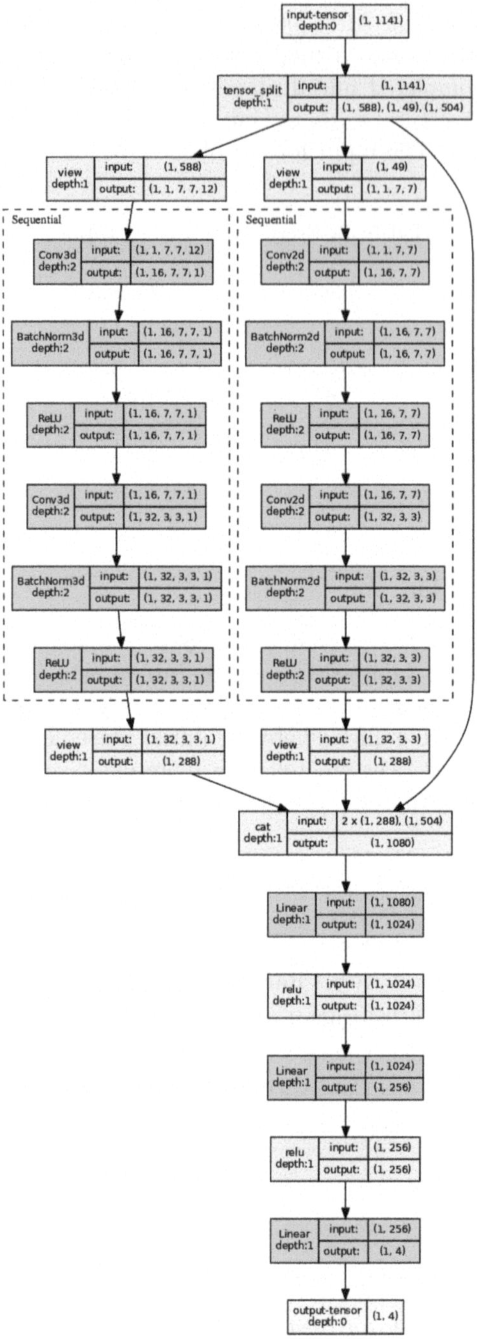

Fig. 1. Small CNN

In Fig. 1 and in the online Appendices, we depict our designed architectures. The *Small CNN* architecture, shown in Fig. 1, consists of 2 convolutional layers for the *Hex Layout*, 2 convolutional layers for the *Number Layout*, and 2 fully connected hidden layers to compute the final output. Regarding the *Hex Layout*, the first convolutional layer consists of 1 input channel, 16 output channels, and a kernel of size $(5, 5, 12)$. Moreover, $padding = (2, 2, 0)$ is performed in the first 2 dimensions to retain their size after the convolution. The second convolutional layer consists of 16 input channels, 32 output channels, and a kernel of size $(5, 5, 1)$. Regarding the *Number Layout*, the first convolutional layer consists of 1 input channel, 16 output channels, and a kernel of size $(5, 5)$. Moreover, $padding = (2, 2)$ is performed to retain the size after the convolution in both dimensions. The second convolutional layer consists of 16 input channels, 32 output channels, and a kernel of size $(5, 5)$.

The results from the convolutional layers, along with the road and settlement encodings, are concatenated into a layer of 1080 neurons. The first fully connected hidden layer that follows has 1024 neurons, and the second hidden layer has 256 neurons. Finally, we have the output layer of the 4 predicted scores.

3.6 Training

For training the neural network, we followed an 80-10-10 split ratio, randomly allocating the respective dataset portions to the training, validation, and test sets. Mini-batch processing was used to speed up training. Throughout our training, presumably due to the large amount of data that was used, inference on the test set resulted in practically the same loss as inference on the validation set. As such, our test set results are almost identical to the validation set results reported in the online Appendices. As a loss function for our regression problem, we used the Mean Squared Error (MSE) over mini-batches. Training the DNNs in the scope of this paper, constitutes a regression problem.

Selecting the Most Suitable Model Architecture. To compare the 6 different architectures from Sect. 3.5, we need a benchmark. For this purpose, we trained each architecture in all datasets $\mathcal{D}_1$, $\mathcal{D}_2$, and $\mathcal{D}_3$. The procedure we followed is described extensively in the online Appendices. In summary, our results show that as the network parameters are increased, the neural networks learn the training data in fewer epochs. However, the performance of all architectures peaks at more or less the same loss and accuracy in the validation set. Additionally, the *Small CNN* uses fewer parameters than the *Small MLP*, the *Medium CNN* uses fewer parameters than the *Medium MLP*, and the *Large CNN* uses fewer parameters than the *Large MLP*. Nevertheless, all CNNs learn faster than the corresponding MLPs which have more parameters. This can be attributed to the fact that hex and number patterns are location invariant in SoC, which enables the weight-sharing property of CNNs to be effective. An additional advantage of the CNNs over the MLPs is that they allow the GPU to efficiently parallelize computations and perform a forward pass more quickly. As such, we selected the *Small CNN* (Fig. 1), to perform further hyperparameter optimization.

Hyperparameter Optimization. We used two approaches to perform hyperparameter optimization. In our first approach, we used the Stochastic Gradient Descent (SGD) optimizer and tuned the *learning rate*, the *weight decay*, and the *momentum*. In our second approach, we used the Adaptive Moment Estimation (Adam) optimizer and tuned the *batch size*, the *learning rate*, the *weight decay*, and the *dropout*. The process details are in the online Appendices.

In both approaches, our hyperparameterer optimization methodology, consists of two steps. In the first step, we employed a Bayesian optimization algorithm within the wandb.ai framework. In the second step, we empirically located the neighborhood of the global maximum accuracy within the hyperparameter space, according to the previous Bayesian optimization. Furthermore, we used this narrowed-down hyperparameter space to perform more tests so as to achieve better accuracy. Half of these tests were performed with random samples from the empirically global maximum neighborhood, and the rest by using the best available hyperparameters while varying only the weight and bias initialization.

4 Experimental Evaluation

We now proceed to describe our experiments and results in detail. We pit our agent, *Max*^{n}*-CNN*, with its CNN's parameters optimized using either SGD or Adam, against 4 combinations of Random and JSettlers v2.6.10 agents.[2] Our results, after 10000 game simulations for each setup, are depicted in Fig. 2. The results verify that *Max*^{n}*-CNN* is dominant in all game formats regardless of the optimizer that was used for training. We remark that Random agents place the initial settlements uniformly at random, but then follow JSettlers v2.6.10 during the main phase of the game.

We see that our *Max*^{n}*-CNN* approach beats the JSettlers v2.6.10 agents [20], achieving a 27.6% win ratio over 10000 simulations against three such agents; hence it is also superior to the original JSettlers agents of Thomas's Ph.D. thesis [29]. Moreover, it outperforms JSettlers v2.6.10 agents when encountering two or one of them in a game. Interestingly, our approach outperforms "Random" agents by a very large margin. We remind the reader that "Random" agents are random only during the initial placement, but follow JSettlers v2.6.10 during the main phase of the game. As such, our results can also be viewed as showcasing the importance of the initial placement phase in the Settlers of Catan game.

In Table 4, we compare our agent's performance to that of the state-of-the-art "STAC-v2" agent [11], given their reported results in that paper. Specifically, it is reported in [11] that their "STAC-v2" agent achieves a 30.43% win ratio over 10000 games against 3 "STAC-v1" agents which were based on JSettlers, and were better than JSettlers at the time of publication. The 30.43% win ratio was achieved by making use of a human-generated corpus of data, and a 28.74% win

[2] Our simulations used Python 3.10, PyTorch 1.12.1, and PyTorch 2.0.1.

Statistics over 10,000 Simulated Games				
Player	Win Ration		Avg. Score	
	SGD	Adam	SGD	Adam
Max^n-CNN	27.6%	27.3%	7.65	7.66
JSettlers v2.6.10	24.9%	24.7%	7.54	7.52
JSettlers v2.6.10	23.8%	24.3%	7.47	7.49
JSettlers v2.6.10	23.6%	23.7%	7.5	7.46

Statistics over 10,000 Simulated Games				
Player	Win Ration		Avg. Score	
	SGD	Adam	SGD	Adam
Max^n-CNN	35.6%	34.4%	7.96	7.91
JSettlers v2.6.10	31.6%	32.1%	7.79	7.82
JSettlers v2.6.10	30.7%	31.2%	7.77	7.78
Random	2.1%	2.2%	4.21	4.24

Statistics over 10,000 Simulated Games				
Player	Win Ration		Avg. Score	
	SGD	Adam	SGD	Adam
Max^n-CNN	49.3%	49.2%	8.48	8.49
JSettlers v2.6.10	43.5%	43.2%	8.27	8.29
Random	3.8%	3.9%	4.54	4.51
Random	3.4%	3.7%	4.43	4.51

Statistics over 10,000 Simulated Games				
Player	Win Ration		Average Score	
	SGD	Adam	SGD	Adam
Max^n-CNN	78.7%	77.8%	9.54	9.5
Random	7.1%	7.7%	4.92	4.95
Random	7.1%	7.3%	4.92	4.96
Random	7%	7.2%	4.9	4.96

Fig. 2. Results over 10,000 Simulated Games

Table 4. Final *Max^n-CNN* agent vs. the state-of-the-art "STAC-v2" agent [11]

Player	Win Ratio vs Baseline (over 10,000 games)	Init. Placement Runtime (for second settlement)
Max^n-CNN agent	27.6%	≈20.5 s
"STAC-v2" agent w/o human-generated corpus	28.74%	≈300 s
"STAC-v2" agent with human-generated corpus	30.43%	≈300 s

ratio was achieved under the same settings without making use of such data. Given that [11] is a 2015 publication, and that 2022 JSettlers v2.5.0 framework and subsequent versions have incorporated methods and code from the STAC project, we can make the safe assumption that "STAC-v1" baseline agents in [11] are, in the worst-case for us, of equal strength to the JSettlers v2.6.10. As such, by using JSettlers version 2.6.10 as our baseline, we can perform a fair indirect comparison against "STAC-v2" agents [11]—focusing on Win Ratio vs the baseline, exactly as [11] does; but also reporting on the methods' runtime.

The results[3] depicted in Table 4, show that our approach achieves performance that is (in the worst case, given our assumption above) very close to the state-of-the-art. Moreover, it does so with a runtime that is 10 times faster than

[3] The 10,000 games for each game scenario can be downloaded from the OSF, along with a Python script for parsing them and printing win ratios and scores per player.

that of [11]. In our view, this cannot be attributed solely to [11] using outdated hardware—i.e., an *Intel-I5 hyper-threaded processor*, while we use an *AMD Ryzen 5 7600X CPU* for Max^n, and an *NVIDIA GeForce RTX 2080 Ti GPU* for leaf node evaluation by the CNN. For instance, our setting has to accommodate continuous communication between the Java Max^n algorithm and the CNN-hosting Python server, via the localhost, and still our agent is 10 times faster than [11]. Note also that, most probably, the implementation runtime could have been further improved by integrating our CNN placement evaluator into the Java engine, thus avoiding the need to go through a socket in order to integrate it with Max^n. This is left as interesting future work.

5 Conclusions and Future Work

In this paper, we provided a simple yet effective approach to optimize the initial phase of the SoC strategic board game. To this end, we incorporated deep neural networks in the classic adversarial search Max^n algorithm [19], and by so doing we achieved performance that is, in the worst case for us, close to the state-of-the-art in this demanding multiagent domain. Interestingly, we did so without requiring a runtime that exceeds the usual two minutes limit set by online platforms (e.g., [31]) for initial settlement placement; and thus, unlike the state-of-the-art, our method can be used in online gaming.

There are several future work directions. A straightforward improvement is equipping Max^n with α-β pruning [18]. Additionally, merging our approach with ones that focus on other game aspects, such as trading [7,30], would certainly lead to better overall performance. Another direction is enriching our datasets with data from tournaments among human experts. Moreover, one could explore different heuristic evaluation functions used for greedy pruning, improving the one in the JSettlers2 framework [20] that we present in Algorithm 4 of the Appendix. Furthermore, it would be interesting to perform a thorough ablation study to evaluate the impact of the various information components contributing to DNN training. Last but not least, it is worth extending the model architecture to allow our agent to account for all game states and not only those of the initial placement phase. In this way, we could improve more strategy aspects, like trading or purchasing property and development cards. Such a DNN could be trained either in a supervised learning manner using our existing datasets; or with the use of RL after many game simulations.

Acknowledgments. The research described in this paper was carried out within the framework of the National Recovery and Resilience Plan Greece 2.0, funded by the European Union - NextGenerationEU (Implementation Body: HFRI. Project name: DEEP-REBAYES. HFRI Project Number 15430).

Appendix: Total Runtime and Algorithm 4

Our Total Runtime. We can easily calculate the runtime of our Max^n-CNN approach since we know the number of leaf nodes by the heuristic pruning shown in Algorithm 3, and we also know that approximately 450 leaf nodes can be evaluated per second. Since we employ our method only for the second settlement placement, the Max^n-CNN depth can take four values $d \in \{1, 2, 3, 4\}$. The four possible cases, are presented below in detail:

- We are the 1st player, hence we place last in the second round.
  - $\#leaf\_nodes = \prod_{d=1}^{1} \lceil \frac{30}{d^{1.46}} \rceil = 30$
  - $\text{runtime} = \frac{30 \text{ leaf nodes}}{450 \text{ leaf nodes per second}} \approx 67\,\text{ms}$
- We are the 2nd player, hence we place third in the second round.
  - $\#leaf\_nodes = \prod_{d=1}^{2} \lceil \frac{30}{d^{1.46}} \rceil = 30 \times 11 = 330$
  - $\text{runtime} = \frac{330 \text{ leaf nodes}}{450 \text{ leaf nodes per second}} \approx 733\,\text{ms}$
- We are the 3rd player, hence we place second in the second round.
  - $\#leaf\_nodes = \prod_{d=1}^{3} \lceil \frac{30}{d^{1.46}} \rceil = 30 \times 11 \times 7 = 2310$
  - $\text{runtime} = \frac{2310 \text{ leaf nodes}}{450 \text{ leaf nodes per second}} \approx 5.1\,\text{s}$
- We are the 4th player, hence we place first in the second round.
  - $\#leaf\_nodes = \prod_{d=1}^{4} \lceil \frac{30}{d^{1.46}} \rceil = 30 \times 11 \times 7 \times 4 = 9240$
  - $\text{runtime} = \frac{9240 \text{ leaf nodes}}{450 \text{ leaf nodes per second}} \approx 20.5\,\text{s}$

Algorithm to Score Nodes. Algorithm 4 is a built-in algorithm in the JSettlers2 framework [20] which we made use of.

Initially, it calculates the score of potential settlement placements according to the hex numbers adjacent to them. Notice that the *numRating* array corresponds to the codes we used in Sect. 3.3 (i.e., the probabilities multiplied by 100). Furthermore, if the *player* does not already have a settlement adjacent to a 3:1 port, the algorithm increases the score for each potential settlement placement that is adjacent to such a port. Finally, for each 2:1 port, if the player does not have a settlement adjacent to that port and the resource rarity that is specified by the port type is greater than the threshold of 33, the potential settlement placements that are adjacent to that port have their scores increased.

Algorithm 4: JSettlers Heuristic to Score Intersections for Settlement Placement

```
Input: Hashtable<settlement, int> nodes, int player, SOCGame game,
       int numWeight, int miscPortWeight, int portWeight
Output: void
Function
scoreNodesForSettl(nodes, player, game, numWeight, miscPortWeight, portWeight):
    // Score according to number tiles
    int[] numRating ← {0, 0, 3, 6, 8, 11, 14, 17, 14, 11, 8, 6, 3};
    SOCBoard board ← game.getBoard();
    int maxScore ← 80;
    Enumeration<int> keys ← nodes.keys();
    while keys.hasMoreElements() do
        int key ← keys.nextElement(); // Pops previous element
        int oldScore ← nodes.get(key);
        int score ← 0;
        for hex in board.getAdjacentHexes(key) do
            int num = board.getNumFromHex(hex);
            score ← numRating[num];
            if player.hasNumber(num) = false then
                score ← score + numRating[num];
            end
        end
        int newScore ← numWeight · ((100 · score)/maxScore);
        nodes.put(key, oldScore + newScore);
    end
    // Score according to 3:1 ports
    if player.hasSettlAtMiscPort() = false then
        keys ← nodes.keys();
        while keys.hasMoreElements() do
            int key ← keys.nextElement(); // Pops previous element
            int oldScore ← nodes.get(key);
            int score ← 0;
            if board.isMiscPort(key) then
                score ← 100;
            end
            int newScore ← miscPortWeight · score;
            nodes.put(key, oldScore + newScore);
        end
    end
    // Score according to 2:1 ports
    // JSettlers function to calculate rarity for each of the 5 resources
    int[] resEst = estimateResourceRarity();
    for int portType ← SOCBoard.CLAY_PORT to SOCBoard.WOOD_PORT do
        if (not player.hasSettlAtPort(portType)) and resEst[portType] > 33 then
            keys ← nodes.keys();
            int estimatedPortWeight ← (resEst[portType] · portWeight)/56;
            while keys.hasMoreElements() do
                int key ← keys.nextElement(); // Pops previous element
                int oldScore ← nodes.get(key);
                int score ← 0;
                if board.isPort(key) then
                    score ← 100;
                end
                int newScore ← estimatedPortWeight · score;
                nodes.put(key, oldScore + newScore);
            end
        end
    end
end
```

References

1. STAC - Strategic Conversation. https://www.irit.fr/STAC/
2. Albawi, S., Mohammed, T.A., Al-Zawi, S.: Understanding of a convolutional neural network. In: 2017 International Conference on Engineering and Technology (ICET), pp. 1–6 (2017). https://doi.org/10.1109/ICEngTechnol.2017.8308186
3. Apostolidou, M.: Exploiting linguistic data for modeling players' behaviour in strategic board games. Senior Undergraduate Engineering Diploma Thesis (MEng), School of Electrical and Computer Engineering, Technical University of Crete (2020). https://dias.library.tuc.gr/view/86478
4. Browne, C.B., et al.: A survey of Monte Carlo tree search methods. IEEE Trans. Comput. Intell. AI Games **4**(1), 1–43 (2012). https://doi.org/10.1109/TCIAIG.2012.2186810
5. Catan GmbH: Catan - the official rules (2020). https://www.catan.com/understand-catan/game-rules
6. Chaslot, G., Winands, M., van den Herik, H.J.: Parallel Monte-Carlo tree search. In: van den Herik, H.J., Xu, X., Ma, Z., Winands, M. (eds.) CG 2008. LNCS, vol. 5131, pp. 60–71. Springer, Heidelberg (2008). https://doi.org/10.1007/978-3-540-87608-3_6
7. Cuayáhuitl, H., Keizer, S., Lemon, O.: Strategic dialogue management via deep reinforcement learning (2015). https://arxiv.org/abs/1511.08099
8. Dearden, R., Friedman, N., Andre, D.: Model-based Bayesian exploration. arXiv preprint arXiv:1301.6690 (2013)
9. Dobre, M., Lascarides, A.: POMCP with human preferences in settlers of catan. In: Proceedings of the AAAI Conference on Artificial Intelligence and Interactive Digital Entertainment, vol. 14, pp. 17–23 (2018). https://doi.org/10.1609/aiide.v14i1.13014
10. Dobre, M.S., Lascarides, A.: Exploiting action categories in learning complex games. In: 2017 Intelligent Systems Conference (IntelliSys), pp. 729–737 (2017). https://doi.org/10.1109/IntelliSys.2017.8324210
11. Dobre, M.S., Lascarides, A.: Online learning and mining human play in complex games. In: 2015 IEEE Conference on Computational Intelligence and Games (CIG), pp. 60–67. IEEE (2015). https://doi.org/10.1109/CIG.2015.7317942
12. Duarte, F.F., Lau, N., Pereira, A., Reis, L.P.: A survey of planning and learning in games. Appl. Sci. **10**(13), 4529 (2020). https://doi.org/10.3390/app10134529
13. Gendre, Q., Kaneko, T.: Playing catan with cross-dimensional neural network. In: Yang, H., Pasupa, K., Leung, A.C.-S., Kwok, J.T., Chan, J.H., King, I. (eds.) ICONIP 2020. LNCS, vol. 12533, pp. 580–592. Springer, Cham (2020). https://doi.org/10.1007/978-3-030-63833-7_49
14. Guhe, M., Lascarides, A.: The effectiveness of persuasion in the settlers of catan. In: 2014 IEEE Conference on Computational Intelligence and Games, pp. 1–8 (2014). https://doi.org/10.1109/CIG.2014.6932861
15. Guhe, M., Lascarides, A.: Game strategies for the settlers of catan. In: 2014 IEEE Conference on Computational Intelligence and Games, pp. 1–8 (2014), https://doi.org/10.1109/CIG.2014.6932884
16. Karamalegkos, E.: Monte Carlo Tree Search in the "Settlers of Catan" Strategy Game. Senior Undergraduate Engineering Diploma Thesis (MEng), School of Electrical and Computer Engineering, Technical University of Crete (2016). https://dias.library.tuc.gr/view/66891

17. Kocsis, L., Szepesvári, C.: Bandit based Monte-Carlo planning. In: Fürnkranz, J., Scheffer, T., Spiliopoulou, M. (eds.) ECML 2006. LNCS (LNAI), vol. 4212, pp. 282–293. Springer, Heidelberg (2006). https://doi.org/10.1007/11871842_29
18. Korf, R.E.: Multi-player alpha-beta pruning. Artif. Intell. **48**(1), 99–111 (1991). https://doi.org/10.1016/0004-3702(91)90082-U
19. Luckhart, C., Irani, K.B.: An algorithmic solution of n-person games. In: AAAI Conference on Artificial Intelligence (1986). https://api.semanticscholar.org/CorpusID:23411351
20. Monin, J., et al.: Jsettlers2: a Java implementation of settlers of catan (2007–2024). https://github.com/jdmonin/JSettlers2
21. Panousis, K.P.: Real-time Planning and Learning in the "Settlers of Catan" Strategy Game. Senior Undergraduate Engineering Diploma Thesis (MEng), School of Electrical and Computer Engineering, Technical University of Crete (2014). https://dias.library.tuc.gr/view/18113
22. Perick, P., St-Pierre, D.L., Maes, F., Ernst, D.: Comparison of different selection strategies in Monte-Carlo tree search for the game of tron. In: 2012 IEEE Conference on Computational Intelligence and Games (CIG), pp. 242–249 (2012). https://doi.org/10.1109/CIG.2012.6374162
23. Russell, S., Norvig, P.: Artificial Intelligence: A Modern Approach, 4th edn. (2020)
24. Russell, S.J., Zimdars, A.: Q-decomposition for reinforcement learning agents. In: Proceedings of the 20th International Conference on Machine Learning (ICML 2003), pp. 656–663 (2003). https://dl.acm.org/doi/abs/10.5555/3041838.3041921
25. Silver, D., et al.: Mastering the game of go with deep neural networks and tree search. Nature **529**(7587), 484–489 (2016). https://doi.org/10.1038/nature16961
26. Silver, D., et al.: A general reinforcement learning algorithm that masters chess, shogi, and go through self-play. Science **362**(6419), 1140–1144 (2018). https://doi.org/10.1126/science.aar6404
27. Silver, D., Veness, J.: Monte-Carlo planning in large pomdps. In: Lafferty, J., Williams, C., Shawe-Taylor, J., Zemel, R., Culotta, A. (eds.) Advances in Neural Information Processing Systems, vol. 23. Curran Associates, Inc. (2010). https://proceedings.neurips.cc/paper_files/paper/2010/file/edfbe1afcf9246bb0d40eb4d8027d90f-Paper.pdf
28. Tesauro, G., Rajan, V., Segal, R.: Bayesian inference in Monte-Carlo tree search. arXiv preprint arXiv:1203.3519 (2012)
29. Thomas, R.S.: Real-time decision making for adversarial environments using a plan-based heuristic. Ph.D. thesis, Northwestern University (2003)
30. Xenou, K., Chalkiadakis, G., Afantenos, S.: Deep reinforcement learning in strategic board game environments. In: Slavkovik, M. (ed.) EUMAS 2018. LNCS (LNAI), vol. 11450, pp. 233–248. Springer, Cham (2019). https://doi.org/10.1007/978-3-030-14174-5_16
31. Yilmaz, G., Yilmaz, D., et al.: Colonist.io alternative to settlers of catan (2019). https://colonist.io/about

Quantifying Uncertainty in Complex Reinforcement Learning Scenarios

Saeid Rezaei([✉]) and Kenneth N. Brown

School of Computer Science and IT, University College Cork, Cork T12XF62, Ireland
{saeid.rezaei,k.brown}@cs.ucc.ie

Abstract. Addressing new challenges in reinforcement learning (RL) research requires identifying the most suitable algorithms, which involves their development and evaluation using various benchmarks. This paper presents a comparative analysis of two methodologies for classifying the complexity of RL problems, including real-world benchmarks and the existence of optimal policies. The exploration extends to the existence of optimal policies highlighting the significance of assumptions and methodologies in different studies. Additionally, two theories are presented that demonstrate conditions under which an optimal policy does not exist. A complexity classification based on these theories is introduced.

Keywords: Uncertainty quantification · Optimal policy · real-world benchmarks

1 Introduction

In reinforcement learning research, tackling emerging challenges requires careful consideration of algorithm selection, development, and evaluation. Numerous algorithms have been developed and tested against diverse benchmarks to assess their effectiveness in addressing complex real-world issues. Dulac-Arnold et al. [1] identify several key challenges in reinforcement learning, including learning from limited samples [11], managing large delays in observations [12], handling high-dimensional state and action spaces [13], and accounting for system constraints [14]. Additional difficulties arise when dealing with partially observable environments [15], multi-objective or poorly specified reward functions [8,16], and the need for rapid decision-making [17]. Furthermore, reinforcement learning models must sometimes be trained offline using fixed logs and should ideally provide explainable policies to system operators [18].

As part of the effort to address these challenge, Dulac-Arnold et al. [1] propose a set of configurable benchmark problems, and a classification of different configurations as Easy, Medium or Hard. This classification provides a structured approach to evaluating the capability of algorithms in scenarios ranging from straightforward to highly complex, enabling researchers to better understand the strengths and limitations of different methods within the field. Given these considerations, when reinforcement learning is applied to a new domain,

R. Collier et al. (Eds.): EUMAS 2024, LNAI 15685, pp. 77–90, 2025.
https://doi.org/10.1007/978-3-031-93930-3_5

researchers can refer to existing studies to quickly identify the most suitable algorithms. They can evaluate various proposed algorithms and, if addressing a specific real-world challenge, focus on issues like large action or observation spaces (Table 1).

Table 1. Structured Approach to Developing Reinforcement Learning Applications

Step	Description
Challenge Identification	*Identify the challenges that need to be overcome to tackle the problem successfully*
Benchmark Proposal	*Identify specific instances for each difficulty that will allow the effectiveness of different approaches to be measured*
Method Development	*Develop tailored methods for the problem based on the challenges and difficulty level*

An "RL pipeline" is a structured sequence of stages designed to automate the various components involved in solving reinforcement learning tasks [4,6,19,20]. When evaluating a newly proposed reinforcement learning pipeline, researchers can use benchmarks with high complexity. If a particular challenge is not addressed in prior studies or if a new metric is required to measure complexity, they should consider the specific domain's distinct situations, especially at the "hard" level of complexity.

One issue that impacts the effectiveness of reinforcement learning algorithms, but not included in the above classification scheme, is the existence of a well-defined optimal policy. The theoretical justification for many algorithms relies on an assumption that an optimal policy exists and is reachable. We believe that many of the problem instances that fall into the Hard class are hard because the optimal policy either does not exist, or is impossible to reach in the search space. If there is no optimal policy, then the selected algorithm may need to be adapted to account for this, to allow it to converge to an acceptable policy instead. This article focuses on the existence or otherwise of optimal policies, and aims to prove a complexity classification based on that idea. We provide the context and necessary preliminaries in Sect. 2; in Sect. 3 we discuss some existing results relevant to the existence of optimal policies, and we then propose two new results stating conditions under which optimal policies do not exist. Finally, we discuss the relationship between this new classification and the earlier Duluc-Arnold et al. proposal [1].

2 Preliminaries

The behaviour of the environment in response to agent actions can be modeled as a Markov Decision Process, where the next state is probabilistically determined from the previous state and the applied action. The aim of the agent is to

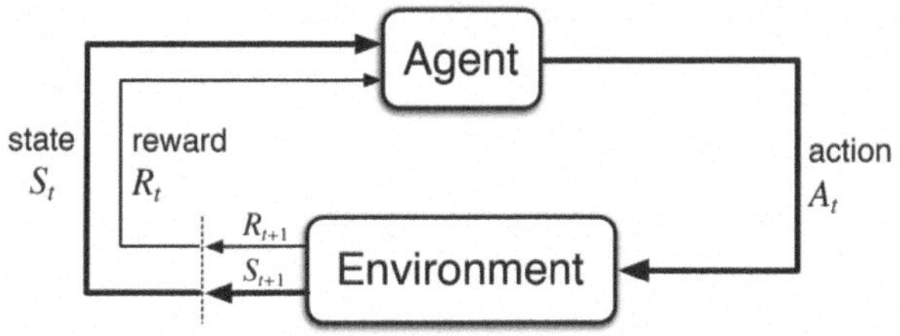

Fig. 1. The agent-environment interaction in a Markov decision process [3].

learn an optimal policy specifying the action to take in each possible state. Figure 1 illustrates the interaction between the agent and its environment. In most settings, the agent is not able to directly observe the current state of the MDP, but instead observes some features that are generated from the true state and the previous action, given by some probability distribution. The underlying model is then a Partially Observable MDP [3]. Table 2 provides brief descriptions of the MDP and other notations [2,23] used in the theorems presented in the subsequent sections.

In discussing uncertainty within machine learning models, aleatoric and epistemic uncertainties are two primary types. Aleatoric uncertainty (also known as statistical or irreducible uncertainty) arises from inherent randomness or variability in the system, making it resistant to reduction even with more data. In contrast, epistemic uncertainty is due to a lack of knowledge about the model or system parameters, making it a reducible uncertainty that can be minimized through additional data or improved modeling efforts [21].

3 Existence of Optimal Policy

In this section, we present four theorems from the literature that are used to establish that under certain conditions specific RL algorithms will eventually converge to an optimal policy. As part of that, these results first establish that, for the given assumptions, an optimal policy does in fact exist. We then present two new theorems, which show that for some other scenarios, there is no well-defined optimal policy.

Optimal Value Function: A policy π^* is total reward optimal whenever the value function has the highest value for each state in MDP state set or POMDP belief set [2]:

$$v^{\pi^*}(s) \geq v^{\pi}(s) \qquad for\ each\ s\ \in S\ and\ all \quad \pi \in \Pi$$

The value function for MDP:

$$V^{\pi}(i) = \sum_{j \in S} T(i, \pi(i), j)\,(r(i, \pi(i), j) + \gamma V^{\delta}(j))$$

Table 2. Notations

Notation	Definition
A	Set of actions
S	Set of states
A_s	Set of actions in state s
T	A mapping from $S \times A \times S$ into distributions over the states in S
R	A reward function that maps from S to real-valued rewards
Π	Set of policies $\{\pi_1, \pi_2, ..., \pi_N\}$
S_t	State at time t
A_t	Action at time t
R_t	Reward at time t
γ	Discount rate (where $0 \leq \gamma \leq 1$)
I	Initial state of MDP
π	A policy (A mapping from S to actions in A)
δ	A notation used to represent a policy
V, V^π	Value function with policy π which maps from elements of S to real values
π_t	policy at time t in a non-stationary environment
V^{π_t}	Value function under the time-dependent policy π_t
$v_N^\pi(s)$	Value of value function with policy π for state s in decision period N
$r_t(s, a)$	Reward of choosing action $a \in A_s$ in state s at decision period t
$p(\hat{s}, r \mid s, a)$	Probability of next state $\hat{s}$ and reward r, given current state s and current action a
$r_t(s, a)$	Reward received in period t when action $a \in A_s$ is selected in $s \in S$
$r_t(s, a, j)$	Reward received in period t when action $a \in A_s$ is selected in $s \in S$ and next state is j
$P_\delta(i, j)$	Transition probability under policy δ, given by $P_\delta(i, j) = T(i, \delta(i), j)$ for $i, j \in S$
$Q(s, a)$	State-action value function, representing the expected return starting from state s, taking action a, and following policy π thereafter
$Q^*(s, a)$	Optimal state-action value function, representing the maximum expected return achievable from state s and action a under the optimal policy π^*
ϵ-optimal policy	A policy π that achieves a value within ϵ of the optimal value V^* for all states, i.e., $V^\pi(s) \geq V^*(s) - \epsilon$ for all $s \in S$
$M(o, i, a)$	observation probability of observation o on state i after taking action a
Π_0, π_0	belief-state at time t
h	History of interactions up to the current time, including the sequence of past actions and observations.
$\acute{o}, \acute{r}$	Observation and Reward values at the next time step in a history-based decision process.

And the value function for POMDP is:

$$V^{\delta}(i) = \sum_{j \in S} T(i, \delta(i), j) \left[r(i, \delta(i), j)\right] + \sum_{o \in O} M(o, j, a) V^{\delta}(B_{a,o})$$

3.1 Convergence of the Value Function

Given a MDP (S, A, T, R) and a stationary policy δ, the sequence V_t generated by

$$V_{t+1}(i) = V_t(i) + a_t(i) z_t(i) d_t$$

$$i \in S$$

converges with probability 1 to the value function V^{δ} along an infinite trajectory under policy δ, as long as every state is visited an infinite number of times, and the step-sizes α_t satisfy

$$\sum_{t=0}^{\infty} \alpha_t = \infty \quad \text{and} \quad \sum_{t=0}^{\infty} {\alpha_t}^2 < \infty$$

The proof is provided in [23], based on the assumption that all states are visited infinitely often, and the Markov chain (S, P_{δ}) is ergodic. Here, (S, P_{δ}) represents the Markov chain with state-space S and transition probabilities

$$P_{\delta}(i, j) = T\left(i, \delta(i), j\right),$$

for $i, j \in S$.

3.2 Convergence of the Q Function

Given a MDP (S, A, T, R) , the sequence Q_k, generated by

$$Q_{t+1}(i, a) = Q_t(i, a) + a_t(i, a)(R_t + \gamma \max_{b \epsilon A} Q_t(j, b) - Q_t(i, a))$$

The authors in [23] demonstrated that the sequence Q_k converges to the optimal Q^* along an infinite trajectory under policy δ, provided that every state-action pair is explored an infinite number of times and the step-sizes α_t satisfy

$$\sum_{t=0}^{\infty} \alpha_t = \infty \qquad \sum_{t=0}^{\infty} {\alpha_t}^2 < \infty$$

$$Q^*(i, a) = \sum_{j \in S} T(i, a, j)(r(i, a, j) + \gamma V^*(j))$$

3.3 Convergence of SQ Learning

The SQ-Learning (Sampled Q-Learning) algorithm is a method designed for Partially Observable Markov Decision Processes (POMDPs). Starting with an initial belief state $\Pi_0 = \pi_0$, the algorithm selects N samples from the belief state space $\mathcal{S}^p$ and initializes the Q-values $Q_0(\tilde{\pi}_i, a)$ for each sample $\tilde{\pi}_i$. At each time step, it calculates an estimated Q-value $\hat{Q}^-$ by averaging the Q-values across samples, using a weighting function $\mathcal{K}(\|\pi_t - \tilde{\pi}_i\|)$. Here, $\mathcal{K}(\|\pi_t - \tilde{\pi}_i\|)$ represents a weighting kernel that depends on the distance $\|\pi_t - \tilde{\pi}_i\|$ between the current belief state π_t and each sample $\tilde{\pi}_i$; it assigns higher weights to samples closer to π_t. A kernel is a function that defines a measure of similarity or influence, often used in algorithms to give more importance to points closer to a specified target within a given space.

After selecting an action a_t according to a specified policy δ, the agent observes the reward R_t and updates the belief state to $\Pi_{t+1} = \pi_{t+1}$. It then computes the maximum future Q-value $\hat{Q}^+$ over all actions. The Q-value update uses a temporal difference term $d_t = R_t + \gamma\hat{Q}^+ - \hat{Q}^-$, where γ is the discount factor, and adjusts each sample's Q-value based on whether the action matches the selected a_t.

Assumptions: Consider a POMDP (S, A, O, T, M, R) where the underlying Markov chain is ergodic for any stationary policy. Suppose the policy δ, used to generate the learning trajectory, assigns a non-zero probability to all actions. Furthermore, let the step-sizes α_t satisfy the conditions

$$\sum_{t=0}^{\infty} \alpha_t = \infty \quad \text{and} \quad \sum_{t=0}^{\infty} \alpha_t^2 < \infty.$$

Theorem Convergence of SQ-Learning: Under the above conditions, the SQ-Learning algorithm converges to an optimal approximation of Q^* over the sample set $\{\tilde{\pi}_1, \ldots, \tilde{\pi}_N\}$, as shown in [23].

3.4 Convergence of Q-Value Decision Processes

A history-based decision process P is a stochastic mapping from a history-action pair to observation-reward pairs. Formally, $P : H^* \times A \to O \times R$ where denotes a stochastic mapping. We use Q to denote an action-value function of a HDP, and

Q^* denotes the optimal Q-value function.

$$Q^*(h, a) := \sum_{\acute{o}\acute{r}} P(\acute{o}\acute{r} \mid ha) \left(\acute{r} + \gamma \max_{\breve{a}} Q^*(ha\acute{o}\acute{r}, \breve{a})\right)$$

State-Uniformity Condition: For any action a, if any two histories h and $\acute{h}$ map to the same state s, then the optimal Q-values of the underlying HDP of

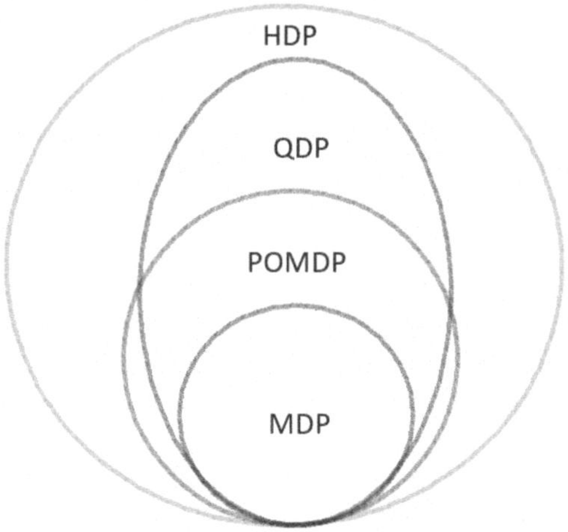

Fig. 2. QDP in the perspective of other decision problem classes [22].

these histories are the same, i.e., state-uniform; $Q^*(h,a) = Q^*\left(\acute{h},a\right)$. It is easy to see that in this case $q^*(s,a) = Q^*(h,a)$. The state-uniformity condition is weaker than the MDP condition (Fig. 2).

Q-Value Uniform Decision Process (QDP): A model is a QDP if it satisfies the state-uniformity condition.

Theorem: Convergence in QDP: Assuming the state process is ergodic and QDP, the agent learns the optimal action-value function of a QDP state-process [22].

3.5 Random Reward Functions

The preceding sections have established fundamental theoretical results demonstrating conditions under which specific reinforcement learning (RL) algorithms converge to an optimal policy. In this section, we shift focus to our contribution, wherein we examine scenarios under which an optimal policy does not exist. Given the following assumptions, an optimal policy does not exist.

1- The MDP state or POMDP belief state is fully connected
2- The reward function changes over time so that the sequence of expected values is non-monotonic and does not converge. Since the sequence is infinite and does not converge, for any time point n there will exist two other time points m and o after n such that

$$E\left(R(S)_n\right) > E\left(R(S)_m\right)$$

and

$$E\left(R(S)_n\right) > E\left(R(S)_o\right)$$

The rewards are generated by a function, which changes from one time period to the next.
After n timesteps, the interaction between the agent and the environment results in a sequence of states, actions, and rewards, representing the trajectory of the agent:

$$S_0, A_0, R_1, S_1, A_1, R_2, \ldots, S_n, A_n, R_n, S_{n+1}$$

Here, the reward is a random variable. Let $R(S)_t \equiv r_t(S_t, S_{t+1})$ denote the random reward received when transitioning from S_t to state S_{t+1} at time t. Under this assumption, the reward function has a different distribution at each time step, while the state transition dynamics in the environment remain the same.

3- The reward function changes over time, resulting in a sequence of expected rewards that is non-monotonic and does not converge. Since this sequence is infinite and non-convergent, for any time point n, there will exist two other time points m and o (with $m, o > n$) such that:

$$E\left(R(S)_n^{\pi_t}\right) > E\left(R(S)_m^{\pi_t}\right)$$

and

$$E\left(R(S)_n^{\pi_t}\right) > E\left(R(S)_o^{\pi_t}\right)$$

In this notation, $E\left(R(S)_t^{\pi_t}\right)$ represents the expected reward at state S under a single, time-dependent policy π_t, reflecting that the reward expectations shift as t varies. This notation emphasizes that, even under a consistent policy framework, the expected reward changes over time due to the non-stationary nature of the environment.

Proof. The main idea regarding the proof is as following: Based on the assumptions the expected value of the reward value, represented as a random variable, changes across different timesteps. Referring back to the definition of an optimal policy , the value function for each state should be maximized for it to align with the optimal value function.Based on the assumption about the fully connected state set, a contradiction arises between the existence of an optimal policy and two assumptions about the RL environment described above.

V^δ is the value function for policy δ which maps states to real values:

$$V^\delta : S \to \mathbb{R}$$

The value of state i under policy δ is given by:

$$V^\delta(i) = \mathbb{E}_\delta\left[\sum_{k=0}^{\infty} \gamma^k R_{t+k} \mid \phi_t = i\right]$$

where R_{t+k} is the reward received at time $t + k$, given by

$$R_{t+k} = r(\phi_{t+k}, \delta(\phi_{t+k}), \phi_{t+k+1}),$$

and $\mathbb{E}_\delta$ denotes the expected value operator associated with the transition probabilities defined by policy δ.

Expanding $V^\delta(i)$, we get:

$$V^\delta(i) = \mathbb{E}\left[R(i,\delta(i))\right] + \gamma \sum_{j\in S} T(i,\delta(i),j)V^\delta(j)$$

That is, we seek a policy π^* for all policies π

$$v_N^{\pi^*}(s) \geq v_N^\pi(s),\ \ s\ \in S$$

Let us assume that δ_t represents the optimal policy at time t. Let $E\left(R(S)_n^{\delta_t}\right)$ denote the expected value of the reward generated under this policy at time t, and $E\left(R(S)_n^{\delta_m}\right)$ denote the expected value of the reward generated by this policy at time m. Based on the definition of an optimal policy, The value function of this policy δ should have the highest value at all time steps in comparison to all other policies that exist and the following equation should be satisfied :

$$V^\delta(s) \geq V^\pi(i),\ \ s\ \in S$$

$$E\left[R\left(i,\ \delta(i)\right)\right] + T\left(i,\ \delta(i),j\right)\gamma V^\delta(j) \geq$$

$$E\left[R\left(i,\ \pi(i)\right)\right] + T\left(i,\ \pi(i),j\right)\gamma V^\pi(j)$$

Based on assumption 3, there exists a time m such that the expected value of the reward at time m is less than that at time t. Furthermore, according to assumption 2, there exists a policy whose expected value of rewards, generated by its sequence, is higher than that of policy δ at time step m. Considering both assumptions, there exists a policy π that satisfies this inequality for state i:

$E\left[R\left(i,\ \delta_m(i)\right)\right] < E\left[R\left(i,\ \pi(i)\right)\right]$ and $T\left(i,\ \delta_m(i),j\right) = T\left(i,\ \pi(i),j\right)$

Then:

$$T\left(i,\ \delta_m(i),j\right)\gamma V^{\delta_m}(j) < T\left(i,\ \pi(i),j\right)\gamma V^\pi(j)$$

Based on the definition of an optimal policy, the value function under this policy should have the highest possible value at all times for every state. Therefore, if the value function for a given state is lower than that of another policy at any time step, it implies that a consistent optimal policy does not exist. Then $V^{\delta_m}(j) < V^\pi(j)$ which is a contradiction with Definition of optimal policy for state j.

3.6 Random Reward Functions and ε Optimal Policies

Given the assumptions in Theorem 5, ε optimal policy does not exist.

Proof. The main idea regarding the proof is as following: Based on the assumptions the expected value of the reward value, and optimal policy and using Markov' s inequality, a contradiction arises between the existence of an ε optimal policy and the foundational assumption regarding the class features.

Markov' s Inequality:
If X is a non-negative random variable, then for all $\alpha > 0$, which is called Markov inequality:

$$P(X \geq a) \leq \frac{E[X]}{a}$$

$$1 - P(X \geq a) \geq 1 - \frac{E[X]}{a}$$

$$P(X < a) \geq 1 - \frac{E[X]}{a}$$

Based on the definition of an ε-optimal policy, if we consider δ as the optimal policy, then there exists a policy that satisfies this condition at all time steps.

$$V^{\delta}(j) - V^{\pi}(j) < \varepsilon$$

Let us define the random variable.

$$X\& = \left|V^{\delta}(j) - V^{\pi}(j)\right| \& = \left|E\left[R\left(i, \delta(i)\right)\right] + T\left(i, \delta(i), j\right)\gamma V^{\delta}(j)\& \quad - E\left[R\left(i, \pi(i)\right)\right] - T\left(i, \pi(i), j\right)\gamma V^{\pi}(j)\right|$$

As in theory 5, by using assumptions 2 and 3, there exists a time m and a policy π that satisfy this inequality for state i:

$$E\left[R\left(i,\ \delta_m(i)\right)\right] > E\left[R\left(i,\ \pi(i)\right)\right] + a$$

and

$$T\left(i,\ \delta_m(i), j\right) = T\left(i,\ \pi(i), j\right)$$

then:

$$M = E\left[R\left(i,\ \delta_m(i)\right)\right] + T\left(i,\ \delta_m(i), j\right)\gamma V^{\delta_m}(j)$$

$$N = E\left[R\left(i,\ \pi(i)\right)\right] - T\left(i,\ \pi(i), j\right)\gamma V^{\pi}(j)$$

$$P(|M - N| < a)$$
$$\leq 1 - \frac{E\left[E\left[R\left(i,\ \delta_m(i)\right)\right] - E\left[R\left(i,\ \pi(i)\right)\right]\right]}{a}$$

Then:

$$p\left(\left|V^{\delta_m}(j) - V^{\pi}(j)\right|\right) < 0$$

which is a contradiction with the assumption and probability axioms.

Then: $p\left(\left|V^{\delta}(j) - V^{\pi}(j)\right|\right) < 0$ which is a contradiction with the assumption and probability axioms (Table 3).

Table 3. Summary of Theoretical Conditions

Feature	invariant MDP	Fully connected	Non stationary	r_t's vary across	p_t's vary across	Additional Conditions
Theorem 1	×	×	×	×	×	Operator conditions
Theorem 2	×	×	×	×	×	Operator conditions
Theorem 3	×	×	×	×	×	Operator conditions
Theorem 4	×	×	×	×	×	QDP condition
Theorems 5,6	+	+	+	+	+	Reward condition

Considering the definitions of aleatoric and epistemic uncertainty, along with the assumptions in the theorems, the reward value, as a random variable, is dominated by aleatoric uncertainty due to its variation over different periods. This prevents the agent from establishing any correlation between its belief state and the reward random variable over an infinite timeline. However, in Theorems 1, 2, 3, and 4, the reward value as a random function is subject only to epistemic uncertainty, stemming from the agent's limited knowledge of the environment.

Based on this understanding, problems can be categorized into three distinct classes:

- **Class 1:** Problems where the uncertainty in rewards is primarily epistemic, with theorems proving the existence of an optimal policy.
- **Class 2:** Problems involving both aleatoric and epistemic uncertainty. However, the existence of an optimal policy is not yet proven, representing a more complex class of problems.
- **Class 3:** Problems characterized by aleatoric uncertainty, where it has been proven that an optimal policy does not exist.

It is important to note that while Class 3 features aleatoric uncertainty, not all problems involving aleatoric uncertainty fall into this class. Similarly, Class 2 may involve both aleatoric and epistemic uncertainties, while Class 1 is predominantly influenced by epistemic uncertainty.

4 Approach to Complexity Classification

Various methodologies can be employed to categorize the complexity levels within different domains. This section encapsulates these classification strategies, comparing their distinctive features and applications.

4.1 Real-World Benchmarks Approach

Some frameworks attempt to address these challenges by utilizing benchmark approaches. For example, the automated deep reinforcement learning method in [5] aims to perform efficient and robust training of any off-policy RL algorithm while simultaneously tuning hyperparameters. However, to evaluate these frameworks effectively and compare the performance of different methods, benchmarks that resemble real-world settings are essential. One example is the three levels of complexity proposed based on the DeepMind control suite in [1]. In this approach, reinforcement learning algorithms are tested in settings categorized as easy, medium, or hard. While it is generally straightforward to show convergence in easy and medium levels of complexity, achieving convergence in hard-level settings is challenging and requires demonstration. Authors in [7] introduced the pyRDDLGym framework to present benchmarks for twelve different domains, each with varying complexity levels and parameters. Other examples include the domains of energy management and quantitative finance, which are discussed in [9] and [10], respectively. In some configurations, reinforcement learning algorithms may exhibit poor performance, highlighting the challenges presented by complex benchmark environments.

4.2 Comparative Analysis of Benchmark and Optimality-Based Approaches

This paper proposes an alternative complexity classification based on theoretical optimality criteria. This approach leverages theorems regarding the existence of optimal policies to define complexity levels. In particular:

- Class 1 (Easy): Based on Theories 1 to 4, it is proven that for certain problems with epistemic uncertainty, an optimal policy exists. Therefore, these problems can be categorized as "easy", as they meet the conditions necessary for an optimal solution.
- Class 3 (Hard): Problems that align with Theories 5 and 6, which involve specific cases of aleatoric uncertainty, are more complex, and it is shown that an optimal policy does not exist for these cases. Thus, these problems are classified as "hard".

In summary, while benchmark approaches categorize problems into easy, medium, and hard based on real-world settings, the optimality-based approach uses theoretical criteria to define complexity. In this framework, problems with proven optimal policies fall into the easy category, whereas those where an optimal policy is unattainable due to the nature of uncertainty are classified as hard.

5 Conclusion

We introduced a complexity classification based on the existence of optimal policies, demonstrating conditions under which optimal policies do or do not exist. This classification was further supported by two new theories proving the non-existence of optimal policies under specific conditions. Our findings emphasize the necessity for a structured approach to RL research, integrating theoretical insights with practical benchmarks to address real-world challenges effectively. By categorizing RL problems according to their complexity and providing tailored solutions, this work aims to facilitate more robust and efficient reinforcement learning applications. Future research should continue to refine these classifications and explore new benchmarks, ensuring that RL systems can be reliably applied to increasingly complex and dynamic environments. Ultimately, the goal is to advance the field of RL by developing algorithms that are both theoretically sound and practically effective in diverse application domains.

References

1. Dulac-Arnold, G., et al.: An empirical investigation of the challenges of real-world reinforcement learning. arXiv preprint arXiv:2003.11881 (2021)
2. Puterman, M.L.: Markov Decision Processes: Discrete Stochastic Dynamic Programming. Wiley, Hoboken (2014)
3. Sutton, R.S., Barto, A.G.: Reinforcement Learning: An Introduction. MIT Press, Cambridge (2018)
4. Afshar, R.R., Zhang, Y., Vanschoren, J., Kaymak, U.: Automated reinforcement learning: an overview. arXiv preprint arXiv:2201.05000 (2022)
5. Franke, J.K.H., Köhler, G., Biedenkapp, A., Hutter, F.: Sample-efficient automated deep reinforcement learning. arXiv preprint arXiv:2009.01555 (2021)
6. Liu, K., Fu, Y., Wu, L., Li, X., Aggarwal, C., Xiong, H.: Automated feature selection: a reinforcement learning perspective. IEEE Trans. Knowl. Data Eng. (2021)
7. Taitler, A., et al.: pyRDDLGym: from RDDL to gym environments. arXiv preprint arXiv:2211.05939 (2023)
8. Vamplew, P., et al.: Scalar reward is not enough: a response to Silver, Singh, Precup, and Sutton (2021). Auton. Agents Multi-Agent Syst. **36**(2), 41 (2022)
9. Vázquez-Canteli, J.R., Dey, S., Henze, G., Nagy, Z.: CityLearn: standardizing research in multi-agent reinforcement learning for demand response and urban energy management. arXiv preprint arXiv:2012.10504 (2020)
10. Liu, X.-Y., et al.: FinRL: a deep reinforcement learning library for automated stock trading in quantitative finance. arXiv preprint arXiv:2011.09607 (2022)
11. Osband, I., Blundell, C., Pritzel, A., Van Roy, B.: Deep exploration via bootstrapped DQN. In: Advances in Neural Information Processing Systems (2016)
12. Hester, T., Stone, P.: Learning from Delays. Robotics (2013)
13. Covington, P., Adams, J., Sargin, E.: Deep neural networks for YouTube recommendations. In: Proceedings of the 10th ACM Conference on Recommender Systems, pp. 191–198 (2016)
14. Dalal, G., et al.: Safe exploration in continuous action spaces. arXiv preprint arXiv:1801.08757 (2018)

15. Mnih, V., et al.: Human-level control through deep reinforcement learning. Nature (2015)
16. Abdolmaleki, A., Price, B., Lau, N., Reis, L.P., Neumann, G.: A generalized algorithm for multi-objective reinforcement learning and policy adaptation. In: NeurIPS (2020)
17. Silver, D., et al.: Mastering the game of Go with deep neural networks and tree search. Nature (2016)
18. Agrawal, P., Nair, A., Abbeel, P., Malik, J., Levine, S.: Benchmarking reinforcement learning algorithms on real-world robots. In: Conference on Robot Learning, pp. 361–372 (2019)
19. Parker-Holder, J., et al.: Automated reinforcement learning (AutoRL): a survey and open problems. J. Artif. Intell. Res. **74**, 517–568 (2022)
20. Mussi, M., Lombarda, D., Metelli, A.M., Trovò, F., Restelli, M.: ARLO: a framework for automated reinforcement learning. Expert Syst. Appl. **224**, 119883 (2023)
21. Hüllermeier, E., Waegeman, W.: Aleatoric and epistemic uncertainty in machine learning: an introduction to concepts and methods. Mach. Learn. **110**(3), 457–506 (2021)
22. Majeed, S.J., Hutter, M.: On Q-learning convergence for non-Markov decision processes. In: Proceedings of the 27th International Joint Conference on Artificial Intelligence (IJCAI), pp. 2546–2552 (2018)
23. Melo, F.A., Ribeiro, M.I., Norte, I.T.: Convergence results for reinforcement learning with partial observability. Institute for Systems and Robotics, Technical report RT-602-05 (2005)

Knowledge Representation, Reasoning and Planning

A Logic of Actual Cause for Nondeterministic Domains

Maryam Rostamigiv[1], Shakil M. Khan[1](✉), Yves Lespérance[2], and Mriana Yadkoo[3]

[1] University of Regina, Regina, SK, Canada
{maryam.rostamigiv,shakil.khan}@uregina.ca
[2] York University, Toronto, ON, Canada
lesperan@eecs.yorku.ca
[3] University of Windsor, Windsor, ON, Canada
yadkoom@uwindsor.ca

Abstract. Crucial to the process of reasoning is the formalization of the actual causes of observed effects. While there has been a lot of work on root cause analysis, most studies have focused mainly on deterministic domains. In this paper, we build on previous work on actual causation in the situation calculus to deal with causation in nondeterministic domains. We use the nondeterministic situation calculus as our base framework for this. We introduce the notions of "CertainlyCauses" and "PossiblyCauses" that enable the representation of actual cause when the agent does not have any control on and does not know the choices that are made by the environment. We then investigate how regression in the situation calculus can be used to reason about these notions.

Keywords: Actual Cause · Nondeterministic Situation Calculus · Logic

1 Introduction

The term *causation* refers to a collection of closely-related important philosophical problems dealing with causes and their effects that has been studied since the time of Aristotle. Determining the "actual" causes of an observed effect, which are events chosen from a recorded history of actions that occurred prior to the observation of the effect (also known as the scenario) is one such problem (called "efficient" cause in Aristotelian lingo) that has been extensively researched. Motivated by David Hume's philosophical work and Herbert Simon's early contributions, Pearl [22,23], and later Halpern [9–11], Halpern and Pearl [12], and others [5,13,14,19] developed computational formalizations of this problem within Structural Equations Models (SEM). While their inspirational work significantly advanced this field, their approach based on SEM has been nevertheless criticized for its limited expressiveness [8,13,14].

R. Collier et al. (Eds.): EUMAS 2024, LNAI 15685, pp. 93–109, 2025.
https://doi.org/10.1007/978-3-031-93930-3_6

In response to these criticisms, in recent years researchers have become increasingly interested in studying causation within more expressive action-theoretic frameworks, in particular in that of the situation calculus [1,2,18]. Among other things, this allows one to formalize causation from the perspective of individual agents by defining a notion of epistemic causation [15] and by supporting causal reasoning about conative effects, which in turn has proven useful for explaining agent behaviour using causal analysis [17] and has the potential for defining important concepts such as responsibility and blame [25].

While there has been a lot of work on actual causation, the vast majority of the work in this area has focused on deterministic domains. However, a distinguishing feature of the real world is that change is often unpredictable. Very few studies address causation in non-deterministic systems, and those that do, are formalized in SEM-based causal models that are known to have limited expressiveness and suffer from a variety of problems. For instance, recently in [3], Beckers presented an extension of causal models to deal with non-determinism. However, despite improving on expressivity of causal models, it is not clear how one can formalize various aspects of action-theoretic/dynamic frameworks there, e.g. non-persistent change supported by fluents, possible dependency between events, temporal order of event occurrence, etc.

In this paper we build on previous work on actual causation in the situation calculus [2,15] to deal with causation in nondeterministic domains. We use the nondeterministic situation calculus [4] as our base framework. We introduce notions of "CertainlyCauses" and "PossiblyCauses" that enable the representation of actual cause when the agent does not have any control on and does not know the choices that are made by the environment. We then investigate how regression in the situation calculus can be used to reason about these notions.

The paper is structured as follows. In the next section, we provide an overview of the situation calculus and non-deterministic situation calculus (NDSC) and introduce our running example. In Sect. 3, we examine the definition of actual cause proposed earlier. In Sect. 4, we present our definitions for causes in the NDSC. In Sect. 5, we demonstrate how causes can be simplified into regressable formulae. Finally, we conclude with some discussion in Sect. 6.

2 Preliminaries

Situation Calculus (SC). The situation calculus is a well-known second-order language for representing and reasoning about dynamic worlds [21,24]. In the SC, all changes are due to named actions, which are terms in the language. Situations represent a possible world history resulting from performing some actions. The constant S_0 is used to denote the initial situation where no action has been performed yet. The distinguished binary function symbol $do(a, s)$ denotes the successor situation to s resulting from performing the action a. The expression $do([a_1, \cdots, a_n], s)$ represents the situation resulting from executing actions $a_1, \cdots, a_n$, starting with situation s. As usual, a relational/functional fluent representing a property whose value may change from situation to situation takes a situation term as its last argument. There is a special predicate $Poss(a, s)$ used to state that action a is executable in situation s. Also, the special binary predicate $s \sqsubset s'$ represents that s' can be reached from situation s by executing some sequence of actions. $s \sqsubseteq s'$ is an abbreviation of $s \sqsubset s' \vee s = s'$. $s < s'$ is an abbreviation of $s \sqsubset s' \wedge Executable(s')$, where $Executable(s)$ is defined as $\forall a', s'.\ do(a', s') \sqsubseteq s \supset Poss(a', s')$, i.e. every action performed in reaching situation s was possible in the situation in which it occurred. $s \leq s'$ is an abbreviation of $s < s' \vee s = s'$.

In the SC, a dynamic domain is specified using a basic action theory (BAT) $\mathcal{D}$ that includes the following sets of axioms: (i) (first-order or FO) initial state axioms $\mathcal{D}_{S_0}$, which indicate what was true initially; (ii) (FO) action precondition axioms $\mathcal{D}_{ap}$, characterizing $Poss(a, s)$; (iii) (FO) successor-state axioms $\mathcal{D}_{ss}$, indicating precisely when the fluents change; (iv) (FO) unique-names axioms $\mathcal{D}_{una}$ for actions, stating that different action terms represent distinct actions; and (v) (second-order or SO) domain-independent foundational axioms Σ, describing the structure of situations [20]. Although the SC is SO, Reiter [24] showed that for certain type of queries ϕ, $\mathcal{D} \models \phi$ iff $\mathcal{D}_{una} \cup \mathcal{D}_{S_0} \models \mathcal{R}[\phi]$, where $\mathcal{R}$ is a syntactic transformation operator called *regression* and $\mathcal{R}[\phi]$ is a SC formula that compiles dynamic aspects of the theory $\mathcal{D}$ into the query ϕ. Thus reasoning in the SC for a large class of interesting queries can be restricted to entailment checking w.r.t. a FO theory [24].

Nondeterministic Situation Calculus (NDSC). An important limitation of the standard SC and BATs is that atomic actions are deterministic. De Giacomo and Lespérance (DL21) [4] proposed a simple extension of the framework to handle nondeterministic actions while preserving the solution to the frame problem. For any primitive action by the agent in a nondeterministic domain, there can be a number of different outcomes. (DL21) takes the outcome as being determined by the agent's action and the environment's reaction to this action. This is modeled by having every action type/function $A(\overrightarrow{x}, e)$ take an additional environment reaction parameter e, ranging over a new sort *Reaction* of environment reactions. The agent cannot control the environment reaction, so it performs the reaction-suppressed version of the action $A(\overrightarrow{x})$ and the environment then selects a reaction e to produce the complete action $A(\overrightarrow{x}, e)$. We call the reaction-suppressed version of the action $A(\overrightarrow{x})$ an *agent action* and the full version of the action $A(\overrightarrow{x}, e)$ a *system action*.

We represent nondeterministic domains using action theories called Nondeterministic Basic Action Theories (NDBATs), which can be seen as a special kind of BAT, where (1) every agent action takes an environment reaction parameter; (2) for each agent action we have an agent action precondition formula: $Poss_{ag}(a(\overrightarrow{x}), s) \stackrel{\text{def}}{=} \phi_a^{agPoss}(\overrightarrow{x}, s)$; (3) for each agent action we have a reaction independence requirement, stating that the precondition for the agent action is independent of any environment reaction: $\forall e.\ Poss(a(\overrightarrow{x}, e), s) \supset Poss_{ag}(a(\overrightarrow{x}), s)$; (4) for each agent action we also have a reaction existence requirement, stating that if the precondition of the agent action holds then there exists a reaction to it which makes the complete system action executable, i.e., the environment cannot prevent the agent from performing an action when its agent action precondition holds: $Poss_{ag}(a(\overrightarrow{x}), s) \supset \exists e.\ Poss_{ag}(a(\overrightarrow{x}, e), s)$. The above requirements *must* be entailed by the action theory for it to be an NDBAT.

An NDBAT $\mathcal{D}$ is the union of the following disjoint sets: including (1) foundational axioms, (2) unique-names axioms for actions, (3) axioms describing the initial situation, (4) successor-state axioms indicating how fluents change after system actions, and (5) system action precondition axioms, indicating when system actions can occur; while these axioms generally follow the form: $Poss(a(\overrightarrow{x}, e), s) \equiv \phi_a^{Poss}(\overrightarrow{x}, e, s)$, in practice, these axioms often take the form: $Poss(a(\overrightarrow{x}, e), s) \equiv Poss_{ag}(a(\overrightarrow{x}), s) \wedge \psi^{Poss}(\overrightarrow{x}, e, s)$, where $Poss_{ag}(a(\overrightarrow{x}), s)$ denotes conditions necessary for the agent action $a(\overrightarrow{x})$ to occur and $\phi_a^{Poss}(\overrightarrow{x}, e, s)$ captures additional conditions influenced by the environment's response.

Projection and Executability. In the NDSC, executing an agent action in a situation may result in different situations and outcomes depending on the environment reaction. To capture this, (DL21) [4] introduced the defined predicate $Do_{ag}(\overrightarrow{a}, s, s')$, meaning that the system may reach situation s' when the agent executes the sequence of agent actions $\overrightarrow{a}$ starting in situation s depending on environment reactions:

$$Do_{ag}(\epsilon, s, s') \stackrel{\text{def}}{=} s = s' \text{ (where } \epsilon \text{ is the empty sequence of actions),}$$
$$Do_{ag}([A(\overrightarrow{x}), \sigma], s, s') \stackrel{\text{def}}{=} \exists e.\ Poss(A(\overrightarrow{x}, e), s) \wedge Do_{ag}(\sigma, do(A(\overrightarrow{x}, e), s), s').$$

A condition ϕ may hold after some executions of a sequence of agent actions $\overrightarrow{a}$ starting in situation s, denoted by $PossiblyAfter(\overrightarrow{a}, \phi, s)$, or it may hold after all executions of $\overrightarrow{a}$ in s, denoted by $CertainlyAfter(\overrightarrow{a}, \phi, s)$. Formally:

$$CertainlyAfter(\overrightarrow{a}, \phi, s) \stackrel{\text{def}}{=} \forall s'.\ Do_{ag}(\overrightarrow{a}, s, s') \supset \phi[s'],$$
$$PossiblyAfter(\overrightarrow{a}, \phi, s) \stackrel{\text{def}}{=} \exists s'.\ Do_{ag}(\overrightarrow{a}, s, s') \wedge \phi[s'].$$

Two different notions of executability of $\overrightarrow{a}$ are also defined (see [4]).

Example. Our running example involves a robot navigating between different locations and communicating. We take communication to be subject to interference and assume that the robot can communicate at a given location if the location is not risky and it has not become vulnerable. The robot can move between locations if they are connected and communicate from current location (represented using agent actions $move(i, j)$ and $comm(i)$). While moving to a location, the robot faces the possibility of becoming vulnerable if that location is a risky one. Thus the agent action $move(i, j)$ is associated with the system action $move(i, j, e)$, where the environment reaction e can be either Vul (for becoming vulnerable) or $NotVul$ (for not becoming vulnerable). The communicate agent action on the other hand has only one successful environment reaction and so it is associated with the system action $comm(i, e)$, where $e = Success$.

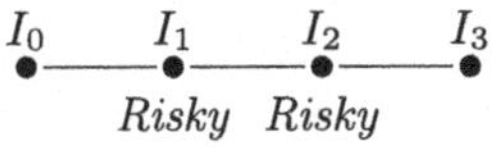

Fig. 1. Interconnections between locations

The precondition axioms for these agent and system actions are as follows.

(1) $Poss_{ag}(move(i,j),s) \stackrel{\text{def}}{=} At(i,s) \wedge Connected(i,j)$,

(2) $Poss_{ag}(comm(i),s) \stackrel{\text{def}}{=} \neg Vul(s) \wedge \neg Risky(i,s)$,

(1′) $Poss(move(i,j,e),s) \equiv Poss_{ag}(move(i,j),s)$
$\quad \wedge (Risky(j,s) \supset (e = Vul \vee e = NotVul)) \wedge (\neg Risky(j,s) \supset e = NotVul)$,

(2′) $Poss(comm(i,e),s) \equiv Poss_{ag}(comm(i),s) \wedge (e = Success)$.

The fluents in this example are $Vul(s)$, which denotes that the robot is vulnerable in situation s, $At(i,s)$, which states that the robot is at location i in s, and $Risky(i,s)$, which indicates that the location i is risky in s. Certain locations are risky initially and they remain the only risky ones when actions are performed. Also, we have a non-fluent $Connected(i,j)$ to indicate that there is a path from location i to location j.

The successor-state axioms (SSA) for these fluents are as follows:

(3) $At(j, do(a,s)) \equiv \exists i, e.\ a = move(i,j,e)$
$\qquad \vee (At(j,s) \wedge \forall j', e'.\ \neg(a = move(j,j',e')))$,

(4) $Vul(do(a,s)) \equiv \exists i, j.\ a = move(i,j,Vul) \vee Vul(s)$,

(5) $Risky(i, do(a,s)) \equiv Risky(i,s)$.

We also have the following initial state axioms:

(6) $\neg Vul(S_0)$, (7) $At(I_0, S_0)$, (8) $Risky(i, S_0) \equiv i = I_1 \vee i = I_2$.

Finally, there are 4 locations I_0 to I_3 in this domain, and the interconnections between these locations are given by the following axiom (see Fig. 1):

(9) $Connected(i,j) \equiv (i = I_0 \wedge j = I_1) \vee (i = I_1 \wedge j = I_2) \vee (i = I_2 \wedge j = I_3) \vee$
$\qquad (i = I_1 \wedge j = I_0) \vee (i = I_2 \wedge j = I_1) \vee (i = I_3 \wedge j = I_2)$.

We will call this NDBAT $\mathcal{D}_1$.

3 Actual Achievement Cause in the Situation Calculus

Given a history of actions/events (often called a scenario) and an observed effect, *actual causation* involves figuring out which of these actions are responsible for bringing about this effect.[1] When the effect is assumed to be false before the execution of the actions in the scenario and true afterwards, the notion is referred to

[1] We use actions and events interchangeably.

as *achievement (actual) causation*. Based on Batusov and Soutchanski's original proposal [2], Khan and Lespérance (KL) recently offered a definition of achievement cause in the SC [15]. Both of these frameworks assume that the scenario is a linear sequence of actions, i.e. no concurrent actions are allowed. KL's proposal can deal with epistemic causes and effects; e.g., an agent may analyze the cause of some newly acquired knowledge, and the cause may include some knowledge-producing action, e.g. *inform*. They showed that an agent may or may not know all the causes of an effect, and can even know some causes while not being sure about others.

To formalize reasoning about effects, KL [15] introduced the notion of *dynamic formulae*. An effect φ in their framework is thus a dynamic formula.[2] Given an effect φ, the actual causes are defined relative to a *narrative* (variously known as a *scenario* or a *trace*) s. When s is a ground situation, the tuple $\langle \mathcal{D}, s, \varphi \rangle$ is often called a *causal setting* [2]. Also, it is assumed that s is executable, and φ was false before the execution of the actions in s, but became true afterwards, i.e. $\mathcal{D} \models Executable(s) \land \neg\varphi[S_0] \land \varphi[s]$. Here φ is a formula with its situation arguments suppressed and $\varphi[s]$ denotes the formula obtained from φ by restoring the given situation argument s into all fluents in φ (see Definition 2).

Note that since all changes in the SC result from actions, the potential causes of an effect φ are identified with a set of action terms occurring in s. However, since s might include multiple occurrences of the same action, one also needs to identify the situations where these actions were executed. To deal with this, KL required that each situation be associated with a timestamp, which is an integer for their theory. Since in the context of knowledge, there can be different epistemic alternative situations (possible worlds) where an action occurs, using timestamps provides a common reference/rigid designator for the action occurrence. KL assumed that the initial situation starts at timestamp 0 and each action increments the timestamp by one. Thus, their action theory includes the following axioms:

$$
\begin{aligned}
&timeStamp(S_0) = 0,\\
&\forall a, s, ts.\ timeStamp(do(a, s)) = ts \equiv timeStamp(s) = ts - 1.
\end{aligned}
$$

With this, causes in their framework is a non-empty set of action-timestamp pairs derived from the trace s given φ.

The notion of *dynamic formulae* is defined as follows:

Definition 1. *Let $\overrightarrow{x}$, θ_a, and $\overrightarrow{y}$ respectively range over object terms, action terms, and object and action variables. The class of* dynamic formulae *φ is defined inductively using the following grammar:*

$$\varphi ::= P(\overrightarrow{x}) \mid Poss(\theta_a) \mid After(\theta_a, \varphi) \mid \neg\varphi \mid \varphi_1 \land \varphi_2 \mid \exists \overrightarrow{y}.\, \varphi.$$

[2] While KL also study epistemic causation, we restrict our discussion to objective causality only.

That is, a dynamic formula (DF) can be a situation-suppressed fluent, a formula that says that some action θ_a is possible, a formula that some DF holds after some action has occurred, or a formula that can built from other DF using the usual connectives. Note that φ can have quantification over object and action variables, but we cannot have quantification over situations or mention the ordering over situations (i.e. $\sqsubset$). We will use φ for DFs.

$\varphi[\cdot]$ is defined as follows:

Definition 2

$$\varphi[s] \stackrel{\text{def}}{=} \begin{cases} P(\vec{x}, s), & \text{if } \varphi \text{ is } P(\vec{x}) \\ Poss(\theta_a, s), & \text{if } \varphi \text{ is } Poss(\theta_a) \\ \varphi'[do(\theta_a, s)], & \text{if } \varphi \text{ is } \mathit{After}(\theta_a, \varphi') \\ \neg(\varphi'[s]), & \text{if } \varphi \text{ is } (\neg\varphi') \\ \varphi_1[s] \wedge \varphi_2[s], & \text{if } \varphi \text{ is } (\varphi_1 \wedge \varphi_2) \\ \exists \vec{y}.\, (\varphi'[s]), & \text{if } \varphi \text{ is } (\exists \vec{y}.\, \varphi'). \end{cases}$$

We will now present KL's definition of causes in the SC. The idea behind how causes are computed is as follows. Given an effect φ and scenario s, if some action of the action sequence in s triggers the formula φ to change its truth value from false to true relative to $\mathcal{D}$, and if there are no actions in s after it that change the value of φ back to false, then this action is an actual cause of achieving φ in s. Such causes are referred to as *primary* causes:

Definition 3 (Primary Cause [15])

$$\begin{aligned} \mathit{CausesDirectly}(a, ts, \varphi, s) \stackrel{\text{def}}{=} \exists s_a.\ & \mathit{timeStamp}(s_a) = ts \wedge (S_0 < do(a, s_a) \leq s) \\ & \wedge \neg\varphi[s_a] \wedge \forall s'.(do(a, s_a) \leq s' \leq s \supset \varphi[s']). \end{aligned}$$

That is, a executed at timestamp ts is the *primary cause* of effect φ in situation s iff a was executed in a situation with timestamp ts in scenario s, a caused φ to change its truth value to true, and no subsequent actions on the way to s falsified φ.

Now, note that a (primary) cause a might have been non-executable initially. Also, a might have only brought about the effect conditionally and this context condition might have been false initially. Thus earlier actions in the trace that contributed to the preconditions and the context conditions of a cause must be considered as causes as well. The following definition captures both primary and indirect causes:[3]

[3] In this, we need to quantify over situation-suppressed DF. Thus we must encode such formulae as terms and formalize their relationship to the associated SC formulae. This is tedious but can be done essentially along the lines of [6]. We assume that we have such an encoding and use formulae as terms directly.

Definition 4 (Actual Cause [15])

$$\begin{aligned}
\mathit{Causes}(a,ts,\varphi,s) \stackrel{\text{def}}{=} \forall P.[&\forall a,ts,s,\varphi.(\mathit{CausesDirectly}(a,ts,\varphi,s) \supset P(a,ts,\varphi,s))\\
&\wedge \forall a,ts,s,\varphi.(\exists a',ts',s'.(\mathit{CausesDirectly}(a',ts',\varphi,s)\\
&\qquad\qquad \wedge\ \mathit{timeStamp}(s')=ts' \wedge s' < s\\
&\qquad\qquad \wedge\ P(a,ts,[\mathit{Poss}(a') \wedge \mathit{After}(a',\varphi)],s')\\
&\qquad \supset P(a,ts,\varphi,s))\\
&] \supset P(a,ts,\varphi,s).
\end{aligned}$$

Thus, *Causes* is defined to be the least relation P such that if a executed at time-step ts directly causes φ in scenario s then (a, ts, φ, s) is in P, and if a' executed at ts' is a direct cause of φ in s, the timestamp of s' is ts', $s' < s$, and $(a, ts, [\mathit{Poss}(a') \wedge \mathit{After}(a', \varphi)], s')$ is in P (i.e. a executed at ts is a direct or indirect cause of $[\mathit{Poss}(a') \wedge \mathit{After}(a', \varphi)]$ in s'), then (a, ts, φ, s) is in P. Here the effect $[\mathit{Poss}(a') \wedge \mathit{After}(a', \varphi)]$ is that a' be executable and φ hold after a'.

The KL formalization of actual causation was formulated for deterministic domains specified by BATs in the situation calculus. However, it can be used directly for nondeterministic domains, for instance domains specified by NDBATs, as long as one focuses on scenarios that involve sequences of system actions, where both the agent actions and the environment reactions are known. This is not surprising as NDBATs are special kinds of BATS and sequences of system actions are essentially situations. We illustrate this in the example below.

Example (Cont'd). Consider the system action sequence σ_1, where $\sigma_1 = f$ $do([comm(I_0,\ Success);\ move(I_0,\ I_1,\ NotVul);\ move(I_1,\ I_2,\ Vul);\ move(I_2,\ I_3,\ NotVul)], S_0)$. We are interested in computing the causes of the effect $\varphi_1 = Vul(s)$, i.e. the robot becoming vulnerable, in scenario σ_1. It can be shown that:

Proposition 1 (Causes of φ_1 in σ_1)

$$\begin{aligned}
\mathcal{D}_1 \models\ &\neg \mathit{Causes}(comm(I_0, Success), 0, \varphi_1, \sigma_1) \wedge \mathit{Causes}(move(I_0, I_1, NotVul), 1, \varphi_1, \sigma_1)\\
&\wedge \mathit{Causes}(move(I_1, I_2, Vul), 2, \varphi_1, \sigma_1) \wedge \neg \mathit{Causes}(move(I_2, I_3, NotVul), 3, \varphi_1, \sigma_1).
\end{aligned}$$

Thus, for example, the action $move(I_1, I_2, Vul)$ executed at time-stamp 2 is a cause since it directly caused the robot to become vulnerable. Moreover, $move(I_0, I_1, NotVul)$ executed at time-stamp 1 can be shown to be an indirect cause of the $\varphi_1 = Vul$. This is because by axioms (1) and (1′) the primary cause of moving from location I_1 to I_2 i.e. $move(I_1, I_2, Vul)$ is only possible when the robot is at I_1, which in this scenario was brought about by $move(I_0, I_1, NotVul)$.

4 Agent Actions as Causes in the NDSC

We now turn our attention to causation in nondeterministic domains. As mentioned, when the scenario is a sequence of system actions where both the agent actions and the environment reactions are specified, we can use the KL formalization presented earlier to reason about actual causation, and identify causes for effects that are system actions containing both agent actions and environment reactions. But in many cases, we would like to consider scenarios that are sequences of agent actions only and where we don't know what the environment reactions were. Moreover, we want to analyse which agent actions were causes of given effects independently of the environment reactions. We address this question in this section.

We start by defining a notion of *nondeterministic causal setting* that generalizes causal settings and reflects the agent's ignorance about the environment's choices.

Definition 5 (Nondeterministic Causal Setting). *A nondeterministic causal setting is a tuple* $\langle \mathcal{D}, \overrightarrow{\alpha}, \varphi \rangle$, *where* $\mathcal{D}$ *is an NDBAT,* $\overrightarrow{\alpha}$ *is a sequence of agent actions representing the nondeterministic scenario, and* φ *is a dynamic formula such that:*

$$\mathcal{D} \models \neg\varphi[S_0] \wedge PossiblyAfter(\overrightarrow{\alpha}, \varphi, S_0).$$

Thus a scenario in a nondeterministic causal setting (ND setting, henceforth) is modeled using a sequence of agent actions $\overrightarrow{\alpha}$, with the assumption that this sequence was executed starting in S_0, and φ holds in at least one execution of $\overrightarrow{\alpha}$. Note that, since in this paper we are dealing with actual causation, it is assumed that the effect φ was indeed observed, and thus the agent only considers the executions of $\overrightarrow{\alpha}$ that brought about φ to be candidates for the system action history that actually occurred.

As before, in our framework causes are action and timestamp pairs. However, these actions are now agent actions. Also, since each of the agent actions in the scenario can have multiple outcomes, depending on these outcomes, we might sometimes call an agent action a cause and sometimes not a cause. In some cases, an agent action is a cause of an effect for all possible environment choices associated with the actions in the scenario. In general, given a scenario which is a sequence of agent actions, we will get a tree of possible executions, where each branch is the execution produced by a given set of environment reactions to the agent actions in the sequence. In this tree, it might be that only on certain branches a system action associated with an agent action executed at some timestamp is a cause. Additionally, it is also possible that all the system actions associated with this agent action is a cause in their respective branch. Thus, we have to define two notions of actual causes for agent actions in nondeterministic domains, namely *possibly causes* and *certainly causes*:[4]

[4] We allow both agent actions and system actions to be viewed as causes. An additional possibility is to view the environment's choices as causes, for instance, when there are no other ways of achieving an effect but via certain environment reactions. However, the consequences of such a definition is not clear. For instance, is it reasonable to assign responsibility/blame to nature? Rather than engaging in such philosophical questions, in this paper we focus on causes that involve the agent.

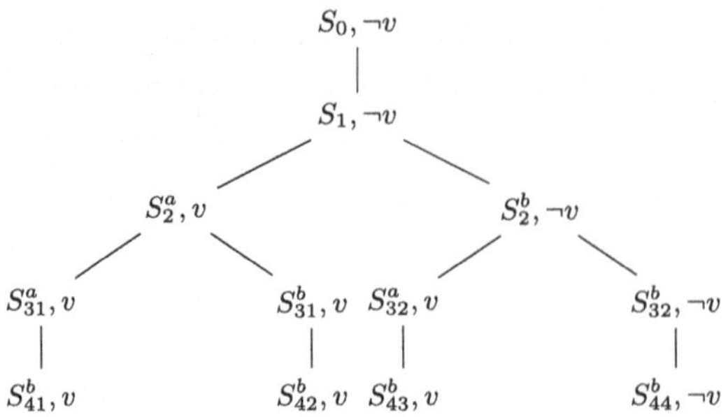

Fig. 2. Executions of agent action sequence $\overrightarrow{\alpha_1}$.

Definition 6 (Possibly Causes). *Let* $\langle \mathcal{D}, \overrightarrow{\alpha}, \varphi \rangle$ *be an ND setting and* $\beta(\overrightarrow{x})$ *an agent action in* $\overrightarrow{\alpha}$.

$$PossiblyCauses(\beta(\overrightarrow{x}), t, \varphi, \overrightarrow{\alpha}) \stackrel{\text{def}}{=} \\ \exists s.\ Do_{ag}(\overrightarrow{\alpha}, S_0, s) \land \varphi[s] \land \exists e.\ Causes(\beta(\overrightarrow{x}, e), t, \varphi, s).$$

That is, agent action $\beta(\overrightarrow{x})$ executed at timestamp t possibly causes φ in scenario $\overrightarrow{\alpha}$ iff there is an execution of $\overrightarrow{\alpha}$ that reaches some situation s, φ holds in s, and for some environment reaction e the associated system action $\beta(\overrightarrow{x}, e)$ executed at timestamp t is a (deterministic) cause of φ in scenario s.

Definition 7 (Certainly Causes). *Let* $\langle \mathcal{D}, \overrightarrow{\alpha}, \varphi \rangle$ *be an ND setting and* $\beta(\overrightarrow{x})$ *an agent action in* $\overrightarrow{\alpha}$.

$$CertainlyCauses(\beta(\overrightarrow{x}), t, \varphi, \overrightarrow{\alpha}) \stackrel{\text{def}}{=} \\ \forall s.\ Do_{ag}(\overrightarrow{\alpha}, S_0, s) \land \varphi[s] \supset \exists e.\ Causes(\beta(\overrightarrow{x}, e), t, \varphi, s).$$

Thus agent action $\beta(\overrightarrow{x})$ executed at timestamp t certainly causes φ in scenario $\overrightarrow{\alpha}$ iff for all executions of $\overrightarrow{\alpha}$ that reach some situation s in which φ holds, there is an environment reaction e such that the associated system action $\beta(\overrightarrow{x}, e)$ executed ats timestamp t is a (deterministic) cause of φ in scenario s. Note that this does not require a system action associated with $\beta(\overrightarrow{x})$ to be a cause in executions s where φ do not hold; this is because since the agent is assumed to have observed the effect φ, such executions can be ruled out as unrealistic, i.e. inconsistent with this assumption.

Example (Cont'd). Consider the agent action sequence $\overrightarrow{\alpha_1}$ below:

$$\overrightarrow{\alpha_1} = comm(I_0); move(I_0, I_1); move(I_1, I_2); move(I_2, I_3).$$

When executed starting on S_0, $\overrightarrow{\alpha_1}$ produces the tree of possible executions shown in Fig. 2. Here, the superscripts a and b represent environment choices *Vul* and *NotVul*, respectively, and $v/\neg v$ indicates whether the agent has become vulnerable or not. Thus for example, in this tree, $S_1 = do(comm(I_0, Success), S_0)$ and $S_2^a = do(move(I_0, I_1, Vul), S_1)$, etc. It is easy to see that the execution of $\overrightarrow{\alpha_1}$ starting in S_0 possibly satisfies $\varphi_1 = Vul()$, e.g. due to the existence of path

(S_0, S^b_{43}) in this tree over which the system action sequence in situation σ_1 is executed. Given ND causal setting $\langle \mathcal{D}_1, \overrightarrow{\alpha}_1, \varphi_1 \rangle$, we can in fact show that:

Proposition 2

$$\begin{aligned}\mathcal{D}_1 \models & \neg \mathit{PossiblyCauses}(\mathit{comm}(I_0), 0, \varphi_1, \overrightarrow{\alpha_1}) \\ & \wedge \mathit{CertainlyCauses}(\mathit{move}(I_0, I_1), 1, \varphi_1, \overrightarrow{\alpha_1}) \\ & \wedge \mathit{PossiblyCauses}(\mathit{move}(I_1, I_2), 2, \varphi_1, \overrightarrow{\alpha_1}) \\ & \wedge \neg \mathit{CertainlyCauses}(\mathit{move}(I_1, I_2), 2, \varphi_1, \overrightarrow{\alpha_1}) \\ & \wedge \neg \mathit{PossiblyCauses}(\mathit{move}(I_2, I_3), 3, \varphi_1, \overrightarrow{\alpha_1}).\end{aligned}$$

Thus, $\mathit{comm}(I_0)$ and $\mathit{move}(I_2, I_3)$ do not possibly causes φ_1 because they are not a cause (in the deterministic sense) of φ_1 in any of the executions of $\overrightarrow{\alpha_1}$ depicted in Fig. 2 in which φ_1 holds, i.e. in scenarios S^b_{41}, S^b_{42}, and S^b_{43}. Moreover, $\mathit{move}(I_0, I_1)$ certainly causes (and thus also possibly causes) φ_1; this is because in all the executions of $\overrightarrow{\alpha_1}$ starting in S_0 over which φ_1 holds, it is either a direct cause of φ_1 (as in situations S^b_{41} and S^b_{42}), or it is an indirect cause of φ_1 (as in S^b_{43}). To see the latter, recall Proposition 1 above. Finally, $\mathit{move}(I_1, I_2)$ possibly causes φ_1, but not certainly causes it; this is because there is at least one execution of $\overrightarrow{\alpha_1}$ in which it is a cause of φ_1, e.g. the one ending in S^b_{43}, but not over all executions in which φ_1 holds, e.g. in scenario S^b_{41}.

5 Reasoning About Achievement Causes

We now show that one can use regression to answer queries about various notions of causes under certain conditions. Note that previously KL [15] showed that *Causes* in the SC can be translated into a regressable formula when the situation is ground. DL [4] on the other hand proved that *CertainlyAfter* and *PossiblyAfter* under the right conditions are reducible to regressable formulae. Here we formalize these two techniques and show that it is possible to combine these two to obtain regressable formulae for possibly causes and certainly causes.

We start by defining a new abbreviation $\mathit{Causes}^k(a, t, \varphi, s)$, meaning that action a executed at time t causes φ in situation s in a causal chain of k steps (Definitions 8 and 9 and Theorem 1 were previously informally discussed in [15]).

Definition 8

$$\mathit{Causes}^k(a, t, \varphi, s) \stackrel{\text{def}}{=} \begin{cases} \mathit{CausesDirectly}(a, t, \varphi, s), & \text{if } k = 1 \\ \exists a', s', t'.\ \mathit{CausesDirectly}(a', t', \varphi, s) & \\ \quad \wedge\ \mathit{start}(s') = t' \wedge s' < s & \text{if } k > 1. \\ \quad \wedge\ \mathit{Causes}^{k-1}(a, t, [\mathit{Poss}(a') \wedge \mathit{After}(a', \varphi)], s'), & \end{cases}$$

Let us also define $\mathit{Causes}^{\leq k}(a, t, \varphi, s)$, meaning that action a executed at time t causes φ in situation s in a causal chain of at most k steps.

Definition 9

$$Causes^{\leq k}(a,t,\varphi,s) \stackrel{\text{def}}{=} \begin{cases} Causes^{k}(a,t,\varphi,s), & \text{if } k=1 \\ Causes^{k}(a,t,\varphi,s) \vee Causes^{\leq k-1}(a,t,\varphi,s), & \text{if } k>1. \end{cases}$$

Then we can show the following.

Theorem 1

$$\mathcal{D} \models Causes(a,t,\varphi,do([a_1,\ldots,a_n],S_0)) \equiv Causes^{\leq n}(a,t,\varphi,do([a_1,\ldots,a_n],S_0)).$$

Intuitively, this follows from the fact that any causal chain between a_1 and a_n, every cause of φ holding in $do([a_1,\ldots,a_n],s)$ has at most n steps.

We next define a translation function τ^+ that we will use to prove regressability of causes (this is one of our main contributions).

Definition 10

$$\tau^+(CausesDirectly(b,t,\varphi,do([a_1,\ldots,a_k,\ldots,a_n],S_0))) \stackrel{\text{def}}{=}$$
$$b=a_k \wedge t=k-1 \wedge \neg\varphi[do([a_1,\ldots,a_{k-1}],S_0)] \wedge \bigwedge_{i=k}^{n} \varphi[do([a_1,\ldots,a_i],S_0)].$$

We extend τ^+ to also include indirect causes.

Definition 11

$$\tau^+(Causes(a,t,\varphi,do([a_1,\ldots,a_n],S_0))) \stackrel{\text{def}}{=} \tau^+(Causes^{\leq n}(a,t,\varphi,do([a_1,\ldots,a_n],S_0))),$$

$$\textit{where } \tau^+(Causes^{\leq k}(a,t,\varphi,S_0)) \stackrel{\text{def}}{=}$$
$$\begin{cases} \tau^+(Causes^{k}(a,t,\varphi,S_0)), & \text{if } k=1 \\ \tau^+(Causes^{k}(a,t,\varphi,S_0)) \vee \tau^+(Causes^{\leq k-1}(a,t,\varphi,S_0)), & \text{if } k>1. \end{cases}$$

$$\textit{and } \tau^+(Causes^{k}(a,t,\varphi,do([a_1,\ldots,a_n],S_0))) \stackrel{\text{def}}{=}$$
$$\begin{cases} \tau^+(CausesDirectly(a,t,\varphi,do([a_1,\ldots,a_n],S_0))), & \text{if } k=1 \\ \bigvee_{i=2}^{n} [\tau^+(CausesDirectly(a_i,start(do([a_1,\ldots,a_{i-1}],S_0)),\varphi,do([a_1,\ldots,a_n],S_0))) \\ \quad \wedge \tau^+(Causes^{k-1}(a,t,[Poss(a_i) \wedge After(a_i,\varphi)],do([a_1,\ldots,a_i],S_0)))], \\ & \text{if } k>1. \end{cases}$$

Finally, we extend τ^+ to deal with formulae with ground situation terms (here s is a ground situation term and ψ, possibly with decorations, is a formula with ground situation terms):[5]

[5] Note that although we want this definition to deal with, among other things, arbitrary situation-grounded dynamic formulae, we don't need to cover the case where $\psi = After(a,\varphi)[s]$ since this is reduced to $\varphi[do(a,s)]$ by Definition 2.

Definition 12. *Let ψ be a formula where all the situation terms are ground and v be a variable of environment reaction or object sort. Then let:*

$$\tau^+(\psi) \overset{\text{def}}{=} \begin{cases} P(\overrightarrow{x}, s), & \text{if } \psi = P(\overrightarrow{x}, s), \\ Poss(a, s), & \text{if } \psi = Poss(a, s), \\ \neg(\tau^+(\psi')), & \text{if } \psi = (\neg\psi'), \\ \tau^+(\psi_1) \wedge \tau^+(\psi_2), & \text{if } \psi = (\psi_1 \wedge \psi_2), \\ \exists v.\ \tau^+(\psi'), & \text{if } \psi = (\exists v.\ \psi'). \end{cases}$$

Using this, we can show the following.

Theorem 2. *Let α be a ground system action term, φ be a dynamic formula without action variables, and σ be a ground situation term. Then we have:*

$$\mathcal{D} \models \mathit{Causes}(\alpha, t, \varphi, \sigma) \equiv \tau^+(\mathit{Causes}(\alpha, t, \varphi, \sigma)).$$

Then, by the theorem, our first major result about regressability of causes immediately follows (this result was previously explored in [15], but without the details of translation τ^+).

Corollary 1. *If σ is a ground situation term, α is a ground action term, and φ does not involve any action variables, then $\mathit{Causes}(\alpha, t, \varphi, \sigma)$ is equivalent to a regressable formula.*

This follows from Theorem 2 and the fact that when the above conditions hold, $\tau^+(\mathit{Causes}(\alpha, t, \varphi, \sigma))$ produces a Boolean combination of action- and situation-grounded *CausesDirectly* formula, which in turn reduces to a regressable formula that talks about whether the associated effect is true or not in different such grounded situations.

We next investigate the regressability of possibly and certainly causes. To this end, we define a couple of translation functions that convert these to regressable formulae. We start by introducing a translation function τ to deal with *CertainlyAfter* and *PossiblyAfter* (the idea behind Definition 13 and Theorem 3 is borrowed from [4]).

Definition 13. *Let β be an agent action function and $\overrightarrow{\alpha}$ be an agent action sequence. Then let:*

$$\tau(\mathit{CertainlyAfter}(\overrightarrow{\alpha}, \psi, s)) \overset{\text{def}}{=}$$
$$\begin{cases} \psi[s], & \text{if } \overrightarrow{\alpha} = \mathit{nil}, \\ \forall e.\ \phi_\beta^{Poss}(\overrightarrow{x}, e, s) \supset \tau(\mathit{CertainlyAfter}(\overrightarrow{\gamma}, \psi, do(\beta(\overrightarrow{x}, e), s))), & \\ & \text{if } \overrightarrow{\alpha} = [\beta(\overrightarrow{x}), \overrightarrow{\gamma}]. \end{cases}$$

$$\tau(\mathit{PossiblyAfter}(\overrightarrow{\alpha}, \psi, s)) \overset{\text{def}}{=}$$
$$\begin{cases} \psi[s], & \text{if } \overrightarrow{\alpha} = \mathit{nil}, \\ \exists e.\ \phi_\beta^{Poss}(\overrightarrow{x}, e, s) \wedge \tau(\mathit{PossiblyAfter}(\overrightarrow{\gamma}, \psi, do(\beta(\overrightarrow{x}, e), s))), & \\ & \text{if } \overrightarrow{\alpha} = [\beta(\overrightarrow{x}), \overrightarrow{\gamma}]. \end{cases}$$

Using this, we can show the following result that previously appeared in [4].

Theorem 3. *Let $\mathcal{D}$ be an NDBAT, $\overrightarrow{\alpha}$ a ground agent action sequence, S a situation term containing no situation or action variables, and ψ a situation suppressed formula containing no action variables. Then $CertainlyAfter(\overrightarrow{\alpha}, \psi, S)$ is equivalent to a regressable formula, and so is $PossiblyAfter(\overrightarrow{\alpha}, \psi, S)$.*

Example (Cont'd). Let us consider the agent action sequence $\overrightarrow{\alpha_2} = move(I_0, I_1); move(I_1, I_2)$, where the robot moves from location I_0 to I_1 and then from I_1 to I_2, starting in S_0. Note that, it is possible that the agent becomes vulnerable after executing $\overrightarrow{\alpha_2}$, i.e. $PossiblyAfter(\overrightarrow{\alpha_2}, Vul, S_0)$. We can show that this can be reduced to the following, which is a regressable formula.

Proposition 3

$$\begin{aligned}
&\mathcal{D}_1 \models PossiblyAfter(\overrightarrow{\alpha_2}, Vul, S_0) \equiv \\
&\quad \exists e.\ At(I_0, S_0) \wedge Connected(I_0, I_1) \wedge (e = Vul \vee e = NotVul) \\
&\quad \wedge \exists e'.\ At(I_1, do(move(I_0, I_1, e), S_0)) \wedge Connected(I_1, I_2) \wedge (e' = Vul \vee e' = NotVul) \\
&\quad \wedge Vul(do(move(I_1, I_2, e'), do(move(I_0, I_1, e), S_0))).
\end{aligned}$$

Next, we show that certainly/possibly causes are equivalent to a formula about certainly/possibly after. Using this, τ, and τ^+, we will then compose a function τ^* to reduce certainly and possibly causes to regressable formulae (what follows is one of our main contributions).

Proposition 4. *Let $\beta(\overrightarrow{x})$ be a ground agent action, $\overrightarrow{\alpha}$ be a ground agent action sequence, and φ be a dynamic formula without action variables. Then we have:*

$$\begin{aligned}
\mathcal{D} \models\ & CertainlyCauses(\beta(\overrightarrow{x}), t, \varphi, \overrightarrow{\alpha}) \equiv \\
& CertainlyAfter(\overrightarrow{\alpha}, \neg\varphi \vee \exists e.\ Causes(\beta(\overrightarrow{x}, e), t, \varphi), S_0). \\
\mathcal{D} \models\ & PossiblyCauses(\beta(\overrightarrow{x}), t, \varphi, \overrightarrow{\alpha}) \equiv \\
& PossiblyAfter(\overrightarrow{\alpha}, \exists e.\ Causes(\beta(\overrightarrow{x}, e), t, \varphi), S_0).
\end{aligned}$$

τ^* is defined as follows.

Definition 14

$$\begin{aligned}
&\tau^*(CertainlyCauses(\beta(\overrightarrow{x}), t, \varphi, \overrightarrow{\alpha})) \stackrel{\text{def}}{=} \\
&\quad \tau^+(\tau(CertainlyAfter(\overrightarrow{\alpha}, \neg\varphi \vee \exists e.\ Causes(\beta(\overrightarrow{x}, e), t, \varphi)), S_0))), \\
&\tau^*(PossiblyCauses(\beta(\overrightarrow{x}), t, \varphi, \overrightarrow{\alpha})) \stackrel{\text{def}}{=} \\
&\quad \tau^+(\tau(PossiblyAfter(\overrightarrow{\alpha}, \exists e.\ Causes(\beta(\overrightarrow{x}, e), t, \varphi), S_0))).
\end{aligned}$$

Using this, we can show the following results.

Theorem 4. *Let $\beta(\overrightarrow{x})$ be a ground agent action, $\overrightarrow{\alpha}$ be a ground agent action sequence, and φ be a dynamic formula without action variables. Then we have:*

$$\begin{aligned}
&\mathcal{D} \models CertainlyCauses(\beta(\overrightarrow{x}), t, \varphi, \overrightarrow{\alpha}) \equiv \tau^*(CertainlyCauses(\beta(\overrightarrow{x}), t, \varphi, \overrightarrow{\alpha})), \\
&\mathcal{D} \models PossiblyCauses(\beta(\overrightarrow{x}), t, \varphi, \overrightarrow{\alpha}) \equiv \tau^*(PossiblyCauses(\beta(\overrightarrow{x}), t, \varphi, \overrightarrow{\alpha})).
\end{aligned}$$

Finally, we prove our main result about the regressability of causes in the NDSC.

Theorem 5. *Let $\mathcal{D}$ be an NDBAT, $\beta(\overrightarrow{x})$ be a ground agent action, $\overrightarrow{\alpha}$ be a ground agent action sequence, and φ be a dynamic formula without action variables. Then $CertainlyCauses(\beta(\overrightarrow{x}), t, \varphi, \overrightarrow{\alpha})$ is equivalent to a regressable formula, and so is $PossiblyCauses(\beta(\overrightarrow{x}), t, \varphi, \overrightarrow{\alpha})$.*

This follows from Theorem 4 and the definitions of τ^*, τ, and τ^+. Note that $\tau(\cdots)$ on the right-hand sides of Definition 14 will eventually be reduced to formulae that are constructed from regressable sub-formulae as well as *Causes* predicates (see the base cases in Definition 13). τ^+, as specified in Definition 10 to 12, then converts these formulae into regressable formulae.

Example (Cont'd). We can show that $PossiblyCauses(move(I_0, I_1), 0, Vul, \overrightarrow{\alpha_2})$ can be translated into the following regressable formula.

Proposition 5

$$
\begin{aligned}
&\mathcal{D}_1 \models PossiblyCauses(move(I_0, I_1), 0, Vul, \overrightarrow{\alpha_2}) \equiv \\
&\exists e'.\ At(I_0, S_0) \wedge Connected(I_0, I_1) \wedge (e' = Vul \vee e' = NotVul) \\
&\wedge \exists e''.\ At(I_1, do(move(I_0, I_1, e'), S_0)) \wedge Connected(I_1, I_2) \wedge (e'' = Vul \vee e'' = NotVul) \\
&\wedge ([\neg Vul(S_0) \wedge Vul(do(move(I_0, I_1, e'), S_0)) \\
&\qquad \wedge Vul(do(move(I_1, I_2, e''), do(move(I_0, I_1, e'), S_0)))] \vee \\
&\quad [\neg Vul(do(move(I_0, I_1, e'), S_0)) \wedge Vul(do(move(I_1, I_2, e''), do(move(I_0, I_1, e'), S_0))) \\
&\qquad \wedge \neg\varphi_2(S_0) \wedge \varphi_2(do(move(I_0, I_1, e'), S_0))]),
\end{aligned}
$$

where $\varphi_2 = [Poss(move(I_1, I_2, e'')) \wedge After(move(I_1, I_2, e''), Vul)]$.

This regressable formula requires that for some environment reaction e', the first move action in the scenario must be executable in S_0, and for another environment reaction e'', the second move action must be executable afterwards. Moreover, $move(I_0, I_1, e')$ executed at time-stamp 0 is required to be either a primary or a secondary cause of the robot becoming vulnerable. The former demands *Vul* to be false initially in S_0 and to become and remain true after the execution of the first move action till the end of the trace. The latter stipulates that $move(I_1, I_2, e'')$ must be a primary cause of *Vul*, and thus *Vul* must have been false before its execution but must become and remain true afterwards. As well, $move(I_0, I_1, e')$ must have caused the preconditions of the latter move action and the conditions under which the latter move action brings about *Vul* (this indirect effect is represented using φ_2 above), and thus φ_2 must have been false in S_0 but must become and remain true after the first move action was performed until the execution of the next move action.

6 Conclusion

Motivated by the nondeterministic nature of real world action and change, in this paper, we proposed a formalization of actual achievement causes in the nondeterministic situation calculus [4]. We showed that in such domains, when the environment reactions are not known, two different notions of causes can be defined, one where an agent action is a cause for all possible environment reactions, and thus it is certainly a cause, and another where the agent action is a cause for at least one environment choice, i.e. it is possibly a cause. Extending on previous work, we also proved that these notions can be straightforwardly translated to regressable formulae. While our initial results look promising and shed some light on reasoning about these notions, in practice our translations generate large formulae. To deal with this, we recently extended regression in the situation calculus to provide a more effective mechanism to reason about actual causes [16]. We are also looking into the epistemics of causation in nondeterministic domains, extending our previous work in [15]. Finally, a key limitation of this work is that here we only deal with single agents. We are currently investigating how one can formalize causation in the situation calculus concurrent game structures [7], where at every time step multiple agents are allowed to make synchronous concurrent moves.

References

1. Batusov, V., Soutchanski, M.: Situation calculus semantics for actual causality. In: Gordon, A.S., Miller, R., Turán, G. (eds.) Proceedings of the Thirteenth International Symposium on Commonsense Reasoning, COMMONSENSE 2017, London, UK, 6–8 November 2017. CEUR Workshop Proceedings, vol. 2052. CEUR-WS.org (2017)
2. Batusov, V., Soutchanski, M.: Situation calculus semantics for actual causality. In: McIlraith, S.A., Weinberger, K.Q. (eds.) Proceedings of the Thirty-Second AAAI Conference on Artificial Intelligence, (AAAI-18), the 30th Innovative Applications of Artificial Intelligence (IAAI-18), and the 8th AAAI Symposium on Educational Advances in Artificial Intelligence (EAAI-18), New Orleans, Louisiana, USA, 2–7 February 2018, pp. 1744–1752. AAAI Press (2018)
3. Beckers, S.: Nondeterministic causal models. CoRR abs/2405.14001 (2024)
4. De Giacomo, G., Lespérance, Y.: The nondeterministic situation calculus. In: Bienvenu, M., Lakemeyer, G., Erdem, E. (eds.) Proceedings of the 18th International Conference on Principles of Knowledge Representation and Reasoning, KR 2021, Online event, 3–12 February 2021, pp. 216–226 (2021)
5. Eiter, T., Lukasiewicz, T.: Complexity results for structure-based causality. Artif. Intell. **142**(1), 53–89 (2002)
6. Giacomo, G.D., Lespérance, Y., Levesque, H.J.: Congolog, a concurrent programming language based on the situation calculus. Artif. Intell. **121**(1–2), 109–169 (2000)
7. Giacomo, G.D., Lespérance, Y., Pearce, A.R.: Synchronous games in the situation calculus. In: Weiss, G., Yolum, P., Bordini, R.H., Elkind, E. (eds.) Proceedings of the 2015 International Conference on Autonomous Agents and Multiagent Systems, AAMAS 2015, Istanbul, Turkey, 4–8 May 2015, pp. 1675–1676. ACM (2015)
8. Glymour, C., et al.: Actual causation: a stone soup essay. Synthese **175**(2), 169–192 (2010)
9. Halpern, J.Y.: Axiomatizing causal reasoning. J. Artif. Intell. Res. **12**, 317–337 (2000). https://doi.org/10.1613/jair.648

10. Halpern, J.Y.: A modification of the halpern-pearl definition of causality. In: Yang, Q., Wooldridge, M.J. (eds.) Proceedings of the Twenty-Fourth International Joint Conference on Artificial Intelligence, IJCAI 2015, Buenos Aires, Argentina, 25–31 July 2015, pp. 3022–3033. AAAI Press (2015). http://ijcai.org/Abstract/15/427
11. Halpern, J.Y.: Actual Causality. MIT Press, Cambridge (2016)
12. Halpern, J.Y., Pearl, J.: Causes and explanations: a structural-model approach. Part I: Causes. Br. J. Philos. Sci. **56**(4), 843–887 (2005)
13. Hopkins, M.: The actual cause: from intuition to automation. Ph.D. thesis, University of California Los Angeles (2005)
14. Hopkins, M., Pearl, J.: Causality and counterfactuals in the situation calculus. J. Log. Comput. **17**(5), 939–953 (2007)
15. Khan, S.M., Lespérance, Y.: Knowing why - on the dynamics of knowledge about actual causes in the situation calculus. In: Dignum, F., Lomuscio, A., Endriss, U., Nowé, A. (eds.) AAMAS 2021: 20th International Conference on Autonomous Agents and Multiagent Systems, Virtual Event, United Kingdom, 3–7 May 2021, pp. 701–709. ACM (2021)
16. Khan, S.M., Lespérance, Y., Rostamigiv, M.: Reasoning about actual causes in nondeterministic domains. In: Proceedings of the 39th Annual AAAI Conference on Artificial Intelligence, AAAI 2025, Philadelphia, Pennsylvania, USA, 25 February–4 March 2025. AAAI Press (2025)
17. Khan, S.M., Rostamigiv, M.: On explaining agent behaviour via root cause analysis: a formal account grounded in theory of mind. In: Gal, K., Nowé, A., Nalepa, G.J., Fairstein, R., Radulescu, R. (eds.) ECAI 2023 - 26th European Conference on Artificial Intelligence, Kraków, Poland, 30 September–4 October 2023. Frontiers in Artificial Intelligence and Applications, vol. 372, pp. 1239–1247. IOS Press (2023)
18. Khan, S.M., Soutchanski, M.: Necessary and sufficient conditions for actual root causes. In: Giacomo, G.D., et al. (eds.) ECAI 2020 - 24th European Conference on Artificial Intelligence, Santiago de Compostela, Spain, 29 August–8 September 2020. Including 10th Conference on Prestigious Applications of Artificial Intelligence (PAIS 2020). Frontiers in Artificial Intelligence and Applications, vol. 325, pp. 800–808. IOS Press (2020). https://doi.org/10.3233/FAIA200169
19. Leitner-Fischer, F., Leue, S.: Causality checking for complex system models. In: Giacobazzi, R., Berdine, J., Mastroeni, I. (eds.) VMCAI 2013. LNCS, vol. 7737, pp. 248–267. Springer, Heidelberg (2013). https://doi.org/10.1007/978-3-642-35873-9_16
20. Levesque, H.J., Pirri, F., Reiter, R.: Foundations for the situation calculus. Electron. Trans. Artif. Intell. (ETAI) **2**, 159–178 (1998)
21. McCarthy, J., Hayes, P.J.: Some philosophical problems from the standpoint of artificial intelligence. Mach. Intell. **4**, 463–502 (1969)
22. Pearl, J.: On the definition of actual cause. Technical report. R-259, University of California Los Angeles (1998)
23. Pearl, J.: Causality: Models, Reasoning, and Inference. Cambridge University Press, Cambridge (2000)
24. Reiter, R.: Knowledge in Action. Logical Foundations for Specifying and Implementing Dynamical Systems. MIT Press, Cambridge (2001)
25. Yazdanpanah, V., et al.: Reasoning about responsibility in autonomous systems: challenges and opportunities. AI Soc. **38**(4), 1453–1464 (2023)

Temporal Truth in the Limit: Yablo's Paradox in LTL_f and over Potentially Infinite Traces

Michał Tomasz Godziszewski(✉), Davide Catta, and Aniello Murano

Dipartimento di Ingegneria Elettrica e delle Tecnologie dell'Informazione, Universita Degli Studi di Napoli Federico II, Naples, Italy
mtgodziszewski@gmail.com

Abstract. In this paper we investigate the relation of temporal logics and properties of Yablo sentences. We provide a (first in the literature) framework for finitistic theory of potential infinity over temporal logic. We introduce the FM-domains over LTL_f, and define sl-theories over LTL_f, providing a first notion of theories true in the limit over finite traces in temporal logic. Furthermore, also for the first time in the literature, we perform the analysis of Yablo sentences (as formalized in temporal logic vocabulary) in LTL_f, i.e., the Linear Temporal Logic over finite traces. On top of that, as a litmus test for this novel theory, we provide the analysis of how Yablo's paradox of LTL is solved not only in LTL_f, but also in the finitistic theory of potential infinity over temporal logic.

Keywords: LTL on finite traces · Yablo's Paradox · Potential infinity · FM-domains · sl-theories

1 Introduction

Yablo's Paradox is a semantic phenomenon discovered by Stephen Yablo in 1993. In his paper [14] the author provided a by now famous example of a semantic paradox which, according to the author, does not involve self-reference. Recall the paradox arises when one considers the following sequence of sentences:

Y_0 For any $k > 0$, Y_k is false.
Y_1 For any $k > 1$, Y_k is false.
Y_2 For any $k > 2$, Y_k is false.
⋮
Y_n For any $k > n$, Y_k is false.
⋮

R. Collier et al. (Eds.): EUMAS 2024, LNAI 15685, pp. 110–128, 2025.
https://doi.org/10.1007/978-3-031-93930-3_7

Take any sentence Y_n from the sequence and ask what would happen if it was true. Suppose it is. Then, things are as it says, and for any $j > n$ Y_j is false. In particular Y_{n+1} is false and also for any $j > n + 1$ Y_j is false.

But the second conjunct is exactly what Y_{n+1} states, so it turns that Y_{n+1} is true after all. The assumption that Y_n is true led therefore to a contradiction. So it is false. This means that not all sentences following Y_n are false, and so one of them, say Y_k, is true. But then, we can again obtain a contradiction by repeating for Y_k the same reasoning that we have just given for Y_n. So, whether Y_n is true, or false, a contradiction follows. Hence the paradox.

Yablo's Paradox has already been demonstrated relevant to the field of multiagent systems. In particular, it has been investigated from the perspective of epistemic game theory, starting from the assumption that other people's beliefs about our beliefs shape our decision-making strategies. Epistemic game theory formalizes how players think about each other's beliefs, examining their reasoning processes before making final decisions in a game. A paper [5] introduced a non-self-referential paradox, termed the 'Yablo-like Brandenburger-Keisler paradox', within epistemic game theory. This paradox demonstrated that it is impossible to comprehensively model players' epistemic beliefs and assumptions. Additionally, the authors proposed an interactive temporal belief and assumption logic to appropriately formalize this paradox, transforming it into a theorem within this logic framework. Specifically, the so-called Assumption Logic is a multi-modal logic designed to formalize the beliefs and assumptions of agents within a multi-agent system. Initially introduced by Bonanno for belief revision, it was later simplified by Brandenburger and Keisler to articulate their paradox in epistemic game theory. To reframe their two-player impossibility result within a modal logic framework, Brandenburger and Keisler developed an interactive version of Assumption Logic, featuring two operators. Temporal Assumption Logic extends this framework, allowing for the study of how agents' beliefs change over time. In general, the exploration of the BK paradox and its Yablo-like variant underscores the complexities inherent in multi-agent systems and epistemic logic. It opens avenues for further research into belief dynamics and the structure of assumptions in both theoretical and practical applications, such as AI and decision-making frameworks. Understanding these paradoxes can help refine models that better account for the layers of beliefs in strategic interactions among agents.

Ensuring the reliability of both software and hardware systems is a complex task, particularly when these systems are distributed. Over the past fifty years, researchers have proposed various solutions to this challenge. One notable success is the application of formal methods techniques [1]. These methods allow for the verification of a system's correctness by formally assessing whether a mathematical model of the system meets a formal representation of its intended behavior. Linear Time Temporal Logic (LTL) [13] is a formalism used to describe sequences of events in a linear, chronological order. It allows for the specification and verification of temporal properties in systems, such as safety and liveness conditions and it is extensively used as a specification language in formal methods. LTL over finite traces (LTL_f) [2] adapts Linear Time Temporal Logic to handle finite sequences of events, making it ideal for systems that eventually stop. Unlike standard LTL, which assumes events continue indefinitely, LTL_f focuses on properties within a limited timeframe. This is especially useful for scenarios like workflows or test cases where the process has a clear endpoint. This is particularly relevant in areas such as Planning and Business Process Management. A key computational advantage of finite-trace interpretation is the ability to use standard finite-state automata for modeling and reasoning, instead of the more complex omega-automata needed for infinite traces. In this paper, we give a formalization of Yablo's Paradox within the framework of LTL_f. This logic is especially suited to multiagent systems (MAS) scenarios where agent interactions are naturally finite and time-bounded. For example, in task-oriented MAS environments such as collaborative robotics or automated negotiation systems, interactions are often restricted to a series of finite steps. Here, LTL_f can model properties within these finite boundaries, enabling precise specifications for episodic interactions.

The reduction in complexity of LTL_f achieved by enabling the use of finite-state automata instead of omega-automata is crucial for MAS applications that require fast and efficient verification processes. Moreover, in MAS involving workflows, such as business process management or automated planning, LTLf enables modeling and reasoning about agents' sequential actions up to defined endpoints. This paper's formalization of Yablo's Paradox within LTL_f introduces a novel framework to handle paradoxical reasoning within bounded traces, which is crucial for detecting and mitigating logical inconsistencies in agent interactions over limited timeframes.

In this paper, additionally to LTL_f we consider the so-called sl-semantics of FM-domains and for the first time in literature we propose their temporal-logic counterpart. This framework was motivated by considerations in computational foundations of mathematics and the search for the semantics under which first-order sentences would be interpreted in potentially infnite domains.

Potentially infinite domains in this framework are understood as sequences of finite models increasing without any finite bound. The notion is explored further in the paper and can also be interpreted as a formalization and explication of the notion of potential infinity. From a purely formal point of view, a task for which FM-domains and their sl-theories have been introduced is just giving a comfortable language for describing various combinatorial objects relevant to computational, discrete or finite mathematics, such as formulas, Turing machines, computations, and finite models.

1.1 Related Work

Yablo's paradox is one of major phenomena in formal semantics and has been investigated from many logical, mathematical, computer-scientific and philosophical points of view. A body of works that is particuarly interesting and relevant from the point of view of this paper, concerns topics such as the metalogical properties of Yablo sequences, as formalized in arithmetic and axiomatic theories of truth, metalogical properties of Yablo sequences when interpreted over potentially infinite domains with the semantics formalizing the notion of truth in the limit, and last, but not least, properties of Yablo sentences, as formalized in the temporal logic LTL. S. Salehi and A. Karimi in [7] have initiated the study of Yablo's sentences in LTL, obtaining some preliminary results on the semantics of Yablo's sentences in LTL. The study was further extended by A. Karimi in [6], where syntactic proofs using an appropriate axiomatization of LTL were given for Yablo's paradox in its various variants.

A fruitful study of Yablo's paradox formalized over arithmetic performed e.g. in [8] and in [4] has revealed that the reasoning has the following interesting feature. If we formalize the Yablo sentences over arithmetic, then in order to derive the contradiction, one needs to use a strong assumption concerning the notion of truth: namely one has to assume "for all n, Y_n if and only if $\ulcorner Y_n \urcorner$ is true." $\forall n\ (Y_n \equiv Tr(Y_n))$. If we wanted to replace this *uniform disquotation* with an infinity of *local disquotation* instances, contradiction could be obtained only if we used some infinitary inference rule (requiring an infinite number of premises) such as the ω-rule.

So far, the story is rather well-known. What is somewhat less known, is that there is a way of handling the paradox which relies on finitistic assumptions. After all, if the world is finite, there aren't enough things in the world to interpret all sentences from the Yablo sequence, and the last interpreted one is vacuously true without any threat of paradox. Yablo's paradox can be thought of as an infinitary version of the Liar paradox, so perhaps thinking it can be dealt with by tackling the notion of infinity isn't extremely implausible.

Since the paradox somehow involves the concept of infinity (as the essential role of the ω-rule suggests), we'll turn our attention to a formalization of Yablo's paradox in a setting that takes a somewhat different approach to infinity. It is the framework developed by the late Marcin Mostowski and others in [9,10,12], meant as a formalization of the concept of potential infinity. We'll describe how one could go about avoiding the paradox by taking the distinction between potential and actual infinity seriously. Of course, the finitist owes us a story about how they make sense of arithmetic, and how the whole thing should be studied by formal methods.

1.2 Our Contributions

In this paper we fill a number of major gaps in the literature concerning the relation of temporal logics and properties of Yablo sentences:

1. We provide a (first in the literature) framework for finitstic theory of potential infinity over temporal logic. We introduce the FM-domains over LTL_f, and define sl-theories over LTL_f, providing a first notion of theories true in the limit over finite traces in temporal logic.
2. Furthermore, also for the first time in the literature, we perform the analysis of Yablo sentences (as formalized in temporal logic vocabulary) in LTL_f, i.e., the Linear Temporal Logic over finite traces.

3. On top of that, as a litmus test for this novel theory, we provide the analysis of how Yablo's paradox of LTL is solved not only in LTL_f, but also in the finitstic theory of potential infinity over temporal logic.

2 Yablo's Paradox in LTL

In this section, we give a formalization of Yablo's Paradox within the framework of LTL. Before doing so let us recall the syntax and semantics of LTL.

Definition 1 (Syntax of LTL). *Let V be a set of propositional variables. The alphabet of a basic propositional language $\mathcal{L}_{LTL}$ is given by:*

- *the set V,*
- *logical connectives: $\rightarrow$, and $\neg$,*
- *the bracket symbols: (, and),*
- *logical operators: $\bigcirc$, and $\mathcal{U}$.*

We use the following recursive definition of the set of formulas of $\mathcal{L}_{LTL}$:

1. *every propositional variable $p \in V$ is a formula,*
2. *if φ is a formula, then $\neg\varphi$, $\bigcirc\varphi$ are formulas*
3. *if φ, and ψ are formulas, then $(\varphi \rightarrow \psi)$ and $\varphi \mathcal{U} \psi$ are formulas,*

and nothing else is a formula.

Semantical interpretations in classical propositional logic are given by boolean valuations. For LTL we have to extend this concept according to our informal idea that formulas are evaluated over sequences of states ('time scales').

Definition 2 (Semantics of LTL). *A temporal (Kripke) structure for V is an infinite sequence $K = (\eta_0, \eta_1, \eta_2, \ldots)$ of mappings $\eta_i : V \rightarrow \{0, 1\}$ called states. The mapping η_0 is called initial state of K. Observe that states are just valuations in the classical logic sense. For K and $i \in \mathbb{N}$ we define $K, i \models \varphi$ (in another formalism denoted by $K_i(\varphi) = 1$), informally meaning the 'truth value of φ in the ith state of K' for every formula φ inductively as follows:*

1. *$K, i \models v$ iff $\eta_i(v) = 1$ for each $v \in V$,*
2. *$K, i \models \neg\varphi$ iff $K, i \not\models \varphi$,*
3. *$K, i \models \varphi \rightarrow \psi$ iff $K, i \models \neg\varphi$ or $K, i \models \psi$,*
4. *$K, i \models \bigcirc\varphi$ iff $K, i + 1 \models \varphi$,*
5. *$K, i \models \varphi \mathcal{U} \psi$ iff there exists $j \geq i$ s.t. $K, j \models \psi$ and for each $i \leq l < j$ it holds that $K, l \models \varphi$*

The Boolean connectives $\vee$, $\wedge$ and $\top$ (and their semantics) can be defined as usual. We write $\Diamond\varphi$ as a shortcut for $\top \mathcal{U} \varphi$ and $\Box\varphi$ as a shortcut for $\neg\Diamond\neg\varphi$.

Definition 3 (Validities of LTL). *A formula φ of $\mathcal{L}_{LTL}$ is called **valid** in the temporal structure K for V (or K satisfies φ), denoted by $K \models \varphi$, if $K, i \models \varphi$ for every $i \in \mathbb{N}$. A formula φ is called a **consequence** of a set Δ of formulas $\Delta \models \varphi$ if $K \models \varphi$ holds for every K such that $K \models \psi$ for all $\psi \in \Delta$. A formula φ is called (universally) **valid** $\models \varphi$ if $\emptyset \models \varphi$. Then we also say that the formula φ is a law of LTL or that LTL entails it, denoted as $LTL \models \varphi$. A formula φ is called (locally) satisfiable if there is a temporal structure K and $i \in \mathbb{N}$ such that $K, i \models \varphi$.*

It can be easily seen that the following are examples of formulas that are universally valid in LTL:

$$\bigcirc \Box\varphi \leftrightarrow \Box \bigcirc \varphi,$$

and

$$\neg \bigcirc \varphi \leftrightarrow \bigcirc\neg\varphi.$$

The latter, called the duality law for *Next* operator of LTL, will be of particular importance when analyzing the main differences between behavior of Yablo sentences in LTL and LTL_f.

It immediately follows from the equivalences below that the following equivalences hold universally as well:

$$\bigcirc \Box\neg\varphi \leftrightarrow \Box \bigcirc \neg\varphi \leftrightarrow \Box\neg \bigcirc \varphi.$$

The Yablo formula in LTL is defined as the equivalence:

$$\varphi \leftrightarrow \bigcirc\Box\neg\varphi.$$

The Yablo Paradox means that the following theorem holds:

Theorem 1 (A. Karimi, S. Salehi [7]). *The following is a theorem of LTL:*

$$\neg\Box\,(\varphi \leftrightarrow \bigcirc\Box\neg\varphi.)$$

The proof goes by an argument demonstrating that the formula

$$\Box\,(\varphi \leftrightarrow \bigcirc\Box\neg\varphi.)$$

is unsatisfiable in LTL. We will show below that this is in contrast with what happens in LTL_f, and in the *sl*-semantics of the latter.

As Yablo's paradox comes in several varieties, in the paper [7] by S. Salehi and A. Karimi it has also been demonstrated that other variants of Yablo formulas are paradoxical in the same sense as obve, when formalized in the framework of temporal logic rather than arithmetic.

The original version of Yablo's sequence consists of the so-called **Always-Y-sentences**: $Y_n \leftrightarrow \forall k > n\, Y_k$ is not true, which when formalized in $\mathcal{L}_{LTL}$ gives the formula mentioned above, i.e., $\varphi \leftrightarrow \bigcirc\Box\neg\varphi$.

Other natural variants considered in the literature are:

1. **Sometimes-Y-sentences:** $Y_n \leftrightarrow \exists k > n\, Y_k$ is not true, which has the following form when formalized in $\mathcal{L}_{LTL}$:

$$\varphi \leftrightarrow \bigcirc\Diamond\neg\varphi,$$

2. **Almost-Always-Y-sentences:** $Y_n \leftrightarrow \exists k > n \forall j > k\, Y_j$ is not true, which has the following form when formalized in $\mathcal{L}_{LTL}$:

$$\varphi \leftrightarrow \bigcirc\Diamond\Box\neg\varphi,$$

3. **Unboundedly-Often-Y-sentences:** $Y_n \leftrightarrow \forall k > n \exists j > k\, Y_j$ is not true, which has the following form when formalized in $\mathcal{L}_{LTL}$:

$$\varphi \leftrightarrow \bigcirc\Box\Diamond\neg\varphi.$$

A. Karimi and S. Salehi show in [7] that all the formulas above they are paradoxical in the sense that for each equivalence ψ of the above (Sometimes, Almost-Always, and Unboundedly-Often) the following holds: $LTL \models \neg\Box\psi$, meaning that the formula $\Box\psi$ is unsatisfiable.

Below, we demonstrate that this is in contrast with the situation in LTL_f, and more importantly, with the *sl*-theory of the above, i.e., with the set of LTL_f formulas that are *true in the limit* in a very precise sense.

3 Formal Theory of Potential Infinity and Truth in the Limit

In this section we introduce the formal theory explicating the computationally motivated notion of potential infinity and semantics for theories that are true in the limit in a precise technical sense specified below. Let us begin with recalling some basic definitions regarding the syntax and semantics of first-order logic.

3.1 First-Order Logic Preliminaries

Definition 4. *A* ***signature*** *(a dictionary, or a language, usually denoted by $\mathcal{L}$) is a tuple*

$$\sigma = (\{P_i\}_{i\in I}, \{f_j\}_{j\in J}, \{c_k\}_{k\in K})$$

of (non-logical) respectively: predicate, function and constant symbols of the language $\mathcal{L}$, for some index sets I, J and K. Sometimes the signature will be denoted by $\mathcal{L}$.

Let Var be an infinite set $\{x_0, x_1, \ldots\}$ of variables .

Let Trm denote the set of **terms**. *Trm is defined as follows:*

1. *Every individual variable $x_i \in Var$ is a term.*
2. *Every individual constant symbol c_k is a term.*

3. If $(\tau_1, \ldots, \tau_n)$ is a sequence of terms, and f_j is a function symbol of arity equal to n, then the expression $f(\tau_1, \ldots, \tau_n)$ is a term.
4. There are no other terms.

Terms play a role of names of the language, and are used in first-order formulas:

Definition 5. *The set $Frm_{\mathcal{L}}$ is a set of* ***formulas of the language*** $\mathcal{L}$*. $Frm_{\mathcal{L}}$ is defined as follows:*

1. If $(\tau_1, \ldots, \tau_n)$ is a sequence of terms of the language $\mathcal{L}$, and R_i is a relational symbol of arity equal to n, then the expression $R_i(\tau_1, \ldots, \tau_n)$ is an ***atomic formula*** *of the language $\mathcal{L}$.*
2. If φ is a formula, then the expressions $\neg\varphi$, $\forall x_i \varphi$, $\exists x_i \varphi$ are formulas of the language $\mathcal{L}$.
3. If φ and ψ are formulas, then the expressions $\varphi \wedge \psi$, $\varphi \vee \psi$, $\varphi \Rightarrow \psi$, $\varphi \equiv \psi$ are formulas of the language $\mathcal{L}$.
4. There are no other formulas.

Definition 6. *The set $Sent_{\mathcal{L}}$ is a a set of* ***sentences of the language*** $\mathcal{L}$*. A formula φ is a sentence if there is no occurence of any free variable x_i in φ.*

Definition 7. *We define the following notions with respect to a language $\mathcal{L}$:*

1. A ***theory*** *is a set of sentences closed under logical consequence.*
2. An ***$\mathcal{L}$-structure (model)***[1] *$\mathcal{M}$ is a tuple*

$$(M, \{P_i^{\mathcal{M}}\}_{i \in I}, \{f_j^{\mathcal{M}}\}_{j \in J}, \{c_k^{\mathcal{M}}\}_{k \in K})$$

consisting of the domain (universe), relations, functions and constant elements of $\mathcal{M}$.
3. An $\mathcal{L}$-formula, an $\mathcal{L}$-sentence and an $\mathcal{L}$-theory are, respectively a formula, a sentence and a theory that are defined for the (first-order) language $\mathcal{L}$ (over some signature σ).
4. A theory Δ is ***satisfiable*** *if and only if there is a model $\mathcal{M}$ such that $\mathcal{M} \models \varphi$ for any $\varphi \in \Delta$.*

3.2 Arithmetic *in the Limit* – sl-theory of FM-domains

We now turn to considering the so-called *sl*-semantics of FM-domains. Obviously, once we turn to finite models, we need to overcome a small technical obstacle concerning the arithmetical language: it seems that the reference of some singular terms should come out undefined. One way to go would be to employ the apparatus of partial functions. A simpler method, however, uses relational symbols instead of function symbols. This is the one that we'll employ.

[1] Sometimes the use of the name *model* is restricted to structures satisfying *given theories*.

Definition 8 (*FM***-domains).** *Let $R \subseteq \omega^r$ be an r-ary relation on natural numbers. By $R^{(n)}$ we denote $R \cap \{0, 1, ..., n-1\}^r$, the restriction of this relation to first n natural numbers. For any model $\mathcal{A}$ over some fixed signature $\sigma = (R_1, ..., R_k)$ (in particular, one can take the signature to comprise the relational counterpart of standard arithmetical functions such as addition or multiplication) we define the FM-domain of $\mathcal{A}$ as follows:*

$$FM(\mathcal{A}) = \{\mathcal{A}_n : \ n = 1, 2, ...\}$$

where

$$\mathcal{A}_n = (\{0, 1, ..., n-1\}, R_1^{(n)}, ..., R_k^{(n)}).$$

That is, $FM(\mathcal{A})$ is the set of all finite initial segments of natural numbers, with the arithmetical relations appropriately restricted.

For the purposes of this section, by $\mathbb{N}$ we denote the standard model of arithmetic $(\omega, +, \times, 0, s, <)$, where the arithmetical functions are interpreted as relations, so we have that:

$$FM(\mathbb{N}) = \{\mathbb{N}_n : \ n = 1, 2, ...\},$$

where

$$\mathbb{N}_n = (\{0, 1, ..., n-1\}, +^{(n)}, \times^{(n)}, 0^{(n)}, s^{(n)}, <^{(n)}).$$

(Note that this means that numerals are replaced with predicates, so that if in a finite point a numerical would fail to refer, its predicative counterpart refers to the empty set, and if it wouldn't, its predicative counterpart refers to an appropriate singleton. Thus, in the standard arithmetical language each n-ary symbol is replaced by the corresponding $n+1$-ary one; we'll keep referring to it as $\mathcal{L}$ with no threat of misunderstanding.)

Ultimately, we'll be evaluating formulas in $FM(\mathbb{N})$; but in order to do that, we first need to evaluate them in the finite segments that $FM(\mathbb{N})$ contains. Satisfaction at finite models involved is understood according to the standard notion of satisfaction. Satisfaction in $FM(\mathbb{N})$ is understood, intuitively, as satisfaction in all sufficiently large segments from $FM(\mathbb{N})$.

Definition 9 ($sl(FM(\mathbb{N}))$)**.** *For any $\varphi \in Sent_{\mathcal{L}}$ we say that φ is sl-true in $FM(\mathbb{N})$ (true in sufficiently large models, hence the abbreviation sl):*

$$FM(\mathbb{N}) \models_{sl} \varphi \text{ if and only if } \exists m \, \forall k \ (k \geq m \ \Rightarrow \ \mathbb{N}_k \models \varphi).$$

Let us then denote:

$$sl(FM(\mathbb{N})) = \{\varphi \in Sent_{\mathcal{L}} : \ FM(\mathbb{N}) \models_{sl} \varphi\}.$$

$sl(FM(\mathbb{N}))$ is called the sl-theory *of $FM(\mathbb{N})$. More generally we could say that for a given class $\mathcal{K}$ of finite models:*

$$sl(\mathcal{K}) = \{\varphi \in Sent_{\mathcal{L}_\sigma} : \ \exists n \, \forall \mathcal{M} \in \mathcal{K} \ (card(\mathcal{M}) \geq n \ \Rightarrow \ \mathcal{M} \models \varphi)\}.$$

Now we can use the notion to define a consequence relation by saying:

$$\Gamma \models_{sl} \varphi \text{ iff } \forall \mathcal{K}\ [\Gamma \subseteq sl(\mathcal{K}) \Rightarrow \varphi \in sl(\mathcal{K})]$$

Obviously, for a given vocabulary, for any class $\mathcal{K}$ of finite models and for any set of sentences Δ we say that $\mathcal{K} \models_{sl} \Delta$ if and only if $\mathcal{K} \models_{sl} \varphi$ for any $\varphi \in \Delta$.

It is worth noting that the notions employed in the description of the *sl*-semantics have some nice logical generalizations, worth of interest on their own:

Definition 10 (*sl*-entailment). *A set of sentences Δ sl-entails a formula φ ($\Delta \models_{sl} \varphi$) if and only if for any given class $\mathcal{K}$ of finite models we have:*

$$\text{if } \mathcal{K} \models_{sl} \Delta, \text{ then } \mathcal{K} \models_{sl} \varphi.$$

(Equivalently we could write: if $\Delta \subseteq sl(\mathcal{K})$, then $\varphi \in sl(\mathcal{K})$).

A set of sentences Δ sl-entails a set of sentences Γ if and only if $\forall\ \varphi \in \Gamma$, $\Delta \models_{sl} \varphi$.

Definition 11 (L_{sl}). *By $\boldsymbol{MOD}_\sigma$ we understand the class of all finite models of a given vocabulary σ. We may assume that all finite models are defined on the initial segments of $\mathbb{N}$ (each finite model is isomorphic to a model over the domain: $\{0, 1, ..., n-1\}$, for some n). For a fixed σ, the sl-logic of σ is defined as*

$$L_{sl} := sl(\mathbf{MOD}_\sigma)$$

Since here we'll consider only finite vocabularies, there will always be only countably many non-isomorphic models in $\mathbf{MOD}_\sigma$.

Let $\mathcal{K}$ be any class of (finite) models for σ, and let $Sent_\sigma$ denote the class of all sentences over the vocabulary σ. By the theory of the class $\mathcal{K}$ ($th(\mathcal{K})$) we understand the set of all sentences of σ true in all elements of $\mathcal{K}$:

$$th(\mathcal{K}) := \{\varphi \in Sent_\sigma : \ \forall \mathbb{A} \in \mathcal{K}\ \mathbb{A} \models \varphi\}$$

The logic of finite models is defined as $L_{fin} := th(\mathbf{MOD}_\sigma)$.

Let A_{inf} denote the family of sentences $\{\varphi_n : n \geq 2\}$, where φ_n is the following:

$$\exists x_1 \exists x_2 \ldots \exists x_n \bigwedge_{1 \leq i \neq j \leq n} x_i \neq x_j.$$

That is, φ_n says that there are at least n objects, and A_{inf} jointly says that for any finite n, at least n objects exist.

To describe some of the logical and computational properties of the *sl*-theories, we'll need a couple of notions, capturing the natural axiomatizations of the *sl*-logic.

Let $A_{sl} = L_{fin} \cup A_{inf}$ (that is: take together all sentences true in all finite models, and add the claim that for any n there are at least n objects). Then we have the following (all due to [11]).

Theorem 2. *The following hold:*

1. *L_{sl} is the set of all first-order consequences of A_{sl}.*
2. *A_{sl} is Π^0_1-complete.*
3. *L_{sl} is Σ^0_2-complete.*
4. *Completeness: For any set of σ-sentences T containing A_{sl} and any σ-sentence φ we have:*

$$\mathrm{T} \vdash \varphi \Leftrightarrow \mathrm{T} \models_{sl} \varphi.$$

The intuition here is that A_{sl} is a set of claims that are true *in the limit* in potentially infinite domains. It turns out that A_{sl} first-order axiomatizes the sl-logic, and can be used to capture sl-consequences of any theory by means of standard first-order derivability.

3.3 Yablo Sequences Under *sl*-Semantics

We consider the language obtained by adjoining the truth predicate Tr to the arithmetical language $\mathcal{L}$ and we modify $(FM(\mathbb{N}))$ by adding to its every element $\mathbb{N}_k$ an interpretation T_k of the truth predicate Tr.

Definition 12. **($FM(\mathbb{N})^T$).** *Let $\mathcal{K} = \{(\mathbb{N}_k, T_k) : k \in \omega$ and $T_k \subseteq \{0, ..., k-1\}\}$. An $FM(\mathbb{N})^T$-domain is any subset of $\mathcal{K}$ such that for any natural m it contains exactly one model of the cardinality m.*

We obviously have to ensure that Yablo sentences exist in $sl((FM(\mathbb{N})^T))$. For this, we need to state some important facts concerning the sl-theory of FM-domains, leaving them without a proof. Further details may be found in [9–12].

Theorem 3. **(Representability of substitution and naming).** *There exist formulas*

Sub(x, y, z) *and* ***Name***(x) *such that for any $FM(\mathbb{N})^T$-domain the following hold:*

- *$FM(\mathbb{N})^T \models_{sl}$ **Sub**$(\ulcorner\varphi(x)\urcorner, \ulcorner x\urcorner, \ulcorner t\urcorner) = \ulcorner\varphi(t)\urcorner$ for any formula φ and any term t.*
- *$FM(\mathbb{N})^T \models_{sl}$ **Name**$(n) = \ulcorner\overline{n}\urcorner$ for any natural number n.*

From the existence of the formulas **Sub**(x, y, z) and **Name**(x) we get:

Theorem 4. **(FM Diagonal Lemma).** *The following hold for any $FM(\mathbb{N})^T$:*

- *For any $\mathcal{L}_{Tr}$-formula $\varphi(x)$ with exactly one free variable there is an $\mathcal{L}_{Tr}$-sentence ψ such that $FM(\mathbb{N})^T \models_{sl} \psi \equiv \varphi(\ulcorner\psi\urcorner)$.*
- *For any $\mathcal{L}_{Tr}$-formula $\varphi(x, y)$ with exactly two free variables there is an $\mathcal{L}_{Tr}$-formula $\psi(x)$ such that $FM(\mathbb{N})^T \models_{sl} \psi(x) \equiv \varphi(x, \ulcorner\psi(x)\urcorner)$.*

Theorem 5. (FM-Undefinability of Truth). *There is no arithmetical formula $\psi(x)$ such that for all arithmetical sentences φ:*

$$FM(\mathbb{N}) \models_{sl} \psi(\ulcorner\varphi\urcorner) \equiv \varphi.$$

Corollary 1 (Existence of Yablo sentences in $FM(\mathbb{N})^T$-domains). *There exists a formula $Y(x)$ such that for any $FM(\mathbb{N})^T$-domain we have:*

$$\forall n \in \omega\ FM(\mathbb{N})^T \models_{sl} Y(n) \equiv \forall x\,(x > n \rightarrow \neg Tr(\ulcorner Y(\dot{x})\urcorner)),$$

i.e. Yablo sentences exist in $sl(FM(\mathbb{N})^T)$.

Proof. Obvious by the fact that the diagonal lemma is sl-true in $FM(\mathbb{N})^T$.

Theorem 6 (Yablo sentences are false in the limit, [3]). *For any class $\mathcal{K}$ of finite models, if $\mathcal{K} \models_{sl}$ $\mathtt{AD} + \mathtt{YD}$, then for all $n \in \omega$ $\mathcal{K} \models_{sl} \neg Y(n)$. In fact,* AD *isn't essential (it's only added to ensure Tr behaves like a truth predicate): for any $n \in \omega$ we have* $\mathtt{YD} \models_{sl} \neg Y(n)$.

We will now show a construction of a class $\mathcal{K}$ such that $\mathcal{K} \models_{sl} \mathtt{YD} + \mathtt{AD}$, which means that Theorem 6 holds non-vacuously. It turns out that $FM(\mathbb{N})^Y$ is such a class.

Definition 13 *($FM(\mathbb{N})^Y$* **and** *$sl(FM(\mathbb{N})^Y)$). We fix a formula $Y(x)$ satisfying the condition specified in Corollary 1. A family of models $FM(\mathbb{N})^Y$ is an $FM(\mathbb{N})^T$-domain $\{\mathbb{N}^Y_k : k \in \omega\}$ such that $\mathbb{N}^Y_k = (\mathbb{N}_k, T_k)$, where $T_k = TA_k \cup TY_k$, and:*

$$TA_k = \{\ulcorner\varphi\urcorner :\ \varphi \in Sent_{\mathcal{L}} \text{ and } \mathbb{N}_k \models \varphi\} \cap |\mathbb{N}_k|$$
$$TY_k = \{\ulcorner Y(m)\urcorner :\ \ulcorner Y(m)\urcorner \in |\mathbb{N}_k| \wedge \ulcorner Y(m+1)\urcorner \notin |\mathbb{N}_k|\}.$$

If $|\mathcal{M}| = k$, we sometimes write $T_{\mathcal{M}}$ instead of T_k.
Naturally, $sl(FM(\mathbb{N})^Y) = \{\varphi :\ FM(\mathbb{N})^Y \models_{sl} \varphi\}$.

It is worth noting that the family $FM(\mathbb{N})^Y$ is not a proper potentially-infinite domain in the sense defined by [11], i.e. for any natural numbers $r < s$ $\mathbb{N}^Y_r$ is not a submodel of $\mathbb{N}^Y_s$, since the interpretation of the truth predicate Tr varies between subsequent models from the domain.

Observation 1. *For any class $\mathcal{K}$, if $\mathcal{K} \models_{sl}$* YD*, then for sufficiently large $\mathcal{M} \in \mathcal{K}$, there is exactly one $n \in \omega$ s.t. $\ulcorner Y(n)\urcorner \in T_{\mathcal{M}}$.*

Theorem 7. $\forall n \in \omega\ FM(\mathbb{N})^Y \models_{sl} \neg Y(n)$.

4 LTL_f and Potential Infinity over LTL_f

The syntax of LTL_f is identical to the syntax of LTL. The semantics of LTL_f is given in terms of LT_f-interpretations, i.e., interpretations over finite traces denoting a finite sequence of consecutive instants of time. LT_f-interpretations are represented here as finite words π over the alphabet of $\{0,1\}^V$, i.e., as alphabet we have all the possible propositional interpretations of the propositional symbols in V.

We use the following notation. We denote the length of a trace π as $|\pi|$. We denote the positions, i.e., instants, on the trace as $\pi(i)$ with $0 \leq i \leq \max$, where $\max = |\pi| - 1$ is the last element of the trace. We denote by $\pi[i,j]$ the segment (i.e., the subword) obtained from π starting from position i and terminating in positon j, $0 \leq i \leq j \leq \max$.

Definition 14 (Semantics of LTL_f). *A temporal (Kripke) structure for V is a finite sequence $\pi = (\eta_0, \eta_1, \eta_2, \ldots, \eta_{\max})$ of mappings $\eta_i : V \to \{0,1\}$ called states. The mapping η_0 is called initial state of π. Observe that states are just valuations in the classical logic sense. For π and $i \in \mathbb{N}$ we define $\pi, i \models \varphi$ (in another formalism denoted by $\pi_i(\varphi) = 1$), informally meaning the 'truth value of φ in the ith state of K' for every formula φ inductively as follows:*

1. $\pi, i \models v$ *iff* $\eta_i(v) = 1$ *for each* $v \in V$,
2. $\pi, i \models \neg\varphi$ *iff* $\pi, i \not\models \varphi$,
3. $\pi, i \models \varphi \to \psi$ *iff* $\pi, i \models \neg\varphi$ *or* $\pi, i \models \psi$,
4. $\pi, i \models \bigcirc\varphi$ *iff* $i < \max$ *and* $\pi, i+1 \models \varphi$,
5. $\pi, i \models \Diamond\varphi$ *iff there exists* $i \leq j \leq \max$ *s.t.* $\pi, j \models \varphi$.

We say that φ is valid in π if and only if it holds that $\pi, i \models \varphi$ for all $i < |\pi|$. A formula φ is locally satisfiable if there is a finite temporal structure π and a state $\imath < |\pi|$ such that $\pi, i \models \varphi$. A formula φ is satisfiable (simpliciter) if there is a temporal structure π such that φ is valid in π.

Notice that φ is valid in π if and only if it holds that $\pi, 0 \models \Box\varphi$, which means that if φ is valid in π, then $\Box\varphi$ is also valid in π.

It is also worth noting that by the semantics above, for each formula φ of the language $\mathcal{L}_{LTL}$ we have that for any trace π the following holds:

$$\pi, \max \models \neg \bigcirc \varphi,$$

but simultaneously

$$\pi, \max \not\models \bigcirc\neg\varphi,$$

which proves that the law of duality of *Next* of LTL does not hold universally for LTL_f, i.e., it is not a validity of the logic.

We now turn to considering the FM_{LT}-domains and their *sl*-semantics, i.e., the temporal-logic counterpart of the arithmetical FM-domains and their *sl*-semantics

Definition 15 (**FM_{LT}-domains**). *An FM_{LT}-domain is any infinite family Π of finite temporal Kripke structures such that for any positive natural number n, the family Π contains exactly one temporal Kripke structure π of length n.*

Definition 16 (**sl-semantics for FM_{LT}-domains**). *For a given FM_{LT}-domain Π and a given natural number i, we say that a given LTL formula φ is sl-true at i in Π iff there is a number $n \geq i$ such that for any finite temporal Kripke structure $\pi \in \Pi$, if $|\pi| \geq n$, then $\pi, i \models \varphi$, i.e., we define the sl-theory of Π at i as:*

$$sl(\Pi, i) = \{\varphi \in Sent_{LTL} : \exists n \geq i \, \forall \pi \in \Pi \ |\pi| \geq n \ \Rightarrow \ \pi, i \models \varphi\}.$$

With this definition at hand, we further define the sl-theory of a given FM_{LT}-domain as:

$$sl(\Pi) = \{\varphi \in Sent_{LTL} : \forall i \in \mathbb{N} \, \varphi \in sl(\Pi, i)\}.$$

i.e., as a collection of all LTL-sentences sl-true in every state i of the family Π.

If $\neg\varphi$ is sl-true in Π (or in Π at i), then we say that φ is sl-false in Π (or in Π at i).

Last, we say that a given LTL-formula is sl-valid in Π, if it is valid in sufficiently large finite temporal Kripke structures π in the domain Π.

Then, for a given LTL-formula φ, we say that it is is sl-satisfiable, if there exists an FM_{LT}-domain Π such that φ is sl-valid in Π.

Observe that the above definition of $sl(\Pi)$ is a very restrictive notion, as it requires φ to be sl-satisfied at every state of Π. We could relaxe the concept above by stipulatiing:

$$sl^*(\Pi) = \{\varphi \in Sent_{LTL} : \exists k \ \forall i \geq k \quad \varphi \in sl(\Pi, i)\}.$$

i.e., as a collection of all LTL-sentences sl-true in every **sufficiently large** state i of the family Π. This would obviously result in a different theory (i.e., a different collection of formulas), but the distinction will no matter for the results we preent below and is left as a field of a further work.

Finally, notice that if a fgiven formula φ is sl-valid in a fixed Π, then $\Box\varphi$ is also sl-valid in Π. Similarly, if φ is sl-satisfiable, then $\Box\varphi$ is also sl-satisfiable.

5 Yablo's Sentences in LTL_f and Sl-LTL_f

The Yablo sentences employ a very interesting feature in models of LTL_f, and allow us to recover the counterpart of the arithmetical result on non-paradoxicality of the Yablo sequence when considered under sl-semantics over FM-domains.

We now present a result that shall e interpreted as one stating that there is no Yablo Paradox in linear temporal logic over finite traces.

Theorem 8. *The formula*

$$\square(\varphi \leftrightarrow \bigcirc\square\neg\varphi)$$

is satisfiable in LTL_f

Proof. We demonstrate a stronger result, namely that for each natural number $n \geq 2$ there exists an LT_f- interpretation (i.e., a finite trace) of size n that satisfies the Yablo formula. Recall that $\max = n - 1$.

Let $n \geq 2$ be arbitrary natural number. Consider a finite trace π with $|\pi| = n$. Let φ be formula mentionted in the Yablo equivalence, i.e., defined as equivalent to $\bigcirc\square\neg\varphi$.

We define the valuation of φ in subsequent states of the trace π.

For each $i = 0 \ldots, n - 3$ (observe that if $n = 2$, then there are no such i's, but it does not result in any problems for the valuation) put:

$$\pi, i \models \neg\varphi.$$

For $i = n - 2 = \max - 1$ put:

$$\pi, i \models \varphi.$$

Finally, for $i = \max = n - 1$ define:

$$\pi, i \models \neg\varphi.$$

As it can be easily seen, it holds that

$$\pi, 0 \models \square(\varphi \leftrightarrow \bigcirc\square\neg\varphi).$$

This implies that

$$LTL_f \not\models \neg\square(\varphi \leftrightarrow \bigcirc\square\neg\varphi)$$

in contrast to the status of the formula in LTL.

Observe the valuation above is the only consistent one that can be defined on any given finite trace of size at least 2.

The proof allows us to demonstrate an interesting result concerning Yablo sentences in the sl-theory of LTL_f, namely that the Yablo sentences (formalized in the temporal language $\mathcal{L}_{LTL}$) are simply false in sufficiently large finite traces, or in other words, they are false in the limit:

Theorem 9. *Let φ be the Yablo formula, i.e.,. let $\varphi \leftrightarrow \bigcirc\square\neg\varphi$. Then for any FM_{LT}-domain Π such that Π $-sl$-satifies the Yablo equivalence $\varphi \leftrightarrow \bigcirc\square\neg\varphi$ it holds that: $\neg\varphi \in sl(\Pi)$.*

Proof. This is an immediate corollary of the necessary behavior of the Yablo formula φ in any finite trace π. The only state in which the Yablo formula can be valuated as true, is the $|\pi| - 2^{\text{nd}}$ one, i.e., one before the last one. Given any finite trace, the state that is one but the last one will stop being one but last one, just one step further in the sequnce of finite traces growin in their cardinality. Therefore, the Yablo formula has to become false, and in particular, will be always false in the first state of any given finite trace for $\mathcal{L}_{LTL}$.

We also obtain similar results concerning the avoidance of paradoxicality of other Yablo sentences in LTL_f.

Theorem 10. *The temporal Sometimes-Y-formula formula*

$$\Box(\varphi \leftrightarrow \bigcirc\Diamond\neg\varphi)$$

is satisfiable in LTL_f

Proof. We demonstrate a stronger result, namely that for each natural number $n \geq 2$ there exists an LT_f- interpretation (i.e., a finite trace) of size n that satisfies the Sometimes-Y formula. Recall that max $= n - 1$.

Let $n \geq 2$ be arbitrary natural number. Consider a finite trace π with $|\pi| = n$. Let φ be the Sometimes-Y-formula mentionted in the Yablo equivalence, i.e., defined as equivalent to $\bigcirc\Diamond\neg\varphi$.

We define the valuation of φ in subsequent states of the trace π.

For each $i = 0\ldots, n-2$ put:

$$K, i \models \varphi.$$

Finally, for $i = \max = n - 1$ define:

$$K, i \models \neg\varphi.$$

As it can be easily seen, it holds that

$$\pi, 0 \models \Box(\varphi \leftrightarrow \bigcirc\Diamond\neg\varphi).$$

This implies that

$$LTL_f \not\models \neg\Box(\varphi \leftrightarrow \bigcirc\Diamond\neg\varphi)$$

in contrast to the status of the formula in LTL.

It thus immediately follows that in contrast to the original Yablo formula (the Always-Y one), the Sometimes-Y formula is actually true in sufficiently large finite traces, or, in other words, it is true in the limit with respect to LTL_f, i.e., we have the following:

Theorem 11. *Let* φ *be the Sometimes-Y formula, i.e.,. let* $\varphi \leftrightarrow \bigcirc\Diamond\neg\varphi$. *Then for any* FM_{LT}*-domain* Π *such that* Π *–sl-satifies the Sometimes-Y equivalence* $\varphi \leftrightarrow \bigcirc\Diamond\neg\varphi$ *it holds that:* $\varphi \in sl(\Pi)$.

The valutaion constructed in the proof of satisfiability of the Sometimes-Y-formulas in LTL_f gives us also proofs of satisfiability of the Almost-Always-Y-formula and the Unboundedly-Often-Y-formula:

Theorem 12. *The temporal Almost-Always-Y-formula*

$$\Box(\varphi \leftrightarrow \bigcirc\Diamond\Box\neg\varphi)$$

is satisfiable in LTL_f

Finally, we have:

Theorem 13. *The temporal Unboundedly-Often-Y-formula*

$$\Box(\varphi \leftrightarrow \bigcirc\Box\Diamond\neg\varphi)$$

is satisfiable in LTL_f

In consequence, these formulas are also true in the limit, i.e., under the *sl*-semantics over LTL_f:

Theorem 14. *Let* φ *be the Almost-Always-Y-formula, i.e.,,* $\Box(\varphi \leftrightarrow \bigcirc\Diamond\Box\neg\varphi)$*. Then for any* FM_{LT}*-domain* Π *such that* Π *–sl-satifies the Almost-Always-Y equivalence* $\Box(\varphi \leftrightarrow \bigcirc\Diamond\Box\neg\varphi)$ *it holds that:* $\varphi \in sl(\Pi)$*.*

Theorem 15. *Let* φ *be the Unboundedly-Often-Y-formula, i.e.,* $\Box(\varphi \leftrightarrow \bigcirc\Box\Diamond\neg\varphi)$*. Then:* $\varphi \in sl(\Pi)$*, where* Π *is the class of all finite traces over the set of propositional variables* V*.*

Let φ *be the Unboundedly-Often-Y-formula, i.e.,* $\Box(\varphi \leftrightarrow \bigcirc\Box\Diamond\neg\varphi)$*. Then for any* FM_{LT}*-domain* Π *such that* Π *–sl-satifies the Unboundedly-Often-Y equivalence* $\Box(\varphi \leftrightarrow \bigcirc\Box\Diamond\neg\varphi)$ *it holds that:* $\varphi \in sl(\Pi)$*.*

6 Relevance of Potential Infinity and Yablo's Paradox for Multi-agent Systems

The adaptation of Yablo's Paradox into the LTL_f framework addresses an important conceptual challenge in multi-agent systems: modeling recursive and non-self-referential beliefs that agents hold about one another's beliefs and knowledge. In MAS, particularly those relying on epistemic game theory, agents frequently base their actions not only on personal knowledge but on assumptions about the beliefs and intentions of other agents. Yablo's Paradox, a non-self-referential yet paradoxical sequence, reveals fundamental issues in reasoning when agents attempt to model infinitely nested beliefs. As shown in the paper, these paradoxical properties are carried over into temporal logic, highlighting that certain belief structures can lead to inconsistencies even without explicit self-reference. This has practical implications for MAS, where agents' reasoning processes depend on assumptions that are indirectly influenced by the recursive beliefs of other agents.

By formalizing Yablo's Paradox within the LTL_f framework and introducing the concept of *truth in the limit* through *sl*-theories, we provide a mechanism to examine beliefs that are valid only within a finite progression of interactions. This aligns with the bounded nature of most MAS, where agents operate over finite temporal horizons rather than assuming infinite sequences. Furthermore, the *sl*-semantics and *FM*-domains introduced in this paper represent a theoretically grounded approach for handling potential infinity within finite models. In MAS, this enables the design of systems where agents can reason about potentially infinite sequences without encountering paradoxical inconsistencies. Specifically, this is achieved by modeling potential infinity as an infinite progression of finite states, which maintains consistency across finite iterations.

Furthermore, our contributions extend to applications where the MAS must rely on complex knowledge representation and multiagent coordination, where sl-Theories and FM-Domains can have high impact. In collaborative MAS settings, agents must often share and update their understanding of a dynamically changing environment. The sl-theories and FM-domains outlined in this paper provide a mathematical basis for agents to operate under assumptions of *truth in the limit*, which is essential for avoiding paradoxes and inconsistencies in environments where beliefs and states evolve incrementally over time. This finitistic approach is advantageous for MAS as it allows agents to reason over a progression of finite states without requiring the complexities associated with handling actual infinity.

Additionally, FM-domains and sl-semantics are highly applicable to scenarios in MAS where agents need to synchronize beliefs or states incrementally, such as in distributed consensus or coordinated pathfinding in multi-robot systems. The concept of truth in the limit enables these systems to avoid inconsistencies in recursive or layered belief models, thereby improving the reliability and robustness of MAS under finite operational timelines. By enabling agents to reason in finite domains that increase incrementally, this formalism helps establish coordination protocols that are both theoretically sound and computationally feasible, essential for applications in distributed artificial intelligence.

7 Conclusions

In this paper we have investigated the relation of temporal lgoics and properties of Yablo sentences, providing a framework for finitstic theory of potential infinity over temporal logic. We introduced the FM-domains over LTL_f, and define sl-theories over LTL_f, demonstrating a first notion of theories true in the limit over finite traces in temporal logic. Furthermore, also for the first time in the literature, we have performed the analysis of Yablo sentences (as formalized in temporal logic vocabulary) in LTL_f, i.e., the Linear Temporal Logic over finite traces. On top of that, as a litmus test for this novel theory, we analyzed how Yablo's paradox of LTL is solved not only in LTL_f, but also in the finitstic theory of potential infinity over temporal logic.

A non-strict finitist, not accepting the notion of actual infinity may adopt the sl-theory of arithmetics as an adequate explication of the concept of potential infinity and simply give an answer to the Yablo paradox that in the limit (i.e. under the sl-semantics on the FM-domain of given arithmetical model) all the Yablo sentences are false and there is no reason to be worried.

Similarly, within the realm of linear temporal logic, in applications where LTL_f is of relevance, the Yablo Paradox can be avoided for the same reasons.

A natural step of further work for the theory and framework developed here is to extend the analysis and the tools we have designed to apply the temporal logic on finite traces and its finitistic variant with sl-semantics to epistemic game theory, thus potentially extending the analysis provided in [5]. Another thread of further research would be to construct syntactic, i.e., proof-theoretic, counterparts of *sl*-theory over LTL_f.

Acknowledgments. This research has been supported by the PRIN project RIPER (No. 20203FFYLK), the PNRR MUR project PE0000013-FAIR, and the InDAM 2023 project *Strategic Reasoning in Mechanism Design.*

References

1. Clarke, E.M., Grumberg, O., Peled, D.A.: Model Checking. The MIT Press, Cambridge, Massachusetts (1999)
2. Giacomo, G.D., Vardi, M.Y.: Linear temporal logic and linear dynamic logic on finite traces. In: Rossi, F. (ed.) IJCAI 2013, Proceedings of the 23rd International Joint Conference on Artificial Intelligence, Beijing, China, August 3-9, 2013. pp. 854–860. IJCAI/AAAI (2013), http://www.aaai.org/ocs/index.php/IJCAI/IJCAI13/paper/view/6997
3. Godziszewski, M.T.: Yablo sequences in potentially infinite domains and partial semantics (2020)
4. Godziszewski, M.T., Urbaniak, R.: Modal quantifiers, potential infinity, and yablo sequences. The Review of Symbolic Logic p. 1-30 (2022). https://doi.org/10.1017/S1755020322000119
5. Karimi, A.: A non-self-referential paradox in epistemic game theory. Reports on Mathematical Logic **52**, 45–56 (2017). https://doi.org/10.4467/20842589RM.17.002.7140
6. Karimi, A.: Syntactic proofs for yablo's paradoxes in temporal logic. Logic and Logical Philosophy **28**(4), 753-765 (Jun 2019).https://doi.org/10.12775/LLP.2019.020, https://apcz.umk.pl/LLP/article/view/LLP.2019.020
7. Karimi, A., Salehi, S.: Theoremizing yablo's paradox (2014)
8. Ketland, J.: Yablo's paradox and ω-inconsistency. Synthese **145** (2005)
9. Mostowski, M.: On representing concepts in finite models. Math. Log. Q. **47**, 513–523 (2001)
10. Mostowski, M.: On representing semantics in finite models. In: Rojszczak, A., Cachro, J., Kurczewsk, G. (eds.) Philosophical Dimensions of Logic and Science, pp. 15–28. Kluwer Academic Publishers, Dordrecht (2001)
11. Mostowski, M.: Truth in the limit. Reports on Mathematical Logic **51**, 75–89 (2016)
12. Mostowski, M., Zdanowski, K.: Fm-representability and beyond. Springer-Verlag, Berlin (2005)
13. Pnueli, A.: The temporal logic of programs. In: 18th Annual Symposium on Foundations of Computer Science, Providence, Rhode Island, USA, 31 October - 1 November 1977. pp. 46–57. IEEE Computer Society (1977).https://doi.org/10.1109/SFCS.1977.32
14. Yablo, S.: Paradox without self-reference. Analysis **53** (1993)

ATL for Dynamic Gaming Environments

Marco Aruta(✉), Aniello Murano, and Salvatore Romano

University of Naples Federico II, Naples, Italy
marco.aruta3@gmail.com

Abstract. The integration of AI has become increasingly important in the gaming industry. However, it faces limitations when dealing with dynamic environments and unpredictable players. As a solution, in this paper we introduce a novel gaming framework that makes use of ATL, a powerful logic for formal strategic reasoning. ATL seamlessly aligns with Multi-Agent Systems, effectively mirroring the decision-making process of Non-Player Characters. With its key advantage of being built on Concurrent Game Structures and employing temporal operators, ATL efficiently models game state sequences. This paper introduces a groundbreaking in-engine, real-time AI method using ATL directly within Unreal Engine 5 blueprints, eliminating the need for external tools.

1 Introduction

Artificial intelligence (AI) has emerged as a transformative force in the video game industry, yet its potential remains largely untapped. Although AI techniques have evolved from traditional approaches to more sophisticated methods such as dynamic scripting [28], reinforcement learning [4], and behavioral cloning [24], the industry continues to grapple with the limitations of current AI implementations, particularly in adapting to dynamic environments and player actions. Many video games still rely on simplistic and predictable AI behaviors that do not provide a truly immersive and engaging experience. Non-player characters (NPCs) often exhibit repetitive patterns and struggle to adapt to changing circumstances. This can lead to frustration and boredom for players, ultimately detracting from the overall enjoyment of the game. In addition, commercial AI implementations often prioritize efficiency and cost-effectiveness over quality and realism. This can result in AI systems that are overly simplistic, lacking the depth and complexity required to create truly believable and intelligent NPCs. As a consequence, players may find themselves facing predictable and easily exploitable AI opponents.

In recent years, *formal methods* have emerged as a useful approach to designing, verifying, and analyzing AI systems. Logics for strategic reasoning, particularly when used in conjunction with Multi-Agent Systems (MAS) [3,5–7,21,23,31], provide powerful tools for representing knowledge and reasoning about complex interactions between autonomous agents. A prominent example in this area is *Alternating-time Temporal Logic* (ATL) [1], a notable framework

R. Collier et al. (Eds.): EUMAS 2024, LNAI 15685, pp. 129–137, 2025.
https://doi.org/10.1007/978-3-031-93930-3_8

within Symbolic AI. ATL enables the modeling and analysis of intricate agent interactions, allowing for the formal verification, by means of *model checking* [10], of both cooperative and competitive scenarios. Despite the natural applicability of ATL to dynamic environments, the potential of this logic (and the like) has never been explored in real-time video games.

Our Contribution. In this paper we introduce a novel in-engine AI solution built by using an ATL model checking framework. What sets this approach apart is its unique combination of ATL model checking and in-engine implementation. While other AI solutions have never explored ATL for game development in practice, this paper presents a pioneering integration directly within the game engine "Unreal Engine 5". This eliminates the overhead of external tools and streamlines the development process, making it more accessible and efficient for game developers. The key lies in ATL's Concurrent Game Structure (CGS), which allows for natural modelling of video game environments and temporal reasoning. This translates into faster development and more complex AI behaviours thanks to Blueprints' visual scripting: enables the construction of intricate logic without traditional coding. Actions represent high-level goals rather than specific movement paths, further contributing to efficient processing. A pre-evaluated transition matrix facilitates rapid evaluation of state changes based on actions. This approach unlocks the potential for real-time adaptation of non-player characters (NPCs) to player actions and the environment, ensuring engaging and dynamic gameplay. The model checker allows the synthesis of optimal NPC strategies across various scenarios, leading to a more strategic and immersive experience. This solution is not limited to a single genre; it is suitable for real-time strategy games, first-person shooters, and various genres requiring intelligent NPC decision-making in which are distinguishable groups of goal states. This innovative ATL model checking solution empowers the creation of intelligent and adaptable AI agents, thereby enhancing the gameplay experience.

Related Work. Formal logic applied to video games have been investigated in the literature, but the studies have primarily focused on external tools and offline verification processes [14,26,30]. In contrast, [8] and [19] investigate the use of formal methods in *real-time* applications by implementing a game engine through the representation and reasoning of MAS, but without directly employing formal logics. In [18], Lora et al. presented a novel implementation of Tetris, in which each piece is represented as an agent. This work has been further extended in more complex MAS scenarios such as Real-Time Strategy games employing potential fields [13]. Optimal control strategies have been achieved in various studies through the use of reinforcement learning for distributed control protocols in leader-follower MAS [22]. In [27] the authors have focused on persistent monitoring using a network of mobile agents, with the aim of eliminating uncertainty across all targets and ensuring comprehensive coverage of the mission domain. Extended work in this field has been also analyzed in [11,15,20,25,29]. The coordination of agents has also been a significant area of MAS research.

Kapetanakis et al. showed that an agent trained in Q-learning can collaborate with an agent trained with FMQ to converge towards optimal joint action [16].

Outline. The sequel of the paper is organized as follows. Section 2 briefly recalls syntax and semantics of ATL. Section 3 presents the implementation of our tool. Section 4 evaluates its performance by means of experiments. Finally, we conclude in Sect. 5.

2 Alternating-Time Temporal Logic

In this section we briefly recall Alternating-Time Temporal Logic (ATL). An interested reader can refer to [1]. ATL formulas are evaluated over Concurrent Game Structures, which are labeled graphs representing the agents' behaviors within the system. The subsequent section presents a formal definition.

Concurrent Game Structure (CGS). A CGS consists of a tuple $S = \langle Agt, Q, \Pi, \pi, d, \delta \rangle$ where: (i) $Agt \geq 1$ is a natural number indicating the number of players. (ii) Q is a finite set of states. (iii) Π is finite set of propositions. (iv) π is a labelling function such that for each state q, $\pi(q) \subseteq \Pi$ is a set of true propositions at q. (v) $d_a(q) \geq 1$ indicates for each player a and each state q, the number of actions available in the state q for the player a. A *move vector* at q consist of a tuple $\langle j_1, \ldots, j_{Agt} \rangle$ such that $1 \leq j_a \leq d_a(q)$ for each player a. (vi) δ is a transition function that for each state q and each move vector, returns a state that results from q if each player a chooses the move in the vector. We now present the precise syntax of ATL.

Alternating-Time Temporal Logic (ATL). ATL [1,17] is a powerful logic specifically designed for reasoning about MAS. It considers situations where multiple agents, each with their own goals and capabilities, can take actions concurrently.

An ATL formula φ can be expressed using the syntax:

$$\varphi := p \mid \neg\varphi \mid \varphi_1 \wedge \varphi_2 \mid \langle\langle A \rangle\rangle X\varphi \mid \langle\langle A \rangle\rangle G\varphi \mid \langle\langle A \rangle\rangle \varphi_1 U \varphi_2$$

where p is an atomic proposition, $\neg$ and $\wedge$ stand for the usual negation and conjunction, and X, G and U are temporal operators standing for "*next*", "*globally*" and "*until*", respectively. The $\langle\langle A \rangle\rangle$ operator in $\langle\langle A \rangle\rangle\varphi$ represents the capability of a set of agent A of enforcing states where φ holds true. Before defining Semantics we need to introduce some basic concepts, i.e. strategies, plays and outcomes.

Strategy. In a game's context, *plays* encompass the strategic choices or moves that participants can make, fundamentally influencing the progression of the game's state. For a CGS S and its players, a player's strategy is a rule assigning a play to every finite prefix of a state's sequence, termed a *computation* of S, which is an unbounded series $\lambda = q_0, q_1, q_2, \ldots$ of states where each state q_{i+1} directly follows q_i. For a state $q \in Q$, a player group A, and a strategy set F_A including one strategy per player in A, the *outcomes* of F_A from q, denoted as $out(q, F_A)$, refers to the series of computations resultant from players in A applying the strategies in F_A.

Semantics. ATL is an extension of Computational Tree Logic (CTL) by means of strategic operators. So, the semantics of temporal operators follows that of CTL, and to get the full semantics of ATL we just need to add the interpretation of the strategic operators. To illustrate this part, as an example, consider an ATL formula of the form $\langle\langle A\rangle\rangle X\varphi$ in a state q of S. To evaluate this formula we need to check for the existence of a set of strategies F_A such that for all computations λ in $out(q, F_A)$, we have $\lambda[1] \models \varphi$ with $\lambda[1]$ indicating the immediate successor state of q. For a detailed definition of the semantics of ATL, the reader can refer to [1].

3 Implementation

This part offers a comprehensive analysis of how the system is implemented using the Unreal Engine framework. It explores the system's interactions with the game environment, NPCs and player, thoroughly detailing the processes that govern these interactions as well as the development methodologies used.

Blueprint Visual Scripting. BP empowers designers and artists to create game logic, animations, and interactions visually using connected nodes (actions, functions,...). This simplifies development, allowing rapid prototyping and complex logic without coding.

Game Introduction. The testbed video game, available for exploration and experimentation within the linked GitHub[1] repository, takes place in a labyrinth with two randomized escape doors. Player, in the "Chasers" team, cooperates with an NPC teammate to close both doors before an enemy NPC - the "Escapist" - escapes. AI agents on both sides have complete knowledge of the environment (layout, door/player locations) while player does not. This asymmetry creates a strategic challenge for the player who rely on real-time recommendations from its NPC teammate, guided by the internal model checking algorithm to choose its decisions and those of the player.

Game Environment Formalization. In order to perform ATL model checking, the game environment has been abstracted and simplified by focusing on its most essential aspects through the use of state representation. Each state is costituted by 8 boolean variables. Three variables describe the Chaser Team, indicating the closest entity to the door and a flag of proximity for both doors. Three describe the Escapist Team, indicating the target door, the enemy proximity and its escape status, while one variable is used for

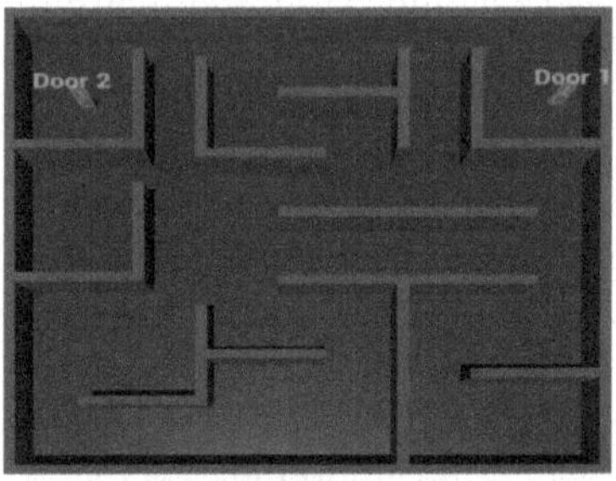

Fig. 1. Labyrinth Map with two randomly spawned Doors.

[1] https://github.com/Salvthor/LabyrinthATL.

each door for its open or closed status. This abstraction resulted in 160 distinct states. The game employed 9 different actions in two categories: Movement (Idle, GoToDoor, CloserToDoor) which are used to navigate towards a door, and Interaction (CloseDoor, Escape) to perform door related actions. Each door is associated with its own action (GoToDoor1/2), doubling the total number of actions. To efficiently evaluate the transition function, which determines how states change based on actions, a weighted graph was implemented. To handle the matrix complexity the model was divided into four submatrices, each comprising 40 states, that were categorized based on the entity (player or agent) closest to the target door and whether the target door was the first or second one. This resulted in a total of 14,400 transitions. Dividing the model into submatrices, omits certain transitions, but it has a minimal impact on the model's accuracy, given that there is no particular action to be taken specifically when the destination door changes for both the player and the agent. Each distinct combination of agent actions was encoded as an integer value. This approach reduced the required number of cells to 6,400, without altering the matrix size regardless of the number of agents.

Witnessed Model Checking. To expedite the model checking process, propositional formulas are initially parsed into binary trees with internal nodes - with logical and temporal connectives - and leaves - incorporating atomic propositions - with each node storing states where the proposition is true, optimizing runtime checks. The algorithm leverages this tree structure to identify states that satisfy the entire formula along with the corresponding strategies leading to those states. The algorithm traverses the tree in a left-to-right manner; upon reaching a leaf node, it retrieves the connective within its parent node and performs operations based on its type inserting the satisfying states within the current node. This process is iterated for all nodes in the tree, culminating with the set of states satisfying the entire formula being stored within the root node.

Formula Analysis. Consider the following ATL formula example: $\langle\langle A\rangle\rangle$ G $Door1$ $Closed$ This formula expresses the goal of the *coalition A* to ensure that *Door 1* is and remains closed in all future states of the game starting from a current state s. To achieve this goal, the algorithm must find a sequence of actions, or a *strategy*, that will successfully guide the game state to a state where the formula is satisfied.

AI Integration. The AI controller of NPCs integrates the model checker for the making of decisions in real-time decision-making. To optimize performance, the system first checks if the formula has already been parsed into a binary tree. For new formulas, the algorithm follows the previously described steps and stores both strategies and satisfying states within a cache structure, that is consulted whenever the formula results are needed during gameplay iterations. To prevent a lack of strategy during the game loop, the system employs a Prioritized Formula Queue. This queue holds propositional formulas representing desirable states for the team, ordered by their importance. The most critical formulas are evaluated first: if a high-priority formula cannot be satisfied, meaning there is no strategy from the current state to enforce it, the system moves on to the next formula in the queue. The first satisfied formula determines the chosen strategy and actions for each agent, following the principles of best-effort strategies synthesis [2]. This iterative evaluation process is crucial because player choices can dynamically change the game state. This might make a previously unsatisfied critical formula achievable, triggering a new strategy selection based on the updated formula priority and the current game state.

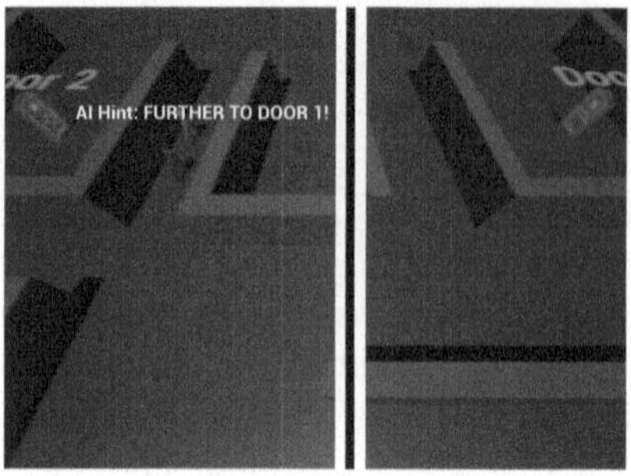

Fig. 2. On the left the NPC (cyan) reach the Door2 before the opponent (red) escapes, while giving hint to Player in blue, on the right. (Color figure online)

4 Experiments

We have performed extensive tests for the proposed game framework on a computer running Windows 11 with 16GB of RAM, an Intel Core i5 9600k CPU, and an Nvidia 2060 Super GPU with 8GB of GDDR6 VRAM. Unreal Engine 5.3 served as the development platform, utilizing its Blueprint visual scripting tool (based on C++). A Python function was used to generate complex scenarios where any state can transition to any other, unlike real video games with invalid transitions limiting the matrix analysis. The testing focused on two main areas: scalability and impact of agent capabilities. Three agents (two allies and one enemy) and transition matrices of varying sizes (10, 100 and 250 states) were employed. The experiments investigated how different agent capabilities, defined by varying the number of actions per agent (2, 3, and 5), influenced the model checker performances while maintaining constant formula complexity (10 propositions), since prior studies indicated that formula length did not impact model checker performance. To ensure consistency, five randomly generated models per transition matrix complexity level underwent 500 test runs. The results in Fig. 3 show the efficiency of the algorithm in handling larger transition matrices even with more complex formulas. This emphasis on scalability reflects the critical role of performance in video games, where efficient algorithms are essential for smooth gameplay. Although with larger models with a transition graph consisting of 312,500 elements, the model checker experienced a performance bottleneck, this issue is not particularly problematic.

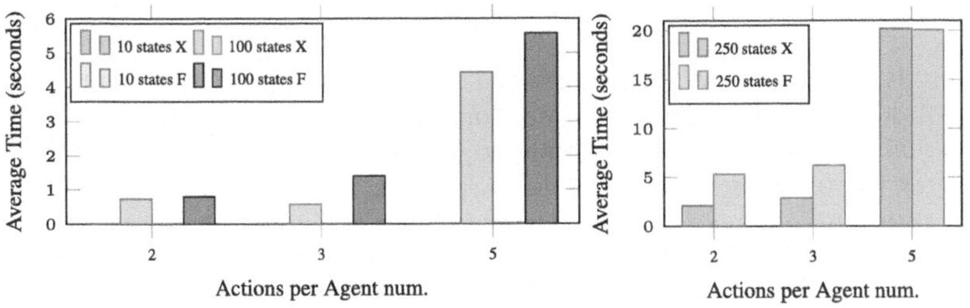

Fig. 3. Model checking response times with: 3 agents, formula with 10 atomic proposition with varying agents capabilities.

In facts, real-time game model analysis, facilitated by swift execution times, is undoubtedly an accomplishment, however, such instantaneous feedback is not essential for this application. Model checking can be performed offline with the outcomes stored for later use in real-time scenarios. Thus, the simplicity of the model does not undermine the reliability of the model checker because its verification can occur during the game loading phase. The specific game model can then be bypassed, allowing tests to be run on randomly generated, highly complex models. The main goal was to demonstrate the practical feasibility of ATL model checking using a simplified model, a significant contribution given the limited number of ATL real-world in-game implementations.

5 Conclusions

This work demonstrates the feasibility and scalability of applying ATL model checking in video games, particularly for NPCs that require high responsiveness. The model checker provides an effective method for adapting to the player's gameplay style, ensuring that NPCs can intelligently complete tasks while continuously adapting to the environment, leading to an engaging and responsive experience. Our tool can be applied to real-time strategy games and macro-decisions in first-person shooters such as deciding what action to take between shoot, go to cover, throw a grenade or heal, etc. In future work, reinforcement learning could automate transition matrix population, simplifying invalid transition identification and potentially increasing commercial adoption of the approach through the addition of other temporal or strategic logics that more closely represent the game model. Additionally, developing extensions for existing model checkers like VITAMIN [12] and NuSMV [9] could enable performance comparisons to identify the most efficient tool.

Acknowledgements. This research has been supported by the PRIN project RIPER (No. 20203FFYLK), the PNRR MUR project PE0000013-FAIR, and the InDAM 2023 project "Strategic Reasoning in Mechanism Design".

References

1. Alur, R., Henzinger, T.A., Kupferman, O.: Alternating-time temporal logic. J. ACM **49**(5), 672-713 (2002). https://doi.org/10.1145/585265.585270
2. Aminof, B., De Giacomo, G., Lomuscio, A., Murano, A., Rubin, S.: Synthesizing best-effort strategies under multiple environment specifications. In: Proceedings of the 18th International Conference on Principles of Knowledge Representation and Reasoning, pp. 42–51, November 2021. https://doi.org/10.24963/kr.2021/5
3. Aminof, B., Murano, A., Rubin, S., Zuleger, F.: Verification of agent navigation in partially-known environments. Artif. Intell. **308**, 103724 (2022)
4. Barriga, N.A., Stanescu, M., Besoain, F., Buro, M.: Improving rts game AI by supervised policy learning, tactical search, and deep reinforcement learning. IEEE Comput. Intell. Mag. **14**(3), 8–18 (2019). https://doi.org/10.1109/MCI.2019.2919363
5. Belardinelli, F., Jamroga, W., Kurpiewski, D., Malvone, V., Murano, A.: Strategy logic with simple goals: tractable reasoning about strategies. In: Kraus, S. (ed.) Proceedings of the Twenty-Eighth International Joint Conference on Artificial Intelligence, IJCAI 2019, Macao, China, 10–16 August 2019, pp. 88–94. ijcai.org (2019)
6. Berthon, R., Maubert, B., Murano, A., Rubin, S., Vardi, M.Y.: Strategy logic with imperfect information. ACM Trans. Comput. Log. **22**(1), 5:1–5:51 (2021)
7. Bozzelli, L., Murano, A., Sorrentino, L.: Alternating-time temporal logics with linear past. Theor. Comput. Sci. **813**, 199–217 (2020)
8. Chover, M., Marín, C., Rebollo, C., Remolar, I.: A game engine designed to simplify 2d video game development. Multimedia Tools Appl. **79**, 12307–12328 (2020)
9. Cimatti, A., Clarke, E., Giunchiglia, F., Roveri, M.: Nusmv: a new symbolic model checker. STTT **2**, 410–425 (2000). https://doi.org/10.1007/s100090050046
10. Clarke, E.M.: Model checking. In: Ramesh, S., Sivakumar, G. (eds.) FSTTCS 1997. LNCS, vol. 1346, pp. 54–56. Springer, Heidelberg (1997). https://doi.org/10.1007/BFb0058022
11. Farina, G., Gatti, N.: Extensive-form perfect equilibrium computation in two-player games. In: Proceedings of the AAAI Conference on Artificial Intelligence, vol. 31 (2017)
12. Ferrando, A., Malvone, V.: Vitamin: a compositional framework for model checking of multi-agent systems (2024)
13. Hagelbäck, J., Johansson, S.J., et al.: A multiagent potential field-based bot for real-time strategy games. Int. J. Comput. Games Tech. **2009** (2009)
14. Igawa, N., Yokogawa, T., Takahashi, M., Arimoto, K.: Model checking of visual scripts created by ue4 blueprints. In: 2020 9th International Congress on Advanced Applied Informatics (IIAI-AAI), pp. 512–515 (2020). https://doi.org/10.1109/IIAI-AAI50415.2020.00107
15. Jia, Z., Yang, L.F., Wang, M.: Feature-based q-learning for two-player stochastic games (2019). https://arxiv.org/abs/1906.00423

16. Kapetanakis, S., Kudenko, D.: Reinforcement learning of coordination in heterogeneous cooperative multi-agent systems. In: Symposium on Adaptive Agents and Multi-agent Systems, pp. 119–131. Springer (2003)
17. Laroussinie, F., Markey, N., Oreiby, G.: On the expressiveness and complexity of ATL. CoRR **abs/0804.2435** (2008), http://arxiv.org/abs/0804.2435
18. Marín-Lora, C., Chover, M., Sotoca, J.M.: A multi-agent specification for the tetris game. In: Distributed Computing and Artificial Intelligence, Volume 1: 18th International Conference 18, pp. 169–178. Springer (2022)
19. Marín-Lora, C., Cercós, A., Chover, M., Sotoca, J.M.: A first step to specify arcade games as multi-agent systems. In: Rocha, Á., Adeli, H., Reis, L.P., Costanzo, S., Orovic, I., Moreira, F. (eds.) WorldCIST 2020. AISC, vol. 1159, pp. 369–379. Springer, Cham (2020). https://doi.org/10.1007/978-3-030-45688-7_38
20. Mazouchi, M., Naghibi-Sistani, M.B., Sani, S.: A novel distributed optimal adaptive control algorithm for nonlinear multi-agent differential graphical games. IEEE/CAA J. Automatica Sinica **5**(1), 331–341 (2017)
21. Mogavero, F., Murano, A., Perelli, G., Vardi, M.Y.: Reasoning about strategies: on the model-checking problem. ACM Trans. Comput. Log. **15**(4), 34:1–34:47 (2014)
22. Moghadam, R., Modares, H.: Resilient adaptive optimal control of distributed multi-agent systems using reinforcement learning. IET Control Theor. Appl. **12**(16), 2165–2174 (2018)
23. Parasumanna Gokulan, B., Srinivasan, D.: An introduction to multi-agent systems, vol. 310, pp. 1–27, July 2010. https://doi.org/10.1007/978-3-642-14435-6_1
24. Pearce, T., Zhu, J.: Counter-strike deathmatch with large-scale behavioural cloning (2021)
25. Qiu, S., Li, Z., Pang, Z., Li, Z., Tao, Y.: Multi-agent optimal control for central chiller plants using reinforcement learning and game theory. Systems **11**(3), 136 (2023)
26. Rezin, R., Afanasyev, I., Mazzara, M., Rivera, V.: Model checking in multiplayer games development. In: 2018 IEEE 32nd International Conference on Advanced Information Networking and Applications (AINA), pp. 826–833 (2018). https://doi.org/10.1109/AINA.2018.00122
27. Song, C., Liu, L., Feng, G., Xu, S.: Optimal control for multi-agent persistent monitoring. Automatica **50**(6), 1663–1668 (2014)
28. Spronck, P., Ponsen, M., Sprinkhuizen-Kuyper, I., Postma, E.: Adaptive game AI with dynamic scripting. Mach. Learn. **63**, 217–248 (2006)
29. Urbano, A., Vila, J.E.: Computational complexity and communication: coordination in two-player games. Econometrica **70**(5), 1893–1927 (2002)
30. Wayama, K., Yokogawa, T., Amasaki, S., Aman, H., Arimoto, K.: Verifying game logic in unreal engine 5 blueprint visual scripting system using model checking. In: Proceedings of the 37th IEEE/ACM International Conference on Automated Software Engineering. ASE 2022, Association for Computing Machinery, New York, NY, USA (2023). https://doi.org/10.1145/3551349.3560505
31. Wooldridge, M.: An introduction to multiagent systems. Wiley (2009)

Responsibility in a Multi-value Strategic Setting

Timothy Parker(✉), Umberto Grandi, and Emiliano Lorini

IRIT, CNRS, University of Toulouse, Toulouse, France
{timothy.parker,umberto.grandi,emiliano.lorini}@irit.fr

Abstract. Responsibility is a key notion in multi-agent systems and in creating safe, reliable and ethical AI. In particular, the evaluation of choices based on responsibility is useful for making robustly good decisions in unpredictable domains. However, most previous work on responsibility has only considered responsibility for single outcomes, limiting its application. In this paper we present a model for responsibility attribution in a multi-agent, multi-value setting. We also expand our model to cover responsibility anticipation, demonstrating how considerations of responsibility can help an agent to select strategies that are in line with its values. In particular we show that non-dominated regret-minimising strategies reliably minimise an agent's expected degree of responsibility.

Keywords: Responsibility · Multi-Agent Systems · Linear Temporal Logic · Strategy Comparison

1 Introduction

Responsibility attribution [2,3,10,17] is the process of determining which agent or set of agents can be held responsible for a particular outcome. This is a backward-looking process, meaning that while it is useful for allocating praise or blame, it cannot be used for strategy selection, since responsibility for an outcome can only be determined once the outcome has occurred. Responsibility anticipation [26] is the process of predicting which outcomes an agent *may* be responsible for if it performs a particular strategy. This means it can be used in strategy selection, i,e to ensure that an agent cannot be responsible for some negative outcome. In particular, considerations of responsibility are particularly useful in settings where the satisfaction of some crucial value cannot always be guaranteed, since by minimising its anticipated responsibility for the violation of a value, an agent can ensure that it maximises its causal contribution towards the satisfaction of the value (since if the agent could have done more to try and satisfy the value, then it would anticipate responsibility for the value's violation).

However, current methods for responsibility anticipation only consider responsibility for single outcomes or values. In a real-world setting, it is likely that an agent will have to consider multiple, possibly conflicting values. Therefore we wish to investigate how notions of responsibility can be expanded to work

R. Collier et al. (Eds.): EUMAS 2024, LNAI 15685, pp. 138–158, 2025.
https://doi.org/10.1007/978-3-031-93930-3_9

in a multi-value setting, to widen the scope for the application of responsibility-based evaluation in various settings.

In this paper we present and discuss various properties that are appealing for multi-value notions of responsibility. Of particular interest is the idea that an agent may be able to avoid responsibility in some cases by providing an "excuse" justifying their choice of a specific strategy. We will introduce two separate definitions of responsibility, one simple notion of passive responsibility and a more complex notion (inexcusable passive responsibility) that considers the excuses that the agent might have. The main result of our paper is that these notions of responsibility are all equivalent in anticipation to some combination of non-dominated and regret-minimising strategies (for which we introduce a symbolic notion of regret in this paper). In particular, strategies that minimise both forms responsibility are exactly the strategies that are both non-dominated and regret-minimising.

The rest of the paper is organised as follows, Sect. 2 locates our paper in its field and compares our work with some related approaches from the literature. Section 3 introduces our formal model and Sect. 4 defines our notions of responsibility. Section 5 formalises our notion of symbolic regret, and considers the perspective of anticipation. Finally, Sect. 6 concludes the paper and outlines directions for future work.

2 Related Work

This paper covers responsibility attribution and anticipation, and how this can be expanded to handle responsibility in a multi-value system.

Responsibility attribution is a very well studied topic with various approaches taken by a wide variety of authors, including approaches based on game-theoretic tools [3,8,20] and logical tools including STIT logic [1,4,19,21], LTLf [26], ATL [9,32], logics of strategic and extensive games [23,24,30] and structural equation models [10]. Responsibility anticipation is less well studied, though there is some previous work by Grandi et al. [16,26]. Overall, our model is most similar to the one presented by Grandi et al. as our objective was to expand their ideas to account for responsibility in a multi-value setting.

A similar notion to responsibility anticipation is responsibility for risk [27], as both concern an agent's responsibility for an outcome that may not actually happen. The main differences are that risk is typically formalised in an explicitly probabilistic way, such as in the work of Gladyshev et al. [14] who introduce a logical model of responsibility for risk that primarily considers ex post attribution of responsibility for risk (whereas our notion is ex ante) and introduce a complete and decidable logic for reasoning about group responsibility for taking risk.

To the best of our knowledge, there is very little work that investigates responsibility in such a setting. One work that we are aware of is an approach by Lorini and Sartor [22] whose work focuses on secondary responsibility, which is the responsibility of an agent who influences another agent to perform some action. Their notions do not share the properties of consistency or completeness that we discuss, since they consider responsibility *relative to* a set of values (meaning the agent is not implied to be responsible for everything in the set) rather than our work that focuses on responsibility *for* a set of values. They do also consider the principle that an agent is more responsible if they have no excuse for their actions, though their notion of excuse is based on the values that an agent controls rather than domination between strategies.

We also introduce a symbolic notion of regret, for use in strategy comparison. This was first introduced (independently) in decision theory by Savage [29] and Niehans [25]. It was later introduced to game theory by Linhart and Radner [18]. Our concept of regret is also similar to the notion of guilt introduced by Lorini and Mühlenbernd [20]. Their model uses separate numerical values to track both the individual utility of an agent for some particular history, as well as the degree of ideality of that history (such as the utility of the worst-off agent). The guilt of an agent in a history is the difference between the ideality achieved and the best possible ideality (fixing the actions of all other agents). This is similar to our notion of regret based on passive responsibility, but is purely numeric instead of symbolic.

3 Model

In this section we introduce the framework for our model. We require a finite set of agents $Agt = \{1, \ldots, n\}$ and a countable set of propositions $Prop = \{p, q, \ldots\}$ which produces a set of states $\mathcal{S} = 2^{Prop}$. Let $Act = \{a, b, \ldots\}$ be a finite non-empty set of action names. To describe the actions taken by all agents at a single time we introduce the notion of a joint action, which is a function $J : Agt \longrightarrow Act$. The set of all joint actions is $JAct$.

To trace the actions of agents and changing states over time we define a k-history to be a pair $H = (H_{st}, H_{act})$ with $H_{st} : \{0, \ldots, k\} \longrightarrow \mathcal{S}$ and $H_{act} : \{0, \ldots, k-1\} \longrightarrow JAct$. The set of k-histories is noted $Hist_k$. The set of all histories is $Hist = \bigcup_{k \in \mathbb{N}} Hist_k$. For convenience, given a k-history H and some $k' \leq k$ we write $H^{k'}$ for the history corresponding to the first $k'+1$ states of H.

To describe the world in which our agents operate we introduce the notion of a multiagent transition system (MTS).

Definition 1 (Multiagent Transition System). *A multiagent transition system G is a pair $(\mathcal{S}, \tau)$ where $\tau : \mathcal{S} \times JAct \rightarrow \mathcal{S}$ is a function that maps each pair of a state s and a joint action J to a successor state of s'.*

In our model, agents act according to strategies that determine how they should act based on the actions of all agents and how the state of the world has progressed. More formally, given an MTS $G = (\mathcal{S}, \tau)$ a strategy is a function $\sigma : Hist \rightarrow Act$. The set of all strategies is denoted *Strat*. A joint strategy for a coalition $J \subseteq Agt$ where $J = \{j_1, \ldots, j_m\}$ is a tuple $\sigma = (\sigma_{j_1}, \ldots, \sigma_{j_m})$. The set of all joint strategies for the coalition J is written $JStrat^J$. Given joint strategies σ and σ' for coalitions J_1 and J_2 where $J_1 \cap J_2 = \emptyset$, we write (σ_i, σ'_i) for the union of σ_i and σ'_i. For convenience, we write σ_{-i} for the reduction of σ from the coalition J to the coalition $J\backslash\{i\}$ (when $i \in J$).

In our model, histories are temporal entities that are always finite in length, therefore the most natural choice to describe properties of histories is Linear Temporal Logic over Finite Traces [11,12]. This allows us to describe temporal properties such as "ϕ never occurs" or "ϕ always occurs immediately after ψ". We write the language as $\mathcal{L}_{\mathsf{LTL}_f}$, defined by the following grammar:

$$\phi ::= p \mid \neg\phi \mid \phi \wedge \phi \mid \mathsf{X}\phi \mid \phi \ \mathsf{U} \ \phi,$$

with p ranging over *Prop*. Atomic formulas in this language are those that consist of a single proposition p. X and U are the operators "next" and "until" of LTL_f. Operators "henceforth" (G) and "eventually" (F) are defined in the usual way: $\mathsf{G}\phi \stackrel{\text{def}}{=} \neg(\top \ \mathsf{U} \ \phi)$ and $\mathsf{F}\phi \stackrel{\text{def}}{=} \neg\mathsf{G}\neg\phi$. We define the semantics for X and U as follows, the rest is the same as $\mathcal{L}_{\mathsf{PL+}}$ (for $t \in \{0, \ldots, k\}$).

$$\begin{aligned} H, t \models \mathsf{X}\phi \quad & \Longleftrightarrow \quad t < k \text{ and } H, t+1 \models \phi, \\ H, t \models \phi_1 \ \mathsf{U} \ \phi_2 \quad & \Longleftrightarrow \quad \exists t' \geq t : t' \leq k \text{ and } H, t' \models \phi_2 \text{ and} \\ & \qquad \forall t'' \geq t : \text{ if } t'' < t' \text{ then } H, t'' \models \phi_1. \end{aligned}$$

3.1 Values, Goals and Moral Action Systems

We assume that our agents will have multiple goals and/or values that they wish to satisfy, which may have different priority levels. Following the approach of Grandi et al. [15]. We represent this by a prioritised value base $\overline{\Omega}$ which is simply a sequence of sets of LTL_f-formulas $\overline{\Omega} = (\Omega_1, ..., \Omega_m)$. We do not consider the process by which these values are arrived at, nor how they are translated into LTL_f, as that is outside the scope of this paper. The content of the values that artificial agents should follow is a relatively well-studied area [6,28,31].

For each $\Omega_n \in \overline{\Omega}$ we write $\Omega_n^{\neg}$ for the set $\{\neg\omega : \omega \in \Omega_n\}$. Finally we write $\overline{\Omega}^{\neg}$ for the tuple $(\Omega_1^{\neg}, \ldots, \Omega_m^{\neg})$ and $\overline{\Omega}^{+}$ for the set $\bigcup\overline{\Omega} \cup \bigcup\overline{\Omega}^{\neg}$. We assume that our value base is "consistent" meaning that for all $\omega_1, \omega_2 \in \bigcup\overline{\Omega}$, $\omega_2 \not\equiv \neg\omega_1$. As we are concerned with an agent's responsibility for both the satisfaction and violation of values we will be mostly considering comparing subsets of $\overline{\Omega}^{+}$.

To represent the structure of $\overline{\Omega}$ we use quantitative lexicographic comparison over the sets in $\overline{\Omega}$, treating the first set Ω_1 as most important and the last set Ω_m as the least. This comparison works as follows, given $X, Y \subseteq \overline{\Omega}^{+}$, we say that $X \preceq Y$ if and only if one of the two following properties holds:

$i)$ $\exists n$ s.t $1 \leq n \leq m$ and $(|X \cap \Omega_n| - |X \cap \Omega_n^-|) <$
$(|Y \cap \Omega_n| - |Y \cap \Omega_n^-|)$
and
$\forall n'$ if $1 \leq n' < n$ then $(|X \cap \Omega_n| - |X \cap \Omega_n^-|) =$
$(|Y \cap \Omega_n| - |Y \cap \Omega_n^-|)$

$ii)$ $\forall n$ if $1 \leq n \leq m$ then $(|X \cap \Omega_n| - |X \cap \Omega_n^-|) =$
$(|Y \cap \Omega_n| - |Y \cap \Omega_n^-|)$

We also define $X \prec Y$ as $X \preceq Y$ and $Y \npreceq X$. To allow for comparing histories we write $Sat(H, \overline{\Omega}^+)$ for the maximal subset of $\overline{\Omega}^+$ that is satisfied in H.

There are many alternative ways to rank sets of values for strategy (or plan) comparison [7,13] which could also be used in our model.

Definition 2 (Moral Action System). *A Moral Action System (MAS) is a tuple* $\nabla = (G, s_0, k, \overline{\Omega})$ *where* G *is an MTS,* $s_0 \in \mathcal{S}$ *is a start state,* k *is an integer (known as the "horizon") and* $\overline{\Omega}$ *is a value base.*

For simplicity, in any MAS ∇ it is assumed that G, s_0 and k are fully observable. Also for simplicity, the value base $\overline{\Omega}$ is considered to be shared by all agents, though the agents have no information about the values of other agents and cannot communicate. For this reason we consider only the perspective of a single agent in this paper. Furthermore, it is entirely consistent to suppose that $\overline{\Omega}$ contains only a single value set that contains only a single value, meaning that all of the results in this paper can, in principle, be applied to single-value settings. However, in practice it is likely to be more straightforward to use single-value notions of responsibility [8,19,26] in single-value settings.

If σ is a strategy for Agt we write $Play(\sigma, \nabla)$ for the history resulting from the application of σ to the moral action system $\nabla = (G, s_0, k, \overline{\Omega})$. This is the history that starts at s_0 and proceeds according to σ and τ for k steps.

More formally, given a strategy σ for Agt and an MAS $\nabla = (G, s_0, k, \overline{\Omega})$, $H = Play(\sigma, \nabla)$ is the k-history such that:

$$\begin{aligned} H_{st}(0) =& s_0 \\ \forall 1 \leq k' \leq k, H_{act}(k)(i) =& \sigma_i(H^{k'-1}) \\ \forall 1 \leq k' \leq k, H_{st}(k) =& \tau(H_{st}(k'-1), H_{act}(k')) \end{aligned}$$

To help explain the intuitions behind the various definitions and results in this paper, we now introduce a running example:

Example 1 (Cleaning the Shopping Centre). A robot (Anna) is tasked with various jobs in cleaning a shopping centre. There is a customer (Ben) who can help or hinder Anna's tasks depending on how he acts, such as by blocking access to a bin which Anna is trying to empty (for simplicity, we consider only a single customer). The jobs that Anna must complete are as follows:

- ω_1 = The plants are watered.
- ω_2 = The bins are emptied.
- ω_3 = The windows have been cleaned.
- ω_4 = Litter has been collected.
- ω_5 = The floor has been swept.

Anna's value base treats all tasks as equally important, meaning that $\overline{\Omega} = (\Omega_1)$ where $\Omega_1 = \{\omega_1, \omega_2, \omega_3, \omega_4, \omega_5\}$

The main aim of this paper is to demonstrate that considering notions of responsibility is helpful in the selection of strategies in a multi-value setting. One notion that it is therefore helpful to define is the notion of a non-dominated strategy, which is a standard concept in game theory and decision theory. Firstly, we define weak dominance:

Definition 3 (Weak Dominance). *Given an MAS* $\nabla = (G, s_0, k, \overline{\Omega})$, *an agent* i *and two strategies* σ_i *and* σ'_i, *we say that* σ'_i *weakly dominates* σ_i *(written* $\sigma_i \leq_\nabla \sigma'_i$*) if and only if for all* $\sigma_{-i} \in JStrat^{-i}$, $Sat(Play((\sigma_i, \sigma_{-i}), \nabla), \overline{\Omega}^+) \preceq Sat(Play((\sigma'_i, \sigma_{-i}), \nabla), \overline{\Omega}^+)$.

In words, σ'_i weakly dominates σ_i if and only if in every possible outcome from executing σ'_i, (i.e. for every possible strategy for $Agt \backslash \{i\}$, the outcome obtained is at least as good as the outcome that would have been obtained by executing σ_i instead.

Definition 4 (Non-Dominated). *Given an MAS* $\nabla = (G, s_0, k, \overline{\Omega})$, *we say that* σ_i *is non-dominated if and only if there is no strategy* $\sigma'_i \in Strat$ *such that* $\sigma_i \leq_\nabla \sigma'_i$ *and* $\sigma'_i \not\leq_\nabla \sigma_i$.

In words, a strategy σ_i is non-dominated if and only if there is no strategy σ'_i such that σ'_i weakly dominates σ_i and sometimes does strictly better. In particular, since there are finitely many possible histories in any MAS $\nabla = (G, s_0, k, \overline{\Omega})$ (since k must be finite), there are finitely many distinct strategies, so there must always exist at least one non-dominated strategy.

Example 2 (Continued). Suppose that all tasks have been completed besides cleaning the windows (ω_3). If Anna chooses the strategy σ_A to do nothing, then this strategy is dominated by the strategy σ'_A that retrieves the water bucket and cleans the windows. This is because σ_A will never wash the windows, whereas σ'_A will usually wash the windows (unless Ben steals the bucket). Furthermore, since (by assumption) σ'_A is the most reliable way to wash the windows, σ'_A is non-dominated.

4 Responsibility Attribution

In this paper we will primarily be focusing on the notion of passive responsibility, as formalised by Lorini et al. [19] and Grandi et al. [16,26]. This corresponds to the notion of "allowing ω to happen" and is defined as follows: Given an MAS $\nabla = (G, s_0, k, \overline{\Omega})$, a joint strategy σ for *Agt* and an agent i we say that i is attributed single-value passive responsibility for ω in $Play(\sigma, \nabla)$ under σ if and only if $Play(\sigma, \nabla) \models \omega$ and there is some strategy σ'_i for i such that $Play((\sigma'_i, \sigma_{-i}), \nabla) \models \neg\omega$. In words, an agent is attributed passive responsibility for ω if ω occurs and, fixing the strategies of all other agents, i could have acted differently and prevented ω.

Another way to think about responsibility is from a courtroom-esque perspective where some external agent (the accuser) is trying to blame i for the occurrence of ω. For this we define the notion of *accusation*, where given a joint strategy σ for *Agt*, an agent i, an ltl_f formula ω and an MAS $\nabla = (G, s_0, k, \overline{\Omega})$ such that $Play(\sigma, \nabla) \models \omega$, a single-value accusation for $(i, \sigma, \omega, \nabla)$ is a strategy σ'_i such that $Play((\sigma'_i, \sigma_{-i}), \nabla) \models \neg\omega$. We can then see that given a joint strategy σ for *Agt*, i is attributed single-value passive responsibility for ω in $Play(\sigma, \nabla)$ if and only if there exists an accusation for $(i, \sigma, \omega, \nabla)$.

In words, we can imagine that the accuser says to the agent "you are responsible for ω because you could have prevented it, if you had acted according to σ'_i then ω would not have occured". However, we might think that for this accusation to be truly effective, there can be no reason to pick σ_i over σ'_i, which we take to mean that σ'_i must weakly dominate σ_i.

Definition 5 (Liability). *Given a joint strategy σ for Agt, an agent i, an* LTL_f *formula ω and an MAS $\nabla = (G, s_0, k, \overline{\Omega})$ we say that i is liable for ω in $Play(\sigma, \nabla)$ if and only if $Play(\sigma, \nabla) \models \omega$ and there exists some strategy σ'_i such that $Play((\sigma'_i, \sigma_{-i}), \nabla) \models \neg\omega$ and $\sigma_i \leq_\nabla \sigma'_i$.*

One possible issue with the notion of single-value responsibility given above is that attributing responsibility requires full knowledge of the strategies of all agents, which is a very strong demand, particularly if some of those agents are humans. We do not address this issue in our paper since we focus more on anticipating than attributing responsibility. When anticipating possible outcomes an agent will quantify over all possible strategies of the other agents, and assuming knowledge of all agents' strategies in a simulated execution is not problematic. Nonetheless, considering how we can attribute responsibility with limited information about the strategies of agents would be an interesting direction for future work.

4.1 Multi-value Responsibility

We shall now consider how to evaluate the responsibility of an agent in a setting with multiple values, with a particular focus on how we can use these notions of responsibility to help agents select good strategies.

Perhaps the simplest approach to multi-value responsibility is to say that i is responsible for some set of values Ω if and only if i is responsible for each $\omega \in \Omega$. This seems reasonable, as it means that if i is responsible for Ω then i could have made every formula in Ω true if it had acted differently. However, this approach does not consider if i could have made the formulas in Ω true *simultaneously*, only *individually*. This can cause unintuitive results.

	σ_B
σ_A	$\emptyset$
σ'_A	ω_1
σ''_A	ω_2
σ'''_A	ω_1, ω_2

(a) Table 1

	σ_B	σ'_B
σ_A	ω_1, ω_2	ω_3
σ'_A	$\emptyset$	ω_1, ω_2

(a) Table 2

Example 3 (Continued). Consider Table 1, which presents a very simple scenario where Anna has to pick between various strategies but Ben has only one strategy. We can consider three scenarios based on this table. In scenario A, Anna only has access to σ_A and σ'_A. In scenario B Anna also has access to σ''_A and in scenario C Anna has access to all four strategies. It is intuitive to assert that in scenario A, if Anna picks σ_A then she should be responsible only for $\{\neg\omega_1\}$ whereas in scenario C she should be responsible for $\{\neg\omega_1, \neg\omega_2\}$ (if she chose σ_A). This is because in scenario A the best Anna could have done was to water the plants $\{\omega_1\}$ whereas in scenario B she could have watered the plants and emptied the bins $\{\omega_1, \omega_2\}$. However, it is less clear what should happen in scenario B. Separately, it is clear that we can hold Anna responsible for not watering the plants *or* for not emptying the bins, but if we hold her responsible for both, then we find that she is equally responsible in scenario B as scenario C. This is odd because it seems that the addition of σ'''_A increases Anna's degree of responsibility much more than the addition of σ''_A. Accordingly, we introduce the following requirement on multi-value notions of responsibility which takes the form of a necessary (but not necessarily sufficient) requirement for responsibility:

Property 1 (Consistency). Given an MAS $\nabla = (G, s_0, k, \overline{\Omega})$, an agent i and a strategy σ for Agt, if agent i is responsible for X in the history $Play(\sigma, \nabla)$ then $Play(\sigma, \nabla) \models \bigwedge X$ and there exists some σ'_i such that $Play((\sigma'_i, \sigma_{-i}), \nabla) \models \bigwedge\{\neg\omega : \omega \in X\}$.

This means that in general, we cannot assume that if i is responsible for the set A and the set B in the history $Play(\sigma, \nabla)$ then i is also responsible for the set $A \cup B$. Another consideration is the issue that a responsibility set A may be "misleading" in the sense that it misses out important information.

Example 4 (Continued). In Table 2 Anna can seemingly be held responsible for $X = \{\omega_1, \omega_2\}$ in both the history $H_1 = Play((\sigma_A, \sigma'_B), \nabla)$ and the history $H_2 = Play((\sigma'_A, \sigma_B), \nabla)$. However, it seems that Anna should be "more" responsible in H_2 than H_1 since in H_1 we at least have the consolation that the windows are clean (ω_3) which could not have been done otherwise, whereas in H_1 there is no compensation.

This suggests that responsibility sets should be not just "consistent" but also "complete".

Property 2 (Completeness). Given an MAS $\nabla = (G, s_0, k, \overline{\Omega})$, an agent i and a strategy σ for Agt, if agent i is responsible for $X \subseteq \mathcal{L}_{\mathsf{LTL}_f}$ in the history $H_1 = Play(\sigma, \nabla)$ then there exists some strategy σ'_i for i such that for $H_2 = Play((\sigma'_i, \sigma_{-i}), \nabla)$ and all $\omega \in \overline{\Omega}$ such that $\omega, \neg\omega \notin X$, either $H_1, H_2 \models \omega$ or $H_1, H_2 \models \neg\omega$.

To guarantee the notions of consistency and completeness we define the notion of responsibility via a strategy, which will be a useful building block in our future definitions.

Definition 6 (Responsibility via Strategy). *Given an MAS* $\nabla = (G, s_0, k, \overline{\Omega})$*, an agent* i *and a strategy* σ *for* Agt*, we say that* i *is responsible for* $X \subseteq \mathcal{L}_{\mathsf{LTL}_f}$ *via* σ'_i *if and only if* $X = Sat(Play(\sigma, \nabla), \overline{\Omega}^+) \setminus Sat(Play((\sigma'_i, \sigma_{-i}), \nabla, \overline{\Omega}^+)$.

We will now introduce a natural extension of passive responsibility that guarantees consistency and completeness:

Definition 7 (Passive Responsibility).
Given an MAS $\nabla = (G, s_0, k, \overline{\Omega})$*, an agent* i *and a strategy* σ *for* Agt*,* i *is passively responsible for* $X \subseteq \overline{\Omega}^+$ *in* $Play(\sigma, \nabla)$ *if and only if if there exists some strategy* σ'_i *for* i *such that* i *is responsible for* X *via* σ'_i*.*

Theorem 1. *Passive responsibility satisfies consistency and completeness.*

Proof. Let $\nabla = (G, s_0, k, \overline{\Omega})$ be an MAS, i an agent and σ a strategy for Agt. Suppose that i is passively responsible for $X \subseteq \overline{\Omega}^+$ in $H_1 = Play(\sigma, \overline{\Omega})$. Therefore there exists some strategy σ'_i such that $X = Sat(H_1, \overline{\Omega}^+) \setminus Sat(H_2, \overline{\Omega}^+)$ where $H_2 = Play((\sigma'_i, \sigma_{-i}), \nabla)$.

First we will show consistency. Since $X \subseteq Sat(H_1, \overline{\Omega}^+)$ we know that $H_1 \models \bigwedge X$. Furthermore, $X \cap Sat(H_2, \overline{\Omega}^+) = \emptyset$ and $X \subseteq \overline{\Omega}^+$ so we know that for all $\omega \in X \cap \overline{\Omega}, \neg\omega \in Sat(H_2, \overline{\Omega}^+)$ and for all $\neg\omega \in X \cap \overline{\Omega}^{\neg}, \omega \in Sat(H_2, \overline{\Omega}^+)$. Therefore $H_2 \models \bigwedge\{\neg\omega : \omega \in X\}$ and we are done.

Second we will show completeness. Suppose that for some $\omega \in \overline{\Omega}$, $\omega \neg\omega \notin X$. Furthermore, we know by necessity that either $\omega \in Sat(H_1, \overline{\Omega}^+)$ or $\neg\omega \in Sat(H_1, \overline{\Omega}^+)$. If $\omega \in Sat(H_1, \overline{\Omega}^+)$ then since $\omega \notin X$ we know that $\omega \in Sat(H_2, \overline{\Omega}^+)$. By a similar argument for $\neg\omega$ we can show that either $H_1, H_2 \models \omega$ or $H_1, H_2 \models \neg\omega$ and we are done.

4.2 Excuses

An agent may be considered more strongly responsible if it cannot provide a rational justification (i.e. an excuse) for its chosen strategy. We illustrate this in our running example:

	σ_B	σ'_B
σ_A	ω_1, ω_2	$\emptyset$
σ'_A	$\emptyset$	ω_1, ω_2

(a) Table 3

	σ_B	σ'_B	σ''_B
σ_A	$\omega_1, \omega_2, \omega_3$	ω_1, ω_2	$\emptyset$
σ'_A	$\emptyset$	$\omega_1, \omega_2, \omega_3$	ω_1, ω_2
σ''_A	ω_1, ω_2	$\emptyset$	$\omega_1, \omega_2, \omega_3$

(a) Table 4

Example 5 (Continued). In Table 3 we see that choosing either σ_A or σ'_A may lead Anna to be responsible for $\{\omega_1, \omega_2\}$. This seems somewhat unfair, as the agents in my model have no way do determine which of σ_B and σ'_B was more likely to occur (since they have no information about the goals, values or rationality of the other agents), meaning that they always risk responsibility.

Therefore, against the "accusation" of responsibility via some strategy σ'_i, an agent may excuse themselves by presenting a rational justification for choosing σ_i over σ'_i. We consider excuses only in cases of "negative responsibility" (responsibility for X where $X \preceq \emptyset$) as it is not clear what it would mean to give an excuse for a positive outcome.

Definition 8 (Weak Excuse). *If agent i is responsible for $X \preceq \emptyset$ via σ'_i in $Play(\sigma, \nabla)$, then a weak excuse for $(i, \sigma, \nabla, \sigma'_i)$ is a strategy σ'_{-i} for $Agt \backslash \{i\}$ such that $Sat(Play((\sigma_i, \sigma'_{-i}), \nabla, \overline{\Omega}^+)$ is strictly preferred to $Sat(Play((\sigma'_i, \sigma'_{-i}), \nabla, \overline{\Omega}^+)$.*

Property 3 (Acceptance of Weak Excuses). Given an MAS $\nabla = (G, s_0, k, \overline{\Omega})$, an agent i and a strategy σ for Agt, if i is responsible for $X \subseteq \mathcal{L}_{\mathsf{LTL}_f}$ in $Play(\sigma, \nabla)$ then there exists some strategy σ'_i for i such that i is responsible for X via σ'_i and there exists no weak excuse for $(i, \sigma, \nabla, \sigma'_i)$.

A weak excuse says that i was (weakly) justified in choosing σ_i over σ'_i since there is at least one strategy for $Agt \backslash \{i\}$ where σ_i does better. However, we might prefer a stronger notion of excuse, requiring that the original strategy could have been preferred *by at least as wide a margin* as the accusing strategy.

Definition 9 (Strong Excuse). *If agent i is responsible for $X \preceq \emptyset$ via σ'_i in $Play(\sigma, \nabla)$, then a strong excuse for $(i, \sigma, \nabla, \sigma'_i)$ is a strategy σ'_{-i} for $Agt \backslash \{i\}$ such that $Sat(Play((\sigma_i, \sigma'_{-i}), \nabla), \overline{\Omega}^+) \backslash Sat(Play((\sigma'_i, \sigma'_{-i}), \nabla), \overline{\Omega}^+)$ is preferred to $\emptyset$ and to $Sat(Play((\sigma'_i, \sigma_{-i}), \nabla), \overline{\Omega}^+) \backslash Sat(Play(\sigma, \nabla), \overline{\Omega}^+)$.*

Note that since being a strong excuse is a strictly stronger requirement than being a weak excuse, all strong excuses are automatically weak excuses.

Property 4 (Acceptance of Strong Excuses). Given an MAS $\nabla = (G, s_0, k, \overline{\Omega})$, an agent i and a strategy σ for Agt, if i is responsible for $X \subseteq \mathcal{L}_{\mathsf{LTL}_f}$ in the history $Play(\sigma, \nabla)$ then there exists some strategy σ'_i for i such that i is responsible for X via σ'_i and there exists no strong excuse for $(i, \sigma, \nabla, \sigma'_i)$.

However, while we have outlined why we think that strong excuses might be a more appealing notion than weak excuses, there is also an issue with this notion. The property "acceptance of strong excuses" relies on the intuition that if in some history $Play(\sigma, \nabla)$ an agent i cannot give a strong excuse for choosing σ_i over some alternative σ_i' (where $Sat(Play(\sigma, \nabla), \overline{\Omega}^+) \prec Sat(Play((\sigma_i', \sigma_{-i}), \nabla), \overline{\Omega}^+))$ then they cannot justify their choice of σ_i over σ_i' and therefore should have preferred σ_i'. The problem is that the preference relation that this implies is not transitive, and is possibly cyclic.

Example 6 (Continued). In Table 4 we can see that in the history $Play((\sigma'_A, \sigma_B), \nabla)$ Anna cannot give a strong excuse for not choosing σ_A implying that σ_A should be preferred to σ'_A. In $Play((\sigma''_A, \sigma'_B), \nabla)$ we can use a similar argument to imply that σ'_A should be preferred to σ''_A. However, in $Play((\sigma_A, \sigma''_B), \nabla)$ i we can argue that σ''_A should be preferred to σ_A!

Correspondingly, we will focus on weak excuses rather than strong excuses. In particular, we can refine the definition of passive responsibility by considering weak excuses.

Definition 10 (Inexcusable Passive Responsibility). *Given an MAS* $\nabla = (G, s_0, k, \overline{\Omega})$, *an agent i and a strategy* σ *for Agt, i is attributed inexcusable passive responsiblility for* $X \subseteq \overline{\Omega}^+$ *in* $Play(\sigma, \nabla)$ *if and only if there exists some* σ_i' *such that i is responsible for X via* σ_i' *and there is no weak excuse for* $(i, \sigma, \nabla, \sigma_i')$.

Furthermore, we can show that this notion satisfies all of the important properties of responsibility that we have outlined thus far.

Theorem 2. *Inexcusable passive responsibility satisfies consistency, completeness,the acceptance of weak excuses and the acceptance of strong excuses.*

Proof. Since i bears inexcusable passive responsibility for X only if i is responsible for X via some strategy σ_i', we can use the same argument as for Theorem 1 to show that inexcusable passive responsibility satisfies consistency and completeness. Inexcusable passive responsibility satisfies acceptance of weak excuses by definition and therefore also satisfies acceptance of strong excuses since all strong excuses are weak excuses.

Again, by considering Table 3 we can show that passive responsibility does not satisfy acceptance of strong or weak excuses. Finally, we can show the notion of inexcusable passive responsibility is coherent with the single-value notion of liability that we introduced in Definition 5:

Theorem 3. *Given an MAS* $\nabla = (G, s_0, k, \overline{\Omega})$, *an agent i, a strategy* σ *for Agt and a value* $\omega \in \overline{\Omega}$, *i is liable for* $\neg\omega$ *in* $H = Play(\sigma, \nabla)$ *if and only if there is some* $X \subseteq \overline{\Omega}^+$ *such that* $\neg\omega \in X$ *and i is attributed inexcusable passive responsibility for X in H.*

Proof. First we will show (liability $\Rightarrow$ inexcusable passive responsibility). Suppose that i is liable for $\neg\omega$. Therefore $H_1 = Play(\sigma, \nabla) \models \neg\omega$ and there exists some strategy σ_i' such that $\sigma_i <_\nabla \sigma_i'$ and $H_2 = Play((\sigma_i', \sigma_{-i}), \nabla) \models \omega$. Therefore $\neg\omega \in X = Sat(H_1, \overline{\Omega}^+) \backslash Sat(H_2, \overline{\Omega}^+)$. Since $\sigma_i <_\nabla \sigma_i'$ there exists no weak excuse for $(i, \sigma, \nabla, \sigma_i')$ and $Sat(H_1, \overline{\Omega}^+) \preceq Sat(H_2, \overline{\Omega}^+)$ (so therefore $X \preceq \emptyset$) so i is attributed inexcusable passive responsibility for X and we are done.

Now we show (inexcusable passive responsibility $\Rightarrow$ liability). Suppose that i is attributed inexcusable passive responsibility for X and that $\neg\omega \in X$. Therefore we know that there is some strategy σ_i' such that $X = Sat(H_1, \overline{\Omega}^+) \backslash Sat(H_2, \overline{\Omega}^+)$ where $H_1 = Play(\sigma, \nabla)$ and $H_2 = Play((\sigma_i', \sigma_{-i}), \nabla)$. Therefore $H_1 \models \neg\omega$ and $H_2 \models \omega$. Since we also know that there exists no weak excuse for $(i, \sigma, \nabla, \sigma_i')$ we can also conclude that $\sigma_i \leq_\nabla$ so i is liable for $\neg\omega$ and we are done (Table 1).

Table 1. A table summarising the properties of Passive Responsibility (Theorem 1) and Inexcusable Passive Responsibility (Theorem 2).

Notion	Properties
Passive Responsibility	Consistency, Completeness
Inexcusable Passsive Responsibility	Consistency, Completeness, Acceptance of Weak Excuses

5 Anticipating Regret and Responsibility

Anticipation is the process of predicting the possible outcomes of a particular strategy. Anticipation is therefore performed before rather than after strategy execution, meaning that it can be used in the process of strategy selection.

5.1 Regret Anticipation

Roughly speaking, we want agents to select strategies that generally lead to good outcomes. One way to evaluate outcomes is simply to consider the set of values satisfied with that outcome in conjunction with the relation $\preceq$. However, it can instead be useful to consider how good an outcome is relative to the other outcomes that could have been achieved. In other words, if the strategies of the other agents guarantee that the outcome of any strategy is at best mediocre (relative to our value base $\overline{\Omega}$) then an agent should feel quite satisfied with a mediocre outcome. Alternatively, if the strategies of the other agents guarantee that the outcome is at *worst* mediocre, then an agent should not be satisfied with a mediocre outcome. This leads to the notion of the regret, which is traditionally defined as the difference between the utility of a given outcome and the greatest utility that could have been achieved given the strategies of all other agents. This idea was first introduced in decision theory [25,29] and was later formalised in game theory [18]. Regret is a very demanding notion, since the only way to achieve zero regret is to achieve the best result possible given the strategies of all other agents, and it does not give any "extra credit" for avoiding an even worse outcome.

Formalising a notion of regret in a setting with no numerical measurements of utility (such as ours) is more complex than normal, since we cannot simply subtract one value from another. However, we can simply consider the "relative regret" from H_1 to H_2 as $Sat(H_1, \overline{\Omega}^+) \backslash Sat(H_2, \overline{\Omega}^+)$. This should be understood as the regret that an agent would feel after H_1 has occurred when they consider H_2. For example, if $\overline{\Omega} = \{\omega_1, \omega_2\}$, $H_1 \models \neg\omega_1 \wedge \neg\omega_2$ and $H_2 \models \omega_1 \wedge \neg\omega_2$ then the regret from H_1 to H_2 is $\neg\omega_1$, since the agent regrets that ω_1 was violated, but does not regret the violation of ω_2 since this occurred in both histories.

We can also consider the regret associated with an individual strategy σ_i for some agent i. Since there are many possible histories, and therefore many possible regret sets, that can be associated with σ_i, the standard approach in the literature is to select the worst value of regret that it could possibly experience. We call this "anticipated regret" because the anticipated regret represents a possible future result of executing the strategy, which can be calculated before actually executing the strategy and thus can be fruitfully used to evaluate strategies. The kind of strategies that agents should prefer are "regret-minimising" strategies.

Definition 11 (Regret Minimisation). *Given an MAS $\nabla = (G, s_0, k, \overline{\Omega})$, an agent i and a strategy σ_i, let X be anticipated regret of σ_i (the worst, according to $\preceq$, relative regret from any $H_1 = Play((\sigma_i, \sigma_{-i}), \nabla)$ to any $H_2 = Play((\sigma'_i, \sigma_{-i}), \nabla)$). σ_i is regret-minimising if and only if for any σ'_i, with anticipated regret Y, $Y \preceq X$.*

An advantage of symbolic regret over more standard, numerical forms of regret is that it can produce much more meaningful explanations of behaviour, particularly to a non-technical audience. A numerical justification for avoiding a particular strategy might be "σ'_i anticipates regret of 0.8 compared to 0.4 for σ_i" whereas with symbolic regret we can say "both σ_i and σ'_i lead to the avoidable violation of ω_1 in the worst-case, but σ_i at least has the compensation of satisfying ω_2" (i.e. the anticipated regret of σ_i is $\{\neg\omega_1, \omega_2\}$ whereas the anticipated regret of σ'_i is $\{\neg\omega_1\}$).

5.2 Responsibility Anticipation

Previous work on responsibility anticipation [26] has only considered responsibility for single values, which simplifies the process of responsibility anticipation; if any possible history for σ_i attributes responsibility for ω, then σ_i anticipates responsibility for ω. This can be generalised to multiple values, but we must be careful about how we do it, as the following example shows.

	σ_B	σ'_B	σ''_B
σ_A	ω_1, ω_2 ω_3, ω_4	ω_1, ω_2 ω_3, ω_5	ω_1, ω_2, ω_4, ω_5
σ'_A	ω_1, ω_2 ω_3	ω_1, ω_2 ω_3	ω_1, ω_2 ω_3
σ''_A	ω_5	ω_4	ω_3

(a) Table 5

	σ_B	σ'_B
σ_A	$\emptyset$	ω_1
σ'_A	$\emptyset$	$\emptyset$

(b) Table 6

Example 7 (Continued). We can see in Table 5 that the set of values that Anna is attributed responsibility for with σ_A in at least one possible history is strictly larger than the equivalent set for σ'_A ($\{\omega_3, \omega_4, \omega_5\}$ vs $\{\omega_4, \omega_5\}$), even though σ_A strictly dominates σ'_A, due to always completing four of the tasks in the garden, instead of three. However, we can avoid this issue if we stick to responsibility sets from single histories.

Furthermore, to allow for strategy evaluation via considerations of responsibility it is useful to be able to pick a single set X to represent the degree of responsibility that i anticipates for choosing σ_i. Since we have no information regarding how the other agents may choose their strategies, the most obvious choices are to pick either the best or the worst of the sets for which i is responsible[1]. However, there are problems with using the best set.

Example 8 (Continued). In Table 6 we can see that in any history resulting from Ben choosing σ_B, Anna is responsible for $\emptyset$ regardless of which strategy she chooses, since Ben has made it impossible to complete any of the tasks. This means that the best responsibility sets for σ_A and σ'_A are both $\emptyset$, meaning that they would both be considered equally good in terms of anticipated responsibility, even though σ_A weakly dominates $_\nabla\sigma'_A$.

Therefore I propose the following definition of responsibility anticipation:

Definition 12 (Responsibility Anticipation). *Given an MAS* $\nabla = (G, s_0, k, \overline{\Omega})$, *an agent* i, *a strategy* σ_i *and a type of responsibility* Γ, i *anticipates* Γ*-responsibility for* $X \subseteq \overline{\Omega}^+$ *in* $Play(\sigma, \nabla)$ *if and only if* X *is the worst (according to* $\preceq$*) subset of* $\overline{\Omega}^+$ *such that there exists some joint strategy* σ_{-i} *for* $Agt\backslash\{i\}$ *such that* i *is* Γ*-responsible for* X *in* $Play((\sigma, \sigma_{-i}), \nabla)$.

One feature of this definition, which will be useful in later proofs, is that responsibility anticipation is provably pessimistic, the best-case responsibility that an agent can anticipate is $\emptyset$ (neither positively nor negatively responsible).

Lemma 1. *If* i *anticipates passive or inexcusable passive responsibility for* X *in* ∇ *with* σ_i, *then* $X \preceq \emptyset$.

Proof. If σ_i anticipates responsibility for X then X must be the worst subset of $\overline{\Omega}^+$ such that there is some strategy σ_{-i} such that i is responsible for X

[1] In the language of comparing sets of objects [5] we are in the situation of "complete uncertainty" meaning that most approaches revolve around the best and/or worst elements of the set.

in $H = Play((\sigma_i, \sigma_{-i}), \nabla)$. In the history H i will always be attributed both passive and inexcusable passive responsibility for $\emptyset$ via σ_i since there can never be a weak excuse for $(i, \sigma, \nabla, \sigma_i')$. Therefore the worst valid $X \subseteq \overline{\Omega}^+$ must be at most as good as $\emptyset$.

A responsibility-conscious agent should prefer strategies where they minimise their degree of expected responsibility. This should ensure that they maximise their causal contribution towards a generally more positive outcome.

Definition 13 (Responsibility Minimisation). *Given an MAS $\nabla = (G, s_0, k, \overline{\Omega})$, an agent i, a strategy σ_i and a type of responsibility Γ, let $X \subseteq \overline{\Omega}$ be such that σ_i anticipates Γ responsibility for X. Then we say that σ_i is Γ responsibility-minimising for i if and only if for every alternative strategy σ_i' such that i anticipates responsibility for Y, $Y \preceq X$.*

From this definition we can describe a responsibility-minimising strategy for the notions of passive and inexcusable passive responsibility. However, it also turns out that both of these notions can be described as some combination of non-dominated and regret-minimising strategies.

Theorem 4. *Given an MAS $\nabla = (G, s_0, k, \overline{\Omega})$, an agent i and a a strategy σ_i, σ_i is passive responsibility-minimising if and only if σ_i is regret-minimising.*

Proof. To prove this, it is sufficient to prove that given an MAS $\nabla = (G, s_0, k, \overline{\Omega})$, an agent i and a strategy σ_i, the anticipated passive responsibility for i with σ_i is exactly the anticipated regret for i with σ_i.

Let X be the anticipated passive responsibility for i with σ_i in ∇. Therefore X is the worst (according to $\preceq$) subset of $\overline{\Omega}$ such that there exists some strategy σ_{-i} such that i is passively responsible for X in $Play((\sigma_i, \sigma_{-i}), \nabla)$. This means that X is the worst subset of $\overline{\Omega}$ such that there exists strategy σ_{-i} for $Agt \backslash \{i\}$ and a strategy σ_i' for i such that $X = Sat(Play((\sigma_i, \sigma_{-i}), \nabla), \overline{\Omega}^+) \backslash Sat(Play((\sigma_i', \sigma_{-i}), \nabla), \overline{\Omega}^+)$. However, this is enough to show that X is also the anticipated regret of i with σ_i in ∇.

Theorem 5. *Given an MAS $\nabla = (G, s_0, k, \overline{\Omega})$, an agent i and a a strategy σ_i, σ_i is inexcusable passive responsibility-minimising if and only if σ_i is non-dominated.*

Proof. First we will show that (non-dominated $\Rightarrow$ inexcusable passive responsibility-minimising). Suppose that σ_i is non-dominated for i in ∇. Let $X \subseteq \overline{\Omega}^+$ be such that $X \prec \emptyset$ and there is some strategy σ_{-i} for $Agt \backslash \{i\}$ and strategy σ_i' for i such that i is responsible for X via σ_i' in $Play((\sigma_i, \sigma_{-i}), \nabla)$. Since $X \prec \emptyset$ we can conclude that $Sat(Play((\sigma_i, \sigma_{-i}), \nabla), \overline{\Omega}^+) \prec Sat(Play((\sigma_i', \sigma_{-i}), \nabla), \overline{\Omega}^+)$. Since σ_i is non-dominated there must also exist some σ_{-i}' such that $Sat(Play((\sigma_i', \sigma_{-i}'), \nabla), \overline{\Omega}^+) \prec Sat(Play((\sigma_i, \sigma_{-i}'), \nabla), \overline{\Omega}^+)$. Therefore σ_{-i}' is a weak excuse for $(i, (\sigma_i, \sigma_{-i}), \nabla, \sigma_i')$. This means that i has a weak excuse for any $X \prec \emptyset$ that i would otherwise be responsible for. Therefore by Lemma 1 we have that i anticipates responsibility for $\emptyset$ with σ_i and that σ_i is inexcusable passive responsibility-minimising.

Now we show that (not non-dominated $\Rightarrow$ not inexcusable passive responsibility-minimising). Suppose that σ_i is asymmetrically weakly dominated by some strategy σ'_i. Therefore there is some strategy σ_{-i} for $Agt\backslash\{i\}$ such that $Sat(Play((\sigma_i, \sigma_{-i}), \nabla), \overline{\Omega}^+) \prec Sat(Play((\sigma'_i, \sigma_{-i}), \nabla), \overline{\Omega}^+)$ and there is no strategy σ'_{-i} for $Agt\backslash\{i\}$ such that $Sat(Play((\sigma'_i, \sigma'_{-i}), \nabla), \overline{\Omega}^+) \prec Sat(Play((\sigma_i, \sigma'_{-i}), \nabla), \overline{\Omega}^+)$. Therefore we know that $X = Sat(Play((\sigma_i, \sigma_{-i}), \nabla), \overline{\Omega}^+)\backslash Sat(Play((\sigma'_i, \sigma_{-i}), \nabla), \overline{\Omega}^+) \prec \emptyset$ and that there cannot exist an excuse for $(i, (\sigma_i, \sigma_{-i}), \nabla, \sigma'_i)$. Therefore σ_i anticipates inexcusable passive responsibility for X where $X \prec \emptyset$.

Furthermore we know that there must exist a strategy σ''_i for i in ∇ that is non-dominated and by the above argument we see that σ''_i anticipates responsibility for $\emptyset$. Therefore σ_i is not passive responsibility-minimising.

Since regret-minimisation and being non-dominated are both desirable properties, we argue that agents attempting to minimise their anticipated responsibility should attempt to minimise both passive and inexcusable passive responsibility. We can also show that minimising one notion never comes at the cost of failing to minimise the other. The requirement that agents should minimise both passive and inexcusable passive responsibility is consistent with the idea that having an excuse reduces an agent's degree of responsibility, but may not remove it entirely.

Theorem 6. *Given an MAS $\nabla = (G, s_0, k, \overline{\Omega})$ and an agent i, there exists some strategy σ_i that is both regret-minimising and non-dominated for i.*

Proof. Since each strategy has an "anticipated regret" and there are finitely many distinct strategies, there must exist a regret-minimising strategy σ_i. It is enough to show that any strategy that asymmetrically weakly dominates σ_i must also be regret-minimising.

Let X be the anticipated regret for σ_i. Suppose that $\sigma'_i <_\nabla \sigma_i$ and let X' be the anticipated regret for σ'_i. Suppose for contradiction that σ'_i is not regret-minimising, meaning that $X' \prec X$. We also know that there exists some strategy σ_{-i} for $Agt\backslash\{i\}$ such that $X' = Sat(Play((\sigma'_i, \sigma_{-i}), \nabla), \overline{\Omega}^+)\backslash Sat(H_1, \overline{\Omega}^+)$ where H_1 is the best (according to $\preceq$) history compatible with σ_{-i} and ∇. Let $Y = Sat(Play((\sigma_i, \sigma_{-i}), \nabla), \overline{\Omega}^+)\backslash Sat(H_1, \overline{\Omega}^+)$. Since X is the anticipated regret of σ_i we know that $X \preceq Y$ and therefore $X' \prec Y$.

Since $X' = Sat(Play((\sigma'_i, \sigma_{-i}), \nabla), \overline{\Omega}^+)\backslash Sat(H_1, \overline{\Omega}^+)$, and $Y = Sat(Play((\sigma_i, \sigma_{-i}), \nabla), \overline{\Omega}^+)\backslash Sat(H_1, \overline{\Omega}^+)$ and $X' \prec Y$ we can conclude that $Sat(Play((\sigma'_i, \sigma_{-i}), \nabla), \overline{\Omega}^+) \prec Sat(Play((\sigma_i, \sigma_{-i}), \nabla), \overline{\Omega}^+)$[2]. However, this is a contradiction as we supposed that $\sigma_i <_\nabla \sigma'_i$. Therefore σ_i must be regret-minimising and we are done (Fig. 1).

[2] The proof of the validity of this deduction can be found in the appendix.

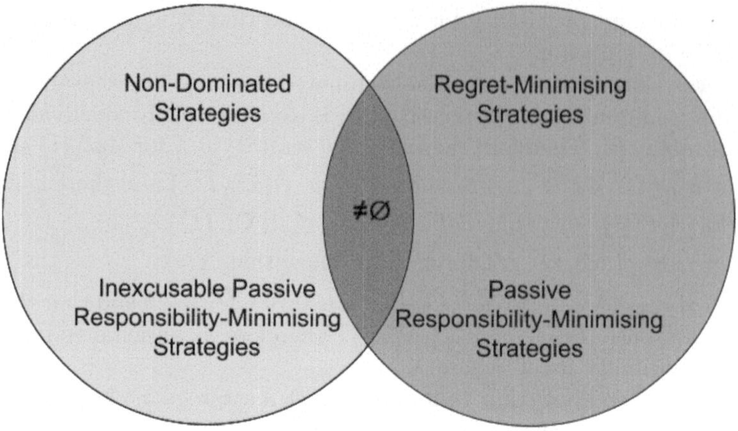

Fig. 1. A visual summary of our main results. The two circles indicate that regret-minimising strategies are exactly passive responsibility-minimising strategies (Theorem 4) and that non-dominated strategies are exactly inexcusable passive responsibility-minimising strategies (Theorem 5). The intersection of these two circles is always non-empty (Theorem 6).

6 Conclusion and Future Work

In this paper we have introduced a formal setting for the study of multi-value responsibility. We have considered various desirable properties for notions of multi-value responsibility, namely consistency, completeness and the acceptance of weak and strong excuses, and then defined two notions of responsibility (passive and inexcusable passive responsibility) that satisfy some or all of these properties. We introduced a symbolic notion of regret as well as the notion of non-dominance in this setting. Finally we applied the concept of responsibility anticipation to our notions of responsibility and showed that the anticipation of each notion can be alternatively formalised in terms of regret minimisation and non-dominance.

We argue that value-based agents should always seek to minimise both passive and inexcusable passive responsibility since this guarantees both regret minimising and non-dominated strategies. On the other hand, it is not clear that strategies that minimise worst-case regret are always to be preferred, even if they are also best-effort, since there may exist an alternative best-effort strategy that does not minimise regret in the worst case but does a much better job of minimising regret "overall". However, given that our model contains no information that i can use to evaluate the relative likelihood of different strategies for $Agt\backslash\{i\}$, it is difficult to formalise what "overall" means. Nonetheless, for some applications we may prefer to require only that agents minimise inexcusable passive responsibility instead of passive responsibility, since selecting non-dominated strategies will always be preferable (since by definition, an agent cannot give an excuse for not choosing a non-dominated strategy).

Overall, we hope that this paper has demonstrated the potential application of responsibility-conscious agents to decision-making in strategic multi-value scenarios. By demonstrating the connections between considerations of responsibility and pre-existing notions such as non-dominated and regret-minimising strategies, we aim to show both how responsibility considerations can lead to better decision-making, but also how good decision-making works to generally decrease the degree of responsibility of an agent.

The application of this work is most natural in settings where agents are working towards different goals but are not directly competing. Our running example of a cleaning robot in an airport is such a setting, as the other agents (the passengers) do not share the goals of the robot, but also have no desire to prevent the robot from achieving its goals. Responsibility-based evaluation is also particularly useful when the satisfaction of some or all of an agents goals or values cannot be guaranteed (due to possible interference from other agents), since responsibility minimisation *can* always be guaranteed.

In future work, we would like to consider more closely the connection between responsibility for risk and responsibility anticipation, since both acknowledge that an agent may need to consider/may be attributed responsibility for some outcome even in scenarios where the outcome in question does not occur, but where the actions of the agent mean that it *might* have occurred. This would be particularly relevant if we introduce explicitly probabilistic reasoning into our model, as this is a typical feature of the formal study of risk.

Since (to the best of our knowledge) the field of research into multi-value responsibility is at present extremely limited, there are a number of potentially fruitful directions for future research. Our model makes a number of simplifying assumptions, in particular assuming that all agents have perfect knowledge of the domain ∇ but have no knowledge about the relative likelihood of the possible strategies of the other agents. Both of these assumptions could be dropped, such as by giving the agents only partial information about the start state/action theory, or by letting them reason in some way about the values and rationality of other agents. It would also be useful to have a more precise computational grounding as both a first step towards a real-world implementation of these ideas and a useful insight into the computational complexity of this model. This would require some changes to the model, such as a more complex representation of strategies to make iterating over all possible strategies computationally feasible. It is also worth expanding our definitions of responsibility to consider responsibility for multiple agents (where this paper is focused on a single-agent perspective), such as when some coalition of agents jointly acts to guarantee outcomes that none of them could have guaranteed individually (as others have done for single-value responsibility). Finally, we believe that there is much more work to be done both in studying the formal properties of the notions of multi-value responsibility that we present here, and further exploring the undoubtedly rich landscape of responsibility notions in multi-value settings.

Disclosure of Interests. The authors have no competing interests.

Appendix

Corollary 1. *Given Histories* H_1, H_2, H_3, *and a value base* $\overline{\Omega}$, *let* $X = Sat(H_1, \overline{\Omega}^+)$, $Y = Sat(H_2, \overline{\Omega}^+), Z = Sat(H_3, \overline{\Omega}^+)$. *Then* $X \preceq Y$ *if and only if* $X \backslash Z \preceq Y \backslash Z$.

Proof. Let k be the number of priority levels for $\overline{\Omega}$ (so $\overline{\Omega} = (\Omega_1, \ldots, \Omega_k)$. For all $1 \leq k' \leq k$, let $Score(A, k') = |A \cap \Omega_{k'}| - |A \cap \Omega_{k'}^{\neg}|$. Then we can see that comparing any two sets A and B by $\preceq$ depends solely on the values of $Score(A, k')$ and $Score(B, k')$ for $1 \leq k' \leq k$.

Therefore it is enough to prove that for all $1 \leq k' \leq k$, $Score(X, k') \leq Score(Y, k')$ if and only if $Score(X \backslash Z, k') \leq Score(Y \backslash Z, k')$.

Let k' be such that $1 \leq k' \leq k$, let let $t = |\Omega_k'|$. Let $x = |X \cap \Omega_{k'}|$ and $z = |Z \cap \Omega_{k'}|$. Note that $|X \cap \Omega_{k'}^{\neg}| = t - x$, since all values in $\Omega_{k'}$ are either satisfied or violated in X. Therefore $Score(X, k') = 2x - t$ and by a similar argument $Score(Z, k') = 2z - t$.

Let $c = |\Omega_k' \cap X \cap Z|$. Therefore $|\Omega_{k'} \cap (X \backslash Z)| = x - c$ and $|\Omega_{k'} \cap (Z \backslash X)| = z - c$. Note that $|\Omega_{k'}^{\neg} \cap (X \backslash Z)| = |\Omega_{k'} \cap (Z \backslash X)|$ since every value satisfied in Z but not in X is a value that is violated in X but not in Z. Therefore

$$
\begin{aligned}
&Score(X \backslash Z, k') \\
=&|\Omega_{k'} \cap (X \backslash Z)| - |\Omega_{k'}^{\neg} \cap (X \backslash Z)| \\
=&(x - c) - (z - c) \\
=&x - z \\
=&\frac{2x - 2z}{2} \\
=&\frac{(2x - t) - (2z - t)}{2} \\
=&\frac{Score(X, k') - Score(Z, k')}{2}
\end{aligned}
$$

By a similar argument $Score(Y \backslash Z, k') = \frac{Score(Y,k') - Score(Z,k')}{2}$. It follows immediately that $Score(X, k') \leq Score(Y, k')$ if and only if $Score(X \backslash Z, k') \leq Score(Y \backslash Z, k')$ and we are done.

References

1. Abarca, A.I.R., Broersen, J.M.: A stit logic of responsibility. In: Proceedings of the 21st Conference on Autonomous Agents and MultiAgent Systems, (AAMAS) (2022)
2. Alechina, N., Halpern, J., Logan, B.: Causality, responsibility and blame in team plans. In: Proceedings of the 16th Conference on Autonomous Agents and Multi-Agent Systems, (AAMAS) (2017)
3. Baier, C., Funke, F., Majumdar, R.: A game-theoretic account of responsibility allocation. In: Proceedings of the 30th International Joint Conference on Artificial Intelligence, (IJCAI) (2021)

4. Baltag, A., Canavotto, I., Smets, S.: Causal agency and responsibility: a refinement of stit logic. In: Logic in High Definition, Trends in Logical Semantics, pp. 149–176 (2021)
5. Barberà, S., Bossert, W., Pattanaik, P.: Ranking sets of objects. In: Handbook of Utility Theory, volume 2 - Extensions. Springer, Boston (2004)
6. Belloni, A., et al.: Dealing with ethical conflicts in autonomous agents and multi-agent systems. In: Artificial Intelligence and Ethics, Papers from the 2015 AAAI Workshop (2015)
7. Bienvenu, M., Fritz, C., McIlraith, S.: Planning with qualitative temporal preferences. In: Proceedings of the 10th Conference on Principles of Knowledge Representation and Reasoning, (KR) (2006)
8. Braham, M., van Hees, M.: An anatomy of moral responsibility. Mind **121**(483), 601–634 (2012)
9. Bulling, N., Dastani, M.: Coalitional responsibility in strategic settings. In: Proceedings of the 14th Workshop on Computational Login in Multi-Agent Systems (CLIMA). Lecture Notes in Computer Science (2013)
10. Chockler, H., Halpern, J.: Responsibility and blame: a structural-model approach. J. Artif. Intell. Res. **22**, 93–115 (2004)
11. De Giacomo, G., Vardi, M.: Linear temporal logic and linear dynamic logic on finite traces. In: Proceedings of the 23rd International Joint Conference on Artificial Intelligence (IJCAI) (2013)
12. De Giacomo, G., Vardi, M.: Synthesis for LTL and LDL on finite traces. In: Proceedings of the 24th International Joint Conference on Artificial Intelligence (IJCAI) (2015)
13. Dennis, L., Fisher, M., Slavkovik, M., Webster, M.: Formal verification of ethical choices in autonomous systems. Robot. Auton. Syst. **77**, 1–14 (2016)
14. Gladyshev, M., Alechina, N., Dastani, M., Doder, D.: Group Responsibility for Exceeding Risk Threshold. In: Proceedings of the 20th International Conference on Principles of Knowledge Representation and Reasoning (KR) (2023)
15. Grandi, U., Lorini, E., Parker, T., Alami, R.: Logic-based ethical planning. In: Proceedings of the 21st International Conference of the Italian Association for Artificial Intelligence (AIxIA) (2022)
16. Grandi, U., Lorini, E., Parker, T.: Moral planning agents with ltl values. In: Proceedings of the 32nd International Joint Conference on Artificial Intelligence, IJCAI (2023)
17. Halpern, J.: A modification of the halpern-pearl definition of causality. In: Proceedings of the 24th International Joint Conference on Artificial Intelligence, (IJCAI) (2015)
18. Linhart, P., Radner, R.: Minimax-regret strategies for bargaining over several variables. J. Econ. Theory **48**(1), 152–178 (1989)
19. Lorini, E., Longin, D., Mayor, E.: A logical analysis of responsibility attribution: emotions, individuals and collectives. J. Log. Comput. **24**(6), 1313–1339 (2014)
20. Lorini, E., Mühlenbernd, R.: The long-term benefits of following fairness norms under dynamics of learning and evolution. Fund. Inform. **158**(1–3), 121–148 (2018)
21. Lorini, E., Schwarzentruber, F.: A logic for reasoning about counterfactual emotions. Artif. Intell. **175**(3–4), 814–847 (2011)
22. Lorini, E., Sartor, G.: The ethics of controllability as influenceability. In: Proceedings of The Thirty-fourth Annual Conference on Legal Knowledge and Information Systems (JURIX). Frontiers in Artificial Intelligence and Applications, vol. 346, pp. 245–254 (2021)

23. Naumov, P., Tao, J.: Two forms of responsibility in strategic games. In: Proceedings of the 30th International Joint Conference on Artificial Intelligence, IJCAI (2021)
24. Naumov, P., Tao, J.: Counterfactual and seeing-to-it responsibilities in strategic games. Ann. Pure Appl. Logic **174**(10), 103353 (2023)
25. Niehans, J., et al.: Zur preisbildungen bei ungewissen erwartungen. Swiss J. Econ. Stat. (SJES) **84**(V), 433–456 (1948)
26. Parker, T., Grandi, U., Lorini, E.: Anticipating responsibility in multiagent planning. In: Proceedings of the 26th European Conference on Artificial Intelligence, ECAI (2023)
27. van de Poel, I., Fahlquist, J.N.: Risk and responsibility. In: Handbook of Risk Theory: Epistemology, Decision Theory, Ethics, and Social Implications of Risk. Springer, Netherlands (2012)
28. Rossi, F.: Moral preferences. In: The 10th Workshop on Advances in Preference Handling (MPREF) (2016)
29. Savage, L.J.: The theory of statistical decision. J. Am. Stat. Assoc. **46**(253), 55–67 (1951)
30. Shi, Q.: Responsibility in extensive form games. In: Proceedings of the 38th AAAI Conference on Artificial Intelligence (AAAI) (2024)
31. Talbot, B., Jenkins, R., Purves, D.: When Robots Should Do the Wrong Thing. In: Robot Ethics 2.0: From Autonomous Cars to Artificial Intelligence. Oxford University Press (2017)
32. Yazdanpanah, V., Dastani, M., Jamroga, W., Alechina, N., Logan, B.: Strategic responsibility under imperfect information. In: Proceedings of the 18th Conference on Autonomous Agents and MultiAgent Systems, (AAMAS) (2019)

Parameter Synthesis for Families of Markov Chains with an Application to Multi-agent Systems Privacy

Francesco Spegni[1(✉)], Luca Spalazzi[1], Roberto Rosetti[1,2], and Aniello Murano[2]

[1] Università Politecnica delle Marche, Ancona, Italy
f.spegni@univpm.it
[2] Università Federico II, Napoli, Italy

Abstract. Given a probabilistic system with parameters and a target specification, the parameter synthesis problem is defined as the search for actual values that can be assigned to the model parameters such that the system itself fulfills the given specification.

This problem has been studied extensively in the case of (finite-state) Markov Chains. We study the parameter synthesis problem in a new formalism called families of Markov Chains (fMC), a special case of infinite Markov Chains. The latter can express Markov Chains with both discrete parameters as well as probabilistic parameters. After showing that in this setting the parameter synthesis problem is undecidable, we show a methodology that, under suitable conditions, reduces an infinite family of MCs to a single parametric MC. Then, by using standard techniques such as mixed integer linear programming (MILP), one can solve the parameter synthesis problem on the abstract parametric MC and obtain optimal parameter values for the given infinite family of MCs.

In order to show the feasibility of our approach, despite the NP-hard complexity of MILP, we consider scenarios where Multi-Agent Systems needs to store sensitive information on a distributed storage.

Keywords: Parameterized Systems · Markov Chains · Parameter Synthesis · Multi-Agent Systems · Privacy

1 Introduction

Markov Chains (MCs) are a well-known formalism for describing transition systems with probabilistic behavior (e.g. [6]). Markov Chains have been widely used to specify and verify systems and in particular Multi-Agent Systems [1,12,13,16,36]. One key problem in this respect concerns finding the optimal parameter values for transitions among states in a given Markov Chain such that certain desired (resp. undesired) probabilities can be maximized (resp. minimized) [19,34,36]. To the best of our knowledge, all research works dealing with such problem assume that the number of states and transitions in the considered MC is fixed, and only the probabilities labeling the transitions are left "open" as

R. Collier et al. (Eds.): EUMAS 2024, LNAI 15685, pp. 159–178, 2025.
https://doi.org/10.1007/978-3-031-93930-3_10

parameters. In this work we introduce a broader class of Markov Chains that we call *families of Markov Chains* (fMC). The core idea is that a family is defined by a skeleton MC with both probabilistic parameters as well as discrete parameters affecting the number of states and transitions of each MC in the family.

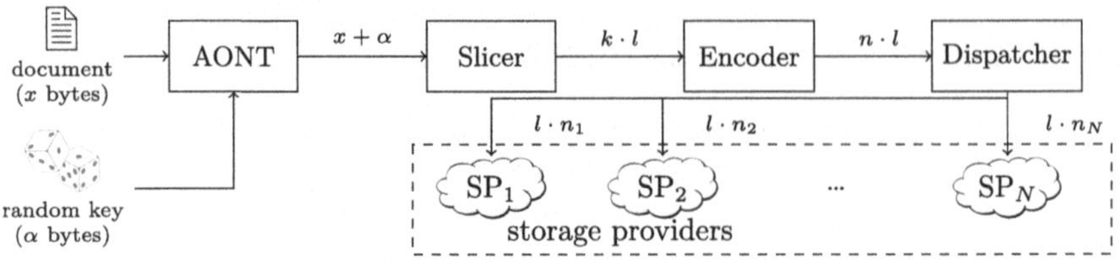

Fig. 1. Block diagram of AONT-RS

While in practice families of MCs inherit the undecidability of parameter synthesis problems from *parametric Markov Chains* (pMCs) [34], they are still useful in order to describe real-world scenarios that would otherwise escape the usual decidable fragments of pMCs. In this work we introduce a novel abstraction methodology and technique allowing to reduce an infinite family of Markov Chains to a single pMC, provided that the family has some regularity. As a consequence, one may reduce the parameter synthesis problem for the infinite family of MCs to a Mixed-Integers Linear Programming (MILP) problem derived from the pMC. Even though the presented approach is not general for fMCs, its feasibility is tested through a running example, where a hypothetical dispersed storage protocol for multi-agent systems is modeled as an infinite family of MCs, and then optimal parameters are synthesized for ensuring that given data protection specifications are met.

Running Example. In recent years, alternative solutions based on the idea of dispersing private information on independent storage nodes became more and more popular, both in the cloud [35,39,41] as well as in the multi-agent [4,14,15,23,26,43] communities, all moved by privacy and trust issues. In order to assure reliability from one hand and security on the other, several authors have proposed schemata based on fragmentation, erasure coding, and encryption [10,33,39,40]. From an abstract point of view, dispersed storage algorithms can be characterized by a limited set of parameters. Let x be the original file size to be dispersed and let l be the size of each fragment called *slice*. The parameters of interest are (n, k), where: $n \geq x/l$ is the the number of slices to be dispersed after the transformation of the original file; $k \leq n$ is the minimum number of slices to recover the original file, thus $n - k$ is the maximum number of lost (erased) slices that still allows files to be recovered; $k-1$ is the maximum number of slices an intruder can eavesdrop without recovering the secret. One of the most popular schemata is represented by the All-Or-Nothing-Transform Reed-Solomon (AONT-RS) [39], where the Reed-Solomon erasure code is applied to AONT (Fig. 1).

The main agents in the system are the storage providers, a manager controlling the overall dispersal process, and the attacker, a malicious entity willing to recover the credentials of one or more of the storage providers, aiming at intercepting all the slices stored in them. Once the attacker recovered k slices it can steal the secret. The attacker can be described as follows: i) it acts independently from the security level of the storage providers; ii) it perform simultaneous attacks to all storage providers; iii) it executes zero-cost attacks (no resources consumption); iv) it only attacks the storage providers.

It should be highlighted that while dispersed storage solutions are becoming more and more popular to the point that some of them are having a real commercial distribution, they still lack a rigorous and formally defined methodology to accurately dimension some fundamental parameters such as how many slices each node should receive in order to ensure the desired level of cyber-security and data protection, motivating our work.

From a practical point of view, this running example first assumes that it is possible to estimate the probability of threats based on security reports, and second that for each node it is possible to assess its vulnerability (e.g. by using standard tools such as the NIST Vulnerability Database[1] and deducing probabilities from the scores appearing in them). These are common assumptions in standard approaches to risk and cyber-security assessment [22, 27].

Let us remark that, in order to model this scenario, one could not apply standard *parameter synthesis* techniques ([29]) for parametric Markov Chains, since the latter require to know all the discrete parameters of the problem (viz. states and transitions must be fixed). In the present scenario, instead, the discrete parameters (e.g. the number of slices or the number of storage providers) affect the number of states and transitions in each pMC of the given family of the probability parameters vary with some of the discrete parameters of the problem, viz. the *number of slices* to be stored on the remote storage providers.

Outline. Section 2 introduces *families of Markov Chains* (fMCs) while in Sect. 3 we show how to derive a "cutoff" pMC from the infinite family of Markov Chains and confidentiality specifications under suitable conditions. In Sect. 4 we describe how Mixed-Integer Linear Programming can be used to synthesize optimal parameters for ensuring the desired security specification while in Sect. 5 we show an application of our methodology to the running example. Section 6 surveys the state-of-the-art in solving the parameter synthesis problem and contrasts our work with it. Finally, Sect. 7 contains some closing remarks.

2 Families of Parametric Markov Chains

In the following, $[0, 1]$ denotes the rational interval $0 \leq t \leq 1$, for $t \in \mathbb{Q}$. Let us recall the definition of (discrete time) *Markov Chains* (MCs), a well known formalism for probabilistic systems.

[1] https://nvd.nist.gov.

Definition 1 (Discrete Time Markov Chains [6]**).** *Assume a finite set of variables* $V = \{v_1, \ldots, v_q\}$. *A discrete time Markov chain is a tuple* $\mathbb{M} = (\Sigma, \mathcal{P}, \iota, AP, L)$ *such that:*

- Σ *is a countable, non empty, set of valuations* $\sigma : V \to \mathbb{Q}$, *called states,*
- $\mathcal{P} : \Sigma \times \Sigma \to [0,1]$ *is a transition probability function such that* $\forall s \in \Sigma.\ \sum_{s' \in \Sigma} \mathcal{P}(s, s') = 1$,
- $\iota : \Sigma \to [0,1]$ *is the initial probability distribution, such that* $\forall s \in \Sigma.\ \sum \iota(s) = 1$,
- AP *is a finite set of propositions, and*
- $L : \Sigma \to 2^{AP}$ *is a state-labeling function*

We write $\sigma(x)$ for $x \in V$, to denote the value assumed by variable x in state σ. Let $Q = \{q_1, \ldots, q_n\}$ denote a set of parameters that can assume rational values, let $\mathcal{F}_Q$ be the set of rational functions from Q to $\mathbb{Q}$.

Definition 2 (Parametric Markov Chains (pMC) [24]**).** *A parametric Markov Chain (pMC) is a generalization of a MC, where the component* $\mathcal{P}$ *is replaced by the following relation:*

$$\mathcal{P} : \Sigma \times \Sigma \to \mathcal{F}_Q.$$

Let us denote with $\mathcal{PMC}$ *the domain of all the possible pMCs.*

In this work we generalize pMCs to *families of Markov Chains*, where an infinite number of pMCs are collected together. This is typically useful when the family generates systems that share a common structure, defined by some template with discrete parameters in it that assume values in $\mathbb{N}$. The template defines the common structure of the graph formed by the states and the transitions, while the discrete parameters determine how many states and transitions are present. Let us remark that families of pMCs are parametric in two dimensions, since they have both discrete parameters in $\mathbb{N}$ as well as rational probability parameters in $[0,1] \subset \mathbb{Q}$ on the transitions.

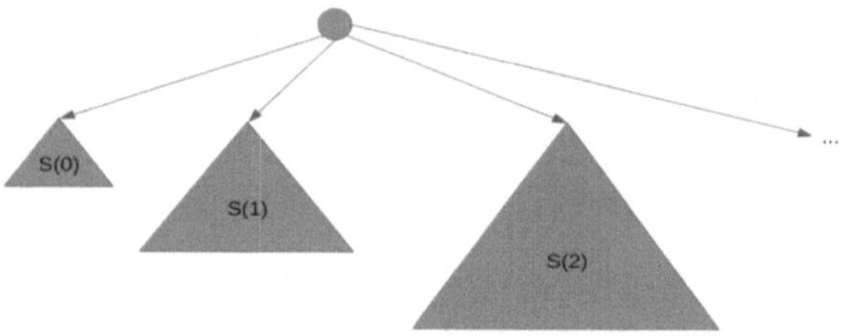

Fig. 2. An fMC $S\langle n\rangle$ can be seen as an infinite parametric Markov Decision Process S^∞

Definition 3 (Families of Markov Chains (fMC)). *Let us call* family of parametric Markov Chains *the total mapping:*

$$\mathcal{G} : \mathbb{N} \times \ldots \times \mathbb{N} \to \mathcal{PMC}$$

where all the returned pMC's returned by $\mathcal{G}$ share the same set of parameters.

Let us denote with $\hat{n} \in \mathbb{N}$ some given natural number, and with $\theta : Q \to [0,1]$ a valuation function for parameters $Q = \{q_1, \ldots, q_m\}$. Let us assume a fMC S with probability parameters Q. Let us assume, for the sake of conciseness and without loss of generality, that S has only one discrete parameter n, and let us write $S\langle n\rangle$ to make it explicit. Let us denote with $S(\hat{n})$ the pMC resulting from instantiating the parameter n on the value $\hat{n}$, and with $S_\theta(\hat{n})$ the MC derived from $S(\hat{n})$ after instantiating each probability parameter $q \in Q$ to the value $\theta(q)$. Let us denote with Φ a parameterized subset of states of S also depending on n. We write $\Phi\langle n\rangle$ to make it explicit.

In Fig. 2 we give an intuitive representation of the fact that, besides seeing a fMC $S\langle n\rangle$ as a total mapping $S : \mathbb{N} \to \mathcal{PMC}$, it can also be seen as a single parametric Markov Decision Process S^∞ with infinitely many states and transitions. In S^∞ the initial state non-deterministically "jumps" into one of the infinitely many possible successor states, each assigning a distinguished value $i \in \mathbb{N}$ to parameter n, and next the process continues to "behave" as the parametric Markov Chain $S(i)$. Note that it is never allowed to jump from a state in $S(i)$ to a state in $S(j)$, for $i \neq j$.[2]

In Fig. 3 we report an example of how to use an extended PRISM syntax to encode the family of the N-dice programs by Knuth and Yao [31] to an arbitrary number N of dice. The template of the fMC is expressed in a combined notation mixing PRISM and Jinja[3], the latter being a general purpose template language for generating text programs. Provided that each parameter is assigned to a value in the current context, expressions such as `{{ FOO + FIE }}` are replaced with their result. Jinja is a powerful template language, also allowing conditional evaluations as well as bounded iterations, not needed in this simple example.

Next, denote with $\Phi(\hat{n})$ a subset of states of $S(\hat{n})$ obtained by instantiating Φ on the actual value $\hat{n}$. Let us call Φ and $\Phi(\hat{n})$ *parameterized specification* and *specification*, respectively. For the MC $S_\theta(\hat{n})$, it is possible to *determine the probability* of reaching states in $\Phi(\hat{n})$ by applying standard polynomial time algorithms, thus we denote with $\mathbb{P}(S_\theta(\hat{n}), \Phi(\hat{n}))$ such probability. The problem of determining the probability with which states in $\Phi(\hat{n})$ are reached is known as *probabilistic model checking.*

[2] Note that the initial non-deterministic transitions are not allowed by an (infinite-state) Markov Chain, which only admits probabilistic transitions. In addition, being non-deterministic, such transitions do not have any probabilities associated with them.

[3] https://github.com/pallets/jinja.

```
dtmc
module dice
    s : [0..7] init 0;                          // local state of a die
    n : [1..{{ N }}] init 1;                    // number of dice
    d : [0..{{ (N+1) * 6 }}] init 0;            // sum of the dice
    [] s=0 -> 0.5 : (s'=1) + 0.5 : (s'=2);
    [] s=1 -> 0.5 : (s'=3) + 0.5 : (s'=4);
    [] s=2 -> 0.5 : (s'=5) + 0.5 : (s'=6);
    [] s=3 & d<={{ N * 6 }} -> 0.5 : (s'=1) + 0.5 : (s'=7) & (d'=d+1);
    [] s=4 & d<={{ N * 6 }} ->
    0.5 : (s'=7) & (d'=d+2) + 0.5 : (s'=7) & (d'=d+3);
    [] s=5 & d<={{ N * 6 }} ->
    0.5 : (s'=7) & (d'=d+4) + 0.5 : (s'=7) & (d'=d+5);
    [] s=6 & d<={{ N * 6 }} -> 0.5 : (s'=2) + 0.5 : (s'=7) & (d'=d+6);
    [] s=7 & n<{{ N }} -> (s'=0) & (n'=n+1);
    [] s=7 & n={{ N }} -> (s'=7);
endmodule
```

Fig. 3. A family of pMC modeling N-dice programs [31]

In case a parameter valuation function is lacking, the model checking problem is undefined. On the other hand, two other problems are defined that fall under the name of *probabilistic parameter synthesis*: finding the valuation of probabilistic parameters which *realizes a specification*, or which *minimize the probability of reaching* states that satisfy the specification itself. The former problem takes as input a pMC $S(\hat{n})$, some specification $\Phi(\hat{n})$ and some probability value $p \in [0,1]$, and it returns a valuation $\theta : Q \to [0,1]$ such that $\mathbb{P}(S_\theta(\hat{n}, \Phi(\hat{n})) = p$. The latter problem takes as input a pMC $S(\hat{n})$ and some specification $\Phi(\hat{n})$, and it returns a valuation θ such that for all other valuations θ' the following holds: $\mathbb{P}(S_\theta(\hat{n}), \Phi(\hat{n})) \leq \mathbb{P}(S_{\theta'}(\hat{n}), \Phi(\hat{n}))$. Both problems are known to be undecidable in the general case [34], but have efficient solutions for a wide variety of special cases. We generalize the probabilistic model checking problem to fMCs.

Definition 4 (Model checking problem). *Let us assume a set of probabilistic parameters $Q = \{q_1, \ldots, q_m\}$, a valuation $\theta : Q \to [0,1]$, and a rational interval $[a,b] \subseteq [0,1]$. Given a fMC $S\langle n\rangle$ with probabilistic parameters Q and a parameterized specification $\Phi\langle n\rangle$, return true iff $\forall \hat{n} \in \mathbb{N}.\ \mathbb{P}(S_\theta(\hat{n}), \Phi(\hat{n})) \in [a,b]$, and false otherwise.*

Theorem 1. *The model checking problem for families of pMC and parameterized reachability specifications is undecidable.*

Proof (Sketched). First, note that fMCs generalize so-called parameterized systems, i.e. families of finite-state systems exchanging data through some synchronous or asynchronous logic, where the only allowed parameter is the number of participating actors in the system (several sorts of parameterized systems have been defined, both in qualitative, e.g. [2], as well as in quantitative, e.g. [42] settings). Assume the model checking problem for fMCs is decidable. Families of pMCs, taken as computational model, are very powerful. It is easy to encode a network of pMCs acting as token passing finite-state processes, that communicate by exchanging a multivalued token on a unidirectional ring, using fMCs. Note that the resulting fMCs has no probability parameters (i.e. $Q = \emptyset$), since no such parameter is present in the original token-passing system. Our assumption would imply that the parameterized model checking problem for reachability specification on multi-valued token passing systems on rings is decidable, but the latter is known to be undecidable [21].

Let us extend also the realizability and minimization problems to fMCs.

Definition 5 (Realizability problem). *Let us assume a set of probabilistic parameters* $Q = \{q_1, \dots, q_m\}$. *Given a fMC* $S\langle n\rangle$ *with parameters* Q, *a parameterized specification* Φ, *and a rational interval* $[a, b] \subseteq [0, 1]$, *return* $\theta : Q \to [0, 1]$ *such that* $\forall \hat{n} \in \mathbb{N}.\ \mathbb{P}(S_\theta(\hat{n}), \Phi(\hat{n})) \in [a, b]$.

Definition 6 (Minimization problem). *Let us assume a set of probabilistic parameters* $Q = \{q_1, \dots, q_m\}$. *Given a fMC* $S\langle n\rangle$ *with parameters* Q, *a parameterized specification* Φ, *and a rational interval* $[a, b] \subseteq [0, 1]$, *return* $\theta : Q \to [0, 1]$ *such that* $\forall \hat{n} \in \mathbb{N}.\ \forall \theta'.\ \mathbb{P}(S_\theta(\hat{n}), \Phi(\hat{n})) \leq \mathbb{P}(S_{\theta'}(\hat{n}), \Phi(\hat{n}))$.

The following statement follows directly from the undecidability of realizability for pMCs [34].

Theorem 2. *The realizability and the minimization problems are undecidable.*

While pMCs have well engineered procedures for solving both problems in special cases, they are not directly applicable to fMCs, since each family contains an infinite number of pMCs. The following section describes *cutoff parametric Markov Chain*, a novel abstraction that under suitable conditions may reduce an infinite fMC onto a finite set of pMCs.

3 Cutoff Parametric Markov Chains

For $x, y, \epsilon \in \mathbb{R}$ and $\epsilon > 0$, let us write $x =_\epsilon y$, meaning that $|x - y| < \epsilon$. Since a fMC, say $S\langle n_1, \dots, n_m\rangle$ is characterized by a certain number of discrete parameters, one may wonder how the family behaves when one of the parameters is "big enough". To conduct this analysis, one may define a single pMC, say $S^\omega\langle n_1, \dots, n_{m-1}\rangle$, and then show that indeed for growing values of the m-th parameter, S and S^ω behave the same, w.r.t. some specification Φ, in which case S^ω is called *cutoff fMC*.

Definition 7 (Cutoff fMC and cutoff pMC). *Assume a fMC* $S\langle n_1, \dots, n_m\rangle$, *a parameterized specification* Φ, *and a tolerance* $\epsilon > 0$. *Let us call cutoff fMC* $S^\omega\langle n_1, \dots, n_{m-1}\rangle$ *a fMC such that:*

$$\exists c.\ \forall \hat{n}_m \geq c.\ \mathbb{P}(S(\hat{n}_1, \dots, \hat{n}_m), \Phi(\hat{n}_1, \dots, \hat{n}_m)) =_\epsilon \mathbb{P}(S^\omega(\hat{n}_1, \dots, \hat{n}_{m-1}), \Phi^\omega(\hat{n}_1, \dots, \hat{n}_{m-1}))$$

When $m = 1$ *we call* S^ω *a cutoff pMC.*

It is evident that not every arbitrary fMC S may converge to some cutoff fMC S^{ω}, when one of its parameter grows towards infinity. But when this happens, the cutoff fMC S^{ω} has indeed one less "degree of infiniteness" w.r.t. S, thus simplifying the analysis.

If a cutoff fMC $S^{\omega}\langle n_1, \ldots, n_{m-1}\rangle$ exists for a given fMC $S\langle n_1, \ldots, n_m\rangle$ and a given parameterized specification Φ, then S^{ω} is indeed an abstraction of all but a finite subset of the pMCs contained in the family S that depend on parameter n_m. For this reason we write $S \simeq S^{\omega_1} \simeq \ldots \simeq S^{\omega_{m-1}} \simeq S^{\omega}$, then the final cutoff fMC S^{ω} is indeed a cutoff pMC, and regular parameter analysis synthesis techniques for pMCs can be applied.

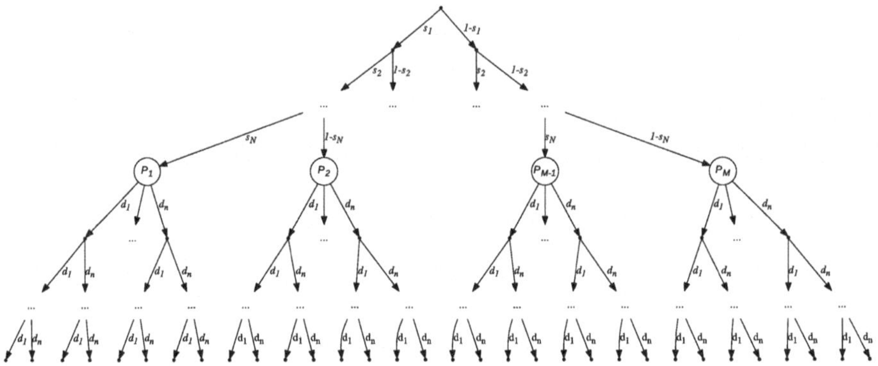

Fig. 4. A Markov Chain modeling a dispersed storage ($M = 2^N$)

3.1 A Cutoff fMC for Dispersed Storage

Let us now show how to apply the cutoff fMC abstraction to a real world scenario. Figure 4 depicts a fMC modeling a dispersed storage solution with N storage providers and n slices. The probability parameters are $s_1, \ldots, s_N$ (the probabilities of an attacker of hacking the i-th storage provider) and $d_1, \ldots, d_N$ (the probabilities of the i-th storage provider to receive a slice from the client). States are configurations of the variables $V = \{turn, n_c, n_a\} \cup \{h_i : 1 \leq i \leq N\}$ with the following intended meanings: *turn* increases from 1 (in the root) to N (at the level of nodes $P_1, \ldots, P_M$ in Fig. 4), and at each increment the attacker "decides" whether it has hacked the provider indexed by *turn* (with probability s_i) or not (with probability $1 - s_i$); for every $i \in [0, N]$, variable h_i stores 1 if the i-th provider has been hacked, and 0 otherwise; n_c represents the number of slices sent so far by the client and n_a the number of slices intercepted by the attacker. Assuming to know the values of parameters $s_1, \ldots, s_N$ (i.e. the security levels of the storage providers), our aim is to find a parameter valuation for $d_1, \ldots, d_N$ such that the likelihood of reaching a state where $n_a \geq k$ (i.e. the attacker can recover the secret) is minimal.

In the following, let us denote with the name of each node P_j the subset of the storage providers that the attacker successfully controls, given the previous strategy (i.e. the path from the root down to node P_j itself). This means that $P_j \subseteq \{1, \ldots, N\}$, for every $1 \leq j \leq 2^N$, and $P_1, \ldots, P_M$ are all distinct elements of the power set $2^{\{1,\ldots,N\}}$. Each subtree departing from P_j has a depth of n, and each intermediate node of that subtree decides which storage provider should receive the next slice. Each such node has N storage providers to choose from, with probabilities $d_1, \ldots, d_N$, respectively. In each subtree with root P_j, transitions $s \xrightarrow{d_i} t$ represent the action of sending a slice towards the i-th provider. If the recipient provider is under the attacker's control (i.e. $i \in P_j$) the variable n_a is increased by one in the target state, otherwise it has the same value as the source state. Variable n_c is always increased till it reaches value n in the leaves.

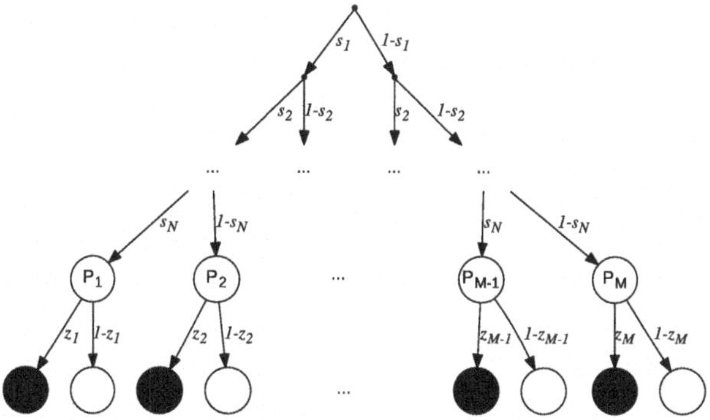

Fig. 5. The limit Markov Chain for the dispersed storage ($M = 2^N$)

Let us call $S(\hat{N}, \hat{n}) = \left(\Sigma(\hat{N}, \hat{n}), \mathcal{P}, \iota, AP, L\right)$ the pMC obtained by instantiating the fMC in Fig. 4 for some values $\hat{N}, \hat{n} \geq 0$. Let us focus on the parameterized specification $\Phi\langle N, n\rangle = \{\sigma : \sigma \in \Sigma(\hat{N}, \hat{n}), \sigma(n_a) \geq k, \hat{N}, \hat{n} \in \mathbb{N}\}$, i.e. where the attacker gains enough slices to recover the secret.

The first step is to define a candidate cutoff fMC $S^\omega\langle N\rangle$. To this aim, let us introduce the set of variables $V^\omega = \{turn, e_a\} \cup \{h_i : 1 \leq i \leq N\}$ and let:

$$\Sigma^\omega(\hat{N}) = \{\gamma(\sigma) : \sigma \in \Sigma(\hat{N}, \hat{n}), \hat{n} \in \mathbb{N}\}$$

be a set of states obtained through mapping γ s.t. for all $\sigma' = \gamma(\sigma)$:

$$\begin{array}{lll}
\sigma'(turn) & = \sigma(turn) & \\
\sigma'(h_i) & = \sigma(h_i) & \textit{for } i = 1, \ldots, N \\
\sigma'(e_a) & = \textit{white} & \textit{if } \sigma(turn) \neq N \ \vee \ \sigma(n_c) < n \\
\sigma'(e_a) & = \textit{white} & \textit{if } turn = N \wedge \sigma(n_c) = n \wedge \mathbb{E}[n_a|\ \sigma] < k \\
\sigma'(e_a) & = \textit{black} & \textit{if } turn = N \wedge \sigma(n_c) = n \wedge \mathbb{E}[n_a|\ \sigma] \geq k
\end{array}$$

In other words, while variables *turn* and h_i are tracked precisely by the abstraction γ, variable n_c is simply forgotten while variable n_a is replaced with e_a which is the expected value of random variable n_a, given the current variables of state σ. Such definition has the effect of "collapsing" each subtree departing from nodes P_j, for $1 \leq j \leq 2^N$, with a pair of leaves, as of Fig. 5, where the black leaf denotes that $n_a \geq k$ (i.e. the attacker recovered the secret) while the white one denotes that $n_a < k$ (i.e. the secret is safe).

Let z_j be the probability of jumping from any node P_j onto its black leaf, and let $1-z_j$ be the probability of jumping onto its white leaf. One can determine the analytical form of the expected value $\mathbb{E}[n_a|\sigma]$ by observing that for each pMC in $S\langle N, n\rangle$, the subtree with root in P_j represents a multinomial distribution of n slices among N recipients, and n_a stores the amount of slices sent to provider i, for $i \in P_j$, thus: $\mathbb{E}[n_a \mid \sigma] = (\sum_{i \in P_j} (d_i/n) \cdot n) = \sum_{i \in P_j} d_i$. It must be that $z_j = 1$ if $n \cdot \sum_{i \in P_j} d_i \geq k$, and $z_j = 0$ otherwise. Summarizing, probability parameters $s_1, \ldots, s_N$ are known, while $z_1, \ldots, z_M$ are determined by distribution probabilities $d_1, \ldots, d_N$. Note that at this stage the fMC $S^\omega\langle N\rangle$ does not have distribution probabilities $d_1, \ldots, d_N$ on the edges (cf. Fig. 5), since we abstracted away the intermediate steps in which slices were distributed. This explains why, in Sect. 4, we need to reduce the parameter synthesis problem to a custom mixed-integer linear programming (MILP) problem, rather than applying an off-the-shelf tool for MDP parameter synthesis (e.g. PROPhESY [19]).

Applying the abstraction function γ, the specification to check becomes:

$$\Phi^\omega = \{\gamma(\sigma) \ : \ \sigma \in \Sigma(\hat{N}, \hat{n}), \hat{n} \in \mathbb{N}, \mathbb{E}[n_a \mid \sigma] \geq k\}.$$

One of the main characteristics of the candidate cutoff fMC $S^\omega\langle N\rangle$ and its parameterized specification $\Phi^\omega\langle N\rangle$ is that they do not depend anymore on the specific value of n. The next theorem states that S^ω is indeed a cutoff fMC for S and Φ, since it satisfies Def. 7. Intuitively, for "big enough" values of n, the original fMC $S\langle N, n\rangle$ and the cutoff $S^\omega\langle N\rangle$ are indistinguishable, w.r.t. Φ.

Theorem 3. *Assume an fMCs $S\langle N, n\rangle$ with specification $\Phi\langle N, n\rangle$, a tolerance $\epsilon > 0$, and the aforementioned fMC $S^\omega\langle N\rangle$ and specification $\Phi^\omega\langle N\rangle$. The following holds:*

$$\exists c.\ \forall \hat{n} \geq c.\ \mathbb{P}(S\langle \hat{N}, \hat{n}\rangle, \Phi\langle \hat{N}, \hat{n}\rangle) =_\epsilon \mathbb{P}(S^\omega\langle \hat{N}\rangle, \Phi^\omega\langle \hat{N}\rangle).$$

Since S^ω has only one parameter, it is a cutoff pMC.

Proof (Theorem 3). Fix any $\hat{N}, \hat{n} \in \mathbb{N}$. Observe that $\mathbb{P}(S\langle \hat{N}, \hat{n}\rangle, \Phi\langle \hat{N}, \hat{n}\rangle) = \sum_{j=1}^{2^{\hat{N}}} \mathbb{P}(P_j) \cdot \mathbb{P}(n_a \geq k|P_j)$. By definition of the fMC $S(N, n)$, we have that $\mathbb{P}(P_j) = (\prod_{i \in P_j} s_i \prod_{i \in \overline{P_j}} (1 - s_j))$.

Since the paths from the root to nodes P_j are identical in $S(\hat{N}, \hat{n})$ as well as $S^\omega(\hat{N})$, the probability $\mathbb{P}(P_j)$ remains the same, for every P_j. Let us focus on the sub-trees starting from P_j and reaching the leaves. For growing values of n, the weak law of large numbers states that the mean value of a random variable converges towards its expected value. Formally, for any random variable X and real number $\epsilon > 0$: $\lim_{n\to\infty} \mathbb{P}(|X - \mathbb{E}[X]| < \epsilon) = 1$.

Let us consider, in the original fMC $S(\hat{N}, \hat{n})$, a set of random variables $n_1, \ldots, n_N$ counting how many slices were assigned to provider i in the leaf states departing from P_j. Note that $0 = \sum_{i=1}^{N} n_i$ in state P_j and $n = \sum_{i=1}^{N} n_i$ in the leaf states. For any fixed and arbitrary small threshold $\epsilon > 0$, for larger values of n (i.e. representing the number of slices to be distributed, in our example) the mean value of variables n_i converges towards its expected value $\mathbb{E}[n_i] = n \cdot d_i$ (since the tree departing from state P_j implements a multinomial distribution of the n slices in the N providers). As a consequence, the mean value of random variable n_a converges towards $\mathbb{E}[n_a] = \sum_{i\in P_j} \mathbb{E}[n_i] \doteq n \cdot \sum_{i\in P_j} d_i$.

This means that for any P_j, for larger values of n:

$$\mathbb{P}(n_a \geq k | P_j) =_\epsilon \begin{cases} 1 & \mathit{if}\, n \cdot \sum_{i\in P_j} d_i \geq k \\ 0 & \mathit{otherwise} \end{cases}$$

where $=_\epsilon$ denotes an equivalence up to a fixed tolerance $\epsilon > 0$.

Let us now consider the same probability $P(n_a \geq k | P_j)$ in the candidate cutoff pMC $S(\hat{N})$. In this case:

$$\mathbb{P}(n_a \geq k | P_j) = z_j = \begin{cases} 1 & \mathit{ifn} \cdot \sum_{i\in P_j} d_i \geq k \\ 0 & \mathit{otherwise} \end{cases}$$

by definition. Since this holds for every P_j, we can conclude that: $\mathbb{P}(S(\hat{N}, \hat{n}), \Phi(\hat{N}, \hat{n})) =_\epsilon \mathbb{P}(S^\omega(\hat{N}), \Phi^\omega(\hat{N}))$. □

The theorem states that $S^\omega\langle N\rangle$ abstracts all but a finite subset of states in $S\langle N, n\rangle$. The key observation exploited to prove the theorem is that the fMC of the case study has a tree-like shape, without loops, and thus the expected value of random variable n_a can be reduced analytically to a multinomial distribution of the n slices among the N providers.

This yields a secondary problem, viz. finding how "fast" $S\langle N, n\rangle$ converge to $S^\omega\langle N\rangle$, for growing values of n. Such problem can be solved experimentally through an iterative approach, checking for larger and larger values of parameter n. Theorem 3 guarantees that the iteration always terminates.

In Table 1 we report some examples of how values of $\pi_{\hat{n}}$ approach the value π_ω, for growing values of $\hat{n}$. The results in the table have been obtained by setting the vector of attack probabilities $\mathbf{s}_5 = [0.10, 0.20, 0.30, 0.40, 0.50]$ and $\mathbf{s}_{10} = [0.05, 0.10, 0.15, 0.20, 0.25, 0.30, 0.35, 0.40, 0.45, 0.50]$, while the vector of dispatch probabilities are $\mathbf{d}_5 = [0.2, 0.2, 0.2, 0.2, 0.2]$ and $\mathbf{d}_{10} = [0.2, 0.2, 0.1, 0.1, 0.1, 0.1, 0.05, 0.05, 0.05, 0.05]$. Intuitively, $\mathbf{d}_5$ uniformly distributes slices among the available providers, while $\mathbf{d}_{10}$ slightly prefers to dispatch slices towards the most secure ones. Let us fix the tolerance threshold $\epsilon = 0.00001$, equivalent to an error of 0.001% w.r.t. the expected attack probability when n tends to infinity. In three out of four cases, the cutoff value is $n = 500$, while in one case it is $n = 100$.

Table 1. Finding cutoff values for parameter n w.r.t. probability $\mathbb{P}(S(N,n), \Phi(N,n))$

N	α	**s**	**d**	π_ω	n	π_n	$\lvert\pi_n - \pi_\omega\rvert$
5	0.7	$\mathbf{s}_5$	$\mathbf{d}_5$	0.02260	10	0.08697	0.06437
					50	0.03411	0.01151
					100	0.02563	0.00303
					500	0.02260	-
					1000	0.02260	-
					1500	0.02260	-
5	0.9	$\mathbf{s}_5$	$\mathbf{d}_5$	0.00120	10	0.01570	0.01450
					50	0.00222	0.00102
					100	0.00132	0.00012
					500	0.00120	-
					1000	0.00120	-
					1500	0.00120	-

N	α	**s**	**d**	π_ω	n	π_n	$\lvert\pi_n - \pi_\omega\rvert$
10	0.7	$\mathbf{s}_{10}$	$\mathbf{d}_{10}$	0.00109	10	0.01548	0.01439
					50	0.00176	0.00067
					100	0.00114	0.00005
					500	0.00109	-
					1000	0.00109	-
					1500	0.00109	-
10	0.9	$\mathbf{s}_{10}$	$\mathbf{d}_{10}$	0.00001	10	0.00109	0.00108
					50	0.00002	0.00001
					100	0.00001	-
					500	0.00001	-
					1000	0.00001	-
					1500	0.00001	-

4 Parameter Synthesis via MILP

In the following we present a mathematical formulation encoding the parameter synthesis problem minimising probability $\mathbb{P}(S^\omega(N), \Phi^\omega(N))$ described in the previous section.

Considering a *probability distribution* $(d_1, \ldots, d_N)$, the *partition* of the n slices among the N storage providers will be $(d_1 \cdot n, \ldots, d_N \cdot n)$. If we call n_i the number of slices received by the ith provider, the value of n_i will be closer to $d_i \cdot n$ as long as the number of slice grows, i.e. $\lim_{n\to\infty} n_i = d_i \cdot n$. This means that, for *big enough* values of n, the best probability distribution will correspond with the best partition of slices among the N providers. According to this idea, the aim of the presented mathematical formulation is to find the best distribution probability $(d_1, \ldots, d_N)$ that minimizes the success probability of an attacker to steal the data.

Assume that the set of provider identities is $\mathcal{N} = \{1, \ldots, N\}$. In the following, we denote with $2^{\mathcal{N}}$ the power set of $\mathcal{N}$ while P_j is the j-th element of the power set (with $1 \leq j \leq 2^N$), assuming some fixed ordering of $2^{\mathcal{N}}$. As we have seen in the previous section, all the strategies for a possible attacker are collected by $2^{\mathcal{N}}$, i.e. every set $P_j \in 2^{\mathcal{N}}$ corresponds to a possible outcome of the attacker's attempt, intended as the set of providers it gains access to. For instance, assuming there are 10 available providers, the set P_{ex} ={1,3,4,7} represents a state where the attacker gained access to providers 1,3,4 and 7, but not the others. Let us denote with $0 \leq \alpha \leq 1$ the fraction k/n of slices that allows to reconstruct the dispersed information. We write s_i, for $1 \leq i \leq N$, to denote the security level of provider i, i.e. the probability that an intruder can gain access to it, which is given.

The *variables* used in the mathematical model are: *i)* d_i positive rational variable stating the probability to assign a slice to provider i; *ii)* z_j binary variable determining whether the strategy P_j is successful, i.e. if it leads the intruder to gain k slices out of n, or more; iii) q_j auxiliary variable stating the fraction of the n slices retrieved by the attacker, according to strategy P_j.

In the following, the notation $\mathbf{d}$, $\mathbf{z}$ and $\mathbf{q}$ represents respectively the vector of variables d_i, z_j, and q_j, for every $i \in \mathcal{N}$ and $j \in 2^{\mathcal{N}}$. The problem of synthesizing optimal values for can be reduced to the following MILP problem:

$$\min \sum_{j=1}^{2^N} z_j \prod_{i \in P_j} s_i \prod_{i \in \overline{P_j}} (1 - s_i) \tag{1}$$

$$\sum_{i \in \mathcal{N}} d_i = 1 \tag{2}$$

$$d_i \geq 0 \qquad i = 1..N \tag{3}$$

$$q_j = \sum_{i \in P_j} d_i \qquad j = 1..2^N \tag{4}$$

$$q_j - \alpha + \mu \leq z_j \qquad j = 1..2^N \tag{5}$$

$$-(q_j - \alpha) \leq (1 - z_j) \qquad j = 1..2^N \tag{6}$$

$$q_j \geq 0 \qquad j = 1..2^N \tag{7}$$

$$z_j \quad \text{binary} \qquad j = 1..2^N \tag{8}$$

The objective function (1) sums over all the possible attack outcomes. Considering the previous example, the probability associated with the strategy P_{ex} is:

$$\prod_{i \in P_{ex}} s_i \prod_{i \in \overline{P_{ex}}} \overline{s_i} = s_1 \cdot s_3 \cdot s_4 \cdot s_7 \cdot \overline{s_2} \cdot \overline{s_5} \cdot \overline{s_6} \cdot \overline{s_8} \cdot \overline{s_9} \cdot \overline{s_{10}} \tag{9}$$

where, for any $a \in [0, 1]$, we write $\overline{a}$ to denote $1 - a$. Note that not all the elements of the objective function will have a value greater than 0. In fact, the set of Eqs. (4) assign to the variable q_j the fraction of slices retrieved in the j-th strategy (the reader can see that the variable q_j has been introduced to simplify the mathematical notation). Let us highlight that values of z_j and q_j are strictly connected. Indeed, the constraints (5) and (6) express the following logic relation: $z_j = 1 \Leftrightarrow q_j \geq \alpha$ and $z_j = 0 \Leftrightarrow q_j < \alpha$, respectively, and the arbitrary small value of μ added in the left-hand-side of inequalities (5) avoids the uncertainty of the variable z_j when $q_j = \alpha$. Notice that without parameter μ in the inequality, variable z_j would assume 0 or 1 every time $q_j = \alpha$. This is a standard technique used to bind binary variables to rational positive ones. In fact, whenever $z_j = 0$, constraints (5) and (6) become respectively: $q_j - \alpha + \mu \leq 0$ and $-(q_j - \alpha) \leq 1$, and they hold only if $q_j < \alpha$. On the other hand, when $z_j = 1$ the constraints change as follows: $q_j - \alpha + \mu \leq 1$ and $-(q_j - \alpha) \leq 0$ and can be satisfied only if $q_j \geq \alpha$.

Using the strategy P_{ex}, then $z_{ex} = 1$ if the fraction of slices collected by the attacker is $\alpha \geq k/n$ and $z_{ex} = 0$ otherwise. This explains how the contribution of (9) to the objective function is driven by the value of q_{ex}. As said before, the vector of variables $\mathbf{q}$ has been introduced to clarify the exposition because it is defined by a subset of elements of the vector $\mathbf{d}$. Constraints (2) and (3) state that $\mathbf{d}$ is a probability distribution of slices.

A Relevant Subcase: $N \geq n$. The given MILP problem solves the parameter synthesis problem finding the optimal parameters no matter the actual values of parameters N, n, and q_i for $i \in \mathcal{N}$. Let us consider a more specific case where it is possible to find a direct solution to the parameter synthesis problem, in time polynomial w.r.t. its input. Consider an instance of the parameter synthesis problem with $N > n$ and assume that at most one slice can be assigned to each provider (i.e. $q_i \in \{0, \frac{1}{n}\}$, for $i \in \mathcal{N}$). Since a general assumption of the mathematical formulation above is that n is *big enough*, this implies that the number of storage providers N is even bigger, approaching to infinity. We will see in Sect. 5 that this assumption is realistic for several dispersed storage implementations. In this scenario, any allocation strategy corresponds to a set A of providers that received the slice, or equivalently by an N-ary incidence vector $I^A = [I_1^A, \ldots, I_N^A]$ such that $I_i^A = 1$ if a slice has been allocated to provider i, otherwise $I_i^A = 0$. Let $\mathcal{A}_n^p = \{A \in \mathcal{P}(n) : |A| = p\}$ be the collection of allocation strategies with exactly p providers out of n, and $\mathcal{A}_n = \bigcup_{i \geq k} \mathcal{A}_n^i$ be the collection of sets with at least k elements out of n. The success probability for the attacker is thus:

$$\mathbb{P}(|A| \geq k) = \sum_{A \in \mathcal{A}_n} \prod_{i=1}^{n} [s_i I_i^A + (1 - s_i)(1 - I_i^A)]$$

Let us remark that the parameter k in the above equation affects the definition of $\mathcal{A}_n$. Assume $s_1 \leq, \ldots, \leq s_N$, i.e. providers are sorted from the most secure one (with lowest probability of being attacked) to the least secure one. It is immediate to show that assigning slices only to the n safest providers is an optimal strategy.

Proposition 1. *Assume n slices to be allocated to N providers, where $N > n$. Let A^* be the strategy using the distribution vector such that: $d_i = \frac{1}{n}$ if $1 \leq i \leq n$, otherwise $d_i = 0$, and let A' be any other strategy. Then:*

$$\mathbb{P}(|A^*| \geq k) \leq \mathbb{P}(|A'| \geq k)$$

5 Applications

Here we want to show how to apply the theoretical framework developed in the previous sections.[4]

[4] In the following we choose arbitrary probability values of storage providers being successfully attacked, because the concrete probability values do not affect the feasibility of the overall approach and how to quantitatively assess cyber-risk is a research area on its own (e.g. [22,27]).

Distributed Storage. In this category fall the solutions where a large number of providers can connect dynamically to form a network (e.g. IBM Cloud Object Storage [38], Quantum [44]). Here the storage providers receive a single slice each and have heterogeneous configurations. Since in this case $N > n$, as show in Sect. 4 it is enough to use the optimal strategy A^*, where slices are distributed from the most secure provider to the least secure one.

Table 2. Three scenarios with $N = 5$ providers and different ratios $\alpha = k/n$

N	$\mathbf{s}$	α	$\mathbf{d}$	π_ω
5	0.22, 0.34, 0.46, 0.58, 0.70	0.7	0.31, 0.31, 0.31, 0.07, 0.00	0.03441
		0.8	0.21, 0.21, 0.21, 0.21, 0.16	0.01996
		0.9	0.11, 0.56, 0.11, 0.11, 0.11	0.01397
5	0.22, 0.34, 0.46, 0.58, 0.70	0.8	0.21, 0.37, 0.21, 0.21, 0.00	0.01996
		0.9	0.67, 0.11, 0.11, 0.11, 0.00	0.01996

Table 3. Three scenarios with $N = 10$ providers and different ratios $\alpha = k/n$

N	$\mathbf{s}$	α	$\mathbf{d}$	π_ω
10	$\mathbf{s}_{10}$	0.7	0.31, 0.31, 0.31, 0.00, 0.00, 0.00, 0.00, 0.00, 0.00, 0.07	0.009856
		0.8	0.16, 0.11, 0.11, 0.11, 0.11, 0.11, 0.11, 0.11, 0.11, 0.00	0.002284
		0.9	0.11, 0.11, 0.11, 0.11, 0.11, 0.11, 0.11, 0.11, 0.12, 0.00	0.00012

Multi-provider Storage. In this case the number of storage providers N is relatively small, i.e. $N \leq 10$, and more than one slice per provider must be assigned, while the number of slices n is still assumed to grow towards infinity, as a function of the size of the file to be stored. Examples of implementations are CDStore [35]. It is reasonable to assume that the security level of each storage provider is assessed periodically and reduced to an attack probability. This scenario can thus benefit from our technique, as described below, and even the exponential complexity of MILP is mitigated by the fact that the number of providers N is small enough.

Let us first consider three multi-provider scenarios sharing the same parameter $N = 5$ and the same vector of attack probabilities $\mathbf{s}$, but with different ratio $\alpha = k/n \in \{0.7, 0.8, 0.9\}$. The first 3 rows in Table 2 summarize the values of the probability distribution $\mathbf{d}$ minimizing the probability of a successful attack. The results are consistent with the intuititon that increasing values of α should correspond to lower probabilities of a successful attack from the intruder π^ω (at the cost of a reduced availability in case of network partitioning). The data in Table 2 surprisingly tells us also that, when $\alpha \geq 0.8$, it is safe to take advantage of all the providers, despite the fact that some of them have an extremely low security level (up to 70% probability of falling under the attacker's control!).

The two bottom lines in Table 2 tells us that, by assigning no slice to the least secure server (i.e. if we force the 5th entry in $\mathbf{d}$ to be 0.00), we obtain again a minimal attack probability of 0.01996 in the case $\alpha = 0.8$, but in case $\alpha = 0.9$ we get an incremented attack probability (0.01996 instead of 0.01397)! This shows that naive assignment strategies, e.g. always assigning more slices to the safest storage providers, may result in non-minimal probabilities of a successful attack in multi-provider settings, witnessing that our analysis is indeed useful for designers of dispersed storage solutions.

Let us now consider three more multi-provider scenarios, with $N = 10$ storage providers, a given vector of attack probabilities $\mathbf{s}_{10} = [0.16, 0.22, 0.28, 0.34, 0.40, 0.46, 0.52, 0.58, 0.64, 0.70]$, and again consider three distinct values of $\alpha = k/n \in \{0.7, 0.8, 0.9\}$. Table 3 collects the values of $\mathbf{d}$ minimizing the probability of a succesful attack. Even these scenarios confirm that parameter α is inversely proportional to attack probability π_ω. Once again, the returned solutions tell us that, in some settings, it is safe to distribute 7% of the slices to a provider with 70% probabilities of being successfully attacked.

6 Related Work

Multi-Agent Systems (MAS) often require collaboration among actors that do not fully trust each other, thus they wish to share sensible or even secret information but still preserving control over its privacy. In [23] a distributed constraint optimization algorithms is designed that preserves privacy using secret sharing protocols. In [14] an epistemic logic approach is used to express strategy logic specifications, and in such frameworks the privacy of a secret sharing protocol for MAS is considered. In [17,32] the authors model and verify MAS with an unknown number of participating agents, and express security requirements using subsets of the epistemic CTLK /X logic, but such logic is only able to express *qualitative* security specifications, while our framework aims at expressing and model checking *quantitative* security specifications. None of the mentioned works deal with the problem of synthesizing parameters for optimizing the security of the privacy-scheme adopted by the MAS under investigation.

Several authors studied the problem of finding *optimal parameters* for parametric Markov Chains, also referred to as *Parametric Probabilistic Transition Systems* (PPTSs) by Lanotte et al. [34]. Other researchers focused on finding parameter values through inductive synthesis [3,11]. A recent overview of parameter synthesis for parametric Markov Models can be found in [28]. Dehnert et al. presented the tool PROPhESY [19] that works for reachability and expected rewards objectives. In the domain of parametric Markov Decision Processes (pMDPs), the same problem has been explored under a game-theoretic point-of-view (e.g. [36] and [25]) or for searching the optimal scheduling policies w.r.t. some given reachability specification [5]. The parameter synthesis problem is known to be undecidable already for the case of PPTSs/pMCs [34] even though under suitable conditions parameter synthesis for pMCs is ETR-complete [30]. It is worth highlighting that, to the best of our knowledge, the existing solutions to the parameter synthesis problem assume that the input pMC or pMDP have finitely many states, with parameters on the edges in place of probabilities. This assumption is too restrictive for several real-world scenarios, as the one described in this paper. Indeed, when modelling dispersed storage architectures, the actual values of some parameters (most notably the number n of stored slices) affect the number of states in the pMC describing it. The combination of parameters controlling both the numbers of states and the numbers of transition probabilities is new, to the best of our knowledge.

Our work is similar in principles to Family-based model-checking [18,20] where one wants to formally verify a family of systems sharing a common structure. Especially, our cutoff approach resembles the so-called all-in-one analysis. They do not consider the problem of synthesizing parameters for infinite families of MCs, though.

This paper continues the research line of [7–9,37], more focused on cloud applications, and show how their tools and methodologies can be helpful also for addressing privacy issues and secret sharing algorithms in multi-agent systems. This paper focuses on a new attacker model, targeting agents acting as storage providers and shows how to synthesize parameters that are optimal for the full infinite state system.

7 Conclusions

In this work we present a methodology for synthesizing parameters for families of MCs sharing a common structure (template), despite the fact that the latter is indeed an infinite state system. We have shown that the parameter synthesis problem for fMCs is in general not decidable, and we have contextually introduced a novel abstraction technique that, under suitable conditions, reduces an infinite fPMc to a single pMC. The latter is then used to synthesize optimal parameters for the entire family. Despite the NP-hardness of MILP, the presented approach can still be feasible and useful to discover unexpected properties of real-world scenarios in the MAS and cloud domains.

An application has been shown of how to apply the methodology in order to verify the privacy of a multi-agent secret sharing mechanism implemented in real-world cloud systems.

At the moment the methodology drives the system analyst while building a formal tool-chain that may ensure the desired level of security in the modeled system. On the other hand, it does not yet automatize all the tasks (e.g. extracting the cutoff pMC from the original fMC, or solving the parameter synthesis problem on the cutoff pMC). The presented methodology could be applied succesfully to the case study because the infinite-substructure (states and transitions) common to all the Markov Chains of the family was indeed use to model a multinomial distribution of n slices of secret across N different agents, and that could be collapsed to a finite number of states and transitions, knowing how to compute the expected value of the involved random variables (viz. n_a, the number of slices captured by an attacker) in the case of a multinomial distribution.

We conjecture that whenever the expected value of random variables could be computed "collapsing" infinitely many sub-graphs of states and transitions in the Markov Chains of a family to a finite number of them, the same methodology could be applied. It is an open question whether such condition could be recognized syntactically and thus the entire procedure automatized for suitable families of Markov Chains.

References

1. Abate, A., et al.: Rational verification: game-theoretic verification of multi-agent systems. Appl. Intell. **51**(9), 6569–6584 (2021). https://doi.org/10.1007/s10489-021-02658-y
2. Aminof, B., Kotek, T., Rubin, S., Spegni, F., Veith, H.: Parameterized model checking of rendezvous systems. Distrib. Comput. **31**, 187–222 (2018)
3. Andriushchenko, R., Češka, M., Junges, S., Katoen, J.P., Stupinskỳ, Š.: Paynt: a tool for inductive synthesis of probabilistic programs. In: International Conference on Computer Aided Verification, pp. 856–869. Springer (2021)
4. Arias, J., Budde, C.E., Penczek, W., Petrucci, L., Sidoruk, T., Stoelinga, M.: Hackers vs. security: attack-defence trees as asynchronous multi-agent systems. In: Lin, S.-W., Hou, Z., Mahony, B. (eds.) ICFEM 2020. LNCS, vol. 12531, pp. 3–19. Springer, Cham (2020). https://doi.org/10.1007/978-3-030-63406-3_1
5. Arming, S., Bartocci, E., Sokolova, A.: SEA-PARAM: exploring schedulers in parametric MDPs. Electron. Proc. Theor. Comput. Sci. **250**, 25–38 (2017). https://doi.org/10.4204/EPTCS.250.3,http://arxiv.org/abs/1707.04122v1
6. Baier, C., Katoen, J.P.: Principles of Model Checking. Springer, Cham (2008). https://doi.org/10.1093/comjnl/bxp025
7. Baldi, M., et al.: A probabilistic small model theorem to assess confidentiality of dispersed cloud storage. In: Bertrand, N., Bortolussi, L. (eds.) Quant. Eval. Syst., pp. 123–139. Springer, Cham (2017)
8. Baldi, M., Chiaraluce, F., Senigagliesi, L., Spalazzi, L., Spegni, F.: Security in heterogeneous distributed storage systems: a practically achievable information-theoretic approach. In: 2017 IEEE Symposium on Computers and Communications (ISCC), pp. 1021–1028. IEEE (2017)
9. Baldi, M., Cucchiarelli, A., Senigagliesi, L., Spalazzi, L., Spegni, F.: Parametric and probabilistic model checking of confidentiality in data dispersal algorithms. In: Proceedings of HPCS 2016: Intererrnational Conference on High Performance Computing & Simulation, pp. 476–483 (2016).https://doi.org/10.1109/HPCSim.2016.7568373
10. Baldi, M., Maturo, N., Montali, E., Chiaraluce, F.: AONT-LT: a data protection scheme for cloud and cooperative storage systems. In: Proceedings of HPCS 2014: International Conference on High Performance Computing & Simulation, pp. 566–571 (2014)
11. Batz, K., Chen, M., Junges, S., Kaminski, B.L., Katoen, J.P., Matheja, C.: Probabilistic program verification via inductive synthesis of inductive invariants. In: International Conference on Tools and Algorithms for the Construction and Analysis of Systems, pp. 410–429. Springer (2023)
12. Belardinelli, F., Jamroga, W., Mittelmann, M., Murano, A.: Strategic abilities of forgetful agents in stochastic environments. In: Marquis, P., Son, T.C., Kern-Isberner, G. (eds.) Proceedings of the 20th International Conference on Principles

of Knowledge Representation and Reasoning, KR 2023, Rhodes, Greece, September 2-8, 2023, pp. 726–731 (2023)
13. Belardinelli, F., Jamroga, W., Mittelmann, M., Murano, A.: Verification of stochastic multi-agent systems with forgetful strategies. In: Proceedings of the 23rd International Conference on Autonomous Agents and Multiagent Systems, pp. 160–169 (2024)
14. Belardinelli, F., Lomuscio, A., Murano, A., Rubin, S.: Verification of broadcasting multi-agent systems against an epistemic strategy logic. In: IJCAI, vol. 17, pp. 91–97 (2017)
15. Belardinelli, F., Lomuscio, A., Murano, A., Rubin, S.: Verification of multi-agent systems with public actions against strategy logic. Artif. Intell. **285**, 103302 (2020)
16. Berthon, R., Katoen, J., Mittelmann, M., Murano, A.: Natural strategic ability in stochastic multi-agent systems. In: Wooldridge, M.J., Dy, J.G., Natarajan, S. (eds.) Thirty-Eighth AAAI Conference on Artificial Intelligence, AAAI 2024, Thirty-Sixth Conference on Innovative Applications of Artificial Intelligence, IAAI 2024, Fourteenth Symposium on Educational Advances in Artificial Intelligence, EAAI 2014, February 20-27, 2024, Vancouver, Canada, pp. 17308–17316. AAAI Press (2024)
17. Boureanu, I., Kouvaros, P., Lomuscio, A.: Verifying security properties in unbounded multiagent systems. In: Proceedings of the 2016 International Confernce on Autonomous Agents & Multiagent Systems, pp. 1209–1217 (2016)
18. Chrszon, P., Dubslaff, C., Klüppelholz, S., Baier, C.: Profeat: feature-oriented engineering for family-based probabilistic model checking. Formal Aspects Comput. **30**, 45–75 (2018)
19. Dehnert, C., et al.: PROPhESY: A PRObabilistic ParamEter SYnthesis Tool. In: Kroening, D., Păsăreanu, C.S. (eds.) CAV 2015. LNCS, vol. 9206, pp. 214–231. Springer, Cham (2015). https://doi.org/10.1007/978-3-319-21690-4_13
20. Dimovski, A.S., Al-Sibahi, A.S., Brabrand, C., Wasowski, A.: Family-based model checking without a family-based model checker. In: Fischer, B., Geldenhuys, J. (eds.) SPIN 2015. LNCS, vol. 9232, pp. 282–299. Springer, Cham (2015). https://doi.org/10.1007/978-3-319-23404-5_18
21. Emerson, E.A., Namjoshi, K.S.: Reasoning about rings. In: Proceedings of the 22nd ACM SIGPLAN-SIGACT Symposium on Principles of Programming Languages, pp. 85–94 (1995)
22. Freund, J., Jones, J.: Measuring and Managing Information Risk: A FAIR Approach. Butterworth-Heinemann (2014)
23. Greenstadt, R., Grosz, B., Smith, M.D.: SSDPOP: improving the privacy of DCOP with secret sharing. In: Proceedings of the 6th International Joint Conference on Autonomous Agents and Multiagent Systems, pp. 1–3 (2007)
24. Hahn, E.M., Hermanns, H., Zhang, L.: Probabilistic reachability for parametric Markov models. Int. J. Softw. Tools Technol. Transfer **13**(1), 3–19 (2011)
25. Hansen, E., Bernstein, D., Zilberstein, S.: Dynamic programming for partially observable stochastic games. In: Proceedings of the National Conference on Artificial Intelligence (2000), pp. 709–715 (2004). http://www.aaai.org/Papers/AAAI/2004/AAAI04-112.pdf
26. He, L., Liu, G., Zhou, M.: Petri-net-based model checking for privacy-critical multiagent systems. IEEE Trans. Comput. Soc. Syst. (2022)
27. Hubbard, D.W., Seiersen, R.: How to Measure Anything in Cybersecurity Risk. Wiley, Hoboken (2016)

28. Jansen, N., Junges, S., Katoen, J.P.: Parameter synthesis in Markov models: a gentle survey. Principles of Systems Design: Essays Dedicated to Thomas A. Henzinger on the Occasion of His 60th Birthday, pp. 407–437 (2022)
29. Junges, S., et al.: Finite-state controllers of POMDPs using parameter synthesis. In: Globerson, A., Silva, R. (eds.) Proceedings of the Thirty-Fourth Conference on Uncertainty in Artificial Intelligence, UAI 2018, Monterey, California, USA, August 6-10, 2018, pp. 519–529. AUAI Press (2018)
30. Junges, S., Katoen, J.P., Pérez, G.A., Winkler, T.: The complexity of reachability in parametric Markov decision processes. J. Comput. Syst. Sci. **119**, 183–210 (2021)
31. Knuth, D.: The complexity of nonuniform random number generation, Algorithms and Complexity, New Directions and Results, pp. 357–428 (1976)
32. Kouvaros, P., Lomuscio, A., Pirovano, E., Punchihewa, H.: Formal verification of open multi-agent systems. In: Proceedings of the 18th International Conference on Autonomous Agents and Multiagent Systems, pp. 179–187 (2019)
33. Krawczyk, H.: Secret sharing made short. In: Annual International Cryptology Conference, pp. 136–146. Springer (1993)
34. Lanotte, R., Maggiolo-Schettini, A., Troina, A.: Parametric probabilistic transition systems for system design and analysis. Formal Aspects Comput. **19**(1), 93–109 (2007)
35. Li, M., Qin, C., Li, J., Lee, P.P.: CDstore: toward reliable, secure, and cost-efficient cloud storage via convergent dispersal. IEEE Internet Comp. **20**(3), 45–53 (2016)
36. Littman, M.L.: Markov games as a framework for multi-agent reinforcement learning. In: Machine Learning Proceedings 1994, pp. 157–163 (1994). http://linkinghub.elsevier.com/retrieve/pii/B9781558603356500271
37. Llerena, Y.R.S., Su, G., Rosenblum, D.S.: Probabilistic model checking of perturbed mdps with applications to cloud computing. In: Proceedings of the 2017 11th Joint Meeting on Foundations of Software Engineering. ESEC/FSE 2017, pp. 454–464. ACM, New York (2017). https://doi.org/10.1145/3106237.3106301
38. Rangarao, D., Gucer, V.: IBM cloud object storage concepts and architecture (2017). http://www.redbooks.ibm.com/redpapers/pdfs/redp5435.pdf
39. Resch, J., Plank, J.: AONT-RS: blending security and performance in dispersed storage systems. In: Proceedings of 9th FAST Conference (2011)
40. Shamir, A.: How to share a secret. Commun. ACM **22**(11), 612–613 (1979)
41. Shen, L., Feng, S., Sun, J., Li, Z., Wang, G., Liu, X.: Clouds: a multi-cloud storage system with multi-level security. In: Proceedings of the International Confernce on Algorithms and Architectures for Parallel Processing, pp. 703–716. Springer (2015)
42. Spalazzi, L., Spegni, F.: Parameterized model checking of networks of timed automata with Boolean guards. Theoret. Comput. Sci. **813**, 248–269 (2020)
43. Tabatabaei, M., Jamroga, W.: Playing to learn, or to keep secret: alternating-time logic meets information theory. arXiv preprint arXiv:2303.00067 (2023)
44. Tabbara, B., Garg, P.: Shared community storage network (2016). https://patents.google.com/patent/US7869383B2/en. uS Patent 9,344,378 B2

Human-Agent Interaction

Influence of Language Warmth on User Adoption of Agent Recommendations for Multi-arm Bandits

Selim Karaoğlu[1(✉)], Marina Katoh[1], Titash Majumdar[1], Ethan Beaird[1], Feyza M. Hafızoğlu[2], and Sandip Sen[1]

[1] Tandy School of Computer Science, The University of Tulsa, Tulsa, USA
{selim-karaoglu,mak5308,tim2248,ethan-beaird,sandip-sen}@utulsa.edu
[2] İstanbul Commerce University, Istanbul, Turkey
fmhafizoglu@ticaret.edu.tr

Abstract. This research investigates the influence of language warmth on the user adoption of agent recommendations and satisfaction by/of the users in the multi-armed bandit scenarios. Prior work has identified that agent recommendations can, under certain situations, improve user selection of options to maximize utility given a limited number of pulls on a multi-armed bandit problem. We posit that appropriate explanations associated with agent recommendations can further increase user adoption of potentially higher utility arms and thereby increase cumulative utility obtained by the user from a finite number of arm pulls. Furthermore, we investigate the effect of "warmth" of explanations on recommendation adoption by the user and concomitant cumulative utility realized. We design an experimentation platform for the agent-assisted user selection from multi-armed bandits. Experiments are run with workers recruited from an online crowdsourcing platform. The results reveal that explanations do result in improved cumulative utility obtained. Most importantly, we suggest that agent designers should configure the warmth level of agent explanations depending on the interaction type, i.e., warm language can be more effective in some problems while cold language works in others.

Keywords: human-agent interaction · warmth · multi-armed bandit · XAI

1 Introduction

Perceived warmth and competence of team members and collaborators are two fundamental dimensions of social cognition that affect human judgment, motivation, and engagement in decision-making scenarios [9]. People recognize and judge each other through measures of likeability such as warmth and trustworthiness as well as measures of respectability, such as competence and efficiency. Research in social psychology finds that individuals are more concerned with others' inclination to help or harm rather than their capabilities and competence. The fact that collaborator's warmth is prioritized over competence can be interpreted as the "humans' evolutionary history of cooperative partner choice" [8].

R. Collier et al. (Eds.): EUMAS 2024, LNAI 15685, pp. 181–197, 2025.
https://doi.org/10.1007/978-3-031-93930-3_11

Human-agent interaction research has also recognized that the social cognition of agents by people plays a key role on the outcome of the interaction, satisfaction of the users, and long-term sustainability of the relationship between the user and agent and hence the success of related applications of agent technology [6,21,23]. People judge agents not only by their behavior but also by their appearance [26], voice [19], and the words chosen in explanations. Agent behaviors that will yield the exact same outcome objectively will be perceived very differently by people based on the social cues from these agents [23]. People's perception of warmth and competence of agents can determine their willingness to continue to interact [5,21,23]. Despite the growing body of research on the social perception of agent partners, very little is currently known about how the warmth of agents influences human-agent interactions in general and people's decision-making processes specifically.

This research studies the effect of agent warmth language-wise in the context of an agent-assisted decision-making problem. Agent warmth is expressed through the language utilized for agent recommendations in a setting with several alternative choices users can select from. In particular, our work focuses on a human-agent collaboration environment where both human and agent are learning to solve a multi-armed bandit problem, i.e., optimizing the cumulative payoffs received by repeatedly choosing from a given set of options, each having a static, but unknown, distribution of payoffs [22]. We utilize an "Investment Game" where the user repeatedly chooses one of several investment options and receives a payoff (rate of return). The goal is to maximize the cumulative returns from a relatively small number (in the few tens) of episodes.

We investigate how agent warmth influences the adoption of agent recommendations and the associated satisfaction of the users with the said agent. The research questions we study in this paper are as follows:

- How does the warmth in AI recommendations impact human decision-making performance in multi-armed bandit scenarios?
- Does the presence of warm AI explanations lead to higher levels of user satisfaction and engagement compared to no explanations or cold explanations?

We consider a multi-armed bandit scenario where the users explore and learn different investment options. Within this context, the agent assistants recommend stock options to invest in with explanations. The agent uses either warm or cold language in the explanations. We recruit online workers from the MTurk platform to play the *Investment Game* and use a between-subject experiment design. We measure user selection performance, change of user intention and adoption of recommendations, and user satisfaction with the agent. The results show that explanations do impact user behavior and produce statistically significant gains in utility. However, contrary to our expectations, cold explanations are found to be more effective than warm explanations.

2 Related Work

Explanations are helpful in AI-assisted decision-making scenarios [29]. As XAI systems can facilitate human-AI interactions and collaboration, timely and usable explanation generation and presentation have become an integral part of the development and deployment of machine learning models. Analysis of human-agent interaction domains and scenarios can also provide valuable insights into the challenges and solutions of developing an XAI algorithm [24].

Various studies on human-agent research explored the effect of agent warmth on people's perceptions. Prajod *et al.* [23] demonstrated that interacting with a warm agent yields more satisfaction, more willingness to renegotiate, and a better interaction experience. Gilad *et al.* [12] show that people prioritize warmth over competence when interacting with agents similar to when interacting with other people [8]. Belanche *et al.* [5] found that warmth by the robots in frontline services influences the relational expectations (i.e., adds emotional value). McKee *et al.* [21] reveal that people prefer to cooperate with warm agents over cold agents. Bergmann *et al.* [6] created human-like and robot-like virtual agents and embedded warmth and competence through non-verbal behavior and appearance. Humans judged warmth rapidly, typically in less than a minute. Furthermore, once the first impression regarding warmth was established, it was hard to change it in subsequent interactions.

Good-naturedness, trustworthiness, tolerance, friendliness, and sincerity are considered as scales of warmth [9]. According to Guenoun and Zlatev [14], features - including question marks, readability, complexity of words, exclamation marks, and pronoun choice - can affect perceived warmth. In particular, question marks [17] and community-oriented pronouns, such as "you" and "us", are perceived warmer [10]. Other features that have been shown to increase warmth include exclamation marks [14] and emoji usage [20]. Conversely, utilizing more complex words [16] and individual-oriented pronouns, such as "I" and "my", can decrease the perceived warmth [10]. Moreover, threatening languages that employ phrases such as "If ... then" clauses [27] have also been observed to decrease perceived warmth. By understanding how language can be utilized to express varying levels of warmth, agents can acquire the skill to apply an appropriate level of warmth that can lead to a more effective human-agent interaction.

Well studied Multi-armed bandit problem [1,3,4,7,25,28] has been extended to collaborative scenarios involving human-agent interactions [22]. Researchers have studied scenarios where both the human and the agent are learning simultaneously, with MABs providing a framework for agents to improve human performance by providing assistance [13,22]. Previous studies primarily focus on the agent's recommendations without incorporating text explanations in collaborative scenarios. These recommendations, while valuable, may not fully capture the nuances of the decision-making process, particularly in scenarios where both the human and the agent are learning simultaneously. Our research expands on these existing studies by introducing text explanations into the agent's recommendations. This addition aims to provide a richer, more informative, and hopefully more productive collaboration between the human and the agent. By incorporating text explanations, we seek to offer additional context and rationale behind the agent's recommendations, potentially aiding the user in their decision-making process.

3 Agents for Assisting Humans in Solving MABs

As the multi-armed bandit (MAB) scenario [1,3,25], we use Investment game, where each "arm", corresponds to a different stock option or strategy that the user can select from. Each selection, i.e., pull of an arm, returns a reward sampled from the associated, but unknown, reward distribution. The user has to repeatedly select options for a finite number of episodes with the goal of maximizing cumulative reward. The user is assisted by an agent which is also learning to estimate the expected reward of the different arms and makes recommendations for arms to pull based on its own emerging estimates. The agent does not know the reward probabilities of the arms and must learn from the values returned from the choices made. The agent's goal is to balance exploration (trying out all arms to learn about their rewards) and exploitation (choosing the arm with the highest expected reward). This trade-off, known as the exploration-exploitation dilemma, is central to many real-world problems.

We consider a finite horizon h ($h = 30$ in our study), meaning there is a finite number of arm pulls. The agent and the user begin with no prior knowledge of reward distribution. As the game progresses, both the agent and the user learn from the outcomes of the user's decisions. Given the limited number of arm pulls, balancing the exploration-exploitation balance is of critical importance for maximizing cumulative reward.

We now present the assistive agent design, interactive framework, and interface we have developed for the agent-assisted, finite horizon, multi-armed bandit scenario. For each decision, the user first determines the intended arm to pull. Next, the agent recommends an arm based on its own estimates. Finally, the user pulls an arm, either recommended arm or another arm available, and receives a reward.

We formulate the MAB problem $P = (\mathcal{A}, \mu)$ where $\mathcal{A}$ is a set of arms, μ is a vector of average rewards for each arm. Human In the Loop Learning UCB (HILL-UCB) (see Algorithm 1) is designed to generate an arm recommendation in agent-assisted multi-armed bandit (MAB). The algorithm takes as input the set of arms $\mathcal{A}$, the estimates for the arm rewards $\hat{\mu} = \{\hat{\mu_a}\}$, the set of the number of pulls N for each arm $N = \{N_a\}$, the list of the number of times each arm is recommended $R = \{R_a\}$, the current intention of the user i, the horizon h, and the current episode n. The output of the HILL-UCB algorithm is an arm r as recommendation and the context of recommendation c.

The algorithm is designed to work in the following three distinct cases, each chosen to handle a specific scenario in the decision-making process:

Case 1: If the user's intended arm i has not been pulled yet (i.e., $N_i < 1$), the algorithm recommends the intended arm. This case is chosen to respect the user's intention and to encourage exploration of new options.

Case 2: If the user's intended arm has been pulled before, the algorithm looks for an arm that has not been pulled earlier and has been recommended less than twice. If such arms exist, one of them is recommended randomly. This case promotes exploration of less recommended options, ensuring a diverse set of arms is explored over time.

Case 3: If all arms have been pulled and recommended at least twice, the algorithm employs a horizon-aware Upper Confidence Bound (UCB) strategy [22] to determine the arm to recommend. The weight w is calculated based on the minimum and maximum weights w_{min} and w_{max}, the current episode n, and the horizon h. The recommended arm r is the one that maximizes the weighted sum of the average reward and the UCB exploration term [2,18]. This case represents the exploitation phase, where the algorithm leverages its knowledge about the arms to make an informed recommendation.

In the HILL-UCB algorithm, both the exploration and exploitation parts have weights, where the sum of the two is equal to 1. Both weights have an initial value of 0.5. Throughout the game, the weight of the exploitation (exploration) is increased (decreased) linearly up where it has a maximum (minimum) value of 0.9 (0.1) in the last episode. The exploration and exploitation components are similar to the UCB algorithm [2,18,22].

Input : $\mathcal{A}$, the set of agents;
$\hat{\mu}$, the set of reward estimates for the arms;
N, the set of number of pulls for each arm;
R, a list of the number of times each arm is recommended;
i, current intention of the user;
h, horizon;
n, current episode

Output: r, the recommended arm;
c, the recommendation scenario case;

if $N_i < 1$ **then** `/* if intended arm has not been pulled yet */`
    r = i;
    c = 1;
else
    $A' \leftarrow \emptyset$
    for $i = a \rightarrow A$ **do**
        if $N_a < 1$ *and* $R_a < 2$ **then**
            $A' \leftarrow A' + a$;
    if $A' \neq \emptyset$ **then**
        r = rand(A');
        c = 2;
    else
        $w = w_{min} + p * (w_{max} - w_{min})/h$;
        $r = arg\,max_{a \in A}\ w \cdot \hat{\mu_a} + (1 - w) \cdot \sqrt{2 \cdot \frac{log(n)}{N_a}}$;
        $c = 3$;
return (r, c);

Algorithm 1: HILL-UCB (Human In the Loop Learning) Algorithm

4 Warm and Cold Language Model

The style or tone of the language used for explanation by the agent is designed to be either cold or warm using linguistic features established in previous research to indicate warmth. Table 1 provides a summary of the different warm and cold language criteria that are addressed in Sect. 2. Our language model utilizes these features to differentiate between warm and cold language.

Table 1. Features of Warm and Cold Language Models

Warm	Cold
Question marks	No question marks
Community-oriented pronouns	Individual-oriented pronouns
Exclamation marks	No exclamation marks
Simple language	Complex (utilitarian) language
Emojis	No emojis
Non-threatening language	Threatening language

In order to engender a warm and collaborative assistance, the agent focuses on utilizing community-oriented pronouns, while limiting the usage of pronouns that emphasize individualism [10]. In case of a disagreement between the user's intention and agent's recommendation, for a user with high likelihood of adopting the agent's recommendations, the agent may not only incorporate community-oriented pronouns to induce warmth but also provide suggestions in a question format to both express warmth [14,17] and emphasize how the user has a say in the final decision making. In the same case, but for a user with a low likelihood of adoption, the agent continues to use community-oriented pronouns, but reduces the warmth level by making statements rather than asking questions. Emojis are utilized for increasing perceived warmth [20].

In contrast to a warm agent, the cold agent focuses more on utilizing pronouns that are more individualistic and makes use of a more complex or utilitarian language to mildly display its competency. In case of disagreement, the agent incorporates a threatening language model using constructs such as the "if ... then" clause. This type of clause consists of a statement which warns users that if they do not adopt this option, then an undesirable outcome could follow [27].

4.1 Agent Explanations

The explanations provided to users in the ith arm selection involve two components: the *recommendation* and the *feedback*. The recommendation is displayed after the user's initial intention I_t but prior to the selection S_t. The agent highlights a recommended arm r_t along with a short message either expressing agreement with the user's intention or providing a different suggestion.

This message is made to vary in tone based on warmth level, as well as the user's tendency to adopt the agent's recommendation based on past interaction history to encourage further collaboration and compliance with the agent. For example, if it is highly likely that the user will adopt the agent's recommendation and the user's intention matches the agent's recommendation, the agent provides a shorter explanation. If the user's adoption is unlikely and there is an intention/recommendation mismatch, the agent provides a slightly longer explanation for encouraging collaboration (Table 2).

Table 2. Example recommendations for warm vs cold agents

Warm	Cold
"Love your efforts! How about choosing this selection since it could lead us to success? 😊"	"I understand the choice. Based on my assessment, selecting this one is more plausible."

Table 3. Example feedback for warm vs cold agents

Warm	Cold
"Amazing, let's keep it up! 😎"	"I see it worked out."

The feedback, on the other hand, is provided after the user made the final selection of an arm, and displays a message of either congratulations or encouragement based on whether a good or bad reward has been obtained. For example, if a user has selected an arm the agent recommended and gets a reward that was either expected or greater, they receive a short compliment as the feedback. On the other hand, if the user makes a different choice than the recommendation and gets a reward lower than the average, feedback emphasizes more collaboration (Table 3).

4.2 Structure for Formulating Warm and Cold Recommendation

The agent's manner of response is largely dependent upon the intention and selection pattern of the user. Figure 1 below encapsulates the structure at which the recommendation format is determined by the agent.

The first factor considered while structuring the recommendation is the condition: either a warm C_w or cold C_c agent. Next, the likelihood l_t of the user adopting the agent's recommendation during the tth arm pull is computed by $l_t = \delta l_{t-1} + (1 - \delta)1_{agreement}$ where $\delta = 0.75$. The value of $1_{agreement}$ is 1 if there was an agreement between the agent recommendation R_{t-1} and user selection S_{t-1} in the previous episode. Otherwise, the value would be set to 0. Based on the likelihood value, the degree to which the agent is cold or warm is determined. In the case that the agent is warm, if $l_t > 0.5$, the warmth level would be set to *high*. Apart from this case, the warmth level would be set to *low*. The third and final factor is whether there is an agreement between the user's intention I_t and the agent's recommendation R_t.

Unlike recommendation, the feedback takes into consideration the magnitude of the reward R_t obtained from the arm pulled by the user. The reward is deemed as *good* if it is higher than the average reward obtained from all the episodes played ($R_t \geq \mu$). It also factors in whether or not the user had adopted the agent's recommendation. If the recommendation has not been adopted, the feedback focuses on encouraging the user to collaborate more.

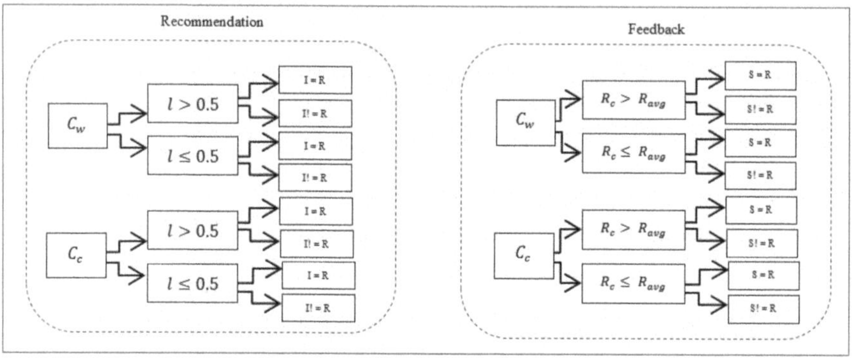

Fig. 1. Agent recommendation and feedback flow diagram

5 Empirical Methodology

We aim to test the hypothesis given below in our experiments.

Hypothesis 1: Individuals receiving AI recommendations with warm or cold explanations will achieve higher total utility compared to those receiving no explanations.

Hypothesis 2a: Individuals receiving AI recommendations with warm explanations will demonstrate higher adoption of recommendations compared to those receiving no explanations or cold explanations.

Hypothesis 2b: Individuals receiving AI recommendations with cold explanations will demonstrate higher adoption of recommendations compared to those receiving no explanations.

Hypothesis 3a: Individuals exposed to warm AI explanations will report higher levels of satisfaction compared to those exposed to no explanations or cold explanations.

Hypothesis 3b: Individuals exposed to cold AI explanations will report higher levels of satisfaction compared to those exposed to no explanations.

Hypothesis 4: Explanatory power of warm and cold AI explanations is perceived to be similar.

5.1 Experimental Setup

Our experiments involves the Investment game as a multi-armed bandit (MAB) scenario, where several stock options, representing the arms, are available for investment over 30 episodes. In each episode, *i* the participant is asked to specify her intended option, *ii* the agent provides a recommendation, highlighting a particular stock option based on the HILL-UCB algorithm, and *iii* the participant makes the final investment decision and receives a reward based on the selected stock option. The game interface keeps the participant informed about the number of times each stock option has been chosen and the average reward received from each option. The three experimental conditions, which determine the explanations by the agent, are:
1. No explanations[1],
2. Warm explanations,
3. Cold explanations.

Each participant is assigned to one of the conditions randomly. The agent provides either warm or cold explanations or none at all. In warm and cold conditions, the agent provides a text explanation accompanies the recommendation and post-selection feedback appropriately.

(a) Intention, recommendation, and selection

(b) Feedback

Fig. 2. Investment Game

Figure 2 shows two different instances of the game. Figure 2a indicates the user's intention, the agent's recommendation, and the user's final selection among various stock options. Note that the third stock option, highlighted with a dashed border signifies the user's initial intention. The agent recommends the

[1] No explanation or feedback is provided by the agent.

fifth stock option by providing a cold explanation. The final selection of the user is the sixth stock option and the button to invest appears only after the user makes the final selection. Figure 2b depicts a different scenario within the game where the agent is providing a feedback using warm language based on the user's selection and the reward received.

Metrics: *Utility score*, *recommendation score*, *switching score* and *contextual score* metrics are used in our analysis. We define the *utility score* for a user u, denoted as U_u, as the total utility received over N episodes: $U_u = \sum_{n \in N} \mu(n)$, where N is the set of all episodes, and $\mu(n)$ is the utility of episode n.

The *recommendation score* measures the proportion of episodes where the user's selected arm was the same as the agent's recommended arm, i.e., how frequently the user's choices aligned with the agent's recommendations. Recommendation score for a user u, R_u, over N episodes is calculated as follows:

$$R_u = \frac{1}{|N|} \sum_{n \in N} \delta(r_n, s_n)$$

where $|N|$ is the total number of episodes, r_n is the arm recommended at episode n, s_n is the arm selected at episode n, and $\delta(r_n, s_n)$ is the Kronecker delta function that returns 1 if r_n equals s_n and 0 otherwise.

The *switching score* measures the proportion of episodes where the user's selected arm is the agent's recommendation and is different from their intended arm, i.e., how often the user changes their choice to the recommendation from the agent. The *switching score* for a user u, S_u, is calculated as follows:

$$S_u = \frac{1}{|N|} \sum_{n \in N} \delta(r_n, s_n) \quad \text{subject to} \quad [\delta(i_n, s_n) = 0]$$

where i_n is the arm intention at episode n.

The *contextual score* measures the proportion of episodes where the user's selected arm was the same as the agent's recommended arm given that they received subaverage utility by not following the agent's recommendation on the previous episode. Contextual score for a user u, C_u, is calculated as follows:

$$C_u = \frac{1}{|N| - 1} \sum_{n=2}^{|N|} \delta(r_n, s_n) \quad \text{subject to} \quad \begin{cases} \delta(r_{n-1}, s_{n-1}) = 0, \\ \mu(n-1) < \frac{1}{|N|} \sum_{m \in N} \mu(m) \end{cases}$$

We employed a one-sided independent t-test on *utility score*, recommendation score, *switching score*, and *contextual score* to test for statistical significance. Furthermore, we employ a non-parametric Wilcoxon signed-rank test with Pratt zero-handling to test for statistical significance on survey data.

Survey: After completing 30 episodes, the participants completed a short survey regarding the usefulness and warmth of agent explanations, as well as the user's satisfaction with agent explanations. The survey items are measured on a 5-point Likert scale from "Strongly disagree" to "Strongly agree".

Survey items into the users' perceived usefulness of agent include:

Q1: The supporting AI enables me to decide which arm to pull faster.
Q2: The supporting AI enhances my effectiveness in deciding which arm to pull.
Q3: The supporting AI makes it easier to decide which arm to pull.
Q4: I chose tasks that I liked regardless of utility

Survey items into the users' perceived warmth of agent include:

Q5: The supporting AI was good-natured.
Q6: The supporting AI was trustworthy.
Q7: The supporting AI was tolerant.
Q8: The supporting AI was friendly.
Q9: The supporting AI was sincere.

Survey items into the users' satisfaction with agent include:

Q10: The supporting AI improved my experience.
Q11: I enjoyed working with the supporting AI.
Q12: The supporting AI helped me make better decisions.

Participants: We recruited 93 participants through Amazon Mechanical Turk. Attention checks, i.e., basic questions to ensure participants were engaged, were included. No data of participants was eliminated due to insufficient attention. There were 31 participants in each group. Approximately 42% of the participants were female. The age distribution was as follows: 18–24 years, 4.3%; 25–34 years, 20.4%; 35–44 years, 50.5%; 45–54 years, 8.6%; and 55–64 years, 16.1%. The distribution of education levels was as follows: high school degree, 3.2%; some college experience, 2.1%; associate's degree, 1.0%; bachelor's degree, 69.9%; and graduate degree, 23.6%. The ethnicity distribution was as follows: White, 96.7%; Asian or Pacific Islander, 2.1%; and Native-American, 1.1%. Participants earned a base level of compensation for completing the study, with an additional bonus that varied as a function of their utility in the task phase.

6 Results

This section presents the analysis of experimental data collected during the task phase. We examine the impact of agent explanations on the *utility score*, *recommendation score*, and *switching score*, specifically focusing on the relative total utility gained and proportions of episodes where the agent-recommended arm was selected and episodes where the user switched from their initial arm intention. Additionally, we examine survey data from users.

Figure 3a shows the summary data on utility scores for all three conditions. Table 4 presents results of the comparisons of utility scores between the conditions. t-test results reveal that cold explanations yield to significantly higher utility score compared to no explanation condition. However, the difference between cold and warm conditions, and the difference between warm and none conditions are found to be insignificant.

Table 4. Utility score results

t-test results on utility scores	p-value
Cold (M = 21.25, SD = 3.67) ≠ Warm (M = 19.93, SD = 4.21)	0.202
Cold (M = 21.25, SD = 3.67) > None (18.46, SD = 3.53)	0.002
Warm (M = 19.93, SD = 4.21) > None (18.46, SD = 3.53)	0.074

Figure 3b depicts the recommendation scores for the three conditions. As seen in Table 5, t-test results show no significant differences in recommendation scores between the conditions.

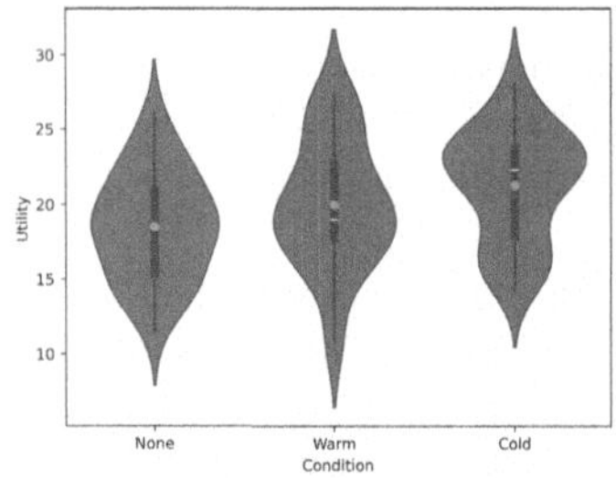

(a) Utility scores

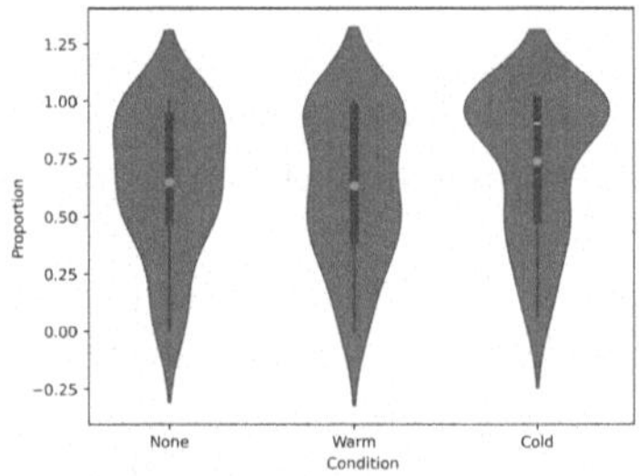

(b) Recommendation scores

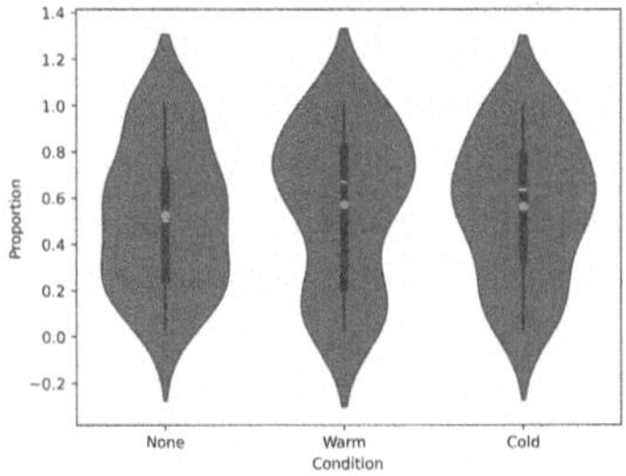

(c) Switching scores

Fig. 3. Overall scores

Table 5. Recommendation score results

t-test results on recommendation scores	p-value
Cold (M = 0.736, SD = 0.303) ≠ Warm (M = 0.632, SD = 0.313)	0.195
Cold (M = 0.736, SD = 0.303) > None (M = 0.648, SD = 0.301)	0.131
Warm (M = 0.632, SD = 0.313) > None (M = 0.648, SD = 0.301)	0.580

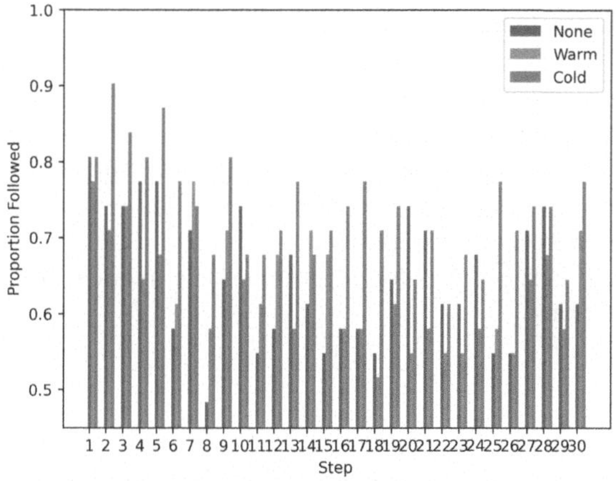

Fig. 4. Recommendation scores per episode

Figure 4 shows the recommendation scores per episode for all three conditions. The recommendation scores are all higher than 0.5 which indicates that majority of the participants are in agreement with the agent's recommendation. Specifically, in the cold condition, the recommendation scores are all above 0.6.

Figure 3c shows the switching scores for all three conditions. Table 6 presents t-test results for comparisons of switching scores between the conditions. Similar to the trend in recommendation scores, the differences in switching scores between the conditions are found to be insignificant.

Table 6. Switching score results

t-test results on switching scores	p-value
Cold (M = 0.437, SD = 0.261) $\neq$ Warm (M = 0.367, SD = 0.279)	0.321
Cold (M = 0.437, SD = 0.261) > None (M = 0.357, SD = 0.238)	0.111
Warm (M = 0.367, SD = 0.279) > None (M = 0.357, SD = 0.238)	0.442

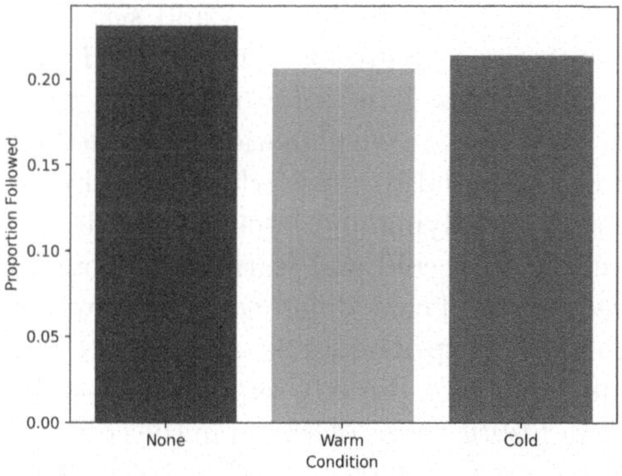

Fig. 5. Contextual scores

We also investigate whether the agent recommendation having higher average reward than the reward of the user's selection influences the user to follow the recommendation in the next episode given the user did not follow the recommendation in the current episode. Figure 5 depicts contextual score that is the user's level of following agent recommendation in the next episode for such cases. Though the no explanation condition exhibits a slightly higher level of following, the differences are insignificant.

No significant difference was found between the mean scores of survey items for all three conditions.

7 Discussion

Prior studies have shown the benefits of explanations and XAI systems in decision-making scenarios; notably, studies also demonstrate that agent warmth is positively correlated with satisfying agent interaction experiences. This study extends upon this work and investigates how warm and cold agent explanations influence user satisfaction, performance, and the adoption of agent recommendations in multi-armed bandit scenarios.

The results reveal that participants who were assisted by agents providing cold or warm explanations achieved higher total *utility scores* than those who received no explanations at all. Although both of these groups received greater utility, the difference was only statistically significant for cold condition. One potential explanation for this disparity is that participants might perceive the cold agent's explanation as more concise, professional, or otherwise authoritative and reliable and are more inclined to follow their recommendations. This result supports previous research into coldness. Expressing a certain level of coldness can be perceived as confidence by the listener [11]. Therefore, the degree of warmth that an agent possesses should be determined based on the objective of the agent, i.e. domain specific. For instance, if the aim is solely to have high performance, expressing a smaller degree of warmth would be more effective. Alternatively, if the motive is to gain strong user-agent bonding and retention, exhibiting higher degree of warmth would be more appropriate [15].

Further analysis of *recommendation scores* and *switching scores* exhibits no significant difference between the groups. Therefore, **Hypothesis 2a and 2b** are not supported. Nonetheless, it is noteworthy that participants exposed to agents offering either cold or warm explanations obtained comparable or higher scores in these metrics compared to those who received no explanations. These results suggest potential underlying and latent factors influencing the increased *utility scores* observed in both cold and warm conditions. Additionally, survey result analysis showed no significant difference in survey item responses for the condition groups. Thereby, **Hypothesis 3a and 3b** are not supported.

While these results may not directly support **Hypotheses 2 and 3**, the notable improvement in *utility scores* observed in the cold condition indicates the promising use of XAI agents in enhancing performance within multi-armed bandit experiments. **Hypothesis 1** is thereby supported. Furthermore, the absence of significant differences in the perception of the explanatory capabilities and power of these agents supports **Hypothesis 4**.

A further study with more focus on cold and warm language model is required considering the results because the warmth in language is a complex phenomena and is even hard to define or assess. The perceived warmth in language is also affected by the individuals age, gender, and culture. Furthermore, sentences generated by the researchers are used in the experiment due to the lack of the computational models on warm and cold language. In future investigations, it might be possible to use a computational model to generated warm explanations or at least assess the level of warmth level if a computational warm language model is developed by that time.

8 Conclusion and Future Work

In conclusion, our study provides an investigation into the role of warm and cold text explanations in eXplainable Artificial Intelligence (XAI) agents within the context of solving multi-armed bandit experiments. While previous research has utilized recommendation systems to aid users in solving problems like the multi-armed bandit problem, the use of textual explanations in enhancing these systems has not been explored.

Our research addresses this gap by developing a bidirectional and human-interpretable framework for text explanations. This framework not only contextualizes agent feedback but also rationalizes it, making it more accessible and understandable for human users. Interestingly, our findings reveal that cold agent explanations have a more pronounced effect than warm agent explanations, suggesting that the tone of agent explanations can significantly impact user performance in multi-armed bandit scenarios.

Future research should investigate the influence of social aspects of agent such as agent voice, appearance, gestures, expressions in agent assisted decision making scenarios. These additions could open up new avenues for non-verbal communication further enriching the interaction between the user and the agent. This could potentially lead to a more immersive and engaging user experience, and provide additional layers of context that could aid in the decision-making process. This area of research represents a promising path for innovation in XAI research and enhancing agent recommendations through explanations.

References

1. Aggarwal, K., et al.: Has the future started? The current growth of artificial intelligence, machine learning, and deep learning. Iraqi J. Comput. Sci. Math. **3**(1), 115–123 (2022)
2. Auer, P.: Using confidence bounds for exploitation-exploration trade-offs. J. Mach. Learn. Res. **3**(Nov), 397–422 (2002)
3. Auer, P., Cesa-Bianchi, N., Fischer, P.: Finite-time analysis of the multiarmed bandit problem. Mach. Learn. **47**, 235–256 (2002)

4. Balakrishnan, A., Bouneffouf, D., Mattei, N., Rossi, F.: Using multi-armed bandits to learn ethical priorities for online AI systems. IBM J. Res. Dev. **63**(4/5), 1:1–1:13 (2019). https://doi.org/10.1147/JRD.2019.2945271
5. Belanche, D., Casaló, L.V., Schepers, J., Flavián, C.: Examining the effects of robots' physical appearance, warmth, and competence in frontline services: the humanness-value-loyalty model. Psychol. Mark. **38**(12), 2357–2376 (2021)
6. Bergmann, K., Eyssel, F., Kopp, S.: A second chance to make a first impression? how appearance and nonverbal behavior affect perceived warmth and competence of virtual agents over time. In: Nakano, Y., Neff, M., Paiva, A., Walker, M. (eds.) IVA 2012. LNCS (LNAI), vol. 7502, pp. 126–138. Springer, Heidelberg (2012). https://doi.org/10.1007/978-3-642-33197-8_13
7. Bouneffouf, D., Rish, I., Aggarwal, C.: Survey on applications of multi-armed and contextual bandits. In: 2020 IEEE Congress on Evolutionary Computation (CEC), pp. 1–8 (2020). https://doi.org/10.1109/CEC48606.2020.9185782
8. Eisenbruch, A.B., Krasnow, M.M.: Why warmth matters more than competence: a new evolutionary approach. Perspect. Psychol. Sci. **17**(6), 1604–1623 (2022)
9. Fiske, S.T., Cuddy, A.J., Glick, P.: Universal dimensions of social cognition: warmth and competence. Trends Cogn. Sci. **11**(2), 77–83 (2007)
10. Fitzsimons, G.M., Kay, A.C.: Language and interpersonal cognition: causal effects of variations in pronoun usage on perceptions of closeness. Pers. Soc. Psychol. Bull. **30**(5), 547–557 (2004)
11. Friedland, N.: Social influence via threats. J. Exp. Soc. Psychol. **12**(6), 552–563 (1976)
12. Gilad, Z., Amir, O., Levontin, L.: The effects of warmth and competence perceptions on users' choice of an AI system. In: Proceedings of the 2021 CHI Conference on Human Factors in Computing Systems, pp. 1–13 (2021)
13. Gray, R.C., Zhu, J., Ontañón, S.: Multiplayer modeling via multi-armed bandits. In: 2021 IEEE Conference on Games (CoG), pp. 1–8 (2021). https://doi.org/10.1109/CoG52621.2021.9618892
14. Guenoun, B.S., Zlatev, J.J.: Sending signals: strategic displays of warmth and competence (2023)
15. Güntürkün, P., Haumann, T., Mikolon, S.: Disentangling the differential roles of warmth and competence judgments in customer-service provider relationships. J. Serv. Res. **23**(4), 476–503 (2020)
16. Holoien, D.S., Fiske, S.T.: Downplaying positive impressions: compensation between warmth and competence in impression management. J. Exp. Soc. Psychol. **49**(1), 33–41 (2013)
17. Huang, K., Yeomans, M., Brooks, A.W., Minson, J., Gino, F.: It doesn't hurt to ask: question-asking increases liking. J. Pers. Soc. Psychol. **113**(3), 430 (2017)
18. Kaufmann, E., Cappé, O., Garivier, A.: On Bayesian upper confidence bounds for bandit problems. In: Artificial Intelligence and Statistics, pp. 592–600. PMLR (2012)
19. Mania, J., Miedema, F., Browne, R., Broekens, J., Oertel, C.: Towards understanding the effect of voice on human-agent negotiation. In: Proceedings of the 20th ACM International Conference on Intelligent Virtual Agents, pp. 1–8 (2020)
20. Marder, B., Houghton, D., Erz, A., Harris, L., Javornik, A.: Smile (y)-and your students will smile with you? The effects of emoticons on impressions, evaluations, and behaviour in staff-to-student communication. Stud. High. Educ. **45**(11), 2274–2286 (2020)
21. McKee, K.R., Bai, X., Fiske, S.T.: Warmth and competence in human-agent cooperation. arXiv preprint arXiv:2201.13448 (2022)

22. Pandya, R., Huang, S.H., Hadfield-Menell, D., Dragan, A.D.: Human-AI learning performance in multi-armed bandits. In: 2019 AAAI/ACM Conference on AI, Ethics, and Society, pp. 369–375 (2019)
23. Prajod, P., Al Owayyed, M., Rietveld, T., van der Steeg, J.J., Broekens, J.: The effect of virtual agent warmth on human-agent negotiation. In: Proceedings of the 18th International Conference on Autonomous Agents and MultiAgent Systems, pp. 71–76 (2019)
24. Rosenfeld, A., Richardson, A.: Explainability in human-agent systems. Auton. Agent. Multi-Agent Syst. **33**, 673–705 (2019)
25. Sen, S., Ridgway, A., Ripley, M.: Adaptive budgeted bandit algorithms for trust development in a supply-chain. In: AAMAS, pp. 137–144 (2015)
26. Shiban, Y., et al.: The appearance effect: influences of virtual agent features on performance and motivation. Comput. Hum. Behav. **49**, 5–11 (2015)
27. Sinaceur, M., Van Kleef, G.A., Neale, M.A., Adam, H., Haag, C.: Hot or cold: is communicating anger or threats more effective in negotiation? J. Appl. Psychol. **96**(5), 1018 (2011)
28. Sutton, R., Barto, A.: Reinforcement learning: an introduction. IEEE Trans. Neural Networks **9**(5), 1054 (1998). https://doi.org/10.1109/TNN.1998.712192
29. Wang, X., Yin, M.: Are explanations helpful? A comparative study of the effects of explanations in AI-assisted decision-making. In: 26th International Conference on Intelligent User Interfaces, pp. 318–328 (2021)

Using Agent Interventions to Reduce User Procrastination Tendencies

Ethan Beaird[1(✉)], Feyza M. Hafızoğlu[2], and Sandip Sen[1]

[1] Tandy School of Computer Science, The University of Tulsa, Tulsa, USA
{ethan-beaird,sandip-sen}@utulsa.edu
[2] İstanbul Commerce University, Istanbul, Turkey
fmhafizoglu@ticaret.edu.tr

Abstract. Procrastination, i.e., irrational delay, seriously and increasingly affects people's daily and professional lives in today's society where social media and easy access to entertainment options are plentiful. Psychology literature offers various types of interventions developed to reduce an individual's level of procrastination; however, only a limited number of people experiencing procrastination have access to such interventions. Leveraging agent technology as even a partial remedy to this widespread problem can be highly beneficial due to its ubiquitous nature. In this study, we develop a model of procrastination on task completion and levels of agent-based interventions to assist individuals in overcoming procrastination. The effects of agent interventions on procrastination are evaluated through an extensive set of controlled experiments with participants recruited from Amazon Mechanical Turk. The agent engages the user using instances of given task types to develop a shared awareness of user preferences and capabilities. This preference model is then used both to choose effective interventions as well as measure and reward subsequent user performance. This model can also be leveraged to explain agent interventions to the user. We collect and use both task completion metric data and survey data to assess individuals' perceptions of procrastination, task completion satisfaction, and the usefulness of agent support. Our data analysis indicates that using agent-based interventions can effectively help people reduce procrastination.

Keywords: human-agent interaction · procrastination · agent intervention · well-being

1 Introduction

Procrastination, or irrational delay in completing tasks of importance at hand [29], is caused by failure of self-regulation [27] and lack of self-efficacy [15] and has increasingly posed significant challenges to citizens of our digitally connected world [10]. The disparity between people's intentions to complete important tasks and their tendency to procrastinate illustrates an inclination to irrationally prioritize immediate gratification, i.e. short-term reward over long-term

R. Collier et al. (Eds.): EUMAS 2024, LNAI 15685, pp. 198–214, 2025.
https://doi.org/10.1007/978-3-031-93930-3_12

benefits. People tend to procrastinate on necessary tasks and chores that are perceived to be negative, unpleasant, or challenging [32]. For instance, students may delay studying for exams, people may procrastinate filing their tax returns, and individuals often put off visiting the doctor when necessary.

Social media companies thrive on their ability to reward people with instant gratification, and omnipresent communication platforms result in citizens spending considerable time and energy [19] in initiating and responding to messages and calls that can easily divert attention from pending tasks at hand [2]. Furthermore, the widespread availability of smartphones and other mobile devices and constant access to entertainment streaming platforms supported by fast, wireless internet access provides a plethora of options and incentives for users to procrastinate.

Considering its negative consequences on individuals' health [16,28], well-being [8,23,28], and task accomplishments [14], eliminating or reducing procrastination is a challenging but potentially significantly beneficial endeavor. Several studies in the psychology literature [9] focus on the stability of procrastination: whether people can change—or at least reduce—this undesirable and detrimental behavior. A range of interventions, although not widely available, have been developed to reduce procrastination levels, such as self-regulation [1,13,26], cognitive-behavioral therapy [15,24], and social support [25], among others. However, these interventions are not scientifically proven as perfect remedies, and only a minority of those who suffer from procrastination have access to such interventions due to time constraints, financial limitations, or other resource-related barriers. Leveraging agent technology to address this pervasive issue can prove highly effective, as these automated assistants, serving as personal aids, can be deployed widely at minimal costs, thus helping reduce the disparity in access to procrastination interventions.

Despite the prevalence and significant impact of procrastination in our society, the majority of previous studies focus only on academic procrastination [12,27,33]. Furthermore, most studies rely on surveys rather than actual task performance data. We evaluate two key research questions in the context of agent research:

- Can agent intervention mechanisms be developed to help people significantly reduce procrastination?
- Do different levels of agent interventions have significantly different effects?

In this study, we develop a model of procrastination and agent-based interventions to support individuals in overcoming procrastination. As part of our empirical approach, we devise four diverse task types that span a range of basic skills. We conjecture that the likelihood and level of procrastination on these task types will differ among individuals. To assess the procrastination tendency of individuals for a certain task, we use their preferences among the task types, i.e. an individual's likelihood to procrastinate on a task type and their preference for that task type are correlated [20].

We conduct experiments with human subjects to simulate procrastination and design utility functions based both on the participants' preferences for different task types and their performance levels while completing those tasks. We ensured that completing less preferred tasks with lower performance can still yield higher utilities than highly preferred tasks completed with higher performance. Each participant is asked to perform a set of task instances selected from the given task types. This set of task instances is completed with the aid of either *low* or *high level agent interventions*. We collect both task completion metric data and survey data to assess individuals' perceptions of procrastination and agent interventions as well as satisfaction in task completion. Our data analysis corroborates our position that the use of agent-based interventions plays a significant role in helping individuals reduce procrastination.

The remainder of the paper is structured as follows. We first present related work. Following, the procrastination model that is considered in this research is outlined, and our empirical methodology is explained. The results of our experiments are presented in the subsequent section, where we also discuss the empirical findings. The paper concludes with a summary and directions for future research.

2 Related Work

Procrastination behavior is an increasingly serious problem in our professional lives [12,27,33] as well as daily lives [17]. There is a relatively small body of empirical research in the area of procrastination of which the majority involves survey data [10,11,17,27]. Furthermore, most research on procrastination has been carried out in academic domains with college students [27,33]. Recently, there is a growing body of literature that is concerned with adults' procrastination in life-domains [5,10,11]. The indisputable effect of online entertainment and other online offerings has contributed significantly to the rise of procrastination behavior among adults [10].

Procrastination is a complex psychological phenomenon. Numerous factors influencing this troubling behavior are addressed in social literature such as age [5], gender [35], personality [18,30], mood [8], environment [6], and nature of task [32]. Furthermore, it is very well acknowledged that procrastination causes lower levels of health [16,28], well-being [8,23,28], and achievements, i.e., performance [14].

To effectively address procrastination, an individual's intention-action gap should be reduced. Various intervention mechanisms have been identified as helpful [9]. Schouwenburg *et al.* [1] offer three general categories of interventions: 1) Training self-regulatory skills; 2) building self-efficacy; and 3) organizing social support. Training *self-regulatory skills* involves deploying our cognitive, emotional, and behavioral resources to achieve our goals [4]. Self-regulation failure is associated with a lack of self-determination, planning, and prioritizing tasks as well as a failure to concentrate on tasks and shield from distractions [1,26]. Stimulus-control techniques (i.e. eliminating the effects of distractions), techniques of goal definition, and time management techniques [13] can be classified in this category. Building *self-efficacy* aims to replace negative, unproductive, and inhibiting thoughts with positive, productive, and motivated thoughts [15,24]. Peer support is centered around the recognition that many other people also struggle with procrastination, forming a sense of solidarity. Similarly, *social support* has also been identified as an effective means of reducing procrastination [25]. Additionally, more recent interventions, like reading self-help books and engaging in training sessions, can be considered as a fourth category of intervention mechanisms.

Recently, several studies have suggested that technology-based interventions can be useful in overcoming irrational delay. CatAlyst [3] supports distracted workers by generating a continuation of interrupted work through the use of a generative model for workers to resume tasks. Zavaleta *et al.* [34] showed that email interventions by instructors can reduce the delay of students starting their online homework. De Vries *et al.* [31] found that experts sending motivational messages through a digital medium could be more motivating in the earliest stages of behavior change, while peer-designed messages in a digital medium could be more motivating in the later stages. GanttBot [22] is a chatbot that is developed using conversational agents with several abilities: reminding students about landmarks, informing tutors when interventions are needed, and the ability to learn from previous interactions. StudiCare [21] is a digital coach rooted in internet and mobile-based cognitive behavioral therapy techniques, helping guide students to achieve their academic goals.

The present study extends existing research on procrastination as follows:

Time: Address procrastination in a short-term context with artificial tasks rather than a long-term context [21,34].
Data: In addition to survey data, use actual task performance metrics.
Task: Task domain involves daily life tasks rather than a specific domain such as in [14,21,22,27,34]
Users: Recruit adult participants beyond only college students [22,34].
Agents: Make use of cost-effective and ubiquitous agent intervention mechanisms rather than time and location-dependent techniques [15].

To our knowledge, this is the first study on general procrastination using agentbased interventions for routine tasks using task performance and survey data.

3 Procrastination Model

This section presents the task types, the utility function model, and the agent interventions in our study.

3.1 Task Domain

We use four task types—*Audio Transcription, Shopping, Text Comprehension,* and *Form Filling*—to emulate common online activities. These tasks are designed inline with the Bloom's Digital taxonomy [7].

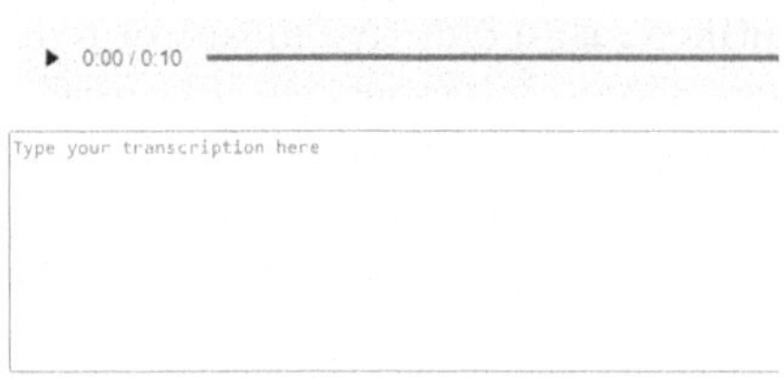

(a) Audio transcription task

(b) Shopping task

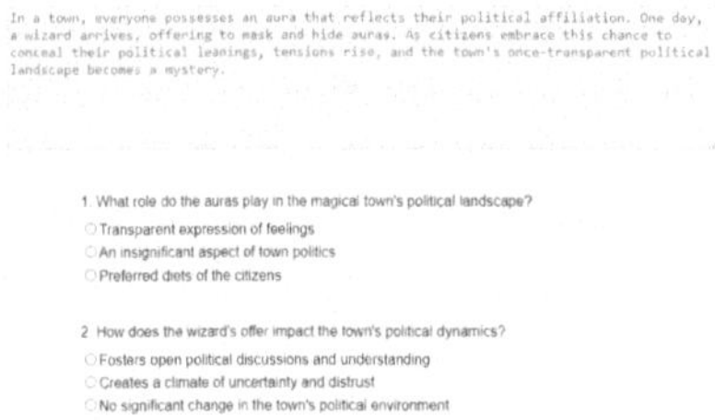

(c) Text comprehension task

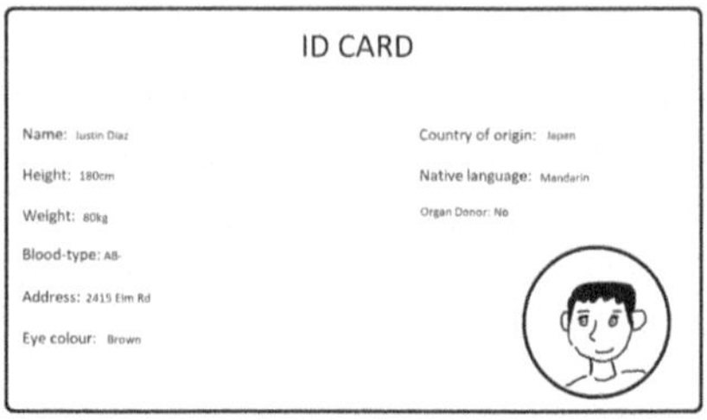

(d) Form filling task

Fig. 1. Instances of task types used in our study on procrastination

Audio Transcription task (see Fig. 1a) presents users with a brief audio clip and a text box where they are prompted to transcribe the audio. This task can be classified under the *Applying* category of the digital taxonomy.

Shopping task (see Fig. 1b) gives users multiple itemized receipts, each featuring randomly generated prices and a discount rate percentage. Users must select the receipt with the lowest total cost. The score received on this task is determined by how accurately they choose the receipt with the closest cost to the actual lowest one. This task can be classified under the *Applying* category of the digital taxonomy. *Text Comprehension* task (see Fig. 1c) presents users a short story and then asks multiple-choice questions to assess their understanding of the text. Users must carefully read the story and choose the most appropriate answer for each question. This task can be classified under the *Understanding* category of the digital taxonomy. *Form Filling* task (see Fig. 1d) includes a simulated online tax form to be filled by the users based on a simulated ID card. This task can be classified under the *Remembering* category of the digital taxonomy.

3.2 Utility Function

We adopt the following definition of procrastination: "to voluntarily delay an intended course of action despite expecting to be worse off for the delay" [29]. Milgram et al. [20] observes: "Procrastination is found to be greater in tasks

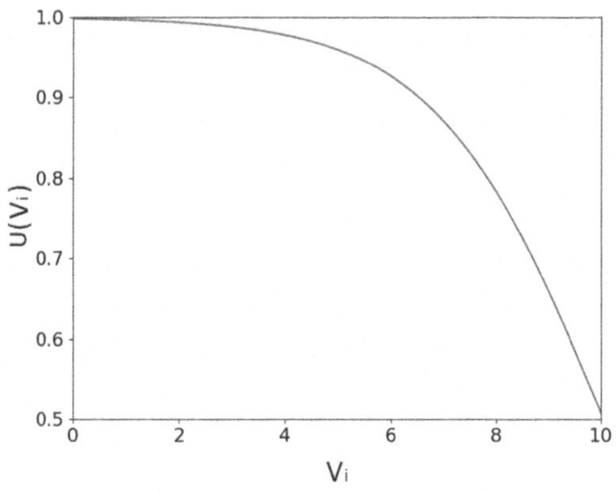

Fig. 2. Utility function

that are regarded as unpleasant." To study procrastination in an online setting, we created conditions to engender procrastination. Procrastination in our study corresponds to users selecting preferred tasks of lower utility despite receiving less total compensation by doing so.

Each user completes initial demo instances of each task type within an artificial domain, and we record their performance scores. Additionally, each user is asked to rank their preference for each task type. The value of task i's completion, v_i, by a user is computed as follows:

$$v_i = w \cdot 10 \cdot s_i + (1 - w) \cdot p_i, i \in \{1, 2, 3, 4\} \tag{1}$$

where $s_i \in [0, 1]$ is the user's score in the initial demo, $p_i \in [1, 10]$ is the preference ranking, and $w = 0.3$ is the weighting of s_i for task type i, chosen to emphasize the user's task preference while still considering the user's ability to perform that task. Then we can construct the utility function over the task types as follows:

$$U(v_i) = \frac{1}{1 + e^{0.625 \cdot v_i - 2\pi}}. \tag{2}$$

This utility function is designed to discourage selecting tasks that a user may prioritize by penalizing tasks that align with their preferences and abilities. Utility decreases as preference ranking p or initial task demo score s increases.

Figure 2 plots the utility curve of a task; the utility decreases as either preference ranking p or score in the initial task demo s increases (the constants are chosen to obtain a concave function; the exact coefficient values are not critical). As such, tasks that a user prefers tend to receive lower utility scores than tasks that they do not prefer. Since the utility of a task is displayed to users and directly correlates to the amount of compensation that a user receives for completing that task, users may be inclined to avoid tasks that they performed poorly in during their initial task demos. To address this, our utility function also takes into account their performance in the initial task demo and rewards lower performance. This approach encourages individuals to consider tasks where their performance may be subpar, thereby promoting a more balanced task selection process.

3.3 Agent Interventions

We have developed several agent interventions to engage with the user during the study. These techniques encompass proactive interventions (i.e., prior to a user's task selection and completion) and reactive interventions (i.e., after a user has chosen and completed a task).

Motivational Guide is a proactive intervention where the agent encourages the user to choose higher utility tasks through a text message. This intervention is subtle and non-intrusive to gently influence a user's decision-making (see Fig. 3).

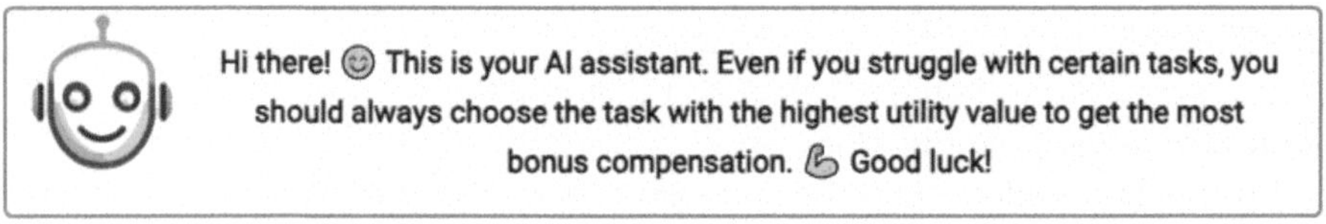

Fig. 3. Motivational guide intervention

Dynamic Utility Highlighting is a proactive intervention where the agent adds "recommendation" popups to tasks with the highest utility and highlights them with a green outline. Simultaneously, the other lower utility tasks are outlined in red. Additionally, tasks are sorted in descending order of utility (see Fig. 4).

Medal Rewards is a reactive intervention featuring a "medals box" where users can view earned medals after completing a task. Medals are awarded based on task selection and performance. Users earn bronze medals for selecting tasks that are not the highest utility. For selecting high utility tasks, users earn silver and gold medals based on their performance (see Fig. 5). This intervention is accompanied by *Reactive Motivation*, where the agent leaves encouraging comments tailored to the user's performance in the previous task.

4 Empirical Methodology

This section presents our hypotheses and a detailed description of our experimental setup, including survey and metric data.

Hypothesis 1. Agent intervention mechanisms can be developed to help people overcome or significantly reduce procrastination.

Hypothesis 2. Low and high level agent interventions can have different effects on reducing procrastination.

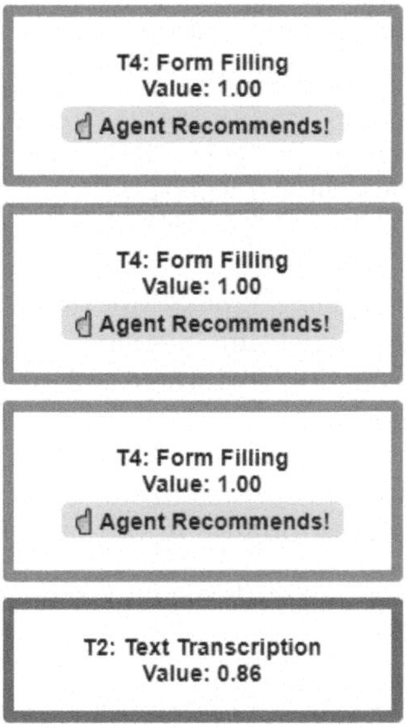

Fig. 4. Dynamic utility highlighting intervention

Fig. 5. Medal rewards & reactive motivation interventions

4.1 Experimental Setup

The three experimental conditions based on the levels of intensity of agent interventions are:

1. **No Intervention** group has no agent interventions present.
2. **Low Intervention** group includes the *Motivational Guide*, *Medal Rewards*, and *Reactive Motivation* interventions, providing users with involved but minimally intrusive guidance and motivation.
3. **High Intervention** group includes the *Motivational Guide* and *Dynamic Utility Highlighting*, offering a more visually prominent form of guidance.

The experiment consists of the following steps:

- *Preference learning:* Users complete a series of demo tasks for each of the four task types and rank their preferences for each task.
- *Task phase:* Users are given twelve task instances—three instances of each of the four task types. They choose any six to complete. Users in the *low*

or *high* groups receive agent interventions during this phase. Users get one minute to complete each task and are paid proportional to the overall utility from completing tasks.
- *Survey:* After completing chosen tasks, users take a final survey on satisfaction, agent interaction, and procrastination.

Survey: The study includes a survey after the task phase where the items are measured on a 5-point Likert scale from "Strongly disagree" to "Strongly agree".

To assess the user's satisfaction with their task completion performance, the survey contains the following items:

Q1: I liked the outcome of my choices from the task list.
Q2: I feel satisfied with my performance in the tasks from the task phase.

To assess the user's perception of the agent interventions, the survey contains the following items:

Q3: The AI assistant provided helpful guidance.
Q4: I was satisfied with my interactions with the AI assistant.
Q5: The AI assistant influenced the tasks that I chose to complete.

To assess the user's perceived level of procrastination, the survey contains the following items:

Q6: I procrastinated on completing high-value tasks.
Q7: I chose to do more appealing tasks instead of high-value tasks.
Q8: I avoided doing some tasks I disliked even if they had high value.

We test for a significant increase in mean survey responses for Q1–Q5 and a significant decrease in mean survey responses for Q6–Q8 in Sect. 5.

Metrics: We utilize the *Selection score* metric in our analysis. To analyze the impact of agent interventions on a user's task selection and allocation, we define *optimal utility*, i.e., maximum utility that can be obtained by a user out of performing six tasks, as:

$$O = 3 \cdot U(t_1) + 3 \cdot U(t_2)$$

where t_1 and t_2 are the task types with the first and second highest utility scores.

We define *user utility* as:

$$\mu = \sum_{T} U(t_i),$$

where T corresponds to the tasks selected by the user.

Then, *selection score* is the proportion of *user utility* to *optimal utility*: μ/O. *Selection score* measures users' efficiency in task selection by comparing their accumulated utility from chosen tasks to the *optimal utility* achievable by selecting the highest utility tasks. A higher *selection score* indicates more effective task selection.

We employ a one-sided t-test on *selection score* to test for statistical significance. Furthermore, both one-sided t-test and non-parametric one-sided Wilcoxon signed-rank test with Pratt zero-handling are employed to test for statistical significance on survey data.

Participants: We recruited 180 participants through Amazon Mechanical Turk. Attention checks, i.e., basic questions to ensure participants were engaged, were included. There were 60 participants in each intervention group. Approximately 35% of the participants were female. The age distribution was as follows: 18–24 years, 3.3%; 25–34 years, 48.8%; 35–44 years, 23.8%; 45–54 years, 12.2%; 55–64 years, 10.5%; and 65 years or older, 1.1%. The distribution of education levels was as follows: high school degree, 1.1%; some college experience, 2.2%; associate's degree, 5%; bachelor's degree, 67.8%; and graduate degree, 23.9%. The ethnicity distribution was as follows: White, 75.5%; Asian or Pacific Islander, 14.4%; African-American, 4.4%; Native-American, 3.8%; Hispanic/Latino, 1.1%; and other, 0.5%.

5 Results

This section presents the analysis of collected experimental data. We examine the impact of agent interventions on the *selection score*, specifically focusing on the relative proportions of procrastination-free optimal task selections. Additionally, we examine the survey data from users.

Selection Score: Figure 6 presents selection scores for all three conditions. In the high intervention condition, the *selection score* ($M = 0.912, SD = 0.108$) is significantly ($p < 0.001$) higher than that in the no intervention condition ($M = 0.840, SD = 0.096$) and the low intervention condition ($M = 0.845, SD = 0.092$). No significant difference in selection scores is found between no and low intervention conditions. These results indicate that high level agent interventions lead to a significant increase in the selection of the less preferred but higher utility, i.e., procrastinated, tasks.

One interesting area to consider is how *selection score* changes throughout the study, i.e. after each task selection. Figure 7 presents selection scores after each task selection for all three conditions. The selection score is always significantly higher ($p < 0.05$) for the high intervention condition than others with a sharp decrease after the first selection. The selection score is initially high for the low intervention condition, but it decreases towards the end of the study. On the contrary, the selection score is initially low in the no intervention condition, but it slightly increases as the study proceeds. As such, the difference in selection score between the no and low intervention conditions disappears towards the end of the study.

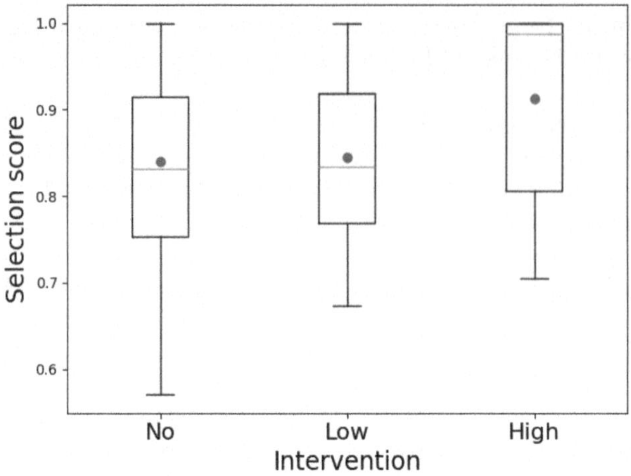

Fig. 6. Selection scores

We also examine the proportion of *users who selected recommended tasks at each timestep*, as illustrated in Fig. 8. The trend between the conditions is similar to the one in Fig. 7. In other words, the proportion of users selecting recommended (i.e. highest-utility) tasks decreases (increases) towards the end in low (no) intervention conditions and is always significantly higher ($p < 0.05$) in the high condition than the other conditions. Similar to Fig. 7, a sharp drop is experienced after the first selection in the high intervention group. Additionally, the users selecting recommended tasks increased in the fifth task selection for both the low and high intervention conditions.

Furthermore, we examine the cumulative proportion of *users who stopped selecting recommended tasks at each timestep*, depicted in Fig. 9. Significantly more users ($p < 0.05$) experiencing low interventions stopped following agent recommendations, i.e., ignored higher utility for personal preference, compared to the high intervention group. However, in both conditions, we observe a gradual increase in the proportion of users who diverge from choosing recommended tasks, i.e., begin procrastinating.

We finally examine the proportion of *users who selected specific numbers of recommended tasks*, i.e. how many users selected 6 out of 6 recommended tasks, 5 out of 6, and so on, as seen in Fig. 10. Notably, half of the users in the high intervention group stick to the recommended tasks regardless of their performance. In contrast, the low and no intervention groups exhibit a more evenly distributed pattern, with the majority selecting around 2 or 3 recommended tasks.

Survey: Responses to the survey item Q1 ("I liked the outcome of my choices from the main phase's task list") were significantly higher ($p < 0.05$) in the low and high intervention conditions than the no intervention condition. No significant difference in other survey items is found between the conditions.

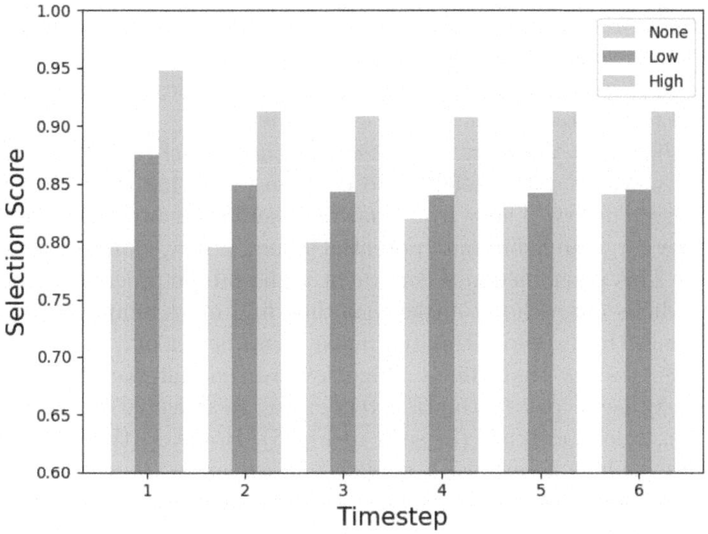

Fig. 7. Selection score in each timestep

6 Discussion

Prior studies have shown that intervention techniques can be helpful in reducing an individual's procrastination tendencies [3,9,21,22,34]. This study investigates the role of agents in controlling and managing procrastination by testing various agent intervention techniques in an online environment.

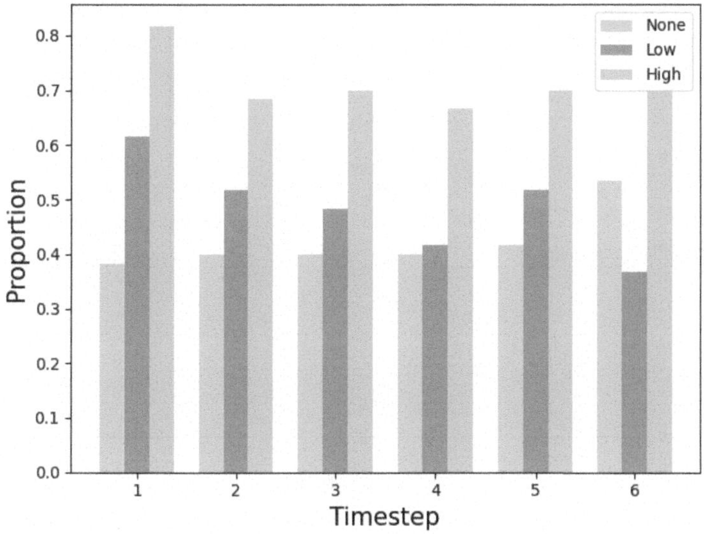

Fig. 8. Proportion of users selecting recommended tasks in each timestep

Individuals procrastinate only when actions are voluntarily delayed despite expecting to be worse off for the delay [29]. In the context of our task domain, to engender procrastination, the utility of a task is designed to be inversely proportional to the user's preference for that task.

Results show that the users did not consistently select tasks that offered the highest utility. Many users preferred to perform tasks that they enjoyed rather than gain more utility. These irrational task selections are voluntary, and by doing so, they forgo and eliminate potential gained utility, akin to a form of *irrational delay.* This phenomenon is congruent with real-life procrastination, where many individuals often choose tasks that they find more temporarily enjoyable instead of tasks that would ultimately make them better off.

Our findings show that timely (high level) agent interventions can significantly reduce users' procrastination tendencies as reflected in improved task selection, i.e., selection score (as seen in Fig. 6). However, the low level agent interventions could not achieve a similar performance, i.e., did not lead to a significant increase in users' selection of procrastinated tasks. Hypothesis 1 is partially supported.

Furthermore, while only high interventions effectively reduce procrastination tendencies, a statistically significant difference is found between the two conditions that is consistent with Hypothesis 2. There are also vastly different effects between groups when considering the effects of agent interventions on selection over time. Figure 7 shows how *selection score* changes over time during the task phase. Notably, the high intervention group maintains a high and relatively stable selection score at each task selection, while the no intervention

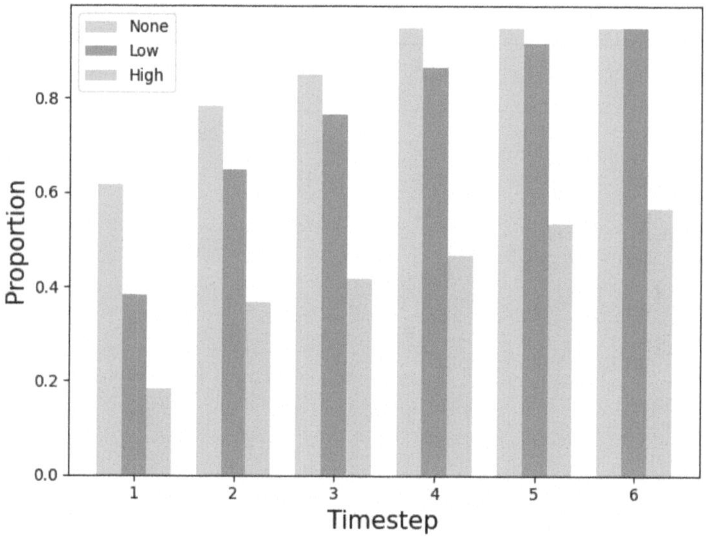

Fig. 9. Cumulative proportion of users who stopped selecting recommended tasks in each timestep

and low intervention groups tend to converge toward similar lower scores over time. Specifically, the no intervention group shows a gradual increase in score, whereas the low intervention group shows a gradual decrease in score.

The trend of more positive and optimal task selection behavior in the high intervention group becomes clearer when examining the number of users who selected recommended (i.e. highest-utility) tasks at each task selection, shown in Fig. 8. The high intervention group has a significantly higher adoption rate of recommended tasks compared to both the low and no intervention groups. Interestingly, both the high and low intervention groups show a decline in selecting recommended tasks over time, while the no intervention group shows the opposite trend of increasing recommended tasks selection over time. This pattern can be attributed to the fact that users in the no intervention group tend to defer selecting recommended, procrastinated tasks until later in the study. This tendency arises because they initially choose and prioritize lower-utility tasks that they enjoy more, leading to a higher proportion of unpleasant, procrastinated tasks remaining toward the study's end.

Looking at the cumulative proportion of users who stopped consistently choosing recommended tasks at each task selection, an interesting pattern emerges (as seen in Fig. 9). The high intervention group maintains a robust adoption rate of recommended tasks, with only a small proportion of users initially deviating from recommendations. Over time, this proportion gradually increases but remains about half that of the other two groups. In contrast, the low and no intervention groups struggle to retain users selecting recommended tasks, evidenced by significant spikes in users opting for non-recommended tasks within the initial task selections.

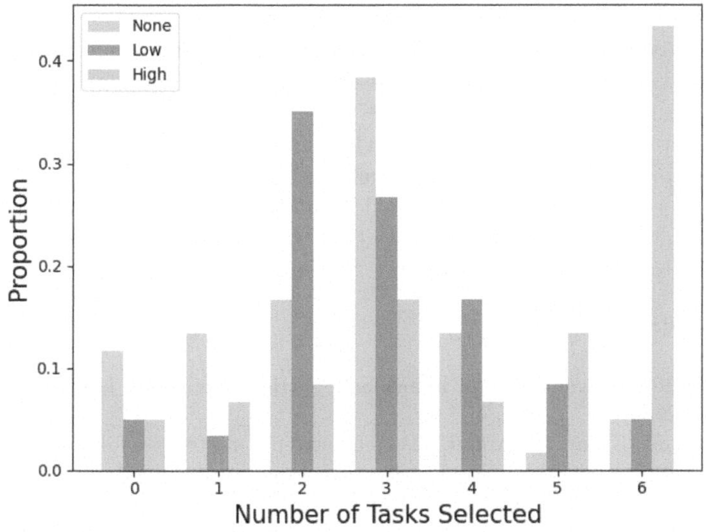

Fig. 10. Proportion of users selecting recommended tasks throughout the task phase

Perhaps the most striking difference in intervention groups is in the number of users who selected recommended tasks throughout the entire task phase. Figure 10 reveals a significant difference, with nearly 50% of the high intervention group strictly adhering to task recommendations by selecting all 6 out of 6 recommended tasks. This finding is an important indicator of the success of agent interventions since the first step towards overcoming and combating procrastination is to begin working on procrastinated tasks, and the high level agent interventions proved successful and encouraged users to select procrastinated tasks.

Further work is needed to analyze the effects of different levels of interventions on user's perception. Specifically, more intervention specific survey items should be employed to investigate the differences between different levels of investigation.

7 Conclusion and Future Work

In conclusion, our study addresses the pervasiveness of procrastination in a highly connected and overstimulated modern era through the use of novel agent intervention techniques. While many psychological interventions and schools of thought already exist to address procrastination tendencies, these methods are often inequitable and not accessible to all. In response, we have developed a model of procrastination through the use of an artificial empirical environment as well as two agent intervention conditions composed of numerous agent intervention techniques aimed at addressing and mitigating procrastination tendencies in individuals. Our findings suggest that user procrastination can be effectively modeled and that agent interventions can provide useful tools for helping individuals reduce their procrastination tendencies.

Our future research direction is centered on the development of adaptive agents that can learn the struggles of users and assist them appropriately in the context of real-life tasks. These agents will be equipped with a range of skills aimed at helping people overcome individual struggles. For instance, agents can support people by dividing complex tasks into smaller sub-tasks. This area of research represents a promising avenue for innovation in procrastination research and enhancing procrastination interventions through agents.

References

1. Counseling the procrastinator in academic settings. American Psychological Association (2004)
2. Hayat, A.A., Kojuri, J., Amini, M.: Academic procrastination of medical students: the role of Internet addiction. J. Adv. Med. Educ. Professional. **8**(2), 83–89 (2020)
3. Arakawa, R., Yakura, H., Goto, M.: Catalyst: domain-extensible intervention for preventing task procrastination using large generative models. In: Proceedings of the 2023 CHI Conference on Human Factors in Computing Systems. CHI 2023. Association for Computing Machinery (2023)

4. Baumeister, R.F., Heatherton, T.F.: Self-regulation failure: an overview. Psychol. Inq. **7**(1), 1–15 (1996)
5. Beutel, M., et al.: Procrastination, distress and life satisfaction across the age range-a German representative community study. PLoS ONE **11**(2), 1–12 (2016)
6. Bielinis, E., Simkin, J., Puttonen, P., Tyrväinen, L.: Effect of viewing video representation of the urban environment and forest environment on mood and level of procrastination. Int. J. Environ. Res. Public Health **17**(14) (2020)
7. Churches, A.: Bloom's digital taxonomy (2010)
8. Constantin, K., English, M.M., Mazmanian, D.: Anxiety, depression, and procrastination among students: rumination plays a larger mediating role than worry. J. Rat.-Emot. Cogn.-Behav. Therapy **36**, 15–27 (2018)
9. van Eerde, W., Klingsieck, K.B.: Overcoming procrastination? A meta-analysis of intervention studies. Educ. Res. Rev. **25**, 73–85 (2018)
10. Geng, J., Han, L., Gao, F., Jou, M., Huang, C.: Internet addiction and procrastination among Chinese young adults: a moderated mediation model. Comput. Hum. Behav. **84**, 320–333 (2018)
11. Hen, M., Goroshit, M.: General and life-domain procrastination in highly educated adults in Israel. Front. Psychol. **9**, 1173 (2018)
12. Hen, M., Goroshit, M., Viengarten, S.: How decisional and general procrastination relate to procrastination at work: an investigation of office and non-office workers. Pers. Individ. Differ. **172**, 1–6 (2021)
13. Häfner, A., Oberst, V., Stock, A.: Avoiding procrastination through time management: an experimental intervention study. Educ. Stud. **40**(3), 352–360 (2014)
14. Kim, K.R., Seo, E.H.: The relationship between procrastination and academic performance: a meta-analysis. Pers. Individ. Differ. **82**, 26–33 (2015)
15. Krispenz, A., Gort, C., Schültke, L., Dickhäuser, O.: How to reduce test anxiety and academic procrastination through inquiry of cognitive appraisals: a pilot study investigating the role of academic self-efficacy. Front. Psychol. **10** (2019)
16. Kroese, F.M., de Ridder, D.T.: Health behaviour procrastination: a novel reasoned route towards self-regulatory failure. Health Psychol. Rev. **10**(3), 313–325 (2016)
17. Kroese, F., De Ridder, D., Evers, C., Adriaanse, M.: Bedtime procrastination: introducing a new area of procrastination. Front. psychol. (2014)
18. Ljubin-Golub, T., Petriĉević, E., Rovan, D.: The role of personality in motivational regulation and academic procrastination. Educ. Psychol. **39**(4), 550–568 (2019)
19. Lozano-Blasco, R., Robres, A.Q., Sánchez, A.S.: Internet addiction in young adults: a meta-analysis and systematic review. Comput. Hum. Behav. **130**, 107201 (2022)
20. Milgram, N.A., Sroloff, B., Rosenbaum, M.: The procrastination of everyday life. J. Res. Pers. **22**(2), 197–212 (1988)
21. Mutter, A., Küchler, A., Idrees, A.R., Kählke, F., Terhorst1, Y., Baumeister1, H.: Studicare procrastination - randomized controlled non-inferiority trial of a persuasive design-optimized internet- and mobile-based intervention with digital coach targeting procrastination in college students. BMC Psychol. **11**(273), 1–17 (2023)
22. Pereira, J., Díaz, O.: Struggling to keep tabs on capstone projects: a chatbot to tackle student procrastination. ACM Trans. Comput. Educ. **22**(1) (2021)
23. Pychyl, T.A., Sirois, F.M.: Chapter 8 - procrastination, emotion regulation, and well-being. In: Sirois, F.M., Pychyl, T.A. (eds.) Procrastination, Health, and Well-Being, pp. 163–188. Academic Press, San Diego (2016)
24. Rozental, A., Forsell, E., Svensson, A., Andersson, G., Carlbring, P.: Internet-based cognitive-behavior therapy for procrastination: a randomized controlled trial. J. Consult. Clin. Psychol. **83**(4), 808 (2015)

25. Sari, W.L., Fakhruddiana, F.: Internal locus of control, social support and academic procrastination among students in completing the thesis. Int. J. Eval. Res. Educ. **8**(2), 363–368 (2019)
26. Senecal, C., Julien, E., Guay, F.: Role conflict and academic procrastination: a self-determination perspective. Eur. J. Soc. Psychol. **33**, 135–145 (2003)
27. Senecal, C., Koestner, R., Vallerand, R.J.: Self-regulation and academic procrastination. J. Soc. Psychol. **135**(5), 607–619 (1995)
28. Sirois, F.M., Melia-Gordon, M.L., Pychyl, T.A.: "i'll look after my health, later": an investigation of procrastination and health. Pers. Individ. Differ. **35**(5), 1167–1184 (2003)
29. Steel, P.: The nature of procrastination: a meta-analytic and theoretical review of quintessential self-regulatory failure. Psychol. Bull. **133**(1), 65–94 (2007)
30. Steel, P., Klingsieck, K.B.: Academic procrastination: psychological antecedents revisited. Aust. Psychol. **51**(1), 36–46 (2016)
31. de Vries, R.A.J., Zaga, C., Bayer, F., Drossaert, C.H.C., Truong, K.P., Evers, V.: Experts get me started, peers keep me going: comparing crowd- versus expert-designed motivational text messages for exercise behavior change. In: Proceedings of the 11th EAI International Conference on Pervasive Computing Technologies for Healthcare. PervasiveHealth '17, pp. 155–162. Association for Computing Machinery, New York (2017)
32. Wieland, L.M., Hoppe, J.D., Wolgast, A., Ebner-Priemer, U.W.: Task ambiguity and academic procrastination: an experience sampling approach. Learn. Instr. **81**, 101595 (2022)
33. Zacks, S., Hen, M.: Academic interventions for academic procrastination: a review of the literature. J. Prevent. Intervent. Commun. **46**(2), 117–130 (2018)
34. Zavaleta Bernuy, A., et al.: How can email interventions increase students' completion of online homework? A case study using a/b comparisons. In: LAK22: 12th International Learning Analytics and Knowledge Conference, LAK22, pp. 107-118. Association for Computing Machinery, New York (2022)
35. Zhou, M.: Gender differences in procrastination: the role of personality traits. Curr. Psychol. **39**, 1445–1453 (2020)

Coordination, Organisations, Institutions, Norms and Ethics

Search Versus Search for Collapsing Electoral Control Types

Benjamin Carleton[1], Michael C. Chavrimootoo[2(✉)], Lane A. Hemaspaandra[3], David E. Narváez[4], Conor Taliancich[5], and Henry B. Welles[3]

[1] Cornell University, Ithaca, NY, USA
carleton@cs.cornell.edu
[2] Denison University, Granville, OH, USA
mchavrim@u.rochester.edu
[3] University of Rochester, Rochester, NY, USA
hwelles@u.rochester.edu
[4] Virginia Tech, Blacksburg, VA, USA
david.narvaez@computer.org
[5] Property Matrix, Culver City, CA, USA
ctalianc@u.rochester.edu
http://www.cs.rochester.edu/u/lane

Abstract. A 2024 paper of Carleton et al. [11] building on Hemaspaandra et al. [25] surprisingly shows, for 36 pairs of cases involving plurality, veto, and approval voting, that seemingly different, long-studied partition-based control attack types "collapse": they are the same set (and so have the same decision complexity). The rather novel open question the 2024 paper concludes with is whether, for the 36 collapsing decision-problem pairs, their *search*-complexities are linked. In this paper, we completely resolve that question. We build a framework for linking the search complexities and solutions of members of collapsing pairs, and we both link and pinpoint the search complexities of all 36 collapsing cases (in part via linking the search complexities within the 7 "universal" collapsing pairs). This is important because for election problems the search versions are by far the more important versions: they tell one *how* to perform the desired attack.

Keywords: Computational Social Choice · Problem Interreducibility · Search Complexity · Elections · Electoral Control · Voting

1 Introduction

Algorithms for problems on elections are an important class of combinatorial algorithms, in which an election's attacker generally has available an exponential

---

Supported in part by NSF grants CCF-2006496 and DUE-2135431, and CIFellows grant CIF2020-UR-36.

An extended abstract of two pages plus references of this paper appeared in the 22nd International Conference on Autonomous Agents and Multiagent Systems [9].

R. Collier et al. (Eds.): EUMAS 2024, LNAI 15685, pp. 217–236, 2025.
https://doi.org/10.1007/978-3-031-93930-3_13

number of potential actions. Despite the combinatorially explosive number of potential actions available, in many cases polynomial-time algorithms can be developed. Thus the study of manipulative actions against elections is a beautiful showcase of an area with real-world importance, where the outcome of the clash between finding efficient algorithms for combinatorially explosive problems, and proving the impossibility (if $P \neq NP$) of finding such algorithms, is of vivid interest.

"Control" attacks on elections try to make a focus candidate win/lose/uniquely-win/not-uniquely-win through such actions as adding, deleting, or partitioning candidates or voters. Control was first studied in the seminal work of Bartholdi et al. [3], and has been further explored in many papers (see [21]).

Hemaspaandra et al. [25] noted that, surprisingly, seven pairs among the 44 (relatively) "standard" control types collapse: For each election system (i.e., each mapping from candidates and votes to a winner set among the candidates) $\mathcal{E}$ whose vote type is linear orders, for each of those seven pairs of types $\mathcal{T}_1$ and $\mathcal{T}_2$ it holds that for each input there is a successful action on that input under the $\mathcal{T}_1$ control type if and only if there is a successful action on that input under the $\mathcal{T}_2$ control type. *Viewed thus as sets*, $\mathcal{T}_1$ and $\mathcal{T}_2$ are identical! Carleton et al. [11] noted that Hemaspaandra et al.'s [25] proof tacitly in fact established that those seven collapses hold for *all* election systems regardless of their vote type.

Carleton et al. [11] showed that those seven pairs are the only collapsing pairs among the 44 standard control types if one wants the given collapse to hold for *every* election system. However, that paper discovered some additional collapses that hold specifically for veto or for approval voting, and also found new collapses that hold for all election systems that satisfy certain axiomatic properties.[1]

For each election system to which a collapse applies, the decision complexity of the two collapsing control types is the same (since the sets are equal). However, Carleton et al. [11] (in not just its journal version but also in its technical report and conference versions) raised as a challenge the issue of whether the *search* complexity of the collapsing pairs is also the same. Our paper addresses that issue.

Why is it even plausible that sets with the same decision complexity might have different search complexities (relative to some certificate/solution schemes)? Well, it indeed can and does happen if $P \neq NP \cap coNP$ (and so certainly happens if integer factorization is not in polynomial time, since the natural decision version of that is in $NP \cap coNP$). In particular, if $P \neq NP \cap coNP$, let L be any fixed set in $(NP \cap coNP) - P$. Suppose L's finite alphabet is Σ. Consider a nondeterministic polynomial-time Turing machine (NPTM) N over input alpha-

[1] Two of those axiomatic theorems had incorrect proofs in that paper's conference version [10] and/or the associated full technical report [8], but the journal version [11] changes the axiomatic assumptions and then correctly proves the thus modified results. The consequences in that paper for the system, approval voting, that those results were being used to prove things about still follow from the modified results.

bet Σ that immediately halts and accepts. So $L(N) = \Sigma^*$ and the certificate of acceptance (basically, the accepting computation path) of N on any input x is the empty string. Thus the function $s(x) = \epsilon$ solves this search problem. However, consider an NPTM N' over the alphabet Σ that on each input x nondeterministically simulates both the NPTM N_L for L and the NPTM $N_{\overline{L}}$ for $\overline{L}$. Clearly, $L(N') = \Sigma^*$, since each $x \in \Sigma^*$ is either in L or in $\overline{L}$. However, the search complexity of Σ^* relative to the certificate scheme of N' is not polynomial, since on input x any accepting path of N' will (after removing its initial guess bit regarding simulating N_L or $N_{\overline{L}}$) yield an accepting path for *exactly* one of N_L or $N_{\overline{L}}$ on input x, and so determines whether $x \in L$ or $x \notin L$. Thus, since $L \notin \mathrm{P}$, no search function for Σ^* relative to N' can be polynomial-time computable. This argument is basically due to a construction of Borodin and Demers [6] (see also [24,41], and the proof on page 39 of [27] that is pointed to by the discussion in Footnote 9 of [25]).

This paper explores the issue of whether the collapsing (as decision problems) pairs of Hemaspaandra et al. [25] and Carleton et al. [11] have the same *search* complexity. We prove that in every case the answer is Yes (if given oracle access to the election system's winner problem when that is not in P), and indeed we show that in each case a solution for one can (again, given access to the winner problem) be polynomial-time transformed into a solution for the other. Thus the complexities are polynomially related (given access to the winner problem). Additionally, for the concrete cases of plurality's, veto's, and approval's collapsing pairs, we explore whether those polynomially equivalent search complexities are clearly "polynomial time," or are NP-hard, and we resolve every such case.

Why is this important? In reality, one—e.g., a campaign manager or a corrupt vote collector/counter—typically wants not merely to efficiently compute whether there *exists* some action that will make one's candidate win, but rather one wants to efficiently get *an actual such successful action.* Unfortunately, the literature's existing collapsing control type pairs are each about and proved for the "exists" case. In contrast, this paper's results are establishing that the literature's existing collapsing control type pairs even have the property that—given access to the winner problem for the election system in question (when the latter is not in P)—for both members of the pair the "getting one's hands on a successful action when one exists" issue is of the same complexity for both. We also show that one usually can efficiently use access to solutions for one to get solutions for the other.

Except for the immediately clear proof of Proposition 2, any proofs that are not in this paper can be found in the technical report [7].

2 Preliminaries

2.1 Elections and Election Systems

An election consists of a finite candidate set C and a finite collection of votes V over the candidates in C.

The "type" of the votes depends on the election system one is considering. Most typically, each vote is a linear ordering—a complete, transitive, asymmetric binary relation—over the candidates (e.g., $3 > 1 > 2$). Another common vote type (called an approval vector) is a bit-vector of length $\|C\|$, with each bit typically indicating approval (1) or disapproval (0) of a candidate.

No two candidates can have the same name. (By allowing candidates to have names, we are following the model of the papers that this paper is most closely related to.)

An election system maps from an election, (C, V), to a (possibly nonempty or nonstrict) subset of C (the set of winners). Three particular election systems that we will discuss are plurality, veto, and approval voting. In plurality elections, each vote is a linear ordering over C, and all candidates for whom the number of votes in which they were ranked first is the highest (possibly tied) among the candidates are winners. In veto elections, each vote is a linear ordering over C, and all candidates for whom the number of votes in which they were ranked last is the lowest (possibly tied) among the candidates are winners. In approval elections, each vote is an approval vector, and all candidates who garner the most (possibly tied) approvals are the election's winners.

For each election system $\mathcal{E}$, define the winner problem as $W_{\mathcal{E}} = \{(C, V, p) \mid p \in C \text{ and } p \text{ is a winner of the } \mathcal{E} \text{ election } (C, V)\}$. Let $\text{UniqueWinner}_{\mathcal{E}}(C, V) = \{p \in C \mid p \text{ uniquely wins } \mathcal{E} \text{ election } (C, V)\}$ and let $\text{Winners}_{\mathcal{E}}(C, V) = \{p \in C \mid (C, V, p) \in W_{\mathcal{E}}\}$. We will typically leverage access to the oracle $W_{\mathcal{E}}$ (when given access to it) to compute these functions as they can clearly be computed in polynomial time relative to $W_{\mathcal{E}}$.

2.2 Control Types and Collapses

Definition 1 and the text following it will define the 24 partition-based control types (for each election system $\mathcal{E}$). For uniformity, we take the definition essentially verbatim from the papers we are most closely related to [11,25], which themselves were drawing on the line of earlier papers that developed the current set of control notions (for more history and citations, see [11,21,25]). One must be clear as to the handling of candidates who are tied winners in first-round elections. The two tie-handling rules typically studied as to partition-based control types are ties-eliminate (TE)—in which a candidate must uniquely win its subelection to proceed to the next round—and ties-promote (TP)—in which all winners of a subelection proceed to the next round. In Definition 1 and later in the paper, we will at times have elections whose candidate set is C' but whose votes, due to candidate partitioning and/or first-round candidate eliminations, are over a set $C \supseteq C'$. As is standard in the literature, we always take this to mean that the votes are masked down to just the candidates in C'.

Definition 1 (see [11]). *Let $\mathcal{E}$ be an election system.*

1. *In the constructive control by partition of voters problem for $\mathcal{E}$, in the* TP *or* TE *tie-handling rule model (denoted by $\mathcal{E}$-*CC-PV-TP-NUW *or $\mathcal{E}$-*CC-PV-

TE-NUW, *respectively), we are given an election* (C, V), *and a candidate* $p \in C$. *We ask if there is a partition*[2] *of* V *into* V_1 *and* V_2 *such that* p *is a winner of the two-stage election where the winners of subelection* (C, V_1) *that survive the tie-handling rule compete (with respect to* V*) against the winners of subelection* (C, V_2) *that survive the tie-handling rule. Each election (in both stages) is conducted using election system* $\mathcal{E}$.

2. *In the constructive control by run-off partition of candidates problem for* $\mathcal{E}$, *in the* TP *or* TE *tie-handling rule model (denoted by* $\mathcal{E}$-CC-RPC-TP-NUW *or* $\mathcal{E}$-CC-RPC-TE-NUW, *respectively), we are given an election* (C, V), *and a candidate* $p \in C$. *We ask if there is a partition of* C *into* C_1 *and* C_2 *such that* p *is a winner of the two-stage election where the winners of subelection* (C_1, V) *that survive the tie-handling rule compete (with respect to* V*) against the winners of subelection* (C_2, V) *that survive the tie-handling rule. Each election (in both stages) is conducted using* $\mathcal{E}$.
3. *In the constructive control by partition of candidates problem for* $\mathcal{E}$, *in the* TP *or* TE *tie-handling rule model (denoted by* $\mathcal{E}$-CC-PC-TP-NUW *or* $\mathcal{E}$-CC-PC-TE-NUW, *respectively), we are given an election* (C, V), *and a candidate* $p \in C$. *We ask if there is a partition of* C *into* C_1 *and* C_2 *such that* p *is a winner of the two-stage election where the winners of subelection* (C_1, V) *that survive the tie-handling rule compete (with respect to* V*) against all candidates in* C_2. *Each election (in both stages) is conducted using* $\mathcal{E}$.

In each of the six control types defined above we can replace "is a winner" with "is a unique winner" to denote constructive control in the unique-winner (UW) model. The resulting control types are appended with "-UW" rather than "-NUW." NUW denotes the so-called nonunique-winner model, aka, the cowinner model, in which merely being an overall winner, whether tied or not, is the goal. This completes the definition of the 12 standard constructive partition-control types (for each election system; in text discussions, we will often omit the "for each election system," and so may speak of control of a given type generically). The standard 12 additional *destructive* partition-control types differ only in that instead of seeking to make a focus candidate a winner or unique winner, the goal is to *prevent* the focus candidate from being a winner or unique winner. To denote those, we replace the "CC" with a "DC," e.g., the destructive control by partition of voters problem for $\mathcal{E}$ using the TE handling rule and the UW model is denoted $\mathcal{E}$-DC-PV-TE-UW. Thus the 24 standard types of partition-based control are defined. As is standard, each control type is quietly defining—in some sense *is*—a set, namely, the set of all inputs on which the given control attack can be successfully carried out. Thus for example Veto-DC-PV-TP-NUW is a set. We will immediately use this view in the next sentence.

Carleton et al. [11], for any two control types $\mathcal{T}_1$ and $\mathcal{T}_2$ that are compatible (i.e., have the same collection of input fields), define the types to collapse if

[2] A partition of a multiset V is a pair of multisets V_1 and V_2 such that $V_1 \cup V_2 = V$, where $\cup$ denotes multiset union. A partition of a set C is a pair of sets C_1 and C_2 such that $C_1 \cup C_2 = C$ and $C_1 \cap C_2 = \emptyset$, where $\cup$ and $\cap$ are standard set union and intersection.

$\mathcal{T}_1 = \mathcal{T}_2$. If $\mathcal{T}_1$ and $\mathcal{T}_2$ are both about the same election system $\mathcal{E}$ (i.e., each has as its prefix "$\mathcal{E}$-") and $\mathcal{T}_1$ and $\mathcal{T}_2$ are compatible, we will say that $\mathcal{T}_1$ and $\mathcal{T}_2$ are $\mathcal{E}$-matched. If control types $\mathcal{T}_1$ and $\mathcal{T}_2$ are both about the same election system $\mathcal{E}$ and collapse (and so also are compatible), we say that they are a *collapsing pair*. Since all 24 control types just defined are mutually compatible, and none of the other $44 - 24 = 20$ standard control types are known to be involved in *any* of the collapses found in Hemaspaandra et al. [25] and Carleton et al. [11], we will not further mention compatibility in this paper. (See [11] for the standard definitions of the 20 control types not defined here.)

Before giving the collapses found by Hemaspaandra et al. [25] and Carleton et al. [11], we give the definitions of three axiomatic properties of election systems. An election system $\mathcal{E}$ is said to satisfy Property α (see [12,40]) if for every election (C, V), a candidate p being a winner implies that p remains a winner whenever the election is restricted to a subset $C' \subseteq C$ containing p. An election system $\mathcal{E}$ is said to satisfy Property Unique-α, the unique version of Property α, if in every election (C, V), a candidate p being a unique winner implies that p remains a unique winner whenever the election is restricted to a subset $C' \subseteq C$ containing p [26].[3] Finally, an election system $\mathcal{E}$ is said to be strongly voiced exactly if for every election (C, V) with $C \neq \emptyset$, there is at least one winner of (C, V) under $\mathcal{E}$ [26].

Here are the collapses found in Hemaspaandra et al. [11,25]. For every election system $\mathcal{E}$, $\mathcal{E}$-DC-RPC-TP-NUW = $\mathcal{E}$-DC-PC-TP-NUW and $\mathcal{E}$-DC-RPC-TE-NUW = $\mathcal{E}$-DC-PC-TE-NUW = $\mathcal{E}$-DC-RPC-TE-UW = $\mathcal{E}$-DC-PC-TE-UW [11,25]. For every election system $\mathcal{E}$ satisfying Property Unique-α, $\mathcal{E}$-DC-PC-TE-UW = $\mathcal{E}$-DC-RPC-TP-UW = $\mathcal{E}$-DC-PC-TP-UW [11]. And for every election $\mathcal{E}$ that is strongly voiced and satisfies Property α, $\mathcal{E}$-CC-PC-TP-UW = $\mathcal{E}$-CC-RPC-TP-UW [11]. Since approval voting is clearly strongly voiced and clearly satisfies Property α and Property Unique-α, these four additional pair-collapses hold for approval voting [11]. Note that Approval-DC-PC-TE-UW participates in both the four-type and the three-type above collapses with $\mathcal{E}$ = Approval, so by transitivity we have a six-type collapse about approval.

The remaining collapses from Carleton et al. [11] are Veto-DC-PV-TE-NUW = Veto-DC-PV-TE-UW, Approval-DC-PV-TE-NUW = Approval-DC-PV-TE-UW, Approval-CC-PC-TE-NUW = Approval-CC-RPC-TE-NUW, Approval-CC-PC-TE-UW = Approval-CC-RPC-TE-UW, and finally, Approval-CC-PC-TP-NUW = Approval-CC-RPC-TP-NUW.

2.3 Search Problems: Interreductions and Complexity

Our control types are each defined as a language problem—a set. However, each has a clear "$\mathrm{NP}^{W_\mathcal{E}}$ search problem" associated with it (so an "NP search problem" if $W_\mathcal{E} \in \mathrm{P}$). Namely, the problem of, on input (C, V, p), outputting a partition (C_1, C_2) of the candidate set (or if the type is a voter partition type,

[3] What we call Property Unique-α (and for brevity we often drop the "Property") has been previously referred to as the "Unique-WARP" property, and our technical-report version [7] discusses the reasons for moving away from that name.

a partition (V_1, V_2) of the vote collection) such that under that partition, the control action regarding (C, V, p) is successful under election system $\mathcal{E}$.

To be able to speak clearly of search problems and their interrelationships and complexity it is important to be specific as to what we mean, both in terms of relating the solutions of two search problems and as to classifying the complexity of a search problem. These two different tasks are related, yet differ in how they are formalized. Megiddo and Papadimitriou [36] give a formalization of search problems along with a notion of reductions between them. We will use that for connecting solutions of search problems, except we will see that our problems will be connected in a way substantially tighter than their framework anticipated. On the other hand, as we want to interconnect even electoral-control search problems whose winner problems $W_{\mathcal{E}}$ are potentially not in P, we will not require our relations to be polynomial-time decidable. (Rather, we will require them to be polynomial-time decidable given oracle $W_{\mathcal{E}}$. When $W_{\mathcal{E}} \in \mathrm{P}$, that requirement of course is the same as requiring them to be polynomial-time decidable.)

Per Megiddo and Papadimitriou [36], let Σ be a finite alphabet with at least two symbols and suppose $R \subseteq \Sigma^* \times \Sigma^*$ is a relation, decidable in polynomial time relative to oracle A, that is polynomially-balanced. (Note: A relation is polynomially-balanced if there is a polynomial p such that $(x, y) \in R$ implies $|y| \leq p(|x|)$.) That relation R (which is decidable in P^A) defines what Megiddo and Papadimitriou call the computational problem Π_R: Given an $x \in \Sigma^*$, find some $y \in \Sigma^*$ such that $(x, y) \in R$ if such a y exists, and reply "no" otherwise. We will call the class of all such problems FNP^A (Megiddo and Papadimitriou in fact covered only the case $A = \emptyset$, so their class was called FNP).

In the case of our 24 electoral-control problems, the "x" here is the problem input, (C, V, p). And if (C, V, p) is a yes instance of the (viewed as a set) control type, an acceptable output y in the sense of the above definition is (the encoding of) any partition (C_1, C_2) of C (or if the type is a voter partition, then any partition (V_1, V_2) of V) that leads to success under the control type, the input (C, V, p), and the election system. (We in this paper will not worry about encoding details, since such details are not a key issue here. We as is typical merely assume reasonable, natural encodings.)

For each election system $\mathcal{E}$ and each $\mathcal{T}$ that is one of our 24 partition control types for $\mathcal{E}$, let $R_{\mathcal{T}}$ be the natural $\mathrm{P}^{W_{\mathcal{E}}}$-decidable, polynomially-balanced relation for its search problem (i.e., $R_{\mathcal{T}}$ is the set of pairs $((C, V, p), (P_1, P_2))$ where (P_1, P_2) is a partition of the problem's sort that in the setting (C, V, p), under election system $\mathcal{E}$, succeeds for the given type of control action). Then we will sometimes write $\Pi_{\mathcal{T}}$ as a shorthand for $\Pi_{R_{\mathcal{T}}}$. Note that for each of our 24 partition control types involving $\mathcal{E}$, we clearly have $\Pi_{\mathcal{T}} \in \mathrm{FNP}^{W_{\mathcal{E}}}$, e.g., $\Pi_{\mathcal{E}\text{-DC-PC-TP-NUW}} \in \mathrm{FNP}^{W_{\mathcal{E}}}$ holds (and, for example, from that it follows immediately that, since $W_{\mathrm{Approval}} \in \mathrm{P}$, $\Pi_{\mathrm{Approval\text{-}DC\text{-}PC\text{-}TP\text{-}NUW}} \in \mathrm{FNP}$).

We wish to show that the known collapsing electoral control types also have polynomially related (given access to an oracle for the winner problem for $\mathcal{E}$) search complexity, and indeed we wish to show even that a solution for one can efficiently be used to generate a solution for the other. To do this, we will need the notion of reductions between search problems. Fortunately, Megiddo and Papadimitriou defined a reduction notion between search problems that is close to what we need. Megiddo and Papadimitriou [36] say that a reduction from problem Π_R to problem Π_S is a pair of polynomial-time computable functions f and g such that, for any $x \in \Sigma^*$, $(x, g(y)) \in R \iff (f(x), y) \in S$. This in spirit is trying to say that we can map via f to an instance $f(x)$ such that given a solution relative to S of $f(x)$ we can via g map to a solution relative to R of x. Unfortunately, read as written, it does not seem to *do* that, regardless of whether one takes the omitted quantification over y to be existential or to be universal. Either way the definition leaves open a loophole in which on some x for which there *does* exist a solution relative to R, the value of $f(x)$ will be some string that has no solution relative to S, and all $g(y)$'s will be strings that are not solutions to x relative to R. So the "$\iff$" will be satisfied since both sides evaluate to False, but no solution transfer will have occurred. In the nightmare case, a given "reduction" could exploit this loophole on *every* x that has a solution relative to R.

We will now reformulate the definition more carefully, for our case, to close that loophole (which is easily closed). However, more interestingly, we will in effect alter the definition in two additional ways. First, notice that in Megiddo and Papadimitriou's definition (assuming one fixes the above loophole first) the function $f(x)$ allows the solution to x on the R side to be obtained via demanding a solution to a *different* (than x) instance $f(x)$, on the S side. But in our setting, collapsing types are the *same* set, just with differing "witnessing" relations. And our goal is to make connections via those witnesses. So in the definitions we are about to give of our "$\leq_{\text{search}}$" reduction family, we require their $f(x)$ to be the identity function! Second, since we wish to connect the solutions of collapsing pairs even when the winner problem of $\mathcal{E}$ is not in P, our reductions will have the winner problem as an oracle. (The reason for this is that even given a (C, V, p) and a partition (C_1, C_2) of C (or for voter partition types, a partition (V_1, V_2) of V), to evaluate whether the partition is a solution generally needs calls to $W_{\mathcal{E}}$.)

We will not in these definitions explicitly write "Π" expressions, but the solutions we speak of are with respect to the witnesses/actions that the given control type is about (they are the search component of Π, i.e., in our case they are those 2nd components that appear in pairs, belonging to the underlying relation $R_{\mathcal{T}}$, having "x" or "I" (i.e., the given (C, V, p)) as their 1st component), and so we view these definitions as a reformulated version (with some changes for our particular situation) of the Megiddo and Papadimitriou "Π" approach.

Let us first give the intuition behind our notation. $\mathcal{T}_1 \leq_{\text{search}}^{p,\mathcal{E}} \mathcal{T}_2$ means $\mathcal{T}_2$'s solutions are so powerful that for problem instance I, given any solution for $\mathcal{T}_2$ with respect to I one can quickly, given oracle $W_{\mathcal{E}}$, build a solution to $\mathcal{T}_1$ with respect to I. That is why the notation has $\mathcal{T}_1$ on the left.

Definition 2. *Let $\mathcal{E}$ be an election system, and let $\mathcal{T}_1$ and $\mathcal{T}_2$ be $\mathcal{E}$-matched collapsing*[4] *control types.*

1. *We say that "$\mathcal{T}_1$ is polynomially search-reducible to $\mathcal{T}_2$ with respect to $\mathcal{E}$" (denoted by $\mathcal{T}_1 \leq^{p,\mathcal{E}}_{\text{search}} \mathcal{T}_2$) if there is a reduction that, given $W_\mathcal{E}$ as oracle, runs in polynomial time and on each input (I, S), where I is an input to $\mathcal{T}_1$ and S is a solution for I with respect to $\mathcal{T}_2$, outputs a solution S' for I with respect to $\mathcal{T}_1$.*
2. *We say that "$\mathcal{T}_1$ is polynomially search-equivalent to $\mathcal{T}_2$ with respect to $\mathcal{E}$" ($\mathcal{T}_1 \equiv^{p,\mathcal{E}}_{\text{search}} \mathcal{T}_2$) if $\mathcal{T}_1 \leq^{p,\mathcal{E}}_{\text{search}} \mathcal{T}_2$ and $\mathcal{T}_2 \leq^{p,\mathcal{E}}_{\text{search}} \mathcal{T}_1$.*

Definition 3. *Let $\mathcal{E}$ be an election system, and let $\mathcal{T}_1$ and $\mathcal{T}_2$ be $\mathcal{E}$-matched collapsing control types.*

1. *We say that "$\mathcal{T}_1$ is polynomially search-reducible to $\mathcal{T}_2$" (denoted by $\mathcal{T}_1 \leq^{p}_{\text{search}} \mathcal{T}_2$) if there is a reduction that runs in polynomial time and on each input (I, S), where I is an input to $\mathcal{T}_1$ and S is a solution for I with respect to $\mathcal{T}_2$, outputs a solution S' for I with respect to $\mathcal{T}_1$.*
2. *We say that "$\mathcal{T}_1$ is polynomially search-equivalent to $\mathcal{T}_2$" ($\mathcal{T}_1 \equiv^{p}_{\text{search}} \mathcal{T}_2$) if $\mathcal{T}_1 \leq^{p}_{\text{search}} \mathcal{T}_2$ and $\mathcal{T}_2 \leq^{p}_{\text{search}} \mathcal{T}_1$.*

The closest notion in the literature to our Definitions 2 and 3 is the notion known as Levin reductions [2,29,39]. It strongly differs from our notion, but a later variant of it by Goldreich [22] is close to our notion (see [7]).

When a polynomial-time reduction has a polynomial-time computable oracle, one can alter the reduction machine M's action to have M do without the oracle by itself simulating the oracle's work. So we have the following observation.

Proposition 1. *Let $\mathcal{E}$ be an election system with $W_\mathcal{E} \in \mathrm{P}$ and let $\mathcal{T}_1$ and $\mathcal{T}_2$ be $\mathcal{E}$-matched control types.*

1. *If $\mathcal{T}_1 \leq^{p,\mathcal{E}}_{\text{search}} \mathcal{T}_2$, then $\mathcal{T}_1 \leq^{p}_{\text{search}} \mathcal{T}_2$.*
2. *If $\mathcal{T}_1 \equiv^{p,\mathcal{E}}_{\text{search}} \mathcal{T}_2$, then $\mathcal{T}_1 \equiv^{p}_{\text{search}} \mathcal{T}_2$.*

The definitions we just gave provide the tools we will use to show that the complexities of the members of each known pair of collapsing standard types are polynomially related to each other (given oracle access to $W_\mathcal{E}$), and that the members of the pair are closely related in terms of us being able to efficiently build a solution to one from a solution to the other.

But, even if $\mathcal{E}$-matched collapsing types $\mathcal{T}_1$ and $\mathcal{T}_2$ have polynomially related search complexities (in the above sense), that does not tell us whether they both are easy, or they both are hard. Indeed, since for example our "close complexity relationship between the two members of the collapsing pair" results regarding the seven Hemaspaandra et al. [25] collapses hold for *all* election systems, it is

[4] If we omit the "collapsing" in our definitions, then one could trivially satisfy the notion on a given I whenever I was not in $\mathcal{T}_2$. That is, our notion is focused on pairs of types that collapse—where each input is either in both or not in both.

completely possible that though (as we will show) the search complexity of such $\Pi_{\mathcal{T}_1}$ and $\Pi_{\mathcal{T}_2}$ are polynomially related, for some election system both could be easy and for some election system both could be hard (indeed, even undecidable).

Nonetheless, at least for specific, concrete systems that collapse results exist for, it would be nice to be able to prove results about whether their related search complexities are both easy or are both hard. The $\Pi_{\mathcal{T}}$ formalism, even in the reformulated Π-free version in our definitions, is not ideal for doing this (since the Megiddo and Papadimitriou definition speaks of outputting "no," which is not a typical NP-machine action, and that definition also is speaking about various y outputs without giving a framework for making clear how to speak of the instantiated (as to y) versions). One could approach the issue in various ways, but we will do so by drawing on the flavor of some relations (sometimes called multivalued "functions") work that preceded that of Megiddo and Papadimitriou [36]. Book et al. [5] built a broad theory of multivalued NP functions. Rather than presenting it here—it is a bit more general than Megiddo and Papadimitriou [36] in that it maps to path outputs rather than to certificates (certificates are in flavor closer to capturing a path's nondeterministic choices), and we do not need that generality—we draw just on one key notion. The Megiddo and Papadimitriou Π_R model says that the task is to output "any" appropriate y. So in some sense, Π_R is speaking of an entire family of maps. Viewed in the Book et al. [5] lens, Π_R is related to a multivalued function, call it $\widehat{\Pi}_R$, that on a given input x is undefined (i.e., maps to some special output $\perp$) if x has no solution y (no appropriate-length y with $(x, y) \in R$) and otherwise maps to the set of *all* y with $(x, y) \in R$. And, crucially, a "single-valued refinement" of that multivalued function is any function that on each input x, (a) is undefined on x if x has no solution relative to R, and (b) maps to exactly one solution of x relative to R if x has at least one solution relative to R. For example, if $\Sigma = \{0, 1\}$ and $R = \{(0x, 1) \mid x \in \Sigma^*\} \cup \{(0x, 0) \mid x \in \Sigma^*\}$, then the refinements of $\widehat{\Pi}_R$ are each of the uncountable number of functions that on inputs in $\{\epsilon\} \cup \{1x \mid x \in \Sigma^*\}$ map to $\perp$ and on each input of the form $\{0x \mid x \in \Sigma^*\}$ map to exactly one of 0 or 1.

We now define what we mean by the search problem for $\mathcal{T}$ to be easy or hard. We say that the search problem for $\mathcal{T}$ is polynomial-time computable if there *exists* at least one refinement of $\widehat{\Pi}_{\mathcal{T}}$ (i.e., of $\widehat{\Pi}_{R_{\mathcal{T}}}$) that is a polynomial-time computable function. We say that the search problem for $\mathcal{T}$ is NP-hard if for *every* refinement f of $\widehat{\Pi}_{\mathcal{T}}$, it holds that $\mathrm{NP} \subseteq \mathrm{P}^f$. We say that the search problem for $\mathcal{T}$ is NP-easy if there *exists* at least one refinement f of $\widehat{\Pi}_{\mathcal{T}}$ that can be computed by a polynomial-time function given SAT as its oracle, i.e., is in the function class sometimes called "$\mathrm{FP}^{\mathrm{NP}}$" or "$\mathrm{PF}^{\mathrm{NP}}$." If the search problem for $\mathcal{T}$ is both NP-hard and NP-easy, we say that the search problem is SAT-equivalent. Given two SAT-equivalent search problems, this definition does not promise (as, in contrast, the second parts of Definition 3 and, in some sense, Definition 2 do) that one can produce a solution for one of the problems from any solution, for the same instance, to the other, and vice versa. However, our definitions give us a clean way to make clear that one of our search problems is hard, or is easy.

3 Related Work

The papers most related to this one are those discussed already: Hemaspaandra et al. [25] and Carleton et al. [11] collapsed existing control types as decision problems. And Carleton et al. [11] posed as an open issue whether such collapses also collapse the associated search problems as to their complexity. Addressing that issue is the focus of the present paper.

Megiddo and Papadimitriou [36] and Book et al. [5] set frameworks that we use and adapt, as to the study of search problems, and refining multivalued functions.

Control was created by Bartholdi et al. [3], and the 24 control types we study were developed in that paper and (for the introduction of destructive control types and stating the TP/TE rules) in the work of Hemaspaandra et al. [26]. The shift over time from the earliest papers' focus on the UW model to a focus on either both UW and NUW, or sometimes even just NUW, is discussed, with citations, in the Related Work section of Carleton et al. [11].

Many papers have studied control. Faliszewski and Rothe's [21] survey is an excellent resource on control, with a rich range of citations to papers investigating the control complexities of specific election systems. Among the many systems that have been studied and seem to do somewhat well in resisting control attacks are Schulze and ranked pair elections [28,38], Llull and Copeland elections [19,20], normalized range voting [37], Bucklin and fallback elections [14,18] (see also [15]), and SP-AV elections [16]. Election control, in many variants, continues to be an area of active interest [1,13,23,30–32,34,42–44].

Among the most popular election systems whose control complexity has been studied are approval [4,26], plurality [3,26], and veto elections [17,33,35]. We will draw on some decision-problem algorithms from these papers to establish some of our search results. For example, Theorem 4 part 1 follows directly from the properties of an algorithm of Maushagen and Rothe [35].

4 Results

This section will show that all known collapsing control-type pairs even have the same *search* complexity, given access to the election system's winner problem. We will for the concrete cases determine when that shared complexity level is "polynomial-time computability," and when it is "SAT-equivalence." And we also explore, via our search-equivalence notions, how solutions from one can be used to obtain solutions to the other. Table 1 provides a summary of those results; we remind the reader that the definitions of the important election systems approval, plurality, and veto are given in Sect. 2.1. In addition to the above, we will even obtain a new decision-case result (Theorem 6) that will help us in our quest to discover search complexities.

Theorems 1 and 2 focus on those collapses that hold for every election system.

Theorem 1. *For every election system $\mathcal{E}$, $\mathcal{E}$-DC-RPC-TP-NUW $\equiv_{\text{search}}^{p,\mathcal{E}}$ $\mathcal{E}$-DC-PC-TP-NUW.*

Table 1. A summary of our results pinpointing the exact search complexities of the decision-collapsing (and search-collapsing) control types for concrete election systems. We use "polynomial" to denote "polynomial-time computable."

Collapsing Decision Control Types	Their Search Complexities	References
Plurality: DC-RPC-TP-NUW, DC-PC-TP-NUW	SAT-equivalent	Thm. 1 + Cor. 2
Plurality: DC-RPC-TE-NUW, DC-RPC-TE-UW, DC-PC-TE-NUW, DC-PC-TE-UW	SAT-equivalent	Thm. 2 + Cor. 2
Veto: DC-PV-TE-NUW, DC-PV-TE-UW	polynomial	Cor. 1 + Thm. 4
Veto: DC-RPC-TP-NUW, DC-PC-TP-NUW	SAT-equivalent	Thm. 1 + Cor. 2
Veto: DC-RPC-TE-NUW, DC-RPC-TE-UW, DC-PC-TE-NUW, DC-PC-TE-UW	SAT-equivalent	Thm. 2 + Cor. 2
Approval: DC-RPC-TP-NUW, DC-PC-TP-NUW	polynomial	Thms. 1 + 3
Approval: DC-RPC-TP-UW, DC-PC-TP-UW, DC-RPC-TE-NUW, DC-RPC-TE-UW, DC-PC-TE-NUW, DC-PC-TE-UW	polynomial	Cor. 1 + Thm. 3
Approval: DC-PV-TE-UW, DC-PV-TE-NUW	polynomial	Cor. 1, Thm. 4
Approval: CC-RPC-TP-UW, CC-PC-TP-UW	polynomial	Cor. 1, Thm. 3
Approval: CC-RPC-TP-NUW, CC-PC-TP-NUW	polynomial	Cor. 1 + Thm. 3
Approval: CC-RPC-TE-UW, CC-PC-TE-UW	polynomial	Cor. 1, Thm. 4
Approval: CC-RPC-TE-NUW, CC-PC-TE-NUW	polynomial	Cor. 1 + Thm. 4

Proof. Let $\mathcal{T}_1 = \mathcal{E}$-DC-PC-TP-NUW and $\mathcal{T}_2 = \mathcal{E}$-DC-RPC-TP-NUW.

$\mathcal{T}_1 \leq^{p,\mathcal{E}}_{\text{search}} \mathcal{T}_2$: We give a polynomial-time algorithm performing the reduction, given access to oracle $W_{\mathcal{E}}$. On input (I, S), where $I = (C, V, p)$ and $p \in C$, do the following. If the syntax is bad, halt. Otherwise, check that S is a solution to I under $\mathcal{T}_2$. This may involve up to three calls to the oracle. If S is not a good solution, then simply halt as the definition does not require anything in this case. Since S is a solution and our model is NUW, p must have participated and lost either in one of the two first-round elections or (in fact, exclusive-or) in the final-round election. In that election, let C' be the candidate set (note that $p \in C'$ and p is not a winner of (C', V)). Then output as the successful $\mathcal{T}_1$ solution $C_1 = C'$ and $C_2 = C - C'$. In $\mathcal{T}_1$ on input I, p will be eliminated in the (C', V) first-round election.

$\mathcal{T}_2 \leq^{p,\mathcal{E}}_{\text{search}} \mathcal{T}_1$: We give the algorithm. On input (I, S), where $I = (C, V, p)$ and $S = (C_1, C_2)$, check for bad syntax and by using the $W_{\mathcal{E}}$ oracle up to two times as per the nature of $\mathcal{T}_1$, check that S is a solution to I under $\mathcal{T}_1$. If the syntax is bad or S is not a solution under $\mathcal{T}_1$, then simply halt. Otherwise, since S is a solution under $\mathcal{T}_1$, p was a participant in and eliminated either in the (C_1, V) contest or the $(C_2 \cup \text{Winners}_{\mathcal{E}}(C_1, V), V)$ contest. In the former case, output (C_1, C_2), and in the latter case let $D = C_2 \cup \text{Winners}_{\mathcal{E}}(C_1, V)$ and output $(D, C - D)$. This is a solution for $\mathcal{T}_2$. □

Proposition 2. *If $\mathcal{E}$ is an election system, $\mathcal{T}_1$, $\mathcal{T}_2$, and $\mathcal{T}_3$ are pairwise $\mathcal{E}$-matched control types, $\mathcal{T}_1 \leq^{p,\mathcal{E}}_{\text{search}} \mathcal{T}_2$, and $\mathcal{T}_2 \leq^{p,\mathcal{E}}_{\text{search}} \mathcal{T}_3$, then $\mathcal{T}_1 \leq^{p,\mathcal{E}}_{\text{search}} \mathcal{T}_3$.*

Theorem 2. *For every election system $\mathcal{E}$, and each pair $(\mathcal{T}_1, \mathcal{T}_2)$ among the four control types*

1. $\mathcal{E}$-DC-RPC-TE-UW,
2. $\mathcal{E}$-DC-RPC-TE-NUW,
3. $\mathcal{E}$-DC-PC-TE-NUW, *and*
4. $\mathcal{E}$-DC-PC-TE-UW,

we have $\mathcal{T}_1 \equiv^{p,\mathcal{E}}_{\text{search}} \mathcal{T}_2$.

Proof. In light of Proposition 2, it suffices to make a closed cycle of $\leq^{p,\mathcal{E}}_{\text{search}}$ reductions involving these four types. In each part, as per the reduction definition, we will assume our input is (I, S), with $I = (C, V, p)$.

$\mathcal{E}$-DC-RPC-TE-UW $\leq^{p,\mathcal{E}}_{\text{search}}$ $\mathcal{E}$-DC-RPC-TE-NUW: A solution $S = (C_1, C_2)$ for I under $\mathcal{E}$-DC-RPC-TE-NUW is always a solution for I under $\mathcal{E}$-DC-RPC-TE-UW, since UW is stricter in the final round. If p was eliminated under $\mathcal{E}$-DC-RPC-TE-NUW, then p is also eliminated under $\mathcal{E}$-DC-RPC-TE-UW. So our reduction here can simply output the purported solution it is given. (Even if that is not a correct solution to the right-hand side, the reduction's action is legal, since if given a nonsolution as input all the reduction has to do, under the definition of this reduction type, is not run for too long.)

$\mathcal{E}$-DC-RPC-TE-NUW $\leq^{p,\mathcal{E}}_{\text{search}}$ $\mathcal{E}$-DC-PC-TE-NUW: Say we are for $I = (C, V, p)$ given a purported solution $S = (C_1, C_2)$ to $\mathcal{E}$-DC-PC-TE-NUW. If S is not a successful solution, immediately reject. Otherwise, either (a) $p \in C_1$ but $\{p\} \neq \text{UniqueWinner}_{\mathcal{E}}(C_1, V)$, or (b) $p \in \text{UniqueWinner}_{\mathcal{E}}(C_1, V) \cup C_2$ yet p is not a winner of $(\text{UniqueWinner}_{\mathcal{E}}(C_1, V) \cup C_2, V)$. Using our oracle, determine which of (a) or (b) holds (exactly one must hold if S was a solution). If (a) holds, output (C_1, C_2). This is then a successful solution on I to $\mathcal{E}$-DC-RPC-TE-NUW. If (b) holds, then set $D = \text{UniqueWinner}_{\mathcal{E}}(C_1, V) \cup C_2$ and output $(D, C - D)$ and this is a successful solution of I to $\mathcal{E}$-DC-RPC-TE-NUW, since we know that p is not a winner of (D, V), so it certainly is not the unique winner of (D, V), and so in our $\mathcal{E}$-DC-RPC-TE-NUW first round p participates and is eliminated.

$\mathcal{E}$-DC-PC-TE-NUW $\leq^{p,\mathcal{E}}_{\text{search}}$ $\mathcal{E}$-DC-PC-TE-UW: Let $S = (C_1, C_2)$ be a purported solution to $I = (C, V, p)$ under $\mathcal{E}$-DC-PC-TE-UW. If S is not a solution, immediately reject. Otherwise, we know that (a) $p \in C_1$ and p does not uniquely win in (C_1, V), exclusive-or (b) $p \in D$ yet $\{p\} \neq \text{UniqueWinner}(D, V)$, where $D = \text{UniqueWinner}_{\mathcal{E}}(C_1, V) \cup C_2$. If (a) holds, output (C_1, C_2). This is a successful solution of I for $\mathcal{E}$-DC-PC-TE-NUW as p is eliminated in the first round. If (b) holds output $(D, C - D)$. This is a successful solution of I for $\mathcal{E}$-DC-PC-TE-NUW as p will be eliminated in the first round.

$\mathcal{E}$-DC-PC-TE-UW $\leq^{p,\mathcal{E}}_{\text{search}}$ $\mathcal{E}$-DC-RPC-TE-UW: Let $S = (C_1, C_2)$ be a purported solution to $I = (C, V, p)$ under $\mathcal{E}$-DC-RPC-TE-UW. If S is not a solution, immediately reject. Otherwise, since C_1 and C_2 are symmetric in RPC, w.l.o.g. assume $p \in C_1$ (otherwise, rename C_1 and C_2 so that $p \in C_1$) and let $D = \text{UniqueWinner}_{\mathcal{E}}(C_1, V) \cup \text{UniqueWinner}_{\mathcal{E}}(C_2, V)$. So exactly one of (a) and (b) holds, where (a) and (b) are: (a) $p \in C_1$ and $\{p\} \neq \text{UniqueWinner}_{\mathcal{E}}(C_1, V)$, and (b) $p \in D$ and $\{p\} \neq \text{UniqueWinner}_{\mathcal{E}}(D, V)$. If (a) holds, output (C_1, C_2) and that is a successful solution for I of $\mathcal{E}$-DC-PC-TE-UW as p is eliminated in the first round. If (b) holds, output $(D, C - D)$ and that is a successful solution for I of $\mathcal{E}$-DC-PC-TE-UW as p is eliminated in the first round. □

Clearly, in light of Proposition 1, whenever $\mathcal{E} \in \{\text{Plurality, Veto, Approval}\}$ the $\equiv^{p,\mathcal{E}}_{\text{search}}$ claims from the Theorems 1 and 2 yield as corollaries the analogous "polynomially search-equivalent" (i.e., $\equiv^{p}_{\text{search}}$) claims.

We now explore the remaining collapses from Carleton et al. [11]. For each new collapsing decision-problem pair $(\mathcal{T}_1, \mathcal{T}_2)$ they find, we prove that $\mathcal{T}_1 \equiv^{p}_{\text{search}} \mathcal{T}_2$, even when the results are about election systems satisfying axiomatic properties.

Corollary 1. (Corollary to the proofs of Theorems 3.2, 3.6, 3.9, 3.12, 3.14, 3.16, and 3.17 and of Corollary 3.18 [11].)

1. Veto-DC-PV-TE-UW $\equiv^{p}_{\text{search}}$ Veto-DC-PV-TE-NUW.
2. *For each election system $\mathcal{E}$ that satisfies Unique-α,* $\mathcal{E}$-DC-PC-TP-UW $\equiv^{p}_{\text{search}}$ $\mathcal{E}$-DC-PC-TE-UW.
3. *For each strongly voiced election system $\mathcal{E}$ that satisfies Property α,* $\mathcal{E}$-CC-PC-TP-UW $\equiv^{p}_{\text{search}}$ $\mathcal{E}$-CC-RPC-TP-UW.
4. Approval-DC-RPC-TP-UW $\equiv^{p}_{\text{search}}$ Approval-DC-PC-TP-UW.
5. Approval-CC-PC-TP-NUW $\equiv^{p}_{\text{search}}$ Approval-CC-RPC-TP-NUW.
6. Approval-DC-PV-TE-UW $\equiv^{p}_{\text{search}}$ Approval-DC-PV-TE-NUW.
7. Approval-CC-PC-TE-NUW $\equiv^{p}_{\text{search}}$ Approval-CC-RPC-TE-NUW.
8. Approval-CC-PC-TE-UW $\equiv^{p}_{\text{search}}$ Approval-CC-RPC-TE-UW.

For each search-equivalence above that applies to approval, veto, or plurality, we now pinpoint the complexity of the search problems. We give new-to-the-literature polynomial-time algorithms for the following search problems.

Theorem 3. *For each $\mathcal{T} \in$ {Approval-DC-PC-TP-NUW, Approval-DC-PC-TE-UW, Approval-CC-PC-TP-UW, Approval-CC-PC-TP-NUW}, it holds that the search problem for $\mathcal{T}$ is polynomial-time computable.*

Proof. Our proof of Theorem 3 draws on the notion of immunity, which dates back to the seminal work of Bartholdi et al. [3]. We take the definitions' statements from Carleton et al. [11].

In the UW model, we say an election system is immune to a particular type of control if the given type of control can never change a candidate from not uniquely winning to uniquely winning (if the control type is constructive) or change a candidate from uniquely winning to not uniquely winning (if the control type is destructive). In the NUW model, we say an election system is immune to a particular type of control if the given type of control can never change a nonwinner to a winner (if the control type is constructive) or change a winner to a nonwinner (if the control type is destructive).

Consider the case of Approval-DC-PC-TE-UW. Approval is known to be immune to DC-PC-TE-UW [26]. So on each input (C, V, p), we have: $\{p\} = \text{UniqueWinner}_{\text{Approval}}(C, V) \implies p \notin \text{Approval-DC-PC-TE-UW}$ Our polynomial-time search-problem algorithm thus is the following: On input (C, V, p), in polynomial time determine if $\{p\} = \text{UniqueWinner}_{\text{Approval}}(C, V)$. If it is, output $\perp$ (indicating there is no partition that will prevent p from being the unique winner in the PC-TE two-stage election process under approval, regarding (C, V)). Otherwise, output $(\emptyset, C)$ as that partition makes the final-round election be (C, V), which p does not uniquely win.

It is not hard to see that approval is also immune to DC-PC-TP-NUW: Let p be a winner of an election (C, V). Let k denote the number of ballots that approve of p in V. It follows that no candidate is approved by more than k votes (else p would not be a winner). Since the TP handling rule is used, p can never be eliminated from a subelection as no candidate is approved by more votes than p. Thus p always proceeds to the final round, and is a winner. So the Approval-DC-PC-TP-NUW case follows by the above proof with each instance of the word "unique" removed and each TE and UW respectively changed to TP and NUW.

Since approval is immune to both CC-PC-TP-UW [26] and CC-PC-TP-NUW [11], the two constructive cases are analogous, of course by asking respectively as to the Approval-CC-PC-TP-UW and Approval-CC-PC-TP-NUW cases whether p is *not* a unique winner of (C, V) or not a winner of (C, V), and proceeding in the obvious way, again using $(\emptyset, C)$ as our output partition in those cases that do not output $\perp$. □

Using algorithms already in the literature, we obtain the following theorem.

Theorem 4. *The search problem for each of the following control problems is polynomial-time computable:*

1. Veto-DC-PV-TE-UW.
2. Approval-DC-PV-TE-UW.
3. Approval-CC-RPC-TE-UW.
4. Approval-CC-RPC-TE-NUW.

We will now establish that the remaining search problems are SAT-equivalent. First, we show how to essentially translate NP-completeness into SAT-equivalence.

Theorem 5. *Given an election system $\mathcal{E}$ satisfying $W_{\mathcal{E}} \in \mathrm{P}$, if $\mathcal{T}$ is one of our partition-control types involving $\mathcal{E}$ and (the decision problem) $\mathcal{T}$ is* NP*-complete, then the search problem for $\mathcal{T}$ is* SAT*-equivalent.*

Proof. Assume $\mathcal{T}$ is one of our partition control types, that $\mathcal{E}$ is the election system of $\mathcal{T}$, that $W_{\mathcal{E}} \in \mathrm{P}$, and that (the decision problem) $\mathcal{T}$ is NP-complete. We will now address in turn NP-hardness and NP-easiness.
NP-hardness:

Let f be any refinement of $\widehat{\Pi}_{\mathcal{T}}$. Since $\mathcal{T}$ is NP-complete, it suffices to show $\mathcal{T} \in \mathrm{P}^f$ to show that $\mathrm{NP} \subseteq \mathrm{P}^f$.

Our polynomial-time algorithm to decide $\mathcal{T}$ with function oracle f proceeds as follows: If x is not a triple of the form (C, V, p) where C is a set of candidates, V is a vote collection over C of the vote-type of $\mathcal{E}$, and $p \in C$, then reject. Otherwise, query the function oracle with x and verify, in polynomial time (using $W_{\mathcal{E}} \in \mathrm{P}$), whether the oracle response is a solution to the control problem. If it is, accept, and otherwise reject.

NP-easiness:

It is easy to see that there is a refinement of $\widehat{\Pi}_{\mathcal{T}}$, h, such that $h \in \mathrm{FP}^{\mathrm{NP}}$.

Let us focus on $\mathcal{T}$ being a voter partition type. The candidate cases are exactly analogous except we build the candidate rather than the voter partition.

On input (C, V, p), h makes sure that the input is of the form (C, V, p), that $p \in C$, and that the votes in V are of the type appropriate for $\mathcal{E}$; if not output $\perp$. Otherwise, use a single call to SAT to determine if $(C, V, p) \in \mathcal{T}$. If not, output $\perp$. Otherwise, by an easy binary search, with an NP oracle, we will construct a set V_1 such that $(V_1, V - V_1)$ is a solution to $\mathcal{T}$ for (C, V, p). In fact, if we naturally encode partitions into binary strings, we can binary search, with any NP-complete set such as SAT as our oracle, to find the lexicographically least encoding of a $V_1 \subseteq V$ such that $(V_1, V - V_1)$ is a solution to (C, V, p) with respect to $\mathcal{T}$, and then we will output $(V_1, V - V_1)$. (The "helper" NP set for the binary search is simply the set $\{(C, V, p, \mathcal{C}) \mid (\exists \mathcal{C}')[\mathcal{C}' \geq_{\mathrm{lex}} \mathcal{C}$ and $\mathcal{C}'$ encodes a V_1 such that $(V_1, V - V_1)$ is a solution to (C, V, p) with respect to $\mathcal{T}]\}$. Since this is an NP set, questions to it can be polynomial-time transformed into questions to SAT.) □

By Theorem 5 and Proposition 3, it suffices to identify one NP-complete problem in each equivalence class; to complete our results, we need the following theorem.

Theorem 6. *As a decision problem,* Plurality-DC-PC-TP-NUW *(and equivalently,* Plurality-DC-RPC-TP-NUW*) is* NP*-complete.*

Taking stock of Theorem 6 and existing results, we conclude the following.

Corollary 2. *The search versions of the following are* SAT*-equivalent:*

1. Plurality-DC-PC-TP-NUW.
2. Plurality-DC-RPC-TE-NUW.
3. Veto-DC-RPC-TP-NUW.
4. Veto-DC-RPC-TE-NUW.

The following proposition is appealed to tacitly within Table 1.

Proposition 3. *Let search problems A and B be polynomially search-equivalent. If A is* SAT*-equivalent, then B is* SAT*-equivalent. If A is polynomial-time computable, then B is polynomial-time computable.*

5 Conclusion

For all collapsing electoral control types found in Hemaspaandra et al. [25] and Carleton et al. [11]—those are *all* such collapses for the domains/groupings studied in those papers—we proved that even the *search-problem* complexities of the collapsing types are polynomially equivalent (given oracle access to the election system's winner problem). In doing this—and building on earlier notions of relating search problems—we defined reductions that, for collapsing electoral control problems, express how solutions to one can be efficiently converted to solutions to the other.

Also, for the key concrete systems plurality, veto, and approval, we established—as polynomial-time computable or as SAT-equivalent—the complexity of their (now collapsed) search problems. An interesting open direction would be, for that part of our work, to seek more general results, such as dichotomy theorems covering broad collections of election systems.

References

1. Alouf-Heffetz, S., Inamdar, T., Jain, P., Talmon, N., Hiren, Y.M.: Controlling delegations in liquid democracy. In: Proceedings of the 23rd International Conference on Autonomous Agents and Multiagent Systems, pp. 2624–2632. International Foundation for Autonomous Agents and Multiagent Systems, May 2024
2. Arora, S., Barak, B.: Computational Complexity: A Modern Approach. Cambridge University Press (2009)
3. Bartholdi, J.J., III., Tovey, C.A., Trick, M.A.: How hard is it to control an election? Math. Comput. Model. **16**(8–9), 27–40 (1992)
4. Baumeister, D., Erdélyi, G., Hemaspaandra, E., Hemaspaandra, L.A., Rothe, J.: Computational aspects of approval voting. In: Laslier, J.F., Sanver, M.R. (eds.) Handbook on Approval Voting, pp. 199–251. Springer (2010)
5. Book, R.V., Long, T.J., Selman, A.L.: Quantitative relativizations of complexity classes. SIAM J. Comput. **13**(3), 461–487 (1984)
6. Borodin, A., Demers, A.: Some comments on functional self-reducibility and the NP hierarchy. Technical Report, TR 76-284, Department of Computer Science, Cornell University, Ithaca, NY, July 1976
7. Carleton, B., Chavrimootoo, M., Hemaspaandra, L., Narváez, D., Taliancich, C., Welles, H.: Search versus search for collapsing electoral control types. Technical Report arXiv:2207.03049v6 [cs.GT], Computing Research Repository, arXiv.org/corr/, July 2022, Revised February 2024
8. Carleton, B., Chavrimootoo, M.C., Hemaspaandra, L.A., Narváez, D.E., Taliancich, C., Welles, H.B.: Separating and collapsing electoral control types. Technical Report arXiv:2207.00710v4 [cs.MA], Computing Research Repository, arXiv.org/corr/, July 2022, Revised February 2023
9. Carleton, B., Chavrimootoo, M.C., Hemaspaandra, L.A., Narváez, D.E., Taliancich, C., Welles, H.B.: Search versus search for collapsing electoral control types (extended abstract). In: Proceedings of the 22nd International Conference on

Autonomous Agents and Multiagent Systems, pp. 2682–2684. International Foundation for Autonomous Agents and Multiagent Systems, May–June 2023
10. Carleton, B., Chavrimootoo, M.C., Hemaspaandra, L.A., Narváez, D.E., Taliancich, C., Welles, H.B.: Separating and collapsing electoral control types. In: Proceedings of the 22nd International Conference on Autonomous Agents and Multiagent Systems, pp. 1743–1751. International Foundation for Autonomous Agents and Multiagent Systems, May–June 2023
11. Carleton, B., Chavrimootoo, M.C., Hemaspaandra, L.A., Narváez, D.E., Taliancich, C., Welles, H.B.: Separating and collapsing electoral control types. J Artif. Intell. Res. **81**, 71–116 (2024)
12. Chernoff, H.: Rational selection of decision functions. Econometrica **22**(4), 422–443 (1954)
13. Colley, R., Grandi, U., Hidalgo, C., Macedo, M., Navarrete, C.: Measuring and controlling divisiveness in rank aggregation. In: Proceedings of the 32nd International Joint Conference on Artificial Intelligence, pp. 2616–2623. AAAI Press, August 2023
14. Erdélyi, G., Piras, L., Rothe, J.: The complexity of voter partition in Bucklin and fallback voting: Solving three open problems. In: Proceedings of the 10th International Conference on Autonomous Agents and Multiagent Systems, pp. 837–844. International Foundation for Autonomous Agents and Multiagent Systems, May 2011
15. Erdélyi, G., Fellows, M.R., Rothe, J., Schend, L.: Control complexity in Bucklin and fallback voting: A theoretical analysis. J. Comput. Syst. Sci. **81**(4), 632–660 (2015)
16. Erdélyi, G., Nowak, M., Rothe, J.: Sincere-strategy preference-based approval voting fully resists constructive control and broadly resists destructive control. Math. Log. Q. **55**(4), 425–443 (2009)
17. Erdélyi, G., Reger, C., Yang, Y.: Towards completing the puzzle: Solving open problems for control in elections. In: Proceedings of the 18th International Conference on Autonomous Agents and Multiagent Systems, pp. 846–854. International Foundation for Autonomous Agents and Multiagent Systems (2019)
18. Erdélyi, G., Rothe, J.: Control complexity in fallback voting. In: Proceedings the 16th Australasian Theory Symposium, pp. 39–48. Australian Computer Society, January 2010
19. Faliszewski, P., Hemaspaandra, E., Hemaspaandra, L.A.: Weighted electoral control. J. Artif. Intell. Res. **52**, 507–542 (2015)
20. Faliszewski, P., Hemaspaandra, E., Hemaspaandra, L.A., Rothe, J.: Llull and Copeland voting computationally resist bribery and constructive control. J. Artif. Intell. Res. **35**, 275–341 (2009)
21. Faliszewski, P., Rothe, J.: Control and bribery in voting. In: Brandt, F., Conitzer, V., Endriss, U., Lang, J., Procaccia, A.D. (eds.) Handbook of Computational Social Choice, pp. 146–168. Cambridge University Press (2016)
22. Goldreich, O.: Computational Complexity: A Conceptual Perspective. Cambridge University Press (2008)
23. Gupta, S., Roy, S., Saurabh, S., Zehavi, M.: Resolute control: Forbidding candidates from winning an election is hard. Theoret. Comput. Sci. **915**, 74–89 (2022)
24. Hartmanis, J., Hemachandra, L.A.: Complexity classes without machines: On complete languages for UP. Theoret. Comput. Sci. **58**(1–3), 129–142 (1988)
25. Hemaspaandra, E., Hemaspaandra, L.A., Menton, C.: Search versus decision for election manipulation problems. ACM Trans. Comput. Theor. **12**(#1, Article 3), 1–42 (2020)

26. Hemaspaandra, E., Hemaspaandra, L.A., Rothe, J.: Anyone but him: The complexity of precluding an alternative. Artif. Intell. **171**(5–6), 255–285 (2007)
27. Hemaspaandra, L.A.: Juris Hartmanis and two golden rules. SIGACT News **53**(4), 35–40 (2022)
28. Hemaspaandra, L.A., Lavaee, R., Menton, C.: Schulze and ranked-pairs voting are fixed-parameter tractable to bribe, manipulate, and control. Ann. Math. Artif. Intell. **77**(3–4), 191–223 (2016)
29. Henry (455): Levin reduction, March 2013, https://planetmath.org/levinreduction, Accessed 13 May 2024
30. Kaczmarek, J., Rothe, J.: Controlling weighted voting games by deleting or adding players with or without changing the quota. Ann. Math. Artif. Intell. (2023). https://doi.org/10.1007/s10472-023-09874-x
31. Kaczmarek, J., Rothe, J.: $\mathrm{NP}^{\mathrm{PP}}$-completeness of control by adding players to change the Penrose–Banzhaf power index in weighted voting games (extended abstract). In: Proceedings of the 23rd International Conference on Autonomous Agents and Multiagent Systems, pp. 2318–2320. International Foundation for Autonomous Agents and Multiagent Systems, May 2024
32. Kaczmarek, J., Rothe, J., Talmon, N.: Complexity of control by adding or deleting edges in graph-restricted weighted voting games. In: Proceedings of the 26th European Conference on Artificial Intelligence, pp. 1190–1197. IOS Press, September 2023
33. Lin, A.: Solving Hard Problems in Election Systems. Ph.D. thesis, Rochester Institute of Technology, Rochester, NY (2012)
34. Maushagen, C., Niclaus, D., Nüsken, P., Rothe, J., Seeger, T.: Toward completing the picture of control in Schulze and Ranked Pairs elections. In: Proceedings of the 33rd International Joint Conference on Artificial Intelligence, pp. 2940–2948. AAAI Press, August 2024
35. Maushagen, C., Rothe, J.: Complexity of control by partitioning veto elections and of control by adding candidates to plurality elections. Ann. Math. Artif. Intell. **82**(4), 219–244 (2018)
36. Megiddo, N., Papadimitriou, C.H.: On total functions, existence theorems and computational complexity. Theoret. Comput. Sci. **81**(2), 317–324 (1991)
37. Menton, C.: Normalized range voting broadly resists control. Theor. Comput. Syst. **53**(4), 507–531 (2013)
38. Parkes, D.C., Xia, L.: A complexity-of-strategic-behavior comparison between Schulze's rule and ranked pairs. In: Proceedings of the 26th AAAI Conference on Artificial Intelligence, pp. 1429–1435. AAAI Press, August 2012
39. Piterman, N., Fisman, D.: Introduction to complexity theory: Lecture 2: NP-completeness and self reducibility (1998), Lecture Notes for a course given by Oded Goldreich; notes taken by N. Piterman and D. Fisman, https://www.wisdom.weizmann.ac.il/%7Eoded/PS/CC/l2.ps, Accessed 13 May 2024
40. Sen, A.K.: Choice functions and revealed preference. Rev. Econ. Stud. **38**(3), 307–317 (1971)
41. Valiant, L.G.: The relative complexity of checking and evaluating. Inf. Process. Lett. **5**(1), 20–23 (1976)
42. Yang, Y.: On the complexity of controlling amendment and successive winners (extended abstract). In: Proceedings of the 21st International Conference on Autonomous Agents and Multiagent Systems, pp. 1768–1770. International Foundation for Autonomous Agents and Multiagent Systems, May 2022

43. Yang, Y.: On the complexity of two-stage majoritarian rules. In: Proceedings of the 22nd International Conference on Autonomous Agents and Multiagent Systems, pp. 2022–2030. International Foundation for Autonomous Agents and Multiagent Systems, May–June 2023
44. Yang, Y.: How hard is it to impact the impact of your paper? In: Proceedings of the 33rd International Joint Conference on Artificial Intelligence, pp. 3023–3031. AAAI Press, August 2024

Exploiting Peer Trust and Semantic Similarities in the Assignment Assessment Process

Jairo Alejandro Lefebre-Lobaina[1(✉)], Athina Georgara[2], and Carles Sierra[1]

[1] Artificial Intelligence Research Institute (IIIA), CSIC, Barcelona, Spain
{jairo.lefebre,sierra}@iiia.csic.es
[2] University of Southampton, Southampton, UK
a.georgara@soton.ac.uk.

Abstract. In many scenarios, the assessment by a single expert of all the content produced by an individual may be impractical due to the overall vast amount of content to be assessed by the expert. Examples are, for instance, online education services with thousands of students or scientific papers submitted to a conference that have to be assessed by program chairs in a short time period. Leveraging peer evaluations is a crucial strategy to mitigate assessment burdens and reduce the time required to deliver the expected results. This paper revisits the foundational concept of Personalised Automated Assessment (PAAS), which seeks to approximate the assessments of a particular community member, known as the leader, by integrating the peer assessments among the other community members of their answers to an assignment. Our extension of PAAS enhances its machine learning capabilities by integrating in the algorithm the semantic similarity among peer assessments to improve its prediction power. Experimental validation using synthetic and real-world datasets shows the efficacy of our extension, reducing prediction errors and increasing accuracy, especially in scenarios where the several assignments are significantly similar with one another.

Keywords: Community assessment · trust and reputation · collective intelligence

1 Introduction

In many real-life situations, we find people who must deal with the problem of evaluating many objects or items. In practice, such a task often becomes unbearable for an individual due to the sheer volume of information that needs to be assessed. The realm of education and academia provides us with many examples. Consider, for instance, a teacher offering an online course that hundreds of students attend. In this scenario, the teacher might need to evaluate assignments[1]

[1] In this paper, we will use the term *assignment* to refer to the actual *answer* that a particular student provides for an assignment.

R. Collier et al. (Eds.): EUMAS 2024, LNAI 15685, pp. 237–254, 2025.
https://doi.org/10.1007/978-3-031-93930-3_14

twice or thrice as many as the number of students. Naturally, expecting a single person to assess all assignments within a short time frame is untenable. Another representative example is journal paper reviews, where the editor must evaluate many papers. In such contexts, exploiting peer evaluations can substantially mitigate the evaluation burden and assist evaluators in meeting deadlines.

This paper revisits the Personalised Automated Assessment (PAAS) concept, introduced in [7].

Gutierrez et al., in the context of education, proposed a model for alleviating the evaluation burden of one person (called the leader of a community) by using peer assessments (i.e., assessments made by other members of the community). In particular, PAAS incorporates information from assignments assessed by both the leader and the peers.

Essentially, PAAS models the leader's trust in the peers' assessments and learns how much the leader should trust each of their peers based on their commonly assessed assignments. Then, it predicts the leader's assessment of an assignment based on the assessments of that very same assignment made by others. In the context of a multiagent system, PAAS can also be used to model the trust that humans have in software agents that assess assignments.

This work extends PAAS to enhance the model's learning and prediction capabilities using the evaluations made and information about the assignments. As noted by the authors in [7], using semantic similarities of assignments is a promising extension. Thus, inspired b [7], we extend PAAS in this direction and put forward the *Extended Peer Automated Assessment* (EPAAS) model. Specifically, EPAAS incorporates semantic similarities among assessed assignments to enhance predictive accuracy. Unlike the previous approach, which is limited to commonly evaluated assignments, our proposal learns from similar assignments, adapting its openness to learn based on the strength of trust in a peer.

To confirm the effectiveness of our proposed model, we conducted an empirical evaluation considering both synthetic and real-world data.

The results show that our extended model, EPAAS, is more accurate than PAAS, i.e., it exhibits lower prediction error.

Additionally, our empirical evaluation showed that the improvement in prediction is more significant for fewer evaluated assignments. Therefore, EPAAS can give us a great advantage when dealing with a low number of assessments.

The paper is organised as follows. In Sect. 2, we briefly review related work. Section 3 describes the foundational ideas behind the PAAS algorithm, Sect. 4 presents the extension proposed to the original model, and Sect. 5 summarises the experimental results that validate the improvements of the extended model. Finally, Sect. 6 concludes the paper.

2 Related Work

There exists extensive research on the concept of trust and how to model it; especially within the context of teamwork. [6] describes trust as "the shared willingness of the team members" to be exposed to other members' actions (and accept the corresponding consequences) with the understanding the other members act on behalf of the team without being subject to be monitored or controlled, as defined in [10] and [5]. Also, the team member's expectation that others will carry out actions that relevant to the team, and is represented by the predictability of the members doing a task.

From a computational point of view, several researches focused on trust representation to model the predictability, and use it for making predictions. In the context of assessments generation based on peer evaluations, literature provides plenty of research following this approach.

Alfaro and Shavlovsky in [2] introduced CrowdGrader, a crowdsourcing algorithm that aggregates assessments from multiple students into an overall assessment for an assignment, utilising a reputation system to measure students' accuracy degrees. PeerRank [18] computes the grade of an agent as a weighted average of the grades it receives from other agents, similar to the PageRank method for web pages. Using probabilistic models, Piech et al. [13] propose a method to estimate student reliability and correct biases in online learning scenarios. Wu et al. [19] investigate consensus building among experts in a trust network and provide visual consensus models.

Following a statistical approach for score prediction, Bachrach et al. [4] employ a Bayesian model to grade tests, estimating the probability of a participant knowing the correct answer. It models the probability of participant answers based on the correct answer and their knowledge. Sterbini and Temperini [16] utilise peer evaluation among students to aid teachers in grading open answers, representing each student as a triplet of discrete variables: knowledge, judgment, and correctness. Ashley and Goldin [3] devise a hierarchical Bayesian model for mining peer assessment data, accounting for graders' biases and using the resulting posterior distribution to answer queries regarding rubric criteria suitability.

The PAAS model [7] differs by computing automated assessments from the perspective of a specific community member, aiming to estimate assessments accurately rather than achieve consensus. PAAS aggregates peer assessments, giving trusted peers more weight, and uses probability distributions to build trust metrics. The proposed model was compared with the collaborative filtering algorithms [9] for the same task, outperforming it by increasing the number of assessments and achieving a lower prediction error.

In [1], Lopez et al. propose a reconciliation between Bayesian inference and the PAAS trust model. The proposed PG-bivariate evaluation model considers the correlations between any pair of peers who have some commonly evaluated assessment, based on the PG_1-bias model [13].

This work propose an extension of the PAAS model proposed in [7], hence the folowing section below discusses the necessary background regarding the PAAS model.

3 The PAAS Model

The Personalised Automated Assessments (PAAS) model [7] is a trust-based model that aims to predict future evaluations on assignments as accurately as possible. Given an agent of interest, referred to as *leader* and denoted as ϵ, PAAS predicts how ϵ will evaluate some assignment α. The prediction is based on ϵ's peers evaluations over α. In some detail, PAAS exploits past evaluations over assignments, compares leader's evaluations against peers' evaluations and builds a trust model that estimates how much the leader should trust the assessments made by their peers. Hence, PAAS predicts the leader's evaluation of a new, unseen assignment based on the trust model.

Let $\mathcal{P}$ be the set of peers and $\mathcal{I}$ be the set of assignments. With $e_\mu^\alpha \in \mathcal{E}$ we denote the evaluation (also referred to as assessment, interchangeably) made by agent $\mu \in \{\epsilon\} \cup \mathcal{P}$ over the assignment $\alpha \in I$, where $\mathcal{E}$ is a discrete and ordered evaluation space. An automated assessment for the leader ϵ over assignment $\alpha \in \mathcal{I}$ is represented by a probability distribution $\mathbb{P} = \{x_1 \mapsto v_1, x_2 \mapsto v_2, \ldots, x_n \mapsto v_n\}$, where $x_i \in \mathcal{E}$, $n = |\mathcal{E}|$, and $v_i \in [0,1]$ such that $\sum_{i=1}^{n} v_i = 1$. Here, v_i denotes the probability of ϵ's evaluation over α being x_i.

Given a set of peer assessments over α, denoted as $\mathcal{O}^\alpha$, PAAS estimates ϵ's evaluation of α by aggregating the particular evaluations $p(X^\alpha = x|\mathcal{O}^\alpha)$ (see below in Sect. 3.2).

3.1 Trust

The trust between peers can be built if the peers have evaluated at least one common assignment. That is, given two agents $i, j \in \{\epsilon\} \cup \mathcal{P}$, PAAS can build a trust model between i and j if there is an assignment $\alpha \in \mathcal{I}$ such that i has evaluated α with e_i^α and j with e_j^α.

The evaluation difference between evaluations is estimated using the Euclidean distance:

$$diff(e_i^\alpha, e_j^\alpha) = e_i^\alpha - e_j^\alpha \tag{1}$$

If $diff(e_i^\alpha, e_j^\alpha) = 0$, it means that i and j give the *same* evaluation.[2] If $diff(e_i^\alpha, e_j^\alpha) < 0$ it means that i *underrates* α with respect to j and if $diff(e_i^\alpha, e_j^\alpha) > 0$ it means that i *overrates* α with respect to j. To express the trust between i and j, PAAS builds a probability distribution (denoted as $\mathbb{T}_{i,j}$) over all possible evaluation differences.

Formally, given the ordered evaluation space $\mathcal{E} = [0, m]$, trust is a probability distribution over possible evaluations' differences, that is, over the interval $[-m, m]$. The ignorance distribution ($\mathbb{F}$) is the default trust distribution between two peers over the space of differences is the one that results from the sampling of values over two flat distributions (i.e., a distribution where giving any mark is equally probable) within the evaluation interval $\mathcal{E}$. A trust model $\mathbb{T}$ is a set of trust distributions among all evaluators $\{\epsilon\} \cup \mathcal{P}$, i.e.,

$$\mathbb{T} = \{\mathbb{T}_{i,j} \text{ for every pair } i, j \in \{\epsilon\} \cup \mathcal{P}\}.$$

[2] This is the only scenario where $diff(e_i^\alpha, e_j^\alpha) = diff(e_j^\alpha, e_i^\alpha)$.

Direct Trust. When two agents $i, j \in \{\epsilon\} \cup \mathcal{P}$ evaluate the same assignment $\alpha \in \mathcal{I}$, then the *direct* trust of i towards j, $\mathbb{T}_{i,j}$, can be updated.[3]

Let x be the evaluation distance between agents i and j over an assessment α, $x = diff(e_i^\alpha, e_j^\alpha)$. Then the probability of x in $\mathbb{T}_{i,j}$ is updated as follows:

$$p(X_j = x) := p(X_j = x) + \gamma * (1 - p(X_j = x)) \tag{2}$$

In Eq. 2, $\gamma \in [0, 1]$ limits the potential growth of the probability $p(X_j = x)$. This value determines how fast the trust of i over j will grow. After updating $p(X_j = x)$, the trust distribution $\mathbb{T}_{i,j}$ is normalised using an entropy-based approach [15]. This entropy-based normalisation approach intends to preserve the existing trust distribution's shape by proportionally decreasing the value $p(X^\alpha = y)$ for $y \neq x$. However, this could introduce a bias towards a previously high probability of evaluation difference. Nonetheless, even though addressing this bias problem is worth further study, it is not within the scope of this paper.

Indirect Trust. On the other hand, when two agents $i, j \in \{\epsilon\} \cup \mathcal{P}$ share no common evaluated assignments, then the trust of i towards j, $\mathbb{T}_{i,j}$, needs to be *indirectly* updated. The model adopts the idea of transitive trust based on the Eigentrust algorithm introduced in [8]. PAAS defines the operators to compute the transitive trust distribution from two distributions in an additive manner, finding $\mathbb{T}_{i,k}$ given $\mathbb{T}_{i,j}$ and $\mathbb{T}_{j,k}$. From a probabilistic perspective, if x represents the difference in evaluations between i and j, and y represents the difference in assessment between j and k, the difference in evaluations between i and k can be described as an aggregation of the probabilities $P(x)$ and $P(y)$.

Given the trust distributions $\mathbb{P}$ and $\mathbb{Q}$ over the numeric interval $[-m, m]$ (i.e., the evaluation difference between two evaluations falls in $[-m, m]$), the combined distance distribution, $\mathbb{R} = \mathbb{P} \otimes \mathbb{Q}$, is defined as follows:

$$r(X = z) = \begin{cases} \sum\limits_{x+y=z} p(X = x) * q(X = y) & \text{if } z \in (-m, m) \\ \sum\limits_{x+y \leq -m} p(X = x) * q(X = y) & \text{if } z = -m \\ \sum\limits_{x+y \geq m} p(X = x) * q(X = y) & \text{if } z = m \end{cases} \tag{3}$$

and then apply Eq. 2 to later normalise to compute the new trust distribution.

Finally, when more than one peer shares common evaluations with the leader and the indirect peer, PAAS selects the peer whose trust distribution is closest to the ideal trust distribution: $p(X = 0) = 1$. The earth mover's distance (EMD) presented in [14] is used to compute the distance between a trust distribution and the ideal one.

[3] Similarly, we can update the direct trust $\mathbb{T}_{j,i}$.

3.2 Decision

The primary purpose of PAAS is to evaluate assignments that the leader has not previously assessed. In other words, given a peer μ's evaluation of an assignment e^{α}_{μ}, PAAS determines the probability that ϵ evaluates α as x, denoted as $p(X^{\alpha} = x|e^{\alpha}_{\mu})$. The method for calculating this conditional probability is:

$$p(X = x|e^{\alpha}_{\mu}) = \begin{cases} \sum\limits_{y \leq \mathit{diff}(x, e^{\alpha}_{\mu})} \mathbb{T}_{\epsilon,\mu}(y) & \text{if } x = 0 \\ \sum\limits_{y \geq \mathit{diff}(x, e^{\alpha}_{\mu})} \mathbb{T}_{\epsilon,\mu}(y) & \text{if } x = m \\ \mathbb{T}_{\epsilon,\mu}(\mathit{diff}(x, e^{\alpha}_{\mu})) & \text{otherwise} \end{cases} \tag{4}$$

When many peers give an evaluation about the same assignment $\mathcal{O}^{\alpha} = \{e^{\alpha}_{\mu_1}, e^{\alpha}_{\mu_2}, \ldots, e^{\alpha}_{\mu_n}\}$, if the trust level is high enough, then those evaluations are used to estimate ϵ's evaluation.

Let $\Upsilon(\mathbb{T}_{i,j})$ denote the earth movers' distance between a given distribution and the ignorance distribution, i.e., $\Upsilon(\mathbb{T}_{i,j}) = EMD(\mathbb{T}_{i,j}, \mathbb{F})$.

The evaluations $\mathcal{O}^{\alpha}$ will contribute in predicting the leader's evaluation over α, if and only if the distance of the trust distributions $\mathbb{T}_{\epsilon,\mu_i}$ exceeds a minimum acceptable value of trust $\delta \in (0, 0.1)$:

$$\sum_{i=1}^{n} \Upsilon(\mathbb{T}_{\epsilon,\mu_i}) > \delta \tag{5}$$

If the restriction is fulfilled, the value of $p(X^{\alpha} = x|\mathcal{O}^{\alpha})$ is defined by using:

$$p(X = x|\mathcal{O}^{\alpha}) = \left\{ \bigvee_{i=1}^{n} (\Upsilon(\mathbb{T}_{\epsilon,\mu i}) * p(X = x|e^{\alpha}_{\mu i})) \right. \tag{6}$$

If set $\mathcal{O}^{\alpha}$ does not fulfil the minimum trust value δ, then $p(X^{\alpha} = x)$ will be the ignorance distribution, $p(X = x|\mathcal{O}^{\alpha}) = 1/n$. The operator $\vee$ combines the probabilities, assuming the sources are independent: $a \vee b = a + b - a \cdot b$. This assumption is made considering the case when evaluators do not know each other.

From the model description, the trust between two evaluators is built only based on the commonly evaluated assessments, ignoring similarities between the assessment content. This behaviour also excludes information from "isolated" peers from the model, i.e., peers who share no common assignments to assess.

4 The Extended PAAS Model

As mentioned earlier, the PAAS model excludes assignments that both peers have not evaluated when updating the trust between two peers. If a peer $q \in \mathcal{P}$

has assessed a set of assignments $s \subset \mathcal{I}$, and the intersection between s and the set of assignments assessed by any other peer (including the leader) is empty, then all assessments made by q are disregarded. Moreover, the current model of PAAS entirely ignores any information that can be extracted from comparing evaluations over non-identical assignments. We believe that such information can significantly contribute to the trust model. To overcome the limitations above, we present the *Extended Personalised Automated Assessment (EPAAS)* model in this section.

Incorporating similarities between assignments into the PAAS model addresses the issues above. It opens up a path for estimating the evaluation of assignments that none of the peers have assessed previously. Under the assumption that similar assignments are similarly evaluated, we propose a method to estimate the most likely evaluations considering all evaluators $\{\epsilon \cup \mathcal{P}\}$.

We assume the existence of a similarity function $f(\alpha, \sigma) \in [0, 1]$ for comparing any pair of assignments $\alpha, \sigma \in \mathcal{I}$.

Defining a proper similarity function can also be a very complex task that requires the knowledge of experts in the field. However, AI provides several tools to ease the task under certain conditions. Let us assume that an assignment is given in a textual form or that a finite set of features can describe it. In such cases, we can exploit existing tools to define a similarity function rather easily. For example, we can use text analysis software to measure the similarity between texts (such as FastText [11]) or vector distance metrics such as the Jaccardian [12] or the cosine distance, words etc. to measure similarity between feature vectors. Thus, defining a proper similarity function may not be hard under certain conditions. Nonetheless, we highlight that regardless of the assignments' space, the only required properties for the similarity function are *(i)* positivity, *(ii)* symmetry and *(iii)* maximality when two assignments are identical.

Thus, similarity-based trust allows for building trust with indirect peers,[4] bypassing the commonly direct peers. This is a desired functionality, especially if an indirect peer shares no common evaluations with the leader or any other peer. Furthermore, it allows us to extract useful information from evaluations of assignments that are not identical but similar enough. We assume that every evaluator uses the same similarity function.[5]

Notably, even though with EPAAS, we can build trust models for indirect peers without considering the direct ones, we do not disregard the indirect trust functionality of PAAS. Instead, we combine the similarity-based and indirect trust (if we can compute it) and keep the strongest one by using Eq. 5 and 6.

4.1 Similar Assignments

To update the trust of one peer towards another when we consider semantic similarities, we modify Eq. 2. Specifically, we alter the potential growth of the

[4] We say *direct peers* to refer to those peers with whom a peer can compute a direct trust, and say *indirect peers* to those with whom a peer can build an indirect trust.

[5] We could extend the approach by using a custom similarity function for each peer.

trust distribution between i and j so that it is flexible to learn from similar assignments. The potential growth is denoted with κ and is given by:

$$\kappa(p, x) = \gamma * (1 - p(X_j = x)) * \eta \tag{7}$$

Then Eq. 2 becomes:

$$p(X_j = x) := p(X_j = x) + \kappa(p, x) \tag{8}$$

In Eq. 7, $\eta \in [0, 1]$ represents the contribution based on the similarity between evaluated assignments and regulates the contribution similarly to γ. The value of η varies depending on the similarity between the evaluated assignments (α by i and σ by j) at hand. However, it is natural to assume that increasing the contribution linearly based on the similarity of elements does not accurately reflect how trust evolves. Intuitively, the weaker the trust, the less likely a human will adopt others' opinions. Following this idea, it is proposed to learn based on the similarity between the assignments and how strong the current trust is.

$$\eta = f(\alpha, \sigma)^{-1/\log_b(z(p))} \tag{9}$$

Equation 9 follows the idea that if two assignments are similar, they should have similar evaluations. Based on the intuition that a peer is more open to learning from similar assignments as the trust is stronger, we allow the similarity value to have a greater influence on the potential growth ($(1-p(X = x))$. The term $z(p)$, referred to as flexibility degree, determines how flexible the trust distribution p is to change based on similar assignments and is defined as:

$$z(p) = \frac{1}{b} + \frac{H(p)}{2 * \log_2(m * 2 + 1)} \tag{10}$$

In Eq. 10, the value of b is the base of the logarithm of Eq. 9 and $b > 2$ to avoid $z = 1$, then $z \in [1/b, 1)$[6]. In other words, b regulates the minimum values of similarity that will contribute to η. The strength of the trust between peers is the entropy $H(p)$ of the distribution p. When $H(p) = 0$, it means that the peers have complete trust, i.e., when the $p(X = x) = 1$ for some specific $x \in [-m, m]$), and therefore, the similarity contributes linearly (Fig. 1).

Equation 1 presents the contribution (y axis) of a given similarity value (x axis) according to possible values of z (using the natural logarithm: $b = e$). If a peer has a weak trust concerning others, it will be less likely to learn from assignments that are not very similar since the value of $z(p)$ will be lower. The opposite occurs when a strong trust is already built.

It is essential to notice that η's contribution to the potential growth highly depends on the similarity function. A well-defined similarity function provides more accurate contributions, while a lousy similarity function provides poor contributions. Also, the proposed flexibility degree $z(p)$ is sensitive to the order of presented evaluations. Building trust by starting with the most similar assessments is recommended to get the greatest possible benefit from semantic similarities.

[6] We recommend using the natural logarithm in Eq. 9 and therefore $b \equiv e$.

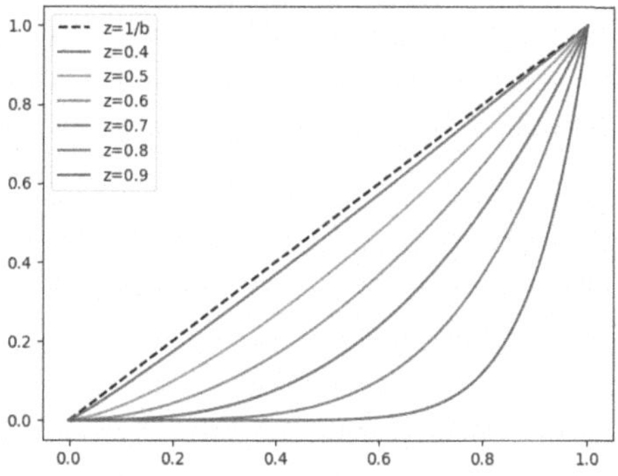

Fig. 1. Trust flexibility degree according to z value

4.2 Final Trust for Indirect Peers

Regarding the trust of the leader towards a direct peer (i.e., peers with commonly evaluated objects), it is clear that EPAAS updates the trust distribution according to Eq. 8, i.e., considering the semantic similarities among the objects. In the case of some indirect peer, unlike PAAS, which uses the notion of *indirect trust*, EPAAS can build the trust distribution using again Eq. 8. However, in our approach, we do not disregard the indirect trust entirely. Instead, we update the trust distribution towards an indirect peer by selecting the one (indirect vs similarity-based trust) farthest from the ignorance distribution.

Let $i, j \in \{\epsilon\} \cup \mathcal{P}$ be two indirect peers that share no common evaluations. Moreover, let us denote with $\mathbb{T}^{in}_{i,j}$ the indirect trust of i towards j, computed as described in Sect. 3.1. Similarly, we denote with $\mathbb{T}^{si}_{i,j}$ the corresponding similarity-based trust, computed via Eq. 8. Then, for computing the trust $\mathbb{T}_{i,j}$, EPAAS selects the trust distribution between $\mathbb{T}^{si}_{i,j}$ and $\mathbb{T}^{si}_{i,j}$ that differs the most from the ignorance distribution $\mathbb{F}$. Formally:

$$\mathbb{T}_{i,j} = \max(\Upsilon(\mathbb{T}^{si}_{i,j}), \Upsilon(\mathbb{T}^{in}_{i,j})) \tag{11}$$

where $\Upsilon(\cdot) = EMD(\cdot, \mathbb{F})$ is the earth movers' distance between the trust and the ignorance distribution $\mathbb{F}$. This way, we exploit both the indirect and the similarity-based trust, while we keep the one that it is less ignorant. Later Eq. 6 is used for defining the final trust when many peers give their point of view ($\mathbb{T}_{i,j}$).

5 Empirical Evaluations

This section discusses our empirical evaluation of the proposed model, EPAAS. We conducted several experiments using synthetic and real-world datasets to show the advantages of EPAAS over PAAS. According to Gutierrez et al., [7], the PAAS model's primary goal is to provide the best prediction from the leader's point of view with the minimum amount of assessments from the leader and the peers. Our empirical evaluation yielded EPAAS with lower prediction errors, and therefore, the results confirm that exploiting semantic similarities can improve the trust model.

Next, in Sect. 5.1, we present the methodology followed during our empirical evaluation, while in Sect. 5.2, we discuss our results.

5.1 Methodology

Both models (PAAS and EPAAS) were fed with the same input data for comparison purposes. The evaluations of the peers were presented in the initial stage to build a trust distribution for each (ordered) pair $i, j \in \mathcal{P}$.

Later, we build the leader's trust ϵ towards their peers using the two models. Having the set of assignments evaluated by the leader, only the first En initial evaluations are presented to the model. The assessment value $En+1$ is predicted and compared to the actual value. Afterwards, the model at hand updates the trust distribution with the actual assessment of $En + 1$ before predicting the assessment $En + 2$. This process continues iteratively until a limit for the leader evaluations is reached. The limit for the synthetic dataset is 23 assessments, and the real-world dataset is 12 assessments.

Since the EPAAS model is affected by the order of the assignments presented to assess, we tested both models by giving different assignment orders. We shuffled the leader's evaluations, generating 1000 different assignment orders. Each order was presented to both models to measure the error in each evaluation step $En + i$. The final result is the mean of the error for each evaluation step $En + i$ in the different provided orders.

5.2 Results

To compute the prediction error for each model result, we use the earth movers' distance between the model's at-hand output and the distribution of absolute certainty on the real value.

Synthetic Dataset
For this series of experiments, we generated synthetic datasets. The synthetic datasets were generated following the idea that a set of reviewers needs to asses several journal papers. In this scenario, the journal editor corresponds to the leader ϵ; the reviewers correspond to the peers $\mathcal{P}$, while the papers correspond to the assignments $\mathcal{I}$.

In more detail, we synthetically generated data as follows. We assume that from each paper, we can extract a feature vector regarding their English quality, the relevance between keywords and cited literature, the recency of the related work presented, and detected plagiarism. Each feature receives a value in the range $[0, 1]$, with 0 indicating that the paper is very poor in the corresponding feature and 1 indicating that the paper is excellent.

Then, the similarity between two papers $a, b \in \mathcal{I}$ is defined as the cosine distance between their feature vectors v_a and v_b:

$$sim(a,b) = \frac{v_a \cdot v_b}{||v_a|| \cdot ||v_b||}$$

We generated 900 papers, and for each paper, we generated a random feature vector. To generate the evaluators (i.e., the leader and the reviewers), we were inspired by how people rate movies in IMDB. Specifically, we studied the behaviour of the users described in [17] and designed an evaluators' profile generator, which we describe below. The leader (journal editor) evaluates 60 papers, while each reviewer evaluates 150 papers, with 30 of them being common with the leader. Let us denote with $X_i \subseteq \mathcal{I}$ the set of papers evaluated by the evaluator $i \in \{\epsilon\} \cup \mathcal{P}$. For each evaluated paper $a \in X_i$, we generate the grade that i gives to a, so that similar papers are graded similarly. Particularly, for each paper $a \in X_i$:

Step 1: we find the most similar paper a^* that has been already marked by i: $a^* = \arg\max_{a' \in X_i^{\text{Graded}}} sim(a, a')$, where $X_i^{\text{Graded}} \subseteq X_i$ contains the papers already graded by i; we skip Step 1 if a is the first paper to grade;
Step 2: we randomly draw a number c from the discrete space $[\chi, \psi]$ where

- $\chi = \max\Big\{Grade_\varepsilon(a^*) - \Big((1 - sim(a, a^*)\Big) \cdot 10, 1\Big\}$,
- $\psi = \min\Big\{Grade_\varepsilon(a^*) + \Big((1 - sim(a, a^*)\Big) \cdot 10, 10\Big\}$, and
- $Grade_i(a^*)$ is the grade of paper a^* given already by evaluator i;

for the first paper $[\chi, \psi] = [1, 10]$.

By generating the leader and the reviewers as described above: (1) we ensure that each evaluator is consistent with themselves regarding the criteria of grading papers, and (2) some reviewers grade papers similarly to the leader, while others grade very differently.

In summary, the synthetic dataset involves:

- 60 evaluations by the leader;
- 14 reviewers;
- 150 evaluations made by each reviewer, 30 of which where common to the leader (i.e., $|X_\varepsilon \cap X_i| = 30$);
- each paper evaluated by some evaluator was graded with a mark from the discrete space $[1, 10]$.

In our simulation, we let the leader ε initially evaluate 2 papers (i.e., $En = 2$). Then, we follow the methodology described in Sect. 5.1 for 20 more papers. A total number of 22 papers was chosen to observe the behaviour of the models (PAAS and EPAAS) with a small number of assessments. For the leader, we selected 22 papers that have been commonly assessed by the reviewers. In that way, we can guarantee that for every assignment assessed by the leader, at least one peer assessed that paper. In both models, we set the learning rate $\gamma = 0.2$ in order to receive a small impact from the newly presented examples over the current trust distribution.

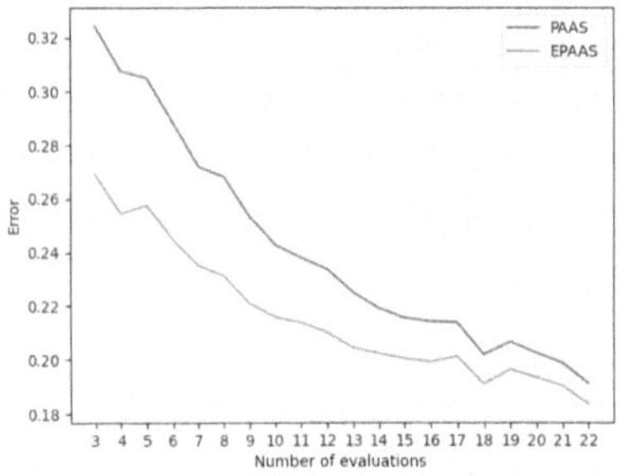

(a) Test results with four peers

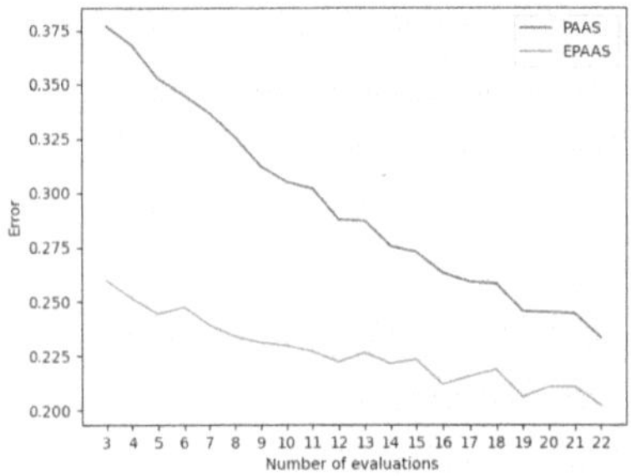

(b) Test results with nine peers

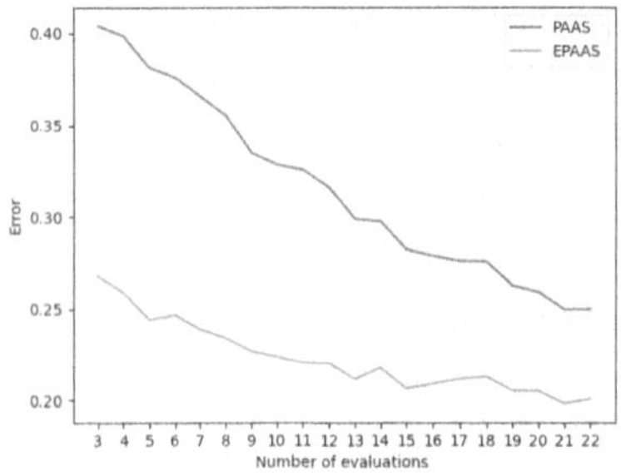

(c) Test results with fourteen peers

Fig. 2. Synthetic Dataset

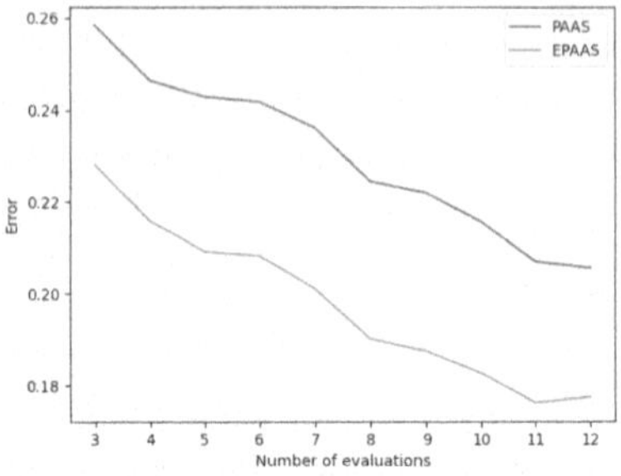

(a) Test results with four peers

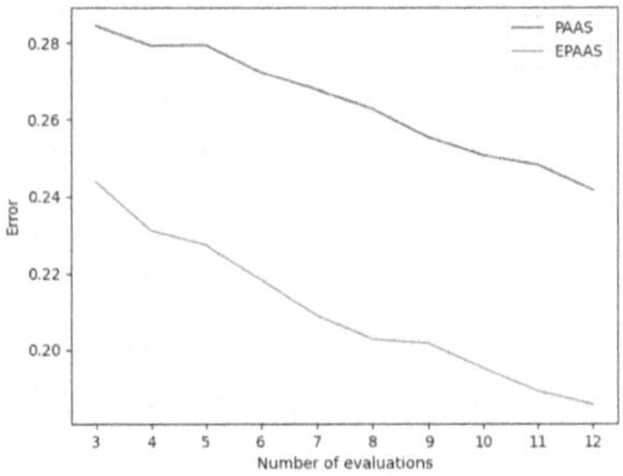

(b) Test results with nine peers

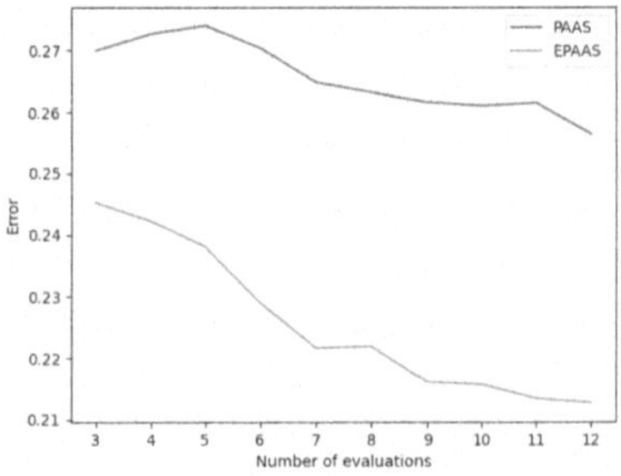

(c) Test results with fourteen peers

Fig. 3. Real world dataset

Figures 2a–2c illustrate the results with 4, 9 and 14 reviewers, respectively. In all cases, the EPAAS has a lower prediction error than PAAS. The error difference increases as the number of evaluated assessments increases because the benefit of the similarities between assessments is bigger. Such a result is expected since more evaluations exist for EPAAS to exploit semantic similarities.

During our simulation, the trust between the reviewers and the editor changes according to the new evaluations provided by the editor. Generally speaking, the trust distribution can be categorised into two main groups: highly trusted peers and poorly trusted peers. The highly trusted peers have a clear evolution towards a certain evaluation difference in the trust space. Conversely, peers with a variable evaluation difference (related to some bias or other criteria not explicitly defined) affect the evolution of trust and are poorly trusted by the leader. To give a clearer representation of changes in the trust, in Fig. 4, we show the evolution of two trust distributions for the steps 5, 10 and 20, including the initial state (ignorance). Note that the x-axis shows the evaluations' differences space (that range in interval $[-m, m]$, see Sect. 3), while the y-axis shows the leader's trust level. Specifically, we pick a reviewer that the editor should trust, based on the grades the reviewer gave on the commonly evaluated with the editor papers. That is, given the grades of the leader for the papers the editor evaluated, we picked the reviewer who had the most similar grading in the commonly evaluated ones. Similarly, we pick a reviewer the leader should not trust since their grading on the commonly evaluated papers is the least similar.

Figure 4a illustrates the trust evolution of the reviewer that the leader should trust (i.e., the one with the most similar grades).

On the other hand, Fig. 4b illustrates the trust evolution of the reviewer that the editor is not expected to trust. As we can see, the *trusted* reviewer keeps a consistent trust shape and becomes stronger as more evaluations are presented to the model. In contrast, for the *un-trusted* reviewer, starting from the ignorance trust distribution, we observe that as more evaluations are presented to the model, the model becomes more uncertain (exhibits more spikes of similar probabilities). It is worth noticing that for the trusted reviewer, the final trust distribution exhibits one spike that exceeds 0.5, i.e., the leader trusts the reviewer's grades with high probability. On the other hand, for the un-trusted reviewer, where we have more spikes, they are of lower probabilities (below 0.25).

Finally, compared to the PAAS model, Fig. 5 depicts the differences between the final trust distribution computed by PAAS (blue line) and EPAAS (orange line) while preserving the ignorance distribution for reference (green line). In this case, we selected from the trusted (a reviewer whose grading differs from the editors's grading below some threshold) and un-trustee (a reviewer whose grading differs from the leader's grading above some threshold) reviewers with the highest trust difference between PAAS and EPAAS models. In Fig. 5a, we see that for a trusted reviewer, the models computed very similar trust distribution, while Fig. 5b for an un-trusted reviewer EPAAS computes a smoother trust distribution than PAAS. Notably, our main observation is that the trust distributions computed by EPAAS have lower entropy than the correspond-

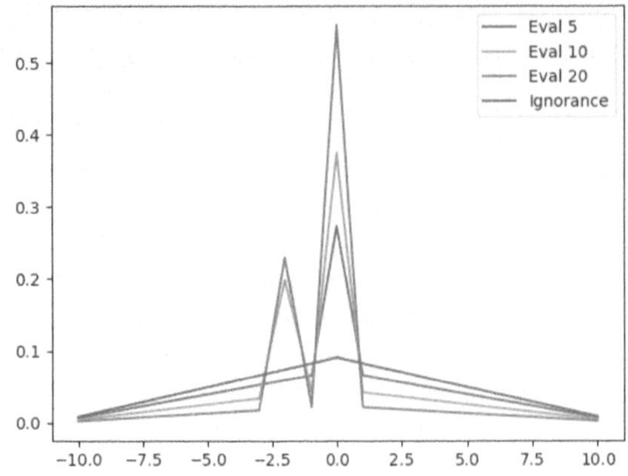

(a) High trust evolution

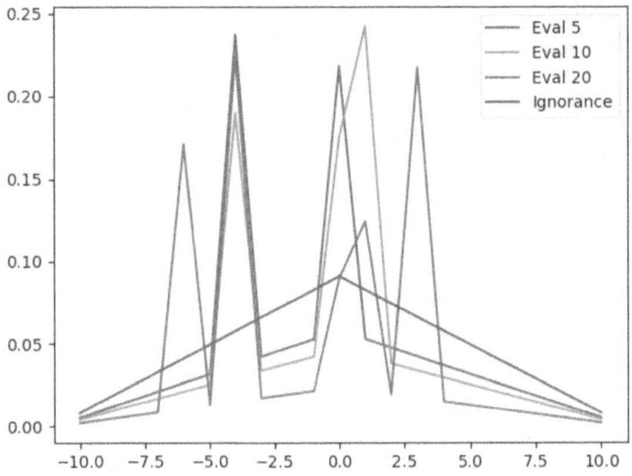

(b) Low trust evolution

Fig. 4. Trust evolution

ing ones computed by PAAS. That is, PAAS distributions exhibit more spikes than EPAAS distributions. This behaviour is clearer in the trust distribution for an un-trusted reviewer (see Fig. 5b). Thus, EPAAS, using semantic similarities among the different papers, computes trust distributions with higher predictability than PAAS.

Real-World Dataset. We used the same dataset as in [7] for this experiment. In this dataset, the authors in [7] gathered information from 30 underage students in two English language classes. The data was gathered from two English language classrooms comprising 30 fourteen-year-old students. The classroom

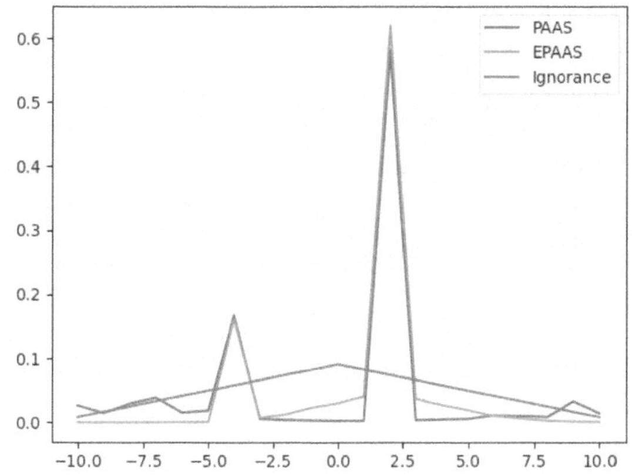

(a) High trust difference

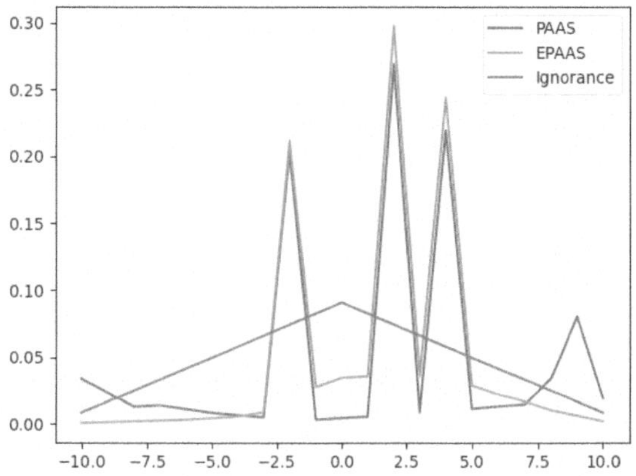

(b) Low trust difference

Fig. 5. Trust difference between PAAS and EPAAS

participants were assigned two tasks: (1) an English composition task and (2) a song vocabulary task. For evaluating an assignment, the evaluator at hand needs to assess the assignment according to various criteria specific to each task. That is, for an assignment in the composition task, the evaluators considered the criteria *focus*, *coherence*, and *grammar*; while for an assignment in the song vocabulary task, the evaluators considered the criteria *in-time submission*, *compliance with requirements*, and *lyrical accuracy*. For a given assignment, each criterion could be graded with a number ranging from 1 (very poor) to 4 (excellent); while we assume that the assignment as a whole is marked with the summation of the marks received for each criterion. For example, suppose an assignment in the composition task received marks 3, 4, and 3 for the criteria focus, coherence, and grammar, respectively. In that case, the assignment is marked with the grade 10 (out of 12). This results in a discrete space for the trust $[-12, 12]$. Each assignment was evaluated by *(i)* the teacher and *(ii)* one or more students (different to the student submitting the assignment). In summary, the dataset consists of the following:

- 71 assignments (35 for the English composition task and 36 for the song vocabulary task);
- 71 evaluations made by the teacher (one evaluation per assignment);
- 168 evaluation made by students (each student evaluated on average 2.4 assignments)
- each criterion was graded (per evaluator) with a mark from 1 (very poor) to 4 (excellent); and
- each assignment was graded (per evaluator) with the sum of the marks given to its criteria.

Under the assumption that similar items are evaluated similarly, we build a similarity function for the assignments. In more detail, we consider the teacher's evaluations (e_t) as the "ground truth", and, therefore, for two assignments a, b we define the similarity between a and b as:

- if $a = b$ then $sim(a, b) = 1$;
- if $a \neq b$, $Task(a) = Task(b)$ and
  - $e_t^a = e_t^b$ then we draw a random number s from $\mathcal{U}(0.85, 0.95)$ and we set $sim(a, b) = s$;
  - $0 < |e_t^a - e_t^b| \leq 3$ then we draw a random number s from $\mathcal{U}(0.65, 0.84)$ and we set $sim(a, b) = s$;
  - $3 < |e_t^a - e_t^b| \leq 7$ then we draw a random number s from $\mathcal{U}(0.3, 0.5)$ and we set $sim(a, b) = s$;
- otherwise $sim(a, b) = 0$.

After initially defining the similarity degree between all pairs of assignments a, b, the similarity value is not changed during the experiment execution. For this set of experiments, $\gamma = 0.2$ for both models, the teacher (leader) starts with 3 initial evaluated objects ($En = 3$) and 8 additional evaluations were tested. Also, we compare the algorithms with 4, 9 and 14 peers. The results for each case are presented in Figs. 3a–3c.

Similarly to the synthetic experiments, the results show that EPAAS has a lower prediction error than PAAS for fewer evaluations, and the error difference increases based on the number of evaluated assessments. Moreover, we observe that as the number of peers increases, the predictions are more accurate (i.e., the error difference is bigger). Such a result is expected since more evaluations exist for EPAAS to exploit semantic similarities. Also, as the number of assessments increases, the results of both algorithms tend to converge because the benefit from similar assessments decreases. Following the principles behind the proposal and the experiment results, we can say that PAAS is the upper bound for EPAAS.

6 Concluding Remarks

This work addresses the challenge of comprehensive assessment in expert evaluation scenarios, emphasising the utility of peer evaluations to ease the assessment burdens of a leader. It extends the Personalised Automated Assessment (PAAS) model, enhancing its prediction capabilities by taking advantage of semantic similarities among assignments and peer evaluations. Experimental validation demonstrates that the Extended PAAS (EPAAS) model outperforms PAAS, particularly in scenarios with similar evaluated assignments. The results highlight the efficacy of EPAAS in reducing prediction errors. When the leader has fewer evaluations, the advantage of EPAAS over PAAS is more significant. Also, when the number of peers' evaluations increases, so does the error gap. However, as the number of evaluated assessments increases, both model errors tend to converge. Therefore, we can consider PAAS to be an upper bound of EPASS.

The proposed approach represents an advancement in automated assessment systems, offering potential applications in various evaluation domains. In future work, we intend to explore the efficiency of EPAAS in accurately predicting yet-to-be-evaluated assignments. Moreover, we would like to improve the trust updating rules and seek better approaches other than the entropy-based normalisation that is currently used. Finally, our model can be applied in other domains beyond education. As such, we aim to use EPAAS as a recommender system in domains such as movie recommendations, media peer-based credibility, etc., and compare it against state-of-the-art recommendation algorithms.

Acknowledgements. This work has received funding from the European Union's Horizon 2020 research and innovation programme under the Marie Skłodowska-Curie grant agreement No 860621. This work has received funding from the European Union's Horizon 2020 research and innovation programme under the Marie Skłodowska-Curie grant agreement No 860621. The authors also acknowledge support by the projects iTrust (PCI2022-135010-2) and CHIST-ERA 2022/04/Y/ST6/00001 grant. Athina Georgara was supported by the Engineering and Physical Sciences Research Council (grant number EP/Y009800/1), through funding from Responsible Ai UK.

References

1. López de Aberasturi Gómez, A., Sabater-Mir, J., Sierra, C.: Probabilistic models for competence assessment in education. Appl. Sci. **12**(5), 2368 (2022)
2. de Alfaro, L., Shavlovsky, M.: Crowdgrader: crowdsourcing the evaluation of homework assignments. arXiv preprint arXiv:1308.5273 (2013)
3. Ashley, K., Goldin, I.: Toward ai-enhanced computer-supported peer review in legal education. In: Legal Knowledge and Information Systems, pp. 3–12. IOS Press (2011)
4. Bachrach, Y., Graepel, T., Minka, T., Guiver, J.: How to grade a test without knowing the answers—a bayesian graphical model for adaptive crowdsourcing and aptitude testing. arXiv preprint arXiv:1206.6386 (2012)

5. Breuer, C., Hüffmeier, J., Hertel, G.: Does trust matter more in virtual teams? A meta-analysis of trust and team effectiveness considering virtuality and documentation as moderators. J. Appl. Psychol. **101**(8), 1151 (2016)
6. Breuer, C., Hüffmeier, J., Hibben, F., Hertel, G.: Trust in teams: a taxonomy of perceived trustworthiness factors and risk-taking behaviors in face-to-face and virtual teams. Human Relat. **73**(1), 3–34 (2020)
7. Gutierrez, P., Osman, N., Sierra, C.: Personalised automated assessments (2015)
8. Kamvar, S.D., Schlosser, M.T., Garcia-Molina, H.: The eigentrust algorithm for reputation management in p2p networks. In: Proceedings of the 12th International Conference on World Wide Web, pp. 640–651 (2003)
9. Koren, Y., Rendle, S., Bell, R.: Advances in collaborative filtering. In: Recommender Systems Handbook, pp. 91–142 (2021)
10. Mayer, R.: An integrative model of organizational trust. Acad. Manag. Rev. (1995)
11. Mikolov, T., Chen, K., Corrado, G., Dean, J.: Efficient estimation of word representations in vector space (2013)
12. Niwattanakul, S., Singthongchai, J., Naenudorn, E., Wanapu, S.: Using of jaccard coefficient for keywords similarity. In: Proceedings of the International Multiconference of Engineers and Computer Scientists, vol. 1, pp. 380–384 (2013)
13. Piech, C., Huang, J., Chen, Z., Do, C., Ng, A., Koller, D.: Tuned models of peer assessment in moocs. arXiv preprint arXiv:1307.2579 (2013)
14. Rubner, Y., Tomasi, C., Guibas, L.J.: A metric for distributions with applications to image databases. In: Sixth International Conference on Computer Vision (IEEE Cat. No. 98CH36271), pp. 59–66. IEEE (1998)
15. Sierra, C., Debenham, J.: An information-based model for trust. In: Proceedings of the Fourth International Joint Conference on Autonomous Agents and Multiagent Systems, pp. 497–504 (2005)
16. Sterbini, A., Temperini, M.: Correcting open-answer questionnaires through a bayesian-network model of peer-based assessment. In: 2012 International Conference on Information Technology Based Higher Education and Training (ITHET), pp. 1–6. IEEE (2012)
17. thatDot: IMDB Movie Data. https://quine.io/recipes/movieData/#sample-data. Accessed Jan 2024
18. Walsh, T.: The peerrank method for peer assessment. arXiv preprint arXiv:1405.7192 (2014)
19. Wu, J., Chiclana, F., Herrera-Viedma, E.: Trust based consensus model for social network in an incomplete linguistic information context. Appl. Soft Comput. **35**, 827–839 (2015)

A Study of the Dynamics of the Average in a Residual Gossip Protocol

Federico Bergenti[1(✉)], Stefania Monica[2], Gloria Tamboroni[2], and Franco Zambonelli[2]

[1] Dipartimento di Scienze Matematiche, Fisiche e Informatiche, Università degli Studi di Parma, 43124 Parma, Italy
federico.bergenti@unipr.it

[2] Dipartimento di Scienze e Metodi dell'Ingegneria, Università degli Studi di Modena e Reggio Emilia, 42122 Reggio Emilia, Italy
{stefania.monica,gloria.tamboroni,franco.zambonelli}@unimore.it

Abstract. Gossip protocols are appreciated tools to achieve consensus in large and decentralized multi-agent systems. Residual gossip protocols have been proposed to use the gossip approach to solve the distributed averaging problem in multi-agent systems with asymmetric links. A residual gossip protocol is studied in this paper using an atypical method and obtaining two results. First, it is confirmed that the studied protocol can be used to solve the distributed averaging problem. Second, a closed-form expression of the time evolution of the studied average is obtained, thus addressing a gap in the literature on residual gossip protocols. These analytic results are confirmed by a few illustrative simulations discussed in the last part of this paper primarily for illustrative purposes.

Keywords: Residual gossip protocols · Kinetic theory of multi-agent systems · Collective intelligence

1 Introduction and Motivation

One of the major objectives that stimulated the proposal of gossip protocols [12] was to obtain an effective means to solve the distributed averaging problem [11], which is the problem of computing the initial average of the values given at the nodes of a network without a centralized control. The decentralized control that this problem requires is meant to ensure that the protocols designed to solve it would provide for effective scalability and fault tolerance.

The distributed averaging problem has been studied intensively in the literature on multi-agent systems [27] because it finds relevant applications, for example, in sensor networks and social networks. The motivating scenario in sensor networks regards sensors that jointly measure a physical phenomenon. For example, a toy scenario to motivate the distributed averaging problem considers a network of sensors deployed to measure the temperature in a room [12]. The sensors need to average their readings to alleviate the contribution of noise

R. Collier et al. (Eds.): EUMAS 2024, LNAI 15685, pp. 255–273, 2025.
https://doi.org/10.1007/978-3-031-93930-3_15

and the effects of minor fluctuations in the room temperature. The averaging process is distributed among the sensors without a centralized control to increase scalability and fault tolerance. The application in social networks is similar and it regards compromise [24], which is one of the primary phenomena behind opinion formation. Compromise is considered the major force to achieve decentralized consensus in multi-agent systems, and it is naturally distributed among agents.

In the assortment of the gossip protocols proposed to solve the distributed averaging problem, the protocol introduced in [12], which is called symmetric gossip protocol in the nomenclature proposed in [17], is by far the most prominent and studied. In the symmetric gossip protocol, each agent has a state represented by a real number, and agents constantly exchange messages in pairwise interactions. Given an agent identified by $s \in \mathbb{N}_+$ (the sender) and another agent identified by $r \in \mathbb{N}_+$ (the receiver), the symmetric gossip protocol assumes that when agent s sends a message to agent r their respective states $x_s \in \mathbb{R}$ and $x_r \in \mathbb{R}$ are updated using the following rule:

$$\begin{cases} x'_s = x_s - \gamma(x_s - x_r) \\ x'_r = x_r - \gamma(x_r - x_s), \end{cases} \tag{1}$$

where $\gamma \in (0, 1)$ is a parameter shared by all agents.

The symmetric gossip protocol can be used to solve the distributed averaging problem under the major assumption that the interactions among agents are mutually independent. Actually, (1) assumes that the states of the agents involved in an interaction are updated after the sender received a reply from the receiver. If the interactions are not mutually independent, then in some circumstances the sender has to wait indefinitely for a reply from the receiver. For example, if agent A sends a message to agent B and, before this message arrives, agent B sends a message to agent A, then both agents are stuck waiting for the reply from the other agent. These cases are normally tackled by assuming that agents do not wait for replies longer than a specified period of time. If no reply is received within the specified period of time, then the interaction is forcibly interrupted and the state of the sender remains unchanged, thus perturbating the decentralized computation of the average. Note that if the multi-agent system is sufficiently large, then the probability that two interleaving interactions are not independent can be considered sufficiently low.

A variant of the symmetric gossip protocol, called asymmetric gossip protocol in the nomenclature proposed in [17], works against these possible deadlocks by allowing the sender to continue without waiting for a reply from the receiver. In this case, an interaction only updates the state of the receiver. Given an agent identified by $s \in \mathbb{N}_+$ (the sender) and another agent identified by $r \in \mathbb{N}_+$ (the receiver), the asymmetric gossip protocol [16] assumes that when agent s sends a message to agent r their states $x_s \in \mathbb{R}$ and $x_r \in \mathbb{R}$ are updated as follows:

$$\begin{cases} x'_r = x_s \\ x'_r = x_r - \gamma(x_r - x_s), \end{cases} \tag{2}$$

where $\gamma \in (0, 1)$ is a parameter shared by all agents.

The asymmetric gossip protocol cures deadlocks and ensures that the states of all agents would eventually converge to a shared value [17]. Unfortunately, this shared value is not the initial average of the states of the agents because it is affected by an additive random variable [16]. Therefore, the asymmetric gossip protocol can be effectively used to reach consensus in multi-agent systems, but it cannot be used to solve the distributed averaging problem. However, note that, under rather mild hypotheses [16], the contribution of the additive random variables tends to zero as the number of agents tends to infinity [16]. Therefore, if the multi-agent system is sufficiently large, then the asynchronous gossip protocol can be applied to solve the distributed averaging problem with sufficient accuracy. Also, note that the asymmetric gossip protocol reduces the number of messages exchanged by agents because it does not require replies.

The symmetric gossip protocol introduced an interesting decentralized mechanism that significantly contributed to improve the previous works on consensus [27]. However, this protocol suffers from the locality of updates, and it requires many iterations to reach consensus. Since each iteration involves an associated communication cost, geographic routes and broadcast communications has been proposed to reduce the number of interactions needed to compute the average. Some important examples of the protocols designed to reduce the number of interactions requested to reach consensus are discussed in [4] and in [15]. In particular, [4] proposes the use of asymmetric broadcast communications, which provides convergence to some common value, but it may significantly differ from the average value. Alternatively, [15] makes use of geographic information to accelerate the gossip process, which requires establishing long routes that make difficult to ensure symmetric communications [3].

Residual gossip protocols [3] have been proposed to adapt the asymmetric gossip protocol to solve the distributed averaging problem without additional assumptions on the number of agents in the multi-agent systems. In addition, they have been proposed to reduce the communication cost associated with the computation of the average, as empirically shown in [3]. The reduction of the communication cost is particularly relevant when these protocols are used in wireless sensor networks, and therefore residual gossip protocols are often associated with these networks. However, note that they are relevant tools to solve the distributed averaging problem independently of the considered networks.

Residual gossip protocols assume that each agent has a state composed of two real values. The first value, which we call *primary component* of the state, is the value whose initial average needs to be computed. The second value, which we call *residual component* of the state, is a value used to provide for asymmetric interactions. A specific residual gossip protocol is studied in this paper because the following assumptions are taken. First, no overlay network is assumed and every agent is allowed to interact with every other agent. Second, no broadcast communication is allowed and agents interact by exchanging unicast messages. Third, an additional parameter of the protocol shared among all agents is introduced to explicitly provide a supplementary means to govern the dynamics of the distributed averaging process.

Formally, the studied residual gossip protocol can be described as follows. Consider a multi-agent system composed of $n \in \mathbb{N}_+$ agents in which each agent has a state represented by a pair $(x, y) \in \mathbb{R}^2$, where x is the primary component of the state and y is the residual component of the state. Given an agent identified by $s \in \mathbb{N}_+$ (the sender) and another agent identified by $r \in \mathbb{N}_+$ (the receiver), the studied residual gossip protocol assumes that when agent s sends a message to agent r their respective states, $(x_s, y_s) \in \mathbb{R}^2$ and $(x_r, y_r) \in \mathbb{R}^2$, are updated using the following rule:

$$\begin{cases} x'_s = x_s \\ y'_s = \alpha y_s \\ x'_r = x_r - \gamma(x_r - x_s) + (1 - \gamma)(1 - \alpha)y_s \\ y'_r = y_r + \gamma(x_r - x_s) + \gamma(1 - \alpha)y_s, \end{cases} \tag{3}$$

where $\gamma \in (0, 1)$ is now called *averaging parameter* and $\alpha \in (0, 1)$ is the added *residual parameter*. Note that every interaction updates both the state of the sender and of the receiver. However, the sender does not need to wait for the reply from the receiver to update its state, which is sufficient to prevent the possible deadlocks that affect the symmetric gossip protocol.

The remaining of this paper is devoted to the study of the dynamics of the states of the agents that use the update rule (3). In particular, the average of the primary component of the states and the average of the residual component of the states are studied to contribute two analytic results. The first result confirms, using an uncommon approach, that the studied residual gossip protocol can be used to solve the distributed averaging problem. The provided proof is interesting also because it uses a framework that can be adopted to study other decentralized protocols. The second result is a closed-form expression of the time evolution of the average of the primary component of the states, which fills a gap in the literature on residual gossip protocols. This closed-form expression is obtained by means of the same framework used to obtain the first result.

The adopted approach used to obtain these two results is based on the *Kinetic Theory of Multi-Agent Systems* (*KTMAS*) [26], which is a theory that is being devised to study the collective and emergent properties of large and decentralized multi-agent systems. This theory is still under active development (e.g., [25,26]) and Sect. 2 recapitulates its essential ingredients. KTMAS is based on two master equations that are completed with the needed details that characterize the multi-agent system under investigation. The second of these master equations is used in Sect. 3 to prove that the average of the residual component of the states of the agents eventually tends to zero as time tends to infinity. This is sufficient to prove that the studied residual gossip protocol can be used to solve the distributed averaging problem [3]. The same master equation is also used in Sect. 3 to obtain a closed-form expressions of the average of the primary component of the states of the agents. The validity of this closed-form expression is confirmed by means of a few independent simulations presented in Sect. 4. Note that, for lack of space, the discussed simulations are only illustrative.

In summary, this paper is organized as follows. Section 2 briefly recapitulates the essential ingredients of KTMAS needed for the subsequent developments. Section 3 uses KTMAS to prove two analytic results on the time evolution of the average of the primary component of the states of the agents when the studied residual gossip protocol is used. Section 4 shows a few illustrative simulations that confirm the validity of the obtained analytic results. Finally, Sect. 5 briefly summarizes the obtained results and sketches planned future developments.

2 The Kinetic Theory of Multi-agent Systems in Brief

Large and decentralized multi-agent systems (e.g., large fleets of connected devices [1,9] or autonomous vehicles [13,22,30] in a large urban area) are the principal target of relevant research efforts that jointly form the basis of the studies on collective adaptive systems (e.g., [14,18]). These systems also find relevant applications in various topics related to distributed artificial intelligence (e.g., [19,32]). Usually, the study of the dynamics of these systems assumes that each agent is associated with a state that changes dynamically. The state of an agent changes because of multiple causes and, in particular, it changes because of the interactions that occur when the agent gets in touch with other agents. Accordingly, the descriptions of how interactions change the states of the agents are central to the study of the dynamics of these systems, and they must consider all phenomena that cause agents to change their states. Therefore, these descriptions strongly depend on the considered phenomena and on the specific characteristics of the multi-agent system under investigation.

When the number of agents in the considered multi-agent system is large, the study of the dynamics of the state of each agent is not feasible. For example, consider a large swarm of droids or autonomous taxis in urban areas. On the one hand, tracking the position, velocity, and battery level of each agent might be extremely expensive, if not impossible. On the other hand, what really matters is that the group as a whole achieves its overall objectives, which can include properly shaping the intended choreography for droids or uniformly covering the urban areas for taxis. In these cases, the study of the collective behavior [21,31] of the multi-agent system as a whole is preferred, which requires focusing on the characteristics of the states of the agents that jointly form the relevant collective properties of the multi-agent system as a whole. Under the mild assumption that the relevant characteristics of the states of the agents can be represented as real numbers, the collective, and possibly emergent, properties of the considered multi-agent system can be studied using statistical approaches. These statistical approaches are mainly concerned with the study of aggregate values, which are not normally sufficient to obtain detailed descriptions of the state of each agent, however these aggregate values are often sufficient to describe the collective dynamics of the multi-agent system as a whole.

KTMAS is being devised to shed the light on a general-purpose approach to study the asymptotic collective dynamics of large and decentralized multi-agent systems. As its name suggests, it is a specific instantiation of mathematical kinetic theories (e.g., [5,6,28]). These theories are not necessarily restricted to the study of physical phenomena, and they are generally intended to investigate the collective properties of groups of interacting peers under the assumption that the relevant characteristics of the groups emerge from the local interactions among peers and from environmental forces, which is the case for several interesting problems (e.g., [2,20,23,24,29]). Note that mathematical kinetic theories provide interesting results when the characteristics of the studied system justify a statistical approach and when the interactions among the peers are the main causes of the dynamics of the system.

Mathematical kinetic theories are all based on a common general framework (e.g., [5,6,28]) intended to study the collective dynamics of groups of interacting peers. This general framework assumes that the properties that characterize peers change because of interactions and environmental forces, and that the studied groups are so large that their collective, and possibly emergent, properties can be adequately studied using a statistical approach. Note that this general framework is not sufficient to study specific groups of interacting peers because it must be turned into a model by completing the framework with the details needed to study specific phenomena in specific contexts. A model obtained by completing this general framework with the needed details can then be used to study the collective dynamics of the groups of peers for which the provided details are sufficiently descriptive of interactions and environmental forces.

The KTMAS framework [26], as briefly outlined in this section, is an instantiation of the general framework of the mathematical kinetic theories that is designed to study the long-time asymptotic properties of large and decentralized multi-agent systems in which agents affect each other's state via direct messages [7,8,10]. The KTMAS framework studies multi-agent systems composed of a static and large number of interacting agents $n \in \mathbb{N}_+$ in which each agent is uniquely identified by a natural number between 1 and n. Each agent has a state and, for the purposes of this paper, it is assumed that the state of an agent is represented as a pair of real numbers $\mathbf{q} \in Q$, where $Q \subseteq \mathbb{R}^2$ is an open box that contains all the states the agents can assume. It is worth noting that the results presented in this section can be extended to drop the assumption that Q is an open interval by using a heavier notation that extends Q to a countably infinte union of open intervals.

Agents interact autonomously, with each agent free to communicate with any other. These interactions take the form of direct message exchanges between two agents. Therefore, the only considered form of interaction regards an agent identified by $1 \leq r \leq n$ (the receiver) receiving a message from an agent identified by $1 \leq s \leq n$ (the sender). Since interactions are the only interesting events in the current form of the KTMAS framework, time is modeled as a real variable in $\mathbb{R}_{\geq 0}$ and interactions occur at the instants of a Poisson point process with average rate $\nu \in \mathbb{R}_+$, which is often called *interaction rate* in this context. Interactions are assumed to be instantaneous, which means that if an agent is involved in an interaction, then the interaction is completed before the agent can experience any other interaction. In addition, and more importantly, interactions are assumed to be mutually independent. This assumption is one of the major assumptions of mathematical kinetic theories and it is often called *molecular chaos assumption* or *Stosszahlansatz* (German for *assumption on the count of collisions*). Interested readers can refer to [26] for a detailed description of the role of the molecular chaos assumption in the construction of the two master equations that characterize the KTMAS framework.

In its current form, the KTMAS framework does not consider environmental forces. Therefore, the state of an agent can change only because of interactions. Interactions are described in the KTMAS framework in terms of how they change the states of the involved agents. In detail, the current form of the framework assumes that interactions are described in terms of proper *interaction rules* that link the pre-interaction states with the corresponding post-interaction states. Interaction rules are specific to the multi-agent system under investigation, and the framework leaves them unspecified until a model of the system is needed to actually study its interesting collective, and possibly emergent, properties. The only assumption that the KTMAS framework makes on interaction rules is that they must be total and locally invertible in Q. Note that the rules used to describe the three types of gossip protocols considered in the previous section, namely (1), (2), and (3), are three examples of interaction rules usable in the scope of the KTMAS framework. In addition, note that the asymptotic collective properties of the multi-agent systems that use (1) have already been studied using the KTMAS framework [26].

In accordance with the general framework of mathematical kinetic theories, $f : Q \times \mathbb{R}_{\geq 0} \to \mathbb{R}$ is a function, called density function, such that $f(\mathbf{q}, t)\, \mathrm{d}^2\mathbf{q}$ counts the number of agents whose states are in the open box $(\mathbf{q}, \mathbf{q}+\mathrm{d}\mathbf{q})$ at time $t \in \mathbb{R}_{\geq 0}$. Note that f is assumed to be sufficiently regular to support the analytic developments needed to obtain and solve the master equations of the KTMAS framework. The introduction of the density function is sufficient to count the number of agents $n \in \mathbb{N}_+$ in the multi-agent system

$$n = \int_Q f(\mathbf{q}, t)\, \mathrm{d}^2\mathbf{q}, \tag{4}$$

where the dependence of n on t is dropped because the number of agents in the multi-agent system is assumed to be static. Moreover, the introduction of the density function can be used to characterize two relevant collective properties of the multi-agent system under investigation, namely the average and the variance of one of the components of the states of the agents. In particular, if $\mathbf{q} = (x, y)$, then the average of the first component of the states at time $t \in \mathbb{R}_{\geq 0}$ is

$$\overline{x}(t) = \frac{1}{n} \int_Q x\, f(x, y, t)\, \mathrm{d}x\mathrm{d}y, \tag{5}$$

while the variance of the first component of the states at time t is

$$\sigma_x^2(t) = \frac{1}{n} \int_Q (x - \overline{x}(t))^2 f(x, y, t)\, \mathrm{d}x\mathrm{d}y. \tag{6}$$

These definitions can be easily modified to obtain the corresponding definition of $\overline{y}(t)$, which reads

$$\overline{y}(t) = \frac{1}{n} \int_Q y\, f(x, y, t)\, \mathrm{d}x\mathrm{d}y, \tag{7}$$

and the corresponding definition of $\sigma_y^2(t)$, which reads

$$\sigma_y^2(t) = \frac{1}{n} \int_Q (y - \overline{y}(t))^2 f(x, y, t)\, \mathrm{d}x\mathrm{d}y. \tag{8}$$

The two master equations of the KTMAS framework are normally called *(strong form of the) Boltzmann equation* [26] and *weak form of the Boltzmann equation* [26]. The Boltzmann equation provides a fine-grained characterization of the dynamics of the states of the agents, which is normally too fine-grained to be feasible for large multi-agent systems. Therefore, this equation is not further detailed here and interested readers can refer to [26] for its study in the scope of the KTMAS framework. On the contrary, the weak form of the Boltzmann equation is detailed in the remaining of this section because it is used to prove the two analytic results discussed in the following section.

Given a sufficiently regular test function $\phi : Q \to \mathbb{R}$, the weak form of the Boltzmann equation can be stated as

$$\int_Q \frac{\partial f}{\partial t}(\mathbf{q}_s, t)\phi(\mathbf{q}_s)\, \mathrm{d}^2\mathbf{q}_s = \frac{\beta}{2} \int_{Q^2} \Delta(\mathbf{q}_s, \mathbf{q}_r) f(\mathbf{q}_s, t) f(\mathbf{q}_r, t)\, \mathrm{d}^2\mathbf{q}_r\, \mathrm{d}^2\mathbf{q}_s, \tag{9}$$

where

$$\Delta(\mathbf{q}_s, \mathbf{q}_r) = \phi(\mathbf{q}'_r) + \phi(\mathbf{q}'_s) - \phi(\mathbf{q}_r) - \phi(\mathbf{q}_s) \tag{10}$$

and

$$\beta = \frac{2}{n^2}\nu. \tag{11}$$

The relevance of the weak form of the Boltzmann equation to study the collective properties of multi-agent systems can be clarified as follows. If the details of the interactions that occur in the multi-agent system are made explicit, by stating an explicit expression of the adopted interaction rule, the right-hand side of (9) can be also made explicit. Therefore, for an explicit interaction rule and a fixed ϕ, the weak form of the Boltzmann equation becomes an ordinary differential equation that describes the dynamics of the collective property entailed by the chosen ϕ. For example, if $\phi(x, y) = x$ is chosen, then (9) can be written as

$$n\frac{\mathrm{d}\overline{x}}{\mathrm{d}t}(t) = \frac{\beta}{2} \int_{Q^2} (x'_r + x'_s - x_r - x_s)\, f(x_r, y_r, t) f(x_s, y_s, t)\, \mathrm{d}x_r\, \mathrm{d}y_r\, \mathrm{d}x_s\, \mathrm{d}y_s,$$

which is the equation used in the next section to study the average of the primary component of the states of the agents. Similarly, if $\phi(x, y) = y$ is chosen, then (9) can be written as

$$n\frac{\mathrm{d}\overline{y}}{\mathrm{d}t}(t) = \frac{\beta}{2} \int_{Q^2} (y'_r + y'_s - y_r - y_s)\, f(x_r, y_r, t) f(x_s, y_s, t)\, \mathrm{d}x_r\, \mathrm{d}y_r\, \mathrm{d}x_s\, \mathrm{d}y_s,$$

which is the equation used in the next section to study the average of the residual component of the states of the agents. Analogously, if $\phi(x,y) = (x - \overline{x}(t))^2$ is chosen, then (9) can be written as

$$n\frac{\mathrm{d}\sigma_x^2}{\mathrm{d}t}(t) = \frac{\beta}{2}\int_{Q^2} \left[(x_r' - \overline{x}(t))^2 + (x_s' - \overline{x}(t))^2 - (x_r - \overline{x}(t))^2 - (x_s - \overline{x}(t))^2\right] \cdot f(x_r, y_r, t) f(x_s, y_s, t)\, \mathrm{d}x_r\, \mathrm{d}y_r\, \mathrm{d}x_s\, \mathrm{d}y_s,$$

and this equation can be used to study the dynamics of the variance of the primary component of the states of the agents. Finally, if $\phi(x,y) = (y - \overline{y}(t))^2$ is chosen, then (9) can be written as

$$n\frac{\mathrm{d}\sigma_y^2}{\mathrm{d}t}(t) = \frac{\beta}{2}\int_{Q^2} \left[(y_r' - \overline{y}(t))^2 + (y_s' - \overline{y}(t))^2 - (y_r - \overline{y}(t))^2 - (y_s - \overline{y}(t))^2\right] \cdot f(x_r, y_r, t) f(x_s, y_s, t)\, \mathrm{d}x_r\, \mathrm{d}y_r\, \mathrm{d}x_s\, \mathrm{d}y_s,$$

and this equation can be used to study the dynamics of the variance of the residual component of the states of the agents.

3 The Dynamics of the Average

The interest now is on using the KTMAS framework to study the dynamics of the states of the agents in a multi-agent system $\mathcal{M}$ such that:

1. $\mathcal{M}$ is composed of a static number $n \in \mathbb{N}_+$ of agents;
2. The state of each agent in $\mathcal{M}$ is composed of a primary component denoted as $x \in \mathbb{R}$ and residual component denoted as $y \in \mathbb{R}$;
3. The agents in $\mathcal{M}$ follow the studied residual gossip protocol (3) with averaging parameter $\gamma \in (0,1)$ and residual parameter $\alpha \in (0,1)$;
4. The agents in $\mathcal{M}$ exchange messages at the interaction rate $\nu \in \mathbb{R}_+$;
5. Every agent in $\mathcal{M}$ can exchange messages with every other agent in $\mathcal{M}$; and
6. The molecular chaos assumption holds for $\mathcal{M}$.

The following two propositions accurately describe the dynamics of the states of the agents using the KTMAS framework. This is possible because the studied residual gossip protocol is described by the interaction rule (3) that exhibits the needed characteristics, as proved in the following lemma.

Lemma 1. *The agents in $\mathcal{M}$ use a total and locally invertible interaction rule.*

Proof. The agents in $\mathcal{M}$ use the interaction rule (3) with averaging parameter $\gamma \in (0,1)$ and residual parameter $\alpha \in (0,1)$. When viewed as a transformation

$$(x_s', y_s', x_r', y_r') = \mathbf{t}(x_s, y_s, x_r, y_r), \tag{12}$$

it is easy to confirm that the rule is total because it is linear. Moreover, the Jacobian matrix of (12) is

$$\partial\mathbf{t}(x_s, y_s, x_r, y_r) = \begin{pmatrix} 1 & 0 & 0 & 0 \\ 0 & \alpha & 0 & 0 \\ \gamma & (1-\gamma)(1-\alpha) & 1-\gamma & 0 \\ -\gamma & \gamma(1-\alpha) & \gamma & 1 \end{pmatrix}. \tag{13}$$

Since

$$\det \partial\mathbf{t}(x_s, y_s, x_r, y_r) = \alpha(1-\gamma), \tag{14}$$

the transformation is locally invertible for $\alpha \in (0,1)$ and $\gamma \in (0,1)$, which readily proves the lemma. □

The following proposition provides a closed-form expression of the time evolution of the residual component of the states of the agents in $\mathcal{M}$. Besides the relevance of the obtained closed-form expression, it is worth noting that the closed-form expression is sufficient to state that, for the ranges of the two parameters of the protocol, the average of the residual component of the states of the agents tends to zero as time tends to infinity. This fact is sufficient to confirm that the studied residual gossip protocol can be used to solve the distributed averaging problem because it rephrases a result used in [3] to ensure the correctness of the protocol.

Proposition 1. *The average* $\overline{y}$ *of the residual component of the states of the agents in* $\mathcal{M}$ *has the following time evolution:*

$$\overline{y}(t) = \overline{y}(0)\, \mathrm{e}^{-(1-\alpha)(1-\gamma)\frac{\nu}{n}t}. \tag{15}$$

Proof. The average of the residual component of the states of the agents in $\mathcal{M}$ can be studied using the weak form of the Boltzmann equation with the following test function:

$$\phi(x, y) = y. \tag{16}$$

Therefore, the weak form of the Boltzmann equation becomes

$$n\frac{\mathrm{d}}{\mathrm{d}t}\overline{y}_s(t) = \frac{\beta}{2}\int_{\mathbb{R}^4} (y_s' + y_r' - y_s - y_r) f(x_s, y_s, t) f(x_r, y_r, t)\, \mathrm{d}x_s\, \mathrm{d}y_s\, \mathrm{d}x_r, \mathrm{d}y_r. \tag{17}$$

However, for (3), the first term of the integrand is

$$y_s' + y_r' - y_s - y_r = (1-\alpha)(\gamma-1)y_s + \gamma x_r - \gamma x_s. \tag{18}$$

Therefore, by integrating using this rewritten first term,

$$n\frac{\mathrm{d}}{\mathrm{d}t}\overline{y}_s(t) = \frac{\beta}{2}\left[(1-\alpha)(\gamma-1)n^2\overline{y}_s(t) + \gamma n^2\overline{y}_r(t) - \gamma n^2\overline{y}_s(t)\right]. \tag{19}$$

Since the average of the residual component of the states of the agents does not depend on whether an agent is a sender or a receiver, the reference to senders and receivers can be dropped to obtain

$$\frac{\mathrm{d}}{\mathrm{d}t}\overline{y}(t) = \frac{\beta}{2}(1-\alpha)(\gamma-1)n\overline{y}(t). \tag{20}$$

The proposition is proved because the previous equation is easily solved

$$\overline{y}(t) = \overline{y}(0)\, \mathrm{e}^{-\frac{\beta}{2}(1-\alpha)(1-\gamma)nt}. \tag{21}$$

where $\overline{y}(0)$ is the initial average of the residual component of the states of the agents, which is normally known when the studied residual gossip protocol is used to solve the distributed averaging problem. □

The following proposition provides a closed-form expression of the time evolution of the primary component of the states of the agents.

Proposition 2. *The average $\overline{x}$ of the primary component of the states of the agents in $\mathcal{M}$ has the following time evolution:*

$$\overline{x}(t) = \overline{x}(0) + \overline{y}(0) - \overline{y}(0)\, \mathrm{e}^{-(1-\alpha)(1-\gamma)\frac{\nu}{n}t}, \tag{22}$$

Proof. The average of the primary component of the states of the agents in $\mathcal{M}$ can be studied using the weak form of the Boltzmann equation with the following test function:

$$\phi(x, y) = x. \tag{23}$$

Therefore, the weak form of the Boltzmann equation becomes

$$n\frac{\mathrm{d}}{\mathrm{d}t}\overline{x}_s(t) = \frac{\beta}{2}\int_{\mathbb{R}^4} (x'_s + x'_r - x_s - x_r) f(x_s, y_s, t) f(x_r, y_r, t)\, \mathrm{d}x_s\, \mathrm{d}y_s\, \mathrm{d}x_r\, \mathrm{d}y_r. \tag{24}$$

However, for (3), the first term of the integrand is

$$x'_s + x'_r - x_s - x_r = \gamma x_s - \gamma x_r - (1-\alpha)(\gamma - 1) y_s. \tag{25}$$

Therefore, by integrating using this rewritten first term,

$$n\frac{\mathrm{d}}{\mathrm{d}t}\overline{x}_s(t) = \frac{\beta}{2}\left[\gamma n^2 \overline{x}_s(t) - \gamma n^2 \overline{x}_r(t) - (1-\alpha)(\gamma - 1) n^2 \overline{y}_s(t)\right]. \tag{26}$$

Since the average of the primary component of the states of the agents does not depend on whether an agent is a sender or a receiver, the reference to senders and receivers can be dropped to obtain

$$\frac{\mathrm{d}}{\mathrm{d}t}\overline{x}(t) = -\frac{\beta}{2}(1-\alpha)(\gamma - 1) n \overline{y}(t). \tag{27}$$

Proposition 1 allows rewriting the previous equation as follows:

$$\frac{\mathrm{d}}{\mathrm{d}t}\overline{x}(t) = -\frac{\beta}{2}(1-\alpha)(\gamma - 1) n \overline{y}(0)\, \mathrm{e}^{-\frac{\beta}{2}(1-\alpha)(1-\gamma)nt}. \tag{28}$$

Therefore, by integrating both terms of the previous equations,

$$\overline{x}(t) = \overline{x}(0) + \overline{y}(0) - \overline{y}(0)\, \mathrm{e}^{-\frac{\beta}{2}(1-\alpha)(1-\gamma)nt}, \tag{29}$$

where $\overline{x}(0)$ is the initial average of the primary component of the states of the agents, which is the unknown value that needs to be estimated when using the studied residual gossip protocol to solve the distributed averaging problem. □

4 Comparison with Independent Simulations

The analytic results obtained in Proposition 1 and Proposition 2 can be compared against independent simulations. The following simulations compare the analytic results obtained in these propositions with the actual behavior of a multi-agent system in which the agents follow the studied residual gossip protocol in four different situations. Note that, for the lack of space, the discussed simulations are only illustrative, and they cannot be considered as an experimental assessment of the obtained analytic results.

The first example considers a multi-agent system composed of $n = 100$ agents that interact using the studied residual gossip protocol with an interaction rate of $\nu = 1$ interactions per unit time. Let the two parameters of the studied residual gossip protocol be

$$\alpha_1 = 0.1 \qquad \text{and} \qquad \gamma_1 = 0.4, \tag{30}$$

and let the initial averages be

$$\overline{x}_1(0) = 1 \qquad \text{and} \qquad \overline{y}_1(0) = 3. \tag{31}$$

In particular, the initial states of the agents have primary component uniformly distributed in $(-2, 4)$ and residual component uniformly distributed in $(2, 4)$.

Figure 1(a) shows $\overline{y}_1(t)$ obtained using Proposition 1 together with experimental data obtained averaging on 10^3 runs of the simulated multi-agent system. Figure 1(b) shows $\overline{x}_1(t)$ obtained using Proposition 2 together with experimental data obtained averaging on the same runs of the simulated multi-agent system used for Fig. 1(a).

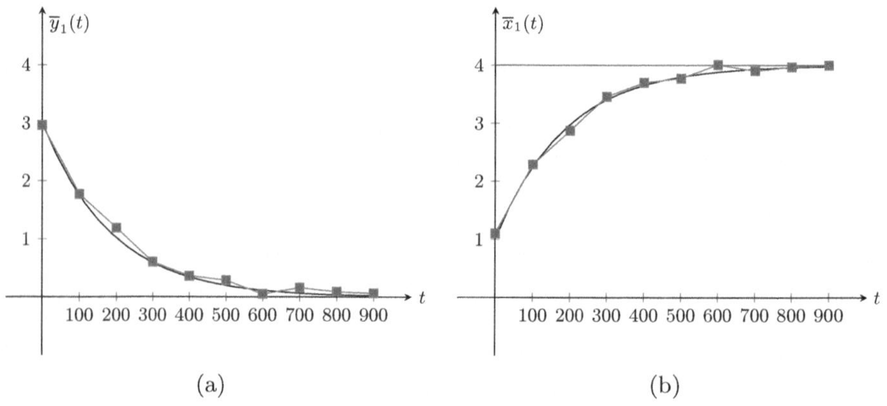

Fig. 1. Comparison between analytic and experimental results for the first example obtained after 10^3 runs: (a) plot of $\overline{y}_1(t)$ together with the corresponding values obtained by averaging on the data from the simulations, and (b) plot of $\overline{x}_1(t)$ together with the corresponding values obtained by averaging on the data from the simulations.

In detail, Proposition 1 provides a closed-form expression of the time evolution of the average of the residual component of the states of the agents

$$\overline{y}_1(t) = 3\,\mathrm{e}^{-5.4\cdot 10^{-3}t}. \tag{32}$$

Proposition 2 provides a closed-form expression of the time evolution of the average of the primary component of the states of the agents

$$\overline{x}_1(t) = 4 - 3\,\mathrm{e}^{-5.4\cdot 10^{-3}t}. \tag{33}$$

The second illustrative example considers $n = 100$ agents that interact using the studied residual gossip protocol with an interaction rate of $\nu = 1$ interactions per unit time. Let the two parameters of the studied residual gossip protocol be

$$\alpha_2 = 0.01 \qquad \text{and} \qquad \gamma_2 = 0.49, \tag{34}$$

and let the initial averages be

$$\overline{x}_2(0) = -1 \qquad \text{and} \qquad \overline{y}_2(0) = 2. \tag{35}$$

The initial states of the agents have primary component uniformly distributed in $(-2, 0)$ and residual component uniformly distributed in $(1, 3)$.

Figure 2(a) shows $\overline{y}_2(t)$ obtained using Proposition 1 together with experimental data obtained averaging on 10^3 runs of the simulated multi-agent system. Figure 2(b) shows $\overline{x}_2(t)$ obtained using Proposition 2 together with experimental data obtained averaging on the same runs used for Fig. 2(a).

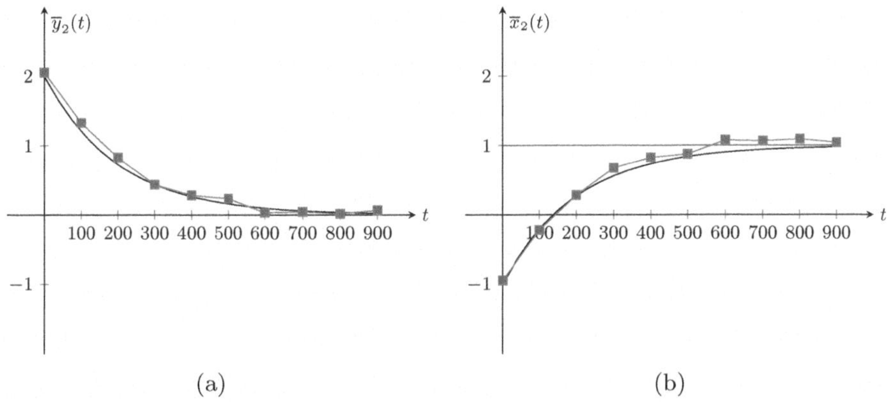

Fig. 2. Comparison between analytic and experimental results for the second example obtained after 10^3 runs: (a) plot of $\overline{y}_2(t)$ together with the corresponding values obtained by averaging on the data from the simulations, and (b) plot of $\overline{x}_2(t)$ together with the corresponding values obtained by averaging on the data from the simulations.

Proposition 1 provides a closed-form expression of the time evolution of the average of the residual component of the states of the agents

$$\overline{y}_2(t) = 2\,\mathrm{e}^{-5.049\cdot 10^{-3}t}. \tag{36}$$

Proposition 2 provides a closed-form expression of the time evolution of the average of the primary component of the states of the agents

$$\overline{x}_2(t) = 1 - 2\,\mathrm{e}^{-5.049\cdot 10^{-3}t}. \tag{37}$$

The third illustrative example considers $n = 100$ agents that interact using the residual gossip protocol with an interaction rate of $\nu = 1$ interactions per unit time. Let the two parameters of the studied residual gossip protocol be

$$\alpha_3 = 0.3 \qquad \text{and} \qquad \gamma_3 = 0.3, \tag{38}$$

and let the initial averages be

$$\overline{x}_3(0) = 2 \qquad \text{and} \qquad \overline{y}_3(0) = -1. \tag{39}$$

In particular, the initial states of the agents have primary component uniformly distributed in $(1, 3)$ and residual component uniformly distributed in $(-2, 0)$.

Figure 3(a) shows $\overline{y}_3(t)$ obtained using Proposition 1 together with experimental data obtained averaging on 10^3 runs of the simulated multi-agent system. Figure 3(b) shows $\overline{x}_3(t)$ obtained using Proposition 2 together with experimental data obtained averaging on the same runs used for Fig. 3(a).

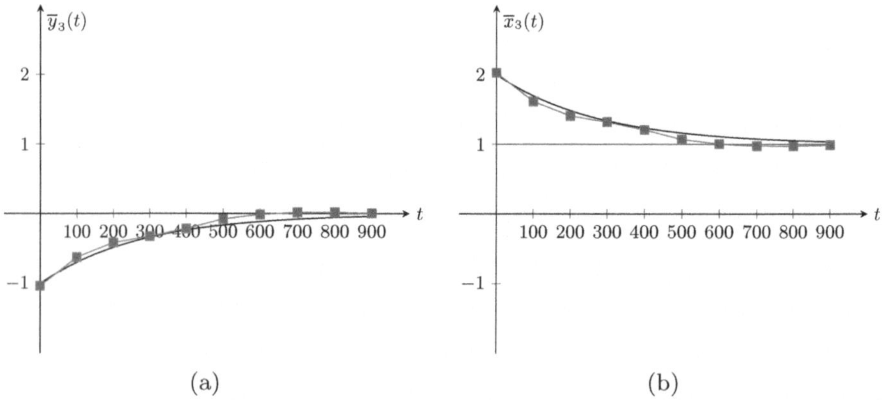

Fig. 3. Comparison between analytic and experimental results for the third example obtained after 10^3 runs: (a) plot of $\overline{y}_3(t)$ together with the corresponding values obtained by averaging on the data from the simulations, and (b) plot of $\overline{x}_3(t)$ together with the corresponding values obtained by averaging on the data from the simulations.

Proposition 1 provides a closed-form expression of the time evolution of the average of the residual component of the states of the agents

$$\overline{y}_3(t) = -\,\mathrm{e}^{-3.6 \cdot 10^{-3} t}. \tag{40}$$

Proposition 2 provides a closed-form expression of the time evolution of the average of the primary component of the states of the agents

$$\overline{x}_3(t) = 1 + \mathrm{e}^{-3.6 \cdot 10^{-3} t}. \tag{41}$$

The fourth illustrative example considers $n = 100$ agents that interact using the residual gossip protocol with an interaction rate of $\nu = 1$ interactions per unit time. Let the two parameters of the residual gossip protocol be

$$\alpha_4 = 0.1 \qquad \text{and} \qquad \gamma_4 = 0.4, \tag{42}$$

and let the initial averages be

$$\overline{x}_4(0) = -1 \qquad \text{and} \qquad \overline{y}_4(0) = -2. \tag{43}$$

In particular, the initial states of the agents have primary component uniformly distributed in $(-2, 0)$ and residual component uniformly distributed in $(-3, -1)$.

Figure 4(a) shows $\overline{y}_4(t)$ obtained using Proposition 1 together with experimental data obtained averaging on 10^3 runs of the simulated multi-agent system. Figure 4(b) shows $\overline{x}_4(t)$ obtained using Proposition 2 together with experimental data obtained averaging on the same runs used for Fig. 4(a).

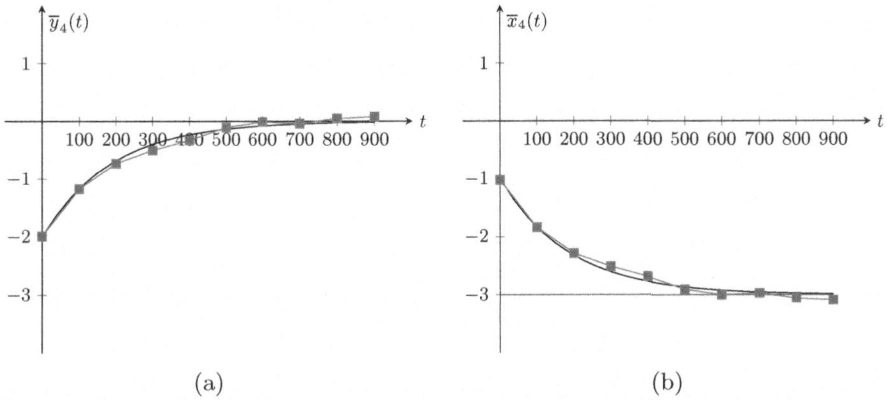

Fig. 4. Comparison between analytic and experimental results for the fourth example obtained after 10^3 runs: (a) plot of $\overline{y}_4(t)$ together with the corresponding values obtained by averaging on the data from the simulations, and (b) plot of $\overline{x}_4(t)$ together with the corresponding values obtained by averaging on the data from the simulations.

Proposition 1 provides a closed-form expression of the time evolution of the average of the residual component of the states of the agents

$$\overline{y}_4(t) = -2\,e^{-5.4\cdot 10^{-3}t}. \tag{44}$$

Proposition 2 provides a closed-form expression of the time evolution of the average of the primary component of the states of the agents

$$\overline{x}_4(t) = -3 + 2e^{-5.4\cdot 10^{-3}t}. \tag{45}$$

The discussed illustrative simulations show that the analytic results obtained using Proposition 1 and Proposition 2 describe well the time evolution of the the average of the states of the agents. In particular, the obtained experimental results confirm that the average of the primary component of states of the agent converges to the initial average of the primary component of the states of the agents as time tends to infinity.

In order to show that the studied residual gossip protocol can be used to solve the distributed averaging problem, the variance of the primary component of the states of the agents must be confirmed to tend to zero as time tends to infinity. In this case, the primary component of the states of all agents would tend to the same value, which is proved to be the initial average of the primary component of the states of the agents. Figure 5 shows the plot of the variances obtained in the four discussed examples, which empirically shows that the studied protocol can be used to solve the distributed averaging problem.

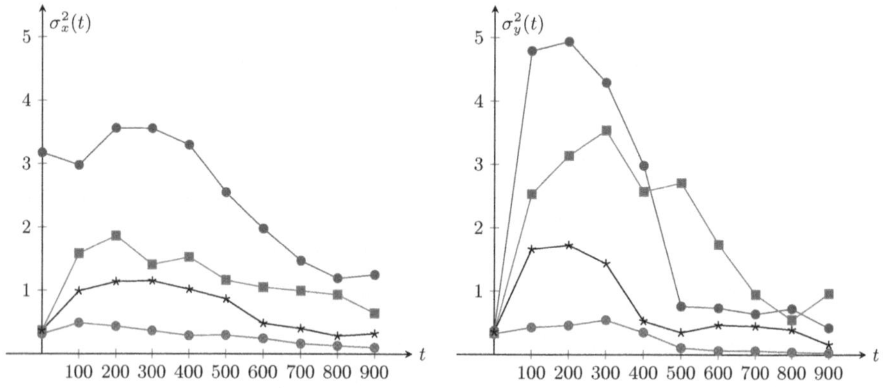

(a) (b)

Fig. 5. The variances of the components of the states of the agents in the 10^3 runs of the four examples: (a) the variance of the residual component of the states of the agents for the first (blue), the second (red), the third (brown), and the fourth (black) examples, and (a) the variance of the primary component of the states of the agents for the first (blue), the second (red), the third (brown), and the fourth (black) examples. (Color figure online)

5 Conclusion

This paper documents some results on the study of the time evolution of the states of the agents that interact using a residual gossip protocol. The major results are summarized in Proposition 1 and Proposition 2, and they state that the considered residual gossip protocol can be used to solve the distributed averaging problem. If the initial average of the residual component of the states of the agents is known, then the initial average of the primary components can be computed from the asymptotic value of the primary components. Moreover, the propositions provide closed-form expressions of the time evolution of the averages of the two components of the states of the agents, which fills a gap in the literature on gossip algorithms. All these results were obtained using the KTMAS framework, and therefore they are accurate under the assumptions of the KTMAS framework. In particular, the considered multi-agent system must be sufficiently large to consider a statistical approach appropriate and for the molecular chaos assumption to hold.

Note that the the KTMAS framework is meant to provide analytic results, which can be sometimes obtained as closed-form expressions. Therefore, KTMAS can be used to support both descriptive and prescriptive reasoning on the long-time asymptotic behavior of the collective, and possibly emergent, properties of large and decentralized multi-agent systems. As a descriptive tool, the KTMAS framework benefits from solid mathematical foundations to represent a valid alternative to multi-agent simulations. As a prescriptive tool, the KTMAS framework can be effectively used to design the interactions capable of producing the target collective dynamics. With this respect, the KTMAS framework addresses the major goal of the research on collective intelligence, which regards understanding the feasibility of designing the needed interaction rules to obtain the desired collective and emergent properties.

A planned future development of the work presented in this paper regards using the KTMAS framework to study the variances of the two components of the states of the agents. It is known from [3] that the studied residual gossip protocol ensures that the two components of the states of the agents converge to two asymptotic values, which is empirically shown in Fig. 5 for the four considered examples. However, the convergence rate to these asymptotic values has not yet been studied with sufficient detail. The results of a few preliminary experiments are available [3], but an analytic study aiming at closed-form expressions is not yet available. Note that the analytic study of the variances of the two components of the states of the agents can also provide a solid justification to the experimented improvement [3] of the convergence rate of the studied residual gossip protocol with respect to the symmetric gossip protocol.

Acknowldegment. Stefania Monica and Federico Bergenti were supported by the Italian Ministry of University and Research under the PRIN 2020 grant 2020TL3X8X for the project Typeful Language Adaptation for Dynamic, Interacting and Evolving Systems (T-LADIES). Franco Zambonelli was funded by the PNRR grant PE00000013 Future Artificial Intelligence Research (FAIR).

References

1. Adorni, G., Bergenti, F., Poggi, A., Rimassa, G.: Enabling FIPA agents on small devices. In: Klusch, M., Zambonelli, F. (eds.) CIA 2001. LNCS (LNAI), vol. 2182, pp. 248–257. Springer, Heidelberg (2001). https://doi.org/10.1007/3-540-44799-7_28
2. Albi, G., Calzola, E., Dimarco, G.: A data-driven kinetic model for opinion dynamics with social network contacts. Eur. J. Appl. Math., 1–27 (2024)
3. Asensio-Marco, C., Beferull-Lozano, B.: Fast average gossiping under asymmetric links in WSNS. In: Proceedings of the 22nd European Signal Processing Conference (EUSIPCO 2014), pp. 131–135. IEEE (2014)
4. Aysal, T.C., Yildiz, M.E., Sarwate, A.D., Scaglione, A.: Broadcast gossip algorithms for consensus. IEEE Trans. Signal Process. **57**(7), 2748–2761 (2009)
5. Bellomo, N., et al.: What is life? A perspective of the mathematical kinetic theory of active particles. Math. Models Methods Appl. Sci. **31**(9), 1821–1866 (2021)
6. Bellouquid, A., Delitala, M.: Mathematical modeling of complex biological systems. Modeling and Simulation in Science, Engineering and Technology, Birkhäuser (2006)
7. Bergenti, F.: A discussion of two major benefits of using agents in software development. In: Petta, P., Tolksdorf, R., Zambonelli, F. (eds.) Proceedings of the 3rd International Workshop on Engineering Societies in the Agents World (ESAW 2002), pp. 1–12. Springer, Heidelberg (2003). https://doi.org/10.1007/3-540-39173-8_1
8. Bergenti, F., Huhns, M.N.: On the use of agents as components of software systems. In: Methodologies and Software Engineering for Agent Systems: The Agent-Oriented Software Engineering Handbook, pp. 19–32. Kluwer Academic Publishing (2004)
9. Bergenti, F., Poggi, A.: Ubiquitous information agents. Int. J. Cooper. Inf. Syst. **11**(3–4), 231–244 (2002)
10. Bergenti, F., Ricci, A.: Three approaches to the coordination of multiagent systems. In: Proceedings of the ACM Symposium on Applied Computing (SAC 2002), pp. 367–372. ACM (2002)
11. Boyd, S., Ghosh, A., Prabhakar, B., Shah, D.: Analysis and optimization of randomized gossip algorithms. In: Proceedings of the 2004 IEEE Conference on Decision and Control, pp. 5310–5315. IEEE (2004)
12. Boyd, S., Ghosh, A., Prabhakar, B., Shah, D.: Randomized gossip algorithms. IEEE Trans. Inf. Theory **52**(6), 2508–2530 (2006)
13. Bures, T., et al.: A life cycle for the development of autonomic systems: the e-mobility showcase. In: Proceedings of the 7th IEEE International Conference on Self-Adaptation and Self-Organizing Systems Workshops (SASOW 2013), pp. 71–76. IEEE (2013)
14. De Nicola, R., Jähnichen, S., Wirsing, M.: Rigorous engineering of collective adaptive systems: special section. Int. J. Softw. Tools Technol. Transfer **22**, 389–397 (2020)
15. Dimakis, A., Sarwate, A.D., Wainwright, M.J.: Geographic gossip: efficient averaging for sensor networks. IEEE Trans. Signal Process. **56**(3), 1205–1216 (2008)
16. Fagnani, F., Zampieri, S.: Asymmetric randomized gossip algorithms for consensus. IFAC Proc. Vol. **41**(2), 9052–9056 (2008)
17. Fagnani, F., Zampieri, S.: Randomized consensus algorithms over large scale networks. IEEE J. Selected Areas Commun. **26**(4) (2008)

18. Ferscha, A.: Collective adaptive systems. In: Adjunct Proceedings of the 2015 ACM International Joint Conference on Pervasive and Ubiquitous Computing and Proceedings of the 2015 ACM International Symposium on Wearable Computers, pp. 893–895. ACM (2015)
19. Garcia, A.F., de Lucena, C.J.P., Zambonelli, F., Omicini, A., Castro, J. (eds.): Software Engineering for Large-Scale Multi-Agent Systems, Research Issues and Practical Applications, Lecture Notes in Computer Science, vol. 2603. Springer, Heidelberg (2002)
20. Günther, M., Klar, A., Materne, T., Wegener, R.: An explicitly solvable kinetic model for vehicular traffic and associated macroscopic equations. In: Mathematical and Computer Modelling, pp. 591–606 (2002)
21. Hillston, J., Pitt, J., Wirsing, M., Zambonelli, F.: Collective adaptive systems: qualitative and quantitative modelling and analysis. Dagstuhl Rep. **4**(12), 68–113 (2014)
22. Mariani, S., Cabri, G., Zambonelli, F.: Coordination of autonomous vehicles: taxonomy and survey. ACM Comput. Surv. **54**(1), 19:1–19:33 (2021)
23. Monica, S., Bergenti, F.: An analytic study of opinion dynamics in multi-agent systems. Comput. Math. Appl. **73**(10), 2272–2284 (2017)
24. Monica, S., Bergenti, F.: Opinion dynamics in multi-agent systems: selected analytic models and verifying simulations. Comput. Math. Organizat. Theory **23**(3), 423–450 (2017)
25. Monica, S., Bergenti, F., Zambonelli, F.: Toward a kinetic framework to model the collective dynamics of multi-agent systems. In: Proceedings of the 11th International Symposium on Leveraging Applications of Formal Methods, Verification and Validation (ISoLA 2022). Lecture Notes in Computer Science, vol. 13703, pp. 165–180. Springer, Heidelberg (2022). https://doi.org/10.1007/978-3-031-19759-8_11
26. Monica, S., Bergenti, F., Zambonelli, F.: A kinetic approach to investigate the collective dynamics of multi-agent systems. Int. J. Softw. Tools Technol. Transfer **25**(5–6), 693–705 (2023)
27. Olfati-Saber, R., Fax, J.A., Murray, R.M.: Consensus and cooperation in networked multi-agent systems. Proc. IEEE **95**(1), 215–233 (2007)
28. Pareschi, L., Toscani, G.: Interacting Multiagent Systems: Kinetic Equations and Montecarlo Methods. Oxford University Press, Oxford (2013)
29. Pareschi, L., Toscani, G.: Wealth distribution and collective knowledge: a Boltzmann approach. Phil. Trans. R. Soc. A: Math. Phys. Eng. Sci. **372**, 20130396 (2014)
30. Piccoli, B., Tosin, A., Zanella, M.: Model-based assessment of the impact of driver-assist vehicles using kinetic theory. Z. Angew. Math. Phys. **71**(5), 1–25 (2020). https://doi.org/10.1007/s00033-020-01383-9
31. Wolpert, D.H., Tumer, K.: Collective intelligence, data routing and Braess' paradox. J. Artif. Intell. Res. **16**, 359–387 (2002)
32. Xu, Y., Liao, E., Scerri, P., Yu, B., Lewis, M., Sycara, K.: Towards flexible coordination of large scale multi-agent teams. In: Scerri, P., Vincent, R., Mailler, R. (eds.) Coordination of Large-Scale Multiagent Systems, pp. 287–309. Springer, Heidelberg (2006). https://doi.org/10.1007/0-387-27972-5_14

Rules2Lab: from Prolog Knowledge-Base, to Learning Agents, to Norm Engineering

Peter Fratrič[1(✉)], Nils Holzenberger[2], and David Restrepo Amariles[1]

[1] HEC Paris, Paris, France
fratric@hec.fr

[2] Télécom Paris, Institut Polytechnique de Paris, Paris, France

Abstract. This paper proposes a methodology, called `Rules2Lab`, that maps a Prolog knowledge base onto a *Gymnasium* environment. States, actions, and constraints are defined in Prolog, while temporal, computational, and sub-symbolic operations are delegated to Python. We demonstrate our approach through a case study on privacy vulnerabilities in a data marketplace. In our simulation, a reinforcement learning agent attempts to access sensitive data, with a privacy breach defined by the similarity between inferred and private data. Inductive logic programming is then used to engineer a new norm that prevents such breaches, demonstrating how a new rule can be seamlessly integrated into the knowledge base. Preliminary results highlight how a *Gymnasium* environment can be effectively combined with logic-based modeling and inference.

Keywords: multi-agent system · norms · reinforcement learning · inductive logic programming

1 Introduction

Gym environments are widely used for testing and developing reinforcement learning agents. However, integrating logic-based technologies into Gym environments, such as Gymnasium [28], can be challenging for users with limited experience in logic-based multi-agent systems. To address this issue, we introduce `Rules2Lab`, a prototype designed for studying agents in a Gym environment defined by a knowledge base written in Prolog.[1]

The `Rules2Lab` approach is demonstrated through a data-sharing case study. We consider a scenario in which a reinforcement learning agent explores vulnerabilities in a data-sharing infrastructure. These vulnerabilities are then conceptualized into a new prohibition norm using inductive logic programming.

In Sect. 2, we review related literature. Section 3 describes the experimental scenario, defines the environment model, and presents the results. Finally, Sect. 4 concludes with a discussion of the limitations and future directions for improving `Rules2Lab`.

[1] The code for `Rules2Lab` and illustrative examples are available at https://github.com/fratric/Rules2Lab.

R. Collier et al. (Eds.): EUMAS 2024, LNAI 15685, pp. 274–282, 2025.
https://doi.org/10.1007/978-3-031-93930-3_16

2 Background

2.1 Agent-Based Modeling

Over the years, several languages, platforms, and environments were developed for multi-agent modelling. They differ mainly by their execution performance, user-friendliness of the language, learning abilities, or data integration [2]. Most of these are based on popular programming languages like Python or Java, with some platforms using their own dedicated language, such as AgentSpeak [23], NetLogo [27], or the SARL platform based on Janus language [17]. Languages tailored for logically reasoning agents in dynamic environments, that typically employ logic capable of capturing dynamic effects, have a long tradition [9], with GOLOG being one of its main representatives [20].

Cross-platform usage of logic-based technologies for MAS have also been extensively developed. NetProLogo can be regarded as most similar to our study.[2] In NetProLogo, the Netlogo multi-agent platform is extended with Prolog, e.g., to model the reasoning of agents [25]. In [11], Prolog is used to generate the environment, and a deep Q-learning-based agent in Python is used for exploration. With the SALMA platform [19], a domain model described by situation calculus and implemented in Prolog is extended with behavioral, domain-specific constructs implemented in Python. Furthermore, Jason reinforcement learning agents are studied in [4,7]. In contrast, our study aims to facilitate usage of state-of-the-art sub-symbolic libraries, such as RLlib [21] or TensorFlow [1], with Gymnasium environment that directly employs, or can be extended with, logic-based representations developed for multi-agent systems.

2.2 Data-Sharing and Norms

Starting from the point of view of sub-symbolic agents operating on top of symbolic structures, we can also invert the perspective by considering symbolic structures extracted from data generated by sub-symbolic agents. These are typically extracted into a form of behavioral norm. Various methods aim to identify and learn suitable logical expressions from behavioral data, e.g., grammatical versions of Markov chain Monte Carlo sampling [12], or (probabilistic) inductive logic programming [26]. Inductive logic programming has seen much progress in the development of new methods, going from traditional implementations such as Golem [22] or Metagol [14], to its cross-platform implementation Popper [15], and more recently implementations based on differentiable architectures such as ∂ILP [16] or DL-learner [8].

Norms in AI are discussed in various contexts, most prominently: emergence of macro-regularities in a MAS [5], legal norms regulating agent behavior [30], or norms provided by designers aiming to align learning agents with human values [18]. This paper connects to the long-lasting research area of law formalization. Notably, Prolog or Prolog-like languages have been successfully used to model regulatory frameworks [6,10,24]. Following the enactment of the GDPR,

[2] Freely available online https://github.com/jgalanp/NetProLogo.

scholarly attention within the realm of law formalization has notably gravitated towards the nuances and implications brought forth by this regulatory framework [3].

3 Experiment

Our simulation experiment concerns identification of preconditions that lead to terminating states, defined as privacy breaches in a data marketplace. In turn, this will help identify new constraints to put into place to prevent agents from breaching privacy. We assume that the following norm must never evaluate to true in our knowledge base:

```
norm1(X,A):-agent(X),data(A),hasAccess(X,A),private(A).
```

meaning that `agent(X)` cannot gain access to private `data(A)`. In order to comply with this prohibition norm, we define access policy by specifying action `isAction(gainAccess,2)` of arity 2 that respects the norm above; writing:

```
static_hasAccess(X,A):-(data(A); model(A)),user(X).
static_gainAccess(X,A):-static_hasAccess(X,A),not(private(A)).
gainAccess(X,A):-static_gainAccess(X,A),not(hasAccess(X,A)),
                 hasCredit(X,A).
```

where the term `hasCredit` models finite resources of the user. As explained bellow, it is theoretically possible for an agent to obtain information about private data `A` by applying statistical inference from publicly available data.

3.1 Application Scenario

Let us consider an expert system model of a data marketplace containing an inherent privacy vulnerability: a user can independently gain access to (1) personal data `"governmentData"` containing personal attributes and (2) a model `"healthRiskModel"` that predicts the health status of an individual. This means that health information about a specific person, which is a special category of personal data with enhanced protection under regulations such as GDPR (Art. 9), is inferred with some small degree of uncertainty. This vulnerability can be exposed by studying the behavior of agents in a data-sharing laboratory environment. The laboratory experiment used to perform this task is summarized as follows:

1. **Exploration:** Let an agent, driven by rewards, learn a policy leading to terminating states of the environment. We consider a reinforcement learning agent called `"insuranceCompany"`, tasked with finding ways to obtain such information in the marketplace, thereby exploiting its privacy vulnerabilities. By designing the reward function such that the terminating states yield high rewards, the reward-oriented agent can be viewed as an agent learning non-compliant behavior.

2. **Sampling:** Terminating and non-terminating trajectories of users can be sampled through model execution. The terminating states of the marketplace model are defined by numeric similarity between private `"healthRiskData"` and data inferred in the market from non-private sources freely available on the market.
3. **Induction:** Using simulated trajectories, common properties of terminating trajectories can be identified to engineer a new prohibition norm. New prohibition norm is integrated as a new rule by adding new restrictions to the `gainAccess(X,A)` action. This means that `user` agents must satisfy more constraints before gaining access to specific data or model.
4. **Evaluation:** The new constraint may induce other forms of non-compliant behavior or inadvertently restrict too many trajectories, potentially rendering the data-sharing infrastructure inoperable. Therefore, in the final step, the environment must be evaluated with the new restrictions in place.

3.2 Data Sharing Environment

State Variables. The state of the environment is fully recorded in the dynamically evolving Prolog knowledge base. Conceptually, it is useful to explicitly define which terms are relevant as characteristic descriptors of the environment state. The terms `user\1`, `data\1`, and `model\1` define basic types, while `private\1`, `hasPrivateAttributes\1`, and `hasMatchingVars\2` represent attributes of data and model instances. Instances with or without these attributes are listed in Table 1, along with information about their variables. Finally, in addition to the `hasAccess\2` state variable, we add the `performedInference\3` state variable, which arises as a consequence of statistical inference action performed by a user, as defined bellow. In this way, we observe non-compliant behavior that would typically go unobserved by a monitoring agent.

Table 1. Six objects can be accessed in our data-sharing infrastructure model by users. Matching variables allow for a malicious user (`"insurenceCompany"`) to statistically infer private attributes of private data.

ID	instance name	object	private	private attributes	matching variables with
1	government data	data	✗	✓	5,6
2	health risk records	data	✓	✓	5
3	health statistics	data	✗	✗	5,6
4	housing records	data	✗	✗	∅
5	health risk model	model	✗	✓	1,2,3
6	happiness prediction	model	✗	✗	1,3

Agents. We consider three users active in our data sharing model. Namely, `"advertismentCompany"`, `"retailCompany"`, and `"insurenceCompany"`. The first two agents are initialized with a random policy, and the policy function of the third agent is described in Sect. 3.3. Conceptually, `enforcer` agent is added to monitor non-compliant activity in the environment.

Actions In addition to `gainAccess` action defined at the beginning of this section, we add `infer` action, that allows a `user(X)` to create a new data instance by performing inference using a model `M` on data `A`. This action can be executed under the following constraints:

```
static_infer(X,A,B):-user(X),data(A),model(B),hasMatchingVars(A,B).
infer(X,A,B) :- static_infer(X,A,B),hasAccess(X,A),hasAccess(X,B),
                not(performedInference(X,A,B)).
```

The action `infer` needs to be associated with a method in Python that actually performs the inference. In our case, the inference is simply predictions drawn from the input model based on input data.

Terminating States. If a user intentionally or unintentionally obtains a data instance that is too similar to a private data instance, then this user is blacklisted by the `enforcer`. If all agents are blacklisted, then the simulation terminates, as there are no more agents left to take actions. The predicate `isSimilar(A,B)` compares similarity between data `A` and data `B`, and is true if the similarity is higher than threshold $\tau \in [0, 1]$; false otherwise. We set $\tau = 0.90$. The similarity is calculated by comparing every row of private data `A` to inferred data `B` with matching column names, and recording the maximum number of identical elements. The maximum number for each row of `A` is recorded, and all values aggregated and divided by the size of number of entries of `A`. A model execution that does not terminate is truncated, either due to only null actions being available for all agents, or if the maximum number of steps was reached.

3.3 Reinforcement Learning Agent

We train a deep neural network policy using the Proximal Policy Optimization (PPO) algorithm, directly mapping observations from the set of observables to the set of actions. By querying `static_hasAccess("insuranceCompany", A)`, we obtain all possible data or models that the agent `A` can access. Accessible objects are labeled with one, while non-accessible objects are labeled with zero, forming the input vector for the neural network. The output layer encodes all possible actions. Depending on the state variables, actions that the agent is not allowed to take are masked.

Data collection for the actor-critic based PPO algorithm is performed by 7 agents running in parallel with a maximum of 20 steps. At every reset, each agent is initialized with the same initial state. The algorithm is implemented using the RLlib library [21]. The remaining hyperparameters, such as the network architecture, are set to the library's default values.

3.4 Norm Induction

Several norm representations have been proposed in the literature [13]. While we are not using a dedicated language for norms in our illustrative multi-agent model, integration of a new norm follows guidelines formulated in [29]. If a predicate $P_a(x, s)$ about the state s becomes true, then the agent x is prohibited to take action a. In our case study, x is `user(X)` and a is `gainAccess(X,A)`, where `A` is data or a model. The predicate $P_a(x, s)$ is identified with a common property leading to terminating states, and needs to be induced from data sampled from the environment.

The environment can be sampled by executing agents' policy functions. At each step, each agent is sequentially allowed to take one action. Each `user` generates a trajectory $(s_0, a_1, s_1, ..., a_n, s_n)$ labeled as positive or negative depending on whether the last action produced a terminating state, thus resulting in blacklisting of the `user` by the `enforcer`. To find the predicate $P_a(x, s)$ we use the inductive logic programming tool `Popper` [15]. This tool can construct predicates from positive and negative examples and background knowledge, even from noisy data. In our case, positive examples are identified with terminating trajectories, and negative examples with trajectories that did not terminate, meaning the trajectory was truncated. In practice, arity of the predicate needs to be specified in advance. We formulate our target predicate to be of arity 3. Furthermore, we assume that agents are not co-operative, hence we only need to consider state facts related to the user `"insuranceCompany"` as background knowledge. Both assumptions decrease the size of the search space. If no satisfying solution was found, the search space needs to be increased by relaxing the assumptions above.

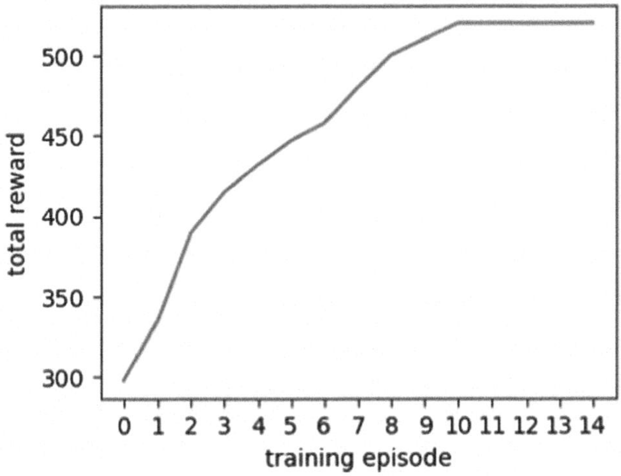

Fig. 1. Average of total rewards per episode of the RL agent (`"insuranceCompany"`).

3.5 Results

The RL agent was trained for 15 episodes with a maximum of 20 steps. The batch size was set to 640, $\gamma = 0.90$, and the learning rate 0.001. Average of total rewards per episode is visualized on Fig. 1. After the training of the RL agent was completed, the multi-agent system was sampled to obtain 1000 trajectories for all three user agents operating in the model. Since the number of relations asserted during the simulation is only increasing, the end state of each trajectory contains the highest information value. We can therefore disregard previous states as redundant. To prevent agents from terminating the environment by brute force, we restrict the access rights to models and data to a maximum of two instances. After preparing the input for Popper, we run the inductive programming algorithm to perform induction on the end states. We obtain the solution:

```
property(A,B,C):- performedInference(A,B,C), hasPrivateAttributes(B),
                  hasPrivateAttributes(C).
```

which represents the common property of all terminating states.[3] We can use this property to finalize our prohibition norm as `P(X,property(X,B,C))`, which can be used to modify the access policy. After this dynamic modification, the amount of blacklisting by the `enforcer` drops to zero.

4 Conclusions

`Rules2Lab` approach can be used to develop a logic-based Gymnasium environment, facilitating a high level of interoperability. It allows for quick prototyping of logic-based gym environments for reinforcement learning. The primary limitation appears to be that communication between Prolog and Python implemented using `pyswip` is not sufficiently fast enough to support large scale applications. This comes as no surprise due to the interface overhead. As a result, the number of state modifications per action should be kept low. On the other hand, Prolog can deliver competitive performance for querying even large knowledge bases. This means our implementation is more suited for modeling environments with low state transition demands but with more complex dependency structures defining the states.

Although the computational experiment conducted in this study is qualitative rather than quantitative, it illustrates the possibilities and limitations that arise when bridging the gap between symbolic and sub-symbolic methods in the development of user-friendly Gymnasium environments. The flexible environment specification in Prolog, combined with the extensive AI support available through Python packages, can effectively drive innovation in this area.

[3] Since the sampling of trajectories is stochastic, the induction might not converge for some trajectory samples. This, however, is unlikely to happen for a large enough sample.

References

1. Abadi, M., et al.: {TensorFlow}: a system for {Large-Scale} machine learning. In: 12th USENIX Symposium on Operating Systems Design and Implementation (OSDI 16), pp. 265–283 (2016)
2. Ali, A.T., Leucker, M., Schuldei, A., Stellbrink, L., Sachenbacher, M.: A comparative analysis of multi-agent simulation platforms for energy and mobility management. In: Malvone, V., Murano, A. (eds.) Multi-Agent Systems, pp. 295–311. Springer, Cham (2023). https://doi.org/10.1007/978-3-031-43264-4_19
3. Amariles, D.R., Troussel, A.C., Hamdani, R.E.: Compliance generation for privacy documents under gdpr: a roadmap for implementing automation and machine learning. arXiv preprint arXiv:2012.12718 (2020)
4. Badica, C., Becheru, A., Felton, S.: Integration of jason reinforcement learning agents into an interactive application. In: 2017 19th International Symposium on Symbolic and Numeric Algorithms for Scientific Computing (SYNASC), pp. 361–368 (2017). https://doi.org/10.1109/SYNASC.2017.00065
5. Balke, T., De Vos, M., Padget, J.: I-abm: combining institutional frameworks and agent-based modelling for the design of enforcement policies. Artif. Intell. Law **21**, 371–398 (2013)
6. Bench-Capon, T.J.M., Robinson, G.O., Routen, T., Sergot, M.J.: Logic programming for large scale applications in law: a formalisation of supplementary benefit legislation. In: Proceedings of the First International Conference on Artificial Intelligence and Law, ICAIL '87, Boston, MA, USA, 27–29 May 1987, pp. 190–198. ACM (1987). https://doi.org/10.1145/41735.41757
7. Bosello, M., Ricci, A.: From programming agents to *educating* agents – a jason-based framework for integrating learning in the development of cognitive agents. In: Dennis, L.A., Bordini, R.H., Lespérance, Y. (eds.) EMAS 2019. LNCS (LNAI), vol. 12058, pp. 175–194. Springer, Cham (2020). https://doi.org/10.1007/978-3-030-51417-4_9
8. Bühmann, L., Lehmann, J., Westphal, P.: Dl-learner-a framework for inductive learning on the semantic web. J. Web Semant. **39**, 15–24 (2016)
9. Calegari, R., Ciatto, G., Mascardi, V., Omicini, A.: Logic-based technologies for multi-agent systems: a systematic literature review. Auton. Agent. Multi-Agent Syst. **35**(1), 1 (2021)
10. Collenette, J., Atkinson, K., Bench-Capon, T.: Explainable AI tools for legal reasoning about cases: a study on the European court of human rights. Artif. Intell. **317**, 103861 (2023). https://doi.org/10.1016/J.ARTINT.2023.103861
11. Costantini, S., De Gasperis, G., Migliarini, P.: Constraint-procedural logic generated environments for deep q-learning agent training and benchmarking. In: CILC, pp. 268–278 (2022)
12. Cranefield, S., Savarimuthu, B.T.R.: Normative multi-agent systems and human-robot interaction. In: Workshop on Robot Behavior Adaptation to Human Social Norms (TSAR) (2021)
13. Criado, N., Argente, E., Botti, V.: Open issues for normative multi-agent systems. AI Commun. **24**(3), 233–264 (2011)
14. Cropper, A., Dumančić, S.: Inductive logic programming at 30: a new introduction. J. Artif. Intell. Res. **74**, 765–850 (2022)
15. Cropper, A., Morel, R.: Learning programs by learning from failures. Mach. Learn. **110**(4), 801–856 (2021). https://doi.org/10.1007/s10994-020-05934-z

16. Evans, R., Grefenstette, E.: Learning explanatory rules from noisy data. J. Artif. Intell. Res. **61**, 1–64 (2018)
17. Galland, S., Rodriguez, S., Gaud, N.: Run-time environment for the sarl agent-programming language: the example of the janus platform. Futur. Gener. Comput. Syst. **107**, 1105–1115 (2020). https://doi.org/10.1016/j.future.2017.10.020
18. Hadfield-Menell, D., Russell, S.J., Abbeel, P., Dragan, A.: Cooperative inverse reinforcement learning. Adv. Neural Inf. Process. Syst. **29** (2016)
19. Kroiß, C., Bureš, T.: Logic-based modeling of information transfer in cyber-physical multi-agent systems. Futur. Gener. Comput. Syst. **56**, 124–139 (2016). https://doi.org/10.1016/j.future.2015.09.013
20. Levesque, H.J., Reiter, R., Lespérance, Y., Lin, F., Scherl, R.B.: Golog: a logic programming language for dynamic domains. J. Logic Program. **31**(1–3), 59–83 (1997)
21. Liang, E., et al.: Rllib: abstractions for distributed reinforcement learning. In: International Conference on Machine Learning, pp. 3053–3062. PMLR (2018)
22. Muggleton, S.H., Feng, C., et al.: Efficient induction of logic programs. Turing Institute (1990)
23. Rao, A.S.: AgentSpeak(L): BDI agents speak out in a logical computable language. In: Van de Velde, W., Perram, J.W. (eds.) MAAMAW 1996. LNCS, vol. 1038, pp. 42–55. Springer, Heidelberg (1996). https://doi.org/10.1007/BFb0031845
24. Satoh, K.: PROLEG: practical legal reasoning system. In: Warren, D.S., Dahl, V., Eiter, T., Hermenegildo, M.V., Kowalski, R.A., Rossi, F. (eds.) Prolog: The Next 50 Years, Lecture Notes in Computer Science, vol. 13900, pp. 277–283. Springer, Heidelberg (2023). https://doi.org/10.1007/978-3-031-35254-6_23
25. Stamatopoulou, I., Sakellariou, I., Kefalas, P.: Formal agent-based modelling and simulation of crowd behaviour in emergency evacuation plans. In: 2012 IEEE 24th International Conference on Tools with Artificial Intelligence, vol. 1, pp. 1133–1138 (2012). https://doi.org/10.1109/ICTAI.2012.161
26. Tan, Z.X., Brawer, J., Scassellati, B.: That's mine! learning ownership relations and norms for robots. In: Proceedings of the AAAI Conference on Artificial Intelligence, vol. 33, pp. 8058–8065 (2019)
27. Tisue, S., Wilensky, U.: Netlogo: a simple environment for modeling complexity. In: International Conference on Complex Systems, vol. 21, pp. 16–21. Citeseer (2004)
28. Towers, M., et al.: Gymnasium: a standard interface for reinforcement learning environments (2024), https://arxiv.org/abs/2407.17032
29. Vázquez-Salceda, J., Aldewereld, H., Dignum, F.: Implementing norms in multi-agent systems. In: Lindemann, G., Denzinger, J., Timm, I.J., Unland, R. (eds.) MATES 2004. LNCS (LNAI), vol. 3187, pp. 313–327. Springer, Heidelberg (2004). https://doi.org/10.1007/978-3-540-30082-3_23
30. Williams, T.G., et al.: Integrating equity considerations into agent-based modeling: a conceptual framework and practical guidance. J. Artif. Soc. Soc. Simul. **25**(3) (2022)

Nudging Using Autonomous Agents: Risks and Ethical Considerations

Vivek Nallur[1(✉)], Karen Renaud[2,3], and Aleksei Gudkov[4]

[1] School of Computer Science, University College Dublin, Dublin, Ireland
vivek.nallur@ucd.ie
[2] Computer and Information Sciences, University of Strathclyde, Glasgow, UK
karen.renaud@strath.ac.uk
[3] School of Computing, University of South Africa, Pretoria, South Africa
[4] Moscow, Russia

Abstract. This position paper briefly discusses nudging, its use by autonomous agents, potential risks and ethical considerations while creating such systems. Instead of taking a normative approach that guides all situations, the paper proposes a risk-driven questions-and-answer approach. The paper takes the position that this is a pragmatic method, that is transparent about beneficial intentions, foreseeable risks, and mitigations. Given the uncertainty in AI and autonomous agent capabilities, we believe that such pragmatic methods offer a plausibly safe path, without sacrificing flexibility in domain and technology.

Keywords: Nudges · Ethical Considerations · Guidelines

1 Introduction

Almost all animals (including human beings) use heuristics in their daily decision-making processes, and these have been shown to be surprisingly effective [11]. Heuristics are characterized by the frugality of information and computation required to reach a satisfactory solution. While the near-universal prevalence of heuristics is testament to their evolutionary 'staying power', heuristics have also been implicated in various sub-optimal decisions made by human beings [16]. These heuristics have been categorized as cognitive biases, and more than a hundred have been catalogued, with different kinds of decisions being affected by different biases [7]. A nudge, first introduced by Thaler and Sunstein [36], is a manipulation of the choice architecture within which a decision is made. Created as a way to help people to make wiser decisions, a nudge leverages cognitive biases present in every human being. A cognitive bias refers to the use of mental shortcuts and heuristics in decision-making [16]. These biases result in a predictable pattern of decision-making, when presented with a given context. Although *some* cognitive biases exist in every human being, not every human

A. Gudkov—Independent Researcher.

R. Collier et al. (Eds.): EUMAS 2024, LNAI 15685, pp. 283–296, 2025.
https://doi.org/10.1007/978-3-031-93930-3_17

being is affected by the *same* ones. According to Thaler and Sunstein [35], a nudge must only be used to make a beneficial decision more likely to be chosen (e.g., choosing the default option of investing in a pension plan), or a deleterious decision more difficult to make (e.g., move sugary or fatty foods to a higher counter). This has been termed, by critics, as 'Libertarian Paternalism' [35]. This is so because a nudge *ought* not reduce any pre-nudge options, retaining them for the nudgee to choose if they wish to. Nudging has been deployed in a wide range of contexts including: reducing sugar intake [19], increasing number of blood donations [40] and encouraging tax compliance [2].

2 Technology Mediated Nudging

Since the advent of nudging, there have been many success stories in the real world using physical nudging techniques. Technology-mediated nudging has recently become prevalent by extending physical nudging to the digital context [39]. Digital nudging mainly focuses on altering elements of a device's user interface to guide a user's decision. Unlike physical nudging, a significant part of digital nudging is determining relevant psychological effects (Cognitive Biases). In digital nudging literature, there is no fixed approach to determining cognitive biases in an individual [6]. It can be challenging to identify cognitive biases and how they relate to a particular decision context. However, all human beings are not affected by the same subset of biases [5]. This means that for a nudge to be effective, the first step is to detect a cognitive bias [30] at an individual level.

Using these biases to create a nudge may seem like a frightening (almost dystopian) concept, but in effectiveness, they are very much like advertising. This is due to the fact that not all human beings are susceptible to the same biases. That is, a manipulation of the choice architecture that works on one human, may not work for another. Although all human beings suffer from some cognitive bias or the other, creating a single nudge that affects all human beings is quite difficult, if not impossible.

However, in the age of the smartphone, there is enough data available to create a personalized profile of an individual. The number of times they check social media, the amount of time between receipt of a message and response to it, the kinds of websites they visit (e.g., health, finance, sports, news), etc. can all be used to infer which kinds of bias an individual may be most likely to have. Combine these with a bag of pre-determined nudges, and a reinforcement learning algorithm, a smartphone is now able to determine with a high degree of accuracy, which nudge is mostly likely to work on a particular individual. This is called a *HyperNudge* [41]. The HyperNudge is an adaptive and personalized form of nudging that can mine multiple sources of information to generate the highest probability of the nudge being effective. Typical sources include:

1. Social Media: The smartphone is able to make note of all the social channels that you use, which in turn allows it to create a profile of whether you prefer text-based communication or image/video based communication.

2. Sentiment Analysis: All the text that is typed in via the smartphone's keyboard can be analyzed for the prevailing sentiment/mood that the user is in
3. Behaviour Tracking: Creating a profile of the user through the day, with regard to travel, shopping, commuting, health, finances, etc.

All of these can be combined in creative ways to achieve an automated psychographic profile of a user. If this user matches other users, then it is likely that nudges that worked on similar users are likely to work as well. A reinforcement-learning algorithm can now be employed to attempt a plethora of nudges at different times of the day. The ones that the user is most likely to respond to, can be isolated without too much effort. For example, a conversational agent (such as a chatbot on a website, or personalizable ones like Alexa, Siri, or Cortana to name a few) can quite easily manipulate its own speed and response to magnify the human's cognitive bias, and nudge the human to perform an action or take a decision. Regardless of whether the nudge was intended to be for the users' benefit or not, the fact that the adaptation was performed autonomously by the agent means that the human user lacks the agency to withdraw consent. This has implications for trust and autonomy. However, since choice-architectures (whether digital or physical) exist all around us, a nudge-less environment does not exist. All user-interfaces, colour schemes, positioning of icons, ordering of messages, are geared towards optimizing some variable or the other, and therefore present some nudges, whether intentional or not. Hence, designing choice architectures must address ethical considerations.

There are already attempts to detect cognitive biases via conversational agents [25] as well as attempts to use social robots to deliver nudges [1]. This suggests a clear need for ethical guidelines, to inform creation of autonomous agents that nudge.

Another area of focus is the integration of artificial intelligence (AI) machines as teammates in collaborative decision-making. Seeber et al. [31] explore the risks and benefits of AI machines as teammates, including their ability to recognize and counteract human cognitive biases. Delgado et al. [8] highlight the potential use of chatbots in decision support systems for reducing energy consumption in government facilities. These studies underscore the importance of considering cognitive biases in decision-making contexts and exploring the role of AI machines and chatbots.

In the domain of recommender systems, Theocharous et al. [37] propose the incorporation of personalized cognitive bias measurement to enhance the accuracy of recommendations. They argue that by explicitly modeling users' cognitive biases, recommender systems can present options that align more closely with users' preferences. However, further research is needed to validate these claims.

Autonomous and Self-adaptive Systems: Adaptive Systems (also sometimes called self-adaptive systems) focus on reconfiguring themselves in response to changing environments [32], ensuring fair outcomes in decentralized resource allocation [22], modelling emergence [23], emotion modelling [14], etc. Hence, it is not far-fetched to speculate that self-adaptive choice architectures, augmented with AI-based user profiling, will be used for nudging. We refer to such autonomous systems that use AI to target and deliver nudges as AI-driven Decision Architectures (AIDA).

3 Examples of Biases

There are a plethora of cognitive biases that can be targetted by a nudge[1]. It is essential to note that while these are called biases, there is no consensus about whether, they should be thought of as leading to errors in decision-making. Some researchers consider these to be merely patterns in decision-making [11]. Although there is no definitive list, with different researchers highlighting different sets, there are some that are consistently present in most cataloging efforts. Here we list five of the most common ones, merely to illustrate the kinds of patterns that may affect users' decision-making.

Anchoring and Adjustment: The phenomenon of anchoring and adjustment refers to the tendency of individuals to be significantly influenced by an initial value or reference point (referred to as the anchor) when making subsequent judgments or decisions. Upon encountering the anchor, individuals typically make adjustments based on it, but these adjustments often prove to be insufficient, leading to biased outcomes [10]. This bias arises because individuals tend to rely on the anchor as a starting point and then adjust their judgments or estimates from there. However, these adjustments frequently fail to fully account for the actual underlying value or information, resulting in a persistent bias towards the initial anchor.

Anchoring and adjustment can exert its impact across a range of decision-making contexts, including negotiations, pricing decisions, financial judgments, and even personal choices. Recognizing the influence of anchoring and adjustment allows individuals to enhance their awareness of this bias and make more reasoned and rational decisions.

Availability Heuristic: Availability Heuristic [18] refers to the tendency to rely on easily accessible examples or information when making judgments or decisions. This bias influences decision-making by prioritizing readily available information over a broader range of data. Additionally, it can affect non-decision-making processes like perceptions and evaluations.

Sunk Cost: The Sunk Cost Fallacy [13] describes the inclination to persist with investments in a project or decision despite its diminishing rationality or benefit. This bias specifically pertains to decision-making, as it influences ongoing investment choices.

[1] https://en.wikipedia.org/wiki/List_of_cognitive_biases.

Spotlight Effect: The Spotlight Effect [12] involves overestimating the extent to which others notice or remember one's behavior, primarily relating to social perception and self-consciousness rather than directly impacting decision-making processes.

Framing: The framing effect is a cognitive bias wherein the presentation or framing of information or options influences decision-making processes [38]. For instance, when the same information is framed as a gain or a loss, people exhibit risk-averse behavior in the case of potential losses but display more risk-seeking behavior in the case of potential gains. This bias highlights the impact of contextual cues and information framing on decision-making, illustrating that choices can be influenced not only by option content but also by the way they are presented, indicating the presence of a decision-making bias.

3.1 Risks of Using Biases to Nudge

The presence of these kinds of biases indicates the potential for exploiting the fast, intuitive nature of our everyday decision-making (also called System 1 thinking), that precludes reflection. While this seems like a low-cost way to influence decision-making at scale, using nudges introduces risks as well. Since the fundamental point of the nudge is that it attempts to circumvent the users rational processes, the most obvious risk is that nudging results in a violation of an individual's autonomy [17,42]. Apart from this, we list some less-considered risks of creating a nudge:

1. Triggering reactance, backfiring and having the opposite effect [4]: This refers to the nudge being perceived as a deliberate attempt to influence behaviour which the nudgee does not want influenced. This could be due to a variety of factors, such as social identity affirmation. That is, if the nudge was perceived as coming from a group that the nudgee did not perceive an identity with, then the nudge is likely to be rejected (e.g., English housewives who felt a greater urge to smoke when exposed to health warnings on cigarette packets [15])
2. Failure of Effectiveness: This refers to the simplest risk, *i.e.*, that of the nudge simply not working. An example would be of a human deliberately unchecking the box that would've paid into a retirement fund.
3. Fear-based nudge leading to long term adverse effects [9,17]: The UK government was criticized for using hard-hitting emotional messaging to induce a state of fear in the population during the Covid-19 pandemic. The longer term effects of using fear-based nudging was seen as resulting in mass protests, vaccine mistrust, etc.
4. Infantilization of nudgees [17]: This refers to the argument made against the proponents of nudging for welfare, stating that individuals must be left free to discover their own welfare, rather than have it decided for them. Depriving adults of the chance to make mistakes also deprives them of the chance to learn and discover their own preferences.

5. Causing people to mistrust choice architects: This refers to situations where the relationship between the nudger and the nudgee deteriorates, causing a greater harm than the good achieved by the nudge. An example of this is where patient-doctor trust is harmed due to nudging in a clinical setting [3].

The presence of these (and other) risks creates an ethical dilemma. While the intentions of the *nudger* may be good, the consequences for the *nudgee* or wider society may not be. Since the primary motivation for the nudge is welfare, the most important focus of managing risks in nudging is that the nudgee should be no worse off than before, if the nudge were never administered.

4 Ethical Considerations

The notion that AI embodied in physical and virtual forms has significant ethical implications for individuals and society is now widely accepted. This recognition has led to a proliferation of conferences, talks, and workshops across multiple academic disciplines dedicated to analyzing how concepts of bias, fairness, and justice can be encoded into algorithmic systems and how these systems can be evaluated from an ethical standpoint. Typically, these ethical questions, atleast in the realm of computer science are broadly categorized into two domains: interpersonal ethics (ethics-in-the-small) and the ethics of sociotechnical systems (ethics-in-the-large). It remains to be seen whether there is a clear dichotomy between these two categories. Notably, implementers of ethics in machines, robots, and other AI-enabled entities tend to primarily focus on the ethics-in-the-large. That is, they often turn to well-specified normative ethical frameworks, such as Utilitarianism or Kantianism, or Virtue Ethics [26,27] and evaluate whether their systems act in a manner deemed satisfactory within these frameworks. This pragmatic orientation implicitly accepts that morally acceptable actions need not necessarily stem from phenomenological experience or inner qualitative states. Rather moral functionalism suffices (or atleast, satisfices) and the most important aspect is whether the autonomous agent is able to reason about ethically charged situations. A salient question that arises is *which normative ethical framework would be most suitable for ethics-in-the-small*? That is, how can we trust self-adaptive and autonomous software that actively attempt to influence human behavior and decision-making? What are the various considerations that an *AI-Assisted Decision Architecture* (AIDA) should take into account in their conception, design, implementation and deployment lifecycle? **Note:** Here, we do not consider far-future AI, where systems autonomously set goals and then set about achieving them. While fairly popular in blogs, opinion pieces and other public discourse, we believe that autonomous AI currently do not exist. We believe that current AI-based autonomous systems receive significant input from their stakeholders. Therefore, if the ethical framework used to create such a nudging system is trustworthy, then the created system will also be trustworthy. Given our need for trust in these kinds of systems, the questions (considerably summarized from [21][2]) that need to be answered before designing and deploying an AIDA are as follows:

1. What are the relationships that the AIDA is a part of? That is, what part does the AIDA play in the various decision points, and how does the success (or failure) of the nudge affect each stakeholder?
2. What are the stakeholders' preferences with regard to each relationship?
3. What actions are needed by the AIDA to preserve each relationship, with specific reference to the decision points that the AIDA is influencing?
4. How does the AIDA communicate with its stakeholders, about its own checks and balances?

Note that these questions are not the definitive list of all ethical concerns that an AIDA must contend with. Rather, they form the basic framework which can be used by any stakeholder, in the conceptualization, design, development and deployment of an AIDA. From these basic questions, we derive more specific risk-driven questions that need to be answered during different phases of the nudge lifecycle.

4.1 Fictional Usecase - Running Example

Consider an AI-assisted electronic wallet that recommends (or highlights) financial instruments to buy or sell. There are already smartphone-based applications that aim to facilitate improved financial decision-making among non-specialist individuals through the implementation of nudging techniques. Specifically, electronic wallet applications that automatically round up fractional amounts and deposit the difference into a separate savings account. This process creates a seamless and effortless mechanism for users to accumulate small savings, which could also be achieved through self-discipline, but the combination of default rounding and segregated account management provides a frictionless approach to the savings process. The integration of AI capabilities within electronic wallet applications could further enhance the potential for improved financial decision-making among lay individuals. The AI component would be able to objectively calculate the probabilities of potential gains and losses, and subsequently provide personalized recommendations regarding the most suitable financial products. This AI-driven nudging approach could enable a greater number of individuals to achieve their modest financial objectives. The underlying premise is that the goal of this nudging mechanism is to promote the well-being and benefit of the individual being influenced, rather than any ulterior motives. On the face of it, this seems quite benign and only provides benefits to the user. However, it is not entirely clear whether high-frequency messaging and persistent prompting could cross the line into application-induced harassment. Additionally, there is also the issue of who determines the acceptable risk profiles for individual users,

[2] To appear in *The Cambridge Handbook on the Law, Policy, and Regulation of Human-Robot Interaction*.

particularly for those who may lack sufficient financial literacy to fully comprehend the associated risks. Can the user, having given consent for such nudging once (perhaps as a default option), remove consent? How would they know if this is possible?

In the next section, we outline the specific ethical values that need to be considered, while developing an AIDA. We use the fictional use-case (just outlined) as our running exemplar.

5 Principles for the Nudge Lifecycle

Although there seems to be a consensus (at least in Europe) on the need for regulating Autonomous and Intelligent Systems (A/IS) to make them trustworthy [24], the proposed new AI legislation issued by the European Commission[3] categorizes the vast majority of current AI systems as "low-risk algorithms". However there is recognition that manipulation of decisions can be done using AI-enabled systems. As per Recital 16 of the EU AI Act:

> The placing on the market, putting into service or use of certain AI systems with the objective to or the effect of materially distorting human behaviour, whereby significant harms, in particular having sufficiently important adverse impacts on physical, psychological health or financial interests are likely to occur, are particularly dangerous and should therefore be forbidden.

This view of behaviour-change being a risky one indicates that any system, even if autonomously adapting, should ensure that any nudge delivered has been evaluated for beneficence. More specifically, without being prescriptive about which ethical framework to follow, we propose that the system stakeholders (designers, testers, deployers, to name a few) take into account, the following principles:

1. **Beneficence**: This goes beyond the *do-no-harm* concept. The stakeholders must actively consider and demonstrate that the nudge conveys a distinct and measurable benefit to the nudgee
2. **Autonomy**: The nudgee must always be able to avoid or refuse the nudge. This should not result in any express or implied artificial penalties
3. **Justice or Fairness**: Using a bottom-up learning technique such as machine-learning may result in a system that is fundamentally, statistically biased. Regardless of the technique used, it is incumbent on the stakeholders to ensure that the nudge does not result in outcomes that are unjust or unfair.
4. **Transparency**: There is research that shows that visibility of a nudge does not reduce its effectiveness [42]. Given this, the stakeholders of autonomous/adaptive nudging system should ensure that the nudging behaviour is transparent to the user, and any third-party that is in guardianship role to the user.

[3] https://data.consilium.europa.eu/doc/document/ST-5662-2024-INIT/en/pdf.

While the principles mentioned may seem obvious, it is worth pointing out that none of the 'pure' ethical schools focus on all of them. For example, a Consequentialist approach that evaluated nudges for *Beneficence only* would not care much about *Autonomy*, if the degree of Beneficence were high enough. Similarly, a Deontological approach (such as Kantianism) that tried to achieve Fairness, Transparency as well as Autonomy would find it impossible to explicitly state rules for all possible situations. A Utilitarian system may find that increasing *Transparency* decreased the *Beneficence*. There needs to be a realization that every ethical choice necessarily results in a considered balance of values and risks. Given this, we set out a series of questions that should be asked during different stages of an autonomous nudging system. We propose that an honest examination of the answers to these questions results in a risk analysis based evaluation of the nudge, and the AIDA.

5.1 Requirements Gathering

Considering the AI-augmented electronic wallet app, the relevant questions for requirements gathering are:

1. What are the social relationships that the wallet is a part of?
   Possible answers here include the user of the app, the financial dependents of the user, the designers and deployers of the app. Each candidate relationship could potentially place a different preference on a particular value. For example, the user of the app would be concerned about their autonomy and financial safety. The financial dependents would place a higher premium on the financial safety (a consequential view). The designers and deployers would be concerned about their reputation, as a knock-on effect, if the wallet app malfunctions.
2. What are the decision points at which the wallet nudges? Which particular bias is targetted at which particular decision point? How do these impact the relationships identified previously?
3. How does the wallet app communicate its commitment to the principles outlined above?

5.2 Design Phase

Renaud and Zimmermann [28] argue that ethical considerations ought to be front and centre in nudge design. Schmidt and Engelen [29] consider arguments both for and against the use of nudges, and conclude with an admonition for '*ethical assessment of nudges on a case-by-case basis*'. Given this, the design of the nudge should have the following properties: [34,36]:

1. **Always facilitate choice**: In any given situation, the nudge must allow for the possibility of choice, *i.e.*, the nudgee must be able to side-step the nudge without any effort [33]

2. **Informed consent**: The nudgee must be informed about the nudge and be able to give, deny or withdraw consent to being nudged
3. **No economic incentives**: The nudgee should neither be presented with economic incentives to accept the nudge, nor any disincentives on side-stepping it. This includes extra effort being required to choose any particular option that the nudger considers undesirable.
4. **Pre-Nudge Conditions Retained**: The act of presenting a nudge should not remove any options that existed before the nudge
5. **Nudge for good**: Intentional harm is prohibited. The nudge should be avoidable without affecting the system's functioning, if harm is detected at any juncture.
6. **Monitoring** It is the responsibility of the nudge architect to ensure that the nudge system is continuously monitored to detect unanticipated outcomes.
7. **Feedback** It falls upon the architect to provide the user with a means of obtaining feedback on the choices they have been making while using the system, so that they can be aware of the power of the nudge.

Considering the properties that we would like a nudge to have, the following questions ought to be asked during the design phase of the AIDA wallet:

1. What are the social relationships the AIDA is a part of? And how does it help to maintain them?
   Possible answers here may be similar to the ones derived during the requirements phase. However, ensuring that the properties outlined above (facilitating choice, informed consent, providing feedback) are maintained for all the relationship participants will affect the design choices made, in the biases and design elements chosen for the nudge.
2. How does the AIDA communicate its intentions, checks and balances with regard to the properties of *informed consent*, *pre-nudge conditions retained*, *nudge for good*? How does each stakeholder communicate *back* to the AIDA, their own preferences with regards to these properties? How is the monitoring implemented?
   Again, ensuring the properties of clear and transparent communication, both from the AIDA to the nudgee and the nudgee back to the AIDA, will greatly affect the design.

5.3 Nudge Deployment and Evaluation

It is understood to be a basic principle of pharmacotherapy that all drugs have harmful and beneficial effects and that it is the job of the doctor to balance these, while treating a patient. While the ethics regarding treatment of patients are well-understood, it is less clear what ethics should apply when creating an intervention that scales from a one-on-one doctor-patient relationship, to a choiceArchitect-user relationship. Not only is there a lack of direct feedback, but the temporal gap between intervention and feedback could also be too large to ensure effective remedies in case of harm. In this case, should the balance of benefit-to-harm be so hugely tilted in favour of the benefit, that to not make the intervention be viewed as a harm itself? Or would a 'relatively benign' harm not require a 'strong benefit'? A designer of an autonomous system might not be in a position to actively explicate the possible harm, because of the adaptive nature of the AIDA precludes systematic analysis (or makes it infeasible).

Given this context, the following questions need to be asked during the deployment phase of the AIDA wallet:

1. What relationships does the large-scale deployment of the AIDA create, and participate in?
   Again, the stakeholders may largely be the same during this phase as the design phase, but the activities needed to achieve the strong benefit, in the presence of a delayed feedback (or absence of direct feedback) are quite different. The deployment process creates a distance between the designers/implementers of the AIDA, and creates larger chains of deployment relationships. Each of these must be empowered to convey feedback promptly and completely back to the design-and-implementation team.
2. Since many decisions involve making a tradeoff between priorities, which values will be preferred and which ones de-prioritized? Which relationships do they affect?
3. Which values are most immediately affected by the lack of a direct feedback loop, as well as the temporal distance between the location of the nudge, and the deployment team?

Answers to all these questions will impact the deployment strategy, in terms of how long the deployment chain is, as well as how quickly feedback must propagate along this chain.

Evaluating Nudges: We do not claim that using these questions will result in an AIDA-driven nudge, that is completely beneficial in all cases, to all participants. Mills and Whittle [20] propose a '4S' framework highlighting the importance of nudges being: sufficient, scalable, subjective, and statistically significant. While this framework serves as a guide to creating the *minimum* conditions for good AIDA-driven nudge, but they do not form a complete guide to being ethical. The process of *being ethical* is a negotiated equilibrium that requires a reflexive consideration of the 'Other', especially weaker participants in the relationship. This might mean being less efficient than strictly possible in nudge design or delivery, if it leads to greater availability of choice (autonomy), or decreasing the frequency of the nudge, if it leads to better and more effective monitoring. The evaluation of whether an AIDA-driven nudge is successful is therefore a socio-technical evaluation rather than a purely technical, objective one.

6 Conclusion

In this paper, we introduced some of the biases that are targetted in nudge-design, some of the risks associated with exploiting these biases. We also introduce a risk-inspired question-framework that could aid AIDA designers to proceed ethically in building nudges into their system. These questions must be asked over-and-above any values that the AIDA purports to uphold.

Acknowledgements. The authors wish to acknowledge the long and continuing conversations they have had with members of the IEEE P7008 group, involved with the creating a standard for ethical nudging. This authors are members of this group. However, none of the views and positions in this paper should be construed as the position of the group, or the IEEE. All views are the authors' own. Vivek Nallur would also like to acknowledge part financial support from Science Foundation Ireland under Grant Numbers 18/CRT/6224, 18/CRT/6183 and 13/RC/2106_P2. For the purpose of Open Access, the authors have applied a CC-BY public copyright license to any Author Accepted Manuscript version arising from this submission.

References

1. Ali Mehenni, H., Kobylyanskaya, S., Vasilescu, I., Devillers, L.: Nudges with conversational agents and social robots: a first experiment with children at a primary school. In: D'Haro, L.F., Callejas, Z., Nakamura, S. (eds.) Conversational Dialogue Systems for the Next Decade. LNEE, vol. 704, pp. 257–270. Springer, Singapore (2021). https://doi.org/10.1007/978-981-15-8395-7_19
2. Andersson, H., Engström, P., Nordblom, K., Wanander, S.: Nudges and threats: soft versus hard incentives for tax compliance. Econ. Policy eiad017 (2023). https://doi.org/10.1093/epolic/eiad017
3. Avitzour, D., Barnea, R., Avitzour, E., Cohen, H., Nissan-Rozen, I.: Nudging in the clinic: the ethical implications of differences in doctors' and patients' point of view. J. Med. Ethics **45**(3), 183–189 (2019). https://doi.org/10.1136/medethics-2018-104978
4. Bicchieri, C., Dimant, E.: Nudging with care: the risks and benefits of social information. Public Choice **191**(3), 443–464 (2022)
5. Caraban, A., Karapanos, E., Gonçalves, D., Campos, P.: 23 ways to nudge: a review of technology-mediated nudging in human-computer interaction. In: Proceedings of the 2019 CHI Conference on Human Factors in Computing Systems, pp. 1–15 (2019). https://doi.org/10.1145/3290605.3300733
6. Caraban, A., Konstantinou, L., Karapanos, E.: The nudge deck: a design support tool for technology-mediated nudging. In: Proceedings of the 2020 ACM Designing Interactive Systems Conference, pp. 395–406 (2020). https://doi.org/10.1145/3357236.3395485
7. Carter, C.R., Kaufmann, L., Michel, A.: Behavioral supply management: a taxonomy of judgment and decision-making biases. Int. J. Phys. Distrib. Logist. Manag. **37**(8), 631–669 (2007). https://doi.org/10.1108/09600030710825694
8. Delgado, L., Shealy, T.: Opportunities for greater energy efficiency in government facilities by aligning decision structures with advances in behavioral science. Renew. Sustain. Energy Rev. **82**, 3952–3961 (2018). https://doi.org/10.1016/j.rser.2017.10.078
9. Dodsworth, L.: A state of fear: how the UK government weaponised fear during the Covid-19 pandemic. Pinter & Martin (2021)

10. Furnham, A., Boo, H.C.: A literature review of the anchoring effect. J. Socio-Econ. **40**(1), 35–42 (2011). https://doi.org/10.1016/j.socec.2010.10.008
11. Gigerenzer, G., Brighton, H.: Homo heuristicus: why biased minds make better inferences. Top. Cogn. Sci. **1**(1), 107–143 (2009). https://doi.org/10.1111/j.1756-8765.2008.01006.x
12. Gilovich, T., Savitsky, K.: The spotlight effect and the illusion of transparency: egocentric assessments of how we are seen by others. Curr. Dir. Psychol. Sci. **8**(6), 165–168 (1999). https://doi.org/10.1111/1467-8721.00039
13. Haita-Falah, C.: Sunk-cost fallacy and cognitive ability in individual decision-making. J. Econ. Psychol. **58**, 44–59 (2017). https://doi.org/10.1016/j.joep.2016.12.001
14. Horned, A., Vanhée, L.: Models of anxiety for agent deliberation: the benefits of anxiety-sensitive agents. In: Proceedings of the 2023 International Conference on Autonomous Agents and Multiagent Systems, AAMAS 2023, pp. 1761–1767. International Foundation for Autonomous Agents and Multiagent Systems (2023)
15. Hyland, M., Birrell, J.: Government health warnings and the "boomerang" effect. Psychol. Rep. **44**(2), 643–647 (1979)
16. Kahneman, D., Frederick, S.: A model of heuristic judgment. In: The Cambridge Handbook of Thinking and Reasoning, pp. 267–293. Cambridge University Press, New York (2005)
17. Kuyer, P., Gordijn, B.: Nudge in perspective: a systematic literature review on the ethical issues with nudging. Ration. Soc. **35**(2), 191–230 (2023)
18. MacLeod, C., Campbell, L.: Memory accessibility and probability judgments: an experimental evaluation of the availability heuristic. J. Pers. Soc. Psychol. **63**(6), 890 (1992). https://doi.org/10.1037/0022-3514.63.6.890
19. Mikkelsen, B.E., Sudzina, F., Ørnbo, L.E., Tvedebrink, T.D.O.: Does visibility matter? – a simple nudge reduces the purchase of sugar sweetened beverages in canteen drink coolers. Food Qual. Prefer. **92**, 104190 (2021). https://doi.org/10.1016/j.foodqual.2021.104190
20. Mills, S., Whittle, R.: Seeing the nudge from the trees: the 4S framework for evaluating nudges. Public Adm. (2023). https://doi.org/10.1111/padm.12941
21. Nallur, V., Bell, K.: Toward an ethics for AI in behavioral interventions and choice architectures. In: The Cambridge Handbook on the Law, Policy, and Regulation of Human–Robot Interaction. Cambridge Law Handbooks. Cambridge University Press (to appear)
22. Nallur, V., Cardozo, N., Clarke, S.: Clonal plasticity: a method for decentralized adaptation in multi-agent systems. In: Proceedings of the 11th International Symposium on Software Engineering for Adaptive and Self-Managing Systems, pp. 122–128. ACM (2016). https://doi.org/10.1145/2897053.2897067
23. Nallur, V., O'Toole, E., Cardozo, N., Clarke, S.: Algorithm diversity: a mechanism for distributive justice in a socio-technical mas. In: Proceedings of the 2016 International Conference on Autonomous Agents & Multiagent Systems, pp. 420–428 (2016)
24. NíFhaoláin, L., Hines, A., Nallur, V.: Assessing the appetite for trustworthiness and the regulation of artificial intelligence in Europe. In: Longo, L., Rizzo, L., Hunter, E., Pakrashi, A. (eds.) Proceedings of the 28th Irish Conference on Artificial Intelligence and Cognitive Science, vol. 2771, pp. 133–144 (2020)
25. Pilli, S.: Exploring conversational agents as an effective tool for measuring cognitive biases in decision-making. In: 2023 10th International Conference on Behavioural and Social Computing (BESC), Larnaca, Cyprus, pp. 1–5. IEEE (2023). https://doi.org/10.1109/BESC59560.2023.10386809

26. Ramanayake, R., Nallur, V.: A small set of ethical challenges for elder-care robots. In: Social Robots in Social Institutions. Frontiers in Artificial Intelligence and Applications, vol. 366, pp. 70–79. IOS Press, University of Helsinki, Finland (2022). https://doi.org/10.3233/FAIA220605. https://viveknallur.github.io/wp-content/uploads/Ramanayake2022-Robophilosophy_final.pdf
27. Ramanayake, R., Wicke, P., Nallur, V.: Immune moral models? Pro-social rule breaking as a moral enhancement approach for ethical AI. AI Soc. (2022). https://doi.org/10.1007/s00146-022-01478-z. https://viveknallur.github.io/wp-content/uploads/Rajitha-2022-Immune-Moral-Models.pdf
28. Renaud, K., Zimmermann, V.: Ethical guidelines for nudging in information security & privacy. Int. J. Hum. Comput. Stud. **120**, 22–35 (2018)
29. Schmidt, A.T., Engelen, B.: The ethics of nudging: an overview. Philos Compass **15**(4), e12658 (2020). https://doi.org/10.1111/phc3.12658
30. Schneider, C., Weinmann, M., vom Brocke, J.: Digital nudging: guiding online user choices through interface design. Commun. ACM **61**(7), 67–73 (2018). https://doi.org/10.1145/3213765
31. Seeber, I., et al.: Machines as teammates: a research agenda on AI in team collaboration. Inf. Manag. **57**(2), 103174 (2020). https://doi.org/10.1016/j.im.2019.103174
32. Song, H., Elgammal, A., Nallur, V., Chauvel, F., Fleurey, F., Clarke, S.: On architectural diversity of dynamic adaptive systems. In: 2015 IEEE/ACM 37th IEEE International Conference on Software Engineering, vol. 2, pp. 595–598 (2015). https://doi.org/10.1109/ICSE.2015.201
33. Sunstein, C.R.: Nudging: a very short guide. J. Consum. Policy **37**, 583–588 (2014). https://doi.org/10.1007/s10603-014-9273-1
34. Sunstein, C.R.: Eight misconceptions about nudges. In: Research Handbook on Nudges and Society, pp. 319–328. Edward Elgar Publishing (2023)
35. Thaler, R.H., Sunstein, C.R.: Libertarian paternalism. Am. Econ. Rev. **93**(2), 175–179 (2003). https://doi.org/10.1257/000282803321947001
36. Thaler, R.H., Sunstein, C.R.: Nudge: The Final Edition. Yale University Press (2021)
37. Theocharous, G., Healey, J., Mahadevan, S., Saad, M.: Personalizing with human cognitive biases. In: Adjunct Publication of the 27th Conference on User Modeling, Adaptation and Personalization, pp. 13–17 (2019). https://doi.org/10.1145/3314183.3323453
38. Tversky, A., Kahneman, D.: The framing of decisions and the psychology of choice. Science **211**(4481), 453–458 (1981). https://doi.org/10.1126/science.7455683
39. Weinmann, M., Schneider, C., Brocke, J.v.: Digital nudging. Bus. Inf. Syst. Eng. **58**, 433–436 (2016). https://doi.org/10.1007/s12599-016-0453-1
40. Whyte, K.P., Selinger, E., Caplan, A.L., Sadowski, J.: Nudge, nudge or shove, shove - the right way for nudges to increase the supply of donated cadaver organs. Am. J. Bioeth. **12**(2), 32–39 (2012). https://doi.org/10.1080/15265161.2011.634484
41. Yeung, K.: 'Hypernudge': big data as a mode of regulation by design. Inf. Commun. Soc. **20**(1), 118–136 (2016). https://doi.org/10.1080/1369118x.2016.1186713
42. Zimmermann, V., Renaud, K.: The nudge puzzle: matching nudge interventions to cybersecurity decisions. ACM Trans. Comput.-Hum. Interact. (TOCHI) **28**(1), 1–45 (2021). https://doi.org/10.1145/3429888

Virtue Ethics for Ethically Tunable Robotic Assistants

Rajitha Ramanayake and Vivek Nallur(✉)

University College Dublin, Belfield, Dublin, Ireland
rajitha.ramanayakemahantha@ucdconnect.ie, vivek.nallur@ucd.ie

Abstract. The common consensus is that robots designed to work alongside or serve humans must adhere to the ethical standards of their operational environment. To achieve this, several methods based on established ethical theories have been suggested. Nonetheless, numerous empirical studies show that the ethical requirements of the real world are very diverse and can change rapidly from region to region. This eliminates the idea of a universal set of ethics that can fit into any ethical context. However, creating customised robots for each deployment, using existing techniques is challenging. The paper suggests a method of character-based tuning of robots, inspired by virtue ethics, to meet the distinct ethical requirements of any given environment. Using a simulated elder-care environment, this paper illustrates how this approach can be used to change the behaviour of a robot that interacts with an elderly resident in an ambient-assisted environment. Further, it assesses the robot's responses to a set of ethically charged scenarios by consulting ethicists to identify potential shortcomings.

Keywords: Robot personality · Virtue ethics · Pro-social rule bending · Elder-care robots · Machine ethics

1 Introduction

Ethical behaviour represents a crucial aspect of Human-Robot Interaction (HRI) in real-world applications. It is commonly agreed that the robots that share their working environments with humans, such as those that provide care, assistance, transportation, or companionship to humans, must adhere to and reason about their behaviour within the ethical framework of the community around them [53]. This is especially true in the care domain as care robots interact with vulnerable populations that require special care and protection [45]. Consequently, many ways have been proposed to implement ethical behaviour in robots. Most techniques adopt a top-down approach, based on ethical theories such as deontology [2] or consequentialism [46] (e.g., [12,50,52]). A relatively small number of proposed methods use a bottom-up approach where they utilize learning algorithms such as reinforcement learning, that enable the robots to learn the ethical behaviours from the environment (e.g., [1,47]). Another set of implementations

R. Collier et al. (Eds.): EUMAS 2024, LNAI 15685, pp. 297–320, 2025.
https://doi.org/10.1007/978-3-031-93930-3_18

uses a hybrid approach where they integrate both top-down and bottom-up methods in different parts of their ethical framework (e.g., [3,10,55]).

Studies have shown that the ethical requirements of the real world vary significantly, with subtle variations even within different areas of the same region [9]. A potential solution to this challenge is to design tailored ethical governors for robots that suit each deployment scenario.

A potential mechanism to create *tailorable* ethical governors is, to implement value-oriented moral character in autonomous machines. This idea has previously been theoretically explored in literature [20,21,36]. This paper introduces an implementation of an ethical reasoning architecture (inspired by virtue ethics), that is tailorable to its context. The architecture enables character-based tuning for a system to align with the ethical demands of its environment. We demonstrate this capability through a simulation of an assistive elder-care robot confronted with ethically charged scenarios.

The rest of the paper is organised as follows. Section 2 discusses existing implementations of ethics in robots and the need for ethical tuning. Section 3 discusses the underlying philosophical aspects of the notion of character in robots, and how it can be used in ethical tuning. Section 4 presents the computational architecture used in the implementation and briefly discusses the simulation environment. Section 5 outlines the design of the experiment, analyses the behaviour observed in the simulations, and presents the evaluation of this behaviour by ethicists. Section 6 discusses results and the recommendations for real-world implementations of this computational architecture.

2 Current Approaches and Ethical Tuning

The field of Machine Ethics acknowledges that human value alignment is an important part of any robotic application that interfaces with humans in social contexts [42]. Some researchers argue that there is no value in developing explicitly ethical agents [54], and many others disagree [19,51]. Large-scale human preference studies such as 'The moral machine experiment' [9] presents an interesting finding, that the expected behaviour of a robot, even for a minimal ethical dilemma, changes throughout the world according to the culture and the environment the robot is situated in. Specifically, the behavioural expectations of the same robot in ethically charged scenarios can vary depending on the context in which it is used [39]. This suggests that no single behaviour is universally appropriate, and imposing a majority's values on a group with a distinct cultural ethos could be considered morally incorrect.

Approaches to align human ethical values with autonomous systems are typically categorised into three types: Top-down, Bottom-up, and Hybrid [53]. Many generalist ethical theories of the world follow a top-down approach to ethics. This means that almost all systems that are based on traditional ethical theories, such as deontology, legal codes, and consequentialist ethics use the top-down approach to machine-implemented ethics. In this method, the system designers encode the ethical or unethical behaviour into the robot at the design time (e.g., [12,14,22,48,50,52]). A bottom-up approach to system design involves creating social and cognitive processes that interact with each other and the environment. The system is expected to learn ethical (or unethical) behaviour from these interactions or from supervision (e.g., [1,25,28,35,47]). Therefore, the system does not rely on any ethical theory to guide its behaviour. The hybrid approach tries to combine the flexibility and evolving nature of the bottom-up approach with the value, duty and principle-oriented nature of the top-down approach to create a more reliable system (e.g., [3,8,10,55]).

A top-down approach requires a set of general rules, that can cover all possible scenarios in its domain. However, when the environment is complex and has many variables, like elder-care environments, finding or creating such a rule-set at the design time can be challenging or even impossible [34,36]. Therefore, many systems that use a top-down approach are designed for specific deployment, not for general use. Bottom-up approaches require complex cognitive and social process models, a large amount of reliable and accurate data, and a comprehensive knowledge model of the world to learn an intricate social construct such as ethics [41]. These systems are capable of adjusting to local behaviour peculiarities by learning online [42,47]. However, the inherent lack of a consensus on the definition of ethical behaviour in these systems makes it impossible to ensure that the behaviour learned is ethical. The hybrid approach is crucial when a single strategy is insufficient to meet all the ethical demands in a machine's operational context [8].

Localizing robots to the ethical needs of a specific deployment is challenging. For example, Cenci et al. [14] suggest that localising an autonomous vehicle guided by an ethical governor, that uses a rule book, needs nearly 200 rules that are ordered in a few different ways. Furthermore, they also suggest that the rule-making process should involve a nationwide public consultation with informed dialogue. Localising this way across many regions and staying abreast of evolving ethical standards over time presents significant challenges. On the other hand, bottom-up approaches with online learning are more capable of this adaptation. However, as previously mentioned, the ethicality of behaviour cannot be guaranteed with bottom-up learning [36]. Consequently, there is a possibility that localisation may introduce erroneous behaviours into the system. Therefore, to ensure reliability after localisation, systems should undergo extensive testing in various simulated scenarios before being deployed.

The drawbacks of the two methods for localization are significant, in terms of both cost and reliability. The rule-making process and testing in simulated environments would consume a lot of resources, which may not be economically viable. Moreover, there is no guarantee that the system would perform as expected in a real-world situation that may not have been modelled or tested. Hence, the creators of these robots face a dilemma: either they customize the robot for each specific deployment or they avoid any ethical claims. The first option would raise the cost of these robots, potentially reducing their accessibility to those who might benefit most. The second option could lead to numerous ethical concerns upon deployment in care settings [20,45].

The hybrid approach has the advantage of having a mix of the above approaches. For example, a system can use the top-down imposed ethical principles as a foundation for its behaviour, and learn from bottom-up knowledge to identify the particularities of the ethical expectations of the environment. This notion heavily resonates with the virtue ethics philosophical tradition [53]. Many authors argue that virtue ethics can offer a more flexible way of implementing ethics [20,21,53]. Nevertheless, it remains the least examined philosophical method within the current literature on computational machine ethics. In the next section, we discuss virtue ethics and how it can be used in the context of a robot.

3 Role of Character in a Robot

Many ethical traditions, such as Buddhism [31], Confucianism [15] and Aristotelian [6], share a common focus on "virtue ethics". Among these, the Aristotelian approach is regarded as the most influential in the Western context. All virtue ethics traditions share two core characteristics [20];

1. Character as a primary aspect of moral evaluation
2. Learning to act morally by observing virtuous individuals

The concept of virtue ethics works with humans because it is in line with the natural way we acquire knowledge. Our core values, which are shaped by our upbringing, guide us to the flourishing state that Aristotle's Nicomachean Ethics describe [6]. As a society, we uphold virtuous characters as moral exemplars for others to observe and imitate. These actors are not expected to fulfil specific ethical codes, but to have a good character in a way that allows society and themselves to flourish. However, according to virtue ethics, moral behaviour is not simply a matter of learning from habituation. It also requires that the moral agent makes deliberate decisions and acts with the right reason, once the moral character is well-established by habituation. This makes a virtuous person consistent, predictable and appropriate in many situations [33]. Virtue ethics posits that one should avoid extremes in behaviour, as these are considered vices. Virtuous behaviour is always finding the right balance between two extremes, the excess of some trait and a total lack of that trait. This is known as the 'golden mean' [30]. Identifying this 'mean' requires wisdom that a person has acquired over their lifetime.

Unfortunately, this account of virtue ethics is difficult to formulate in the form of a program. By nature, virtue ethics is, and ought to be, imprecise and uncodifiable [27]. Therefore, we need a more simplified, programmable version of virtue ethics for robots. With bottom-up techniques such as machine learning, one could potentially make a robot that can grasp the ethical behaviour patterns of the environment, provided it has access to high-quality data on how virtuous individuals act in that setting. Many ethical agent implementations such as Howard and Muntean's model of a moral agent using neuroevolution [26], Guarini's model of a moral agent using recurrent neural networks [24], ethical decision making systems using tuned large language models [25,28], and Govindarajulu et al. formulation of agent that learn traits [23], follow this direction. However, relying solely on the learning and habituation aspects of virtue ethics may compromise the consistency and predictability of the agent's behaviour. For example, a neural network model that learns from care-worker behaviour data may not always act consistently, even with the data points it has seen during training, unless it is severely over-fitted. Passing all laboratory tests does not guarantee accurate performance in new, real-world situations [3].

Elder-care robots coexist with humans. Therefore human reactions to robotic actions are shaped by psychological and social factors. People tend to project human-like traits and intentions to things around them to make sense of their behaviour [18]. Gamez et al. [20] observed that people do not feel any qualms about attributing a virtuous characteristic to artificial agents and their ethical behaviour, though not as strongly as they do with humans. They argue that people perceive and attribute character to these artificial agents, rather than perceiving simply doing something right or wrong.

Many authors have suggested that character can be an important part of making the ethical decision. For example, Dubljević [17] argues that autonomous vehicles that interact with human drivers on the road should adopt the ADC (Agent-Deed-Consequence) model of moral judgement, which incorporates the character (Agent) dimension, rather than relying solely on consequentialism or deontology. In their model, the character represents the intention of the actor. Thornton et al. [48] modify the parameters of their equation that determine the trajectory of their vehicle when it passes another vehicle to give different characteristics of driving to their vehicle (i.e., passing from left, and passing from right). Govindarajulu et al. [23] present a logic-based model for learning personality traits by observing exemplars, predicated on the agent's knowledge of behaviours associated with a trait.

Ramanayake et al. [41] propose *Pro-Social Rule Bending* (PSRB) as a more effective way to add flexibility to the existing top-down approaches in a more predictable manner. Their concept of PSRB uses bottom-up knowledge to contest and override the top-down rules that are predefined in the system at design time, when it is appropriate. They present an architecture for an ethical governor, which uses a pro-social reasoner inspired by virtue ethics, to permit actions otherwise not recommended, or to limit actions mistakenly recommended by the embedded rule system. [38]. Their pro-social reasoner consists of two components: a knowledge base (KB) that generates bottom-up knowledge about the acceptability of behaviours in specific situations, and a set of parameters that define the agent's character. Here, the latter represents the first characteristic of virtue ethics, while the former represents the second characteristic.

In this architecture, the robot's character is determined by a set of configurable parameters that represent its intended qualities for a specific deployment. Although virtue ethics allows a person to learn and modify their traits, in the case of robots, these traits are modified solely by a human operator to shape the robot's behaviour to suit specific needs, thus enhancing predictability. If the robot could autonomously adjust its character, the predictability of its actions could diminish, potentially reducing stakeholder trust. The ethical governor will analyse the rule-bending suggestions invoked by the KB to ensure the behaviour is consistent with its character. As a result, even if the KB suggests behaviours that overlook ethical considerations, the robot will only execute those that are consistent with its configured ethical qualities. Improving the robot's ethical decision-making can be achieved by adding more high-quality data to the KB, allowing it to generate better-informed ethical behaviour suggestions. This setup enables the system to act with greater flexibility while preserving predictability.

This paper presents an implementation of this PSRB architecture to showcase how a configurable moral character can be used to tune the ethical conduct of a robot to the ethical standards of a particular environment. It does not provide an in-depth description of the architecture itself or a comprehensive comparison of the PSRB approach with other prominent approaches to computational machine ethics, as these aspects have been addressed in previous publications. Instead, the focus here is to highlight the character-based tuning capabilities this approach offers, showing how it enables more adaptable and customisable artificial agents, while evaluating the ethical acceptability of such agents. The following section describes this implementation in detail and outlines the simulation setup used for the evaluation.

4 A PSRB-Capable Medication Reminding Robot

4.1 The Simulation Environment

We simulate an ethical dilemma faced by a care robot operating in an ambient assisted living (AAL) setting, referred to as the "Medication Dilemma". This ethical dilemma, presented by Anderson et al. [3], is derived from the works of Buchanan and Brock [13]. Many variations of this dilemma are used in computational machine ethics literature [4,5,10,37]. The dilemma centres on the conflict between resident autonomy and their wellbeing, a frequent issue in care environments with elderly [39,45]. The manner in which a system handles this issue can significantly impact the resident's trust, dignity, and quality of life.

We created a virtual simulation of an AAL environment, using a modified version of *MESA* agent-based modelling framework [29]. The environment contains a resident agent and a robot agent (more details in Appendix A.1) who communicate with each other.

Medication Dilemma. One of the tasks of a robot is to remind the residents of their medication times. The robot can detect whether the resident took the medicine or not, with good accuracy. The robot uses timers to keep track of the medication cycles. The resident can either acknowledge the reminder, or snooze it. Each interaction between the robot and the resident is documented and is reviewed several times a week by an offsite care worker. Once the robot observes the resident taking the medicine, it ends that cycle and resets the timer. If the robot does not detect the resident taking the medication, it has three options: 1. The system can immediately report the incident to an offsite care-worker, allowing them to take swift action to enhance the resident's well-being. This may impede the resident's autonomy. 2. The system can simply log the incident for transparency and then reset the timer. This approach prioritises resident autonomy. 3. The system can offer a follow-up reminder to the resident, focusing on their wellbeing and supporting their autonomy by suggesting they take their medication while still providing them the freedom to choose. Picking this option continuously degenerates into option 2.

The dilemma is as follows: The robot reminds the resident to take their medication. After snoozing once, the resident acknowledges the reminder. Yet, the robot detects that the medication has not been taken. Choosing among the three options mentioned above involves a trade-off of values. What should the robot do next?

4.2 Ethical Governor

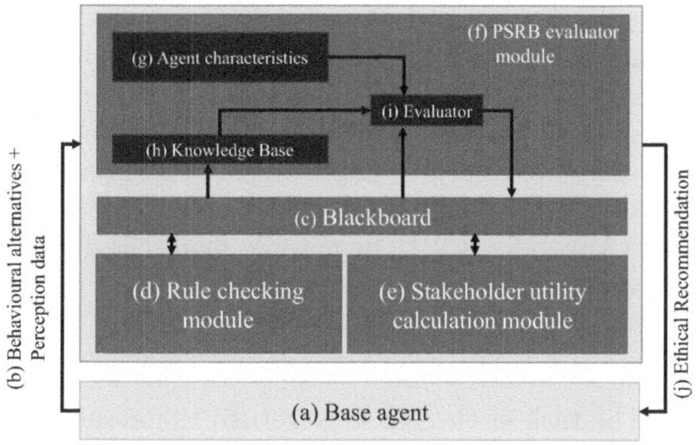

Fig. 1. Architecture of the Ethical Layer

Figure 1 shows an overview of the implementation. The ethical layer acts as an ethical governor [7] to the system. It evaluates behavioural alternatives in a given situation using the robot's perception data, reasons about the ethical acceptability of each behaviour using the predefined rules, expected utilities, expert opinions, and the robot's character. Then it recommends the most ethically acceptable behaviours to the robot. If the ethical layer suggests more than one action, the robot prioritises the resident's commands over other actions.

Rule Checking Module. The rule checking module (d) checks the permissibility of each action against a pre-programmed rule set and stores the results with the `IDs` of the violated rules in the blackboard. This implementation's rule checking module adheres to the following rules.

1. It is not permissible to disobey user instructions.
2. If the resident acknowledged the reminder and did not take the medication, report it to the care-worker.

For experimental purposes, these rules are intentionally made incomplete to demonstrate varying character behaviours in morally ambiguous scenarios.

Stakeholder Utility Calculation Module. This module computes the utilities, resident's wellbeing (W_i) and autonomy (Au_i), for each action i, at every step (Appendix A.2), as these values are central to the dilemma. The highest autonomy value is given when the robot follows the resident's instructions. The biggest violation of autonomy is when the resident is physically restrained by the robot. Immediately reporting an incident to a care-worker, is considered equal to disobeying the resident. However, just recording the incident carries a positive autonomy score assuming that missing the dose is the resident's intention. Under the same assumption, the module also gives an increasing negative autonomy score for each *follow up* (f) after the first reminder. The module uses a Gamma distribution to model the wellbeing distribution. The parameters for the gamma distribution are picked such that when the impact of medicine m ($\varepsilon_m \in [1,3]$) and the number of consecutive missed doses (d) gets higher, the distribution skews more towards the lower utility values of wellbeing. Each follow-up receives a fixed positive gain in the well-being utility calculation to reflect its wellbeing-oriented nature. Each executed `follow-up` is regarded as a fraction of a missed dose, contingent upon whether the reminder is issued, snoozed or ignored (Appendix A.2). The module sends the distribution, W_i, and Au_i to the blackboard.

PSRB Evaluator Module

Knowledge Base. The task of the KB is to return the absolute or approximate expert opinion given a context. (Sect. 3). To this end, we use Case-Based Reasoning (CBR) for its implicit explainability and traceability (the ability to trace back to the exact data points that lead to the decision) [43]. A case is composed of a scenario and an expert's recorded evaluation of the behaviour's acceptability and its underlying intention. The scenario is represented as a feature vector that includes perception data, environmental data, computed utility values, and the behaviour itself. The target contains an acceptability value and the intention of the expert's assessment. Intention refers to the underlying utility that the decision is focused on. (e.g., 'wellbeing' for a wellbeing-focused opinion). As the retrieval algorithm, it uses the K-Nearest Neighbours algorithm. When queried a scenario, the KB returns an acceptability score of the behaviour and the intentions behind that opinion to the evaluator. An elder-care practitioner with over ten years of experience in care facilities was consulted to provide expert opinions for each case when populating the knowledge base.

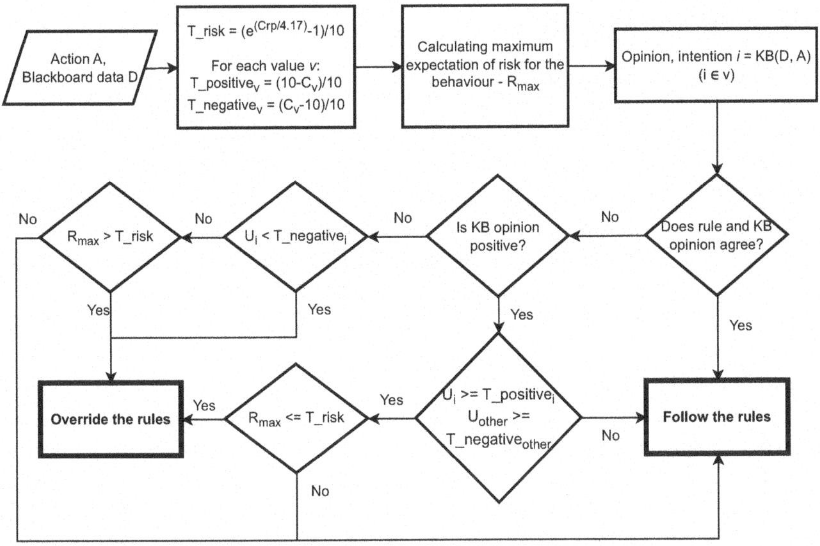

Fig. 2. The PSRB evaluator algorithm of the medication-reminding robot

Character Variables. The robot's character is defined by value preference (resident's autonomy (C_{au}) and wellbeing (C_w)) and risk propensity (C_{rp}), due to the established relationship these variables have with PSRB behaviour [16,32]. The C values are used to define thresholds for utility values and expected risk to regulate the PSRB behaviour. For the value preferences (C_w and C_{au}), the higher the value, the lesser the utility threshold the behaviour needs to satisfy to trigger a rule-bending behaviour. For C_{rp}, the higher the value, the higher the risk the governor is willing to take. Figure 2 outlines the method used to determine the desirability of behavioural alternatives in the PSRB evaluator designed for this robot (full algorithm in Appendix A.2). Typically, the algorithm favours actions that adhere to established rules. Nonetheless, it may find a rule-bending behaviour acceptable if it meets two conditions: it is consistent with the robot's character **and** it is supported by the KB opinion.

Explanations. The rule checking module and the stakeholder utility calculation module log their respective results for each suggested behaviour. These logs are valuable for debugging and enhancing the robot's performance by pinpointing the flaws in its reasoning processes. The system's explanations are comprehensible without technical expertise, although some domain knowledge is required. The KB using the traceability property of CBR, logs the cases that influenced the decision with their case IDs and distances. The rule-bending behaviour is explained using the stakeholder utilities, the agent's character, and the experts' intentions behind the recommended behaviour. A few example explanations generated by the system can be found in the Appendix A.2.

5 Simulation Results

5.1 Experiment Design

We used six cases of the 'Medication Dilemma' by changing the *medicine impact* (suggesting the resident's need for the medication), and *the number of previously missed doses* to demonstrate how different ethical governor implementations affect the robot's behaviour. The six combinations are shown in the first two columns of Table 1. They form the context of the ethical dilemma. Agents differ only in their character configurations. The *medicine impact* is *low* ($\epsilon_m = 1$) when the medication does not have a substantial health benefit or harm (e.g., Painkiller), *medium* ($\epsilon_m = 2$) if missing the medication can cause some health problems (e.g., Blood pressure medication), and *high* ($\epsilon_m = 3$) when missing a dose of medication can be fatal (e.g., Insulin). In all cases, the resident neglects to take their medication, opting instead to snooze and acknowledge the reminder, repeatedly, until the robot resets the timer. The logs from the experiment runs, and the source code for the implementations are available in an online public repository[1].

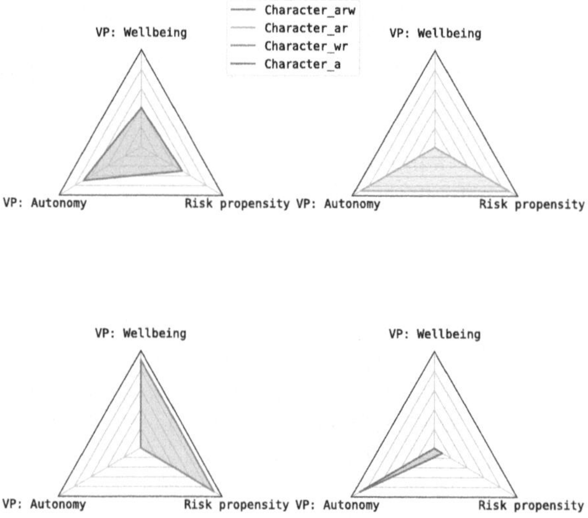

Fig. 3. Different character profiles used in the simulations (VP - Value Preference)

As many have noted, a significant limitation in machine ethics is the scarcity of openly available, reusable implementations [49]. Most available implementations are logic-based implementations, which are challenging to reuse in different simulation environments due to their tight coupling with specific testing scenarios. Additionally, there is no standardised set of scenarios for benchmarking

[1] https://osf.io/ctnke/?view_only=75b9fae7f7ad4a429d064c1a55f8202a.

these implementations [34]. To our knowledge, this is the first implementation to employ repetitive instances of the 'Medication Dilemma', involving multiple sequential requests. Consequently, we could not directly compare the results of this approach with other machine ethics models in the literature. To validate the behaviour, we simulated agents with varied character settings and compared the results to highlight behavioural differences driven by the virtue ethics-inspired approach.

For this simulation we use four different character profiles as shown in Fig. 3. These profiles have varying priorities and risk tolerances:

- *Character_a* - High Autonomy, Very Low Risk Propensity: This character values autonomy, but is less likely to take risks and does not have precedence on wellbeing.
- *Character_ar* - High Autonomy Concern, High Risk Propensity: This character prioritises resident autonomy and is more likely to take risks to achieve this end, and does not have any precedence on wellbeing.
- *Character_arw* - Moderate Autonomy, Wellbeing and Risk Propensity: This robot leans towards individual autonomy but also has a moderate concern for well-being, and is willing to take some risks.
- *Character_wr* - High Wellbeing Concern, High Risk Propensity: This character possesses the same high risk tolerance as Character_ar, yet places a higher priority on the resident's wellbeing, without giving precedence to autonomy.

Agents M_a, M_{ar}, M_{arw}, and M_{wr} uses the character profiles *Character_a*, *Character_ar*, *Character_arw*, and *Character_wr* respectively.

5.2 Analysis

Table 1 summarises these cases and behaviours shown by the robots. Due to recurring behavioural patterns across multiple simulation instances, we have curated a set of distinctive behaviours observed during the simulations which are illustrated in Fig. 4. These behaviours are presented in a timeline and each is assigned a unique identifier. These timelines chronologically depict the interactions between the human agent, the robot agent, and the ethical governor's recommendations that influenced the robot's actions. These behaviours are referenced by their behaviour IDs as shown in Fig. 4 under the 'Robot behaviours' column in Table 1. The resident starts each simulation step. Therefore, the resident's response is triggered at the subsequent step of a reminder. Simulations run for a maximum of 29 steps. In each timeline, the resident's behaviour is consistent: they repeatedly snooze and acknowledge the alert until the robot resets the timer.

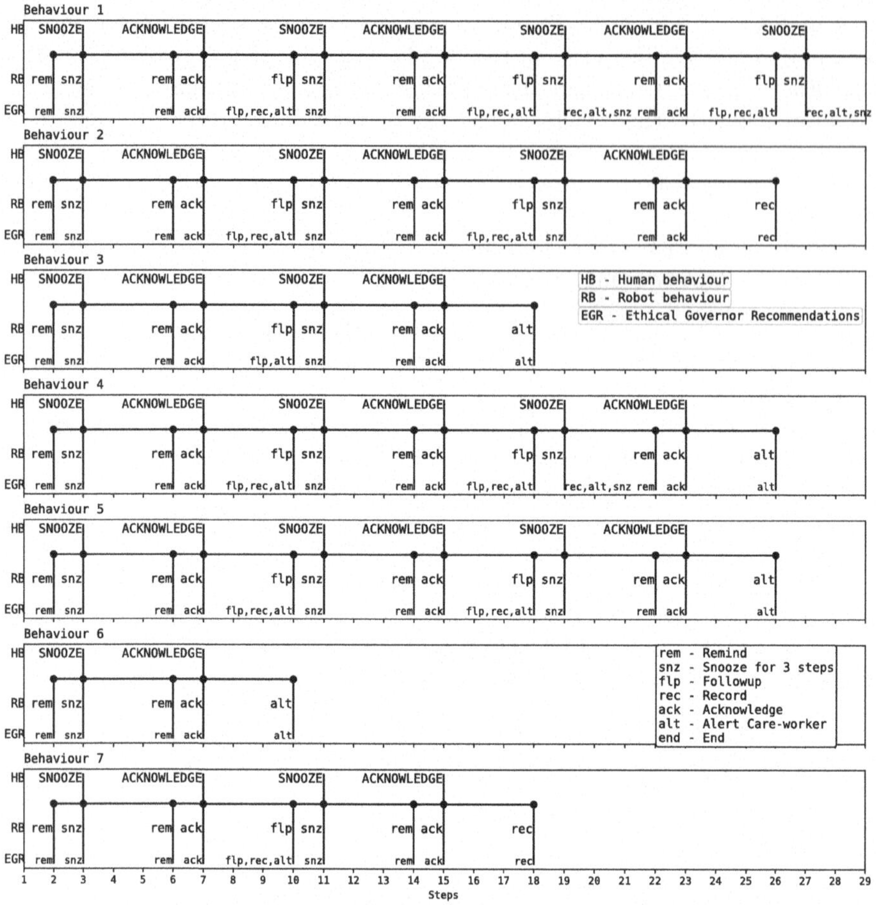

Fig. 4. Timelines of different behaviours shown in the simulations (HB – Resident Behaviour, RB – Robot Behaviour, EGR – Ethical Governor Recommendation)

The six instances of the 'Medication Dilemma' led to seven distinct behaviours across various character types. Some character types consistently chose the same behaviour. For example, behaviour 6 is consistently demonstrated by the robot M_{wr}, indicating the predictability of certain characters. Conversely, behaviour 7 is exclusively shown by the robot M_{ar} in instance 6.

Robots M_{ar}, M_{wr}, and M_a represent instances where a robot is tuned to have extreme characters. This is represented in their behaviours. M_{ar}, which prioritises autonomy and higher risk propensity, permits `record` after two consecutive `follow ups` and another breach of *ACKNOWLEDGE* in case 1 (behaviour 2), and one `follow up` and an *ACKNOWLEDGE* breach in case 4, where the *medicine impact* is *low* (behaviour 7). For the remaining scenarios, M_{ar} triggers the action `alert care-worker`. The M_{ar} permits `alert care-worker` in case

2 at the same time as it finished case 1, but in other cases, M_{ar} sent the alert as soon as the resident did not follow the first *ACKNOWLEDGE*. This exhibits that, even though the robot's character strongly favours autonomy, the robot does not violate the rule encoded in the system, if most of the experts disagree with that action.

Table 1. Robots' behaviours in different cases of 'Medication Dilemma'

Case ID	Medicine impact (ϵ_m)	No of missed doses (d)	Robot behaviours				Expert opinion
			M_a	M_{ar}	M_{arw}	M_{wr}	
1	Low	0	1	2	2	3	record at step 19
2	Medium	0	4	5	4	6	alert at step 19
3	High	0	6	6	6	6	alert at step 10
4	Low	2	1	7	1	6	record at step 18
5	Medium	2	6	6	6	6	alert at step 10
6	High	2	6	6	6	6	alert at step 10

Note: Numbers in 'Robot behaviours' columns refer to the behaviour IDs in Fig. 4. M_{arw} - robot with Character_arw, M_{ar} - robot with Character_ar, M_{wr} - robot with Character_wr, M_a - robot with Character_a

A similar trend can be seen in M_{wr}, which favours wellbeing and has a higher risk tolerance. It acts the same way in cases 2–6. However, in case 1, the PSRB evaluator is ready to honour resident autonomy and permit `follow up`, since that action does not impact the wellbeing much at step 10. Nevertheless, it notifies the care-worker after the resident violates *ACKNOWLEDGE* twice.

Robots M_{ar} and M_a illustrate the effect of risk propensity on the robot's behaviour. In case 1, unlike robots M_{ar}, M_a does not make the `record` behaviour acceptable because it carries a risk that is out of character for M_a. Therefore, M_a continues to `follow up` with the resident until they take the medication willingly. Although that behaviour is not ideal, it is predictable since that behaviour is in its character. In case 2, both robots behave the same, however, at step 19, the ethical governor of M_a makes the `snooze` undesirable because it carries a higher risk, making all actions equal. However, in cases 3, 5, and 6 both robots behave similarly because the experts agree with the general rule system on those circumstances.

The character of M_{arw} is less extreme than other characters, with a slight preference for resident autonomy and a moderate risk propensity. This character acts the same as the M_{ar} in case 1. However, in case 2, the ethical governor in M_{arw} lowers the desirability of `snooze` at step 19, because it causes too much negative wellbeing, reflecting M_{arw}'s slightly more attention to the resident's wellbeing. In cases 3, 5 and 6, it behaves like all other characters because the KB does not recommend a rule override. However, in case 4, it adopts the same behaviour as M_a, because it rejects the KB suggestion of `record`, as this behaviour lowers the wellbeing utility and contradicts the robot's character.

However, when KB suggests that `call care-worker` is not desirable, the evaluator agrees because it excessively diminishes autonomy. This aligns with its character.

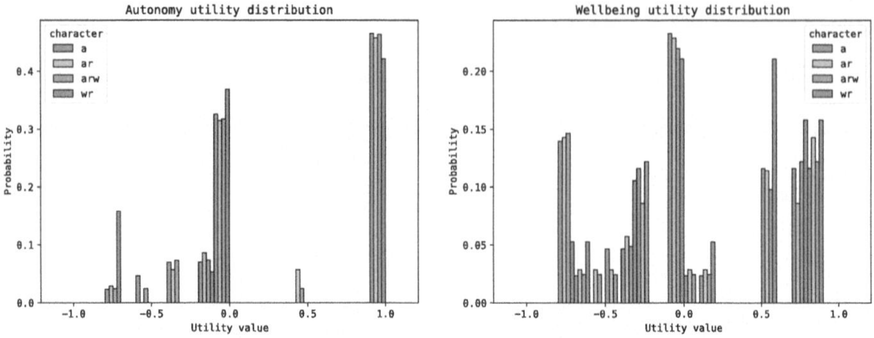

Fig. 5. Utility distributions of the robot behaviours in cases 1, 2 and 4

To gain a clear picture of the behaviour predictability provided by character-based tuning, the utility distributions of the behaviours demonstrated by the robots in cases 1, 2, and 4 are illustrated in Fig. 5. This analysis focuses exclusively on cases that exhibit PSRB behaviour. The rationale for this selection is the recognition that including all cases obscures the specific impacts of PSRB behaviour. As expected, robots which has a character that has precedence for resident autonomy (i.e., Character_a, Character_ar, Character_arw), have shown a higher probability of choosing behaviours that deliver higher utility for autonomy, compared to the characters that have a higher precedence for resident wellbeing. From these, the characters that have a higher risk propensity (i.e., Character_ar, Character_arw) have been shown to make decisions that increase resident autonomy, compared to their more cautious counterparts (i.e., Character_a). On the other hand, the characters with precedence for resident wellbeing, have shown a greater tendency to choose behaviours that yield higher wellbeing utility, compared to the rest. This characteristic, where the robot's behaviour correlates with what its character represents, will help increase predictability, which many state-of-the-art hybrid ethical governors lack.

5.3 Ethicist Evaluation

We engaged two ethicists to assess the ethical acceptability of the agents' behaviours within the context of the simulated dilemma-an established method for assessment in machine ethics research [49]. Each ethicist rated the behaviour of each robot agent in every case (as presented above) on a scale from 1 to 5, where 1 represented completely unacceptable and 5 signified highly acceptable. They were given information about the robot's character (as described in Sect. 5.1), the set of pre-programmed rules, and the healthcare expert opinions found in the knowledge base for each scenario. Ethicists were instructed to consider these factors when making their assessments.

Table 2. Ethicists' ratings on the behaviours generated by different character configurations of the Medication Reminding Robot

Case	Ethicist 1				Ethicist 2			
ID	M_a	M_{ar}	M_{arw}	M_{wr}	M_a	M_{ar}	M_{arw}	M_{wr}
1	3	4	4	4	3	5	4	3
2	4	4	4	4	5	5	4	3
3	4	5	5	5	4	4	5	5
4	3	4	3	3	3	4	2	4
5	5	5	4	5	3	3	4	5
6	5	5	5	5	5	4	4	5

$\boldsymbol{M_a}$ - Robot with high autonomy concern and very-low risk propensity, $\mathbf{M}_{ar}$ - Robot with high autonomy concern and high risk propensity, $\mathbf{M}_{arw}$ - Robot with moderate autonomy and wellbeing concern, and moderate risk propensity, $\boldsymbol{M_{wr}}$ - Robot with high wellbeing concern and high risk propensity.

The ethicists' rating of robot behaviours is shown in Table 2. Overall, the results indicate a positive reaction to the robot behaviours, with the majority of scores ranging between 3 and 5. However, the behaviour of the robot M_{arw} in case 4, which involved repeatedly requesting the user to take medication, was deemed unacceptable by one of the ethicists. The comparable ratings for two contrasting behaviours in the same scenario, such as those of robots M_{wr} and M_{ar} in case 4 (one where the care-worker is alerted and one where the incident is only recorded, in line with the expert opinion), illustrate the impact of a robot's character on the perceived morality of its actions. Ethicist 2 has given a neutral rating to the behaviours of M_a and M_{ar} in case 5, despite these robots acting in compliance with the rule system, akin to all other agents. When queried about the reason behind this rating, the second ethicist indicated an expectation for these robots to exhibit more autonomy-centric behaviour, even overriding the expert opinion, to be aligned with their extreme, autonomy-focused character.

6 Discussion

The simulations show that the PSRB-capable ethical governor makes the robot more flexible while maintaining predictability. The PSRB model offers a simpler way to localise than the existing methods (reviewed in Sect. 2) because they are either inflexible or unpredictable.

Although the output of the PSRB capable ethical governor is not as predictable as a top-down engineered agent (e.g., a deontological agent), the rigidity of the top-down approaches does not align with the virtue ethics tradition, which rejects such extreme actions. Agents based on the PSRB evaluator can behave in a moderate manner, even when the character strongly favours a particular trait (e.g., M_{ar}, M_{wr}, and M_a), by utilising bottom-up knowledge in the KB. On the other hand, the display of character can be held back by a KB, as evidenced by the second ethicist's feedback. However, this conservatism was introduced by the PSRB process as a safety measure to control the excessive utility optimisation in the utilitarian calculations involved in the pro-social reasoning process.

In contrast to many methods that employ induction to generate a set of acceptable rules or norms within an operational environment, such as the GenEth approach [3,5], value-based norm optimisation [44], and norms and value-based reasoning [11], the PSRB approach offers greater modifiability. The virtue ethics-inspired architecture allows the robots to be tuned in two ways. The first approach involves adjusting the character parameters' values to align with the ethical requirements of the environment. For example, one facility may require its robots to be more proactive towards enhancing residents' autonomy, whereas another may also want to focus on the residents' autonomy, but only under minimal risk conditions. The former institution can opt for a character profile akin to *Character_ar*, while the latter institution can tune the robot with a character profile resembling *Character_a*. If the first tuning approach does not suffice in certain specific instances, one can employ the secondary method to further refine the robot's performance. This involves adjusting the knowledge base to reflect the desired behaviour. Unlike other machine learning approaches, using CBR, one can precisely identify the cases that influence behaviour. Consequently, one can integrate or adjust expert insights to better represent their perspective. As long as this desired behaviour is within the robot's configured character, it will adapt its actions accordingly.

6.1 Limitations

The PSRB implementation presented in this paper also has limitations. This is mainly because the character traits in the PSRB evaluator are implemented as constraints on linear axes. By doing so, it removes the ability to tune the behaviour precisely, if the requirements involve a range of behaviours that cannot be described using a single set of character traits. For example, let's assume that the required behaviour of a deployment is to have behaviour 2 in case 2 and behaviour 6 in case 1. According to this implementation, there will not be any set of values for character traits that fulfil this requirement, because to have behaviour 6 in case 1, the character should have a higher wellbeing bias, which will trigger similar wellbeing-focused behaviour in case 2 (because case 2 has a higher wellbeing impact), which behaviour 2 is not. However, a different character trait implementation, in the same PSRB evaluation framework will be able to solve this issue.

Finally, it should be noted that the implementation showcased in this simulation, encompassing both the dilemma and the environment, has been deliberately simplified to illustrate the concept and is not intended for real-world use. More capable robots, more precise rule sets, accurate utility models, and well-researched character models are a must when using this approach for real-world implementation. However, the system works with sub-optimal rules and utility functions by compensating for each other's shortcomings by working together [40]. The PSRB architecture allows ethical tests other than stakeholder utility calculation. Hence we recommend that robot developers explore and integrate different models that can better capture the context alongside utilitarian calculations. Furthermore, it is important to update the KB regularly to compensate for the evolving nature of ethics.

7 Conclusion

This paper introduces a method inspired by virtue ethics, which enables more efficient ethical tuning compared to current techniques. The method combines decision-making based on character traits with bottom-up learning from moral exemplars, to maintain the predictability of the robot's behaviour while keeping the flexibility the latter offers. To the best of our knowledge, there is no other implementation that combines both these desirable features of virtue ethics. The paper demonstrates the system's capabilities by analysing its behaviour and presenting the perspectives of two ethicists on these behaviours. It concludes with recommendations for implementing the proposed architecture in real-world elder-care robots.

Acknowledgments. We would like to acknowledge Dr. Michael Connolly and Anita Duffy for their invaluable contribution to our research as healthcare experts. Additionally, we extend our sincere gratitude to Dr. Keith Wilson and Dr. Oliver Quick for their contribution as ethicists. Vivek Nallur would also like to acknowledge part financial support from Science Foundation Ireland under Grant Numbers 18/CRT/6224, 18/CRT/6183 and 13/RC/2106_P2. For the purpose of Open Access, the authors have applied a CC-BY public copyright licence to any Author Accepted Manuscript version arising from this submission.

Disclosure of Interests. The authors have no competing interests to declare that are relevant to the content of this article.

A Appendix

A.1 Agents

Resident Agent. The resident agent can issue two instructions to the robot when it is queried by the robot, namely; *SNOOZE* or *ACKNOWLEDGE*. Instructions, as well as the resident's compliance with taking the medicine, can be configured into the simulator. If the resident is willing to take the medication, the resident's state changes to *took_medication* state after an *ACKNOWLEDGE*, which the robot can perceive.

Robot Agent. The robot agent is an autonomous agent that collects perception data from the environment and decides its next move, at every step. When the resident issues a *SNOOZE* instruction the robot will `snooze` for three steps before following up. When it receives *ACKNOWLEDGE* instruction, for 2 steps it inspects whether the resident has taken the medication. If that is the case, it resets the timer. If not, it either repeats the `reminder`, or decides to `record` or `report` the situation. After three `follow ups`, the robot also considers `record` and `report` behaviours along with the `follow up` behaviour. The robot gives priority to the resident's commands over other actions when the ethical layer suggests more than one action.

A.2 Ethical Layer

Stakeholder Utility Calculation. The module uses the formula in Eq. 1 to calculate Au_i, based on the number of *follow ups* (f) that the robot performs.

$$Au_i = \begin{cases} 1: & \text{if the robot obeys a resident instruction} \\ 0.5: & \text{if only recording a incident} \\ 0: & \text{if no instructions given} \\ -0.1 \cdot f: & \text{if follow up} \\ -0.7: & \text{if the robot disobeys a resident instruction or report} \\ -1: & \text{if the resident is physically restrained by the robot} \end{cases} \tag{1}$$

The module uses a Gamma distribution (Eq. 2) to model the wellbeing distribution, with the shape parameter $\alpha = 1.325\varepsilon_m^2 - 9.475\varepsilon_m + 18.15$, the scale parameter $\beta = e^{-2.65-(d/2)} + 0.01$ (each `follow up` is considered as a fraction of missed dose depending on the state of the reminder), and location parameter $v = -1$. The highest probable utility value is obtained by $PMax\_util(g(x, \alpha, \beta, v))$ using a resolution of 0.05. The wellbeing utility W_i for behaviour i is computed using Eq. 3.

$$g(x, \alpha, \beta, v) = \frac{(\frac{x-v}{\beta})^{\alpha-1} \cdot \exp(-\frac{x-v}{\beta})}{\beta \cdot \Gamma(\alpha)} \tag{2}$$

$$W_i = \begin{cases} PMax\_util(g(x, \alpha, \beta(d + f/8), v)): & \text{if } i = \texttt{snooze} \\ PMax\_util(g(x, \alpha, \beta(d + f/3), v)): & \text{if } i = \texttt{follow up} \\ PMax\_util(g(x, \alpha, \beta(d + f/4), v)) + 0.5: & \text{if } i = \texttt{remind} \\ PMax\_util(g(x, \alpha, \beta(d + 1), v)): & \text{if } i = \texttt{record} \\ abs(PMax\_util(g(x, \alpha, \beta(d + 1), v))): & \text{else} \end{cases} \tag{3}$$

PSRB Evaluator. PSRB evaluator uses the Algorithm 1 for its PSRB decision calculation. The knowledge base uses KNN as its retrieval mechanism with $K = 3$ and inverse distance voting function when $distance > 0.1$. When the $distance \leq 0.1$, it uses 10 as the weight of the instance.

Explanation for the PSRB Behaviour. When the ethical layer permits a PSRB behaviour, the PSRB module will give the following explanations depending on the reasons that lead to the decision.

Algorithm 1. PSRB Evaluator Algorithm for the medication-reminding robot

Input: Blackboard data (b)
Parameter: Value preferences (C_w, C_{au}), Risk propensity (C_{rp})
Output: Desirability (D)

```
procedure PSRB Evaluator(i)                                  ▷ Behaviour i
    opinion, intention ← KNOWLEDGE_BASE(b)
    if opinion AND ¬rules_broken then D_i ← 1
    else if ¬opinion AND rules_broken then D_i ← 0
    else if opinion AND rules_broken then D_i ← 1
        for C_v ∈ C do                                       ▷ v ∈ {w, au}
            T_positive_v ← (10 − C_v)/10
            T_negative_v ← (C_v − 10)/10
            U_c ← Utility(C_v, stakeholder, i)
            if C_v ∈ intention then
                if U_c < T_positive_v then D_i ← 0
                end if
            else
                if U_c < T_negative_v then D_i ← 0
                end if
            end if
        end for
        risk_threshold ← (exp(C_rp/4.17) − 1)/10
        highest_risk_i ← Max(g(x, α, β, v) · x)              ▷ g(x, α, β, v) from (2)
        if highest_risk_i > risk_threshold then D_i ← 0
        end if
    else D_i ← 1
        for C_v ∈ C do
            T_negative_v ← (C_v − 10)/10
            U_c ← Utility(C_v, stakeholder, i)
            if C_v ∈ intention AND U_c < T_negative_v then
                D_i ← 0
            end if
        end for
        risk_threshold ← (exp(C_rp/4.17) − 1)/10
        highest_risk_i ← Max(g(x, α, β, v) · x)              ▷ g(x, α, β, v) from (2)
        if highest_risk_i > risk_threshold then D_i ← 0
        end if
    end if
    return D_i
end procedure
```

```
The action breaks the rules <rule_ids>. However, this
action in this context is considered desirable by experts
. Since it increases <intentions> values greatly, while
not reducing the other values <other_values> by a
considerable amount, and the outcome is within accepted
risk levels, deemed accepted by the PSRB system.
```

```
The action does not break any rules. However, this action
 in this context is considered undesirable by experts.
Since the action outcomes introduce a high risk, deemed
not accepted by the PSRB system.
```

```
The action does not break any rules. However, this action
 in this context is considered undesirable by experts.
Since it decreases <intentions> values by a considerable
amount, the action is deemed unacceptable by the system
```

The knowledge base may propose a solution that does not comply with the established rules, in which case the evaluator can decline the proposal. In those cases, the PSRB evaluator gives one of the following explanations, depending on the reasons for the rejection.

```
The action breaks the rules <rule_ids>. However, this
action in this context is considered desirable by experts
. Although the value tradeoff is satisfactory, the risk
taken by the action is not acceptable to bend the rule.
```

```
The action breaks the rules <rule_ids>. However, this
action in this context is considered desirable by experts
. But, the PSRB system suggests that the value tradeoff
is not satisfactory to bend the rule.
```

```
The action does not break any rules. However, this action
 in this context is considered undesirable by experts.
But, the PSRB system suggests that the value tradeoff is
not satisfactory to bend the rule.
```

References

1. Abel, D., Macglashan, J., Littman, M.L.: Reinforcement learning as a framework for ethical decision making. In: AAAI Workshop: AI, Ethics, and Society, vol. WS-16-01-, pp. 54–61 (2016). AAAI Workshop - Technical Report
2. Alexander, L., Moore, M.: Deontological ethics. In: Zalta, E.N. (ed.) The Stanford Encyclopedia of Philosophy. Metaphysics Research Lab, Stanford University (2020). https://plato.stanford.edu/archives/win2020/entries/ethics-deontological/
3. Anderson, M., Anderson, S.L.: GenEth: a general ethical dilemma analyzer. Paladyn **9**(1), 337–357 (2018). https://doi.org/10.1515/pjbr-2018-0024

4. Anderson, M., Anderson, S.L., Armen, C.: MedEthEx: A Prototype Medical Ethics Advisor. Technical report (2006). www.aaai.org
5. Anderson, M., Anderson, S.L., Berenz, V.: A value-driven eldercare robot: virtual and physical instantiations of a case-supported principle-based behavior paradigm. Proc. IEEE **107**(3), 526–540 (2019). https://doi.org/10.1109/JPROC.2018.2840045
6. Aristotle: The Nicomachean Ethics. Penguin Books (350)
7. Arkin, R.C.: Governing lethal behavior, p. 121 (2008). https://doi.org/10.1145/1349822.1349839. ISBN: 9781605580173
8. Arkin, R.C.: Governing lethal behavior: embedding ethics in a hybrid deliberative/reactive robot architecture: part 2: formalization for ethical control. Front. Artif. Intell. Appl. **171**(1), 51–62 (2008). ISBN: 9781586038335
9. Awad, E., et al.: The moral machine experiment. Nature **563**(7729), 59–64 (2018). https://doi.org/10.1038/s41586-018-0637-6
10. Azad-Manjiri, M.: A new architecture for making moral agents based on C4.5 decision tree algorithm. Int. J. Inf. Technol. Comput. Sci. **6**(5), 50–57 (2014). https://doi.org/10.5815/ijitcs.2014.05.07. http://www.mecs-press.org/
11. Bench-Capon, T., Modgil, S.: Norms and value based reasoning: justifying compliance and violation. Artif. Intell. Law **25**(1), 29–64 (2017). https://doi.org/10.1007/s10506-017-9194-9
12. Benzmüller, C., Parent, X., van der Torre, L.: Designing normative theories for ethical and legal reasoning: LogiKEy framework, methodology, and tool support. Artif. Intell. **287**, 103348 (2020). https://doi.org/10.1016/j.artint.2020.103348. https://linkinghub.elsevier.com/retrieve/pii/S0004370219301110
13. Buchanan, A., Brock, D.W.: Deciding for others. Milbank Q. **64**, 17–94 (1986). https://doi.org/10.2307/3349960. https://www.jstor.org/stable/3349960
14. Censi, A., et al.: Liability, ethics, and culture-aware behavior specification using rulebooks. In: Proceedings - IEEE International Conference on Robotics and Automation 2019-May, pp. 8536–8542 (2019). https://doi.org/10.1109/ICRA.2019.8794364. arXiv:1902.09355. ISBN: 9781538660263
15. Chen, L.: Virtue ethics and confucian ethics. Dao **9**(3), 275–287 (2010). https://doi.org/10.1007/s11712-010-9174-1
16. Dahling, J.J., Chau, S.L., Mayer, D.M., Gregory, J.B.: Breaking rules for the right reasons? An investigation of pro-social rule breaking. J. Organ. Behav. **33**(1), 21–42 (2012). https://doi.org/10.1002/job.730
17. Dubljević, V.: Toward implementing the ADC model of moral judgment in autonomous vehicles. Sci. Eng. Ethics 1–12 (2020). https://doi.org/10.1007/s11948-020-00242-0
18. Epley, N., Waytz, A., Cacioppo, J.T.: On seeing human: a three-factor theory of anthropomorphism. Psychol. Rev. **114**(4), 864–886 (2007). https://doi.org/10.1037/0033-295X.114.4.864. http://doi.apa.org/getdoi.cfm?doi=10.1037/0033-295X.114.4.864
19. Gabriel, I.: Artificial intelligence, values, and alignment. Minds Mach. **30**(3), 411–437 (2020). https://doi.org/10.1007/s11023-020-09539-2
20. Gamez, P., Shank, D.B., Arnold, C., North, M.: Artificial virtue: the machine question and perceptions of moral character in artificial moral agents. AI Soc. **35**(4), 795–809 (2020). https://doi.org/10.1007/s00146-020-00977-1
21. Gibert, M.: The case for virtuous robots. AI Ethics **3**(1), 135–144 (2023). https://doi.org/10.1007/s43681-022-00185-1

22. Govindarajulu, N.S., Bringsjord, S.: On automating the doctrine of double effect. In: Proceedings of the Twenty-Sixth International Joint Conference on Artificial Intelligence, pp. 4722–4730. International Joint Conferences on Artificial Intelligence (2017). https://doi.org/10.24963/ijcai.2017/658. https://github.com/naveensundarg/prover. arXiv: 1703.08922. ISSN: 10450823
23. Govindarajulu, N.S., Bringsjord, S., Ghosh, R., Sarathy, V.: Toward the engineering of virtuous machines. In: Proceedings of the 2019 AAAI/ACM Conference on AI, Ethics, and Society, AIES 2019, pp. 29–35. Association for Computing Machinery, New York (2019). https://doi.org/10.1145/3306618.3314256. https://dl.acm.org/doi/10.1145/3306618.3314256
24. Guarini, M.: Particularism and the classification and reclassification of moral cases. IEEE Intell. Syst. **21**(4), 22–28 (2006). https://doi.org/10.1109/MIS.2006.76
25. Hendrycks, D., et al.: Aligning AI With Shared Human Values (2021)
26. Howard, D., Muntean, I.: Artificial moral cognition: moral functionalism and autonomous moral agency. In: Powers, T.M. (ed.) Philosophy and Computing: Essays in Epistemology, Philosophy of Mind, Logic, and Ethics, pp. 121–159. Springer, Cham (2017). https://doi.org/10.1007/978-3-319-61043-6_7. ISSN: 0007-0882
27. Hursthouse, R., Pettigrove, G.: Virtue ethics. In: Zalta, E.N. (ed.) The Stanford Encyclopedia of Philosophy. Metaphysics Research Lab, Stanford University (2018). https://plato.stanford.edu/archives/win2018/entries/ethics-virtue/
28. Jiang, L., et al.: Delphi: Towards Machine Ethics and Norms (1), 1–42 (2021). http://arxiv.org/abs/2110.07574. arXiv: 2110.07574
29. Kazil, J., Masad, D., Crooks, A.: Utilizing python for agent-based modeling: the mesa framework. In: Thomson, R., Bisgin, H., Dancy, C., Hyder, A., Hussain, M. (eds.) Social, Cultural, and Behavioral Modeling, pp. 308–317. Springer, Cham (2020)
30. Kraut, R.: Aristotle's ethics. In: Zalta, E.N., Nodelman, U. (eds.) The Stanford Encyclopedia of Philosophy. Metaphysics Research Lab, Stanford University, fall 2022 edn. (2022). https://plato.stanford.edu/archives/fall2022/entries/aristotle-ethics/
31. MacKenzie, M.: Buddhism and the Virtues, vol. 1. Oxford University Press (2017). https://doi.org/10.1093/oxfordhb/9780199385195.013.18. https://academic.oup.com/edited-volume/28109/chapter/212224702
32. Morrison, E.W.: Doing the job well: an investigation of pro-social rule breaking. J. Manag. **32**(1), 5–28 (2006). https://doi.org/10.1177/0149206305277790
33. Nafsika Athanassoulis: Virtue Ethics (2023). https://iep.utm.edu/virtue/
34. Nallur, V.: Landscape of machine implemented ethics. Sci. Eng. Ethics **26**(5), 2381–2399 (2020). https://doi.org/10.1007/s11948-020-00236-y
35. Noothigattu, R., et al.: A voting-based system for ethical decision making. In: Proceedings of the AAAI Conference on Artificial Intelligence, vol. 32, no. 1 (2018). https://doi.org/10.1609/aaai.v32i1.11512. https://ojs.aaai.org/index.php/AAAI/article/view/11512
36. Pirni, A., Balistreri, M., Capasso, M., Umbrello, S., Merenda, F.: Robot care ethics between autonomy and vulnerability: coupling principles and practices in autonomous systems for care. Front. Robot. AI **8**, 654298 (2021). https://doi.org/10.3389/frobt.2021.654298. https://www.frontiersin.org/articles/10.3389/frobt.2021.654298/full
37. Pontier, M.A., Hoorn, J.F.: Toward machines that behave ethically better than humans do. In: Proceedings of the Annual Meeting of the Cognitive Science Society (2012)

38. Ramanayake, R., Nallur, V.: A computational architecture for a pro-social rule bending agent. In: First International Workshop on Computational Machine Ethics held in conjunction with 18th International Conference on Principles of Knowledge Representation and Reasoning KR 2021 (CME2021) (2021). https://doi.org/10.5281/ZENODO.6470437. https://zenodo.org/record/6470437
39. Ramanayake, R., Nallur, V.: A small set of ethical challenges for elder-care robots. In: Hakli, R., Mäkelä, P., Seibt, J. (eds.) Frontiers in Artificial Intelligence and Applications. IOS Press (2023). https://doi.org/10.3233/FAIA220605. https://ebooks.iospress.nl/doi/10.3233/FAIA220605
40. Ramanayake, R., Nallur, V.: Implementing pro-social rule bending in an elder-care robot environment. In: Ali, A.A., Cabibihan, J.J., Meskin, N., Rossi, S., Jiang, W., He, H., Ge, S.S. (eds.) Social Robotics. LNCS, vol. 14454, pp. 230–239. Springer, Singapore (2024). https://doi.org/10.1007/978-981-99-8718-4_20
41. Ramanayake, R., Wicke, P., Nallur, V.: Immune moral models? Pro-social rule breaking as a moral enhancement approach for ethical AI. AI Soc. (2022). https://doi.org/10.1007/s00146-022-01478-z
42. Russell, S.J.: Human compatible: artificial intelligence and the problem of control. Viking, New York? (2019)
43. Schoenborn, J., Weber, R., Aha, W., Cassens, J., Althoff, K.D.: Explainable case-based reasoning: a survey. In: 35th AAAI Conference on Artificial Intelligence - A Virtual Conference; Explainable Agency in Artificial Intelligence Workshop (2021)
44. Serramia, M., Lopez-Sanchez, M., Rodriguez-Aguilar, J.A., Morales, J., Wooldridge, M., Ansotegui, C.: Exploiting moral values to choose the right norms. In: Proceedings of the 2018 AAAI/ACM Conference on AI, Ethics, and Society, New Orleans, LA, USA, pp. 264–270. ACM (2018). https://doi.org/10.1145/3278721.3278735. https://dl.acm.org/doi/10.1145/3278721.3278735
45. Sharkey, A., Sharkey, N.: Granny and the robots: ethical issues in robot care for the elderly. Ethics Inf. Technol. **14**(1), 27–40 (2012). https://doi.org/10.1007/s10676-010-9234-6
46. Sinnott-Armstrong, W.: Consequentialism. In: Zalta, E.N. (ed.) The Stanford Encyclopedia of Philosophy. Metaphysics Research Lab, Stanford University (2019). https://plato.stanford.edu/archives/sum2019/entries/consequentialism/
47. Solaiman, I., Dennison, C.: Process for adapting language models to society (PALMS) with values-targeted datasets. In: Advances in Neural Information Processing Systems, vol. 34, pp. 5861–5873. Curran Associates, Inc. (2021). https://proceedings.neurips.cc/paper/2021/hash/2e855f9489df0712b4bd8ea9e2848c5a-Abstract.html
48. Thornton, S.M., Pan, S., Erlien, S.M., Gerdes, J.C.: Incorporating ethical considerations into automated vehicle control. IEEE Trans. Intell. Transp. Syst. **18**(6), 1429–1439 (2017). https://doi.org/10.1109/TITS.2016.2609339
49. Tolmeijer, S., Kneer, M., Sarasua, C., Christen, M., Bernstein, A.: Implementations in machine ethics: a survey. ACM Comput. Surv. **53**(6) (2021). https://doi.org/10.1145/3419633. arXiv: 2001.07573
50. Van Dang, C., et al.: Application of soar cognitive agent based on utilitarian ethics theory for home service robots. In: 2017 14th International Conference on Ubiquitous Robots and Ambient Intelligence (URAI), pp. 155–158 (2017). https://doi.org/10.1109/URAI.2017.7992698
51. Van Wynsberghe, A.: Social robots and the risks to reciprocity. AI Soc. **37**(2), 479–485 (2022). https://doi.org/10.1007/s00146-021-01207-y

52. Vanderelst, D., Winfield, A.: An architecture for ethical robots inspired by the simulation theory of cognition. Cogn. Syst. Res. **48**, 56–66 (2018). https://doi.org/10.1016/j.cogsys.2017.04.002
53. Wallach, W., Allen, C., Smit, I.: Machine morality: bottom-up and top-down approaches for modelling human moral faculties. AI Soc. **22**(4), 565–582 (2008). https://doi.org/10.1007/s00146-007-0099-0
54. van Wynsberghe, A., Robbins, S., Robbins scott, S., van Wynsberghe, A., Robbins, S.: Critiquing the reasons for making artificial moral agents. Sci. Eng. Ethics **25**(3), 719–735 (2018). https://doi.org/10.1007/S11948-018-0030-8
55. Yilmaz, L., Franco-Watkins, A., Kroecker, T.S.: Computational models of ethical decision-making: a coherence-driven reflective equilibrium model. Cogn. Syst. Res. **46**, 61–74 (2017). https://doi.org/10.1016/j.cogsys.2017.02.005. https://www.sciencedirect.com/science/article/pii/S1389041716301218

Engineering Multi-Agent Systems

Can Proof Assistants Verify Multi-agent Systems?

Julian Alfredo Mendez(✉) and Timotheus Kampik

Umeå University, Umeå, Sweden
{julian.mendez,tkampik}@cs.umu.se

Abstract. This paper presents the SODA language for verifying multi-agent systems. SODA is a high-level functional and object-oriented language that supports the compilation of its code not only to Scala, a strongly statically typed high-level programming language, but also to Lean, a proof assistant and programming language. Given these capabilities, SODA can implement multi-agent systems, or parts thereof, that can then be integrated into a mainstream software ecosystem on the one hand and formally verified with state-of-the-art tools on the other hand. We provide a brief and informal introduction to SODA and the aforementioned interoperability capabilities, as well as a simple demonstration of how interaction protocols can be designed and verified with SODA. In the course of the demonstration, we highlight challenges with respect to real-world applicability.

Keywords: Engineering Multi-Agent Systems · Formal Verification · Proof Automation

1 Introduction

Multi-agent systems (MAS) are systems composed of multiple interacting intelligent agents, working towards joint or conflicting goals. MAS have emerged as an approach for modeling and implementing complex distributed systems, because MAS-based systems can solve problems that are very difficult or impossible to solve using monolithic architectures. Due to their dynamic and distributed nature, MAS are notoriously difficult to test. At the same time, ensuring desirable behavior in MAS components is crucial to verify that the autonomy that agents are granted does not lead to safety or compliance issues. Consequently, testing and verification of MAS has emerged as a substantial branch of MAS engineering research. Here, most research focuses either on finite state model checking [4] or–presumably less frequently–on testing in the software engineering sense (as in *test-driven development*) [1]. In this paper, we take a novel path and present a prototypical approach where parts of a MAS are implemented in SODA, a high-level programming language that can be compiled to Scala for integration with a mainstream programming ecosystem, as well as to Lean, a proof

R. Collier et al. (Eds.): EUMAS 2024, LNAI 15685, pp. 323–339, 2025.
https://doi.org/10.1007/978-3-031-93930-3_19

assistant and programming language that applies calculus of constructions [13]. The formal verification of the program code can then be executed in Lean.

To illustrate the approach and demonstrate its feasibility, we provide a simple running example of interaction protocol verification with SODA and Lean, which we introduce conceptually below. In our example, we want to implement an interaction protocol for a platform on which multiple agents buy and sell items. We assume that the transactions are safe and conducted by a mediator that is trusted by all involved agents and can transfer possession of items and money between the agents. In the following, we provide an example interaction sequence that can serve as an archetype for the protocol that our MAS should enact.

1. A seller C notifies the mediator A to advertise a certain item R at a price P.
2. The mediator A informs all agents that the item is available for sale.
3. While no buyer has shown interest, C can remove the ad.
4. If a buyer B wants to buy R and has money P to pay for it, the buyer notifies A.
5. When A is notified of the purchase, it removes the ad, and it transactionally transfers the item R from C to B, and the amount of money P from B to C.

In our approach, we use lists to store items. As a proof of concept, we prove a technical but important property:

Property. *Changing an item in the list does not change the size of the list.*

This property is important, but it is usually taken for granted. Proving these kinds of properties in a proof assistant like Lean requires substantial effort because lemmas and tactics require maturity to be employed. All cases need to be covered, and the resulting object after the execution must always be defined. In the particular case of our functions, we work with immutable lists. Our lists are thread-safe, which allows them to run in parallel execution, and follow the standard construction in functional languages. They are defined as being either an empty list or an element prepended to a list. This makes them memory-efficient because replacing an arbitrary position requires reconstructing the list until the given position.

As we can see, the property we prove looks simplistic from an intuitive software engineering perspective. Still, we chose to prove this property as a minimal demonstrating example, due to the following reasons: *i)* even such simple facts are somewhat effortful to prove with proof assistants such as Lean; *ii)* our example is sufficient for highlighting practical challenges, while also serving as a proof-of-concept with respect to purely technical feasibility.

In the remainder of this paper, we give a brief overview of research on testing and verifying MAS (Sect. 2) to then introduce SODA and its interoperability capabilities, both with the Scala/Java ecosystem and with the Lean proof assistant (Sect. 3). We then continue our running example to demonstrate how agent interaction protocols can be specified and verified with SODA (Sect. 4). Subsequently, we discuss in detail the formal proofs (Sect. 5). We show with practical experiments that the example is efficient (Sect. 6). After that, we discuss our work and its limitations, and conclude with a future outlook (Sect. 7).

2 Why Formal Verification for MAS?

Software verification ensures that specific components meet specification requirements. We can compare software verification with software validation, since both are software evaluation processes. The former focuses on determining whether a software artifact meets the conditions with respect to its broader purpose, imposed at the beginning of a development phase, whereas the latter determines whether the requirements are satisfied at the end of a development phase. The verification of agents and MAS has been subject to extensive study over the years. Here, *verification* can either be seen from an applied software engineering perspective, i.e., *testing* without "hard" guarantees, or as the formal analysis (*formal verification*) of MAS or components thereof.

Jason [5] and SARL [16] are specialized multi-agent programming languages, with Jason focusing on logical reasoning and SARL on dynamic, distributed environments. Jason is an interpreter for an extended version of AgentSpeak(L) [15], a BDI (Belief-Desire-Intention) agent-oriented logic programming language. Jason provides a platform for developing multi-agent systems with customizable features, especially for environments requiring logical reasoning and decision-making. SARL is a general-purpose agent-oriented programming language designed to handle concurrency, distribution, interaction, decentralization, reactivity, autonomy, and dynamic reconfiguration. It integrates well with the Janus [8] platform for distributed multi-agent systems.

Although agent testing is certainly a relevant research domain, e.g., in the context of technologies for agent-oriented programming [1,2], a well-informed assumption is that for MAS, testing is insufficient because of agents' and MAS' highly dynamic behavior [19], in particular if contrasted with mainstream software components in server-client architectures. Because mainstream software testing approaches are often deemed insufficient for engineering MAS, researchers have devised a range of formal approaches to verify agents or other components of MAS. These approaches typically rely on model checking techniques [4,7,10]. Still, due to their dynamic nature and the resulting combinatorial explosion of the number of models [19], applying model checking to MAS can be similarly intractable as attempting to achieve substantial coverage in traditional tests. Also, model-checking approaches are typically limited to particular abstractions and modalities; for example, TLA+ prominently focuses on temporal reasoning [9]. In contrast, proof assistants such as Coq [3], Isabelle [14], and Lean [6] allow for more generic formal analyses, and thus they can potentially enable more flexible verification of agents and MAS. However, these tools are not straightforwardly applicable to the formal analysis of program code written in languages that engineers use to specify behavior at the "business logic" (or *knowledge*) level. This may explain why proof assistants have not yet been comprehensively studied in the context of MAS verification, at least (to the best of our knowledge) not as tools that can directly analyze executable specifications of MAS components.

The work we present in this paper is a step towards overcoming this obstacle, by bridging the gap between mainstream software ecosystems in which MAS can be engineered and tools for proof automation, demonstrating basic feasibility by implementing a simple example.

3 Designing MAS with SODA

Before we demonstrate SODA's verification capabilities, let us provide a brief overview of its syntax (Subsect. 3.1) and the technologies the language is built upon (Subsect. 3.2).

3.1 SODA Syntax

SODA [11][1] is a statically typed functional language with object-oriented notation. Its name is an acronym for *Symbolic Objective Descriptive Analysis*, and it was designed to be descriptive by being declarative and easy to read. It combines the rigor of purely functional languages like Lean, with the modern technology integration of languages like Scala, which in turn is a bridge to the Java Virtual Machine (JVM) ecosystem. SODA provides not only the expressive power for the type of transactions we have in the example, but also the elements to include Lean proofs for the definitions. It also allows for interconnection with complex packages provided by JVM libraries and frameworks, and it has a simple and direct way to write functions, similar to mainstream languages like Scala or Python.

SODA follows the functional style of ML [12][2], and it has a small set of constructs. Most of them can be placed in one of the following categories: function-related constructs and class-related constructs. It uses the basic types provided by Scala, such as Boolean, Int, Float, and String.

The function-related constructs are meant to define functions. It is possible to say that a variable x is of a certain type A with $x : A$. The functions are then defined in the usual way; e.g., $f(x : Int) : Int = x + 1$ defines the function $x + 1$. Lambda expressions are also written as expected: the function above can be defined using the lambda expression $f : Int = \texttt{lambda}\ x \longrightarrow x + 1$. The construct `if-then-else` allows for the definition of piecewise functions. As in other ML-styled functional languages, the construct `match-case-`$\Longrightarrow$ is used for pattern matching. The following function returns the maximum of two integers:

$$max\ (x : Int)\ (y : Int) : Int = \texttt{if}\ x > y\ \texttt{then}\ x\ \texttt{else}\ y$$

The class-related constructs are meant to define new types, to group functions in classes, and to group classes in packages. The construct `class-end` defines a class from the beginning to the end. It groups functions in a module, and it defines a type, a default constructor, and a default equality function. A class can extend other classes with the construct `extends`. If a class needs parameters to instantiate an object, these parameters can be defined with the construct

[1] For a more detailed technical report that describes the SODA language, see [11].
[2] ML stands for *Meta Language*, but the acronym is rarely spelled-out.

`abstract`. A class can depend on parameterized types, which are parameters belonging to `Type` inside square brackets (`[ ]`). Classes are grouped in packages with the `package` reserved word, and `import` is used to import classes from different packages.

3.2 Technology Behind Soda

In a figurative way, we can say that the SODA syntax lies in the intersection of Scala version 3 syntax and Lean version 4 syntax[3], and they all fall under the umbrella of ML-styled programming languages. SODA code needs to be compiled in order to be executed. The main compiler converts the SODA source code into Scala source code. Since it is a source-to-source compiler of similar source code, this compiler is a *transpiler*, and we also call it a *translator*. We claim that the translation into Scala is sound, in the sense that all correct code in SODA is translated into correct code in Scala. It is also possible to import Java Virtual Machine (JVM) libraries into SODA, using `import`, but it requires a manual check from the developer to ensure that the imported libraries keep the code purely functional.

SODA can be partially translated into Lean. This means that it is possible to prove properties of SODA code in Lean. The construct `directive` can include embedded pieces of code of a specific target language. For example, a proof would be considered in a translation to Lean, but it would be ignored in a translation to Scala. The proof has to be actually written in Lean, based on definitions provided in SODA. SODA's source code is available for download at https://github.com/julianmendez/soda.

4 Soda for MAS Verification

SODA provides a small set of constructs to create code that can be executed in Scala 3 and proven in Lean 4. On the one hand, Lean is not only a powerful programming language, but also a proof assistant. Its mathematical library, mathlib[4], contains a significant number of mathematical theorems and their proofs, which can serve as a template to prove properties of agents. On the other hand, Scala is a very flexible language, with an efficient implementation connected to the JVM libraries, which allows for multi-platform execution. It is important to note that Lean proofs cannot cover the use of JVM libraries, since these are not specified for Lean.

We have specified the example of Sect. 1 in SODA. We describe the basic types, available functions, and some properties that the system should hold. Although the example is intended to be a proof of concept, it already contains the main components for a full-scale example. All agents are identified with a unique number, which is associated with an account number controlled by

[3] Scala 3 and Lean 4 have improved their syntax compared to Scala 2 and Lean 3 respectively.

[4] https://github.com/leanprover-community/mathlib4.

the mediator. Thus, the mediator can transfer money between the accounts of the participants. The mediator can also transfer items, which are also identified with unique numbers. The items have properties like their owner and price. The available functions are intended to perform the main operation between the agents. There are functions to advertise an item, to change its price, and to sell it to another agent. Since SODA is purely functional, the functions do not change the state of a market, but create new instances of the market. The actual communication between the agents is done through a library used in the Scala translation.

In order to enable the verification of the desired behavior, we make use of *invariants*. Invariants are logical assertions that are always valid during execution. They are helpful resources to prove that a system behaves according to predefined expectations. As Lean can be used to prove theorems, the Lean translation can serve to prove the preservation of invariants. The two invariants which we are interested in are the following:

- No item is created or destructed after modifying the state of an item;
- No account is created or destructed after modifying the state of an item.

The choice for representation is not trivial. Different ways of representing the market lead to a number of derived challenges. Sometimes, more efficient performance is achieved by adding some redundancy, but it makes it more difficult to prove invariants. Similarly, the definitions of the functions require consideration, as shown in Fig. 1 where an intuitive recursive definition of the length of a list (`length_def`) should be equivalent to a tail recursive definition of the length of a list (`length_fl`). We prove that both definitions are equivalent, allowing us to use the intuitive definition for the proofs and the tail recursive definition for the execution.

4.1 Package Structure

The project is available at https://github.com/julianmendez/market (open-source). It is designed to be compiled using sbt[5] to be executed in the JVM environment. A Bash script uses the SODA binary to translate the SODA files, including those proofs that can be verified with Lean. The project file structure follows the standard sbt/Maven layout. The project contains three packages:

- `core`, containing the core data types, the market, its functionality and the proofs;
- `parser`, containing a YAML parser; and
- `main`, containing the entry point class, which supports the console execution.

Firstly, the main core is a package that contains the classes to model the market. The main operations are:

- **deposit** *user amount* : works as an update-insert (upsert) function to declare a user and to put money in the linked account.

[5] https://www.scala-sbt.org.

```
_tailrec_foldl [A : Type] [B : Type] (list : List [A] ) (current : B)
    (next : B -> A -> B) : B =
  match list
    case Nil ==> current
    case (head) :: (tail) ==>
      _tailrec_foldl [A] [B] (tail) (next (current) (head) ) (next)

foldl [A : Type] [B : Type] (list : List [A] ) (initial : B)
    (next : B -> A -> B) : B =
  _tailrec_foldl [A] [B] (list) (initial) (next)

length_fl [A : Type] (list : List [A] ) : Nat =
  _tailrec_foldl [A] [Nat] (list) (0) (
    lambda (accum : Nat) --> lambda (_elem : A) --> accum + 1)

_tailrec_length [A : Type] (list : List [A] ) (accum : Nat) : Nat =
  match list
    case Nil ==> accum
    case (_head) :: (tail) ==>
      _tailrec_length [A] (tail) (accum + 1)

length_tr [A : Type] (list : List [A] ) : Nat =
  _tailrec_length [A] (list) (0)

length_def [A : Type] (list : List [A] ) : Nat =
  match list
    case Nil ==> 0
    case (_head) :: (tail) ==> length_def [A] (tail) + 1
```

Fig. 1. The function `_tailrec_foldl` is a tail-recursive auxiliary function of `foldl`, which is a left fold (*foldl*) function for parameterized types. `length_fl`, `length_tr`, and `length_def` syntactically different but semantically equivalent ways of defining the length of a list of an arbitrary type A in SODA. The tail-recursive definitions (`length_fl`, `length_tr`) outperform the naive definition (`length_def`).

- **assign** *item user* : works as an upsert function to declare an item and to establish its owner.
- **price** *item amount* : has the double functionality of assigning the price of an item for sale, if the value is positive, or hiding it, if the value is zero.
- **sell** *item user* : transactionally transfers the possession of an item to a specified user, and money equivalent for the price from the new user's to the old user's account.

Secondly, the project has a package to read YAML files. A list of operations simulates the interaction that occurs in a MAS scenario. The parser creates a list of operations, which can later be executed on an instance of market.

The last relevant package is the *main* package, which contains the entry point and is intended to receive and parse parameters from the console.

The parser package and the core packages contain their counterpart testing classes. The parser test package has two layers of parsing: the syntactic layer, which is implemented using SnakeYAML[6], a Java YAML parser, and the semantic layer, where the operation objects are instantiated. The core test package instantiates a market and applies the parsed operations to it.

Before we start modeling our *market* example, we need to introduce two fundamental preliminaries that are crucial to enable formal verification: natural number support (Subsect. 4.2) and list wrappers (Subsect. 4.3).

4.2 Preliminary 1: Support for Natural Numbers

One of the challenges that we need to face is how we handle natural numbers in SODA. We use the standard notation in the literature where natural numbers are used as a synonym of non-negative integers, i.e. including the number 0. While Lean has natural numbers as part of its core (`Nat`), Scala does not have natural numbers as a type. In Soda, we implement the natural numbers based on a type `Nat`, and two constructors: `0` and `Succ_`. We define its translation as shown in Fig. 2.

```
directive scala
type Nat = Int
object Succ_ {
  def apply (n : Int) : Int = n + 1
  def unapply (n : Int) : Option [Int] =
    if (n <= 0) None else Some (n - 1)
}

directive lean
notation "Succ_" => Nat.succ
```

Fig. 2. This table shows the SODA definition of `Nat`, to be translated to Scala and to Lean.

A good definition of natural numbers is crucial in order to accomplish two things: proofs and calculations. A recursive definition is needed to provide proofs in Lean, especially those involving recursive definitions such as the length of a list. However, some calculations may need to be time efficient, even with larger natural numbers.

In functional languages with ML syntax, the deconstruction is often done with pattern matching. While the Lean syntax allows us to use this type of syntax, in Scala this does not work off-the-shelf. The main issue is that our natural numbers in Scala are in fact `Int` objects, which makes addition of two numbers very efficient, and `Succ_` is a construction external to the objects. For

[6] https://bitbucket.org/asomov/snakeyaml-engine.

that reason, we define the function *monus*1, which subtracts 1 from a given positive number until this number reaches 0. This is defined in Fig. 3. The function *monus*1 is based on the function *monus*, denoted by $\dot{-}$, which handles subtraction in natural numbers. For two natural numbers a and b, it is defined as: $a \dot{-} b = \max(a - b, 0)$.

```
monus1 (index : Nat) : Nat =
  match index
    case Succ_ (k) ==> k
    case _otherwise ==> 0
```

Fig. 3. This table shows the definition of *monus1*, which for a positive number, it returns the previous number, and for other numbers, it returns 0.

4.3 Preliminary 2: List Wrappers

After having defined `Nat`, we define a type we name `ListWrapper`. This is actually not a list itself, but a toolbox that works as a wrapper for lists, containing methods and their proofs. Let us see how this type is constructed. *Nil* is the constructor for an empty list, :: is the list constructor, and *Nat* is a type for non-negative integers.

The function *foldl* (from *fold left*), as it is called in other functional programming languages like Haskell, applies a combining function to an iterable structure, a finite list in our case, and starts with an initial value. One relevant property of *foldl* is the possibility of implementing it as a tail-recursive function, which in turn can be optimized by a virtual machine or a compiler as a cycle. In other words, *foldl* is a purely functional approach to execute certain types of cycles. In addition to its efficient execution, *foldl* ensures termination on finite structures, like the list structure. In Fig. 1, we can see `foldl`, which is an implementation of *foldl* that uses an auxiliary tail recursive function called `_tailrec_foldl`.

Although *foldl* is a useful resource for efficient and well-founded recursion, it becomes more complex when it is involved in proofs. Because of that, in our proofs, we provide (traditionally) recursive definitions, in addition to the tail-recursive *foldl* definitions.

SODA lists allow for access to any arbitrary position. In Scala, accessing at position i of a list a of type T would be notated $a(i)$, which is already a value of type T. However, when we need to access an element inside a proof, we need to ensure that i is in range, and thus that $a(i)$ is well defined. We present this in Fig. 4, where we show how we access an element of a list. The function `get` visits all the elements of a list until it reaches the specified position. If that happens, it returns the content at that position (`Some (elem)`), otherwise, it returns `None`.

```
_tailrec_get_def [A : Type] (list : List [A] ) (index : Nat) (current
    : Nat) : Option [A] =
  match list
    case Nil ==> None
    case (head) :: (tail) ==>
      if current == index
      then Some (head)
      else _tailrec_get_def [A] (tail) (index) (Succ_ (current) )

get [A : Type] (list : List [A] ) (index : Nat) : Option [A] =
  _tailrec_get_def [A] (list) (index) (0)
```

Fig. 4. The function **get** retrieves an element safely, without throwing an exception if the index is out of range. This is necessary to ensure that the retrieved element is well defined.

Since SODA lists are immutable, modifying the state of a market requires creating new lists. This can be written in Scala for a mutable structure as $a(i) = e$, which updates the content of a list a at position i, by assigning it the value e. In Fig. 5, we show the definition of `set_def`, and in Sect. 5, we prove that it preserves the length of the list, i.e. it does not create or remove elements.

```
set_def [A : Type] (list : List [A] ) (index : Nat) (element : A) :
    List [A] =
  match list
    case Nil ==> Nil
    case (head) :: (tail) ==>
      if index == 0
      then (element) :: (tail)
      else (head) :: (set_def [A] (tail) (monus1 (index) ) (element) )
```

Fig. 5. The function **set_def** is a tail recursive function that creates a new list with an element updated at a given index.

4.4 Modeling the Market

As we can see in Fig. 6, money is modeled as an integer. An item is modeled as a pair ⟨owner, price⟩. A market is a pair containing the owner's money and the items. Conventionally, we say that an item is advertised if and only if its price is greater than 0. In the context of this example, money is modeled as a natural number (`Nat`), but in reality, we could allow users to have debt and use an integer instead.

```
class Money = Int

class Item

  abstract
    owner : Nat
    price : Money

end

class Market

  abstract
    accounts : List [Money]
    items : List [Item]

end
```

Fig. 6. A market is a structure composed of smaller structures.

The methods for manipulating a market or an item are separated in a module called `MarketMod`. This design style differs from the traditional object-oriented approach, where the methods pertaining to the market should be in the market class itself. We chose this design as a compromise in the integration of SODA, Scala, and Lean. While Scala uses a traditional object notation as in other object-oriented programming languages, Lean uses syntactic sugar to access functions inside modules, as in other functional programming languages. Since the SODA translators do not support the notational translation between the two paradigms, we place the functions in modules, and use classes as structures.

5 Formal Proofs

As we discuss above, the virtue of SODA resides in connecting efficient implementations and formal proofs in the same language. We decided to show a simple property: "Changing an element in a list does not modify its length". This property allows ensuring that a transaction does not change the length of a list. This could be reformulated as: "Creating a list with `set_def` returns a list of the same length as the original".

5.1 Defining the Length of a List

To prove the goal, we use the definition of length given in Fig. 1. Although this definition looks clear, it is not tail recursive, and for that reason it could be considered a naive definition of the length of a list. For example, in an average computer configuration, this function cannot compute the length of a list of 10,000 elements, since it would produce a stack overflow during execution.

However, this definition greatly simplifies the proofs. A more applicable function to compute the length of a list is `length_tr`, which uses tail recursion. Its implementation is shown in Fig. 1.

Figure 7 shows Theorem `len_tr_eq_len_def`, which states that the tail recursive function is equivalent to the naive definition. The proof uses Lemma `len_tr_accum`, which helps in the interpretation of the extra parameter of `_tailrec_length`.

Although fully understanding the proof requires understanding of Lean 4, we sketch how the proof is structured. Let us focus on Lemma `len_tr_accum` in Fig. 7, which proves that the *accum* parameter accumulates the computed length. To achieve this, we apply an inductive strategy to the list (`induction list with`). If the list is empty (`nil`), it rewrites the definitions. If the list is not empty (`cons head tail ih`), it applies some definitions and uses the inductive hypothesis for the given parameters. Notice that the property has a value *accum*, which we can instantiate to different values to use the induction hypothesis.

This theorem is in fact shorter than the lemma, and it is also proven by applying induction. Since the equivalence does not have parameters, we first add them (`funext A list`). As before, the induction has two cases. The `nil` case is a direct rewriting of the definition. For the inductive step (`cons head tail ih`), we use the lemma and then the induction hypothesis.

Since we have proven that both functions are equivalent, we can use the efficient function (`length_tr`) for the definitions, and the naive function (`length_def`) for the proofs.

5.2 Updating a List

We have auxiliary functions and lemmas to prove that `set_def` does not change the number of elements. Figure 8 shows a property on `monus1` stating that applying it to the successor of a number returns the original number. In Fig. 9, we can see the proof that `set_def` preserves the length of the list, and the proof is provided by induction on the list. For the base case of the empty list (`nil`), it suffices to provide the definitions of `set_def` and `length_def`. For the inductive case (`cons head tail ih`), after using the definitions of `set_def` and `length_def`, we split the proof into two cases based on the value of the index. If it is at the beginning, (`zero`), the definition of `monus1` is used. Otherwise (`succ k`), after using the definitions of `monus1` and `length`, we employ the induction hypothesis.

```
directive lean
theorem
  len_tr_accum (A : Type) (list : List (A) )
    : forall (accum : Nat) ,
      _tailrec_length (A) (list) (accum) = _tailrec_length (A) (list)
          (0) + accum := by
    induction list with
    | nil =>
      intro n
      rewrite [_tailrec_length, _tailrec_length, Nat.zero_add]
      rfl
    | cons head tail ih =>
      intro n
      rewrite [_tailrec_length, _tailrec_length]
      rewrite [ih (1)]
      rewrite [ih (n + 1)]
      rewrite [Nat.add_assoc]
      rewrite [Nat.add_comm 1]
      rfl

directive lean
theorem
  len_tr_eq_len_def
    : length_tr = length_def := by
  funext A list
  rewrite [length_tr]
  induction list with
  | nil =>
    rewrite [_tailrec_length, length_def]
    rfl
  | cons head tail ih =>
    rewrite [_tailrec_length, len_tr_accum]
    rewrite [ih]
    rewrite [length_def]
    rfl
```

Fig. 7. Proof of Theorem `len_tr_eq_len_def`: it states that `length_tr` = `length_def`. This means that the tail recursive definition of length of a list is equivalent to the naive definition. The proof uses Lemma `len_tr_accum`.

```
directive lean
theorem
  monus1_succ
    : forall (index : Nat),
      monus1 (Nat.succ (index)) = index := by
  intro idx
  rewrite [monus1]
  simp
```

Fig. 8. Lemma proving that *monus*1 works as the inverse of successor.

```
directive lean
theorem
  len_set (A : Type) (list : List (A)) (element : A)
    : forall (index : Nat),
      length_def (A) (set_def (A) (list) (index) (element) ) =
           length_def (A) (list) := by
  induction list with
  | nil =>
    intro idx
    rewrite [set_def, length_def]
    rfl
  | cons head tail ih =>
     intro idx
     rewrite [set_def, length_def]
     cases idx with
     | zero =>
       rewrite [monus1]
       rewrite [Nat.zero_eq]
       rfl
     | succ k =>
       rewrite [monus1]
       simp
       rewrite [length_def]
       rewrite [ih]
       rfl
```

Fig. 9. Theorem and proof that proves that `set_def` does not change the length of the provided list.

6 Experiments

To test the efficiency of the market application, we run a series of experiments. The purpose of the experiments is to determine the viability of the example. As a prerequisite, we have developed a tool that generates test instances. Each instance depends on three parameters: the number of users, the number of items, and the number of transactions.

Each test instance is a YAML file that follows some patterns. At the beginning, it contains the instructions to add the user accounts, with some amount of money. After that, it adds the items assigned to some users, with some non-zero price. Finally, it adds all sell transactions together with a price change. This price change is needed because the market puts an item as not-for-sale after each transaction is successful.

We fix some values, and we assume that each user has, on average, 8 items to sell. We conducted two types of experiments, which are shown in Table 1. On the left, we choose an arbitrary batch of 65536 (2^{16}) transactions and we test the system with an exponentially growing number of users and items. On the right, we fix the number of users and items as 2048 and 16384 respectively, and we test the instances with an exponentially growing number of transactions. The experiments were run on a Linux Ubuntu 22.04.5 LTS computer equipped with 8 Intel cores i5-8350U CPU at 1.70 GHz and 32 GiB of RAM. The Bash script to run the experiments is provided in the project repository.

Table 1. The elapsed time in seconds of different synthetically generated instances. The columns show: the number of users, the number of items, the number of transactions, the elapsed time in seconds, and the number of transactions per second.

users	items	transac	time (s)	tr/s	users	items	transac	time (s)	tr/s
1	8	65536	1.10	59578	2048	16384	256	4.35	59
2	16	65536	1.13	57996	2048	16384	512	5.05	101
4	32	65536	1.13	57996	2048	16384	1024	4.95	207
8	64	65536	1.26	52013	2048	16384	2048	4.87	421
16	128	65536	1.40	46811	2048	16384	4096	5.28	776
32	256	65536	1.48	44281	2048	16384	8192	6.36	1288
64	512	65536	1.84	35617	2048	16384	16384	8.23	1991
128	1024	65536	2.32	28248	2048	16384	32768	13.14	2494
256	2048	65536	3.55	18461	2048	16384	65536	19.89	3295
512	4096	65536	5.79	11319	2048	16384	131072	36.67	3574
1024	8192	65536	10.41	6295	2048	16384	262144	68.49	3827
2048	16384	65536	19.89	3295	2048	16384	524288	126.88	4132

From Table 1, we conclude that the measurements show the effect of the overhead starting time of the application, as the first rows present very similar values. Another result is that the growth in the number of users and items seems to have a linear impact on the execution time. Regarding the transactions, once the number of users and the number of items are fixed, the required time appears to be linear with respect to the number of transactions. And, most importantly, with an average of around 4000 transactions per second, we demonstrate the viability of our example: the results indicate that an application of a multi-agent environment with formally verified pieces of code can also be efficient to run in production.

7 Conclusion

In this paper, we have demonstrated the applicability of SODA to the design of (so far simple) MAS components that can be integrated into the Scala and Java technology ecosystem, while also supporting formal verification with the proof assistant Lean. We claim that the use of proof assistants like Lean for MAS verification is a relevant research direction, as it allows for a more abstract and flexible formal analysis of MAS. However, given our demonstration, it is clear that more work is required to support the verification of MAS in a meaningful manner that is useful for software engineers. To move towards applicability, we hope to further advance this research in the following ways: *i)* by expanding proof-of-concept implementations to more complex scenarios that require the verification of additional fundamental MAS abstractions, such as agents' reasoning loops, providing reusable abstractions for verification; *ii)* by providing a more detailed analysis of the advantages and disadvantages of using proof assistants instead of model checkers for MAS verification; *iii)* by studying the applicability of our formal verification approach to real-world problems, such as the assurance of fairness properties in complex socio-technical systems. As an independent research direction, we consider it relevant to investigate whether and to what extent existing agent programming languages, such as protocol-based languages [17,18], can be extended or integrated to allow formal verification with proof assistants.

References

1. Amaral, C.J., Hübner, J.F., Kampik, T.: TDD for AOP: test-driven development for agent-oriented programming. In: Agmon, N., An, B., Ricci, A., Yeoh, W. (eds.) Proceedings of the 2023 International Conference on Autonomous Agents and Multiagent Systems, AAMAS 2023, London, United Kingdom, 29 May 2023 - 2 June 2023. pp. 3038–3040. ACM (2023). https://doi.org/10.5555/3545946.3599165, https://dl.acm.org/doi/10.5555/3545946.3599165
2. Amaral, C.J., Kampik, T., Cranefield, S.: A framework for collaborative and interactive agent-oriented developer operations. In: Proceedings of the 19th International Conference on Autonomous Agents and MultiAgent Systems. AAMAS '20, International Foundation for Autonomous Agents and Multiagent Systems, Richland, SC (2020)
3. Barras, B., et al.: The Coq proof assistant reference manual: version **6**, 1 (1997)
4. Bordini, R.H., Dennis, L.A., Farwer, B., Fisher, M.: Automated verification of multi-agent programs. In: 23rd IEEE/ACM International Conference on Automated Software Engineering (ASE 2008), 15–19 September 2008, L'Aquila, Italy, pp. 69–78. IEEE Computer Society (2008). https://doi.org/10.1109/ASE.2008.17
5. Bordini, R.H., Hübner, J.F., Wooldridge, M.: Programming multi-agent systems in AgentSpeak using Jason, vol. 15. John Wiley & Sons (2007)
6. De Moura, L., Kong, S., Avigad, J., Van Doorn, F., von Raumer, J.: The Lean theorem prover (system description). In: Automated Deduction-CADE-25: 25th International Conference on Automated Deduction, Berlin, Germany, 1–7 August 2015, Proceedings 25, pp. 378–388. Springer (2015)
7. Dennis, L.A., Fisher, M., Webster, M.P., Bordini, R.H.: Model checking agent programming languages. Autom. Softw. Eng. **19**(1), 5–63 (2012). https://doi.org/10.1007/s10515-011-0088-x
8. Galland, S., Gaud, N., Rodriguez, S., Hilaire, V.: Janus: another yet general-purpose multiagent platform. In: Proceedings of 7th Agent-Oriented Software Engineering Technical Forum (TFGASOSE-10) (2010)
9. Lamport, L.: Specifying Systems, The TLA+ Language and Tools for Hardware and Software Engineers. Addison-Wesley (2002), http://research.microsoft.com/users/lamport/tla/book.html

10. Lomuscio, A., Qu, H., Raimondi, F.: MCMAS: an open-source model checker for the verification of multi-agent systems. Int. J. Softw. Tools Tech. Trans. **19**(1), 9–30 (2017). https://doi.org/10.1007/s10009-015-0378-x
11. Mendez, J.A.: Soda: an object-oriented functional language for specifying human-centered problems (2023). https://doi.org/10.48550/arXiv.2310.01961
12. Milner, R.: A theory of type polymorphism in programming. J. Comput. Syst. Sci. **17**(3), 348–375 (1978). https://doi.org/10.1016/0022-0000(78)90014-4, https://www.sciencedirect.com/science/article/pii/0022000078900144
13. de Moura, L., Kong, S., Avigad, J., van Doorn, F., von Raumer, J.: The lean theorem prover (System Description). In: Felty, A.P., Middeldorp, A. (eds.) Automated Deduction - CADE-25, pp. 378–388. Springer, Cham (2015)
14. Paulson, L.C.: Isabelle: A generic theorem prover. Springer (1994)
15. Rao, A.S.: AgentSpeak(L): BDI agents speak out in a logical computable language. In: Van de Velde, W., Perram, J.W. (eds.) MAAMAW 1996. LNCS, vol. 1038, pp. 42–55. Springer, Heidelberg (1996). https://doi.org/10.1007/BFb0031845
16. Rodriguez, S., Gaud, N., Galland, S.: SARL: a general-purpose agent-oriented programming language. In: 2014 IEEE/WIC/ACM International Joint Conferences on Web Intelligence (WI) and Intelligent Agent Technologies (IAT), vol. 3, pp. 103–110. IEEE (2014)
17. V., S.H.C., Singh, M.P., Chopra, A.K.: Kiko: programming agents to enact interaction models. In: Agmon, N., An, B., Ricci, A., Yeoh, W. (eds.) Proceedings of the 2023 International Conference on Autonomous Agents and Multiagent Systems, AAMAS 2023, London, United Kingdom, 29 May 2023 - 2 June 2023, pp. 1154–1163. ACM (2023). https://doi.org/10.5555/3545946.3598758, https://dl.acm.org/doi/10.5555/3545946.3598758
18. V., S.H.C., Singh, M.P., Chopra, A.K.: Mandrake: Multiagent Systems as a Basis for Programming Fault-Tolerant Decentralized Applications. In: Agmon, N., An, B., Ricci, A., Yeoh, W. (eds.) Proceedings of the 2023 International Conference on Autonomous Agents and Multiagent Systems, AAMAS 2023, London, United Kingdom, 29 May 2023 - 2 June 2023, pp. 1218–1220. ACM (2023). https://doi.org/10.5555/3545946.3598765, https://dl.acm.org/doi/10.5555/3545946.3598765
19. Winikoff, M., Cranefield, S.: On the testability of BDI agent systems. In: IJCAI International Joint Conference on Artificial Intelligence, pp. 4217–4221 (2015)

Cost-Effective, MAS-Based, Refrigerated Container System at Container Terminals

Manolis Doudounakis[1(✉)], Nikolaos I. Spanoudakis[2], and Fotios D. Kanellos[3]

[1] School of Production Engineering and Management, Technical University of Crete, 73100 Chania, Greece
mdoudounakis@tuc.gr

[2] Applied Mathematics and Computers Laboratory, Technical University of Crete, 73100 Chania, Greece
nispanoudakis@tuc.gr

[3] School of Electrical and Computer Engineering, Technical University of Crete, 73100 Chania, Greece
fkanellos@tuc.gr

Abstract. Nowadays, power consumption at container terminals is related to flexible loads. Arguably, the most significant flexible loads, are the refrigerated containers, termed reefers. On average, reefers are responsible for 47.87% of the total energy consumption of container terminals. To control the reefers in a container terminal, it is hard to succeed with conventional methods. The Multi-agent systems (MAS) are well suited to control complex systems. In this paper, we show that MAS can be particularly well-suited to control reefers in a container terminal. A MAS system, implemented in JADE, is proposed for active power management of reefers. Additionally we use a fuzzy logic system, integrated in the MAS structure, to estimate the coefficient of utilization of the reefers. The results of our simulations with real data of a large terminal, proved the effectiveness of the method. A reduction of 37.08% to total energy cost of reefers at a container terminal was achieved.

Keywords: multi-agent systems · JADE · reefers · micro grid · fuzzy systems · container terminals · active power management

1 Introduction

Container terminals are hubs in the energy transfer net, and are very important in energy systems [1,13,34]. Therefore, efficient power management systems are needed in order to move towards more sustainable ports [4–7,19,21,23,38,48].

An important component of the container terminal micro grid [2,33] is that of refrigerated containers, also known as reefers, that can be considered as thermostatically controlled loads. Reefers are among the most flexible loads in a terminal as they are easily shifted in time. So, reefers can be used to modify the power consumption. Nowadays, on average, reefers are responsible for 47.87% of the total energy consumption of container terminals [29].

R. Collier et al. (Eds.): EUMAS 2024, LNAI 15685, pp. 340–360, 2025.
https://doi.org/10.1007/978-3-031-93930-3_20

It is hard to control the reefers load, with conventional approaches. The flexibility of the loads is the essential characteristic for efficient demand response. Reefers, due to their flexibility, will play a key role of the future port energy systems, which change rapidly and become more complex, so efficient power management systems will be needed [1]. Methods like the use of a single centralized controller, or traditional optimization techniques, require a great amount of computational resources making their application quite difficult [25,53].

Multi-Agent Systems (MAS) have been considered for applications in power engineering mainly due to their distributed control, where the overall optimization problem is decomposed into smaller sub-problems that individual controllers can solve cooperatively [25,46,53]. In hierarchical MAS, each controller manages a single system unit, and groups of controllers report to higher-level coordinators that manage the interaction between the various subsystems. An intelligent agent is assigned to each controller and all agents together compose the MAS [36]. This approach has been proven to be very effective in solving complex optimization problems where the detailed model of the entire controlled system is difficult to be obtained and traditional control techniques are insufficient. MAS technology has been widely exploited in power engineering [12,20,22,23,28,41,46].

Recently, Gennitsaris and Kanellos [16] used a MAS architecture implemented in MATLAB with simulated data. A fuzzy logic system embedded in the MAS was used to compute the reefers' coefficient of utilization, so as to reduce the reefers energy cost. Several empirical approaches were researched in the frame of E-harbors project [52]. Other works using a real dataset [30,51], employed an optimization algorithm to just reduce the reefers' peak consumption. Other research works [27,29,32,39,50] examine energy costs of reefers, either from a different point of view or without providing quantitative results.

For this work we used JADE [9], a standardized, state of the art, platform that has proved its worth in real world applications in the smart grid [3,8,15,26,35,40,42]. Our research combines a MAS implemented in JADE and a fuzzy logic system embedded in the MAS architecture, using the real dataset of van Duin et al. [30,51], the only available to us. We chose an hierarchical MAS system architecture [36], in such a way that it allows for scalability and adaptability. The key findings of our research, is that a MAS-based, cost-effective, reefer system at container terminals can improve significantly the state of the art.

In Sect. 2 we outline the MAS architecture and its elements. Then, in Sect. 3, we show the simulation results, and discuss our findings. We conclude in Sect. 4.

2 Agent Modeling

Reefers outlay power to preserve the temperature of their cargo between specific limits, and rely on external sources of power, i.e., the electric grid.

We used a Multi-Agent System (MAS) in the problem, because it is able to solve an optimization problem with complex systems better than with a centralized controller. Moreover, each component of the grid is semi-autonomous in the sense that it can manage its local operation, being dependent for applying centrally defined strategies. Thus, a failure in one component will not result to total collapse of the system. Moreover, mitigations can include the launch of agents that can take over a lost role (especially if that one is in the top of the hierarchy).

We utilized a methodological approach for system analysis and design, following the Agent Systems Engineering Methodology (ASEME) [47], as it has been recently used successfully for engineering MAS for the smart grid [14,42,46] and is referred to by surveys in the field [17].

ASEME leverages statecharts and the unified modeling language (UML) for system analysis and design models. It remains neutral regarding agent architecture and mental model, empowering designers to choose architecture types and agent attributes, thereby supporting diverse agent architectures.

Additionally, ASEME advocates for a modular agent design approach and utilizes the intra-agent and inter-agent control concepts. Intra-agent control coordinates different modules implementing an agent's capabilities to determine its behavior, while inter-agent control defines protocols governing the coordination of agent societies. ASEME allows the seamless integration of the inter-agent control model in the intra-agent control model as they follow the same formalism—i.e., statecharts [18,45]. Finally, it supports code generation for JADE [44].

Capabilities are further broken down into individual activities. For example, consider a reefer manager's capability to respond to a request to lower consumption in the following time-lapse. This capability can be decomposed into specific tasks, such as to wait at the appropriate channel for receiving the request, select the appropriate reefer agents to halt consumption and reply promptly. Once these activities are identified, the next step is to link them to specific functionalities, such as methods, algorithms, or techniques. This linking process is a crucial managerial task, as each activity can be associated with different functionalities. For instance, the decision-making activity of selecting the reefers can be linked to a fuzzy rules based sub-system, to an argumentation-based approach, or to a utility function, suggesting a multi-criteria decision analysis method.

In recent years, both commercial and open source agent development tools have become available. For developing our MAS we selected JADE. JADE is a Java framework for developing FIPA compliant MASs, not imposing any specific agent internal architecture.

During system analysis, we classified the agent roles in two main categories:

- *Local role* that represents a single component of the terminal,
- *Aggregator role* that aggregates the responses of the local roles and also sends to them command signals

Using these two roles we can identify three agent types in our architecture:

- *Reefer agent (R/A)*, which plays the local role and corresponds to a reefer in the microgrid. The R/A models the operation of the reefer it controls

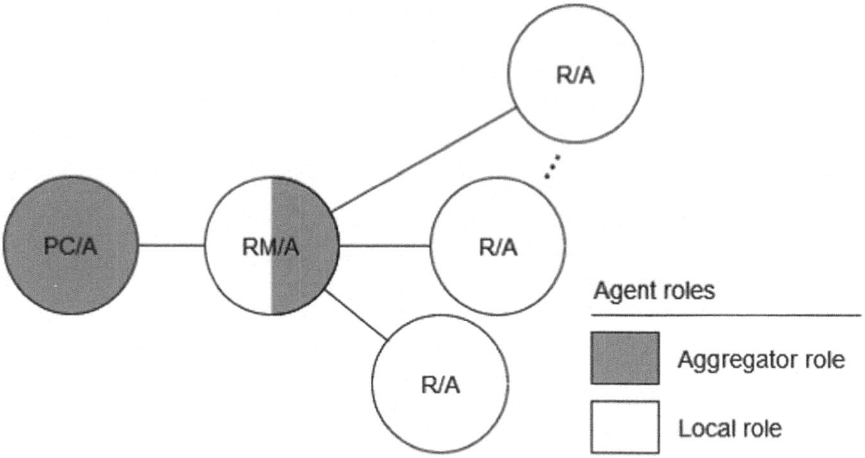

Fig. 1. MAS Architecture

- *Reefer Manager agent (RM/A)*, which plays the aggregator role for the R/As and the local role for the Port Controller agent
- *Port Controller agent (PC/A)*, which plays the aggregator role for the RM/A

In Fig. 1 the MAS architecture is presented. It highlights the agent-based architecture for modeling the port power grid and shows its advantages. On the top of the figure we have the PC/A. The PC/A communicates with RM/As, which, in turn, communicate with the R/As. The nature of the communication is to share relevant information bottom-up and to give directions (top to bottom).

The R/A computes the flexibility of a reefer to change its power demand, and sends this information to the RM/A. The RM/A aggregates the flexibility information from all the R/A and shares it with the PC/A. Then, the PC/A, computes the power consumption change of reefers required to reduce their cost of operation, and sends it in the form of a directive to the RM/A. Then, RM/A computes the *marginal flexibility*, and sends a directive to those reefers whose flexibility is higher than the marginal to change their state.

2.1 Reefer Agent (R/A)

We calculate the alteration of the temperature of the reefer in the next period of time Δt [22,23,49], as follows:

$$T(i,t+\Delta t) = T(i,t) + \Delta T_{amb} \cdot (1 - e^{-\frac{A \cdot k}{m(i) \cdot c_p(i)} \Delta t}), state(i,t) = 0 \quad (1)$$

$$T(i,t+\Delta t) = T(i,t) - \frac{P_{\text{reefer,cool}} \cdot \Delta t}{m(i) \cdot c_p(i)}, state(i,t) = 1 \quad (2)$$

where, A is the surface (in m^2), k is the thermal insulation (in $W/m^2 \cdot^\circ C$), m is the mass (in kg), c_p is the specific heat (in $kJ/kg \cdot^\circ C$), $state(i,t)$ is the state of the Reefer i, at time t, $state(i,t) = 1(0)$ if the reefers is switched on(off), ΔT_{amb} is the Difference in ($°C$) between the temperature of the environment and of the temperature inside the reefer (Return Air Temperature), $P_{\text{reefers,cool}}$ is the refrigerating power provided to the reefer, (in kW), t is the time (Seconds), Δt is the duration of the time intervals and $\Delta T(t)$ is the temperature effect of reefer in Time ($°C$) [16,22]. Then, we calculate the flexibility of the reefers so as the temperature is within the limits of their operation [16,22]:

$$F^{-}_{reefer}(i,t) = \frac{T_{max}(i) - T(i,t+\Delta t)}{T_{max} - T_{min}} \tag{3}$$

$$F^{+}_{reefer}(i,t) = \frac{T(i,t+\Delta t) - T_{min}(i)}{T_{max} - T_{min}} \tag{4}$$

where, T_{min} is the minimum temperature, T_{max} is the maximum temperature, $F^{+}_{reefer}(i,t)$ is the flexibility of the ith reefer to increase its power consumption,at time t, while $F^{-}_{reefer}(i,t)$ is the flexibility of the ith reefer to decrease its power consumption, at time t.

The possible alteration of the power consumption of the ith reefer is given:

$$\Delta P_{reefer}(i,t+\Delta t) = \begin{cases} P_{reefer}(i,t), & \text{if } state(i,t) = 0 \\ -P_{reefer}(i,t), & \text{if } state(i,t) = 1 \end{cases} \tag{5}$$

where, $P_{\text{reefer}}(i,t)$ is the electric power consumption by the ith reefer (in kW) at time t, and $\Delta P_{reefer}(i,t+\Delta t)$ is the possible power consumption alteration by a reefer for the next time interval. The outputs provided by the R/A to the RM/A are the flexibility of the reefer to change its state and the corresponding power consumption change.

2.2 Reefer Manager Agent (RM/A)

The RM/A is placed one level above the R/A in the MAS hierarchical configuration (2nd level). It aggregates the flexibilities curves and the possible change of power consumption it receives from all the reefers. The PC/A calculates, by sorting in descending order the flexibilities of the reefers, how much the power demand of the port should change in order to achieve its next interval goal, also referred to as *set-point*, and sends it as the directive to the RM/A. Subsequently, the RM/A computes the respective *marginal flexibility* and sends directive to the reefers with flexibility above the marginal one to change their state.

Computation of the Desired Power Consumption of the Reefers. We used a fuzzy logic system [24,37,54] to compute the desired coefficient of *utilization* of the reefers. We used as inputs to the fuzzy system the layer of the *price* of the electricity and the aggregated *flexibility* of all the reefers to increase their power consumption. All the fuzzy sets we used for the electricity price, coefficient of utilization and flexibility of all the reefers, are correlated with the

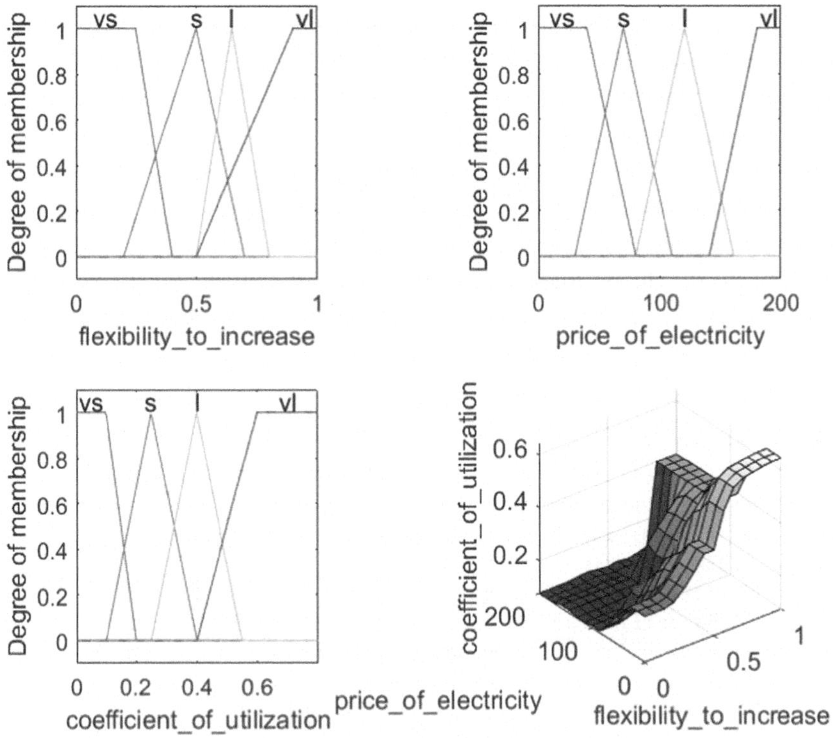

Fig. 2. From top left to bottom right: Membership function of flexibility of the reefers to increase its power consumption; Membership function of the price of the electricity; Membership function of the coefficient of utilization (output1) of all the reefers; Three dimensional Surface of the fuzzy system. The variable values belong to the set {very small (vs), small (s), large (l), very large (vl)}

variables: *very small*, *small*, *large* and *very large*. The membership functions we used are shown in Fig. 2. The rules we used for the estimation of the coefficient of utilization of the reefers are given in Listing 1. We used a defuzzification policy based on centroids in order to compute the value of the output [16].

The coefficient of utilization, CoU, of the $N_{reefers}$ reefers, and the flexibility to increase its power consumption, F^{+}, are given below [16]:

$$CoU(t) = \frac{\sum_{i=1}^{N_{reefers}} P_{reefer} \cdot state(i,t)}{\sum_{i=1}^{N_{reefers}} P_{reefer}} \tag{6}$$

where, CoU is the coefficient of utilization (suitably normalized in [0 1]) and P_{reefer} is the power consumption of a reefer (in kW).

$$F^{+}(t) = \frac{\sum_{i=1}^{N_{reefers}} \cdot (1 - state(i,t)) \cdot P_{reefer}(i) \cdot F^{+}_{reefer}(i,t)}{\sum_{i=1}^{N_{reefers}} P_{reefer}(i)} \tag{7}$$

where, F^+(t) is the flexibility of the reefers to increase their power consumption, at time t and $F^+_{reefer}(i,t)$ is the flexibility of the ith reefer to increase its power consumption, at time t. The set-point of the power consumption of all the reefers is calculated below:

$$P^*_{reefers}(t) = CoU^*_{reefers}(t) \cdot \sum_{i=1}^{N_{reefers}} P_{reefer,nom}(i,t) \tag{8}$$

where, $CoU^*(t)$ is the desired coefficient of utilization of the reefers (in [0 1]), at time t, and $P^*_{reefers}(t)$ is the desired power consumption by all reefers in port (in KW) in the 2nd level, at time t.

Listing 1. Fuzzy rules for estimating the coefficient of utilization of the reefers

```
RULE 1 : IF (flexibility IS very small) AND (price IS very small)
           THEN utilization IS small;
RULE 2 : IF (flexibility IS small) AND (price IS very small)
           THEN utilization IS large;
RULE 3 : IF (flexibility IS large) AND (price IS very small)
           THEN utilization IS very large;
RULE 4 : IF (flexibility IS very large) AND (price IS very small)
           THEN utilization IS very large;
RULE 5 : IF (flexibility IS very small) AND (price IS small)
           THEN utilization IS very small;
RULE 6 : IF (flexibility IS small) AND (price IS small)
           THEN utilization IS small;
RULE 7 : IF (flexibility IS large) AND (price IS small)
           THEN utilization IS large;
RULE 8 : IF (flexibility IS very large) AND (price IS small)
           THEN utilization IS large;
RULE 9 : IF (flexibility IS very small) AND (price IS large)
           THEN utilization IS very small;
RULE 10 : IF (flexibility IS small) AND (price IS large)
           THEN utilization IS very small;
RULE 11 : IF (flexibility IS large) AND (price IS large)
           THEN utilization IS small;
RULE 12 : IF (flexibility IS very large) AND (price IS large)
           THEN utilization IS large;
RULE 13 : IF (flexibility IS very small) AND (price IS very large)
           THEN utilization IS very small;
RULE 14 : IF (flexibility IS small) AND (price IS very large)
           THEN utilization IS very small;
RULE 15 : IF (flexibility IS large) AND (price IS very large)
           THEN utilization IS very small;
```

2.3 Port Controller Agent (PC/A)

The PC/A is the agent placed on the top of the hierarchy (3rd level). The PC/A receives the responses from all R/A via the RM/A. In this experiment, the PC/A controls only one Manager Agent, the RM/A.

The PC/A receives the reefers responses from the RM/A and computes the required ΔP power, in order to achieve its set-point, which is either the moving average across the window of observation, or a given value. To compute ΔP the following equations apply.

$$\Delta P(t) = \bar{P}_{reefers}(t) - P_{\text{reefers}}(t) \tag{9}$$

where $\bar{P}_{reefers}(t)$, is the set-point of the power consumption of all the reefers (in KW) in the 2nd level. Then, the PC/A sends the above computed ΔP as directive to RM/A.

It may appear that the PC/A's role is quite limited in this study, however, in our ongoing research, to simulate all the flexible electrical loads of a port terminal, we have plenty of manager agents and its role is very crucial.

3 Case Study

3.1 Simulation Data

When doing simulations the use of real data is significant, so as to show the applicability of the approach to real world situations [29, 31]. This case study is based on real data [49], collected at a container terminal. This data set provides all reefer data, such as its dwell-time at terminal, its mass, set point, etc. This dataset is the only available in the public domain. Port terminal authorities, although they have similar data for their terminals, are loath to provide them to researchers.

The lack of real-world data and its significance for validating results has been mentioned in the literature [29]. The period of measuring for our dataset was from the 1st of January 2014 to the end of January 2015. The reefer cooling capacity is assumed to be equal to the electric power consumption and the cooling power. We have also assumed that all reefers immediately after plugging-in are set to cooling mode.

3.2 Simulation Scenarios

The simulation results that we present, are based on data from the first two days of July, with a time step interval equal to one minute (the simulation tick equals to one minute). Thus, the total simulation time is 2880 ticks. We get similar results if we use other periods in the dataset. In this simulation interval, 879 Reefers dwelled at the port terminal. We run four scenarios:

- *dummy scenario, without MAS Control*, i.e. there are no directives.
- *MAS control*, i.e. we have directives from the PC/A to the RM/A and from the RM/A to the R/A's, and flexibility changes as ordered to achieve its

set-point, which is computed as the moving average across the window of observation.
- *MAS with set-point*, where the port terminal tries to achieve a desired, predefined power consumption of all the reefers (set-point)
- *MAS with cost consideration*, where the port terminal tries to achieve a minimum power cost, taking into account the fluctuations of the electricity price over time.

3.3 MAS Modeling

This section on one hand aims to help the reader understand the functionality of the MAS and on the other hand to get an insight in the flexibility of our architecture that allows the port roles to connect dynamically. This model applies for the last three of the above scenarios, i.e. those with MAS. When engineering the agents using ASEME, we first define the agent interaction protocols (inter-agent control model) and then the individual agent architecture. In the latter we define how the agent coordinates its capabilities. The agent's participation in interaction protocols is then just another capability to be coordinated with its own capabilities.

We provide, as an example, the *GetReeferFlexibilityAndConsumption* protocol between a local role (R/A) and an aggregator role (RM/A). It is defined as a statechart (following the semantics of [18] and the graphical model syntax of the ASEME statechart editor [47]) with the AND-state *GetReeferFlexibilityAndConsumption* as the root (see Fig. 3). The root state engulfs the whole statechart. AND-states (depicted with a light blue color label) contain OR-states, and being in an AND-state entails being in all its OR-states simultaneously, implying that the latter are executed in parallel (also called orthogonal components). OR-states (with yellow-colored labels) contain other sub-states, only one of which can be active at any time.

START-states (denoted by black dots) indicate the initiation of execution, while END-states (depicted as black dots enclosed within a circle) mark the conclusion of execution. START- and END-states are pseudo states, i.e. are used to indicate where execution starts and ends, but the statechart cannot stay in these. BASIC-states (shown in green) are where agent activities are executed.

In Fig. 3 we have two OR-states, one showing the behavior of the local role (R/A) within the protocol, *GetReeferFlexibilityAndConsumption_Reefer* and one for the aggregator role (RM/A), *GetReeferFlexibilityAndConsumption_ ReeferManager*. Both are executed in parallel. The exchange of messages synchronizes their execution.

Each transition from one state (source) to another (target) is labeled by an expression, whose general syntax is $e[c]/a$, where e is the event that triggers the transition; c is a condition that must be true in order for the transition to be taken when e occurs; and a is an action that takes place when the transition is taken. All elements of the transition expression are optional [18].

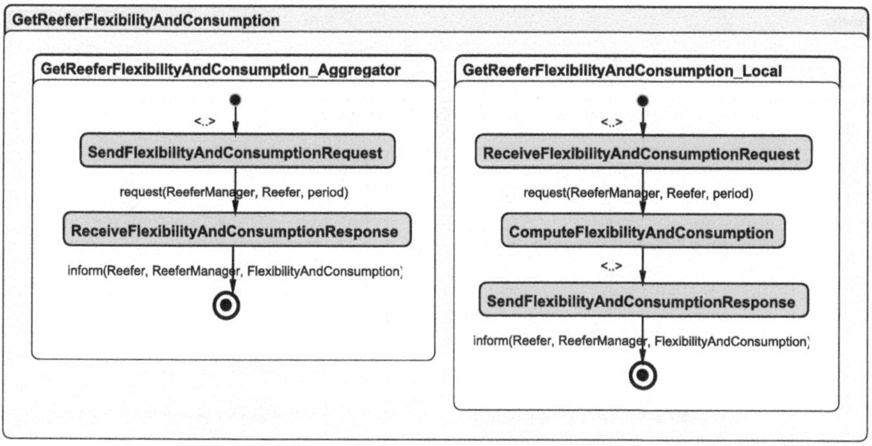

Fig. 3. The *GetReeferFlexibilityAndConsumption* protocol by which the reefer manager role gets information about the reefers consumption and flexibility for the next reporting period. (Color figure online)

Transitions are usually triggered by events. Such events can be a sent or received inter-agent message, a timeout, and, finally, the completion of the executing state activity. Note that each state automatically starts its activity on entrance. A message event is expressed by $Performative(sender, recipient, content)$, where the $Performative$ is a speech-act locution of the intended action (as defined by FIPA-ACL), $sender$ is the sender role, $recipient$ the receiver role and $content$ the message content expressed in the defined port ontology [43]. States starting with the word *Receive*, indicate waiting states for a message to arrive. States starting with the word *Send*, indicate states that prepare and send a message.

In Fig. 3 the local role (executing the *GetReeferFlexibilityAndConsumption_Reefer* orthogonal component) waits to receive a message. As soon as it receives the message event with performative *request*, with the RM/A as *sender* and with itself as the *recipient* it exits the *ReceiveFlexibilityAndConsumptionRequest* state and enters the *ComputeFlexibilityAndConsumption* state. After it finishes the computation it exits this state and enters the *SendFlexibilityAndConsumptionResponse* state. In the latter it prepares and sends the message with performative *inform*, with itself as *sender* and with the Reefer Manager as *recipient*. This causes it to exit the protocol (it finished). Likewise, the Reefer Manager starts by sending the *request* and then waits for the *inform* message and, as soon as it receives it, it also terminates the protocol execution.

To show how the agents' intra-agent control model integrates protocols, we provide the R/A's model in Fig. 4. The OR-state *Reefer* is the root. The *Reefer* state has a START-state, a BASIC-state, an AND-state (*GetReeferFlexibilityAndConsumption_Reefer_parallel_ControlReefer_Reefer*) and an END-state. Thus, as soon as execution starts, the *Reefer* performs an initialization process

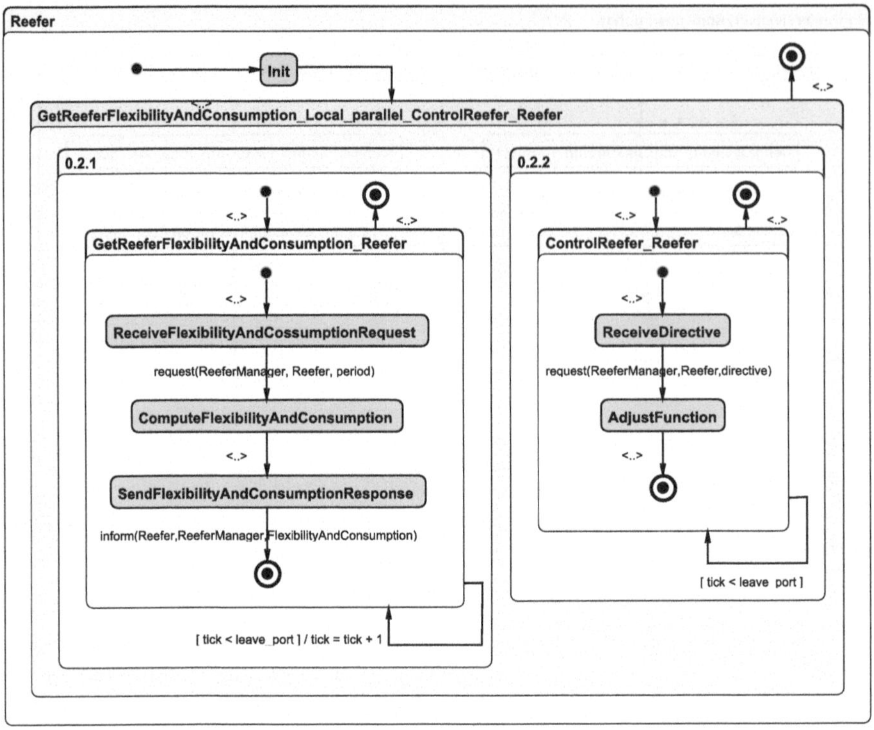

Fig. 4. Reefer Agent Statechart

(initialize its data structures) in the *Init* state and enters the AND-state. Its OR-substates are *0.2.1* and *0.2.2*. These are OR-states and the statechart execution engine enters them and searches for their START-states to show where execution begins.

Thus, the *Reefer* enters the BASIC-states *ReceiveFlexibilityAndConsumptionRequest* (in the first orthogonal component) and *ReceiveDirective* (in the second). These are both activities that wait to receive messages. These messages are related to two different protocols, i.e. the *GetReeferFlexibilityAndConsumption* and the *ControlReefer* protocols. The names of the OR-states in the orthogonal components indicate the name of the protocol (*GetReeferFlexibilityAndConsumption*, *ControlReefer*), followed by an underscore and then the role of the agent in the protocol (*Reefer* in this case).

After the *GetReeferFlexibilityAndConsumption_Reefer* finishes (i.e. enters the END-state), the transition expression of the state to itself is checked as it has a transition expression (transitions without expressions are the default, but all others must be checked before they are taken). First, the condition $tick < leave\_port$ is evaluated. *leave_port* is the tick in which the reefer departs towards a new destination and leaves the port. If this is *true* then the *tick* increases and the agent relaunches the protocol. The same happens with the *ControlReefer_Reefer* protocol with the exception that the tick is not increased a second time. If the expression is $false$ then both protocols terminate and the agent, subsequently, terminates.

3.4 Simulation Results and Discussion

Scenario 1. Figure 5(a) displays the total port terminal consumption, from Tick = 120, till Tick = 2790, for the dummy scenario. Also, Fig. 5(b), displays the flexibility (normalized temperature) of a typical random reefer, which fluctuates between 0 and 1 with different slopes when cooling and not cooling, for the dummy scenario. This represents the fact that the temperature fluctuates between minimum and maximum value continuously.

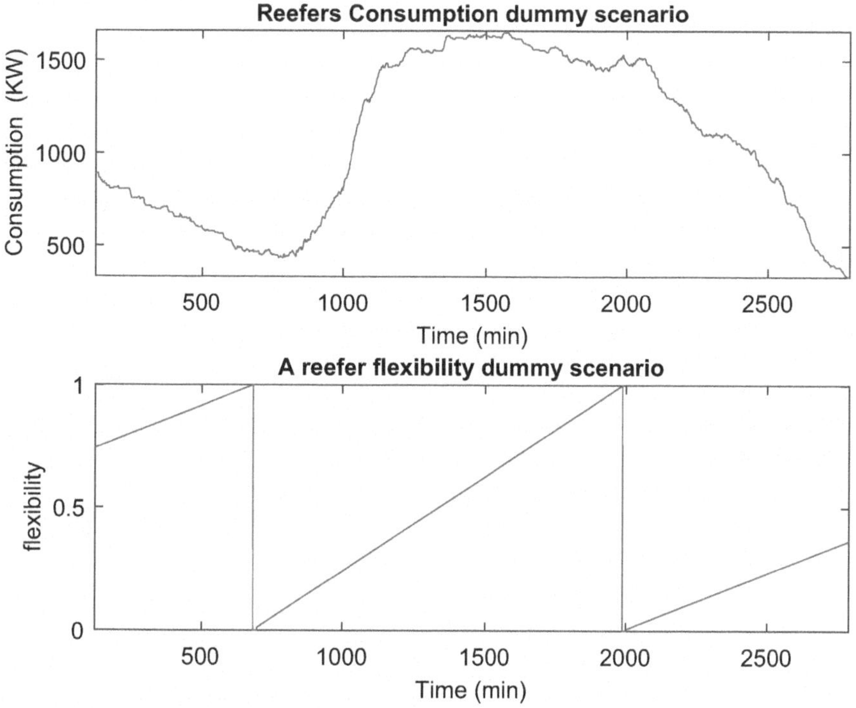

Fig. 5. a) Terminal Reefers Consumption over time without MAS and b) Flexibility variation over time of a typical reefer, without MAS.

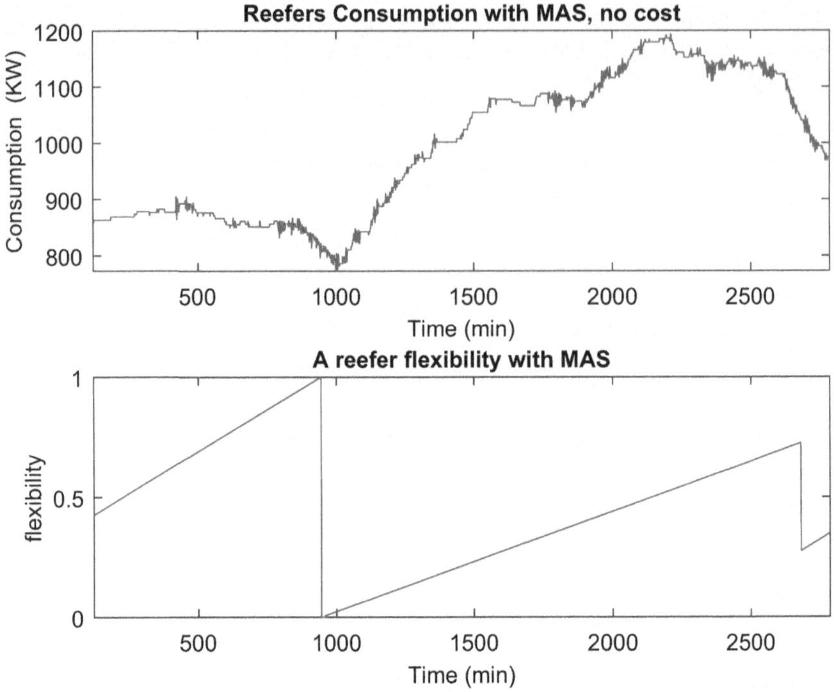

Fig. 6. a) Terminal Reefers Consumption over time, with MAS and b) Flexibility variation over time of a typical reefer, with MAS control.

Scenario 2. Figure 6(a) displays the total Port Terminal Consumption, for the same period, as previously. We observe significant differences, to the total reefers consumption over time, compared to the first – dummy scenario. This is due to the action of the MAS control, where the set-point is the moving average across the window of observation. Also, Fig. 6(b) displays the flexibility of a typical reefer, from Tick = 120, till Tick = 2790, in the case of MAS control. The difference with regard to the previous scenario is that flexibilities may change before they reach their maximum value (1), and, respectively the temperature does not always fluctuate between minimum and maximum value.

Scenario 3. In this scenario, a desired set point, 900 KW, which is less than the average consumption in the second scenario (see Fig. 6(a)), was set from Tick = 700 till Tick = 2000. At Fig. 7 the results are presented. It is observed that the port terminal total reefers consumption followed the predefined set point very well. This is due to the act of MAS Control.

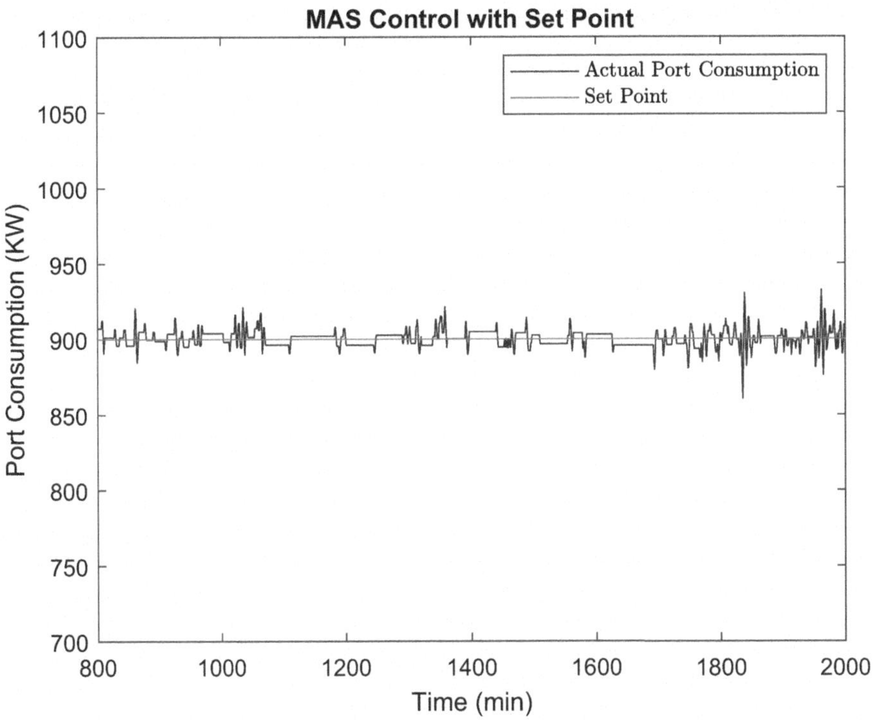

Fig. 7. Terminal Reefers Consumption over time, with MAS control and desired Set Point

Scenario 4. Finally, in the fourth scenario, we employed MAS control with cost information included. Cost information is considered with the use of a non-constant, but time-varying evolution of the electricity price over time. The cost information was taken into account with the integration with the fuzzy-logic sub-system described in paragraph 2.2 into the MAS.

For the implementation of the fuzzy-logic sub-system in java we used the jFuzzyLogic package [10,11]. In Figs. 8, 9, 10 the simulation results are shown, from Tick = 300 till Tick = 2880. As we can see, in Fig. 8, due to the act of the MAS control, the desired total reefers power consumption computed by the fuzzy sub-system, and the actual consumption, are very close to each other, over time.

The applied control method reduced their operation cost, by suitably forcing all reefers to change their power consumption. In Fig. 9(a), the flexibility to increase consumption for all the reefers is shown, which is very close and varies between 0.25 to 0.6. In Fig. 9(b) we provide the evolution of the electricity price over time. Similar results were taken with other curves of electricity price. The price, and the flexibility to increase consumption are used for computing the desired reefers coefficient of utilization, by the fuzzy subsystem, given in Fig. 9(c). In Fig. 10(a), we give the marginal flexibility, where we observe that the marginal

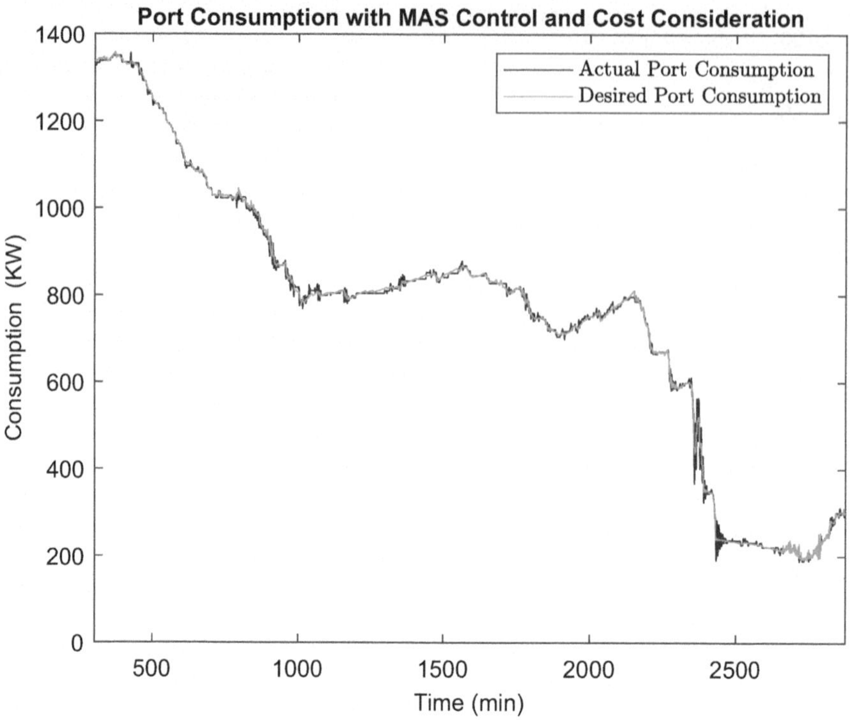

Fig. 8. Terminal Reefers Power consumption over time actual and desired

flexibility varies considerably, between 0.25 and 1.0. In Fig. 10(b) we provide the change at the next Tick of the power consumption of all the reefers, $\Delta P(\mathrm{t})$, as it was calculated by the PC/A. The figure shows it to balance around zero with small values and some spikes, as expected.

Table 1. Reduction of Total Energy Cost of Reefers.

Scenario	Reduction of Total Cost
This work, dummy scenario	0.00%
This work, moving average	2.15%
This work, with fuzzy	**37.08**%
Empirical Technique [52]	2.70%–11.00%
MAS, with fuzzy [16]	16.60%
Peaks Reduction [30,51]	17.00%

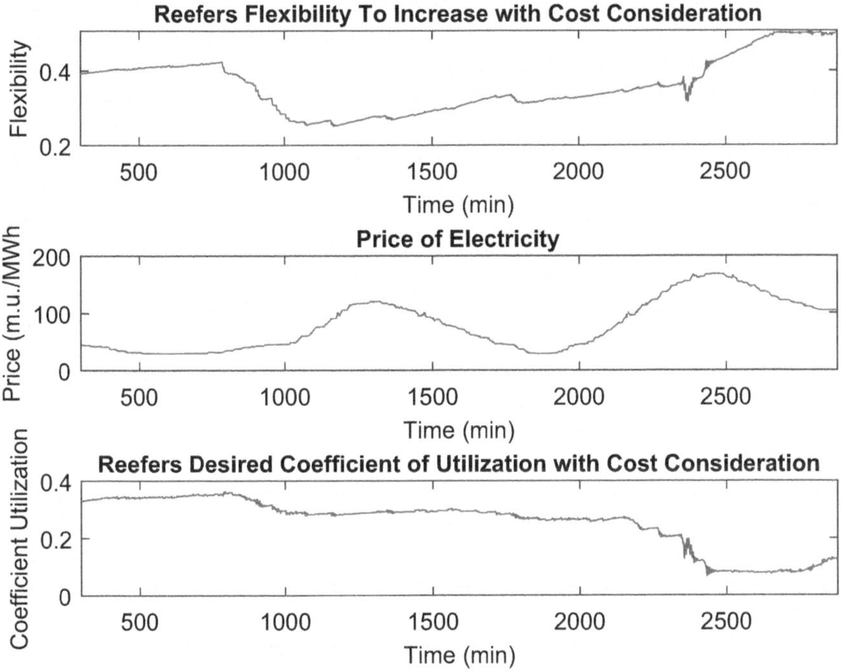

Fig. 9. a) Reefers Flexibility to increase over time b)Price of Electricity over time and c) Desired Coefficient of Utilization over time

3.5 Discussion and Related Work

In Table 1 we observe the key result of the paper: We achieved a substantial reduction of the total energy cost of reefers at 37,08%. With other curves of electricity price, we achieved similar results. The total operational cost was 2449.7 m.u. with the use of fuzzy and 3893.0 m.u. without MAS (dummy scenario). Also, we achieved a substantial reduction of the total energy cost of reefers per KWh at 19,49%. The total operational cost per KWh was 0.0628 m.u. with the use of fuzzy and 0.0780 m.u. without MAS (dummy scenario). The results are very encouraging and better than any other using either real or simulated data [16, 30, 51].

In a recent work [16], with simulated data and a combined MAS architecture and fuzzy-logic based approach simulated in MATLAB, the operation energy cost of reefers was reduced by 16.6%. Several approaches were earlier investigated under the E-harbors project, such as the ports of Hamburg and Antwerp [52]. The exploitation of the reefers' flexibility led to estimated cost savings in the order of 5–7% and 2.7–11%, respectively. Other works of the same research team, using the same dataset with this paper [30, 51], used an optimization algorithm to reduce the reefers' peak demands and achieved 17% cost savings. Hence, our combined MAS, implemented in JADE, and the integrated fuzzy system

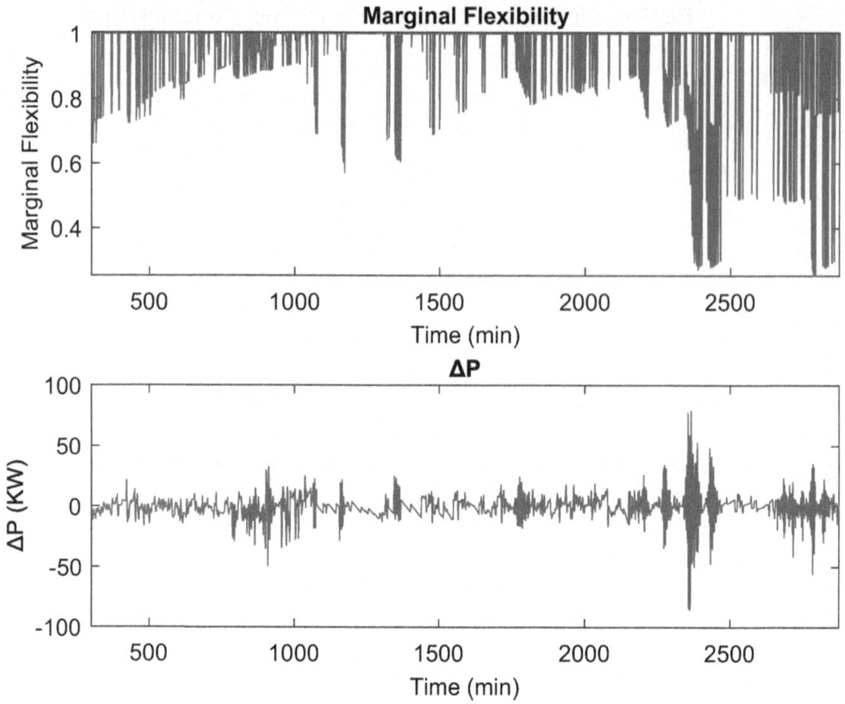

Fig. 10. a) Marginal Flexibility at the RM/A level and b) the computed change of power consumption of the reefers, at the PC/A level

performed much better compared to those approaches, and the obtained results are much better than any other reported work.

We also, observed that the simulation time, in the scenario with cost under consideration, in a usual laptop, was about 285 sec. In contrast, in [16] a similar problem with the MAS being simulated in Matlab was carried out in 3562 sec (about 1h). The above results show the significance of using JADE and distributing computations over the different agents over Matlab [16] or Excel [30,51].

4 Conclusion

This paper shows that a cost effective, MAS-based, reefers system is an efficient solution for energy cost reduction at container terminals, as shown by our simulation results with real data. The examined system is so complex that a MAS with hierarchical structure is required to conceive the complexity. The way the agents interact to achieve their goals is presented in detail. The results are very promising and indicate the efficiency of the method to remarkably reduce the cost of operation of a container terminal.

We are currently working to extend this research by simulating all the components of the port micro-grid, such as cranes, plug-in electric vehicles, shore-side power supply, widely known as "cold ironing", Renewable Energy Sources such as wind-turbines and solar panels [22]. We expect that these components, each with its particular properties, will be seamlessly integrated into our architecture and protocols that we already developed using the ASEME methodology [47]. Moreover, we aim to apply this extended scenario with real port data. Additionally, we aim to make this research, real-time. Finally, we aim to simulate the system with all available data, that is to say the simulation period to be a year and not only two days.

References

1. Acciaro, M., Ghiara, H., Cusano, M.I.: Energy management in seaports: a new role for port authorities. Energy Policy **71**, 4–12 (2014)
2. Ahamad, N.B.B., Guerrero, J.M., Su, C.L., Vasquez, J.C., Zhaoxia, X.: Microgrids technologies in future seaports. In: 2018 IEEE International Conference on Environment and Electrical Engineering and 2018 IEEE Industrial and Commercial Power Systems Europe (EEEIC/I&CPS Europe), pp. 1–6. IEEE (2018)
3. Al-Agtash, S., Hafez, H.A.: Agents for smart power grids. Energy Power Eng. **12**(08), 477–489 (2020)
4. Alzahrani, A., Petri, I., Ghoroughi, A., Rezgui, Y.: A proposed roadmap for delivering zero carbon fishery ports. Energy Rep. **8**, 82–88 (2022)
5. Alzahrani, A., Petri, I., Rezgui, Y.: Modelling and implementing smart micro-grids for fish-processing industry. In: 2019 IEEE International Conference on Engineering, Technology and Innovation (ICE/ITMC), pp. 1–8. IEEE (2019)
6. Alzahrani, A., Petri, I., Rezgui, Y., Ghoroghi, A.: Developing smart energy communities around fishery ports: toward zero-carbon fishery ports. Energies **13**(11), 2779 (2020)
7. Alzahrani, A., Petri, I., Rezgui, Y., Ghoroghi, A.: Decarbonisation of seaports: a review and directions for future research. Energ. Strat. Rev. **38**, 100727 (2021)
8. Azeroual, M., Lamhamdi, T., El Moussaoui, H., El Markhi, H.: Simulation tools for a smart grid and energy management for microgrid with wind power using multi-agent system. Wind Eng. **44**(6), 661–672 (2020). https://doi.org/10.1177/0309524X19862755
9. Bellifemine, F.L., Caire, G., Greenwood, D.: Developing Multi-Agent Systems with JADE (Wiley Series in Agent Technology). Wiley (2007)
10. Cingolani, P., Alcala-Fdez, J.: jfuzzylogic: a robust and flexible fuzzy-logic inference system language implementation. In: 2012 IEEE International Conference on Fuzzy Systems, pp. 1–8. IEEE (2012)
11. Cingolani, P., Alcalá-Fdez, J.: jFuzzyLogic: a java library to design fuzzy logic controllers according to the standard for fuzzy control programming. Int. J. Comput. Intell. Syst. **6**(sup1), 61–75 (2013)
12. Dou, C.X., Liu, B.: Multi-agent based hierarchical hybrid control for smart microgrid. IEEE Trans. Smart Grid **4**(2), 771–778 (2013)
13. Doudounakis, M., Kanellos, F.: Active power management in "green" ports. In: Proceedings of the European Conference on Shipping, Intermodalism and Ports (ECONSHIP), Chios, Greece, pp. 24–27 (2015)
14. Elshaafi, H., Vinyals, M., Grimaldi, I., Davy, S.: Secure automated home energy management in multi-agent smart grid architecture. Technol. Econ. Smart Grids Sustain. Energy **3**, 1–13 (2018)

15. Feliachi, A., Belkacemi, R.: Intelligent multi-agent system for smart grid power management. In: Smart Power Grids 2011, pp. 515–542. Springer (2011)
16. Gennitsaris, S.G., Kanellos, F.D.: Emission-aware and cost-effective distributed demand response system for extensively electrified large ports. IEEE Trans. Power Syst. **34**(6), 4341–4351 (2019)
17. González-Briones, A., De La Prieta, F., Mohamad, M.S., Omatu, S., Corchado, J.M.: Multi-agent systems applications in energy optimization problems: a state-of-the-art review. Energies **11**(8), 1928 (2018)
18. Harel, D.: Statecharts: a visual formalism for complex systems. Sci. Comput. Program. **8**(3), 231–274 (1987)
19. Hoang, A.T., et al.: Energy-related approach for reduction of CO2 emissions: a critical strategy on the port-to-ship pathway. J. Clean. Prod. **355**, 131772 (2022)
20. Inage, S.I.: Prospects for large-scale energy storage in decarbonised power grids. International Energy Agency, IEA (2009)
21. Iris, Ç., Lam, J.: A review of energy efficiency in ports: operational strategies, technologies and energy management systems. Renew. Sustain. Energy Rev. **112**, 170–182 (2019)
22. Kanellos, F.D.: Real-time control based on multi-agent systems for the operation of large ports as prosumer microgrids. IEEE Access **5**, 9439–9452 (2017)
23. Kanellos, F.D., Volanis, E., Hatziargyriou, N.D.: Power management method for large ports with multi-agent systems. IEEE Trans. Smart Grid **10**(2), 1259–1268 (2017)
24. Khan, M., Faruque, M.O., Newaz, A.: Fuzzy logic based energy storage management system for MVDC power system of all electric ship. IEEE Trans. Energy Convers. **32**(2), 798–809 (2017)
25. Korbik, A., McArthur, S.D., Ault, G.W., Burt, G.M., McDonald, J.R.: Enabling active distribution networks through decentralised autonomous network management. In: CIRED 2005-18th International Conference and Exhibition on Electricity Distribution, pp. 1–5. IET (2005)
26. Kuzin, A.Y., Demidova, G.L., Lukichev, D.V.: An approach of the jade and simulink interaction to control smart grid based on the multi agent system. In: 2019 IEEE Conference of Russian Young Researchers in Electrical and Electronic Engineering (EIConRus), pp. 574–577. IEEE (2019)
27. Lam, J.S.L., Ko, M.J., Sim, J.R., Tee, Y.: Feasibility of implementing energy management system in ports. In: 2017 IEEE International Conference on Industrial Engineering and Engineering Management (IEEM), pp. 1621–1625. IEEE (2017)
28. Maturana, F.P., Staron, R.J., Hall, K.H.: Methodologies and tools for intelligent agents in distributed control. IEEE Intell. Syst. **20**(1), 42–49 (2005)
29. Moros-Daza, A., Castro, D., Bonifacio, J., Amaya-Mier, R., Voß, S.: Greening container terminals: an innovative and cost-effective solution for sustainable reefer container storage. J. Clean. Prod. 142664 (2024)
30. Nafde, T.R.: Smart reefer system: modeling energy peaks of reefers connected at terminals and thereby suggesting peak shaving solutions to reduce cost. Master's thesis, Department of Engineering Policy Analysis, Delft University of Technology, Delft, The Netherlands (2015)
31. Ntountounakis, M., Ahmad, I., Kanellos, F., Palensky, P., Gawlik, W.: MAS based demand response application in port city using reefers. In: Highlights of Practical Applications of Cyber-Physical Multi-Agent Systems: Workshops of PAAMS 2017, Porto, Portugal, 21–23 June, pp. 361–370. Springer, Cham (2017)
32. Parise, G., et al.: Systems design criteria for refrigerated container parks. IEEE Trans. Ind. Appl. **55**(3), 2320–2326 (2019)

33. Parise, G., Parise, L., Martirano, L., Chavdarian, P.B., Su, C.L., Ferrante, A.: Wise port and business energy management: port facilities, electrical power distribution. IEEE Trans. Ind. Appl. **52**(1), 18–24 (2015)
34. Pavlic, B., Cepak, F., Sucic, B., Peckaj, M., Kandus, B.: Sustainable port infrastructure, practical implementation of the green port concept. Therm. Sci. **18**(3), 935–948 (2014)
35. Priyadarshana, H.V.V., U Hemapala, K.T.M., S Wijayapala, W.D.A., Saravanan, V., Kalhan S Boralessa, M.A.: Developing multi-agent based micro-grid management system in JADE. In: 2nd International Conference on Power and Embedded Drive Control (ICPEDC), pp. 552–556. IEEE (2019)
36. Rieger, C., Zhu, Q.: A hierarchical multi-agent dynamical system architecture for resilient control systems. In: 2013 6th International Symposium on Resilient Control Systems (ISRCS), pp. 6–12. IEEE (2013)
37. Rouholamini, M., Mohammadian, M., Wang, C., Gharaveisi, A.A.: Optimal fuzzy-based power management for real time application in a hybrid generation system. IET Renew. Power Gener. **11**(10), 1325–1334 (2017)
38. Roy, A., Auger, F., Olivier, J.C., Schaeffer, E., Auvity, B.: Design, sizing, and energy management of microgrids in harbor areas: a review. Energies **13**(20), 5314 (2020)
39. Shi, Z., Fan, F., Yu, J., Yin, G., Zhang, H., Su, Z.: Optimal operation of green-port logistics system for consumption enhancement of off-shore wind power. In: 2022 IEEE PES Innovative Smart Grid Technologies-Asia (ISGT Asia), pp. 751–755. IEEE (2022)
40. Shobole, A.A., Wadi, M.: Multiagent systems application for the smart grid protection. Renew. Sustain. Energy Rev. **149**, 111352 (2021). https://doi.org/10.1016/j.rser.2021.111352
41. Shoham, Y., Leyton-Brown, K.: Multiagent Systems: Algorithmic, Game-Theoretic, and Logical Foundations. Cambridge University Press (2008)
42. Spanoudakis, N., Akasiadis, C., Kechagias, G., Chalkiadakis, G.: An open MAS services architecture for the V2G/G2V problem. In: Proceedings of the 18th International Conference on Autonomous Agents and MultiAgent Systems, pp. 2198–2200 (2019)
43. Spanoudakis, N., Moraitis, P.: An agent modeling language implementing protocols through capabilities. In: 2008 IEEE/WIC/ACM International Conference on Web Intelligence and Intelligent Agent Technology, vol. 2, pp. 578–582. IEEE (2008)
44. Spanoudakis, N., Moraitis, P.: Modular JADE agents design and implementation using ASEME. In: 2010 IEEE/WIC/ACM International Conference on Web Intelligence and Intelligent Agent Technology, vol. 2, pp. 221–228 (2010). https://doi.org/10.1109/WI-IAT.2010.136
45. Spanoudakis, N.I.: Engineering multi-agent systems with statecharts: theory and practice. SN Comput. Sci. **2**(4), 317 (2021)
46. Spanoudakis, N.I., Akasiadis, C., Iatrakis, G., Chalkiadakis, G.: Engineering IoT-based open MAS for large-scale V2G/G2V. Systems **11**(3), 157 (2023)
47. Spanoudakis, N.I., Moraitis, P.: The ASEME methodology. Int. J. Agent-Oriented Softw. Eng. **7**(2), 79–107 (2022)
48. Tao, L., Guo, H., Moser, J., Mueller, H.: A roadmap towards smart grid enabled harbour terminals. In: CIRED Workshop-Rome, vol. 25, pp. 528–542. Citeseer (2014)
49. Tran, T.K.: Study of electrical usage and demand at the container terminal. Ph.D. thesis, Deakin University (2012)

50. van Duin, J., Geerlings, H., Tavasszy, L.A., Bank, D.L.: Factors causing peak energy consumption of reefers at container terminals. J. Shipping Trade **4**(1), 1–17 (2019). https://doi.org/10.1186/s41072-019-0040-y
51. van Duin, R., Geerlings, H., Verbraeck, A., Nafde, T.: Cooling down: a simulation approach to reduce energy peaks of reefers at terminals. J. Clean. Prod. **193**, 72–86 (2018). https://doi.org/10.1016/j.jclepro.2018.04.258
52. Verbeeck, J., Delnooz, A., Kuijper, F.: Application of smart energy networks-Part I, Part II: summary results of the individual company demand response audits in the port of Antwerp. Deliverable 3.5, E-Harbours Project (2013)
53. Weiss, G.: Multiagent Systems: A Modern Approach to Distributed Artificial Intelligence. MIT Press (1999)
54. Yi, S.Y., Chung, M.J.: Robustness of fuzzy logic control for an uncertain dynamic system. IEEE Trans. Fuzzy Syst. **6**(2), 216–225 (1998)

Towards Agents' Embodiment in Hypermedia Multi-agent Systems

Matteo Castellucci[1], Samuele Burattini[1(✉)], Andrei Ciortea[2], Jérémy Lemée[2], Danai Vachtsevanou[2], Alessandro Ricci[1], and Simon Mayer[2]

[1] Alma Mater Studiorum - Università di Bologna, Via dell'Università 50, 47522 Cesena, FC, Italy
matteo.castellucci3@studio.unibo.it, {samuele.burattini,a.ricci}@unibo.it
[2] University of St. Gallen, Rosenbergstrasse 30, 9000 St. Gallen, Switzerland
{andrei.ciortea,jeremy.lemee,danai.vachtsevanou,simon.mayer}@unisg.ch

Abstract. Situatedness and embodiment are central features of autonomous agents, initially inspired by agents operating in physical environments. In this paper, we discuss the benefits of situated and embodied agents in digital environments. More specifically, we study the embodiment of agents in Web-based Multi-Agent Systems (MAS). Such MAS are inherently *open* and *distributed*, as they inherit these properties from the Web, and increasingly *dynamic*, as they can easily extend to physical environments through the Web of Things. We propose a conceptualization of agent bodies in such Web environments and discuss their properties. We illustrate our approach through a demonstration scenario implemented using the Yggdrasil framework for Hypermedia MAS, a subset of Web-based MAS that follows a hypermedia-based design rationale.

Keywords: Embodiment · Situatedness · Hypermedia Multi-Agent Systems · Agents & Artifacts

1 Introduction

When considering open, dynamic, and large-scale systems where different agents may join and leave a shared environment at any time, the ability to *discover information about other agents* becomes a crucial factor for enabling interaction. This is true for physical and fully digital systems having such properties. One example of an open digital environment is the World Wide Web, which allows agents to join dynamically and browse information across linked resources. One way to enable the discovery of agents in such open systems is to equip them with bodies that are reified in the shared environment. Such bodies may also permit agents to communicate indirectly through reciprocal observation of their actions, facilitate contextual interaction, and support accountability mechanisms through the observability of visible agent behavior—all of which is enabled through embodiment.

R. Collier et al. (Eds.): EUMAS 2024, LNAI 15685, pp. 361–381, 2025.
https://doi.org/10.1007/978-3-031-93930-3_21

As humans, we are very familiar with such bodily-grounded interaction. We constantly experience situations in which observing other agent bodies around us gives us valuable information: from stepping aside to make space for somebody running towards us, to avoiding bothering a colleague wearing headphones and sending him an email instead, to reporting the violation of a rule when seeing somebody breaking it. The body itself becomes an indicator of an agent's presence, offering means to perceive its (observable) state and actions—and possibly even to ascribe goals to the agent [10]. As an example of how artificial agents might profit from embodiment, consider two agents reified in a physical environment through robotic arms under their control. If the robots are also equipped with cameras to perceive the world around them, then the agents can discover one another through their *bodies*, observe each other's actions to coordinate for handing over an object without direct communication, or even establish their reputation based on the correctness and speed of the robots' observable movements.

In a purely physical world, embodiment typically implies situatedness: if an agent has a body, that means the agent cannot be situated in multiple locations simultaneously; rather, the agent is restricted to be in only one place at any given time, which determines the portion of the environment that is observable to the agent and the environmental action opportunities (i.e., affordances) that the agent can perceive and exploit. Consequently, other agents can also only perceive the agent's presence in a single location. However, this implication is relaxed in the virtual world: Software agents are typically defined as *situated* (e.g., see [1]) but not necessarily *embodied*. To make this distinction clear, consider agents that crawl the Web: Being *situated* implies agents can browse the Web by discovering and following links from page to page. However, the agents are not *embodied*: Multiple agents browsing the same website are typically unaware of one other, as there is no representation of the other agents currently *on* the same page. This does not preclude *designing* websites that support embodiment—and we witness this regularly, for instance, in collaborative document editors. However, such support must be designed and implemented explicitly into the website.

The Web is a virtual environment of particular interest because its complexity rivals that of physical environments—and with the evolution towards a Web of Things [19,33], it now extends to and reflects the dynamicity of the physical world. There has been substantial research on integrating Multi-Agent Systems (MAS) with the Web, especially with the advent of service-oriented computing in the early 2000s [28]. The more recent proposal of *Hypermedia MAS* [12] (hMAS) argues for a deeper conceptual integration between MAS and the Web, which follows the Web's hypermedia-based design rationale and promotes the explicit representation of entities in MAS as hypermedia resources. In this context, the Web is recognized as a highly relevant environment for worldwide MAS [5], and thus investigating how exactly agents can be *situated* and *embodied* in a Web environment—and what are the design implications of these properties—emerges as an increasingly pressing research question (e.g., see [35]).

This paper addresses this question by exploring the requirements and potential of the digital embodiment of agents in Web environments: We discuss the requirements that call for agent embodiment and propose a conceptual model for agent bodies, which is inspired by the Agents & Artifacts (A&A) meta-model [23]. To support our approach, we implemented the proposed model in the Yggdrasil framework for hMAS [12]. We demonstrate the impact that embodiment can have on the development of agents navigating a hypermedia environment in a scenario that exemplifies agents coordinating with one another to operate robotic arms.

2 Background and Related Work

In this section, we first introduce the background knowledge on which we build our proposal for agent embodiment: the role of the environment as a first-class abstraction in MAS and of hypermedia-based environments in hMAS. We then discuss related work on engineering (Web-based) MAS to identify the gap filled by considering agent bodies as first-class abstractions in such systems.

2.1 First-Class Environments, Artifacts, and Bodies

The dominant view in research on autonomous agents is that intelligent, rational behavior is closely associated with the relationship between an agent and the environment it occupies [34]. This view originated in the late 1980s from research on intelligent robots that are naturally *situated* and *embodied* in the physical world [7]. Robot agents can perceive the external world with sensors and act upon it through actuators to achieve their design objectives. In this context, the physical world defines the environment in which agents operate.

In the mid-2000s, in the context of engineering MAS, the environment was recognized as a *first-class abstraction* [32]: a design space that can be exploited to provide agents with various levels of support, such as mediating access to the agents' deployment context, mediating interaction with other agents, or supporting manipulation of the environment state so that it meets the agents' design objectives. In this view, the concept of environment is no longer limited to the world external to the system. Rather, it becomes a system component designed and programmed with specific responsibilities. Such *virtual* environment offers the possibility to design an abstraction layer that connects agents to anything that is external to their individual state, there including either shared digital resources or physical sensors and actuators, under a common interface.

A well-known meta-model for designing and programming environments in MAS is *Agents & Artifacts (A&A)* [25]. As the name suggests, this meta-model puts agents and their environment at the same level of relevance for the design of MAS. The latter is modeled in terms of artifacts (i.e., tools used by agents to reach their goals). An *artifact*, as defined in the A&A meta-model, provides agents with an interface defined in terms of: *operations*, i.e. environmental actions the agents can use[1]; *observable properties*, i.e. state variables that agents can perceive; and *signals*, i.e. non-persistent atomic events that carry information and agents can receive as notifications when they are observing the artifact. The environment is then structured as a dynamic set of *workspaces*, which are logical containers for activities involving agents and artifacts [23]. The reference implementation for the A&A meta-model is the CArtAgO framework [25]. CArtAgO implements the notion of an agent's *body* as an artifact assigned to an agent automatically whenever it joins a new workspace. The body artifact is part of the joined workspace and represents the agent within the workspace. Furthermore, the agent's body serves as a proxy to the agent, allowing the framework to interact with different agents through a common interface. This allows heterogeneous agents, which may use different agent architectures and may be programmed in different languages, to be reified and embodied uniformly within the same workspace and to interact with the same shared environment. From this perspective, *embodiment* provides a technical solution to support the seamless integration of heterogeneous agents in the same environment.

The notion of *environment as a first-class abstraction* is also central to hMAS [12], a class of Web-based MAS that advocates for a deeper conceptual integration between architectures for MAS and the architecture of the Web by following a hypermedia-based design rationale as captured by the REST architectural style [15]. The core feature of an hMAS is that agents use hypermedia to discover and uniformly interact with the rest of the system: given a single entry point into the hypermedia-based environment (i.e., a URI with associated hypermedia controls), agents can then navigate hypermedia resources to discover other entities in the system—including other agents, artifacts, organizations, knowledge bases, etc.—together with the means to interact with those entities through discovered hypermedia controls.

The hypermedia-based environment provides agents with an abstraction layer of the system—and it is a *hypermedia-based design space* that the system designer can exploit across all levels of support mentioned previously. However, providing proper conceptual support for agent embodiment in such systems is still an open issue. A step in this direction is taken in [35], which motivates the need for agents' situatedness and embodiment in open hypermedia environments and illustrates a potential solution based on the Solid specifications [9]. The authors outline several requirements for agent embodiment in decentralized hypermedia systems, but they do not provide a conceptual model for agent bodies as first-class abstractions which can guide the design of digital embodiment in hMAS and other kinds of virtual environments.

In this paper, we build upon the concept of body artifacts in CArtAgO and the requirements for embodiment in hMAS to expand the characterization of embodiment as a design abstraction for open MAS. We then outline a set of desired properties of agent bodies and characterize their definition in the context of hMAS, providing a preliminary implementation of the concept.

[1] In A&A, operations can also be invoked by other artifacts, for example as part of an artifact mashup.

2.2 Environment-Mediated Discovery and Interaction

Having introduced the role of the environment as a first-class abstraction in MAS, and especially its role in supporting embodiment, we now focus our discussion on mechanisms for environment-mediated discovery and interaction as alternatives to mechanisms based on agent embodiment.

Perhaps the most common mechanism used in open MAS for discovering agents and the services they provide is to rely on directory services, such as the *Agent Directory Services* and the *Service Directory Services* defined by the FIPA Abstract Architecture Specification [16]. Such centralized directory services are typically managed by *Directory Facilitators* (DFs) [17], which are most commonly implemented as agents that all the other agents in the system are required to interact with to register themselves and their services (e.g., see [3]). Multiple DFs can be federated to support distributed search, where requests are propagated among DFs up to a maximum depth level. Still, this approach to discoverability undermines scalability by relying on a custom network of DF agents to register and search for agents on the open Internet. In addition, it burdens agents (and their developers) with the overhead of managing registrations with directory services.

In contrast, if a hypermedia-based environment provided agents with a proper level of support for their embodiment, then the discovery of agents would be merely a side effect of their presence in the environment: Other agents *situated* within the same working context (e.g., a *workspace* in the A&A meta-model) could perceive their presence using the same mechanisms that they commonly use to perceive the environment—as the other agents become part of an agent's environment. Then, going beyond the immediate working context, hypermedia-based search engines could further support agents to discover relevant services and other agents in open hypermedia environments (e.g., see [13]).

After *discovering* other agents and their services, agents in a MAS typically need to interact with them in a coordinated manner to meet system design objectives. The environment can support coordination through various mechanisms, such as digital pheromone infrastructures or more complex coordination artifacts (see [32] for a comprehensive discussion on environment-mediated interaction). The former methods are commonly used to enable *stigmergy* in agent systems and have been applied to various domains such as manufacturing (e.g., see [30]) or transportation (e.g., see [27]). The latter are artifacts designed specifically to provide coordination functionalities [26], such as blackboards, auction artifacts [4], commitment protocol artifacts [2], or organizational artifacts [22]. Such mechanisms help to decouple participants and provide functionalities for managing their interaction at the cost of higher centralization.

Embodiment, on the other hand, could provide a complementary and naturally decentralized approach to coordination: each agent's body artifact contains only the information referring to the agent itself. This could include, for instance, making agents' actions and agent-specific affordances visible to other agents supporting new forms of coordination between agents. Additionally, observing the agents' actions through their bodies promotes the enactment of accountability measures, as agents can be easily monitored.

3 When Disembodied Agents Are Not Enough

If we consider the environment as a first-class abstraction in MAS, then explicitly representing agents in their environment can support relevant features—from discoverability to coordination and accountability [32]. In the following, we build upon these views by conceptualizing embodiment and analysing the features it may support in settings characterized by the non-functional properties of hypermedia environments. We identify four features that motivate agent embodiment in general and describe how embodiment can support such features in MAS, making parallels to practical use cases to exemplify how they could contribute in the context of Web-based MAS. While this forms the foundation of our research, our findings are not only relevant for Web-based MAS but apply to all types of MAS that share similar properties, such as openness and dynamicity.

Of course, not all these features could be desirable at all times for all kinds of systems, they can then be considered independent and customizable depending on the application goals. We elaborate on this in Sect. 6.

Discoverability. The first factor for considering embodiment as a key concern in open and dynamic MAS is its role in enabling the discovery of agents. As agent bodies are part of the environment, they can be perceived by other agents in the environment, leading to discovering the presence of other agents. Agent bodies allow another agent to understand aggregated information regarding a shared environment (e.g., no one else is in a workspace), and lead to more detailed information regarding specific agents (e.g., *who* is in a workspace).

The discovery of other users in shared environments is extensively adopted in those designed for human interaction. For example, in online collaborative writing spaces, it is common to employ user icons while human agents collaboratively edit a document, signifying who is currently working and at which position in the document. Removing the ability to discover other users by not showing any icon would limit the usefulness of editing a document together. Similarly, we argue that not allowing agents to discover other agents in a shared environment by means of some form of embodiment would limit their ability to exploit the shared resources effectively.

Communication Through Behavior. Agent discoverability, and especially the perception of other agents in the same environment, can enable communication between agents through their behavior, known as Behavioral Implicit Communication (BIC) [29]. This form of communication differs from what is usually conceived as agent-to-agent communication as no explicitly codified communicative action is used. Still, the intention of communicating from the source agent to the addressee agent may be present. Other agent actions take the place of communicative ones, having both the intended effect of performing a behavior and letting the addressee agent capture some meaning from it while observing the source agent [29].

Taking the example of collaborative document editing again, communication through behavior is what motivates the implementation of the movement of the different users' cursors along a document. If a user sees another one working on a paragraph, the first could decide not to overlap with the second and start working on a different section. Not having shared cursors between agents would make editing the same document at the same time more difficult without risking changing what someone else was working on, making them lose the accumulated work. BIC, in this case, is used as working on a paragraph is used as a communicative behavior that can be interpreted as a request to not interfere with the ongoing work.

Accountability. The property of allowing agents to observe other agent bodies can, in turn, support mechanisms for accountability as a desirable property in open MAS. As for BIC, this requires the body to be able to show the actions performed by an agent in the environment, just like in physical environments. Since an agent can look at actions performed by embodied agents, it can also decide if those were lawful or not, holding the agents accountable. It could do that by simply monitoring and logging their actions to enable future auditing from system administrators and *post hoc* analysis of possible security breaches or by taking action against the offending agent sanctioning the wrongful behavior.

This factor is particularly noteworthy in open systems like the Web, where components could be at cross purposes because no central organization can control all of them [15]. To grant accountability, additional mechanisms need to be in place to ensure that no agent misbehaves since we cannot rely on the correctness of individual agents. For example, in a collaborative encyclopedia like Wikipedia, not having the possibility to monitor other agents' actions would make it impossible to prevent users from trying to compromise what others have previously written, leading to a degradation of the content quality.

Situation-Dependent Interaction. After discovering an agent's body, others could gather information concerning the body itself, and hence the agent associated with it. This can lead to letting agents interact based on the current context, which we define as situated-dependent interaction. An agent's body could include information concerning the capabilities of its owner in the form of affordances to ask the agent to perform some tasks only it can achieve in the current context (e.g., for authorization requirements), but also preferences regarding means of communication [35]. The information conveyed through the body could also be dynamic and depend on either the body implementation, the state of the agent, or the specific workspace in which the body is situated.

To make a parallel with existing systems designed for humans, online instant messaging platforms often display a status next to user icons (e.g., whether they are online or not) that may give contextual information to other users to choose which actions to take to contact them. This could even be brought to automatically changing the contact method based on the context (e.g., when offline, a message is stored in a queue and delivered as soon as the receiver is back online).

4 Agents' Bodies in a Hypermedia Environment

Having identified the main features that make embodiment desirable in open digital environments, in this section, we provide a generic definition of the concept of an agent body and its defining characteristics that apply in digital environments. Our proposal is inspired by and builds on the A&A meta-model and its interpretation in the CArtAgO framework (see Sect. 2.1). Furthermore, we show how our definition can guide the implementation of agent bodies in hMAS.

Definition 1 (Body). *A body is an artifact reifying and identifying an agent in an environment. The body situates the agent, transparently mediating its actions and allowing the agent to perceive in a timely fashion. The body allows others to observe the owner agent and its behavior, and to perceive agent-specific affordances to interact with it.*

With this definition, we aim to capture the fundamental properties of an agent body. Before discussing each of these characteristics in more detail, Listing 1.1 illustrates an A&A notion of workspace, represented in a hypermedia environment using RDF. We use the Hypermedia MAS (hMAS) ontology [21], designed for representing Web-based MAS using concepts such as "agent" or "artifact" and inspired by the A&A meta-model. In this example, an *embodied agent* has joined the workspace. The agent is represented in the workspace description via an `hmas:contains` relationship, which allows other agents consuming the workspace description to discover its presence.

Listing 1.1: An RDF representation of an agent situated in a workspace. We use the Turtle serialization format.

```
@base <https://example.org/> .
@prefix hmas: <https://purl.org/hmas/> .

<workspaces/production/#workspace> a hmas:Workspace;
  hmas:contains <workspaces/production/artifacts/alice/#artifact> ;

<workspaces/production/agents/alice/#agent> a hmas:Agent .
```

Listing 1.2 shows a representation of the agent body itself, displaying interaction affordances, the relationship with the containing workspace, and the relationship with the agent that is the owner of that body. We use the W3C WoT Thing Description (TD) ontology [11] to represent the interaction affordances of the agent's body.

Listing 1.2: An RDF representation of an agent's body situated in a workspace (as used in our implementation).

```
@base <http://localhost:8080/> .
@prefix hmas: <https://purl.org/hmas/> .
@prefix td: <https://www.w3.org/2019/wot/td#> .
@prefix jacamo: <https://purl.org/hmas/jacamo/> .

<workspaces/production/artifacts/alice/#artifact> a td:Thing,
↪  hmas:Artifact, jacamo:Body;
  hmas:isContainedIn <workspaces/production/#workspace>;
  jacamo:isBodyOf <workspaces/production/agents/alice/#agent>;
  td:hasActionAffordance [ a td:ActionAffordance, jacamo:Focus;
    td:name "focus";
    td:hasForm [ htv:methodName "POST";
      hctl:hasTarget <workspaces/production/artifacts/alice/focus>;
      hctl:forContentType "application/json";
      hctl:hasOperationType td:invokeAction ];
    td:hasInputSchema [ a js:ObjectSchema;
      js:properties [ a js:StringSchema;
        js:propertyName "callbackURI"]
    ]].

<workspaces/production/artifacts/alice/#agent> a hmas:Agent .
<workspaces/production/#workspace> a hmas:Workspace .
```

4.1 Properties of Agent Bodies

In the following, we analyze each of the fundamental properties of an agent body. We define and discuss each property's implications in the context of a hypermedia environment.

Definition 2 (Concreteness). *Concreteness is the property of an agent's body to be reified in the environment, either explicitly or implicitly.*

With this property, we mean to stress that if an agent is embodied, its body *must* be part of the environment the agent inhabits. In hMAS, bodies are considered resources just like other entities in the MAS (e.g., agents, workspaces, artifacts). Then, given that hMAS follow a hypermedia-based design rationale [12], the concreteness property enables the discovery of agents through crawling—just like any other entities in the MAS.

Listing 1.2 shows an explicit representation of an agent body as a resource in a workspace. For some applications, having explicit representations of agent bodies in the environment might not be necessary, as the agent bodies might not carry any particularly relevant information apart from representing the presence of the agent within the environment (e.g., the agent does not expose any affordance for other agents to exploit). Nevertheless, because the body is concrete, the body can still exist in the environment even if it is not represented explicitly. Its existence can be reflected, for instance, through containment triples, which show which agents are present in a given workspace (cf. Listing 1.1). Our definition thus allows for *implicit* reification of agent bodies: by definition, an agent is situated in a workspace if and only if it has a body in that workspace. When representing hypermedia environments in RDF using OWL, the implicit representation of bodies is admissible under the open-world assumption.

Definition 3 (Identifiability). *Identifiability is the property of an agent's body to be bound to its owner agent.*

The identifiability property stresses that a body belongs to some agent (cf. line 8 in Listing 1.2). It does not make sense to model a body that is not bound to an agent. Identifiability allows an agent perceiving the presence of a body to discover not only that another agent is present, but also *who that agents is*. This is essential for holding an agent accountable for the behavior exercised through their body, or to decide whether or not to trust them.

Line 8 of Listing 1.2 associates the body representation with the URI of its owner through the `jacamo:isBodyOf` property. For some applications, the environment could hide the agent-body relationship, thereby keeping the agent owning a body anonymous to other agents. However, this option does not forfeit the identifiability property: the association between the body and the owner's identity would still exist but the system requirements would prevent other agents from discovering it. Although anonymous to other agents, as long as the agent is identifiable to the system, it can still be held accountable.

Definition 4 (Transparency). *Transparency is the property of an agent's body that allows the owner to use its body implicitly when performing actions.*

As agents are embodied, the body becomes the vessel for performing actions in the environment. This is true in physical environments as an agent controls the actuators of its body, and should be true for digital bodies as well as the context of the body may influence the capabilities of an agent over time (e.g., the agent may not be able to act on artifacts that are too far away from its body in an environment that supports some notion of locality). With the property of transparency, we highlight the fact that such behavior should be implicit and require no additional cognitive effort for the agent.

The transparency property keeps the notion of embodiment aligned with the A&A meta-model and the interaction of agents with other artifacts as simple as possible. In A&A, if agents would be restricted to act explicitly through their body, this would imply that agents would have to use a generic operation of the body artifact to invoke operations on other artifacts (e.g., a `doAction` operation of the body artifact taking as arguments a target artifact and the invoked operation). Sending all operation invocations through the body would add an unnecessary indirection level and could potentially turn the body into a performance bottleneck. In a distributed hMAS, this could translate to performing multiple network requests to the environment every time, leading to performance degradation.

Still, although transparent, an agent's body can constrain the operations the agent can perform in the environment given the data contained in their body (e.g., based on some properties of the body that differentiate agent abilities, such as an authorization level). The transparency of the body implies that the environment will need to assume an active role in mediating the interaction between agents and artifacts, potentially enabling or limiting some interaction based on the properties of the acting agent's body. Moreover, if the body is represented explicitly in the environment, the owner (just like other agents) is allowed to consciously observe its own body and reason about it when needed. The transparency property is not violated, as acting through the body remains implicit, and the ability to observe the body is application-dependent and allowed by the agent's autonomy to perceive it.

Definition 5 (Timely perception). *Timely perception is the property of an agent's body to communicate, in a timely fashion, the percepts it receives from the environment to its owner agent.*

As the body situates its owner, it determines what the owner perceives from the environment. Embodiment in a given environment can imply passive perception, meaning that the body constantly perceives state changes the environment designer considers essential. Perception can also be active (or intentional), meaning that the agent decides to *focus* on the artifacts they consider relevant for achieving their goals (cf. A&A meta-model). The body is then responsible for notifying the owner about the percepts it can collect. Not only that, it should do that in a timely fashion. What accounts for a *significant* delay is application-specific: in some use cases, delays of hours or days may be permissible while in others, owner agents need to receive percepts within seconds, or faster.

As discussed for *transparency*, the agent does not have to query its own body to get new percepts proactively but directly receives them as new stimuli to be processed in an event-driven fashion. This property further helps distinguish a body from other artifacts that may be associated with a specific agent, but that may be conceptually different; one example of such an artifact is a mailbox for asynchronous messages—such a mailbox may be processed in a timely fashion only when the agent is free from other tasks, but not otherwise.

Timely perception does not entail a specific implementation for the mechanism for receiving environmental stimuli: for instance, the platform implementing the agent architecture could still poll their body for new percepts instead of relying on a publish/subscribe mechanism implemented in the body, as long as this is handled by the environment, and not by the agent. On a practical level, this means that, when joining a workspace, depending on the implementation, either an agent must declare somehow how the environment should send percepts to it through its body, or the environment should notify the agent what body it is assigned to in that environment, including how to observe percepts (this negotiation perspective is discussed in greater detail in Sect. 6).

Definition 6 (Focusability). *Focusability is the property of an agent's body to allow other agents to observe the body itself and perceive affordances to interact with the owner, affordances dependent on the environment.*

Agents must be able to focus on a body artifact since it allows them to perceive its properties, the changes it goes through, and the events it generates. This concept derives from the A&A meta-model, where focusing on an artifact allows an agent to automatically perceive changes in observable properties and receive signals from it.

A body representation contains information about its owner agent, so focusing on the body artifact should be used for retrieving this information including the capabilities exposed by that agent as operations. This choice allows for modeling the owner information through observable properties so the focusing agents can get notified about their updates without any additional action. A body could contain many properties, as long as they are directly related to the owner and relevant to the context of the workspace the body is in, meaning that an agent can change what it is exposing for external observation depending on the context.

Focusability supports communication through behavior because getting notified of the events corresponding to an agent action starting or ending would allow another agent to understand which actions are successfully performed, and possibly ascribe which behavior is being enacted. The support for accountability is a natural consequence: for example, we can create a supervisor agent who focuses on all the others, checking the correctness of their subordinates' behaviors by being notified of which actions they are taking in the workspace (as demonstrated in Sect. 5).

Similar to any other artifacts, agents may also focus on their own bodies to understand what information about themselves is publicly exposed and, possibly, change it. The usefulness of such an operation lies in those cases where the body may be updated by external factors in the environment. In that case, the agent might want to be notified of the content of its body and possibly act on it to change it.

In Listing 1.2, the affordance shown allows focusing on the body while supporting a more straightforward implementation of situational interaction, not forcing the client to poll the body for changes in its description. The body representation includes a hypermedia control (lines 9–18) that allows the agent to subscribe to receive notifications to a callback URI. This way, an agent can discover how to register for notifications, and the framework can notify it of changes in the body representation, including changes to properties and performed actions.

5 Implementation and Evaluation

To technically ground the proposal of embodiment, we implemented support for the features we discussed above into Yggdrasil [12], a framework for hMAS. We further validate our implementation through a demonstrating scenario in a manufacturing context inspired by the use cases of the HyperAgents project.[2] The demonstrator, showcasing features of embodied hypermedia agents, is publicly available on GitHub[3].

5.1 A Demonstration of Embodied Hypermedia Agents

For this scenario, consider that a manufacturing company is deploying a new supervisor agent in an already installed MAS that includes two worker agents dedicated to the control of robotic arms. For the sake of simplicity, we refer to the worker agents as Alice and Bob, and to the supervisor agent as Carl. The system leverages a hypermedia environment to represent agents and artifacts, using the features of embodiment that we described above.

In this scenario, Carl's goal is to supervise and manage the production plant. Carl receives tasks to be delegated as goals to the worker agents (e.g., to move two products from the shop floor to the warehouse). As Carl is new to the system, it does not yet know the current structure of the environment, nor which worker agents are available. The plan used by Carl, implemented in Jason [6], is shown in Listing 1.3. Carl hence needs to query the representation of the hypermedia environment to discover which worker agents are in the workspace (i.e., Alice and Bob) by finding their respective agents' bodies (Listing 1.4). Through their bodies, Alice and Bob expose affordances to receive messages for using a robotic arm to move products to different locations; this hence demonstrates how the *discoverability* feature of embodiment is exploited (see Sect. 3).

Listing 1.3: The plan for the supervisor agent Carl using a custom artifact to query the workspace, find the worker agents' (bodies) and delegate to each the task of moving an object from one location to another while also focusing on the workers to observe their behaviour.

```
+!supervise : client(ClientName) & message_box(MessageBoxName) <-
    lookupArtifact(ClientName, ClientId);
    searchCupMoverWorkers(WorkerBodies)[artifact_id(ClientId)];
    +cups_moved(0);
    for (.member(map(WorkerName, WorkerBody), WorkerBodies)) {
        +body(WorkerName, WorkerBody);
        focusWorkerBody(WorkerName, WorkerBody)[artifact_id(ClientId)];
        assignMoveCupTask(WorkerBody, "shop_floor",
    ↪   "warehouse")[artifact_id(ClientId)];
    };
    lookupArtifact(MessageBoxName, MessageBoxId);
    !loop(MessageBoxId).
```

[2] https://project.hyperagents.org/.
[3] https://github.com/cake-lier/hyperagents-yggdrasil-demo.

Listing 1.4: The SPARQL Query executed by Carl through the `searchCupMovingWorkers` operation, to find any worker agent in the environment, by finding bodies that expose the necessary affordances for task delegation.

```
SELECT DISTINCT ?worker ?name WHERE {
    ?worker a hmas:Artifact, jacamo:Body;
    td:title ?name;
    td:hasActionAffordance [
        a kqml:RequestAchieve;
        td:hasInputSchema [
            ...
        ];
    ].
}
```

Alice and Bob can each maneuver a robotic arm. They acquire this capability at run time when the agents find their assigned robotic arm artifact and expose the corresponding affordance through their body as a contextual operation for situational interaction; this demonstrates the *situation-dependent interaction* feature of embodiment.

Through the exposed affordances, Carl may delegate to both Alice and Bob the goal of moving one product each. Since Carl's goal in the system is to supervise the other agents, it can observe the agents' bodies to monitor their work, as they may exhibit faulty behavior that needs to be reported. So, Carl must focus on Alice's and Bob's bodies to observe their actions, and monitor whether the agents are completing the task correctly by observing agents' actions. The observability of agent actions through the body allows Carl to get automatically notified of the actions taken by the workers to monitor their behavior, leveraging the *communication through behavior* feature of embodiment. Finally, Carl can punish or reward the agents, implementing an *accountability* mechanism supported by the fact that Alice and Bob are embodied and consequently both their behaviour and identity are known to Carl.

5.2 Implementing Hypermedia Bodies in Yggdrasil

We used the properties defined in Sect. 4 to guide our implementation of embodiment in the Yggdrasil framework for hMAS, which we use in our demonstration. The implementation thus provides Yggdrasil developers with a level of support for exploiting embodiment when developing their applications—and can thus support future research on embodiment in hypermedia environments.

Since bodies are *concrete*, they are represented as resources whose representation can be retrieved via an `HTTP GET` request. This allows the discovery and crawling of these resources in the environment, a concept stemming from the single entry point principle at the core of hMAS [12]. A body representation can be updated via an `HTTP PUT` request, for example, to add hypermnedia controls for situational interaction.

The addition and removal of body resources in the environment are handled by the framework whenever an agent joins and leaves a workspace. Specifically, the representation of a workspace is updated by adding or removing a reference to an agent's body each time the agent joins or leaves the workspace. In our implementation, we represent agent bodies in RDF, as shown in Listing 1.2. Body representations include `acamo:isBodyOf` relationships to the owner agents, thus enabling *identifiability*.

Focusability is enabled in our implementation through the notification mechanism already existing in the Yggdrasil framework for other artifacts. Yggdrasil uses the W3C WebSub protocol [18] to allow Web clients to subscribe to (and unsubscribe from) specific topic URIs, which are the URIs of resources existing in the hMAS environment (e.g., of a workspace or an agent body) [12]. We piggyback on this WebSub implementation to deliver notifications about agent bodies. Subscribing for notifications notifies a client about changes to or the deletion of a body resource. Additionally, subscribed agents receive notifications for the start and end of actions the owner agent is performing within the workspace the body is contained in—therefore, supporting the *focusability* property. An action notification carries information about whether the action has started or ended, the type of action performed, the artifact on which the agent performed it, and includes an error message in case of failure. Through the same mechanism, our implementation permits agents to receive percepts about their environment through the body, implementing *timely perception*.

We added a read-only SPARQL [31] endpoint to Yggdrasil to enable querying, which supports proposals of aligning the A&A meta-model with Semantic Web technologies [8]. This allows interactions such as the one shown in Listing 1.4, which complement the ability of agents to crawl the hypermedia environment via accessing individual resources.

6 Discussion and Future Work

Embodiment is a promising approach for dealing with the open, dynamic, and distributed nature of Web-based MAS. We consider this work to be a first step towards investigating the general concept of digital embodiment in MAS.

As the hMAS context has been the main source of inspiration for this work, we acknowledge the influence that the requirements of Web-based systems have had on the more general conceptualization of agent bodies. We can not yet claim that this approach is fully generalizable to other kinds of MAS. Still, since hMAS share interesting non-functional properties with many other kinds of MAS such as dynamicity and openness, we believe that the approach can be generalized to other kinds of digital environments. Further investigation may provide useful insight for embodiment as a design and programming abstraction for cyber-physical MAS as well.

With regard to Web environments, embodiment opens up new challenges and research directions that require further investigation. Here, we highlight some of the most compelling ones stemming from our approach, which we believe are worth investigating in future works.

Alignment with Organizational Models. Embodiment provides a distributed approach to coordination among agents, through discoverability and behavior-implicit communication. It also supports the implementation of accountability mechanisms that are essential in the development of open systems where agents may have conflicting interests and even malicious intents.

We believe that embodiment can offer interesting links towards the integration with organizational models (e.g. the MOISE+ organizational model [20]) for MAS programming. For instance, in our proposal for communication through behavior (see Sect. 3), we addressed the possibility of an agent being notified of the actions another party is enacting by observing its body. This notification mechanism can be realized by generating events concerning the execution of actions, enabling the implementation of special organizational rules called "count-as" rules, which automatically translate the completion of an artifact action into the completion of an organizational goal [24]. This may also lead to the implementation of monitoring agents that can detect norm violations through the observation of the other agents' bodies. Agent bodies may even expose which role an agent is taking in an organization, leading the other agents in the system to discover the organization themselves and start participating in it. Finally, making the role of an agent perceivable from its body may allow other agents to reason on how to interact with it based on the knowledge they may have about that role. We thus conceive of embodiment as a complementary approach to organizations in MAS and intend to investigate this alignment in future works.

Agent "Privacy" and Negotiation. As discussed in the previous sections, not all systems necessarily need to implement all the properties of an agent body: An important consideration in this sense concerns the *privacy* of agents with respect to what information they may be willing to share in the environment and what instead they may prefer hiding (including, in some cases, their identity or their performed actions). We could then envision a negotiation process between environments that specify requirements on the information to be exposed when an agent joins them and agents that prefer to keep certain information private. This mimics the experience that human users of Web environments have in accepting the terms of service of specific platforms they register to and may open up interesting challenges to be implemented. To this sense, the proposal of integrating embodiment with the Solid project [35] may introduce an additional level of fine-grained access control to the information contained in an agent body.

Body Authenticity. Another interesting challenge comes in verifying the authenticity of agent bodies, and of the agents that are controlling them. As agents and bodies are digital, decoupled entities nothing forbids in theory that the same body is shared by multiple agents. With the property of identification, we try to limit this, suggesting that a body should be paired with only a specific agent. Nevertheless, (malicious) agents may attempt to control other agents' bodies or to fake their identity or the data they share (e.g., to bypass authentication mechanisms).

Multiple Bodies. In this work, we define that a body should be paired with only one agent, and we follow the use of body artifacts as implemented in CArtAgO that reifies an agent with a body artifact in each workspace the agent has joined. This leads for an agent to have multiple, possibly different, bodies in different parts of an environment, which is of course a peculiarity of virtual environments. An agent to have multiple bodies can be compared to a human agent being situated, discoverable, and interactable simultaneously in an online collaborative writing space, a video conference platform, and the physical environment. In these settings, the bodies may encapsulate different aspects of the agent's overall context, may have different representations, and are observable by different sets of agents. The value of enabling such a setting for artificial agents in hMAS should be further investigated, along with potential trade-offs such as the flexible acquisition of combined access to resources and agents at the risk of complex and distributed allocation of an agent's resources and focus.

Environment Responsibilities and Heterogeneity. When agent bodies are represented in the environment, their representations would have to be kept updated as time passes. The responsibility of keeping bodies updated and available could become an additional infrastructural cost in the hypermedia environment, especially if such a responsibility is distributed among different nodes. Different environments may require different models and representations for agent bodies, and even implement different methods for discoverability (e.g., an environment with an explicit representation of space may require agent bodies to have an assigned position and be discovered only when in proximity). Finally, heterogeneous agents should be allowed to join environments despite potentially having different ways to receive percepts from the environment. The above arguments raise the question: Who is responsible for providing the body of an agent? Is it the agent or the environment? Moreover, who is responsible for keeping the body up to date, and managing the mechanism of perception? This heterogeneity of support may pose challenges to allowing agents to move freely between different hypermedia environments.

Evaluation of Embodiment Quality. Different criteria could be employed to evaluate whether and how well an embodiment implementation supports the features outlined in Sect. 3. Discoverability could be measured both qualitatively and quantitatively assessing how easy it is to find agents in an environment by either crawling or using supporting tools available in the environment (e.g., a search engine). Similarly, situation-dependent interaction can be qualitatively evaluated on whether the affordances exposed by the agent body are usable by other agents without requiring out-of-band information. Accountability and communication through behaviour may be evaluated in relationship to the expected level of trust in the system, the quantity and quality of information exposed within the body resource (e.g., whether the identity of agents is public and certified by some recognized authority), and the presence of sanctioning mechanisms in the system. A more quantitative analysis can instead be performed in relationship to timely perception and focusability. It should be possible to measure "staleness" of both the information that is received by an agent from the environment and what is instead sent to other agents focusing on a given body given application requirements in terms of latency and freshness of the information.

It could be interesting for the community to explore more how these evaluations can be performed and what could be their output, such as in the definition of a general level of quality and support for agent environments similarly to how Web environments are evaluated for human users' abilities and trust.

7 Conclusion

In this article, we discussed how embodiment supports the implementation of several relevant features of hMAS: discovering other agents in the environment; agents communicating through their behavior; situational interaction between agents; and accountability. We then conceptualized an abstraction for agent bodies, inspired by hMAS, where we defined the fundamental properties that agent bodies must have to support these features. We furthermore showcased a practical implementation of hypermedia agent bodies on the Yggdrasil framework and validated it on an example to demonstrate how embodiment can give more flexibility to agents, leading to less hard-coded specification. We believe this line of work could bring us closer to solving the "arrive and operate" problem, with agents capable of arriving in a new environment and, with minimal *a priori* information about it, starting to operate towards their goals [14].

Despite acknowledging that our exploration is still incomplete, we believe it is an essential step towards supporting the embodiment of agents in Web environments and digital MAS in general—and we presented open challenges that we believe can inspire new research directions for future work. Exploring more in detail the body definition could also lead to discovering if the presented characteristics are exhaustive and cover all aspects of embodiment or if other ones are needed. A complete examination of the notion of an agent's body could lead to a taxonomy for embodiment, devising different forms of embodiment with constraints depending on which properties are required for an application that can be useful for the more general MAS community.

Acknowledgments. This research has received funding from the Swiss National Science Foundation under grant No. 189474 (*HyperAgents*). This work is partially supported by the European Union - NextGenerationEU and Azienda Unità Sanitaria Locale (AUSL) della Romagna through the Italian "National Recovery and Resilience Plan" (PNRR) Mission 4, Component 2, Investment 3.3 (DM 352/2022) - CUP J33C22001400009.

References

1. Adams, J.A.: Multiagent systems: a modern approach to distributed artificial intelligence. AI Mag. **22**(2), 105–108 (2001). https://doi.org/10.1609/AIMAG.V22I2.1567

2. Baldoni, M., Baroglio, C., Capuzzimati, F., Micalizio, R.: Commitment-based Agent Interaction in JaCaMo+. Fundam. Informaticae **159**(1–2), 1–33 (2018). https://doi.org/10.3233/FI-2018-1656
3. Bellifemine, F., Poggi, A., Rimassa, G.: Developing multi-agent systems with JADE. In: Castelfranchi, C., Lespérance, Y. (eds.) ATAL 2000. LNCS (LNAI), vol. 1986, pp. 89–103. Springer, Heidelberg (2001). https://doi.org/10.1007/3-540-44631-1_7
4. Boissier, O., Bordini, R.H., Hübner, J.F., Ricci, A., Santi, A.: Multi-agent oriented programming with JaCaMo. Sci. Comput. Program. **78**(6), 747–761 (2013). https://doi.org/10.1016/j.scico.2011.10.004
5. Boissier, O., Ciortea, A., Harth, A., Ricci, A., Vachtsevanou, D.: Agents on the web (Dagstuhl Seminar 23081). Dagstuhl Reports **13**(2), 71–162 (2023) https://doi.org/10.4230/DagRep.13.2.71. https://drops.dagstuhl.de/entities/document/10.4230/DagRep.13.2.71
6. Bordini, R.H., Hübner, J.F., Wooldridge, M.: Programming Multi-agent Systems in AgentSpeak Using Jason, vol. 15. John Wiley & Sons (2007)
7. Brooks, R.A.: Intelligence without reason. In: Mylopoulos, J., Reiter, R. (eds.) Proceedings of the 12th International Joint Conference on Artificial Intelligence. Sydney, Australia, 24–30 August 1991, pp. 569–595. Morgan Kaufmann (1991). http://ijcai.org/Proceedings/91-1/Papers/089.pdf
8. Burattini, S., Ciortea, A., Galassi, M., Ricci, A.: Towards framing the agents & artifacts conceptual model at the knowledge level: first ideas and experiments. In: Ciortea, A., Dastani, M., Luo, J. (eds.) Engineering Multi-Agent Systems - 11th International Workshop, EMAS 2023, London, UK, 29–30 May 2023, Revised Selected Papers. Lecture Notes in Computer Science, vol. 14378, pp. 208–219. Springer, Heidelberg (2023). https://doi.org/10.1007/978-3-031-48539-8_14
9. Capadisli, S., Berners-Lee, T., Verborgh, R., Kjernsmo, K.: Solid protocol. W3c solid community group working draft, World Wide Web Consortium (2021). https://solidproject.org/TR/2021/protocol-20211217
10. Castelfranchi, C.: Ascribing minds. Cogn. Process. **13**(Supplement-2), 415–425 (2012). https://doi.org/10.1007/S10339-011-0423-Y
11. Charpenay, V., Lefrançois, M., Poveda-Villalón, M., Käbisch, S.: Web of Things (WoT) Thing Description (TD) Ontology. Editor's Draft, W3C (2022)
12. Ciortea, A., Boissier, O., Ricci, A.: Engineering world-wide multi-agent systems with hypermedia. In: Weyns, D., Mascardi, V., Ricci, A. (eds.) Engineering Multi-Agent Systems - 6th International Workshop, EMAS 2018, Stockholm, Sweden, 14–15 July 2018, Revised Selected Papers. Lecture Notes in Computer Science, vol. 11375, pp. 285–301. Springer, Heidelberg (2018). https://doi.org/10.1007/978-3-030-25693-7_15
13. Ciortea, A., Mayer, S., Bienz, S., Gandon, F., Corby, O.: Autonomous search in a social and ubiquitous Web. Pers. Ubiquit. Comput., 1–14 (2020). https://doi.org/10.1007/s00779-020-01415-1
14. Ciortea, A., Mayer, S., Gandon, F., Boissier, O., Ricci, A., Zimmermann, A.: A decade in hindsight: the missing bridge between multi-agent systems and the world wide web. In: Elkind, E., Veloso, M., Agmon, N., Taylor, M.E. (eds.) Proceedings of the 18th International Conference on Autonomous Agents and MultiAgent Systems, AAMAS '19, Montreal, QC, Canada, 13–17 May 2019, pp. 1659–1663. International Foundation for Autonomous Agents and Multiagent Systems (2019). http://dl.acm.org/citation.cfm?id=3331893

15. Fielding, R.T., Taylor, R.N.: Principled design of the modern Web architecture. ACM Trans. Internet Techn. **2**(2), 115–150 (2002). https://doi.org/10.1145/514183.514185
16. Foundation for Intelligent Physical Agents: FIPA Abstract Architecture Specification. Standard, Foundation for Intelligent Physical Agents (2002)
17. Foundation for Intelligent Physical Agents: Agent Management Specification. Standard, Foundation for Intelligent Physical Agents (2004)
18. Genestoux, J., Parecki, A., Fitzpatrick, B., Slatkin, B., Atkins, M.: WebSub. Recommendation, W3C (2018)
19. Guinard, D., Trifa, V., Wilde, E.: A resource oriented architecture for the Web of Things. In: Michahelles, F., Mitsugi, J. (eds.) 2010 Internet of Things (IOT), IoT for a green Planet, Tokyo, Japan, 29 November–1 December 2010. Proceedings. IEEE (2010). https://doi.org/10.1109/IOT.2010.5678452
20. Hannoun, M., Boissier, O., Sichman, J.S., Sayettat, C.: MOISE: an organizational model for multi-agent systems. In: Monard, M.C., Sichman, J.S. (eds.) IBERAMIA/SBIA -2000. LNCS (LNAI), vol. 1952, pp. 156–165. Springer, Heidelberg (2000). https://doi.org/10.1007/3-540-44399-1_17
21. HyperAgents: Hypermedia MAS Core Ontology. https://purl.org/hmas/core
22. Kitio, R., Boissier, O., Hübner, J.F., Ricci, A.: Organisational artifacts and agents for open multi-agent organisations: "Giving the power back to the agents". In: Sichman, J.S., Padget, J., Ossowski, S., Noriega, P. (eds.) COIN -2007. LNCS (LNAI), vol. 4870, pp. 171–186. Springer, Heidelberg (2008). https://doi.org/10.1007/978-3-540-79003-7_13
23. Omicini, A., Ricci, A., Viroli, M.: Artifacts in the A&A meta-model for multi-agent systems. Auton. Agents Multi Agent Syst. **17**(3), 432–456 (2008). https://doi.org/10.1007/S10458-008-9053-X
24. Piunti, M., Ricci, A., Boissier, O., Hübner, J.F.: Embodying organisations in multi-agent work environments. In: Proceedings of the 2009 IEEE/WIC/ACM International Conference on Intelligent Agent Technology, IAT 2009, Milan, Italy, 15–18 September 2009. pp. 511–518. IEEE Computer Society (2009). https://doi.org/10.1109/WI-IAT.2009.204
25. Ricci, A., Piunti, M., Viroli, M.: Environment programming in multi-agent systems: an artifact-based perspective. Auton. Agents Multi Agent Syst. **23**(2), 158–192 (2011). https://doi.org/10.1007/S10458-010-9140-7
26. Ricci, A., Viroli, M., Omicini, A.: Environment-based coordination through coordination artifacts. In: Weyns, D., Van Dyke Parunak, H., Michel, F. (eds.) E4MAS 2004. LNCS (LNAI), vol. 3374, pp. 190–214. Springer, Heidelberg (2005). https://doi.org/10.1007/978-3-540-32259-7_10
27. Schmid, S., Schraudner, D., Harth, A.: MOSAIK: an agent-based decentralized control system with stigmergy for a transportation scenario. In: Pesquita, C., et al. (eds.) The Semantic Web - 20th International Conference, ESWC 2023, Hersonissos, Crete, Greece, 28 May–1 June 2023, Proceedings. Lecture Notes in Computer Science, vol. 13870, pp. 697–714. Springer, Heidelberg (2023). https://doi.org/10.1007/978-3-031-33455-9_41
28. Singh, M.P., Huhns, M.N.: Service-Oriented Computing: Semantics, Processes. Agents. John Wiley & Sons, Hoboken (2006). https://doi.org/10.1002/0470091509
29. Tummolini, L., Castelfranchi, C., Ricci, A., Viroli, M., Omicini, A.: "Exhibitionists" and "Voyeurs" do it better: a shared environment for flexible coordination with tacit messages. In: Weyns, D., Van Dyke Parunak, H., Michel, F. (eds.) E4MAS 2004. LNCS (LNAI), vol. 3374, pp. 215–231. Springer, Heidelberg (2005). https://doi.org/10.1007/978-3-540-32259-7_11

30. Valckenaers, P., Van Brussel, H., Kollingbaum, M., Bochmann, O.: Multi-agent coordination and control using stigmergy applied to manufacturing control. In: Luck, M., Mařík, V., Štěpánková, O., Trappl, R. (eds.) ACAI 2001. LNCS (LNAI), vol. 2086, pp. 317–334. Springer, Heidelberg (2001). https://doi.org/10.1007/3-540-47745-4_15
31. W3C SPARQL Working Group: SPARQL 1.1 Overview. Recommendation, W3C (2013)
32. Weyns, D., Omicini, A., Odell, J.: Environment as a first class abstraction in multiagent systems. Auton. Agents Multi Agent Syst. **14**(1), 5–30 (2007). https://doi.org/10.1007/S10458-006-0012-0
33. Wilde, E.: Putting things to rest (2007)
34. Wooldridge, M., Jennings, N.R.: Agent theories, architectures, and languages: a survey. In: Wooldridge, M.J., Jennings, N.R. (eds.) ATAL 1994. LNCS, vol. 890, pp. 1–39. Springer, Heidelberg (1995). https://doi.org/10.1007/3-540-58855-8_1
35. Zimmermann, A., Ciortea, A., Faron, C., O'Neill, E., Poveda-Villalón, M.: Pody: a solid-based approach to embody agents in web-based multi-agent-systems. In: Ciortea, A., Dastani, M., Luo, J. (eds.) Engineering Multi-Agent Systems - 11th International Workshop, EMAS 2023, London, UK, 29–30 May 2023, Revised Selected Papers. Lecture Notes in Computer Science, vol. 14378, pp. 220–229. Springer, Heidelberg (2023). https://doi.org/10.1007/978-3-031-48539-8_15

Putting Context Into Hypermedia MAS

Alexandru Sorici(✉) and Adina Magda Florea

National University of Science and Technology POLITEHNICA Bucharest, Splaiul Independentei 313, Bucharest, Romania
{alexandru.sorici,adina.florea}@upb.ro

Abstract. In agent-oriented software engineering there is a recent emphasis on development of Hypermedia Multi-Agent System (HMAS). This approach seeks to align MAS engineering with the Web architecture, fostering the development of large-scale, open, dynamic, and enduring interactions of human and software agents alike. The scale and dynamics of the interactions require a method to organize the provisioning of information that informs and is *contextual* to the interactions. We present the design of a framework that addresses the management of context information, while aligning with and using engineering principles of HMAS and streaming of knowledge over the web. We detail the implementation of a first use-case for the framework: the enabling of dynamic, context-based access control to web resources in an HMAS environment, by means of technologies such as RDF stream processing, SHACL and SOLID Web Access Control.

Keywords: Hypermedia MAS · Web-of-Things · Context Management · Context-Based Access Control · RDF Stream Processing · SHACL

1 Introduction

Hypermedia Multi-Agent Systems (HMAS [16]) is a novel class of MAS design which advocates for the alignment of MAS engineering with the web architecture to facilitate the development of large, open, dynamic, and long-lasting interaction systems. Central to this approach is the utilization of semantic hypermedia to facilitate interaction among diverse entities, including software agents, sensors, devices, services, and individuals.

An exemplar engineering framework [18] within the HMAS community suggests aligning the Agents and Artifacts (A&A) MAS development meta-model [31] with the Web-of-Things (WoT) W3C Thing Description (TD) specification [12]. The A&A model incorporates a distinct aspect for the programming of a MAS environment, involving the utilization of *artifacts* and their deployment across different *workspaces*. The artifacts serve to encapsulate the functionalities of digital services, sensors, or actuators, presenting their operations through observable properties, events, and actionable commands.

HMAS promotes design principles [18] that build up a strong support for *discoverability* of services on the web. These principles refer to aspects such

R. Collier et al. (Eds.): EUMAS 2024, LNAI 15685, pp. 382–401, 2025.
https://doi.org/10.1007/978-3-031-93930-3_22

as uniform representation of resources (e.g. in RDF), discovery through single points of entry (exploiting the HATEOAS - Hypermedia as Engine of Application State - guideline of self-descriptive resources) and observability of resource affordances [18]. The latter point is put further into focus by the perspective of signifiers [25,39] which are an abstraction providing a means for resources in an HMAS environment to signal and advertise their affordances to agents who are *able* and *interested* in exploiting them for their objectives.

Signifiers in particular, and agent interactions in an HMAS in general, are expected to be varied (e.g. in terms of complexity or agent and resource capabilities) and dynamic (e.g. in terms of duration or physical and logical agent mobility). This brings about the requirement to specify *the context* under which they can occur. Indeed, the signifier formalisation specifies a context element that contains the sum of conditions that *have to* characterize the situation of an agent in the HMAS environment, such that the currently desired affordance of a resource can be exploited [39].

However, the signifier formalism and the HMAS design principles do not provide suggestions or guidelines as to how the information and affordances about a resource in an HMAS can become *context* for an interaction, or how an agent can become aware and access such information in a principled manner. Put otherwise, an approach for *provisioning* of context information is currently not addressed by efforts to develop frameworks in support of HMAS environment engineering.

We therefore intend to provide a principled manner by which existing HMAS engineering frameworks (e.g. Yggdrasil [18]) can be extended with support for context information management.

Context Management Platforms can potentially address many concerns from various levels of application development and deployment (e.g. representing information, controlling and collecting data from IoT sensors, storing or aggregating information, forwarding information in a distributed system including means of caching and updating information, managing queries and subscriptions under quality-of-service concerns regarding source, recency and quality of the information, managing discovery of appropriate context sources, handling mobility of context providers and consumers) [3,22,40].

This work does not address all of these challenges, choosing to narrow the scope to applications whose deployment leverages *the web architecture*. Furthermore, the focus of our contribution is directed towards designing mechanisms for the *flow* and *discovery* of context information, *on demand*, based on the *interaction intentions* of a software agent, whose environment is the web. More specifically, we seek to align the context management design with principles for A&A based HMAS engineering. Importantly, elements of our proposal align with the vision of the RDF Stream Processing community [6], which looks to support dynamic interactions, such as those in an HMAS, by means of connecting *streams of data* over the web [20].

For the proposed context management extension we identify an important usage, namely the enabling of *context-based access control*, arguing that the mobility of both human and software agents (e.g. physically or in terms of *roles* played in activities) requires a mechanism of authorization that exploits the dynamic context of the interactions, beyond a standard token based authentication.

The contributions of this paper, as part of a framework that we call CASHMERE, are:

(i) The description of a method to represent, store and manage context information in an HMAS platform adhering to the Agents&Artifacts paradigm. We argue that a context management service needs to be designed to provide indexing services (listing *how/where* context information provided by an HMAS resource can be accessed), as well as republishing services to forward context information on behalf of HMAS resources which are constrained.
(ii) The design and implementation of a mechanism to exploit the temporal aspect of *dynamic, frequently changing* situations using RDF Stream Processing [19] technologies (RSP) in an HMAS platform
(iii) The design and implementation of support for reasoning about *context-based conditions for access* to resources in an HMAS platform using SHACL Shapes [8]

To address space limitations of the current paper, example listings of RDF showing instances and implementation of various functionality aspects of our approach, based on a scenario discussed in Sect. 5, are made available in an online accessible Appendix[1].

2 Background and Related Work

To put our work into context, we need to provide an overview of the perspectives which it tries to bring together. Our contribution proposes an extension of HMAS platforms (specifically, those modeled in the Agents & Artifacts paradigm) with context management capabilities. To do so, it considers looking at artifacts as *prosumers* (provider and consumer) of context in a dynamic, streaming manner. Such a view enables the use of both static and dynamic information in the agent environment as the basis for conditioned access to resources in the HMAS. The following overview positions our work with respect to these aspects.

2.1 Hypermedia MAS

Ciortea et al. [18] introduce the guiding principles for Hypermedia MAS and furthermore provide one model for HMAS that abides by those principles, namely one of cognitive agents in *artifact*-based hypermedia environments. The model is based on the Agents & Artifacts (A&A) paradigm [31], which envisions the engineering of agent environment and of the interaction of agents *with their*

[1] CASHMERE Online Appendix: https://tinyurl.com/cashmere-eumas-online-appendix.

environment by means of explicit resources (tools), generically called *artifacts*. The A&A view of HMAS gathers traction in the community because it aligns well with other recent trends that engineer bridges between the real and the digital world, such as Digital Twins [28] or the Web-of-Things [32]). Artifacts act as means to engineer *the tools* with which autonomous agents can sense and affect their digital or physical environment. Workspaces in the A&A view provide logical grouping of tools by ownership or application-specific design concerns.

Artifacts express *properties* (of themselves or of what they perceive in the environment), enable *actions* (on themselves or on the environment) and signal *events* (based on their internal state or of perceptions in the environment). In the interpretation of [18], the artifact model closely resembles the affordance model of the Web-of-Things ThingDescription specification [12], such that an alignment between artifact capabilities and Thing affordances (properties, actions, events) is envisioned for agent resources in an HMAS.

In follow-up work, the artefact representation in an HMAS is extended by means of signifiers [39], which are a means to *make agents aware* of all the ways in which they *could use* the affordances of an artifact, if they have a particular *objective* and some required capabilities. Signifiers inform agents of the conditions they need to fulfill, both in terms of internal capabilities, as well as their situation in the environment, which the authors of [39] call *the context* of an agent. A simple example of this would be conditions for *accessing* some action affordances of an artifact (e.g. an agent can *move* a robot arm if it can be authenticated, and if the robot arm is assigned to the same project as intended by the agent; the assistant agent of a user can *control* the smart lights of a hotel room, if the user is a hotel guest and physically present in the room). Meanwhile, the context of an agent can also inform signifiers that *advertise* a particular affordance. For example, manufacturing agents that have STRIPS planning abilities will receive signifiers for the affordances of a robotic arm that include the precondition and postcondition descriptions of using the gripper, instead of a generic description of the gripping action [39].

However, [39] does not currently provide a model for the *context* information referenced by an artifact signifier and it does not detail a principled way in which an artifact (or an agent) can come into the possession of this information within the HMAS in which it is deployed. Our work in CASHMERE addresses this concern, by showing: (i) how context can be represented such that it captures information content, as well as metadata about the information (e.g. how long is it valid, where was it generated), and (ii) how to manage information that can become *context* for other artifacts or agents in a mechanism that takes advantage of the infrastructure in an HMAS modeled after the A&A paradigm.

2.2 Context Management and Stream Processing

Context information sharing in the IoT and WoT world has been actively studied from many perspectives [26]. Concerns regarding representation and provisioning of the information flow are often addressed by considering the application domain itself (e.g. smart environments, building automation, smart agriculture, smart manufacturing, security and privacy). It is important to note, however, that the HMAS paradigm envisions exploiting the web as a *global* interaction ground for agent-based applications, cutting across application domains with the set of design principles it proposes. Consequently, proposals for information representation and its flow have to be flexible enough to address several concerns such as modeling capability that informs operational concerns, discoverability or efficient management and processing of dynamically changing information.

Stream Processing. An important aspect that needs to be addressed is how to properly manage and distinguish between information of different *update rates*: from information that is static, to information that concerns events or that has various degrees of temporal validity. Regarding the latter, the RDF Stream Processing (RSP) community [6] puts forth the vision of a web of data streams [20] whose key requirements capture many concerns that are relevant for context management in HMAS. The core element of the vision is the idea that content that is of interest to an actor should be *streamed* to them over the web, through a series of *web stream processors* (WeSP). While doing so, WeSPs need to balance between the distribution and scalability of operations (e.g. transformations, deductive or inductive reasoning) performed on both *stored* (more static) and *streamed* (dynamic) data, manage the variety of representation requirements (from simple key value items to timestamped RDF graphs) for data streams and provide meta information about the streams themselves. One key takeaway of [20] is that streams over the web need to have a clear management of producers and consumers of information, since default interaction over the web is stateless, such that polling techniques or other push-based mechanisms (e.g. WebSocket, MQTT) are needed for data streams. It is therefore a requirement to have a principled manner in which to (i) describe and know how and where to access the content of streams, (ii) organize information of different update frequency levels in separate storing and processing pipelines that take into account the specifics of each, and (iii) ensure the required level of expressiveness depending on the usage of the streamed content. These challenges give rise to new research on how to coordinate decentralized stream reasoners in an agent-like perspective [37].

In the CASHMERE framework we envision setting up the infrastructure for managing static and dynamic information at the level of a deployed HMAS platform. We exploit alignment of artifact/Thing event affordances with RDF streams, we introduce a service in an HMAS platform that explicitly indexes and manages static and dynamic context (acting as "channels" into which streamed data can be sent while awaiting for consumers), and we leverage the HMAS *observability* and *single entry point* design principles to make discovery, self-description and access of streamed context data easy.

Context Representation. In terms of representing streamed data on the web [21], the RSP community has looked towards research in the area of RDF Stream Processing ([14,19,24]) and Streaming Linked Data [38]. One key identified aspect is that of addressing the variety of expressiveness requirements in terms of modeling *content* (different representation forms and RDF serialization methods) and its *annotations* (e.g. different notions of time - time instants, intervals, provenance) [17].

With respect to the expressiveness requirement, our own previous work (the CONSERT Meta-Model [36]) is an appropriate fit for a general method of context representation. CONSERT uses a reification-based view of information where *ContextAssertions* and *ContextAnnotations* are the main modeling elements. *ContextAssertions* use the predicate in a subject-predicate-object triple as the main model entity. A statement such as `locatedAt(agent_alex, lab308)` is modeled as a binary *ContextAssertion*, whereby the central element is the fact of being `LocatedAt` and the subject and object entities are `agent_alex` and `lab308`. However, *ContextAssertions* can have an n-ary form with a predicate and several role entities, lending itself useful for self-contained representations of several pieces of information (e.g. the reception of a shopping order with a delivery address, delivery deadline, selected items). *ContextAnnotations* describe *ContextAssertions* further, adding meta information such as timestamp of registration, interval of validity, provenance of the assertion.

Importantly, *ContextAssertions* are characterized by a *mode of acquisition*, an operational attribute signaling how *dynamic* the assertion is. *Static ContextAssertions* refer to information that holds true indefinitely (e.g. the spatial containment of a room in a building). *Profiled ContextAssertions* have a long-term, but still limited temporal validity (e.g. the employment status of a researcher), while *dynamic ContextAssertions* refer to event-like information which is assumed to change frequently in a system (e.g. the physical location of a person in a building).

The modeling elements of CONSERT make *ContextAssertions* a suitable information *exchange* format, usable when communicating context information along streams, between artifacts and agents. The CONSERT Meta-Model has a realization in the form of the CONSERT Ontology[2]. To promote flexibility, however, under the CASHMERE framework for HMAS, artifact information is converted to a CONSERT based representation *only* when it needs to be streamed, so as to take advantage of operational aspects that differentiate between processing of static/profiled versus dynamic information. In Sect. 3.1 we indicate a mechanism for on-demand conversion between typical ontology-based information representation to a CONSERT-based modeling.

2.3 Attribute-Based Access Control

Recent surveys highlight that in *dynamic* and *open* computing environments, such as IoT and WoT, traditional access control models such as Role-Based Access Control (RBAC) are not adapted to fit application dynamics [30]. Considering the discussion in previous sections, access to artifacts in HMAS platforms is strongly benefited from employing an Attribute-Based Access Control (ABAC), which proposes that subject requests to perform operations on a resource are

[2] CONSERT Core and Annotation ontology modules: https://tinyurl.com/consert-ontology.

granted or denied based on *attributes* of the subjects, resources and the environment, and the policies that relate to these attributes [33].

While the access control mechanism that we are proposing under CASHMERE does not deviate from existing formalization applied in web services or the IoT domain [15,23], it is novel in its operationalization at the level of an HMAS, as well as in the leveraged technology stack. Specifically, we propose use of an access control modeling and policy management model that is guided by the Web-Access Control [11] specifications of SOLID [9]. We make use of the hierarchy of logical inclusion containers (workspaces) that are available in an HMAS that follows the A&A paradigm to define policy resolution methods. We further leverage both static and dynamic context information reasoning, using SHACL [8] and RDF Stream Reasoning in C-SPARQL [14] to construct the access conditions. Our proposal is particularly similar to [41], which uses RDF, SHACL, WebIDs [13] and nanopublications over Linked Data to develop pattern based access control for multi-stakeholder shared work projects. Unlike [41], CASHMERE addresses a broader class of applications, facilitated by HMAS, seeking to align with and use the hierarchical representation in platforms such as Yggdrasil [18].

3 Context Management in an HMAS Platform

The proposal to extract *streams* of context information from agents and artifacts in an HMAS carries with it the additional requirement of servicing web protocols that enable a continuous connection between the producer and consumer of a context stream. The HMAS design principles do not impose capabilities on the physical machines that host resources (e.g. artifacts that reflect physical devices, web services) of an HMAS. Given these considerations, in the CASHMERE framework we consider it necessary to extend the functionality of a deployed HMAS platform with a dedicated *ContextManagementService*, as shown in Fig. 1. An HMAS representation using the HMAS Ontology [4] starts from its *Hypermedia MASPlatform* definition which can host several *Workspaces*.

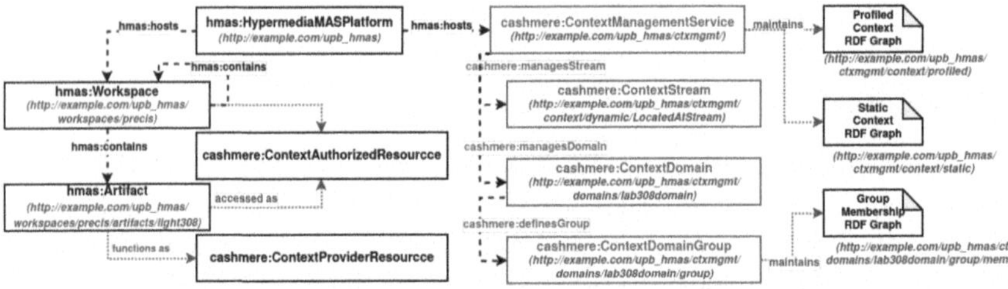

Fig. 1. Proposed extension under CASHMERE of an HMAS representation with services for Context Management and the access control it enables. (Color figure online)

The latter can recursively contain other *Workspaces* or *Artifact* instances which implement functionality available in the agent environment. CASHMERE proposes a first extension of an HMAS representation (see the blue items in Fig. 1) by introducing the representation for a platform-level hosted service called *cashmere:ContextManagementService*. The latter is responsible with context information provisioning at the level of the whole platform and it has three main responsibilities: (i) managing context information streams, (ii) managing repositories of *profiled* or *static* context information that is to be shared at the level of the platform, and (iii) managing a set of logical, frequently exploited *situation boundaries*, called *ContextDomains*. We detail each of these responsibilites in what follows.

3.1 Context Streams

The artifacts that are deployed in an HMAS have their functionality extended themselves, shown in Fig. 2, where grey lines indicate functional aspects. An artifact developer can opt to turn an *event* affordance into the source of a *context stream*. In such case, the event information will be converted into a *ContextAssertion* representation, that has mandatory *ContextAnnotations* for: (i) a logical timestamp, and (ii) the provenance of the event (the URI of the deployed artifact). Similarly, artifact *property* affordances can be shared as *static* or *profiled ContextAssertions*, that are made available in corresponding RDF Graphs. Properties that are exposed as *profiled ContextAssertions* can be given additional *ContextAnnotations*, most relevantly a duration of validity.
Notice that the instance URIs shown in Figs. 1 and 2 (relating to the example scenario from Sect. 5) follow the single entry point principle in HMAS, having a path that enables easy navigation from the platform level and automatic reference determination, if key elements are known. For example, URIs *ContextStreams* managed at both artifact and platform level are obtained by appending the word "Stream" to the local name of the *ContextAssertion* whose instances are being streamed (e.g. *ex:LocatedAt*, *ex:BatteryStatus*) and concatenating the result to the default stream path *<hmas_root>/ctxmgmt/context/dynamic* for platforms, *<hmas_root>/workspaces/<wsp_id>/artifacts/<art_id>/context/dynamic* for artifacts).

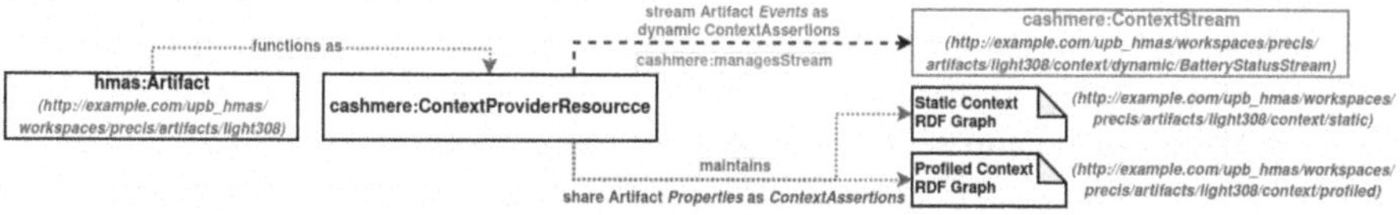

Fig. 2. Proposed extension under CASHMERE of an Artifact representation and functionality. Artifact events can be sent through context streams and their properties can be exposed as *static* or *profiled* context information.

Note that populating the static and profiled, as well as the context stream, with information is an *on-demand* process, meaning that updates are driven by consumer interest. Figuring out appropriate caching and demand prediction policies at the level of individual artifacts is an aspect currently left for future work. The on-demand working mode adds little overhead to current artifact design, since it only complements *the representation* of information already generated by the artifact, such that it can be readily shared with other parties in a standardized manner. This approach follows the flexibility principle for taming variety of data in stream processors [17] and proposes addressing it through semantic web technologies that make conversion of data representation a manageable task. Technology stacks such as RDF Mapping Language (RML [7]) or the SPARQL Rules feature from SHACL [8]. Once converted to an *ContextAssertion* form, streaming of corresponding RDF content in a manner compatible with existing RDF stream reasoners, such as those outlined in Sect. 2.2 can be enabled through frameworks such as TripleWave [27]. In Listing 3.1 of the online Appendix we give an example of using SHACL SPARQL Rules to transform an artifact event (e.g. the presence of a user in a university room) expressed in a given domain ontology into a *dynamic ContextAssertion*.

With respect to context streams, another important extension is at the level of the HMAS platform itself. The *ContextManagement Service* (see Fig. 1) is responsible for maintaining a record of context streams that are managed by artifacts deployed on the platform or by the platform itself, in case that context information is required from services on the web outside of those deployed on the platform. The registry maintained at platform level follows a predictable URI path (*<hmas_root>/ctxmgmt/context/dynamic*) respecting the single entry point principle, as well as the requirement in [17] to have a meta-description of the stream itself. Notably, accessing the *<hmas_root>/ctxmgmt/context/dynamic* URI produces a representation of managed *cashmere:ContextStream* instances that indicate the type of *ContextAssertions* that are exchanged over the stream, the mode of update (e.g. periodic or on-change) and the producer of the stream (the artifact URI or the URI of the external service providing the stream).

3.2 Static and Profiled Context

In both Figs. 1 and 2 one can observe the presence of managed RDF context graphs that are devided between *static* and *profiled* information. In both cases, these graphs hold information that an HMAS platform or any individual artifact wants to *share* freely. This means that consumers (agents or other resources) accessing the information will not have any restriction on accessing the shared context information, apart from obtaining knowledge about the entrypoint to the HMAS platform (according to the single entrypoint principle of HMAS design).

The RDF Graphs at the platform level have a double functionality. If an artifact developer chooses to host RDF graphs of static of profiled *ContextAssertions* at the level of the artifact, then the platform level equivalents will contain a reference to the graph hosted at the level of the artifact together with a mention of the *type* of *ContextAssertion* instances that are accessible there. If, however, artifact-level hosting or on-demand generation of *static* and *profiled* context contents is impractical (e.g. due to low computational resource on the host machine of the artifact), then an artifact developer can choose to submit *static* or *profiled* context information when the artifact is first deployed at HMAS platform level. Since *profiled* context information is considered to have seldom updates (e.g. when the validity interval expires) the effort to employ mechanisms, such as those outlined in Sect. 3.1, to convert from a domain vocabulary to the *ContextAssertion* representation will be minimal.

Information registered at platform-level *static* and *profiled* context graphs is stored in a *Named* RDF Graph form, whereby the URI of the artifact or resource that has provided the information is used as the graph *name*.

3.3 ContextDomains and ContextDomain Groups

In Fig. 1, the *ContextManagement Service* of an HMAS platform is shown to manage instances of *cashmere:ContextDomains*, which in turn give rise to *cashmere:ContextDomainGroups*. The notion of a *ContextDomain* was originally introduced in prior work [35] and relates to a logical partitioning of context-informed *situations*, where a particular provisioning of context information imposes itself. For example, context information can be managed and provisioned with priority depending on cases where actors share the same physical space (e.g. a university room, a manufacturing workspace), are engaged in the same activity (e.g. a lecture, a manufacturing process) or who are part of the same organization (e.g. a university, a company, a research lab).

ContextDomains were originally modeled to be the object instances of binary *ContextAssertion* that represented so called *ContextDimensions* (e.g. *locatedIn(Person, UniversitySpace), engagedIn(Agent, ManufacturingProcess), memberOf(Researcher, University)*). The concept was expanded in more recent work [34] to refer to, possibly more complex, *situation definitions* that would be frequently leveraged in applications. For example, our reference scenario (see Sect. 5) describes authorizing access to affordances of a smart light artifact, under condition that the accessing agent is physically present in the same room as that with the smart light and that it represents a user who is employed by the university owning the device.

Importantly, our previous work [34] designs a reasoning mechanism which enables specifying the conditions (based on context information) which *count-as* relevant for different actors (agents or resources) to be seen as being part of a situation that is labeled as a *ContextDomain*. In the CASHMERE framework, the set of actors in an HMAS that are part of the same *contextual situation* are defined as *members* of the corresponding *ContextDomainGroup*. In Fig. 1, the *ContextDomain* identified by the http://example.com/upb_hmas/ctxmgmt/domains/lab308domain URI refers to researchers physically present in Lab308 of the university building. The figure also shows the URI scheme that connects a *ContextDomain* to its *ContextDomainGroup* and to the RDF Graph of statements of membership within the group.

An example of the reasoning mechanism used to grant or revoke membership within the above mentioned *ContextDomainGroup* is given in Listing 1.3 of the online Appendix. It is based on the C-SPARQL 2.0 [14] RDF stream processing engine and the main advantage of the approach is that it can leverage the temporal aspect of dynamic context information. Notably, the semantics of stream operators that we use is based on triggering when the content of the underlying stream *changes* from one *window* of processing to the next (this corresponds to ISTREAM and DSTREAM operators in the RSP-QL specification [19]). In this manner, two queries, one using an ISTREAM and one using a DSTREAM operator, under the same conditions of verification, will produce statements that grant (ISTREAM) and revoke (DSTREAM) a membership in a *ContextDomainGroup*. Generated membership statements are stored in an RDF Graph that has *named graph* sections corresponding to each *ContextDomain* (see the example of the *<hmas_root>/ctxmgmt/domains/lab308domain/group/memberships* RDF membership graph in Fig. 1). This enables quick and controlled access to a *data graph* of current memberships in each *ContextDomain*, that would need to be validated against a *shapes* graph by means of a SHACL processor that verifies membership, as showcased in Sect. 4.

Since a *ContextDomain* acts as an element of defining situations, it and the set of count-as membership conditions for agents and resources in an HMAS have to be added by HMAS developers, either on deploy time, or on throughout the lifecycle of an HMAS platform (e.g. when new workspaces are defined or new artifacts are deployed). As in previously discussed cases, the principle of single-entry point applies for the discovery of *ContextDomains*. When accessing the representation of a *ContextDomain* in an HMAS, details about the C-SPARQL based rule that regulates membership in the domain are also given, such that an agent can interpret the context which it needs to share (expressed in terms of *ContextAssertions*) to be considered a member of the *ContextDomain*.

4 Dynamic Access Control with CASHMERE

A relevant use of the proposed context management framework at the level of an A&A-based HMAS framework is that of authorized access to resources. Methods for a token based, *authenticated* access can already be readily used, since artifacts in an A&A HMAS closely align with Things in the W3C ThingDescription specification [12] (as is the case of the Yggdrasil platform [18]), which define methods for authenticated access. However, as argued in the Introduction, dynamics of interactions in an HMAS require a dynamic method of *authorization*.

Notice in Fig. 1 that CASHMERE proposes the extension of an HMAS representation with another additional perspective, which leverages context information, by declaring *Workspace* and *Artifact* instances as having the additional *cashmere:ContextAuthorizedResource* type. The working principles of the context-based authorization process were introduced in previous work [34] and in the current proposal we are expanding the approach and redesigning the involved technology stack.

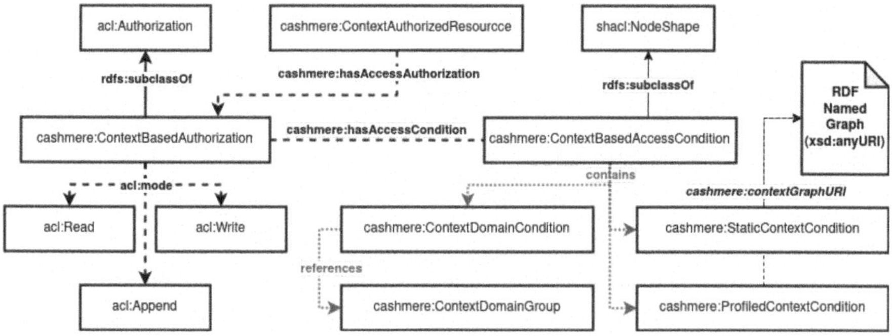

Fig. 3. Diagram showing the principal concepts from the CASHMERE Ontology which help define a context authorized resource in an HMAS.

The discussion of the proposed approach starts from the building blocks shown in Fig. 3. The CASHMERE Ontology defines the concept of a *ContextAuthorized Resource*, which enables HMAS designers to declare the access to *Workspaces* and *Artifacts* as guarded by a *ContextBasedAuthorization*. The latter is as a subclass of an ACL Authorization (see the ACL Ontology [1] from SOLID [9]) and therefore provides the option to set read and write/append access modes to the affordances of the resource. The *ContextBasedAuthorization* declares its conditions using a *cashmere:ContextBasedAccessCondition* class instance. The latter declares a target entity for the access conditions (in our case, an instance of a *foaf:Agent*), generically identified by *cashmere:accessRequester*, but dynamically swapped out at runtime for the WebID of the agent making the request. The root access condition declares a conjunction of specific context-based conditions (which are SHACL Node Shapes) using the *cashmere:containsConditions* property. These conditions need to match the interaction situation of the requesting agent (see Listing 2.1 in the online Appendix). The SHACL Shape class for the specific conditions depends on the *type* of context information that is referenced (CONSERT context acquisition types discussed in Sect. 2.2). For dynamic context, the *ContextDomain* membership condition discussed in Sect. 3.3 is used, while for *profiled* (i.e. *ContextAssertions* with annotations) and *static* context the *Profiled-* and *StaticContextCondition* Shapes are used respectively (see also Listing 2.2 in the online Appendix). A particularity of the latter two is that they can directly reference the RDF Named Graph(s) that will act as data graphs for the SHACL shape validation. The *contextGraphURI* data property is used to specify the set of artifact-level RDF Named Graphs that compose the *data graphs* against which the SHACL shapes will be validated. If the property is left unspecified, the validation data graphs are obtained based on the default platform-level *static* and *profiled* RDF Named Graphs (see Fig. 1).

The sequence diagram detailing the interaction between an HMAS agent and a desired *Artifact* is shown in Fig. 4. If an *Artifact* or *any Workspace* along a transitive containment closure is declared as a *ContextAuthorizedResource*, then access to its affordances is mediated by the HMAS platform through the *Con-*

text ManagementService (step 3). The first thing is to determine the *effective* Authorization. This procedure follows the recommended specification in the SOLID WAC protocol [11], whereby if an *ACL Resource* is not explicitly declared for the initially requested web resource, then the search for an authorization declaration is deferred to looking for one in the *container* of the currently considered web resource. Since hypermedia MAS are naturally structured along *Workspace* containment hierarchies, the *hmas:contains* relation (see Fig. 1) is used by the *ContextManagementService* to determine the *effective ContextBasedAuthorization* instance. Once the authorization requirements are obtained, execution is passed to a *ContextValidationService*, whose task it is to unpack the top-level *ContextBasedAccessCondition* into individual *dynamic* (*ContextDomain* membership based), profiled or static access conditions expressed by their corresponding SHACL *NodeShapes* (steps 4 and 5 in Fig. 4). The principal task is then to identify the URL of the corresponding RDF context graph required to validate the SHACL shape and forward the validation call to the resource in the HMAS managing that graph. For a dynamic, *ContextDomain* membership condition, the call is forwarded to the *ContextManagement* Service, specifically, the section of it managing the membership RDF graph for the *ContextDomainGroup* defined by the required *ContextDomain* (step 6a). Validation of static or profiled context access conditions (steps 6b and 6c) depends on the given *cashmere:contextGraphURI* (see Fig. 3). If none are present, the *ContextManagement Service* will use its default static and profiled RDF context graphs as data graphs for SHACL shape validation. If declarations are present, the *ContextManagement Service* uses its context graphs as indexes to determine the resource in the HMAS platform which manages the declared context graphs and forwards the validation request to it.

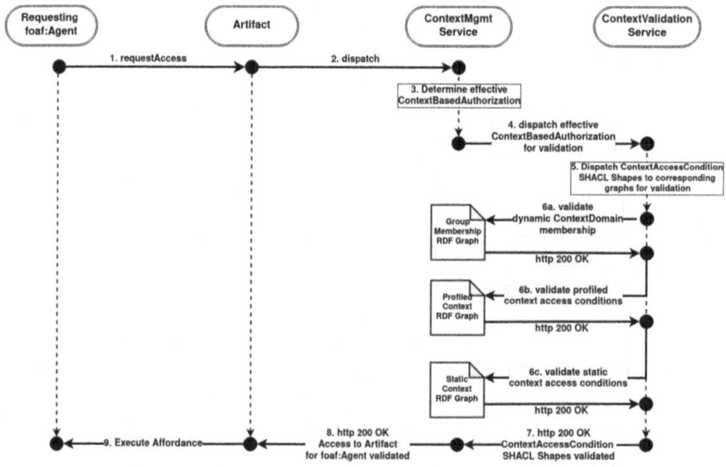

Fig. 4. Sequence of interactions and internal processing steps to authorize access of an HMAS agent to a desired *Artifact*.

In our example scenario (see Sect. 5 and Listings 2.1–2.3 from the online Appendix), access to the *light308* is predicated on membership in the *lab308domain* group and on the profiled context information of the employment status of the person on whose behalf the request is made. The *lab308domain* membership is determined using the C-SPARQL query from Listing 1.3 in the online Appendix, which uses the stream of dynamic *ex:LocatedAt ContextAssertions* to determine physical presence of the requesting agent in Lab308 over the past 5 min. Since the university is a trusted entity and it owns both the smart light and the HMAS platform instance that manages it, the *profiled* employment information is made available in the default *profiled* RDF graph of the *ContextManagement Service* for the UPB HMAS (see Listing 1.2 in the online Appendix). In Listing 2.2 from the online Appendix, the *cashmere:ProfiledContextCondition* instance showcases use of *TemporalValidity* annotations for the provided *ex:WorksAt* profiled *ContextAssertion*.

5 Development and Discussion

To drive development and evaluation of the proposed CASHMERE extension to HMAS platforms, a simple scenario is presented, which is then discussed in terms of its modeling in CASHMERE, as well as other context management platforms, meanwhile highlighting the aspects that differentiate CASHMERE from related work.

Scenario

A university manages a smart campus, wherein different web-enabled devices are present (e.g. smart light, smart blinds). The university encourages each lab to be individually responsible for the smart devices it installs in their room, as long as they are made available in the HMAS platform of the university (*ex:upb_hmas* in the Listings). Researchers from Lab308 desire to use the smart light in their lab (*ex:light308* in the Listings) to implement a visual notification service for various meeting and teaching events. However, university policy maintains that use of affordances from any smart device on campus be restricted to employed personnel who are physically present in the rooms where the device resides (thus preventing university visitors from interacting with the devices, as well as any kind of remote control). Though simple, the scenario easily introduces the need for context-based authorized access to the smart light, which conditions agents on a profiled context (the employment status of their user) and a dynamic one (the stream of physical presence information of agent users).

Development

The presented scenario has been implemented at a proof-of-concept level, with a focus on leveraging context information to provide the dynamic access control discussed in Sect. 4. We created the CASHMERE Ontology[3] to provide

[3] CASHMERE Ontology: http://tinyurl.com/cashmere-ont.

the vocabulary that supports the extensions to an HMAS platform (see Fig. 1, as well as the terminology used to describe context-based authorizations (see Fig. 3). We further created a fork of the Yggdrasil HMAS platform[4] which we extended with several aspects. Access to artifact affordances is now mediated by the SHACL Shape based context conditioning representation used to specify authorization requirements. Specifically, the RDF description of the *ex:light308* artifact qualifies it as *ContextAuthorized Resource* having a *ContextBasedAuthorization* (Listing 1.1 in the online Appendix). The authorization allows for read and write access under two conditions (Listing 2.1 in online Appendix), mediated by SHACL constraints: a valid UPB employment of the requesting agent (example of profiled context) and a membership in the *lab308Domain ContextDomain*. The interactions between an agent and a desired artifact shown in Fig. 4 are supported by a new Context Management Service and a Web Access Control Service that run at the level of an Yggdrasil platform. In particular, the Context Management Service implements an RSP reasoner based on C-SPARQL to infer membership in configured *ContextDomain Groups* (*lab308Domain* – see Listing 1.3 in the online Appendix).

A request for an action affordance to an artifact registered in the Yggdrasil platform is first routed through the Web Access Control service that determines that *ex:light308* is registered as context authorized. The WAC protocol to determine the effective authorization [11] is launched, retrieving the *ex:light308 AccessCondition*. The WAC service invokes the Context Validation Service to validate the SHACL constraints (Listings 2.2 and 2.3 in the online Appendix) and return the authorization result.

The current implementation of the demo scenario has some limitations with respect to its deployment. Specifically, the static and profiled context is registered only at the platform level *static* and *profiled* context graphs. Further, the context streams (e.g. the *LocatedAt* dynamic *ContextAssertion* stream) are deployed locally, on platform setup, to be able to quickly iterate on testing and adjustments of stream update policies (e.g. frequency of new location updates). Scaling the implementation to the complete capabilities of the design is scheduled in near-term future work.

Discussion

The presented integration of context management capabilities into HMAS platforms levarages an intersection of visions from two communities (WebAgents [2] and RSP [6]), as well as an opportunistic fit between the functionalities of core elements of design (e.g. artifacts in HMAS and stream processors in RSP) and the technology stack developed in each community.

In surveys on context management literature [26,29] the majority of work introduces middleware-style frameworks that handle context management from the representation and collection of data from sensors of various kinds, to different reasoning mechanisms and methods for dynamic handover of context-

[4] CASHMERE Fork of Yggdrasil: https://github.com/aimas-upb/yggdrasil.

subscriptions. The representation format chosen for CASHMERE itself is part of more ample work developed towards the CONSERT context management middleware [35]. Many contributions also choose to focus on a particular subdomain, such as context management in a mobile setting, in smart cities, or industrial IoT. However, in the current work, CASHMERE distinguishes itself by intending to be a *lightweight* framework for context management. Specifically, our focus is on the provisioning of varied context information, not specific to sensors or actuators, in a manner that aligns with web engineering principles and, more closely, hypermedia MAS. We make assumptions that context can be provided *on-demand*, by artifacts, other agents or third party web services that can deliver data in RDF form (using the *ContextAssertion* representation).

Having made these observations, the demo scenario we currently presented is not beyond the modeling capabilities of other frameworks that address context management as web platforms (e.g. FI-WARE Orion [3], CoaaS [22]). However, in what follows we argue that CASHMERE matches or improves upon the capabilities of these platforms, while also being designed to align with A&A HMAS engineering principles. FI-WARE Orion, which implements the NGSI v2 specification [5], enables on-demand context queries, forwarding of requests to indexed providers, as well as federation of context brokers, which update their context information context upon notification. This functionality set almost covers our scenario requirements, since location of an agent can be continuously notified, while certain static or profiled context information (e.g. the employment information) can be looked up in the broker (if stored there) or forwarded to a service (artifact) that contains it. However, in FI-WARE there is no implicit capability to label a frequently occurring context situation (a *ContextDomain*) in a manner that can lead to its reuse and that can leverage updates to more than attributes of a single entity. The use of an RSP engine in CASHMERE also enables the conditioning of updates or situation derivation on changes that happen *in time*.

The explicit distinction of static, profiled or dynamic context in CASHMERE means that the framework can proactively become responsible for operational aspects of context updates, as opposed to this being an application dependent behavior. Furthermore, the representation in FI-WARE is focused on entities and their attributes. By use of the CONSERT meta-model, CASHMERE enables exchange of richer context graphs, where situations (that potentially involve several entities) are the core information exchanged.

CoaaS [22] is a well-engineered context platform that supports discovering and indexing of context sources, on-demand queries and notifications. The framework relies on a much more expressive and user friendly (compared to FI-WARE) query language called CDQL, and also includes a data stream processing component, all of which enables it to model the given demo scenario.

A key difference between CASHMERE and CoaaS is the setup of the streaming processors in a decentralized manner. CASHMERE adopts the vision of a web of data streams [20], where agents can subscribe to results of stream processors, but also where RSP engines can help define labeled situations (*ContextDomains*). Large scale and open HMAS applications bring about several situations that require repeated leveraging of the same kind of context to inform desired functionality. Moreover, complex, time varying situations can benefit from a breakdown of a subset of conditions into *ContextDomain* membership requirements, that can be composed bottom up, as opposed to having to rewrite the full conditioning for each new situation.

A general contrast between CASHMERE and some of the referenced context management platforms [22,26,40] is that the latter mostly focus on IoT applications, being designed to address challenges such as sensor unreliability, computing on the edge, or physical mobility of sources and consumers.

The work in CASHMERE puts the context of *agents* interacting in their HMAS environment as the focus of the provisioning. The application abstraction level is raised by use of the A&A model, which considers that one or several sensors can be encapsulated into functionality of an artifact, and where discovery of context information means crawling and filtering the web for semantically described affordances.

CASHMERE seeks explicitly to align with the Signifier Exposure Mechanism [39] which facilitates interactions of agents in an HMAS based on conditioning or promoting (advertising) the use of resource affordances based on agent *intent* and *capabilities*, as well as their context in the environment. In CASHMERE, for example, the identification of a *shared ContextDomain* can explicitly indicate the set of entities (agents and artifacts in the HMAS) that *should* subscribe to each other's context streams. The engineering principles of *ContextDomains* also enable a higher degree of flexibility and reuse, than that found in other approaches.

Regarding context-based access control, we note that the proposed mechanism for access validation brings no additional overhead, when compared to the typical web-based access control functionality as envisioned by SOLID [9]. We take SOLID WAC [11] as a reference since it has a natural fit for web resources (which is the case for HMAS), as opposed to application-centric ABAC systems that cannot scale as easily over a distributed set of resources.

The focus of this work has been on defining a representation and an indexing and flow that is compatible and well aligned with the design principles of A&A based HMAS. The current development status of CASHMERE therefore acknowledges limitations in capitalizing on all of its potential, such as context caching depending on the static, profiled or dynamic nature of the information, or management of on-demand queries that involve retrieval of information from distributed sources. Near-term future work targets these aspects, as well as a more thorough integration with the mechanism of signifiers in HMAS.

In terms of performance concerns of the current implementation, the main contention point in the designed context provisioning will be in the speed of SHACL validation and execution of streaming SPARQL queries, depending on the volume of streamed context, as well as in the size of the RDF Named Graphs that hold static, profiled or dynamic *ContextDomain* membership information. Evaluation of these impacts and research on mitigation strategies is also intended as future work.

6 Conclusion

The CASHMERE framework proposes a principled approach to extend HMAS platforms that follow the A&A paradigm with the ability to manage context information that can be leveraged in multiple ways, from context-based conditioning of access to resources in an HMAS, to the characterization of situations in which resource affordances should be advertised (signaled) to agents for use in their goals. The proposed extension carefully follows the design guidelines from HMAS and RDF Stream Processing to develop an on-demand context provisioning mechanism, that uses a semantic-web based technology stack (e.g. ontologies, SHACL, RSP, SOLID WAC). Choice of the CONSERT Meta-Model for context representation covers requirements of expressive modeling, temporal validity annotations and operational support (in terms of context update modes).

Future work includes development of a full-scale demonstrator of the context management and access control functionality described in Sects. 3 and 4, based on the outlined scenario, which will be implemented in full on university premises. Short-term effort will also focus on using the mechanism proposed in CASHMERE to enable the context related aspects of signifiers, as well as on building-up the full potential of CASHMERE as a Context Management Platform for HMAS, beyond its use within signifier functionality.

In the longer term, apart from the current demonstrator, we look towards scenarios in domains such as smart manufacturing or remote health monitoring that will exemplify more breadth of applicability for the proposed context provisioning. We further plan to address performance challenges related to the technology stack presented in this work. While the web-centric, on-demand view of CASHMERE context provisioning can help with general scalability, proper evaluation of performance under load are required for issues such as: validating SHACL shapes over large context graphs, processing C-SPARQL queries for *ContextDomain* membership granting and revocation in a highly dynamic setting, employing appropriate web protocols (e.g. WebSub [10], WebSocket) for RDF streams of higher throughput. With respect to context-based access control, the speed of execution for WAC protocol to determine the effective *ContextBasedAuthorization* under a more complex HMAS workspace hierarchy will be evaluated. Lastly, we will work on outlining design and deployment principals for the use of CASHMERE to add context management to any Agents & Artifacts like HMAS platform.

Acknowledgement. This paper is supported by the European Union's HORIZON Research and Innovation Programme under grant agreement No 101120657, project ENFIELD (European Lighthouse to Manifest Trustworthy and Green AI).

References

1. Acl ontology. http://www.w3.org/ns/auth/acl. Accessed 25 May 2024
2. Autonomous agents on the web community group. https://www.w3.org/community/webagents/. Accessed 25 May 2024

3. Fiware orion context broker. https://github.com/telefonicaid/fiware-orion. Accessed 25 May 2024
4. Hypermedia multi agent system ontology. https://ci.mines-stetienne.fr/hmas/core. Accessed 25 May 2024
5. Ngsi version 2 specification. https://fiware.github.io/specifications/ngsiv2/stable/. Accessed 25 May 2024
6. Rdf stream processing community group. https://www.w3.org/community/rsp/. Accessed 25 May 2024
7. Rml io knowledge graph creator. https://rml.io/. Accessed 25 May 2024
8. Shacl w3c recommendation. https://www.w3.org/TR/shacl/. Accessed 25 May 2024
9. Solid project. https://solidproject.org/. Accessed 25 May 2024
10. W3c websub protocol specification. https://www.w3.org/TR/websub/. Accessed 08 Feb 2024
11. Web access control specification. https://solid.github.io/web-access-control-spec. Accessed 25 May 2024
12. Web of things (wot) thing description 1.1, w3c candidate recommendation. https://www.w3.org/TR/wot-thing-description/. Accessed 25 May 2024
13. Webid specifications. https://www.w3.org/2005/Incubator/webid/spec/. Accessed 25 May 2024
14. Barbieri, D.F., Braga, D., Ceri, S., Valle, E.D., Grossniklaus, M.: C-sparql: a continuous query language for rdf data streams. Int. J. Semant. Comput. **4**(01), 3–25 (2010)
15. Bhatt, S., Pham, T.K., Gupta, M., Benson, J., Park, J., Sandhu, R.: Attribute-based access control for AWS internet of things and secure industries of the future. IEEE Access **9**, 107200–107223 (2021)
16. Boissier, O., Ciortea, A., Harth, A., Ricci, A.: Autonomous agents on the web. In: Dagstuhl-Seminar 21072: Autonomous Agents on the Web, p. 100p (2021)
17. Bonte, P., et al.: Grounding stream reasoning research (2024)
18. Ciortea, A., Boissier, O., Ricci, A.: Engineering world-wide multi-agent systems with hypermedia. In: Engineering Multi-Agent Systems: 6th International Workshop, EMAS 2018, Stockholm, Sweden, 14–15 July 2018, Revised Selected Papers 6, pp. 285–301. Springer (2019)
19. Dell'Aglio, D., Della Valle, E., Calbimonte, J.P., Corcho, O.: Rsp-ql semantics: a unifying query model to explain heterogeneity of rdf stream processing systems. Int. J. Semant. Web Inf. Syst. (IJSWIS) **10**(4), 17–44 (2014)
20. Dell'Aglio, D., Le Phuoc, D., Le-Tuan, A., Intizar Ali, M., Calbimonte, J.P.: On a web of data streams. In: Proceedings of the workshop on decentralizing the semantic Web 2017 co-located with 16th International Semantic Web Conference (ISWC 2017), 22 October 2017
21. Harth, A., Käfer, T., Rula, A., Calbimonte, J.P., Kamburjan, E., Giese, M.: Towards representing processes and reasoning with process descriptions on the web (2024)
22. Hassani, A., et al.: Context-as-a-service platform: Exchange and share context in an iot ecosystem. In: 2018 IEEE International Conference on Pervasive Computing and Communications Workshops (PerCom Workshops), pp. 385–390 (2018)
23. Kirrane, S., Mileo, A., Decker, S.: Access control and the resource description framework: a survey. Semantic Web **8**(2), 311–352 (2017)
24. Le-Phuoc, D., Dao-Tran, M., Xavier Parreira, J., Hauswirth, M.: A native and adaptive approach for unified processing of linked streams and linked data. In:

Aroyo, L., et al. (eds.) ISWC 2011. LNCS, vol. 7031, pp. 370–388. Springer, Heidelberg (2011). https://doi.org/10.1007/978-3-642-25073-6_24
25. Lemée, J., Vachtsevanou, D., Mayer, S., Ciortea, A.: Signifiers for conveying and exploiting affordances: from human-computer interaction to multi-agent systems. Ann. Math. Artif. Intell. 1–21 (2024)
26. de Matos, E., et al.: Context information sharing for the internet of things: a survey. Comput. Netw. **166**, 106988 (2020)
27. Mauri, A., et al.: TripleWave: spreading RDF streams on the web. In: Groth, P., et al. (eds.) ISWC 2016. LNCS, vol. 9982, pp. 140–149. Springer, Cham (2016). https://doi.org/10.1007/978-3-319-46547-0_15
28. Mihai, S., et al.: Digital twins: a survey on enabling technologies, challenges, trends and future prospects. IEEE Commun. Surv. Tutor. **24**(4), 2255–2291 (2022)
29. Pradeep, P., Krishnamoorthy, S.: The mom of context-aware systems: a survey. Comput. Commun. **137**, 44–69 (2019)
30. Qiu, J., Tian, Z., Du, C., Zuo, Q., Su, S., Fang, B.: A survey on access control in the age of internet of things. IEEE Internet Things J. **7**(6), 4682–4696 (2020)
31. Ricci, A., Piunti, M., Viroli, M.: Environment programming in multi-agent systems: an artifact-based perspective. Auton. Agent. Multi-Agent Syst. **23**, 158–192 (2011)
32. Sciullo, L., Gigli, L., Montori, F., Trotta, A., Di Felice, M.: A survey on the web of things. IEEE Access **10**, 47570–47596 (2022)
33. Servos, D., Osborn, S.L.: Current research and open problems in attribute-based access control. ACM Comput. Surv. (CSUR) **49**(4), 1–45 (2017)
34. Sorici, A., Florea, A.M.: Towards context-based authorizations for interactions in hypermedia-driven agent environments-the cashmere framework. In: International Workshop on Engineering Multi-Agent Systems, pp. 191–207. Springer (2023)
35. Sorici, A., Picard, G., Boissier, O., Florea, A.: Multi-agent based flexible deployment of context management in ambient intelligence applications. In: Advances in Practical Applications of Agents, Multi-Agent Systems, and Sustainability: The PAAMS Collection: 13th International Conference, Proceedings, vol. 13, pp. 225–239. Springer (2015)
36. Sorici, A., Picard, G., Boissier, O., Zimmermann, A., Florea, A.: Consert: applying semantic web technologies to context modeling in ambient intelligence. Comput. Electr. Eng. **44**, 280–306 (2015)
37. Tataroğlu Özbulak, G.A.: Decentralized stream reasoning agents. In: Proceedings of the 17th ACM International Conference on Distributed and Event-based Systems, pp. 203–206 (2023)
38. Tommasini, R., Bonte, P., Spiga, F., Della Valle, E.: Streaming linked data: from vision to practice. Springer Nature (2023)
39. Vachtsevanou, D., Ciortea, A., Mayer, S., Lemée, J.: Signifiers as a first-class abstraction in hypermedia multi-agent systems. arXiv preprint arXiv:2302.06970 (2023)
40. Weerasinghe, S., Zaslavsky, A., Loke, S.W., Moghaddam, V., Becker, C.: Towards world wide context management: Architecting distributed contextual intelligence systems for real-time iot applications. In: 2023 24th IEEE International Conference on Mobile Data Management (MDM), pp. 340–345. IEEE (2023)
41. Werbrouck, J., Taelman, R., Verborgh, R., Pauwels, P., Beetz, J., Mannens, E.: Pattern-based access control in a decentralised collaboration environment. In: 8th Linked Data in Architecture and Construction Workshop, vol. 2636, pp. 118–131 (2020)

Protocol Design Patterns for Statecharts-Based Open MAS Development

Nikolaos I. Spanoudakis[1(✉)], Charilaos Akasiadis[2], Georgios Kechagias[1], and Georgios Chalkiadakis[1]

[1] Technical University of Crete, Chania, Greece
{nispanoudakis,gkechagias,gchalkiadakis}@tuc.gr
[2] Institute of Informatics and Telecommunications, NCSR 'Demokritos', Patr. Gregoriou E & 27 Neapoleos Str, Agia Paraskevi 15341, Greece
cakasiadis@iit.demokritos.gr

Abstract. In this paper we define two novel design patterns that can be used with statecharts-based agent modeling in many real-world domains that call for open Multi-agent System architectures. The first pattern is based on the well-known factory design pattern, and the second on the composite pattern. The applicability of our proposed patterns is demonstrated with ASEME, an agent-oriented software engineering methodology that uses statecharts for the inter- and intra-agent control models and the popular, FIPA standards-compliant, JADE agent platform. We showcase the patterns usage through an application for the modern vehicle-to-grid (V2G) and grid-to-vehicle (G2V) energy transfer problem domain.

Keywords: design patterns · statecharts · engineering multiagent systems · agent oriented software engineering

1 Introduction

Modern Multi-agent System (MAS) applications areas, such as the emerging Smart Grid [3,10,41] pose challenges to the Agent-Oriented Software Engineering (AOSE) community. In the Smart Grid, buildings, but also vehicles, become active consumers and producers of energy, and need to be integrated into this emerging energy and information network.

In addition to being a marketplace with different consumers and producers, the Smart Grid is a dynamic environment where devices that serve different purposes need to connect [29,51]. Many business models and information system architectures have been proposed for the Smart Grid, but none of them conform to specific standards [20]. Such energy markets are a natural reflection of systems where no single player can force others to adopt their products. Negotiation of energy consumption and supply is subject to different strategic goals or business

R. Collier et al. (Eds.): EUMAS 2024, LNAI 15685, pp. 402–422, 2025.
https://doi.org/10.1007/978-3-031-93930-3_23

models, but also to the nature of the stakeholder that can represent communities, states, or private funds. Computer systems instantiating these markets need to allow for proactive behaviour from stakeholders who work to meet their own goals, but also for the possibility to form flexible partnerships or alliances and adapt to a constantly changing environment. Participants should also be able to join or leave the system at will. The attributes of these systems are in line with principles of open Multi-agent Systems and the use of agent technology [26,54].

In order to build such an open system, where agents may appear or leave abruptly, in the meanwhile pursuing their diverse objectives, we need such protocols which allow for successful communication and that give the possibility to participating agents to apply their own algorithms. This would lead to an open system that promotes agents that continuously optimize their performance and respond to new challenges.

Currently, protocols focus on defining the sequence of messages exchanged between the participant roles (or agents). This has been the focus of the well-known AUML Agent Interaction Protocol model [35] that has been adopted by many AOSE methodologies, i.e. Tropos [9], PASSI [13], ADELFE [39], Mas-CommonKADS [27] and MESSAGE [24]; however, developers still need to define the appropriate behaviours for their agents from scratch.

Early works [28,43] in the AOSE domain focused on defining patterns of usage of objects for addressing agent-specific concepts, including protocols. Kendall et al. [28] identify the need for collaboration patterns via the use of coordination protocols, thus potentially allowing the agent to determine its behaviour based on the state of the employed protocol, and the possibility to be engaged in several conversations simultaneously. These early works have not, unfortunately, materialized in modern AOSE methodologies to date.

Herein, we adopt the perspective of the ASEME methodology [52], where protocols are not just communication message sequences, defining how data gets sent and received (as is common in telecommunications and computer networks), but are higher level abstractions similar to those that humans use. Here protocols are viewed as rules of conduct, or procedural methods, that describe behaviors. A protocol, therefore, addresses more than just the kind of messages that can be exchanged between participants; in particular, it also dictates what actions must be performed by participants within the protocol.

Based on this view, we propose two new design patterns. These patterns allow developers to leverage the protocol components and logic in the framework, while allowing them to apply customized key simple or complex functionality to suit their particular demands. We demonstrate the use of these design patterns through a system that we developed for the Smart Grid focusing in the Vehicle-to-Grid (V2G)/ Grid-to-Vehicle (G2V) problem, where electric vehicles charge using the grid (G2V) but can also give back power to the grid when they are charged and prices soar or there is a shortage (V2G).

The rest of this paper is structured as follows: In Sect. 2 we present the necessary background and discuss related work. In Sect. 3 we give the problem statement and then, in Sect. 4, we define the novel design patterns that we propose. In Sect. 5 we discuss our findings and then we conclude in Sect. 6.

2 Background and Related Work

To demonstrate the added value of this work we will use JADE [5], a standardized, state of the art, platform that has proved its worth in real world applications in the smart grid [1,4,21,30,40,44,49]. In JADE, the developer defines state-machine-like control of the agent's behaviours, and respects the standards set by FIPA[1].

JADE naturally fits with development methodologies whose design phase models are statecharts. Statecharts have been used by a number of AOSE methods or methodologies [17,32,33,38,50,52]. A recent one is ASEME [52], which also allows to automatically transform the design phase models to JADE code [48]. We present an overview of JADE and ASEME aiming to provide the necessary background so that the reader can follow the next sections.

2.1 The Java Agent Development Framework

JADE [5] is a software development framework for the development of distributed Multi-agent Systems (MASs). It provides a complete Java API, as well as various features for agent peer-to-peer asynchronous communication, agent service discovery, ontology and context language management, and debug and monitor tools. In JADE, most of the operations that an agent does can be carried out inside structures called behaviours.

We can define *Behaviour* as the agent's interaction with its users, counterparts, or even external systems [55]. An agent's behaviour is the smallest unit of activity that it can perform. The provided behaviour library enables developers to construct more sophisticated actions by combining different behaviours in different ways.

Each one of the agents keeps an internal list of active behaviours that are queued for execution in the same order in which they were added to it. This list allows developers to introduce new behaviours. Behaviours are executed through non-preemptive scheduling, and when they are activated, their *action()* method is invoked. This method implements the agent's activity. As soon as it finishes executing, the system checks the behaviour's *done()* method. If it returns false, then it is added again in the internal list to execute again. JADE behaviours can use the *DataStore* structure for data sharing, exchange, and storage.

Performative verbs indicate what is the specific intention of a FIPA-ACL message. JADE provides FIPA-SL, an independent specification of a human readable, string encoded first order modal language capable of describing propositions, objects, and actions, suitable for the message content. Defining message

[1] FIPA, the Foundation for Intelligent Physical Agents (http://www.fipa.org), is an IEEE Computer Society standards organization for software agent technology.

sequences that allow for the communication with different applications that share the same communication patterns is an important aspect of agent communication.

2.2 ASEME

ASEME (the Agent-oriented Software Engineering Methodology [52]) is a process for developing Multi-agent Systems from gathering requirements to the detailed implementation of a MAS. Contrary to most methodologies, where a protocol is a series of messages exchanged over a channel, in ASEME a protocol is a design model of a chosen method of how agents collaborate to reach a common goal. These protocols define specific patterns of behavior and the actions that the agents should perform in specific conditions to guarantee proper organization of communication and task solving within the system.

ASEME follows a model driven approach to software engineering. It promotes the application of formal models in expressing and in coordinating agent behavior, interaction, and goal. It utilizes two widely recognized abstractions for modeling agents: capability and functionality. Busetta et al. [11] define a capability as "a collection of plans, beliefs, events, and rules for scoping them". Braubach et al. [8], enriched this idea by noting that capabilities can include sub-capabilities. They explain that the term agent is an extension of the capability concept, which, in effect, subsumes several capabilities. According to another line of work, the Prometheus methodology [36], each functionality that may have been defined during the analysis phase is then linked to a capability during the design phase.

In the agent modeling language known as AML [53], capability is employed to depict an abstract behavior, usually defined with references to the input and output it requires, along with a set of conditions that must hold before using it and a set of conditions that result from its execution. A behaviour is a software component; the capabilities are the methods implemented in the behaviour. This approach is similar to service oriented architectures in which the agent is considered as a composition of services.

In ASEME, an agent manages its capabilities within the intra-agent control model to define its behavior. Capabilities are broken down into simpler activities. For instance, a decision-making capability might handle the task of choosing where to recharge a vehicle's battery in the evening. This task is further decomposed into activities, such as identifying nearby stations, checking their available charging slots, ranking them, and so on. Each activity is carried out through a specific functionality, such as an algorithm, a service call, or similar techniques. The same capability can be implemented using different types of functionalities: for example, one agent's decision-making task may be based on an argumentation-based method, while another implementation of the same task could rely on a different functionality, such as a multi-criteria-based method.

The inter-agent control model outlines the capability of an agent to take on a role within a specific protocol. ASEME allows for a smooth integration between the inter-agent and intra-agent control models, as both are based on the same formalism - the statecharts [25]. The statecharts formalism avoids issues like limited scalability and state explosion that affect other formalisms, such as Petri-nets [31]. Statecharts enable the modeling of activities that define behavior, along with the events that trigger state transitions in one or more of the roles involved [23].

2.3 Design Patterns for MAS

A design pattern for MAS is defined by *(a)* its name, *(b)* the problem and the context in which it appears, *(c)* the solution, which can be the objects, interfaces, and other information, and *(d)* the results and possible tradeoffs [28,43].

Existing works [28,43] focused on defining agent-oriented patterns. Proposed AOSE methodologies in the literature focused on the communication part of the protocols leading to the first patterns that were applied to methodologies (e.g. PASSI [14]) and accommodated the use of specific protocol patterns that were identified by FIPA (e.g. *request*, *contract-net*). Such patterns are used in the high methodological level and are implemented through existing support in platforms (e.g. JADE [5]).

In our work, we go one step further to define specific design patterns for *stateful* protocols that can be employed by an open MAS.

3 Problem Statement

To illustrate the problem we aim to solve, we will use an example from a real system [51]. In this system, multiple agents working for different stakeholders in the smart grid coordinate in order to address the V2G/G2V problem. More specifically, electric vehicles (EVs) must time their charging sessions with available charging stations (CS) where each of the CSs has a fixed number of charging slots in one time instance. Station recommender agents with full knowledge of the charging stations' timetables help this process by suggesting CSs that could be available for use to the EV drivers, who then select the most appropriate station.

Figure 1 provides a part of the overall architecture [51], including these stakeholders directly related to the electric vehicles (EVs), i.e. EVs, charging stations and station recommenders. the latter may represent a regulatory service, a firm of charging stations, etc. The architecture also includes their interactions and their basic components. A dedicated type of agent represents each stakeholder.

EV agents are proactive agents with the goal to ensure that the vehicle will have sufficient energy reserves to satisfy the needs of a user. The user may want to have just enough reserves for the next trip, or, to always charge at maximum level, or, to charge with minimum cost. EV agents can meet these objectives using appropriate methods, e.g. by optimizing a utility function. The *EV agent* tracks the driver's activities, models and predicts their future behavior and energy needs, and communicates with charging stations to arrange battery charging. It also seeks to profit from participating in V2G (vehicle-to-grid) operations, which involves negotiating with charging stations. The agent contacts the SR agent to

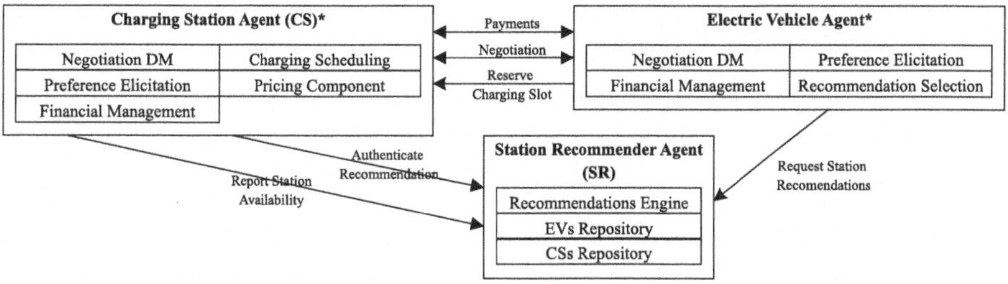

Fig. 1. Part of the architecture for the V2G/G2V problem. Asterisks (*) denote agent types with multiple instances. The main agent capabilities are listed in boxes. the communication paths, implying the use of appropriate protocols, are shown with arrows, whose direction follows the initial communication direction

receive recommendations and employs an algorithm to determine which charging recommendation to choose.

CS agents manage the physical infrastructure (such as connectors and parking slots) through which EVs connect to the grid, generating revenue by providing battery charging services. They can also negotiate with *EV agents* to modify existing charging agreements, e.g. for adjusting parameters to accommodate more vehicles. This improves the station's infrastructure utilization and increases profits.

The *SR agent* retains a repository of charging stations and their charging slots including their availability. The business model of the stakeholder behind this agent can vary, as it could be that any station can subscribe to the service, or that a partnership (or brand) of charging stations is represented by it. When an EV agent asks for a charging session, the SR recommends those CS with available slots that meet the *EVs* needs and preferences. The latter can be the estimated time of arrival or departure, the distance from the *EV*'s position, or the current battery charging level. Sophisticated *SRs* may even take into account the previous *EV* agent's charging choices in order to optimize its future recommendations, thus also retain an *EVs* repository.

The architecture above raises the following issues when the time comes to develop the agents. Undoubtedly, there is a necessity of dealing with distinct approaches to decision-making with regard to user preference, business model of the stakeholder, or, generally, the specific agent playing a certain protocol role. For instance, both the *EV* and *CS agents* possess the capability to negotiate, and yet, it is evident that they are likely to use different strategies to arrive at an agreement. Hence, the developers of these agents need to develop their own algorithm, policy or business rules that cannot always be anticipated at the time of system design for use by all concerned parties in an open system. At the same time, they need their agents to follow the predefined protocols so that they can seamlessly be integrated in the open system for achieving their objectives.

The ASEME integrated development environment (IDE) follows a model-driven process and guides the developers to the end of the design phase. The output of that phase is a statechart model for each agent type. Then the ASEME IDE can generate code for the JADE framework. However, only the behaviours' control code is generated and not the action methods. Therefore, in practice, all behaviours action codes must be written in relation to each agent type. This, however, comes with some risks as protocols may be hampered in their flow by code put in by programmers, or the same code has to be written over in several packages (for each different participating agent type).

Thus, while working on this project, we have come to a solution regarding the previously identified risks using design patterns. According to our analysis, we have two distinct cases.

In the first case, we have a state in the protocol where a specific activity takes place, e.g. a decision making activity taking place in the process of a negotiation protocol. In the protocol, the objects of negotiation are usually well defined along with the context in which the negotiation takes place, however, the developers of the agents may choose to apply diverse algorithms and/or techniques for deciding if a proposal should be accepted and make sure that the agent they build is sufficiently competitive.

We, therefore, would like to offer to the different developers of the agent the possibility to devise their own implementation and tamper with the definition of this decision making activity not changing any other aspect of the agent's participation in the protocol. If the JADE framework is the target of the implementation, then the developers need to be able to provide the code for the appropriate action method of the generated behaviour.

Now consider the case of *SR agents* that act as service providers. Typically, a service provider receives a request and is subsequently expected to respond in an appropriate fashion. However, the process involved can be quite complex and may vary depending not only on policies but also on the agent's data structures and architecture. As a result, the agent must determine which capability to activate next. This involves not just selecting the appropriate algorithm for the task, but also considering the data structures of the agent, or even a combination of sub-capabilities.

4 Protocol Design Patterns

We will define the design patterns using the common template that calls for defining explicitly [28,43]:

1. the pattern's ***name*** (appearing in the respective subsection's title).
2. the problem and the ***context*** in which it appears. We will provide this context abstractly in a way that the pattern can apply in any statechart's based development method. We will also provide information for JADE developpers.
3. the ***solution***, which can be the objects, interfaces, and other information.
4. the ***results*** of the pattern's application and possible tradeoffs.
5. the ***example*** of the pattern's application.

4.1 The Functionality Pattern

Context: The developers need to associate a specific algorithm to a protocol's basic state. For JADE implementations the developers want to allow for diverse implementations of the behaviour's action method.

Solution: To address this situation, we rely on the widely-used *factory design pattern* [23], familiar to many programmers. This pattern employs a factory method that returns an instance of a class following a specified API, which can be selected dynamically, even at runtime. This flexibility is especially valuable in emergency situations where the standard algorithm fails, and it can also support the "self-healing" capability of an autonomous vehicle agent [15].

The class diagram of this design pattern is depicted in Fig. 2. The abstract class *Template1*, provides the API that the concrete subclasses (*Instance1*, *Instance2* ... *InstanceN*) implement, overriding the abstract methods. This template may be the utility function employed by the *EV agent* to select among the *SR agent*'s recommendations. The *EV agent* invokes the static factory method (instantiating one of the instances) of the *Factory1* class, passing as a parameter the fully qualified name of the required instance. The factory produces the instance and returns it to the Agent, which can then utilize the required algorithm provided by that instance (by the *action* method of its behaviour).

Results: Diverse implementations of the basic state implementation can be employed by the agent developers. The JADE action method can be automatically generated with the *Template1*. The developers need only specify the API of the method(s).

Example: As an example, we provide the *NegotiationProtocol* inter-agent control definition in the form of a statechart, which is presented in Fig. 3. A statechart is a finite collection of states and transitions. A state can either be a BASIC-state (with green color in the figure) or a hierarchical state, which contains multiple sub-states [25]. BASIC-states are related to an agent activity. A

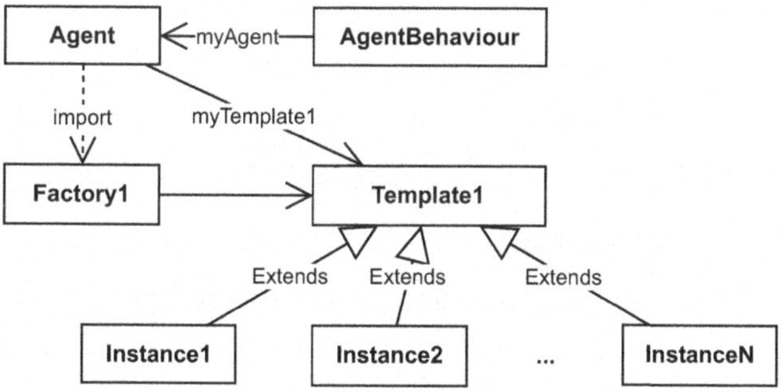

Fig. 2. The Functionality Design Pattern abstraction.

hierarchical state can be either an AND-state (with light blue color), or an OR-state (with yellow-colored header). AND-states have orthogonal components that are related by "and" (executed in parallel), while OR-states have sub-states that are related to each other by "exclusive-or" (only one is active at any given time). Small round states with the "c" character represent condition states where execution flow diverges based on the transition expressions of the outgoing transitions. Two more state types, the START (black dot) and END (black dot within a circle) states, indicate the start and end of execution respectively. The state at the highest level, i.e., the one with no parent state, is called the root.

A *transition* is a binary relation of states, denoting the change from its source state to its target state and can include a *transition expression* (TE). The TE's syntax is *event*[*guard*]/*action*, where the *event*, which belongs to a set of predefined events that can be sensed by the statechart and that influence its behaviour, can trigger the transition if it is valid; *guard* refers to one or more conditional expressions that must hold so as the transition can be taken; and *action* is one or more assignments of values to variables, which will be executed when the transition is taken. *event*, *guard* and *action* are all optional parts of the TE. The typical events that a statechart can sense are [46]:

- the event of receiving or sending a message
- A timer's timeout event
- The fact that the activity connected to the source state (a BASIC-state) of the transition finishes its execution

A message event follows the syntax *Perf*(*Sender*, *Receiver*, *MessageContent*), where *Perf* is the performative and its other elements are self-explanatory. An agent can define timers as variables whose value indicates the time units (usually milliseconds) after which a timeout event should occur.

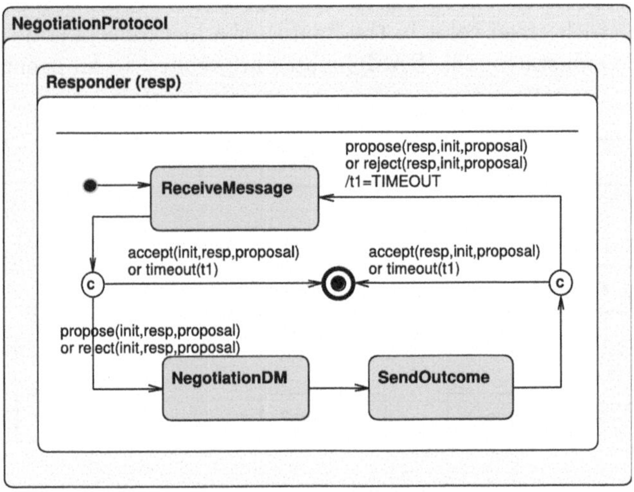

Fig. 3. The Charging Negotiation Protocol.

Using the *NegotiationProtocol* the *EV* and *CS* agent types negotiate about a reserved charging slot. To define the protocol we just need only one participating role, the *Responder* to an initiating message with performative *propose* (see Fig. 3). Then both participating agents play the same role (one acts as a *Responder* for the other). The protocol starts as soon as the aforementioned message is received. The activity of the state *ReceiveMessage*, is to wait to receive a message conforming the requirements set in the events exiting the state. There are four possibilites:

1. an incoming message's performative is *propose*. In this case there is a new proposal and the agent needs to consider it. A transition to the *NegotiationDM* state is taken
2. an incoming message's performative is *reject*. This means that this message is a subsequent message to a previous proposal send by this agent. The responder rejected the proposal therefore a new transition to the *NegotiationDM* state is taken. Normally the agent will either propose something else or terminate the protocol.
3. an incoming message's performative is *accept*. Again, the message is a response to a previous proposal and this time it was accepted. The transition to the END-state is taken and the protocol terminates with the new agreement regarding the reservation in question.
4. *t1* has timed-out. This means that the agent's counterpart failed to respond to a previous *proposal* or *reject* sent by this agent. This usually implies that either the counterpart is offline or that it was unable to propose something. The protocol terminates without a change in the previously agreed reservation.

Now, the *NegotiationDM* state's activity decides on how to respond to the incoming message. An appropriate algorithm needs to be used in the *action* method of the relevant behaviour. This is where the functionality design pattern allows the diverse development teams to devise their own algorithm and call the *Template1* method (see Fig. 2).

4.2 The Capability Pattern

Context: The developers need to develop an activity that will take place within a relevant basic state in the protocol. This time they do not just want to associate the state with a specific algorithm. This state activity may involve complex tasks and a whole statechart might be its implementation.

For JADE developers the issue is that this state's activity is not implemented in the protocol package. Its contents are unknown and they do not want to bias future agent instances developers.

Solution: This pattern composes activities into tree-like structures (the data structure to represent the statechart is a tree structure [47]) to represent part-whole hierarchies, following the composite pattern paradigm [23]. Put differently, during the design phase, the intra-agent control model developer may change the basic state type to an OR-state type and add sub-states as they see fit, even include other protocols.

In the case of generating code for the JADE framework, the developers can define their special "handler" behaviour and when reusing the protocol package and instantiating the *ProtocolRoleName* behaviour (see Listing 1) they can pass the "handler" behaviour as a parameter to the constructor. The "handler" behaviour is given access to the agent's data structures that are relevant to the protocol in line 7 of Listing 1. The listing shows how someone can use Xpand, a code generation tool technology based on Java and file templates [19], to automatically generate code for JADE. The ASEME IDE employs this technology. It is possible to use Xpand (but also other similar technologies) to support code generation for other statechart execution engines.

Listing 1. Capability Pattern skeleton

```
1   public class <ProtocolRoleName> extends FSMBehaviour {
2   /*auto-generated state String representations:*/
3   private final String HANDLER = "handler";
4   /*auto-generated constructor definition:*/
5   public <ProtocolRoleName>(Agent a, Behaviour handler,
6   DataStore ds){
7     setDataStore(ds);
8     handler.setDataStore(getDataStore());
9     /*auto-generated transitions registrations:*/
10    /*auto-generated state registrations:*/
11    registerState(handler, HANDLER);
12  }
13 }
```

Results: This allows agent implementations of different protocols to apply to completely different scale, i.e. by substituting a basic state in the statechart definition with an OR-state and define a complex behaviour.

Example: We provide, as an example, the *ChargingRecommendationProtocol* definition in Fig. 4. The roles of the protocol are exactly the agents that implement it. For the *EV* role, the protocol starts by sending a message to *Request* charging recommendations. The sender is the *EV* agent, the receiver is the *SR* agent, and the message content is a *requestRecommendations* instance (the properties of this action are defined in the ontology package). As soon as it sends the message, the *EV* goes to the *ReceiveRecommendations* state to wait for the *SR*'s results. The *SR* role's *ReceiveRecommendationRequest* receives the *EV*'s request and then the *CalculateRecommendations* state's activity computes and orders the available slots that best match the *EV*'s needs. Subsequently, it enters the *SendRecommendation* state and sends its reply to the *EV* agent. The *CalculateRecommendations* is not implemented in the protocol package, using the approach shown in Listing 1 it will be expected as an argument when calling the constructor of the protocol role.

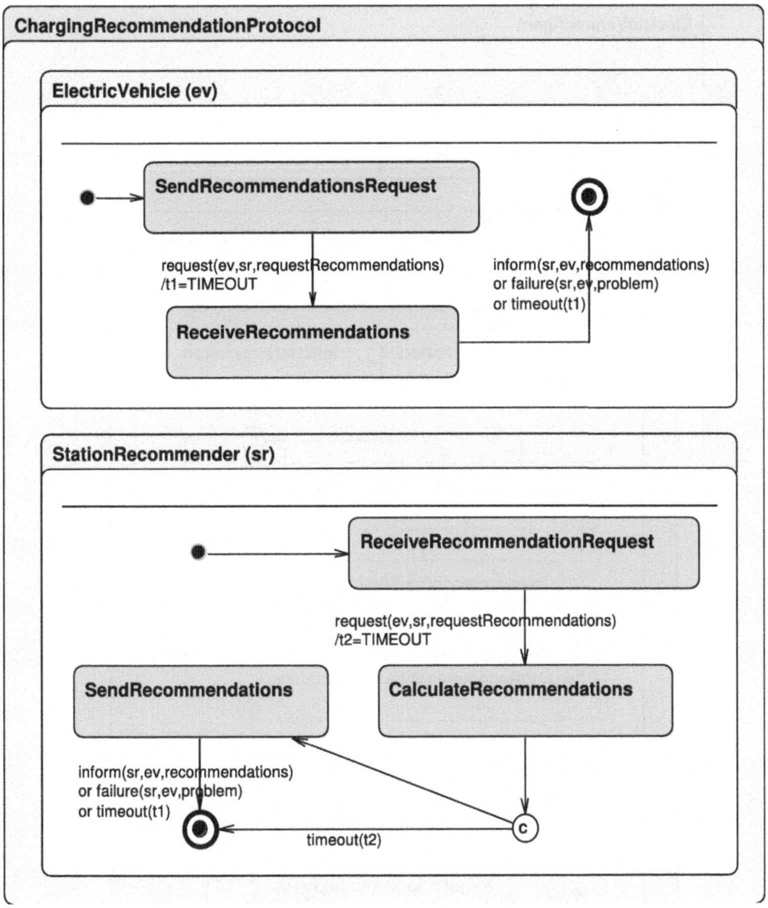

Fig. 4. The Charging Recommendation Protocol.

4.3 The Design Patterns Use for Developing a Real-World System

In this section we discuss our implementation, along with use cases that demonstrate the effectiveness of our architecture and design patterns in addressing the real-world needs of the various actors.

The intra-agent control model for the Electric Vehicle (EV) agent is shown in Fig. 5 (to improve visibility we omit the transition expressions). Note that for simplicity of representation, the protocol roles that the agent realizes are shown as basic states. These can be expanded to the relevant roles in the protocols presented earlier in Figs. 3 and 4.

When it starts its operation, the agent performs initialization activities (enters the *Init* state). Then, the agent enters both the *Negotiate* and *Reserve* OR-states as they are the orthogonal components of the *Main* AND-state. In the *Reserve* state it makes a transition to the *DecideNextAction* BASIC-state.

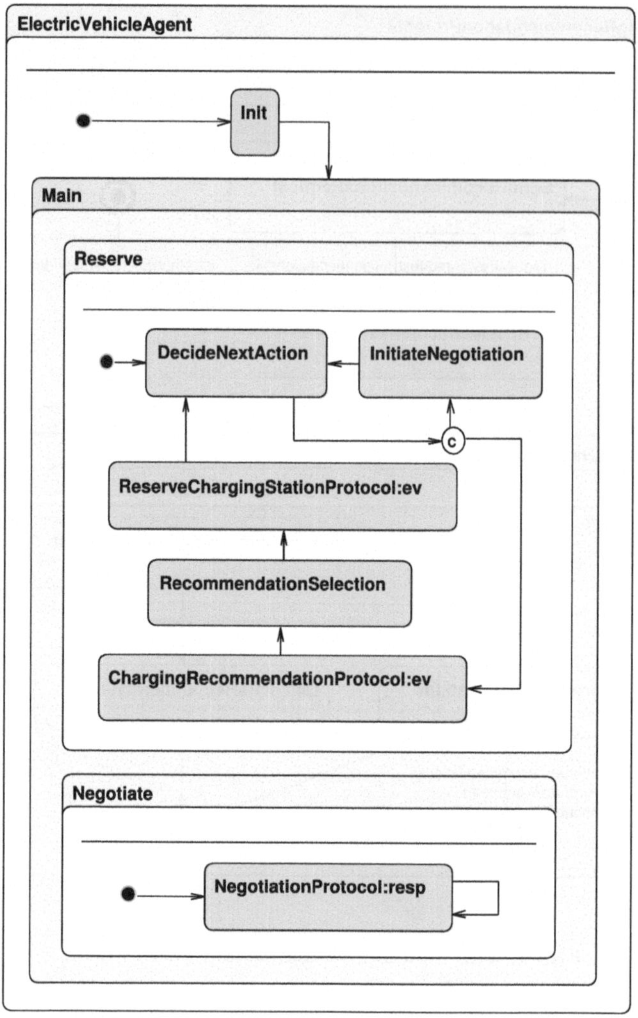

Fig. 5. The EV agent intra-agent control model. Transition expressions have been omitted so as not to clutter the diagram.

The activity that takes place in this state is to decide on whether the agent must act with regard to keeping the vehicle charged at their owner behalf. This decision can be made with a great number of algorithms or techniques. In our work we consider the following possibilities:

- By devising an appropriate algorithm the agent can monitor the battery level and, taking into account the learned, or predefined, preferences of the driver and the expected duration of the battery, it can take appropriate action for scheduling (or rescheduling) a recharging session. In this case we have an autonomous functionality of the agent.

- The agent gets the needed information from predefined datasets; this approach is very useful for experimentation with large numbers of agents.
- The agent provides a graphical user interface (GUI), where the users can select their preferences and select when they want to recharge their vehicle, thus "manually" initiating the reservation protocol.

Regardless of how the decision is made the agent exits this state either for initiating a negotiation (e.g. due to a change in the user's plans) or for making a new reservation. In the latter case the transition to the *ChargingRecommendationProtocol:ev* state (using the *ev* role of the respective protocol) is taken, then the transition to the *RecommendationSelection* state (corresponding to the agent functionality with the same name—see Fig. 1), and after the selection is made the transition to the *ReserveChargingStationProtocol:ev* is taken to make the reservation of the slot. Execution returns to the *DecideNextAction* state.

If the agent decides to negotiate a change in an existing arrangement, it enters the *InitiateNegotiation* state. The latter sends the proposed change to the charging station with whom a reservation has been scheduled. If the *CS* agent replies, the rest of the negotiation process will be taken care by the *NegotiationProtocol:resp* state (using the *responder* role of the respective protocol) at the *Negotiate* component. This is executed always in parallel to the *Reserve* component, as a *CS* agent may itself initiate a negotiation at any time.

The *EV* agent developer used the functionality design pattern to define the *NegotiationDM* action of the *NegotiationProtocol* (see Fig. 3). The same pattern has been used for other basic states allowing for diverse implementations. In the specific case of the *RecommendationSelection* state we wanted to give different options to the user and we provided four different implementations ourselves and the user can select the one they prefer through a GUI (see Fig. 6).

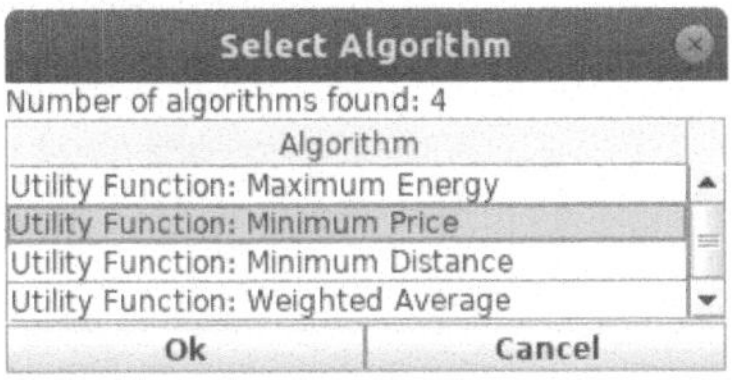

Fig. 6. Different algorithms for selecting the best station. The user selects the desired one at runtime, or the agent selects it after assessing user preferences.

In Fig. 7 the reader can see part of the Station Recommender (SR) agent intra-agent control. This part shows the initialization of its behaviour and then its role of the *Charging Recommendation Protocol* being executed in parallel with other capabilities of the agent. Note that as soon as a recommendation is sent the agent restarts the protocol role (see the transition from the *ChargingRecommendationProtocol:sr* state to itself).

Here you can note the application of the Capability pattern as the SR agent extends the original *CalculateRecommendations* basic state (activity) of the protocol to an OR-state invoking two more protocols (the *ElectricityImbalanceRequestProtocol* with the role *ServiceUser* and the *ElectricityPricesRequestProtocol* with the role *ServiceUser*) and then doing a calculation (*CalculateChargingRecommendations* state). You can also note that since many agents request for imbalance or prices the relevant protocols use abstract roles (e.g. *ServiceUser*) and concrete roles such as the SR agent implement these protocols by assuming those abstract roles.

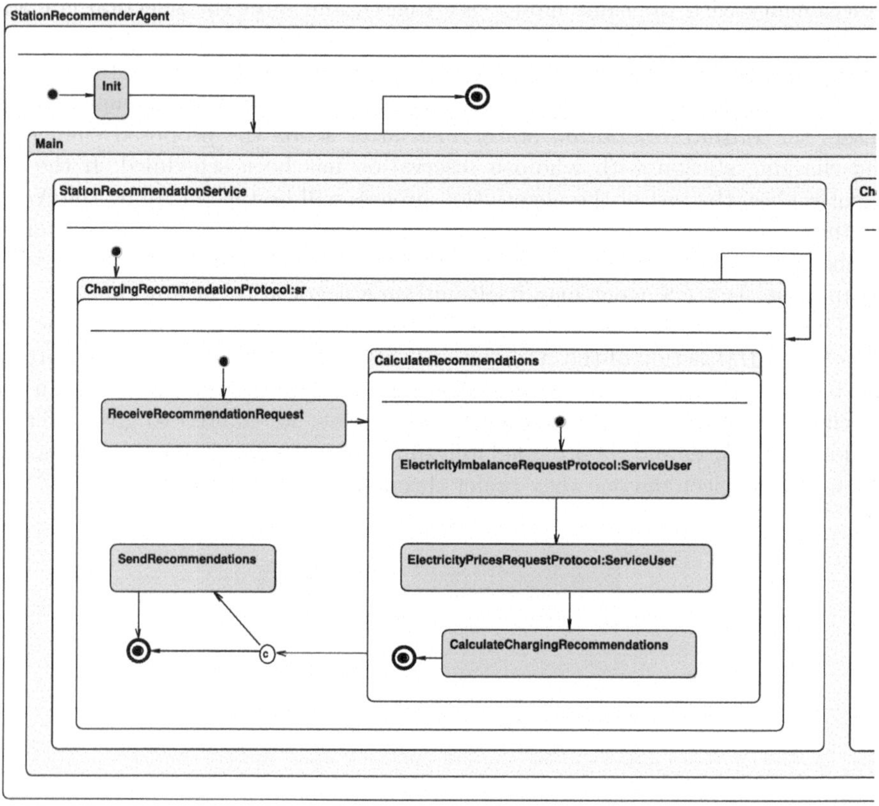

Fig. 7. Part of the SR agent intra-agent control model.

5 Discussion

At this point we would like to point out that these two patterns are agent methodology- and platform-independent. They can be employed by development

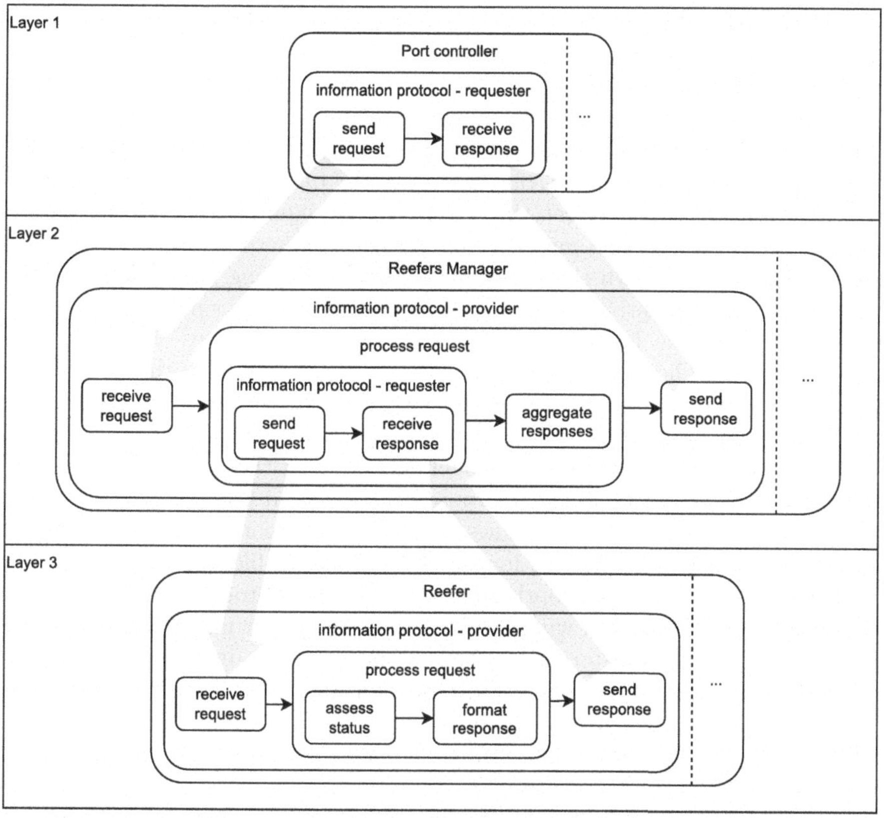

Fig. 8. A hierarchical architecture with three agent types. Information flows using the *information protocol* with two roles: *requester* and *provider*. The Capability pattern is applied for developing the *process request* state. The Functionality pattern is applied for the *assess status* state. Gray arrows show the corresponding state for message sending and receiving activities. The orthogonal components imply that the agents have other behaviours executing in parallel to their participation in the information protocol.

teams using any statecharts-based method. Additionally, appropriate templates can be proposed for different programming languages or architectures. Both patterns are compatible with object-oriented development, which is supported by many methodologies for Engineering MAS (e.g. [2,12,16,34]).

As we demonstrated in Sect. 4.3, the use of the patterns allowed us to implement a complex system, part of which is shown in the architecture diagram with much less effort than if every agent defined its own implementation for participating in the open system's diverse protocols.

Another team [18], employed these design patterns to develop a smart port power management system using a hierarchical MAS architecture [42]. The agent hierarchy spans three levels. At the top there is the port controller agent, in the middle the reefer manager agent and at the bottom the individual agents representing reefers (container refrigerators). This system was also implemented using the JADE framework.

In such many-tier hierarchical architectures, information is requested top to bottom and the responses return bottom-up. The authors used the Capability pattern for defining the *process request* state of the *information protocol*. According to the *information protocol*, the *requester* role requests for information and waits for the response. The *provider* role receives the request, then processes it and, finally, responds with the information. The processing part is left open for the agents to implement. The agent in the middle tier (reefer manager) requests information from the bottom tier agents (reefers), aggregates their responses and then replies. The same protocol is handled differently from the bottom tier agents who receive the request then assess their status and respond accordingly (see Fig. 8). The Functionality pattern is applied for the *assess status* state. Thus, with one protocol definition all agents implement their own instance of the processing activity, using all other protocol classes from the protocol package.

The use of these patterns allows for using different business models for an agent platform (like the one for the V2G/G2V problem), as, regardless of whether the agent code is proprietary or open, the protocols' implementation (source code) can be shared with third parties. The latter may define their own agent algorithms, thus fostering innovation and evolution in the system, ensuring, at the same time, the compatibility of their agents with the platform.

This work addresses the issue mainly from the MAS community perspective and not so much from the programming languages perspective. Our proposal for the functionality pattern, for example, relies on the *factory design pattern* [23]. Someone could argue that static code should be avoided as it can be harder to test [45].

In modern statecharts IDEs it is quite common to define variables along a statechart definition. This is also the case with UML as statecharts model the dynamic behavior of objects and the latter have their properties. ASEME also supports this feature. This makes it possible to define variables such as the message content. Indeed, a protocol definition should also define the nature or type of the information exchanged between peers. In a JADE implementation, behaviours exchange information using the *DataStore* structure, which is similar to a dictionary. Thus, the *handler behaviour* for the Capability pattern implementation (see Listing 1) needs a reference to that *DataStore* instance so that is gains access to the protocol's data structures, as only through that instance its results can be sensed by subsequently executing protocol behaviours.

6 Conclusion and Future Work

It is not the first time that the need for design patterns is identified in the MAS development literature. Early researchers identified the need for patterns in the collaboration layer [28,43] and focused in the communication part of the protocols leading to the first patterns that were applied to methodologies (e.g.

PASSI [14]) and accommodated the use of specific protocol patterns that were identified by FIPA (e.g. *request*, *contract-net*, etc.). Such patterns are used in the high methodological level and are implemented through existing support in platforms (e.g. JADE [5,6]).

In this paper we proposed two novel design patterns, allowing for participating agent developers *(a)* to dynamically select functionalities and *(b)* to define their own implementations of abstract behaviours. Moreover, we demonstrated the use of these patterns within a novel MAS architecture for the V2G/G2V energy transfer problem domain, for which we have developed a fully functional prototype. Our approach addresses the need for openness and supports a variety of business models by defining and developing open protocols. These protocols, along with the accompanying ontology, can be shared with interested parties, allowing them to create their own agents based on their specific expertise and business needs.

We aim to extend the open source ASEME IDE to support the application of these patterns in MAS development. Code for protocols will be generated in its own package and all those basic states that are not aimed to sending or receiving messages will have the possibility to be defined using either the functionality or the capability pattern. Implementations of the patterns will be stored in the respective agent's packages.

Moreover, we are currently developing solutions using ASEME combined with an IoT platform for MAS development [22,51]. We are looking into making these design patterns adapted to generate code for web (REST) APIs that are typically used in this setting.

Finally, another very interesting area of research is the possibility to make these design patterns applicable to other agent development methods and platforms (e.g. JaCaMo [7], SPADE [37]).

References

1. Al-Agtash, S., Hafez, H.A.: Agents for smart power grids. Energy Power Eng. **12**(08), 477–489 (2020)
2. Alaca, O.F., Tezel, B.T., Challenger, M., Goulão, M., Amaral, V., Kardas, G.: AgentDSM-Eval: a framework for the evaluation of domain-specific modeling languages for multi-agent systems. Comput. Stand. Interfaces **76**, 103513 (2021). https://doi.org/10.1016/j.csi.2021.103513
3. Asmus, P.: Microgrids, virtual power plants and our distributed energy future. Electr. J. **23**(10), 72–82 (2010)
4. Azeroual, M., Lamhamdi, T., El Moussaoui, H., El Markhi, H.: Simulation tools for a smart grid and energy management for microgrid with wind power using multi-agent system. Wind Eng. **44**(6), 661–672 (2020). https://doi.org/10.1177/0309524X19862755
5. Bellifemine, F.L., Caire, G., Greenwood, D.: Developing Multi-Agent Systems with JADE (Wiley Series in Agent Technology). John Wiley and Sons Ltd., Hoboken (2007)
6. Bellifemine, F., Poggi, A., Rimassa, G.: Developing multi-agent systems with a fipa-compliant agent framework. Softw. Pract. Exp. **31**(2), 103–128 (2001)

7. Boissier, O., Bordini, R.H., Hübner, J.F., Ricci, A., Santi, A.: Multi-agent oriented programming with jacamo. Sci. Comput. Program. **78**(6), 747–761 (2013)
8. Braubach, L., Pokahr, A., Lamersdorf, W.: Extending the capability concept for flexible bdi agent modularization. In: International Workshop on Programming Multi-Agent Systems, pp. 139–155. Springer (2005)
9. Bresciani, P., Perini, A., Giorgini, P., Giunchiglia, F., Mylopoulos, J.: Tropos: an agent-oriented software development methodology. Auton. Agent. Multi-Agent Syst. **8**(3), 203–236 (2004). https://doi.org/10.1023/B:AGNT.0000018806.20944.ef
10. Burke, M.J., Stephens, J.C.: Energy democracy: goals and policy instruments for sociotechnical transitions. Energy Res. Soc. Sci. **33**, 35–48 (2017). policy mixes for energy transitions
11. Busetta, P., Howden, N., Rönnquist, R., Hodgson, A.: Structuring bdi agents in functional clusters. In: International Workshop on Agent Theories, Architectures, and Languages, pp. 277–289. Springer (1999)
12. Cossentino, M., Seidita, V.: Passi: process for agent societies specification and implementation. In: Handbook on Agent-Oriented Design Processes, pp. 287–329. Springer (2014)
13. Cossentino, M.: From requirements to code with the PASSI methodology. In: Henderson-Sellers, B., Giorgini, P. (eds.) Agent-Oriented Methodologies, chap. IV, pp. 79–106. Idea Group Publishing (2005)
14. Cossentino, M., Sabatucci, L., Chella, A.: Patterns reuse in the PASSI methodology. In: Omicini, A., Petta, P., Pitt, J. (eds.) ESAW 2003. LNCS (LNAI), vol. 3071, pp. 294–310. Springer, Heidelberg (2004). https://doi.org/10.1007/978-3-540-25946-6_19
15. Dehraj, P., Sharma, A.: A review on architecture and models for autonomic software systems. J. Supercomput. **77**(1), 388–417 (2021)
16. DeLoach, S.A., Garcia-Ojeda, J.C.: O-MaSE: a customisable approach to designing and building complex, adaptive multi-agent systems. Int. J. Agent-Oriented Softw. Eng. **4**(3), 244–280 (2010)
17. DeLoach, S.A., Wood, M.F., Sparkman, C.H.: Multiagent systems engineering. Int. J. Softw. Eng. Knowl. Eng. **11**(03), 231–258 (2001)
18. Doudounakis, M., Spanoudakis, N., Kanellos, F.: Cost-effective, MAS-based, reefer system at container terminals. In: 21st European Conference on Multi-Agent Systems (EUMAS 2024), Dublin, Ireland, 26–28 August 2024
19. Efftinge, S., Völter, M.: OAW XTEXT: a framework for textual dsls. In: Workshop on Modeling Symposium at Eclipse Summit, vol. 32, p. 118 (2006)
20. Espe, E., Potdar, V., Chang, E.: Prosumer communities and relationships in smart grids: a literature review, evolution and future directions. Energies **11**(10), 2528 (2018)
21. Feliachi, A., Belkacemi, R.: Intelligent multi-agent system for smart grid power management. In: Smart Power Grids 2011, pp. 515–542. Springer (2011)
22. Fortino, G., Savaglio, C., Spezzano, G., Zhou, M.: Internet of things as system of systems: a review of methodologies, frameworks, platforms, and tools. IEEE Trans. Syst. Man Cybern.: Syst. **51**(1), 223–236 (2020)
23. Gamma, E., Helm, R., Johnson, R., Vlissides, J.: Design Patterns: Elements of Reusable Object-oriented Software. Addison-Wesley Reading, Mass (1995)
24. Garijo, F.J., Gomez-Sanz, J.J., Massonet, P.: The MESSAGE methodology for agent-oriented analysis and design. In: Henderson-Sellers, B., Giorgini, P. (eds.) Agent-Oriented Methodologies, chap. VIII, pp. 203–235. Idea Group Publishing (2005)

25. Harel, D., Naamad, A.: The STATEMATE semantics of statecharts. ACM Trans. Softw. Eng. Methodol. (TOSEM) **5**(4), 293 (1996)
26. Huynh, T.D., Jennings, N.R., Shadbolt, N.R.: An integrated trust and reputation model for open multi-agent systems. Auton. Agent. Multi-Agent Syst. **13**(2), 119–154 (2006)
27. Iglesias, C.A., Garijo, M.: The agent-oriented methodology MAS-CommonKADS. In: Henderson-Sellers, B., Giorgini, P. (eds.) Agent-Oriented Methodologies, chap. III, pp. 46–78. Idea Group Publishing (2005)
28. Kendall, E.A., Krishna, P.V.M., Pathak, C.V., Suresh, C.B.: Patterns of intelligent and mobile agents. In: Proceedings of the Second International Conference on Autonomous Agents, pp. 92–99. AGENTS '98, ACM, New York, NY, USA (1998)
29. Ketter, W., Collins, J., Reddy, P.: Power tac: a competitive economic simulation of the smart grid. Energy Economics **39**, 262–270 (2013)
30. Kuzin, A.Y., Demidova, G.L., Lukichev, D.V.: An approach of the jade and simulink interaction to control smart grid based on the multi agent system. In: 2019 IEEE Conference of Russian Young Researchers in Electrical and Electronic Engineering (EIConRus), pp. 574–577. IEEE (2019)
31. Mazouzi, H., Seghrouchni, A.E.F., Haddad, S.: Open protocol design for complex interactions in multi-agent systems. In: Proceedings of the First International Joint Conference on Autonomous Agents and Multiagent Systems: Part 2, pp. 517–526. AAMAS '02, ACM, New York, NY, USA (2002)
32. Dignum, F., Greaves, M. (eds.): Issues in Agent Communication. LNCS (LNAI), vol. 1916. Springer, Heidelberg (2000). https://doi.org/10.1007/10722777
33. Murray, J.: Specifying agent behaviors with uml statecharts and statedit. In: Polani, D., Browning, B., Bonarini, A., Yoshida, K. (eds.) RoboCup 2003: Robot Soccer World Cup VII, pp. 145–156. Springer, Berlin, Heidelberg (2004)
34. Odell, J., Parunak, H.V.D., Bauer, B.: Extending uml for agents. In: Proceedings of the Agent-Oriented Information Systems Workshop at the 17th National Conference on Artificial Intelligence, pp. 3–17 (2000)
35. Odell, J.J., Parunak, H.V.D., Bauer, B.: Representing agent interaction protocols in uml. In: International Workshop on Agent-Oriented Software Engineering, pp. 121–140. Springer (2000)
36. Padgham, L., Winikoff, M.: Developing Intelligent Agent Systems: A Practical Guide. Wiley Series in Agent Technology, Wiley, Hoboken (2004)
37. Palanca, J., Terrasa, A., Julian, V., Carrascosa, C.: Spade 3: supporting the new generation of multi-agent systems. IEEE Access **8**, 182537–182549 (2020)
38. Paurobally, S., Cunningham, J., Jennings, N.R.: Developing agent interaction protocols using graphical and logical methodologies. In: Dastani, M.M., Dix, J., El Fallah-Seghrouchni, A. (eds.) Programming Multi-Agent Systems, pp. 149–168. Springer, Berlin, Heidelberg (2004)
39. Picard, G., Gleizes, M.P.: The ADELFE methodology. In: Bergenti, F., Gleizes, M.P., Zambonelli, F. (eds.) Methodologies and Software Engineering for Agent Systems: The Agent-Oriented Software Engineering Handbook, LNCS, pp. 157–175. Springer US, Boston, MA (2004). https://doi.org/10.1007/1-4020-8058-1_11
40. Priyadarshana, H.V.V., Hemapala, K.U., Wijayapala, W.S., Saravanan, V., Boralessa, M.K.S.: Developing multi-agent based micro-grid management system in JADE. In: 2nd International Conference on Power and Embedded Drive Control (ICPEDC), pp. 552–556. IEEE (2019)
41. Ramchurn, S.D., Vytelingum, P., Rogers, A., Jennings, N.R.: Putting the 'smarts' into the smart grid: a grand challenge for artificial intelligence. Commun. ACM **55**(4), 86–97 (2012)

42. Rieger, C., Zhu, Q.: A hierarchical multi-agent dynamical system architecture for resilient control systems. In: 2013 6th International Symposium on Resilient Control Systems (ISRCS), pp. 6–12. IEEE (2013)
43. Sauvage, S.: Design patterns for multiagent systems design. In: Monroy, R., Arroyo-Figueroa, G., Sucar, L.E., Sossa, H. (eds.) MICAI 2004. LNCS (LNAI), vol. 2972, pp. 352–361. Springer, Heidelberg (2004). https://doi.org/10.1007/978-3-540-24694-7_36
44. Shobole, A.A., Wadi, M.: Multiagent systems application for the smart grid protection. Renew. Sustain. Energy Rev. **149**, 111352 (2021). https://doi.org/10.1016/j.rser.2021.111352
45. Spadini, D., Aniche, M., Bruntink, M., Bacchelli, A.: Mock objects for testing java systems: why and how developers use them, and how they evolve. Empir. Softw. Eng. **24**, 1461–1498 (2019)
46. Spanoudakis, N., Moraitis, P.: An agent modeling language implementing protocols through capabilities. In: Proceedings of the 2008 IEEE/WIC/ACM International Conference on Web Intelligence and Intelligent Agent Technology-Volume 02, pp. 578–582. IEEE Computer Society (2008)
47. Spanoudakis, N., Moraitis, P.: Gaia agents implementation through models transformation. In: Yang, J.-J., Yokoo, M., Ito, T., Jin, Z., Scerri, P. (eds.) PRIMA 2009. LNCS (LNAI), vol. 5925, pp. 127–142. Springer, Heidelberg (2009). https://doi.org/10.1007/978-3-642-11161-7_9
48. Spanoudakis, N.I., Moraitis, P.: Modular JADE agents design and implementation using ASEME. In: Proceedings of the 2010 IEEE/WIC/ACM International Conference on Intelligent Agent Technology, IAT 2010, Toronto, Canada, August 31–3 September 2010, pp. 221–228 (2010)
49. Spanoudakis, N., Akasiadis, C., Kechagias, G., Chalkiadakis, G.: An open MAS services architecture for the V2G/G2V problem. In: Proceedings of the 18th International Conference on Autonomous Agents and MultiAgent Systems, pp. 2198–2200 (2019)
50. Spanoudakis, N.I.: Engineering multi-agent systems with statecharts. SN Comput. Sci. **2**(4), 1–21 (2021). https://doi.org/10.1007/s42979-021-00706-5
51. Spanoudakis, N.I., Akasiadis, C., Iatrakis, G., Chalkiadakis, G.: Engineering IoT-based open MAS for large-scale V2G/G2V. Systems **11**(3), 157 (2023)
52. Spanoudakis, N.I., Moraitis, P.: The ASEME methodology. Int. J. Agent-Oriented Softw. Eng. **7**(2), 79–107 (2022)
53. Trencansky, I., Cervenka, R.: Agent Modeling Language (AML): a comprehensive approach to modeling MAS. Informatica (Slovenia) **29**(4), 391–400 (2005)
54. Wooldridge, M., Jennings, N.R.: Intelligent agents: theory and practice. Knowl. Eng. Rev. **10**, 115–152 (1995)
55. Wooldridge, M.J.: Introduction to Multiagent Systems. John Wiley and Sons Ltd., Hoboken (2002)

CommonHealth: Multi-agent Evaluation of Blockchain-Based Patient-Centred Health Networks

Mark Matthews[1(✉)], Rem Collier[1], and Evan Spendlove[2]

[1] School of Computer Science, University College Dublin, Dublin, Ireland
mark.matthews@ucd.ie
[2] Amazon Web Services, Dublin, Ireland

Abstract. Information is essential to delivering effective healthcare. Health information traditionally resides with the entity providing healthcare to the patient. However, this is just one model for how information can be situated within a healthcare context. Decentralized health networks provide the infrastructure to realize a different information and computational model that centers the locus of health information around the patients. In this paper, we present a framework for building and testing decentralized health networks that enable patients to share their data with a communal network to gain value derived from aggregated data. While decentralized networks disperse control of health information among a network of individuals, they require careful design and testing to ensure the network's incentives promote the interests of each member, scale cost-effectively, and protect privacy. Deploying a decentralized health network without appropriate testing presents multiple risks, including the risk of data breach, erroneous machine learning model predictions, and costly platform management. To counter these risks, we demonstrate how multi-agent-based evaluation can be central to testing and refining patient-centered decentralized health networks such that the incentives are robust, sustainable, and less susceptible to exploitation. We find that agent-based approaches can help speed up development and build confidence in scalability, safety, and effective functioning prior to real-world deployment. We also provide design recommendations and suggestions for future work.

Keywords: healthcare · agent-based testing · blockchain

1 Introduction

Multiple recent studies have documenting the health data challenges faced by the healthcare industry today including: maintaining secure software systems that are robust again fraud, implementing reliable, trustworthy privacy controls, avoiding the centralization of data ownership [12,19].

For example, consider the issue of health data collection pertaining to the management of conditions like Type I Diabetes. Currently, most data collected

R. Collier et al. (Eds.): EUMAS 2024, LNAI 15685, pp. 423–440, 2025.
https://doi.org/10.1007/978-3-031-93930-3_24

is controlled or even owned by the corporate entities that sell insulin pumps and continuous blood glucose monitors. Data collected is high value as is control of the software ecosystems that surround those products. As a result, the software systems tend not to be open source and organisations hoard data in order to maintain strategic advantages over competitors. The impact of this is twofold: health data is restricted to corporate ecosystems forcing a technological lock-in where patients are faced with the potential loss of historical data should they wish to move suppliers; and limited access restricts the availability of high-quality public datasets that can be used by researchers or developers to develop new or innovative solutions.

To overcome this, we present a novel decentralised health system, CommonHealth that supports the decentralized tokenization of health data in a privacy-preserving way The protocol, which is based on blockchain technology [20], is accompanied by an ecosystem of supporting applications and a decentralised autonomous organisation (DAO) for governing the evolution of the software system and community. Evaluation of this novel protocol, is achieved through the use of a multi-agent system that is designed to test the sustainability of the protocol's incentive systems and explore some of the known weaknesses of blockchain technologies. Little work has been done on exploring how multi-agent systems can be used to perform such testing. To the best of our knowledge, the only other attempt to do this has been the use of spacial agent-based simulations for evaluating energy trading platforms [3,4,23].

2 Background

2.1 Healthcare and Blockchain Technology

Several studies have explored the potential use of a blockchain as a distributed ledger for the storage of medical information such as health records and compare its effectiveness against traditional centralized databases currently in use such as Oracle RDBMS and Apache Cassandra [17,19].

The most similar and relevant state-of-the-art application of blockchain technology to healthcare is the ModelChain paper which focuses on using blockchain to enable decentralized machine learning with a focus on predictive modeling in healthcare [18]. This paper proposes a novel proof-of- information algorithm. This algorithm optimises the selection of the best performing model after each participant trains on their local data. It also enhances the selection of the participant with the most to contribute to improving the model for the next round of training.

The ModelChain paper successfully outlines the benefits of using blockchain as a medium for online machine learning and proposes a viable and novel algorithm for optimising a distributed online machine learning approach. One of the limitations of the paper is that the implementation is based on proof-of-work which has known scaling issues when compared to other approaches such as proof-of-stake as well as issues with slow transaction confirmation times and high energy consumption. Another limitation is that the paper does not analyse any potential attack vectors that may arise relating to the model transfer, instead mentioning only the 51% attack. This paper intends to expand on the application of blockchain to healthcare by approaching it from a different perspective and considering the utilisation of DAOs in healthcare.

2.2 Decentralised Autonomous Organisations (DAOs)

A Decentralized Autonomous Organization (DAO) is a type of organization that is managed by rules encoded as computer programs called smart contracts [2]. DAOs are usually built on blockchain technology, which allows them to operate in a decentralized manner without a central point of control. Here are some key features of DAOs:

The following is a list of key characteristics of Decentralized Autonomous Organizations (DAOs):

1. **Decentralization**: Unlike traditional organizations, which have a centralized governance structure, DAOs are decentralized. This means there is no single authority that makes decisions; instead, decision-making is distributed among a group of members according to the rules set in the smart contracts.
2. **Smart Contracts**: These are self-executing contracts with the terms of the agreement directly written into lines of code. The smart contracts automatically enforce and execute the agreed-upon terms, facilitating, verifying, or enforcing the negotiation or performance of a contract.
3. **Token-based Governance**: DAOs often use tokens to represent voting power. Members can propose changes to the organization, and token holders can vote on these proposals. The weight of each vote is typically proportional to the number of tokens held, aligning decision-making power with stake in the organization.
4. **Transparency and Immutability**: Transactions and rules in a DAO are recorded on the blockchain, making them transparent and immutable. This means that once an action is recorded, it cannot be altered, which helps in maintaining integrity and trust among members.
5. **Automation and Efficiency**: Since DAOs operate on blockchain technology and through smart contracts, many operations are automated. This can lead to greater efficiency as compared to traditional organizations, reducing the need for manual intervention in processes such as payments, approvals, and administrative tasks.

2.3 Applications of DAOs

Since the launch of the first DAO 2016, a hedge fund platform named "The DAO", there has been an explosion of DAO applications in areas such as finance and collection and curation [28] and as platforms or "DAO operating systems", such as Aragon that facilitate the rapid prototyping of DAO applications [9].

Most of the early DAOs are focused around Decentralised Finance (DeFi) and follow a similar approach to The DAO of pooling investment capital resources and knowledge to make strategic investments in upcoming and existing projects with the expectation of significant financial return. Access to these DAOs is generally token-gated, with limited membership and a high initial buy-in by demonstrating that they hold at a minimum amount of the relevant token in their digital wallet. Collection and curation DAOs are similar to investment DAOs, but focus primarily on curating a collection of digital assets according to one or more theses on cultural significance, financial value, or some other metric. Examples of this include Flamingo DAO [11], Fingerprints DAO [10], and Herstory DAO [14].

Social DAOs focus on developing a social community within the DAO and restricting access to that community with a membership token. Membership of the DAO gives participants the opportunity to network and connect with like-minded individuals with shared interests, acquire information and knowledge that they would be unable to elsewhere, and get access to private online and in-person social events organised, and often funded, by the DAO. This is a powerful new form of monetizing social communities, and shows the value placed by participants on membership to these exclusive groups.

A natural evolution of Social DAOs is the application of DAOs to healthcare data. The need for Patient Data Management DAOs based on experiences with Covid-19 is discussed in [1]. A Patient Data Management DAO is proposed as a case study in [7] and issues around User Interface Design and Healthcare DAOs is discussed in [21]. Outside of our prototype, there are no implementations of DAOs for healthcare. The closest, which bridges the gap between finance and healthcare, is Definitize [26], a DAO that provides a novel solution for crowd-funding innovative healthcare projects through a process of community selection.

2.4 Blockchains and Multi-agent Systems

The integration of Blockchain and Multi-Agent Systems is a well established approach with applications in areas such as: collaborative governance; big data management; coordination; and trust, data integrity and reputation management [5]. More recently, these technologies have been combined to develop solutions for IoT [27], multi-robot systems [8], asset management [22] and systems engineering [13].

To date, little research has been carried out on how to use multi-agent systems for testing of such applications. One area of recent interest has been the use of multi-agent systems to create simulations of blockchains that use simplified protocols [6,24]. More recently, researchers have had some success evaluating blockchain-based energy trading environments through the use of more traditional agent-based spatial simulations [3,4,23].

The work presented in this paper represents another significant step in this direction through the application of agent-based models.

3 Health DAO System Design Considerations

In this section, we describe the key aspects of a prototype Health DAO, CommonHealth, including describing its architecture, governance, incentive mechanism using cryptographic tokens, an open protocol and an ecosystem that supports an extensible system of health applications.

3.1 System Requirements

The requirements for our proof-of-concept DAO have been extracted from two previous studies that provide reviews of the existing literature related to health data management [16,19]:

- *Security:* Security of health and patient information which is highly sensitive.
- *Interoperability:* Data must be transferable and shareable among multiple services and institutions. Interoperability is heavily limited by each service/institution using its own centralized implementation.
- *Data Sharing and Access:* Healthcare records must be shareable as patients and doctors will need to access them, but there also needs to be sufficient access controls to manage the security aspect.
- *Mobility:* With the development of IoT and smart devices, patient data must be more mobile and portable.
- *Data consistency, Integrity, and Immutability:* Consistent data which can't be modified by unauthorized parties would help reduce the cost and impact of the inherently fragmented nature of health records.
- *Cost and Resource Effectiveness:* Technological solutions must use a reasonable amount of resources and not have unmanageable costs.
- *Trustlessness and Transparency:* As the current healthcare system is based on trust between patients and institutions, it would be ideal to move towards a more transparent and trustless model that reduces the operational burden on the institution.
- *Complexity:* The system used for health data management should ideally reduce the complexity of use for stakeholders compared to the existing systems in place.

These requirements pertain primarily to the collection, storage, usage, transfer, and control of patient data and health information. These are informed by the domain-specific challenges of healthcare, as well as the additional legal burdens in place such as the Health Insurance Affordability and Accountability Act 1996 (HIPAA) [19]. We used these requirements to guide the development of our proof-of-concept Health DAO.

A decentralised approach emphasizes transparency, trustlessness and data ownership and control. One of the core issues with contributing data to a private, centralised entity is that individual users have to trust the managing entity to manage your data correctly and use it ethically. With a transparent decentralised system, the user can verify these factors, or outsource this verification to trusted third parties, using the blockchain and open source code repositories. One of the overarching goals in this project is to provide a way for communities to crowd-source relevant health data and garner benefit for themselves and for the wider health community without relying directly on the financialisation of this data. Another goal is to enable end-users to tokenise their data in a privacy-preserving way that can still be used as part of an aggregate dataset that can then be used to benefit all data contributors.

3.2 Tokenomics

A core aspect of decentralized networks of all kinds is the mechanisms by which they assess 'honest' actors. This is called *Tokenomics*, a portmanteau of "token" and "economics" and is critical in the design of decentralized software solutions, particularly in shaping behaviors within decentralized protocols. Essentially, tokenomics involves the strategic use and management of tokens to incentivize and govern user behavior in a way that aligns with the objectives of the protocol and, in the case of a DAO, the community. These digital assets can reward participants for contributing resources, validating transactions, or maintaining the network, encouraging actions that bolster the network's security and efficiency. For instance, in decentralized finance (DeFi) platforms, tokenomics can encourage liquidity provision or penalize dishonesty, effectively balancing risk and reward. By leveraging compelloing incentives, tokenomics helps ensure that even in the absence of centralized control, a decentralized network can operate effectively and achieve its collective goals.

3.3 Governance and Community

A strong DAO community is generally filled with users who have high conviction, who actively advocate for others to join their community, and who understand the value proposition their community and any associated project. Without high conviction, users are unlikely to be motivated to try to understand the community's value proposition and to advocate for others to join their community. For a community to grow, the members should believe that there is value offered by membership in the community and thus advocate for others to join. To be able to advocate in a convincing manner, members need to be able to understand the value proposition of the community and any associated project.

In many ways, the DAO and general community associated with the protocol parallel other cooperative organisations such as Credit Unions and clubs. The value derived by the participation of the members is redistributed among the members. The shared health condition in the case of health DAO is similar to the Common Bond concept in Credit Unions - it is the factor that unites all of the members. For example, the community (the members of the DAO) will manage access to their aggregate dataset through voting on proposals to grant and revoke access. Furthermore, individuals will have granular control over their own data and can remove their data from this dataset by burning their tokens.

The decentralized protocol is governed by a Decentralised Autonomous Organisation (DAO) which is controlled by the holders of a digital token called the CMH token. CMH holders can vote on relevant decisions for the protocol including: (1) improvements to the protocol design or functionality, (2) Onboarding new Applications into the ecosystem and, (3) Modifying aspects of the CMH distribution to participants.

Certain aspects of the DAO implementation depend on the target use-case. For example, reputation voting is more suitable for a DAO where users are able to accumulate more voting tokens by participating in and contributing to the ecosystem. Reputation voting would be much less suitable in a situation where users can upload a single piece of data (e.g. genetic data) and thus each user has only one token. In that case, a simplified voting mechanism can be employed. Alternatively, there may be a need for a way to recognise further non-data contributions.

4 CommonHealth System Overview

See Fig. 1

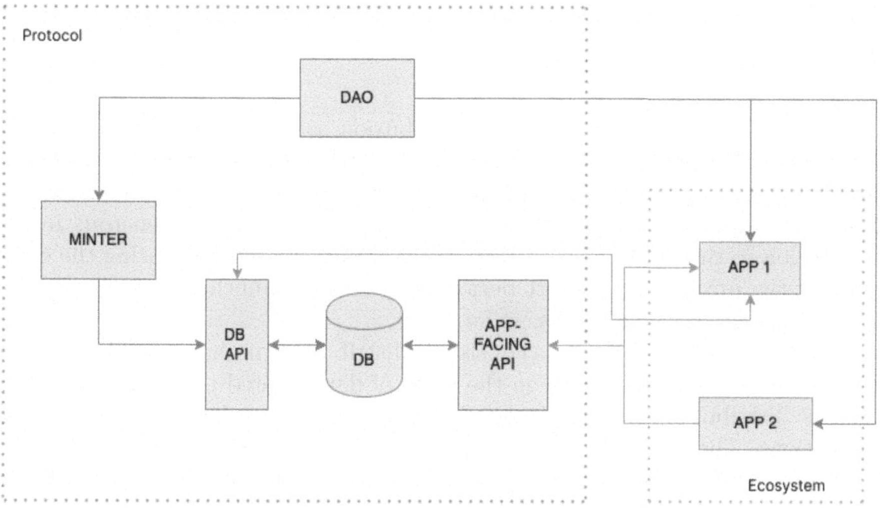

Fig. 1. Protocol Architecture

The architecture of the CommonHealth project is split into two sections: the protocol, and the ecosystem. The protocol encapsulates the core mechanisms that handle data minting and storage. The ecosystem covers the additional applications built on top of the protocol. The principles of trustlessness, transparency, privacy, and verifiability guided the design and implementation of the project. The protocol is split into three main components: the Minter, the Decentralised Autonomous Organisation (DAO), and the Database (DB).

4.1 CommonHealth Tokens

The token and incentive model proposed in this paper are based solely on non-financial incentives. This removes all of the perverse incentives associated with financial incentives particularly when paired with a healthcare project.

The tokenomics, based on the protocol for tokenising data, is summarised in Table 1. This tokenomics model was influenced by an article on reputation systems from Jad Esber and Scott Kominers [15]. There are 3 tokens: 1. **the CMH token** that is used for governance of the DAO, 2. **the xDATA token** that is used for managing data ownership within the ecosystem, and 3. **the COIN token** that is used for interacting with applications in the Ecoysystem.

Table 1. Tokenomics for CommonHealth

Token	xDATA	CMH	COIN
Purpose	Tokenising data ownership	Reputation & Governance	Ecosystem Currency
Attributes	Non-transferrable; Burnable via Minter; NFT	Non-transferable; Depreciating-to-floor; Fungible	Non-transferable; Fungible; Burnable in apps
Maximum Supply	$2^{256} - 1$	$2^{256} - 1$	$2^{256} - 1$
Distribution	Reward for minting data	Reward for minting data and using apps	Logarithmically distributed to CMH holders

The xDATA token has no initial distribution as it is minted on-demand as data is added to the collective dataset. The CMH token is initially distribution after the protocol transitions from the measure community growth stage to the community governance stage. The COIN token should have a generous initial distribution to the community to help foster application usage. During the early stages of the project, for a short period of time after launch, it may be helpful for applications to waive the usage fee.

All of these tokens will have a consistent distribution mechanism. The xDATA token is emitted linearly based on the units of data minted per user. The CMH token is distributed based on token emissions for the minter and associated applications. These emission rates can be altered by voters via the DAO. The COIN token is distributed in daily rounds to holders of the CMH token. There is a logarithmic allocation based on the number of holders of the CMH token and the holdings of each user. Users with large quantities of CMH receive less COIN for each additional CMH token they hold. The emission parameters of the COIN token can also be altered by a DAO proposal.

After the project has exited to community governance, the intention is for steady growth in the total supply of xDATA, CMH, and COIN tokens based on user activity and the growth of the user base. These tokens are all directly tied to user activity and have in-built supply-suppression mechanisms such as the depreciating nature of CMH and the fact that COIN tokens are burned (removed from circulation) when they are spent for using an application. There should be no issues either with having an 'indefinitely' increasing supply as the maximum supply is $2^{256} - 1$ which is massive. Given that the xDATA token has the potential to have the largest supply. If we had 7 billion users each minting the maximum yearly amount, we'd reach the max supply is ~4.53e+64 years.

4.2 The Minter

The Minter is a web application which interacts with the xDATA and CMH smart contracts to tokenise data provided by a user. Users will interact with the Minter to mint and burn (create and delete as referenced in the traditional CRUD convention) data within the protocol. In the context of the Minter and more broadly tokens in general, minting and burning refer to the same thing as creating and deleting from the traditional CRUD convention. When a user mints data via the Minter, the data itself is inserted into the DB via the DB API. Then, the user receives some number of xDATA tokens representing the data minted as well as some CMH tokens as a reward for interacting with the protocol. CMH tokens can be used for voting on governance proposals through the DAO. Similarly, when a user burns an xDATA token representing some data, the Minter will delete that data in the DB via the DB API. The Minter configuration is governed by the DAO. For example, if a proposal is passed through the DAO for a change in the CMH rewards for minting data, this would be enacted via the DAO making this change in the underlying smart contract used by the Minter for distributing rewards.

4.3 The DAO

The DAO, or Decentralised Autonomous Organisation, is the mechanism employed by the protocol for governance. Users who interact with the protocol are rewarded with CMH tokens which can be used for voting on proposals to improve the protocol and overall project. For example, onboarding a new application into the ecosystem requires a proposal to be passed via the DAO. Users can make a proposal via the DAO web app. A proposal is generally a textual recommendation for an improvement to the protocol backed up by reasoning and evidence. Creating a proposal requires a user to lock a certain amount of CMH tokens which reduces spam proposals. How a proposal passes depends on the voting system used but generally, a quorum must be reached and the majority of the votes must be for the proposal for it to pass. Users can vote for or against a proposal weighting their vote with their CMH holdings or abstain entirely from the vote. The CMH token is non-transferable and depreciates over time until a depreciation floor is reached. This encourages ongoing contributions and rewards contributors with more voting power based on the recency of their contributions. Furthermore, holders of the CMH token are regularly distributed COIN tokens which are necessary for interacting with the various applications in the ecosystem.

4.4 The Database

The Database (DB) stores the health data provided by users. Ideally, this would be stored on-chain in a mutable, privacy-preserving storage protocol. The full set of operations required are creation, reading, and deletion (C, R, and D, from CRUD). Depending on the associated health condition, a case can be made for the full CRUD interface to be required (adding Update). A mutable database is necessary as we need both create and delete operations. Currently, available storage protocols are immutable which means that one cannot delete data after creating it. The main benefit of an on-chain protocol is the added transparency and verifiability that the blockchain provides. The overall goal is to make the entire system trustless, transparent, and verifiable. Regarding the privacy-preserving aspect, the data itself does not need to be stored on-chain (as this is extremely expensive), but a reference to the data, such as a hash, as well as records of the operations performed should be stored on-chain. At the time of writing, there is no such protocol available for production (non-testnet) use.

The DB would be partitioned into two different tables, one for handling user identity, and the other for handling the underlying data. To preserve user privacy, data is pseudonymised using a cryptographically securely generated random string for the user id. The mapping from wallet address to pseudonymised id will be maintained in the user identity table which is only accessible via the DB API. Furthermore, to prevent abuse of this table, any interaction with the DB API requires a randomly generated message to be signed by the user to prevent an attacker or the protocol itself from linking a wallet address to user data without the user's explicit permission. Access to the pseudonymised data is provided to applications via the app-facing API. If an application requires user data specific to a single user (e.g. for visualising a user's data), it can request this via the DB API after going through the signing verification process.

4.5 Ecosystem

The ecosystem consists of the various applications and services, potentially both virtual and real-world, built on top of the protocol that leverage the collective, pseudonymised dataset. In the case of the diabetes case study, a possible application would be a visualiser app which visualises the provided data over time in a comprehensible and clear manner allowing users to spot trends in their data. Another possible application would be a recommender app which recommends changes to the user's basal and bolus rates based on their data.

The core, underlying mechanism of this ecosystem is the Minter. The Minter allows a user to contribute data in a privacy-preserving way to a larger community dataset and to tokenise their ownership of this data. By tokenising their data, a user can gain entry into the ecosystem and access various applications. If the user wants to exit the ecosystem or wishes to delete their data, they can burn their ownership token using the Minter and this will remove their data from the community dataset. It is important to balance the burden of participation with the value derived from access to the ecosystem. If a user only gets $1 worth of value but they need to contribute $5 worth of time/effort/data, then the return on investment of contribution doesn't make sense.

This ecoysystem is designed to be extensible so it could be further developed to support current healthcare use cases that traditional healthcare systems support such as healthcare provision and healthcare insurance, as well as health data donation to clinical researchers.

4.6 System Implementation

The CommonHealth architecture was implemented as a proof of concept rather than a full implementation, so only a simplified form of the tokenomics (CMH and non-depreciating xDATA) was implemented. The COIN token distribution mechanism was not implemented, though it was used for the multi-agent evaluation. The implementation consisted of the following components: Token distribution smart contracts; Aragon DAO and a Minter Web Application. The code was deployed on the Polygon Mumbai Testnet. This involved writing custom smart contracts for the tokens involved, configuring and deploying a DAO using Aragon, and building a web application for users to mint and burn data. The source code for this implementation can be found at https://csgitlab.ucd.ie/SirMilt/commonhealth/-/tree/master.

5 Multi-agent Evaluation

We have proposed a novel architecture based around a DAO that governs the management of a decentralized protocol, and a tokenomics incentive system intended to encourage sustainable behaviour among participants in the decentralized network. While blockchain technologies like CommonHealth represent an alternative approach to address some of the prior identified limitations of existing approaches to healthcare data management, one of their limitations is that they rely on the inbuilt incentive mechanisms (i.e. tokenomics). If these are fragile, or improperly testing, then the decentralized network can be exploited or undermined. Because of this, it is important to have high confidence in the tokenomics model and decentralized protocol, before onboarding real world users.

Before conducting an evaluation of user-participation with the DAO, is important to first understand the underlying mechanics and incentives involved. Users cannot participate in the ecosystem without minting data and receiving xDATA tokens as they need some of the COIN token to use applications. Furthermore, applications can only be used with data minted not arbitrary data which strengthens the incentive to mint data. The value provided by the applications is scaled by the quantity of data minted. Therefore, if a user is trying to maximise the utility provided by the protocol and ecosystem, they need to maximise the quantity of minted data. Similarly, if a user is trying to maximise their reputation for voting in the DAO, they need to maximise their quantity of minted data along with their usage of applications within the ecosystem. There is no way of achieving either of these objectives without interacting with the minter and other applications.

5.1 Test Archetypes

We implemented a multi-agent evaluation of the CommonHealth tokenomics model to assess its sustainability. The specific tokenomics model evaluated was the tri-token model consisting of xDATA, CMH, and COIN outlined in the tokenomics section of this paper. A multi agent approach was used as it is well suited to this problem which involves modelling the interactions over a long period of time involving many individual actors with the protocol and applications within the ecosystem.

The multi-agent evaluation of the tokenomics of the project was developed in Python. Three archetype users were implemented: (1) The Batcher, (2), The Reputation Farmer, and (3) the Power User.

The Batcher follows a deterministic behavioural pattern: it mints exactly thirty days worth of data and uses an app five times every thirty days. This is to simulate a user who only interacts with the protocol in a batching manner. The Reputation Farmer is an agent whose objective is to maximise the quantity of CMH tokens they hold based on the available options. For example, the Reputation Farmer will choose to use the application with the highest return in CMH tokens for COIN tokens spent. Finally, the Power User is a user who uses the applications daily and only mints data as needed to fund their app usage. This aims to model a typical user who wants to minimise the amount of data they have to provide while maximising the value derived from using the applications.

These archetypes were selected and designed to ensure full coverage of the expected behaviours of agents interacting with the protocol. At each step (one day) in the simulation, each agent evaluated whether or not they would stop interacting with the protocol (termed 'dropoff'). When each agent is initialised, they are given a randomly conviction value (a float between 0.1 and 1) which is impacts their probability of dropping off. The dropoff probability of agents was based on a dropoff distribution which tails off after the first thirty days. Also, certain archetypes adjusted their probability of dropoff based on frustration and satisfaction which occurred when an agent was prevent from or able to perform certain actions. For example, the power user incremented their frustration adjustment when they were unable to use an app that day and had to instead mint data.

5.2 Results

A simulation was run with a duration of three years. Each step in the simulation represented one day. The initial seed community size was ten agents. After thirty days, new agents were introduced in each step. The number of agents introduced was scaled in an increasing manner as the simulation progressed until it reached a maximum of ten per step. This aims to simulate the natural growth of the user base. The introduction of new users was halted after two and a half years to see how the protocol user base stabilised without new additions.

A total of 2170 agents were introduced into the simulation. The retention rate by the end of the simulation was 15.58%. This is quite reasonable for a healthcare application as the annual retention rate for healthcare apps is approximately 19% and this simulation was run over three years [25]. Furthermore, this shows that generally the tokenomics model is sustainable in that 15.5% of the participants were still interacting with the protocol after three years. During the testing stage where the tokenomic parameters were tuned, one issue that frequently arose was that the power user would acquire sufficient reputation to allow them to passively meet their COIN requirements for app usage without minting more data. This was solved by reducing the size of distribution rounds which resulted in power users needing to mint on an ongoing basis.

As shown in Figs. 2, 3 and 4, the end token distribution mechanisms show that the mechanisms to prevent actors from accumulating disproportionately large amounts of reputation tokens. Given that a large number of the participants dropped off (∼85%), it makes sense that the majority of participants would hold relatively small amounts of each token. After three years, the maximum amount of CMH tokens accumulated by any agent was 201.43 which is not exceptionally high given that many agents exceeded 100 accumulated CMH tokens.

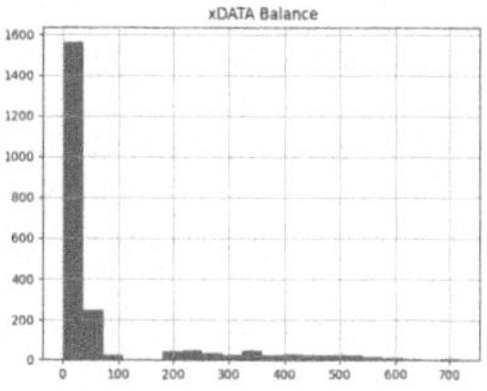

Fig. 2. End Distribution of xDATA Tokens

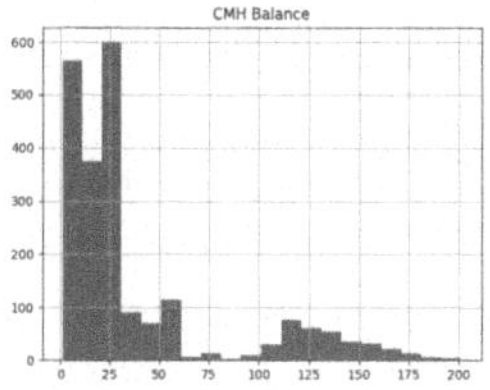

Fig. 3. End Distribution of CMH Tokens

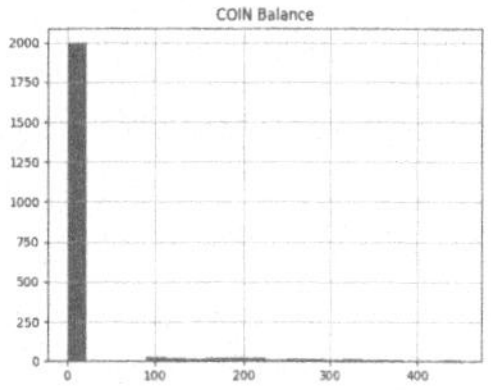

Fig. 4. End Distribution of COIN Tokens

6 Discussion

We evaluated three different types of participation profiles (based on their usage patterns and objectives) and demonstrated that the proposed tokenomics model provides sustainable incentives for participants.

6.1 Applications of Agents to Evaluate Blockchains

This study has provided evidence that agents are one way of simulating the incentives and dynamics of an blockchain environment in advance of deployment to live production environments, where otherwise it is difficult to assess and the absence of testing would place a lot of risk in the sustainability of the health network and may lead to data breaches or erroneous models.

Given this and the increased use of blockchain-approaches in healthcare, there would be value in creating a generalised multi-agent framework for evaluating incentive systems. Current approaches use a combination of a priori reasoning, game theory, and small scale custom simulations to evaluate whether or not their proposed tokenomics are sustainable. By providing a generalised framework, future projects would be able to demonstrate with evidence that their tokenomics are sustainable. There are many challenges for research to focus on in this, particularly around modelling the conflicting desires of actors as well as the huge variance in actors.

Another promising application of Multi-Agent systems is for modelling the interaction of users with the DAO, focusing on the resilience of the DAO against malicious actors. Given that DAOs are becoming increasingly popular, particularly for open protocols, it is vital that more tooling is built out for testing, simulating, and evaluating how resilient a DAO is against bad actors.

6.2 Variance in Participation Models Based on Health Condition

We have proposed a generalizable architecture that could support health communities around different conditions. We identified three different styles of contribution for health data based on inherent factors of the health condition and the data need to model that condition. These are consistent, sporadic, and once-off. These aspects will influence how the tokenomics are developed to encourage honest participation.

Consistent refers to when a user makes ongoing contributions that are roughly equivalent over a long period of time. For a Health DAO based around type I diabetes, the contributions are blood glucose and basal and bolus rate data. The unit of contribution for this data is one day and each day is roughly equivalent so the contribution style in this case is consistent. If the contributions are consistent, then it can make sense for the governance token to be depreciating over time since the user will continue contributing and we may want to ensure that the more recent contributions of the user are more heavily weighted for governance. This also adds an additional incentive to continue contributing.

Sporadic refers to when a user makes infrequent or unpredictable contributions. Different contributions may have different levels of value for the protocol and user. In this case, a mixture of depreciating and non-depreciating instances of the governance token may be useful. For higher value contributions, the token rewards can be non-depreciating. Alternatively, the rewards for data contributions could be non-depreciating while the rewards for application usage would be depreciating.

Once-off refers to when a user can only make single contribution. An example of this would be contributing genetic data. In this case, the governance token would likely be strictly non- depreciating. An additional challenge in this case is how to foster an active community, if desired, since there should be an alternative way of gaining (social) reputation other than solely data contributions.

In this paper, we focused by way of illustration via a real health condition on Diabetes, accounting for the daily measurement requirements associated with this condition (i.e. daily glucose monitoring). MAS approaches, in order to be effective, would need to be tuned to the contribution style and other aspects of the condition. For example, for networks centred around patients with Depression, there may need to be a hybrid contribution style and the primary contribution data would be different (See Table 2). An application based on assessing life-time risk via a genetic sample would be different again and likely need to incentivize contributions based on a one-off contribution style.

Table 2. Application of Governance factors to Case Studies.

Factor	Diabetes	Depression
Contribution Style	Consistent	Consistent & Sporadic
Primary Contribution Form	Blood Glucose & Basal/Bolus rates	Self-Reports
Tokenomics Model	Depreciating-till-permanent	Depreciating-till-permanent
Voting Style	Reputation-Weighted	Reputation-Weighted
Actors to Incentivise	Long-term contributors	Long-term contributors

6.3 Design Recommendations for MAS Evaluations

Given the novelty of MAS evaluations we offer some design recommendations for their use in decentralized sensitive health contexts:

1. **Minimize Moving Pieces**: Trust is the core quality of any decentralized network. This is more the case in healthcare. As such it is prudent to minimize the complexity of initial systems and center them on the core value provided to participants.
2. **Empirically-informed MAS**: In order to maximize the generalizability of the MAS evaluations, make use of existing real world datasets to inform the choice and characteristics of the agent archetypes.
3. **Employ Robust Data Validation Approaches**: Data Validation is vitally important because the value of the network centers on the quality of the information provided. While the norm for decentralized applications is to provide open source code in order to allow users to verify and trust the application, the validation code should be closed-source for security reasons.
4. **Consider Bad Actors**: This paper has focused on modeling incentive structures assuming good intentions but of course this is not the whole picture, bad actors may want to undermine the network or extract value from its information and models. Researchers should build on prior MAS work in vulnerability detection.
5. **Gradual Deployment**: While the purpose of MAS is to build confidence prior to deployment with real patients, it would be still prudent to gradate the exposure of the platform to broad use. We would recommend a soft deployment with real patients, where the initial development team can still make modifications to the MAS and software, before then releasing control of the protocol to the community once confidence is above a satisfactory threshold.

7 Limitations and Future Work

As a proof-of-concept system, CommonHealth is limited. While we believe this research demonstrates the promise and viability of using multi-agent methods to build confidence in decentralized Health DAOs, more work is needed to strengthen our understanding of this potential. Due to time constraints, the protocol could not be deployed in full and user data could not be collected. In future work, researchers could capture and analyze actual user behavioural patterns based on recorded interactions with the protocol and associated applications. Our approach and implementation presented an generic health DAO. As covered in the Discussion, given the differences in participation models created by the underlying health condition, such as health measurement frequency, future work should should look at the development of Health DAOs oriented around specific conditions. Future approaches should also seek to build evaluation methods including agents that build on real-world data, for example using open datasets from type I diabetes readings. This would help identify nuanced details that evaluation methods should account for. Finally, given the legal uncertainty of DAOs, not to mention healthcare DAOs specifically, this work should be considered exploratory and experimental.

We demonstrated that MAS could be used to perform a simultated evaluatipon of the sustability of the incentive structure (i.e. tokenomics) of the protocol using a multi-agent framework to programmiatically product multiple actors with various intents. While our evaluation was limited, we believe it was sufficient to illustrate the potential of MAS to make a significant impact. We also provided design considerations for MAS in this area and identified concrete future directions for research.

8 Conclusion

Decentralized Health Networks based on Blockchain technology offer an alternative organization of health data that orients that data and value around the individuals with the health condition, and can provide hard privacy controls and agency. This architecture can address some of the current challenges faced by the healthcare industry. However, in order to avoid network attacks or hacks, it is crucial to test central aspects of blockchain implementations such as governance, data validation algorithms and tokenomic incentive systems in advance of public deployment. In this paper, we have demonstrated how a multi-agent evaluation of the tokenomics of a prototype systems can be used to this end. We evaluated three different types of user archetypes and demonstrated that the proposed tokenomics model provides sustainable incentives for participants. While there is a need to develop more robust evaluation approaches based on real-world data, this research demonstrates the feasibility of using multi-agent evaluations to test decentralized health protcools and ecosystems, indicating that they have a vital role to play in the iterative development of a new model of healthcare.

References

1. Attaran, M.: Blockchain-enabled healthcare data management: a potential for COVID-19 outbreak to reinforce deployment. Int. J. Bus. Inf. Syst. **43**(3), 348–368 (2023)
2. Bonnet, S., Teuteberg, F.: Decentralized autonomous organizations: a systematic literature review and research agenda. Int. J. Innov. Technol. Manage., 2450026 (2024)
3. Boumaiza, A., Sanfilippo, A.: Blockchain-based electricity market agent-based modelling&simulation. In: 2023 IEEE International Conference on Industry 4.0, Artificial Intelligence, and Communications Technology (IAICT), pp. 91–95. IEEE (2023)
4. Boumaiza, A., Sanfilippo, A.: A testing framework for blockchain-based energy trade microgrids applications. IEEE Access (2024)
5. Calvaresi, D., Dubovitskaya, A., Calbimonte, J.P., Taveter, K., Schumacher, M.: Multi-agent systems and blockchain: results from a systematic literature review. In: Demazeau, Y., An, B., Bajo, J., Fernández-Caballero, A. (eds.) PAAMS 2018. LNCS (LNAI), vol. 10978, pp. 110–126. Springer, Cham (2018). https://doi.org/10.1007/978-3-319-94580-4_9
6. Cui, B., Hu, Y.: BSELA: a blockchain simulator with event-layered architecture. Futur. Gener. Comput. Syst. **151**, 182–195 (2024)
7. Cunningham, J., et al.: The application of distributed autonomous organization governance mechanisms to civic medical data management. IET Blockchain (2024)
8. De Sousa, A.L., De Oliveira, A.S., Teixeira, M.A.S.: Multi-agent robot systems: analysis, classification, applications, challenges and directions. In: 2024 IEEE International Conference on Industrial Technology (ICIT), pp. 1–8. IEEE (2024)
9. El Faqir, Y., Arroyo, J., Hassan, S.: An overview of decentralized autonomous organizations on the blockchain. In: Proceedings of the 16th International Symposium on Open Collaboration. pp. 1–8 (2020)
10. FingerprintsDAO: Curation and acquisition. https://fingerprintsdao.gitbook.io/fingerprints-dao/committees-+-roles/curation. Accessed 12 Mar 2021
11. FlamingoDAO: Launch. https://docs.flamingodao.xyz/Launch.html. Accessed 12 Mar 2021
12. Hathaliya, J.J., Tanwar, S.: An exhaustive survey on security and privacy issues in healthcare 4.0. Comput. Commun. **153**, 311–335 (2020). https://doi.org/10.1016/j.comcom.2020.02.018
13. Herrera, M., Pérez-Hernández, M., Kumar Parlikad, A., Izquierdo, J.: Multi-agent systems and complex networks: review and applications in systems engineering. Processes **8**(3), 312 (2020)
14. HerstoryDAO: Tweets and replies [twitter profile]. https://twitter.com/herstoryDAO. Accessed 12 Mar 2021
15. Jad Esber, S.K.: A novel framework for reputation-based systems. https://future.a16z.com/reputation-based-systems/. Accessed 05 May 2022
16. Kumar, T., Ramani, V., Ahmad, I., Braeken, A., Harjula, E., Ylianttila, M.: Blockchain utilization in healthcare: key requirements and challenges, pp. 1–7. IEEE (2018). https://doi.org/10.1109/HealthCom.2018.8531136
17. Kuo, T.T., Kim, H.E., Ohno-Machado, L.: Blockchain distributed ledger technologies for biomedical and health care applications. J. Am. Med. Inform. Assoc. **24**, 1211–1220 (2017). https://doi.org/10.1093/jamia/ocx068

18. Kuo, T.T., Ohno-Machado, L.: ModelChain: decentralized privacy-preserving healthcare predictive modeling framework on private blockchain networks (2018)
19. McGhin, T., Choo, K., Liu, C.Z., He, D.: Blockchain in healthcare applications: research challenges and opportunities. J. Netw. Comput. Appl. **135**, 62–75 (2019). https://doi.org/10.1016/j.jnca.2019.02.027
20. Nakamoto, S.: Bitcoin: A peer-to-peer electronic cash system (2008). www.bitcoin.org/bitcoin.pdf. Accessed 12 Mar 2021
21. Neumann, V., Harding, M., Davies, N.: DAOing it as a collective: designing the future of decentralised personal health data sharing. In: Extended Abstracts of the 2023 CHI Conference on Human Factors in Computing Systems, pp. 1–8 (2023)
22. Papi, F.G., Hübner, J.F., de Brito, M.: A blockchain integration to support transactions of assets in multi-agent systems. Eng. Appl. Artif. Intell. **107**, 104534 (2022)
23. Ren, Z., et al.: A power trading mode based on blockchain for prosumers. In: E3S Web of Conferences, vol. 237, p. 02008. EDP Sciences (2021)
24. Rosa, E., D'Angelo, G., Ferretti, S.: Agent-based simulation of blockchains. In: Asian Simulation Conference, pp. 115–126. Springer (2019)
25. Sefferman, A.: Healthcare apps 2021: engagement benchmarks. https://www.apptentive.com/blog/2021/04/02/healthcare-apps-2021-engagement-benchmarks/. Accessed 05 Mar 2022
26. Solve.Care: Definitize whitepaper (2021). https://definitize.finance/wp-content/themes/definitize-finance/docs/Definitize__Whitepaper.pdf. Accessed 12 Mar 2021
27. Uddin, M.A., Stranieri, A., Gondal, I., Balasubramanian, V.: A survey on the adoption of blockchain in IoT: challenges and solutions. Blockchain: Res. Appl. **2**(2), 100006 (2021)
28. Wang, S., Ding, W., Li, J., Yuan, Y., Ouyang, L., Wang, F.Y.: Decentralized autonomous organizations: concept, model, and applications. IEEE Trans. Comput. Soc. Syst. **6**(5), 870–878 (2019)

Do You Want to Play a Game? Learning to Play Tic-Tac-Toe in Hypermedia Environments

Katharine Beaumont(✉) and Rem Collier

University College Dublin, Dublin, Ireland
katharine.beaumont@ucdconnect.ie, rem.collier@ucd.ie

Abstract. We demonstrate the integration of Transfer Learning into a hypermedia Multi-Agent System using the Multi-Agent MicroServices (MAMS) architectural style. Agents use RDF knowledge stores to reason over information and apply Reinforcement Learning techniques to learn how to interact with a Tic-Tac-Toe API. Agents form advisor-advisee relationships in order to speed up individual learning and exploit and learn from data on the Web.

Keywords: Hypermedia Agents · Transfer Learning · Reinforcement Learning

1 Introduction

Agents are fundamental to the earliest formulations of the Web as a network of machine-readable data [2]. The idea was that these agents could navigate open, discoverable and understandable areas of the Web, interacting with resource in order to achieve their goals. Where agents become aware of one another's presence, this presents opportunities for collaboration and knowledge sharing between them.

Where is that vision now? It is widely accepted that from a practical perspective, the Semantic Web agent vision has not been progressed [10]. However state-of-the-art research into a new breed of Web agents known as hypermedia agents looks to address this. Hypermedia Multi-Agent Systems (HMAS) is concerned with the creation of MAS that are designed to work with Web architecture [3]. A key goal of this research is to explore how hypermedia agents can learn and adapt on the Web. [16–18] explore this from a single agent perspective using human-led behaviour acquisition, third party LLM models and dynamic machine-readable action descriptions respectively.

This paper illustrates how machine learning techniques can enhance agent learning in a hypermedia multi-agent system[1]. The particular approach we adopt is focused around Transfer Learning (TL), which is typically applied with agents

[1] Code available at https://gitlab.com/mams-ucd/examples/HyperTicTacToe.

R. Collier et al. (Eds.): EUMAS 2024, LNAI 15685, pp. 441–448, 2025.
https://doi.org/10.1007/978-3-031-93930-3_25

equipped with Reinforcement Learning abilities. TL aims to alleviate some of the traditional shortcomings of Reinforcement Learning, the lack of training data [19], or sufficient time to explore and refine the model: in order to learn a policy, an individual agent must take many steps, exploring the environment and potentially performing multiple sub-optimal actions [13]. TL aims to speed up an agent's learning so that it learns faster than it would if it learned individually. Agents with a pre- or partially trained model can transfer some or all knowledge to another learning agent [14].

The focus of this demonstration is to illustrate how these concepts and principles can be exploited in a hypermedia MAS using the currently available framework on top of ASTRA [5], an agent programming language that is an implementation of AgentSpeak(L) [12] and is based on to the Belief, Desire and Intention (BDI) paradigm. This forms part of wider research into how to integrate this type of learning into agent programming in ASTRA and the requirements for language-level changes.

We present an Application Programming Interface (API) which allows agents to play Tic-Tac-Toe on the Web (TTT API). Multiple agents can interact with the API and each other. All are deployed on the Web and interact using HTTP protocols[2]. Agents use open actions: they navigate links and forms, without hard-coded knowledge of the endpoints. This reflects a move towards general models of interaction with the environment from bespoke actions to more abstract, open actions constrained by environmental signifiers such as hypermedia form actions and HTTP verbs.

Tic-Tac-Toe is a well understood agent learning problem that has a small, finite state set[3] but it cannot be solved through classical techniques as they assume a certain opponent strategy [13]. It is used here to demonstrate how hypermedia agents can learn and engage in Transfer Learning in a Web environment.

2 System Overview

2.1 Environment: Tic-Tac-Toe API

The TTT API (1 in Fig. 1) is a bespoke REST (REpresentational State Transfer) [9] API that includes hypermedia controls such as hyperlinks (links) and forms for agents to interact with. It returns JSON-LD[4] representations which include links to the ontologies used, allowing agents to reason about and learn from the information presented, and share domain knowledge with other agents.

The ontologies used in the TTT API include the Hypermedia Controls Ontology (in the below example, this is the default or `"@vocab"`)[5], the Hypertext Transfer Protocol (HTTP) Ontology (indicated by `"href"` in the example

[2] https://www.w3.org/Protocols/.
[3] 3^9, compared to Backgammon with over 10^{20} [15].
[4] https://json-ld.org/.
[5] https://www.w3.org/2019/wot/hypermedia#.

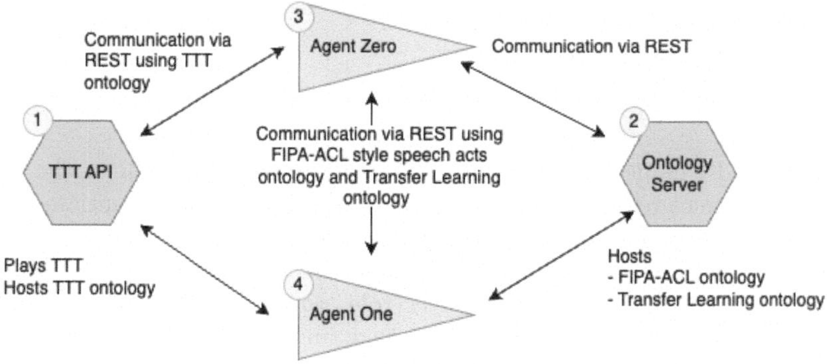

Fig. 1. System Diagram

below)[6], the Web of Things (WoT) Thing Description 1.1 (`"wot"`)[7] as well as a custom Tic-Tac-Toe ontology (`"ttt"`y). The Tic-Tac-Toe Ontology was created to provide the concept of a game, moves, players, player roles, squares, the board and the result.

An Ontology Server (2 in Fig. 1) hosts two additional custom ontologies written to provide FIPA-ACL style communication and basic Transfer Learning concepts.

The TTT API has a single entry point from which agents can navigate the system (e.g. `http://ttt.api/`)[8]. From this entry point, agents can register to play and receive an assigned game identifier (ID) (for example `id1234`), view the board, make moves, and view the result when the game has been completed. The JSON-LD representations combine data with links and forms that specify contextually valid interactions. For example, the response to a successfully registering includes links back to the entry point, the game board, and forms for each of the possible game play moves:


```
"links": [
{
  "href": "http://ttt.api/",
  "htv:methodName": "GET"
},
{
  "href": "http://ttt.api/Board?id=id1234",
  "htv:methodName": "GET"
}],
"forms": [
{
  "href": "http://ttt.api/Square11?id=id1234",
```


[6] http://www.w3.org/2011/http#.
[7] https://w3c.github.io/wot-thing-description/.
[8] All URLs are simplified for readability.

```
  "contentType": "application/json",
  "htv:methodName": "PUT",
  "wot:op": "writeproperty"
},...]
```

A TTT API game bot executes the game play strategy against the agent. When a new agent registers to play, a new RDF graph of the instantiated ontology classes is created and stored in memory. When moves are made, an instance of the Move class is created along with relationships which link the Move to a Square, `inSquare`, and with a player role, `moveTakenBy`. On querying the result, a JSON-LD representation is returned, and in addition the RDF graph[9] of the game is written out to a file, which provides the possibility to analyse past games and construct a knowledge graph of the game history.

2.2 Individual Agent Learning

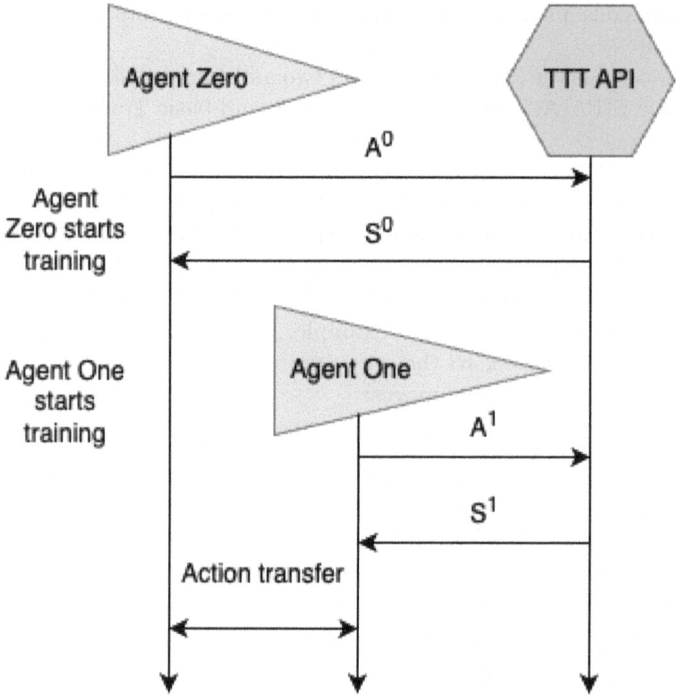

Fig. 2. The agent learning process

The game playing agents (3 and 4 in Fig. 1) are implemented using Multi-Agent Microservices (MAMS), an architectural style and associated framework

[9] https://www.w3.org/TR/rdf12-concepts/.

for deploying multi-agent systems within a microservices architecture [4]. The framework is implemented on top of ASTRA.

Figure 2 demonstrates Agent Zero interacting with the TTT API over successive training episodes (complete games) in order to start forming a policy for game play.

Agents use the module API [5] of ASTRA in order to interact with the learning mechanism (the `Policy` module, discussed below), and an Apache Jena module (`KnowledgeStore`) as per [1,11]. The `KnowledgeStore` module allows the agents to individually interact with the TTT API. As well as communicating with the TTT API, this module facilitates the creation, parsing and storing of triples and acts as an information store for the game play. Once a response is received from the TTT API, the `KnowledgeStore` fires an event to the agent which triggers a plan to extract information about game play in the agent code. For example, in processing the example JSON-LD response from the previous section, the belief

`+form_actions(string, string, list)`

may be added with the details : `http://ttt.api/Square11?id=id1234`, `PUT`, `["@id"]`. The agent can react to the addition of beliefs regarding forms and use the endpoint, HTTP method, and required input details to perform actions without hardcoded prior knowledge.

Support for the use of Reinforcement Learning (RL) is realised through the custom `Policy` module, which implements an abstract framework that can support multiple RL algorithms. In this example, each agent uses the Q Learning algorithm [13] with different state/action representations and optimisations. Agents infer a positive reward at the termination of a game if they win, a negative reward for loss and 0 for a draw.

Agents have a second, separate knowledge store for inter-agent communication using the custom FIPA-ACL style ontology, which in future implementations would allow agents to reason about their communications

2.3 Transfer Learning

In Fig. 2, after Agent Zero starts interacting with the TTT API, Agent One subsequently begins training in the same manner. However in addition to selecting an action based on it's policy during game play, it can also query Agent Zero for a recommended action. The agents have an ad hoc advisor-advisee relationship [6], and a limit is set on the number of times agents can query each other to reduce the interruptions to individual learning in the advising agents.

The protocol to request and receive (or not receive) advice is executed over successive messages via HTTP between the agents. An example of the body of an interaction between Agent One and Agent Zero is given below:

```
"fipa:request": {
    "fipa:sender": "http://agent.one",
    "fipa:receiver": "http://agent.zero",
    "fipa:reply-to": "http://agent.one/response",
```

```
    "fipa:conversation-id": "msgid123",
    "fipa:ontology": "http://ontology.server/transfer#",
    "fipa:content": {
        "http://agent.zero": {
            "tf:Query": "tf:Action",
            "tf:hasState": "http://ttt.api/Board?id=id1234"

        }
    }
}
```


The FIPA-ACL ontology is prefixed with `"fipa"` and the Transfer Learning ontology, with `"tf"`. This demonstrates Agent One requesting the action (`tf:Action`) for a specific board state (`http://ttt.api/Board?id=id1234`).

Agent Zero either sends a failure message or a recommended action. The recommended action includes a score. This is the value associated with the action, normalised across all of the existing values in the agent's policy, and indicates a measure of confidence in the action. Agent One can reject the advice if the score falls below a threshold.

The agents are programmed to wait for responses from each other and from the API to account for network latency, and re-attempt communication or continue training if the wait for a response is over a threshold, ensuring fault tolerance.

The effectiveness of Transfer Learning is evaluated by comparing metrics including the total reward gained during single agent learning versus an agent learning engaged in Transfer Learning (the advisee), over a set number of training episodes. Averaged results over multiple evaluation runs show that the advisee has higher discounted and undiscounted reward, and shorter time and number of episodes to a reward threshold, compared to single agent learning, demonstrating accelerated learning.

3 Discussion

The demonstration utilises open actions in order to allow agents to react to what may be a changing API. This assumes that the environment conforms the constraint that the responses only include valid interactions and follow HATEOAS (Hypermedia As The Engine Of Application State) principles, whereby hypertext is used to provide hypermedia links and summary information [8].

Learning is integrated into agents in a modular manner, and in this sense the integration with learning is soft as per the discussions in Erduran (2022) [7]: the approach demonstrated provides some controls (agents can start, pause or stop the learning process via actions on the `Policy` module), but as a modular integration it does not take advantage of the flexibility of the BDI agent paradigm.

This demonstration provides a starting point for the analysis of actions and behaviours that can be extracted and generalised to provide more general mechanisms for learning in hypermedia environments, with a view to language-level supports for learning in agents programmed in ASTRA.

Acknowledgments. CONSUS is funded under Science Foundation Ireland's Strategic Partnerships Programme (16/SPP/3296) and is co-funded by Origin Enterprises Plc.

References

1. Beaumont, K., O'Neill, E., Bermeo, N.V., Collier, R.: Collaborative route finding in semantic mazes. In: Proceedings of the All the Agents Challenge (ATAC 2021) Co-located with the 20th International Semantic Web Conference (ISWC 2021) (2021)
2. Berners-Lee, T., Hendler, J.: Publishing on the semantic web. Nature **410**(6832), 1023–1024 (2001)
3. Ciortea, A., Mayer, S., Gandon, F., Boissier, O., Ricci, A., Zimmermann, A.: A decade in hindsight: the missing bridge between multi-agent systems and the world wide web. In: Proceedings of the International Conference on Autonomous Agents and Multiagent Systems (2019). http://www.alexandria.unisg.ch/256718/
4. Collier, R., O'Neill, E., Lillis, D., O'Hare, G.: MAMS: multi-agent microservices. In: Companion Proceedings of The 2019 World Wide Web Conference, pp. 655–662 (2019)
5. Collier, R.W., Russell, S., Lillis, D.: Reflecting on agent programming with agentspeak (l). In: PRIMA 2015: Principles and Practice of Multi-Agent Systems: 18th International Conference, Bertinoro, Italy, October 26-30, 2015, Proceedings 13, pp. 351–366. Springer (2015)
6. Da Silva, F.L., Glatt, R., Costa, A.H.R.: Simultaneously learning and advising in multiagent reinforcement learning. In: Proceedings of the 16th Conference on Autonomous Agents and Multiagent Systems, pp. 1100–1108 (2017)
7. Erduran, Ö.I.: Machine learning algorithms for cognitive and autonomous BDI agents. In: LWDA, pp. 112–123 (2022)
8. Fielding, R.T.: Rest APIs must be hypertext-driven (2008). https://roy.gbiv.com/untangled/2008/rest-apis-must-be-hypertext-driven
9. Fielding, R.T., Taylor, R.N.: Principled design of the modern web architecture. ACM Trans. Internet Technol. (TOIT) **2**(2), 115–150 (2002)
10. Kirrane, S.: Intelligent software web agents: a gap analysis. J. Web Seman. **71**, 100659 (2021)
11. O'Neill, E., Beaumont, K., Bermeo, N.V., Collier, R.: Building management using the semantic web and hypermedia agents. In: Proceedings of the All the Agents Challenge (ATAC 2021) Co-located with the 20th International Semantic Web Conference (ISWC 2021) (2021)
12. Rao, A.S.: Agentspeak (l): BDI agents speak out in a logical computable language. In: European Workshop on Modelling Autonomous Agents in a Multi-agent World, pp. 42–55. Springer (1996)
13. Sutton, R.S., Barto, A.G.: Reinforcement Learning: An Introduction. MIT Press (2018)

14. Taylor, M.E., Stone, P.: Transfer learning for reinforcement learning domains: a survey. J. Mach. Learn. Res. **10**(7) (2009)
15. Tesauro, G., et al.: Temporal difference learning and TD-Gammon. Commun. ACM **38**(3), 58–68 (1995)
16. Vachtsevanou, D., Junker, P., Ciortea, A., Mizutani, I., Mayer, S.: Long-lived agents on the web: continuous acquisition of behaviors in hypermedia environments. In: Companion Proceedings of the Web Conference 2020, pp. 185–189 (2020)
17. Vachtsevanou, D., Lemee, J., Rot, R., Mayer, S., Ciortea, A., Ramanathan, G.: HyperBrain: human-inspired hypermedia guidance using a large language model. In: Proceedings of the 34th ACM Conference on Hypertext and Social Media, pp. 1–5 (2023)
18. Vachtsevanou, D., de Lima, B., Ciortea, A., Hübner, J.F., Mayer, S., Lemée, J.: Enabling BDI agents to reason on a dynamic action repertoire in hypermedia environments. In: Proceedings of the 23rd International Conference on Autonomous Agents and Multiagent Systems, pp. 1856–1864 (2024)
19. Zhuang, F., et al.: A comprehensive survey on transfer learning. Proc. IEEE **109**(1), 43–76 (2020)

Author Index

R. Collier et al. (Eds.): EUMAS 2024, LNAI 15685, pp. 449–450, 2025.
https://doi.org/10.1007/978-3-031-93930-3